Transdisciplinary

Play-Based
Intervention

Other products available in the [TPBA Play-Based TPBI] system include:

- **Transdisciplinary Play-Based Intervention: Guidelines for Developing a Meaningful Curriculum for Young Children**
  by Toni W. Linder, Ed.D.

- **Transdisciplinary Play-Based Assessment and Intervention: Child and Program Summary Forms**
  by Toni W. Linder, Ed.D.
  shrink-wrapped package of 5 complete pads, each including all key forms of the *TPBA* and *TPBI* manuals:
  - Instructions to All Forms *and* Child/Family Identification Sheet (1 page)
  - Cognitive Observation Worksheet (8 pages) *and* Summary Sheet (2 pages)
  - Social-Emotional Observation Worksheet (8 pages) *and* Summary Sheet (2 pages)
  - Communication and Language Observation Worksheet (10 pages) *and* Summary Sheet (2 pages)
  - Sensorimotor Observation Worksheet (8 pages) *and* Summary Sheet (2 pages)
  - Cumulative Summary Sheet (1 page)
  - Team Ideas for Play (TIP)/Team Assessment of Play (TAP) Sheet (4 pages)
  - Play-Based Curriculum Planning Sheet: Infant/Toddler (1 page)
  - Play-Based Curriculum Planning Sheet: Preschool/Kindergarten (2 pages)

To order, contact Paul H. Brookes Publishing Co., P.O. Box 10624, Baltimore, Maryland 21285-0624 (1-800-638-3775).

Transdisciplinary *Play-Based* Intervention

Guidelines for Developing a Meaningful Curriculum for Young Children

by

Toni W. Linder, Ed.D.
Professor
School of Education
University of Denver
Denver, Colorado

with invited contributors

·P·A·U·L·H·
BROOKES
PUBLISHING Co

Baltimore • London • Toronto • Sydney

Paul H. Brookes Publishing Co.
P.O. Box 10624
Baltimore, Maryland 21285-0624

Typeset by Brushwood Graphics, Inc., Baltimore, Maryland.
Manufactured in the United States of America by
BookCrafters, Chelsea, Michigan.

First printing, September 1993.
Second printing, February 1996.
Third printing, October 1997.

Library of Congress Cataloging-in-Publication Data

Linder, Toni W., 1946–
    Transdisciplinary play-based intervention: guidelines for developing a meaningful
curriculum for young children / by Toni W. Linder; with invited contributors.
        p.   cm.
    Includes bibliographical references and index.
    ISBN 1-55766-130-8
    1. Transdisciplinary Play-Based Intervention.   I. Title.
RJ53.T7L65   1993
305.23′1′0287—dc20   93-426
                                                                                                                      CIP

British Library Cataloguing-in-Publication data are available from the British Library.

Contents

About the Author

Toni W. Linder, Ed.D., is Professor and Coordinator of Graduate Studies at the University of Denver. Dr. Linder is the chair of the Early Childhood Special Education and the Child and Family Studies graduate programs. She has experience as an educator and an administrator of programs for children with special needs as well as programs for children who are at risk. Dr. Linder consults nationally on issues related to assessment and intervention with young children and their families. Dr. Linder is the parent of a 5-year-old son, a 19-year-old stepson, and a 22-year-old stepdaughter.

Also contributing to this volume:

Anita C. Bundy, Sc.D., O.T.R., F.A.O.T.A., is Associate Professor in the Department of Occupational Therapy at Colorado State University in Ft. Collins, Colorado. Dr. Bundy has extensive experience working with children and adults who have disabilities, both in clinical and school settings. She is the author of numerous articles and the co-author of two books.

Jane C. O'Brien, M.S.O.T., O.T.R., is Instructor in the Department of Occupational Therapy at the Medical University of South Carolina in Charleston, South Carolina. She has several years' experience working with young children and their families and has been the recipient of a number of grants designed to bring innovation to service delivery.

Carol Lay, Ed.D., is a licensed psychologist in private practice. Her specialty is the treatment of children and adolescents. Prior to becoming a psychologist, Dr. Lay was a special educator. She was on the faculty of the School of Education, University of Denver, and prior to that, the educational consultant in the Child Psychiatry Clinic, University of Colorado Health Sciences Center, where she was also a teacher of children with emotional disabilities. Dr. Lay is a frequent speaker on issues of social-emotional development for parent and school groups. She is also the parent of a teenager and a toddler.

Sandy Patrick, M.S., CCC-SLP, has been a speech-language pathologist for 12 years. She has provided diagnostic and therapeutic services for children in hospitals, clinics, and educational settings. She has worked with a variety of age groups and disorders and is currently supervising students at the University of Colorado Communications Disorders Clinic and working on several grant programs. Ms. Patrick is committed to children and families and always strives to find the most efficacious service delivery model.

The transdisciplinary play-based assessment Observation Guidelines contained in this volume were developed by Toni W. Linder, Susan Hall, Kim Dickson, and Paula Hudson. They originally appeared in *Transdisciplinary Play-Based Assessment: A Functional Approach to Working with Young Children* (Linder, 1990) and subsequently in the revised edition (Linder, 1993), the companion to this volume.

Preface

Agradual evolution has been taking place in the field of early childhood special education, school psychology, occupational and physical therapy, speech-language therapy, and related fields. Influenced by research and professional literature, parental pressure, legislation, and policy changes, assessment and intervention have been moving toward more naturalistic approaches with young children and their families. The "who, what, when, and where" of intervention is changing. The people who work with young children with disabilities or with children who are at risk for developmental concerns not only are specialists and parents, but increasingly include regular educators and child care staff. Children with special needs are now included in regular classrooms, preschools, and child care centers, in addition to specialized programs. Intervention is viewed as a process that should take place in all of the child's natural environments, which expands intervention to the home and community and broadens it to encompass the whole day. If intervention is to take place across all of the child's environments, with numerous persons responsible for implementation, it makes sense that intervention should be a natural process that is comfortable, pleasurable, and easy to implement.

Transdisciplinary play-based intervention (TPBI) has evolved in response to these changes in the field. After the publication of *Transdisciplinary Play-Based Assessment* (Linder, 1990), the author had the opportunity to provide training in the TPBA model around the United States. The reaction to TPBA was gratifying. Parents and persons from all disciplines responded positively to a functional, naturalistic model for determining what the child is ready to learn and how the child learns best. Comments always included statements such as, "It makes so much sense to assess a child through observation of his or her play. Does this approach translate into intervention?" This reaction was heard so many times that the author decided to develop a few simple guidelines or principles that could be contained in a small handbook on play intervention. The idea for a small handbook has grown into the present volume.

The author solicited contributions from colleagues and respected experts in the field of early intervention for the various domain chapters. Carol Lay, Ed.D., a colleague in private practice who has expertise in working with young children with emotional and behavior disorders, worked with the author in writing the chapter on social and emotional intervention. Sandy Patrick, M.S., CCC-SLP, who has expertise in working both with young children with disabilities and with children who are at risk for developmental delay, contributed the chapter on communication and language intervention. Anita C. Bundy, Sc.D., O.T.R., a nationally recognized expert in play and motor therapy with young children, contributed the chapter on sensorimotor intervention, along with Jane C. O'Brien, M.S.O.T., O.T.R. who has extensive clinical experience working with young children with motor deficits or delays. Each of these individuals spent a great deal of time preparing thoughtful and comprehensive recommendations, the result of which is somewhat larger than a "small handbook."

The intent of this book is to provide practitioners and parents with principles, guidelines, and practical suggestions for incorporating play and other pleasurable activities into the daily life of the child. The format was developed to complement the TPBA process, so that after the child was assessed with the TPBA guidelines, the team could refer to what the child was currently doing and generate intervention ideas that would facilitate continued learning and developmental progress. Intervention implications are addressed across the cognitive, social-emotional, communication and language, and sensorimotor domains, with the intent that the team will integrate all developmental areas. Examples are provided throughout the text to illustrate how the various strategies can be implemented and how the recommended approaches relate to recommendations in other developmental domains.

The suggestions and guidelines presented in this book can be used in any setting and with many different curricula or philosophical orientations. However, the author and other contributors to the book believe strongly that a play-based orientation is best for working with young children and their families. To assist in implementation of a play-based model, suggestions and examples are offered in each chapter of what intervention might look like for children with varying levels of ability. Recommendations are made for home, center, and school environments. The guidelines contained in Chapters 8–11, the TPBI Planner, should be helpful to both parents and professionals across disciplines. The Planner reproduces the Observation Guidelines from *Transdisciplinary Play-Based Assessment* and provides the link between assessment and intervention. (*Transdisciplinary Play-Based Assessment* has been released in a revised edition with the publication of this volume.)

In addition to guidelines for intervention and recommendations for specific types of activities, *Transdisciplinary Play-Based Intervention* offers a format for development of plans for intervention in home, center, school, and community environments. Team Ideas for Play (TIP) Sheets and Team Assessment of Play (TAP) Sheets allow the team, which includes the family, to generate play intervention strategies and monitor the changes in the child across activities and environments. Curriculum planning sheets are also included to assist teams in incorporating TPBI into the curriculum. Examples of how TPBI is used in a storybook curriculum are presented as well.

Transdisciplinary play-based intervention is a natural, functional intervention process that builds upon the child's play skills and incorporates strategies to promote positive developmental changes into each aspect of the child's life. It is a process that "makes sense" philosophically and pragmatically. TPBI is a family-oriented process that directly involves the parent in the decision-making about what type of intervention feels comfortable for their family. TPBI is also a child-oriented approach that sees the child's motivations and pleasurable interactions with the environment as keys to learning. In addition, TPBI is a team process that encourages transdisciplinary sharing and cross-disciplinary intervention.

It is the author's hope that *Transdisciplinary Play-Based Intervention* will, in some small way, contribute to the growing trend to make intervention for young children and their families less intrusive, more responsive and sensitive to individual strengths, and more of a partnership with families. Intervention does not have to be something we "do" to children and families. It should build meaningful relationships and lasting skills and processes that generalize across people, events, and environments. Intervention can and should be fun.

Toni W. Linder
1993

REFERENCES

Linder, T.W. (1990). *Transdisciplinary play-based assessment: A functional approach to working with young children*. Baltimore: Paul H. Brookes Publishing Co.

Linder, T.W. (1993). *Transdisciplinary play-based assessment: A functional approach to working with young children* (rev. ed.). Baltimore: Paul H. Brookes Publishing Co.

Acknowledgments

Transdisciplinary Play-based Intervention is the result of contributions from many parents, teachers, therapists, and other professionals who care about children and families. I would like to express my gratitude to all of those who gave me ideas and suggestions and who encouraged me to write this book.

I thank each of the contributors to this volume, Anita C. Bundy, Sc.D., O.T.R., Carol Lay, Ed.D., Sandy Patrick, M.S., CCC-SLP, and Jane C. O'Brien, M.S.O.T., O.T.R., for their enormous efforts. Each of their chapters turned out to be much more than a "typical" chapter, and I appreciate their persistent efforts and major contribution to this book. All of our work in this volume builds upon the foundation laid in *Transdisciplinary Play-Based Assessment*. My appreciation of the efforts of Susan Hall, Kim Dickson, and Paula Hudson, who contributed to *TPBA*, grows each day.

The material that comprises this book was field tested in a small program that is a consortium effort of Denver Public Schools, Sewell Child Development Center, and the University of Denver. My thanks go to Cheryl Caldwell and Heidi Heissenbuttal of Sewall and Tish Castro and Richie Strickland at Bradley Elementary School who made the program possible and to each of the therapists and teacher assistants who have been involved in field testing various aspects of TPBI. Colleen Murphy, Caroline Sweitzer, Mary Sue Johnson, Yaruba Bryant, Mary Zahniser, and Bevin Rolfs are all talented individuals with great ideas, who contribute much to the lives of children. A special thanks goes to Mary Dodd, the teacher in the program, who has been patient and tolerant of the many times I asked if we could "just try this and see how it works." And, of course, I cannot forget all of the children in the program and the families who have participated. Most of the pictures of children in this book are of children from the preschool.

I also thank my friend and colleague Dr. Jill Miller for her professional advice on the chapter "Facilitation of Social-Emotional Development" and for her support and encouragement through the various stages of writing this book. She and my friend Ann Kiley, the "steam room support group," helped me see clearly through the occasional mind fog.

I extend my gratitude to Sikha Sibanda, our secretary in the College of Education at the University of Denver, who has helped me innumerable times to meet deadlines. She now knows the people at Federal Express well.

To Kathy Boyd and Melissa Behm at Paul H. Brookes Publishing Co. my deepest thanks and warmest regards. They were positive, supporting, encouraging, and demanding—as needed. Kathy will probably be seeing the letters TPBA and TPBI in her sleep for years to come.

And finally, a big hug and a kiss go to my husband Fred, who woke up every morning and rolled over to find my side of the bed empty. He also found a warm seat in front of his computer, which I'm sure was no consolation. Without his support and encouragement, this book would not have been possible.

To my mother,
who let me dress as Dale Evans
and Roy Rogers
and put me on the Happy Trail to play
and
to Fred, Lisa, Justin, and Adam
who have taught me that play
is critical at every age!

Transdisciplinary

Play-Based

Intervention

TPBA Play-Based TPBI

1

A Review of Transdisciplinary Play-Based Assessment

Transdisciplinary play-based assessment (TPBA) is a functional assessment process designed for children between infancy and 6 years of age. TPBA examines a child's performance across all areas of development while he or she interacts with a play facilitator, parent(s) or caregiver(s), and a peer or group of peers. By following the child's lead, the facilitator keeps the child interested and motivated, thus encouraging optimal levels of performance. As the facilitator helps the child make transitions among play areas and play materials, an observing transdisciplinary team notes the child's skills, behaviors, and learning and interaction styles. These observations lead to an assessment of the child across cognitive, social-emotional, communication and language, and sensorimotor domains (Linder, 1993).

The TPBA model and process are described in detail in *Transdisciplinary Play-Based Assessment: A Functional Approach to Working with Young Children* (revised edition) (Linder, 1993). For the purposes of this volume, TPBA is reviewed in this chapter.

HOW DOES TPBA WORK?

The TPBA model was designed to examine a child's developmental skills, underlying developmental processes, learning style, and interaction patterns. Because children are different in each of these areas, TPBA is unique and flexible, taking into consideration each child's characteristics and needs. However, in all cases, the TPBA revolves around the observations made by a transdisciplinary team who observe a carefully planned play session that generally lasts for an hour to an hour and a half. The content of the assessment, the team members who plan and observe the play session, the session itself, and the questions addressed differ depending on the child being evaluated.

Each TPBA begins with information-gathering. The child's parent(s) or caregiver(s) provide information about his or her development and behavior patterns. For the purposes of this volume, *caregiver(s)* refers to person(s) other than parents who are primarily responsible for the child. This may include a foster parent, grandparent, or another relative. Based on the information collected about the child, the play session is planned. This planning includes structuring the session so the child can be observed across the four developmental domains, arranging toys and playthings to entice the child to play using various skills and strategies, and determining which team members will play the roles of play facilitator and parent facilitator. Videotaping of the session is recommended, as the tape is helpful during post-session analysis and in discussions with parents and other professionals. Documentation of progress throughout the child's program is also enhanced through video updates.

Phases of the TPBA Play Session

The play session is divided into six phases that may be re-ordered to meet the developmental and behavioral needs of the individual child (Table 1). The process is meant to be flexible and responsive; for example, some children may need or want to engage in motor play first, a snack might be added to the house area, or a peer might join the child in motor play. Generally, however, the play facilitator begins Phase I with *unstructured facilitation*, during which the child leads the play and the play facilitator imitates, models, and expands the child's play. The facilitator watches to see what the child does spontaneously before modeling for the child. "Wait time," or observing the child and waiting for a response, is important. Moving the child into turn-taking with the facilitator is also emphasized. If the child is an infant or has difficulty with separation, a parent or caregiver remains with the child until the child feels comfortable with the adult moving away.

Structured facilitation, which is used during Phase II, is provided to incorporate aspects of play that the child did not spontaneously initiate. Using transition techniques that allow the child to feel as if he or she is still in control, the play facilitator entices the child to move to different toys, areas, materials, and activities. The play facilitator may engage in parallel play with a different toy, play a game with the parent, or use a transition object to lure the child to a new activity. During an activity, the play facilitator may also attempt different types of interactions to ascertain which techniques are most successful in promoting higher-level problem-solving.

Depending on the child's developmental level, observation of peer interaction can provide insight into social interactions. A peer is introduced in Phase III to enable observation of *child–child interaction*. The peer, who may be familiar to the child, should have slightly higher-functioning abilities than the child being assessed. A peer of the same sex as the child being assessed is also preferred. The play facilitator waits and watches to see the interactions that take place spontaneously between the children. The play facilitator then may structure the environment with toys or prompts so as to encourage interaction. If a child is currently in a program or group child care setting, observations of the child's actions in a group may prove useful. These observations may be done at a separate time. For the child who is not yet at a developmental level in which he or she is interested in peers, this phase may be omitted. Siblings do not substitute for peers. Interactions with siblings may also be observed and may provide useful information, but peer interactions are frequently different in nature. Insights derived from observation of the child's interactions assist in planning social arrangements in the classroom.

During Phase IV, *parent–child interaction* is observed in both unstructured and structured play. Just as parent(s) learn about their child from observing the child's interactions with the facilitator, the team can learn much from observing the parent's interactions with the child. If the child spends a great deal of time with a specific caregiver, observations of caregiver–child interactions may also be useful. The child may communicate uniquely, initiate or respond differently, demonstrate varying social interactions, and play at a dissimilar developmental level than was observed with the play facilitator. When patterns or interactions are then analyzed to determine which interaction styles elicit higher levels of performance, the information gained is helpful to both the parent(s) or caregiver(s) and the rest of the team.

As indicated previously, the parent(s) or caregiver(s) are also asked to leave the room at some time during the assessment to allow the team to observe separation and reunion behaviors. If separation is difficult for the child, this aspect of the assessment is reserved until the end of the

Table 1. Sample format of a TPBA play session

Phase	Types of play	Time (minutes)
I	Unstructured facilitation	20–25
II	Structured facilitation	10–15
III	Child–child interaction	5–10
IV	Parent/caregiver–child interaction	
	A. Unstructured	5
	B. Separation	
	C. Structured	5
V	Motor play	
	A. Unstructured	5–10
	B. Structured	5–10
VI	Snack	5–10
	Total time:	60–90

session. Responses on the part of the child (or parent/caregiver) may help the team to make decisions about the appropriateness of home-based or center-based programs or the supports needed by parents or caregivers concerning separation issues. Concerns about interaction patterns may require follow-up assessment.

Phase V includes unstructured and structured *motor play*. Depending on the child's age and developmental level, the motor play can be done in the playroom or in a "motor area" if one is available. An outdoor play area may also be utilized. Again, the child's spontaneous preferences are observed. The child usually gravitates to those areas that are pleasurable and in which he or she functions more proficiently. The play facilitator, following the child's lead, may imitate the child or engage in a reciprocal game, such as throwing a ball or rocking in a boat. An obstacle course may be set up to require the child to maneuver over, around, and through different pieces of equipment and tactile materials in a fun "lion hunt" or other fantasy adventure. Especially for children who have been involved in individual therapy, the motor area must entice the child into functional activity. If the activity feels like therapy, the child may be hesitant, fearful, and resistant to movement. The physical or occupational therapist may want to be involved with the child during this time if a "hands-on" examination is desired. However, after much practice, most facilitators can become proficient at getting the child to move through various positions and movement experiences. In this way, the child does not have to adjust to new people in the assessment process.

The final phase, Phase VI, of the TPBA is a *snack*, which enables the team to screen for oral motor difficulties and conduct developmental observations related to fine motor skills, social interactions, language usage, and other adaptive skills. The snack may be done during the play session in the "house" area or may be set up at the end of the play session as a "treat." Inclusion of the parent(s) or caregiver(s) and/or the peer(s) provides an additional opportunity to examine social skills. This piece should be viewed as an oral motor screening, as intrusive examination of the mouth is not conducted.

Observation Guidelines

Included in *Transdisciplinary Play-Based Assessment* (Linder, 1993) are systematic observation guidelines for cognitive, social-emotional, communication and language, and sensorimotor development. A chapter related to each developmental domain includes observation questions, age tables, worksheets, and Summary Sheets.

The domain guidelines are divided into categories and are primarily stated in the form of questions. Questions encourage the team members to address qualitative aspects of "how" the child performs, not just "if" the child performs a task. Worksheets assist team members in documenting behaviors associated with categories listed in the guidelines, while age ranges are included to assist the team in determining deveopmental levels for specific skills. A Summary Sheet for each domain provides space for recording the strengths observed and the needs related to intervention. Space is also included for judging whether the child's skills are age-appropriate and qualitatively adequate.

Each team member elects to observe the child's skills in one or more of the developmental areas during the play session. Team members may choose to observe the area related to their specific discipline or to watch the child's play in a different area. Rotating the areas observed allows each of the team members to acquire knowledge and expertise for all areas and leads to more holistic observations.

Who Can Be Assessed with TPBA?

TPBA was designed to work with all children with developmental functioning between infancy and 6 years of age. Younger infants have been successfully assessed with TPBA as well. This includes children at risk and those with and without disabilities.

Who Conducts a TPBA?

TPBA is implemented by a transdisciplinary team, which is generally composed of the child's parents or primary caregivers and representatives from various disciplines. Because the TPBA addresses four domains (cognitive, social-emotional, communication and language, and sensorimotor), the team should include professionals and paraprofessionals from these fields.

Like the TPBA itself, the team conducting the assessment and planning the intervention will be different for each child. For this reason, anyone with knowledge of the child's development may be invited to participate. It is most important that the team members communicate continually prior to and throughout the child's intervention progam.

How Are Parents or Caregivers Involved in a TPBA?   Parents or caregivers are very important members of the TPBA team. They participate throughout the process. Before the play session, parents or caregivers complete checklists and provide information about the child's developmental status. This information is then used to plan the play session. During the session, parents or caregivers may observe along with the other team members and/or participate in the play. After the assessment and throughout the intervention process, parents and caregivers help to plan and implement a program for the child and the family.

Where Is a TPBA Conducted?

A TPBA can be conducted in any creative play environment. What is important is that the environment include toys and playthings that will facilitate exploratory, manipulative, and problem-solving behaviors, emotional expression, and language skills. Because appropriate materials are usually available in preschool or infant intervention rooms, these settings are often used. However, the child's home may be used as the TPBA site if items in the home are supplemented by other items provided by the team.

How Can a TPBA Be Modified?

Aspects of the TPBA can be modified or omitted depending on the type of child being assessed, the age of the child, the information needed, and the requirements of the state. The composition of the team and the roles various team members play may also be changed depending on the skills of team members and the needs of the child being assessed. The process may also be modified to complement other assessment approaches that are required.

The TPBA guidelines provide a systematic structure for observation and discussion of cognitive, social-emotional, communication and language, and sensorimotor development. The discussion of the child's performance and determination of needs is meant to be a team process and should include a discussion of information obtained through other assessment processes as well. All children do not need the same battery of tests and procedures. In fact, standardizing the assessment process defeats the purpose of assessment, which is to look at each child as an individual with different strengths and needs. Toward this end, diverse assessment methods are needed.

The comparison of a child's developmental progress with other children of the same age through the use of standardized instruments may be needed in order to make reasonable determinations about the child's developmental status. However, the selection of appropriate instruments is critical, and no decisions should ever be made on the basis of test scores alone. The inclusion of a process that includes observation of play, such as the one recommended in *Transdisciplinary Play-Based Assessment* (Linder, 1993), can provide a more accurate portrayal of the child's abilities and also lay the foundation for intervention. Use of a play-based assessment process links naturally to a play-based intervention approach.

Analysis of the TPBA

Following the play session, the team can meet briefly with or without the parents or caregivers to review their observations and initial findings. (Most parents are ready to leave with their child after the play assessment, as they know there will be future meetings to discuss the individualized family service plan [IFSP] or individualized education program [IEP]. Many programs also provide the family with a copy of the TPBA videotape.) At this or a subsequent meeting, the team reviews the TPBA guidelines, which provide structure for observation of development, while observing the videotape (if available), and completes the summary form to determine the child's strengths and needs with regard to intervention. If the assessment is being used to determine eligibility for a program, the rating and justification sections of the form are also completed.

Team interaction is critical for analysis. To save time, the team members may complete their assigned sections independently, but discussion of the summary sheets by all disciplines is essential. This process ensures the integration of information and cross-disciplinary input into the child's intervention program. The interrelationship between developmental areas thus becomes clear, and integrated planning can occur.

WHY DOES TPBA WORK?

TPBA is effective for several reasons that are best explained when compared to traditional assessment procedures. Generally, traditional assessment procedures do not promote the child's optimal performance and may result in inaccurate conclusions concerning his or her current developmental status and abilities. Discussed here are the advantages of TPBA over such traditional assessments.

Natural Environments

The TPBA play session is conducted in a natural, relaxed, and stimulating environment to promote the child's comfort and optimal performance. When the play session is held in the child's home or in a room much like those he or she has seen in child care or preschool settings, the child is more likely to use typical language, to manipulate items comfortably, and to interact with the play facilitator or peers naturally. The child is usually surrounded by toys and materials that he or she has seen before. Making such arrangements is facilitated by the pre-play session information-gathering conducted with the parent(s) or caregiver(s). These arrangements tend also to enhance development of rapport between the child and the facilitator.

Rapport with Examiner

In traditional assessments, a number of examiners may interact with the child. Each has a different approach and each is reacted to differently by the child, which may bias results regarding the child's developmental status and abilities. With TPBA, there is only one examiner (the play facilitator) with whom the child develops a rapport.

The role assumed by the play facilitator in TPBA differs from that assumed by examiners in traditional assessments. Rather than taking the lead and casting the child as the follower as in traditional assessments, the play facilitator in a TPBA follows *the child's lead*, imitating, modeling, suggesting, and only occasionally requesting.

Flexibility of the Model

Unlike standardized tests, the TPBA model is flexible enough to allow variations dependent on the individual child's characteristics and needs. Different types of toys and playthings may be provided, environmental conditions may be varied, the language used by the facilitator may be adapted, and the sequence and content of the session may be altered to enhance the child's performance and put him or her at ease. These changes can be planned based on the child's developmental level, disability or impairment, and interests.

Holistic Approach to Assessment

Unlike most assessment processes, TPBA does not assess the child by discipline. Although representatives from various disciplines are involved, their roles in the assessment process may vary. These roles are determined in the planning session before the play session. The primary roles include: 1) the child facilitator, who plays with the child and elicits developmental behaviors; 2) the parent facilitator, who sits with the parent and discusses the behaviors being seen compared to those observed at home; 3) observers, who watch the child's play and take notes on observed behaviors; and 4) a video camera operator, who records the session for later discussion and use with the intervention team and parents.

Parental or Caregiver Involvement

In TPBA, parents or caregivers observe and participate in the play session, which can be beneficial for both the child and the parent(s) or caregiver(s). The parent(s)' or caregiver(s)' presence contributes to the child being at ease and performing at optimal levels.

Parent or caregiver involvement on the transdisplinary team also enhances the TPBA results. While observing the play session and participating in the post-session analysis, they may uniquely contribute because of their special relationships to the child. Finally, in contrast to traditional assessments, because parents or caregivers witness and take part in the assessments, they may better understand the reasons for the professionals' recommendations and may more effectively assist in intervention.

Integration with Other Approaches

TPBA was designed as part of a multilevel evaluation and assessment process. The information the TPBA yields can often be integrated with what may have been learned earlier from other tests and family input. When combined, all of this information can be used to formulate an IFSP or an IEP.

Figure TPBA is a child-oriented process in which the facilitator follows the child's lead.

What Does TPBA Yield?   Following the play session, the team is often able to compile summary information about the child's developmental status and skills and abilities in each of the four domains. The team members will also have insight concerning some of the child's behaviors and the way he or she learns and interacts with others.

Identification of Service Needs   The information gleaned while watching the child during the play session and on the videotape and from analyzing observations based on the TPBA guidelines can lead to the identification of strengths and areas of concern in each of the four domains. Combining these results with the use of age ranges on skill items and team members' professional judgment assists in the determination of the type and amount of services needed.

Development of Intervention Plans   As mentioned previously, IFSPs and IEPs can be developed based on how the child functions in the various play situations and with the play facilitator, parent(s) or caregiver(s), and peer(s). Because the parent(s) or caregiver(s) are involved in the TPBA, the IFSP and/or IEP is more likely to be functional and meaningful to them.

Evaluation of Progress   The TPBA process can be used to evaluate the child's progress on an ongoing and year-end basis and to update the child's objectives as needed. TPBA results can be used to meet federal legislation stipulations requiring yearly reviews for IEPs and semiannual reviews for IFSPs. The TPBA process may be repeated each year for pre- or postevaluation.

WHAT HAPPENS AFTER A TPBA?

After the team, which includes the parents or caregivers, has developed the child's goals and objectives, the ways in which these goals and objectives will be accomplished must be considered. This is where the transdisciplinary play-based intervention approach can be useful. The team can use the guidelines provided in this text to develop a functional and practical program for the child at home and/or at school. In addition, the TPBI approach provides a process model for developing activities, curriculum, and ongoing assessment procedures for monitoring the child's progress.

REFERENCE

Linder, T. W. (1993). *Transdisciplinary play-based assessment: A functional approach to working with young children* (rev. ed.). Baltimore: Paul H. Brookes Publishing Co.

I

The Fundamentals of TPBI

2

An Introduction to Transdisciplinary Play-Based Intervention

Transdisciplinary play-based intervention involves the child in an enjoyable process from which an individualized and meaningful curriculum can be developed. Designed to provide intervention guidelines and suggestions for the parent(s), caregiver(s), and other facilitating adult(s), TPBI is effective for children from infancy to 6 years of age. TPBI ensures that the child's present skills are consistent and qualitatively sound and encourages higher developmental levels of behavior in cognitive, social-emotional, communication and language, and sensorimotor domains.

WHAT IS TRANSDISCIPLINARY PLAY-BASED INTERVENTION?

Transdisciplinary play-based intervention (TPBI) is a natural extension of transdisciplinary play-based assessment (TPBA) (Linder, 1993). Like the assessment process, TPBI is flexible, holistic, and dynamic. Based on the Observation Guidelines provided for each developmental domain in *Transdisciplinary Play-Based Assessment* (Linder, 1993), TPBI begins with an understanding of the child's developmental skills, underlying developmental processes, learning style, and interaction patterns. This information, combined with knowledge about the child's interests and the family's goals for development, is used by a team that includes the parent(s) and representatives from a variety of disciplines to create an intervention plan.

The TPBA and TPBI processes are cyclical in nature. Outcomes of the transdisciplinary play-based assessment lead directly into planning transdisciplinary play-based intervention strategies and curricula. Integration of continued observational information within the intervention process results in ongoing modification of objectives and, consequently, strategies for working with individual children. This cyclical assessment–intervention process, which is conducted in the child's natural environments, results in a dynamic, responsive approach to working with children and families.

The purpose of transdisciplinary play-based intervention is to strengthen developmental processes and increase functional skills across the cognitive, social-emotional, communication and language, and sensorimotor domains. The intent is to relate domains and integrate intervention strategies into an inclusive curriculum. For example, during a team planning discussion, the child's abilities to sequence and organize actions and ideas in dramatic play (in the cognitive domain) might be related to the child's sequencing of communicative acts (in the communication and language domain) and turn-taking and imitation with peers (in the social-emotional domain). In turn, the child's need for stability in order to use fine motor skills (in the sensori-motor domain) might be related to his or her dramatic play skills and social interactions. The transdisciplinary process encourages the team to develop strategies that reflect the interrelated nature of the child's abilities and disabilities.

WHY USE TPBI?

Transdisciplinary play-based intervention is an effective approach to intervention that can be incorporated into the child's and family's daily routine. A flexible process, TPBI guidelines can be transferred from home to infant and toddler or preschool programs, and for the most part do not require the acquisition of special toys or play materials. TPBI encourages the use of household items and situations the child encounters daily as play materials and opportunities for playful interaction.

TPBI is based on theories related to child growth and development: 1) children learn by engaging and acting upon their environment (Piaget, 1962); 2) children learn through social interactions involving communication and problem-solving (Vygotsky, 1962, 1978); 3) skills are acquired in increments (Fischer, 1980); 4) play provides a window into the child's inner world (Freud, 1958, 1973); 5) responsiveness and encouragement of the child's autonomy on the adult's part are keys to development (Erikson, 1950); 6) children learn by observing those they admire and care about (Bandura, 1977, 1986); 7) emotions influence and intensify learning

TPBI can be utilized by all persons who interact with the child.

(Campos, Caplovitz, Lamb, Goldsmith, & Stenberg, 1983); and 8) the quality, quantity, fluidity, use, organization, generalization, and intent of the child's thoughts and actions are important to functioning (Lewis & Starr, 1979). These theories contribute to a philosophy of intervention that is child-centered, family-focused, peer-oriented, culturally and developmentally relevant, and based on pleasurable play interactions. (The theoretical and philosophical bases for TPBI are discussed further in Chapter 4.)

To Implement Intervention Plans

When making the transition from assessment to intervention, TPBI requires consideration of the objectives featured in the child's individualized family service plan (IFSP) or individualized education program (IEP). From these objectives, specific strategies are developed by the team. These strategies are designed to work as part of the child's daily routine.

To Plan Intervention and To Evaluate Progress

TPBI features two helpful forms that can be modified according to the child's needs and/or a center's requirements. These forms, called the Team Ideas for Play (TIP) Sheet and the Team Assessment of Play (TAP) Sheet, can be used to generate ideas to meet intervention objectives and to monitor the child's progress.

To Serve as a Basis for Curriculum Development

TPBI can be incorporated into any curriculum model that is congruent with the theoretical and philosophical basis of the process. This text proposes the use of the TPBI model with a storybook curriculum. Forms and description of the curriculum planning process are included in this volume. However, TPBI can be integrated into other home-based and center-based curricular approaches.

To Build a Transdisciplinary Team

TPBI requires the communication and problem-solving of a team of professionals and parents. The process of team building is not always an easy one, but the procedures outlined will assist teams in developing stronger team communication and expanded parental involvement in the planning and intervention process. The resulting cooperative team effort, implemented through an integrated therapy model, provides a mechanism for ongoing communication among team members and consequently more effective intervention.

WHO CAN RECEIVE INTERVENTION?

The TPBI process can be used with children with developmental functioning between infancy and 6 years of age. TPBI was designed for children who have disabilities, children at risk, and children without disabilities.

WHO CAN CONDUCT TPBI?

The intervention process is intended to be implemented by a transdisciplinary team that includes the parent(s) or caregiver(s). The composition of the child's team is determined by his or her individualized needs and the family's goals for development. In most cases, however, representatives from the cognitive, social-emotional, communication and language, and sensorimotor fields are included in the team. The TPBI guidelines suggest that each member of the team become familiar with the goals and developmental levels of *all* of the domains, as this approach makes it possible for the team to consider the whole child rather than the child's needs in a specific area. The advantages of a transdisciplinary approach to intervention are discussed in more detail in Chapter 4.

HOW ARE PARENT(S) OR CAREGIVER(S) INVOLVED?

The role of parent(s) or caregiver(s) is carried over from their input in the TPBA process. The child's primary caregiver(s) are usually his or her parent(s); however, care for some children may be provided by grandparents, foster parents, or other individuals. In such instances, these persons should be involved in both the TPBA and TPBI processes.

As members of the intervention team, parents or caregivers participate in the development of the TIP Sheet and the implementation of the intervention strategies derived from the form. Some parents and caregivers may opt to complete TAP Sheets as home-based intervention proceeds; others may prefer that a home visitor complete this portion of the process. The extent of the family's involvement is always their decision.

WHERE IS TPBI CONDUCTED?

TPBI can be implemented in almost any play environment using whatever play materials and opportunities are at hand. For the purposes of this volume, the discussion of play environments focuses on the home, infant and toddler, and preschool and kindergarten center-based programs.

WHAT DOES THE TPBI PROCESS INVOLVE?

TPBI is an ongoing planning process that begins when programmatic decisions are made with the family. After completing the TPBA, the team will have determined at what levels the child is functioning in each of the domains and how the child best interacts and learns. The TPBI Planner (see Chapters 8–11) then can be used to identify principles for intervention and the specific types of play materials and opportunities that will enhance and promote the child's development. The suggestions in the TPBI Planner can be matched with the highest level of performance observed and the areas of readiness determined in the TPBA observations. These suggestions are used as a basis for problem-solving and generating other alternatives that will be useful in the home and/or school environment.

As objectives are written for the child, alternative approaches to intervention that correspond to these objectives are written on the TIP Sheets for home and school. These are adapted to meet the family's needs and desires for involvement in home play activities and interaction opportunities. For example, suggestions for interactions relating to language objectives might be incorporated into mealtimes, shopping, television time, and bedtime if the parents or caregivers indicate that these were natural times for them to interact with the child. Early interventionists, teachers, and therapists also incorporate these ideas into the curriculum used for intervention. They might, for instance, make suggestions for incorporating these same language objectives into the sensory play center, the dramatic play area, snacktime, and gross motor play.

As the intervention progam is implemented, the process is monitored through the use of TAP Sheets (see Chapter 5). Observation intervals are determined by the team and parents or caregivers. These forms allow the observing parents, caregivers, or team members to document the child's progress on individual objectives across various times of the day. This information can then be discussed by the team to determine if the child is making progress. If the child has accomplished objectives and is generalizing skills and processes across the day, settings, and people, a new objective can be written better to meet the child's current functioning level. If the objective is not being met, the team must discuss whether the objective is appropriate for the child and whether other intervention strategies should be tried to facilitate progress. Thus, the TPBI process continuously evaluates the effectiveness of the intervention for each child in a program. Periodic re-evaluations using transdisciplinary play-based assessment can also be done for pre- and post-intervention comparisons.

Another aspect of TPBI involves the curriculum development process. Forms are included for team planning of a play-based storybook curriculum (see Chapter 7). As new planning sheets are developed based on the cultural and developmental needs and interests of the child, the team develops an individualized curriculum that can be used and adapted for future groups of children.

Transdisciplinary play-based intervention is, thus, an individualized planning process for specific children and their families, for groups of children involved in a classroom curriculum, and for teams working with children and families. The process can be adapted to meet the unique needs of each participant in the intervention process.

REFERENCES

Bandura, A. (1977). *Social learning theory.* Englewood, Cliffs, NJ: Prentice Hall.

Bandura, A. (1986). *Social foundations of thought and action: A social cognitive theory.* Englewood Cliffs, NJ: Prentice Hall.

Campos, J.J., Caplovitz, K.B., Lamb, M.E., Goldsmith, H.H., & Stenberg, C. (1983). Socioemotional development. In M.M. Haith & J.J. Campos (Eds.), *Handbook of child psychology: Volume 2. Infancy and developmental psychobiology* (4th ed.) (pp. 783–915). New York: John Wiley & Sons.

Erikson, E.H. (1950). *Childhood and society.* New York: Norton.

Fischer, K.W. (1980). A theory of cognitive development: The control and construction of hierarchical skills. *Psychological Review, 87,* 477–531.

Freud, A. (1958). Child observation and prediction of development: A memorial lecture in honor of Ernst Kris. *Psychoanalytic Review of the Child, 13,* 97–98.

Freud, A. (1973). *The writings of Anna Freud, Vol. 7. Normality and pathology in childhood.* New York: International Universities Press.

Lewis, M., & Starr, M.D. (1979). Developmental continuity. In J.D. Osofsky (Ed.), *Handbook of infant development.* New York: John Wiley & Sons.

Linder, T.W. (1993). *Transdisciplinary play-based assessment: A functional approach to working with young children* (rev. ed.). Baltimore: Paul H. Brookes Publishing Co.

Piaget, J. (1962). *Play, dreams, and imitation in childhood.* New York: Norton.

Vygotsky, L. (1962). *Thought and language.* Cambridge, MA: MIT Press.

Vygotsky, L. (1978). *Mind in society: The development of higher psychological processes.* Cambridge, MA: Harvard University Press.

3

Traditional Intervention and Transdisciplinary Play-Based Intervention

A Comparison

In *Transdisciplinary Play-Based Assessment* (Linder, 1993), the difference between traditional assessment and transdisciplinary play-based assessment was illustrated through the eyes of a child. The process of transdisciplinary play-based intervention may also be understood by comparing a more traditional intervention approach with that of the TPBI—again through the eyes of a child.

TRADITIONAL INTERVENTION

You are a 3-year-old in a preschool classroom. Empty tables are placed around the room with chairs tucked under them. In one corner, pieces of carpet are arranged on the floor in a half-circle. A toy stove and sink are in another area with pots, pans, and dishes. Toys are on shelves around the room. Children are quiet as they enter the room, hang their coats, and go to sit on their carpet squares. The teacher's assistant, Lois, is sitting in the middle of the circle, looking at books with the children. You approach the circle and try to remember which square is yours. You sit down next to your friend Celia and start to show her the toy you got at McDonald's last night. Miss Johnson, the teacher, sits down in front of the children and tells you to put your toy in your pocket and move to your square. You put the toy in your pocket, but stay where you are. You look down at the floor and feel sad because you have done something wrong. You don't know where you should move. Lois takes you by the hand and says, "This one is yours. It is a red one. Can you say red?" You repeat, "Red" and sit on the square.

The teacher gets out the calendar and asks, "What day is it today?" Everyone shouts out something different. You don't say anything. The teacher points to David and says, "That's right, David. It's Tuesday. Yesterday was Monday. Today is Tuesday. Let's look at our calendar and see what day it is." Pointing to the number on the calendar, Miss Johnson says, "Yesterday was January 25th, so today is----?" It is quiet. No one speaks. Finally, José says, "Five." Miss Johnson says, "No, not five. It is January 26. Let's all say that. It's Tuesday, January 26." Numerous mumbling sounds intermingled with recognizable words and numbers are heard. "Is it cold or hot?" the teacher continues. You say, "Cold or hot," repeating what you just heard. Miss Johnson is always asking you to say what she just said. "Is it hot, Chanda?" she asks. "No," you say looking down and feeling silly. "No," replies Miss Johnson, "It is *cold* outside. Let's all say, 'It is Tuesday.'"

Everyone repeats, "It is Tuesday." "January," says Miss Johnson. "January," everyone says. "26th," says Miss Johnson. "26th," say the children. "And it is cold outside," continues Miss Johnson. "Cold outside," the children repeat.

You have been fidgeting during this activity. You don't want to say all these things. You have found that toy in your pocket and have slid back off your carpet square and started to play with it. Miss Johnson starts to sing the welcome song. It's okay and kinda fun at first 'cause you know the words. But you have to wait a long time for them to sing "welcome" to you 'cause your square is almost at the end. At last they sing, "Welcome Chanda," and you smile and join in.

Finally, it is time to get up. The teacher tells you to go to the art table with Lois. Lois is waiting at the art table with paper placed on the table in front of each chair. Five other children also are told to go to the art table with Lois. Each sits in front of a piece of blue construction paper. Lois gives everyone three white circles of different sizes. "What is something you do in the winter?" asks Lois. Joey says, "Ski." Ricardo says, "Go to the store." You say nothing. "Well," replies Lois, "some people do those things, and some people build a snowman. We're going to build a snowman! You have three white circles, a big circle, a middle-size circle, and a little circle. When you put them on top of each other, like mine, you have a snowman." Lois helps everyone glue the big circle on the bottom, the middle-size circle in the middle, and the small circle on the top. Then she gives everyone a black crayon to draw eyes, a nose, and a mouth— just like on hers. You feel bad 'cause your snowman doesn't look like Lois's. You tried to make eyes, but it just looks all scribbly. How did she make those marks? Lois then gives everyone a picture of a snowman from a coloring book to color. When everyone at the table has finished (which took a while 'cause Marcus was really slow), Lois tells you all to go over to the "motor area" to play bean bag throw. You notice that your friend Celia is coming to make a snowman now and you'd like to stay and help her, but Lois says, "Go over with Miss Johnson and see if you can hit the box." Miss Johnson has everyone line up and take turns throwing the bean bag into the box. You miss the box every time, but Miss Johnson smiles and shouts, "Great! Good try!" (She obviously can't see very well.) While you are standing at the back of the line, Willy starts poking you and trying to get your toy out of your pocket. You cry and yell, "No!" Miss Johnson takes the toy and puts it on her desk. She puts Willy in "timeout" and tells you not to bring toys to school if you don't want other kids to play with them.

After bean bag throw, the children are brought back to the tables for snack. Everyone has to say, "Juice, please," "I want a cracker," and "Thank you." After you clean up your space, Miss Johnson says you may pick a play area in which to play. Celia is going to the kitchen, so you go there, too. You and Celia play in the kitchen for a while. Miss Johnson and Lois are busy with children playing with puzzles and coloring. You watch Celia and do what she does.

After what seems like just a few minutes, Miss Johnson calls you to come back to the carpet square. This time you get it right. At least you think it's right. No one tells you to move. This is language group. Miss Johnson shows pictures and asks kids what is the name of the thing in the picture. When it is your turn, she asks, "What is this?" You know what it is. Mommy uses it to make that hot, dark stuff that she says you can't have. You look at Miss Johnson and smile. "It is a coffee pot," says Miss Johnson. Say "Coffee pot." "Towee ot," you say. "No. Say C-C-coffee p-p-pot." "Towee ot." you try again. "Jason," says Miss Johnson, "You say coffee pot." "Coffee pot," spurts Jason. You don't like Jason.

Just then, Miss Annie comes to get you and take you down the hall for therapy. She rolls you over a ball, has you walk on a balance beam, swings you in a big net, and has you climb over a big plastic hill. Then she takes you back to the classroom.

You are back in time for singing. You try to make your fingers move like everyone else's, but it's hard. It's a nice song about a bunny and you try to sing a few of the words. Then it is time for the "good-bye" song, and Mom is there to get you. Good. Now you can go home and play!

Limitations of Traditional Intervention

The previous scenario combines facets from many different traditional models of intervention. The hallmark of most of these models is that intervention is teacher-directed with many unrelated activities that "work" on specific skills. Children are often placed in groups and are told to perform certain tasks. The teacher provides direction, correction, and praise for successful performance. As the groups are often large, the children must wait for their turn to perform. Areas are arranged with materials that are to be used in specific ways. Worksheets, puzzles, stringing beads, and paper and coloring activities are common activities. Therapy is conducted outside of the classroom.

Teacher-Directed Environment   The environment in the traditional intervention model may at first glance look very similar to a TPBI environment (see p. 21 and Chapter 6). The toys and materials may be similar. But the arrangement, availability, and use of the toys and materials are very different. Opportunities for choice, variety, repetition, and child-directed interactions are limited.

One of the disadvantages of traditional approaches is that children are always told what to do and how to do it. Children who are never given the opportunity to make choices and plan activities may never learn how to take initiative. Children need to know how to design their own play activities and be able to modify materials and experiences creatively to suit their own interests and developmental needs. The environment in traditional models, however, is structured for the child to achieve specific results. The content of what a child learns is controlled. Toys and materials are set out for the child with a definite purpose. Success is achieved by using the materials in prescribed ways. The room is usually arranged with a large group area and small group areas for table work. Toy areas are restricted to distinct places in the room.

Skills-Driven Curriculum   The content of what is taught in most traditional intervention programs is derived from items missed on various assessment instruments. A child who misses an item, for instance, "Knows three colors," now has learning this item (the three colors) as an objective. Color activities are arranged and colors are presented, questioned, and practiced until the child can identify three. Whether knowledge of colors is functionally relevant or important to the child is not questioned. Activities in the curriculum are frequently derived from books or activity cards that address specific skills on the assessment checklist. Activities may be planned around language, motor, or cognitive skills. Functionality, interrelatedness of areas, or interests of the child may be a minor consideration. Many curricula for children with severe disabilities have tasks broken down into minute steps so that each activity is a series of mini-activities that lead to the final shaped behavior.

Global Educational Goals   A typical preschool class designed for children without disabilities, however, may offer a variety of activities for groups of children, but not have specific goals or objectives in mind. Activities in the "regular education" preschool model are usually teacher directed, as well. The children may be rotated through a variety of centers or activities. The teacher in the regular preschool setting has more global educational goals and believes that children will learn by being exposed to different activities. Consequently, the benefit the child derives from each activity is left to chance. Such an approach may serve the typically developing child (a questionable premise), but the needs of the child with disabilities may be lost in such a setting. Individual modifications and facilitation techniques addressing each child's unique abilities and readiness are required to enhance each child's developmental, educational, and therapeutic progress.

Adult-Dominated Interactions   Adults in the traditional intervention models are directive. They tell children what to do and how to do it. They ask many "closed" questions (ones with one "right" answer). As a result of the adult-dominated-interactions, the language opportunities available to children are restricted to those in which they respond to direct requests, thus limiting the potential language usage. Adults have control over where the children are in the room and what they are doing at any given moment in time. Attention is directed toward certain items and away from any materials that might compete for attention. Behavior management is important, as loss of control means no learning is taking place. There is a definite hierarchy in the classroom, with each player having a prescribed role. The role of the child is to respond passively to the requests of the adults in the room.

Segregated Therapy   Therapy is also directed and is usually done outside of the classroom in a special therapeutic environment with more toys and materials designed to elicit particular responses. Therapeutic goals and processes are viewed as distinct entities and are not integrated into the classroom curriculum. Therapy methods may also emphasize nonfunctional approaches that are successful only in the therapy rooms, but do not translate into behavioral changes in the child's real life activities. For example, the speech-language therapist may be able to get the child to make the appropriate sounds in words using a mirror and reinforcement, but as soon as the child leaves the therapy room, the articulation errors return. The occupational therapist may be able to increase tone using bouncing and stimulating actions, but by the time the child returns to the classroom, his or her tone is again diminished. When sitting at the table to perform fine motor tasks, the low tone once again interferes with the child's stability, which is needed to be able to use both hands together successfully.

TRANSDISCIPLINARY PLAY-BASED INTERVENTION

You are the same 3-year-old in the preschool classroom. When you enter the room, you stand and look around trying to decide where to go first. Kids are playing in different areas of the room. Your friend Celia is in the house area so you decide to go there. The teacher's assistant, Lois, is also playing there. She is all dressed up in a hat and coat and is carrying a purse. She says she came by for dinner. You and Celia make her dinner. Boy, is she hungry! She asks for fruit and vegetables, meat, and a drink. You and Celia find everything in the refrigerator and the cupboard. Lois then gets sleepy, so you put her to bed.

Miss Johnson blinks the lights to tell everyone to clean up and come to circle. You sit next to Celia while Miss Johnson reads a book about a mitten. It is the same book she read yesterday, so you remember the story and can answer when she asks, "What do you think is going to happen next?" After the story, you and the other children choose whether to act out the story, play with blocks and little animals, play in the "snow" in the water table, or make something in the art area. You want to crawl in the mitten like yesterday. (It is really a sleeping bag, but you pretend it is a mitten like in the book.) You go to the story area. You and the other children pretend to pull wood on a sled through the forest, lose your mitten, and be animals crawling into the mitten. Miss Annie helps you think about the next part of the story—how to get through the woods, over logs, under a tunnel, and into the mitten. Sometimes the other therapist, Miss Felicia, comes to play, too. You wish she were here today. She's funny. After crawling through the woods and into the mitten several times, you decide to make a mitten at the art table.

Using different materials, you trace around your hand, cut out the mittens, and sew them together with a big needle and thread. Lois helps you hold the mittens together and move the needle up and down. After that, you decide to go to the "sensory" area. In the water table, which is full of white packing peanuts and different colors and sizes of mittens, you find animals hidden in the peanuts and fit them into the mittens—just like in the story. You then wander over to the quiet corner and punch the green button on the tape recorder so you can listen to the story again while you look at the pictures in the book. You can hear Miss Johnson's voice reading the story and saying, "Turn the page," when you need to look at the next picture.

Intervention built upon the child's interests and motivation are more effective than traditional interventions.

At snacktime, you play funny games with your fingers and mouth, make silly noises, and sing songs. You get to help set the table with one plate for each place. You eat carrots like the rabbit in the story. You even get to peel them with a peeler.

At the end of playtime, Miss Johnson calls you together to sing songs and do fingerplays. You sing a song about the little kittens who lost their mittens. You get to tell what your favorite play activity was today. You say you liked crawling in the sleeping bag. The teacher writes down what you say on a piece of paper to take home to Mommy and Daddy. You wonder if Daddy will let you play in his sleeping bag at home. When Mommy comes, you run and hand her the note and say, "Mommy, Daddy bag?" She looks at the note and says, "You like crawling into the sleeping bag? Well, I'll bet Daddy will let you play with his sleeping bag." You leave with a big smile on your face.

Strengths of Transdisciplinary Play-Based Intervention

The difference between traditional intervention models and TPBI can be summarized in six words—child-motivating, child-directed, individualized, interaction-focused, integrated, and holistic. These key words describe the advantages of the transdisciplinary play-based intervention approach.

Child-Motivating Environment The TPBI environment is one that is adjusted to satisfy children's interests. Thematically related areas of content reinforce concepts and maximize the motivational aspects of play. Materials are self-motivating to promote exploration. Cultural bias can be eliminated through the use of child-initiated selection among multidimensional activities. The contents of the curriculum, materials, and play opportunities are intended to be designed around the cultural backgrounds and interests of children.

Child-Directed Curriculum   The TPBI approach views the child as central to the curriculum and the play environment. By making activities child-directed to the extent to which the child is capable, the incentives for child initiation and participation are inherent within a given play activity. Motivating the child to engage in an endeavor becomes less of an issue when the child is choosing the toys, materials, and/or activities with which he or she will play. Play (interspersed with eating) is the most motivating enterprise for a child of any age. Capitalizing on what is motivating to the child ensures focused attention, exploration, and problem-solving and encourages the child to question and conceptualize at a higher level. Mastery motivation, or the child's goal-orientation and persistence, is critical to long-term success and is promoted by allowing the child to choose a goal and pursue it. Problem-solving is enhanced as different approaches to the same materials are encouraged. In the TPBI approach, motivation to perform comes from within, not from without (internal versus external rewards) as much as possible.

Of course, there are times when the adult will want the child to move to a new play area after a period of time, to engage in a different activity, or to play in a more appropriate manner. The child's interests and motivations are then used to encourage the child to *want* to shift his or her focus. The adult may move a motivating play object to a new area, engage others that are of interest to the child, model for the child, or use other methods of enticement. The key point is to capture the child's interest and encourage modification of behavior first through the child's internal motivation system and use external supports only as necessary. This contrasts sharply with more traditional approaches to curriculum, where the adult is in control.

Individualized Objectives   Although most intervention programs are individualized (i.e., they identify individual goals and objectives for children), many of these objectives become bureaucratic fodder for the file. They are written at the time of the staffing and are not referred to again until it is time for the child's review. In regular education preschool programs, only the children with identified special needs may have educational objectives. In the TPBI process, the development of objectives is appropriate for all children. Objectives are not just written, but are integrated into the curriculum. The individualization process is magnified by continuing the TPBA observation process in the classroom, allowing objectives to be modified or rewritten as needed.

Another distinction of TPBI is that the objectives that are written are not only related to skills, but also to underlying developmental processes. For instance, the child may have as an objective, "will link three actions into a sequence." This objective can be addressed in any play activity in which the child engages (e.g., at the water table, in the theme area, in the art area). If the child learns to link three actions in sequence in all play activities, he or she will have also increased his or her attention span and problem-solving. Language may also increase, as the child has additional actions on which to comment. Fine motor skills may also be increased through the addition and practice of increased actions. The longer and more varied the play sequence, the more likely it is that the activity will draw peer interaction. Developing individualized objectives related to learning processes thus heightens the potential for increased skills acquisition across all developmental domains.

Interaction-Focused Activities   In the TPBI approach, the relationship with adults is less hierarchical and more reciprocal than in traditional models. The adults actively play and experiment along with the children. Participation replaces direction; facilitation replaces direct teaching, and functional use of skills replaces practice of isolated skills. Practice comes through repetition of desired activities and outcomes—pleasurable repetition for the joy of seeing desired results. The communication between children and adults is a focus within the curriculum. Not only are the language and communication efforts of the child important, but the communication *between* children and adults and children and other children is paramount. The emphasis is not just on the language a child produces, but the quality and amount of communication manifested in interactions. The interactions between adults and children are thus of a different nature than those found in typical programs. The adult uses communication strategies to encourage child-initiation and maintenance of dialogue, not just production of words and phrases.

Integrated Therapy   In many traditional intervention models, the child is removed from the group to attend individual therapy. The therapist may or may not communicate with the teaching staff about what is taking place in therapy. Consequently, the child may practice skills in a nonfunctional environment and have difficulty transferring the skills to other environments. Also, persons who interact with the child may not learn the therapeutic techniques that would assist the child in generalizing the skills to diverse settings. Transdisciplinary play-based intervention provides a format for ongoing team training. Each team member continues to gain knowledge and skills in intervention through discussions about individual children.

Holistic Approach   TPBI is a holistic approach to intervention. Developmental, educational, and therapeutic aspects of intervention are viewed as interrelated and synergistic. Attention to one developmental area in isolation is less effective than holistic approaches and may, in fact, be detrimental to the child's total development. For example, "working" on language without consideration of cognitive level and the social context of communication may encourage the child to "perform" and respond to set questions, but not use language appropriately or functionally with other children and adults. For this reason, the continuing input and involvement of a team of professionals and the parents is critical to the development and implementation of a transdisciplinary, holistic program for the child. Ongoing communication and problem-solving with parents is essential to the effectiveness of the program. Integration of parents onto the transdisciplinary team ensures the functionality of the program at home and school.

Inclusive Classrooms   Another aspect of integration is the importance of including children of many developmental levels and abilities in the classroom. It is critical that all children have peers that provide role models and associates in play. Older or higher-functioning peers act as "play facilitators," demonstrating higher-level cognitive skills such as acting out sequences in dramatic play; social skills such as playing together cooperatively; language skills such as carrying on a conversation; and motor skills such as maneuvering through obstacle courses. No matter how hard they try, adults are not large children and cannot be a replacement for admired peers.

CONCLUSION

Transdisciplinary play-based intervention, like its counterpart transdisciplinary play-based assessment, is meant to provide a method for interacting with children and promoting their development using techniques that are responsive to the needs of young children and their families. TPBI contributes a means for developing a curriculum for children that is not only child-centered, individualized, interactional, integrated, and holistic but also fun.

REFERENCE

Linder, T.W. (1993). *Transdisciplinary play-based assessment: A functional approach to working with young children* (rev. ed.). Baltimore: Paul H. Brookes Publishing Co.

4

Play-Based Intervention and the Transdisciplinary Process

The use of play in curricula for young children is not a new idea. The use of play as an intervention approach with young children with disabilities is a more recent concept. The combination of a play-based curriculum and a transdisciplinary staffing model is a somewhat radical concept. This chapter examines play and the transdisciplinary process as a basis for intervention. Presentation of the definition of play and how play is viewed in the literature leads to a discussion of how play supports development. Examination of the theoretical underpinnings of the transdisciplinary play-based intervention approach helps to establish the rationale for the contribution of play to the development of the young child. The philosophy of TPBI derives from these theories, evidence from research, and current understandings of the needs of and recommended practices for infants, toddlers, preschoolers, and kindergartners.

Also in this chapter, the transdisciplinary process is addressed. The justification for a transdisciplinary team approach and the composition of the team is discussed. Developing a well-functioning transdisciplinary team is a complex process that presents personal, interpersonal, and administrative challenges. Persons initiating the transdisciplinary process should be mindful of these issues and confront them directly.

The TPBI approach is in accordance with the mandates of PL 102-119, the Individuals with Disabilities Education Act Amendments of 1991, and its predecessor, PL 99-457, the Education of the Handicapped Act Amendments of 1986, which amended PL 94-142, the Education for All Handicapped Children Act of 1975. (All of these laws are now referred to as *the Individuals with Disabilities Education Act [IDEA]*.) In combination, these laws mandate, among other things, a free appropriate public education in the least restrictive environment, the provision of related services, the extension of educational guarantees to preschool-age children ages 3–5, the requirement for multidisciplinary evaluation, and the expectation that parents are equal partners in the development of the child's program plan. Part H of IDEA, the program for infants and toddlers, mandates that each state develop a statewide system for serving infants and toddlers. This system must include a multidisciplinary evaluation of the child and the family's strengths and needs and result in the development of an individualized family service plan (IFSP).

This legislation implies the need for several programmatic features that are consistent with the philosophy and approach of TPBI. First, programs must be provided in an inclusionary model whenever possible. TPBI can be conducted in segregated or inclusive settings, but is most effective in an inclusionary model in which typical peers can provide models and facilitate play.

Second, the requirement of team involvement and provision of related services is also compatible with TPBI. In fact, the use of a transdisciplinary team exceeds the requirements of the law, providing a higher level of team participation and the integration of related services in the inclusionary model. And, finally, TPBI is a family-focused as well as child-focused process, making the involvement of families in the child's program an inherent part of program planning. The need for a family-focused program also supports the need for a transdisciplinary team, as most individuals working with young children with disabilities have not been taught the skills necessary to work with families. When the transdisciplinary process is used, team members who have these skills can support other team members in learning to work better with the child in the context of the family.

PLAY-BASED INTERVENTION

Play is the child's most natural activity, and research has shown that play encourages cognitive, or thinking, skills (Almy, Monighan, Scales, & VanHoorn, 1984; Pepler & Ross, 1981; Piaget, 1962; Rubin, Fein, & Vandenberg, 1983; Smilansky & Shefatya, 1990; Vygotsky, 1967; Yawkey, Jones, & Hrncir, 1979), social-emotional development (Burns & Brainerd, 1979; Connolly & Doyle, 1984; Curry & Arnaud, 1984; Smilansky & Shefatya, 1990); communication and language abilities (Garvey, 1977; Heath & Mangiola, 1991; Nicholich, 1977; Pellegrini, 1981; Smilansky, 1968), and movement proficiency (Athey, 1984; Bundy, 1991; Musselwhite, 1986). Therefore, play-based intervention should be an effective approach with children who have disabilities. The TPBI approach provides intervention guidelines for each of these four domains. The following pages help to define play and review the tenets and underpinnings for its use in intervention.

What Is Play?

Numerous definitions of play have been offered in the literature. Perhaps Gottfried (1985) summarizes these definitions best by noting that play is easier to recognize than to define, as no single behavior or set of behaviors encompasses the many forms of play.

> Evidence indicates that play is related to children's social and emotional development. It is an important indicator of children's language and symbol systems, and of the meanings children give to persons, places, and events. It is also an index of children's imagination, curiosity, motivation, preferences, interests, and persistence. (Gottfried, 1985, p. xix)

Play can take many forms, including the following:

- Sensorimotor play, in which the child uses his or her senses to examine and manipulate objects
- Functional play, in which the child relates objects in appropriate ways
- Constructive play, in which the child attempts to create something
- Dramatic play, in which the child represents actions and events
- Games with rules, in which the child follows prescribed guidelines

Some forms of play are object-oriented, while others do not involve the use of objects. Play can be child-initiated and child-structured or adult-initiated and adult-structured. Play can involve the child in isolation, in proximity to others, or in social interaction with others. Play can be verbal or nonverbal. The content and style of play reflect the cultural values of the child's family.

Neumann (1971) identifies play on the basis of a continuum, with three elements demonstrating lesser to greater degrees of expression. The level of locus of control (i.e., freedom to choose), internal determination of reality, and intrinsic motivation combine to determine where on the play–nonplay continuum a specific behavior falls. Others add that play is pleasurable, valued by its participants, spontaneous, and voluntary (Bundy, 1991). Rubin et al. (1983) summarized six traits most frequently identified in literature regarding play. These traits are the following: 1) intrinsic motivation, 2) attention to means rather than ends, 3) control of the stimulus, 4) ability to act out nonliteral or pretend actions, 5) freedom from externally imposed rules, and 6) active participation by the player.

Through play, the child acquires, practices, and adapts skills in all developmental areas. The importance of play to development is reviewed in *Transdisciplinary Play-Based Assessment* (Linder, 1993). As Bundy (1991) states, "If play is the vehicle by which individuals become masters of their environment, then play should be among the most powerful of therapeutic tools" (p. 61). Several critical aspects that underscore the power of play are summarized here. Play requires the child to direct activity and make choices (Hohmann, Banet, & Weikert, 1979) and encourages discrimination of relevant and irrelevant information (Athey, 1984), problem-solving (Pellegrini, 1984; Sharp, 1970), and mastery motivation (Morgan & Harmon, 1984). The development of memory (Saltz & Johnson, 1974), classification and spatial understanding (Johnson, Ershler, & Lawton, 1982; Rubin & Maioni, 1975), and abstract thinking (Sigel, 1993; Vygotsky, 1978) are stimulated in play. In addition, play encourages the development of social understanding (Mead, 1975), promotes understanding of inner processes, desires, issues, and anxieties (Bettelheim, 1987), and enables the child to practice cultural roles and mores (Erikson, 1950). In play, the child also masters the phonological, syntactic, and semantic rules of language (Athey, 1984; Garvey, 1977) and uses language in increasingly more sophisticated (Heath & Mangiola, 1991; Smilansky, 1968) and socially appropriate ways (Pellegrini, 1981). Motor development is also influenced positively by play, as the child gains greater fluidity and accuracy of movement through practice in play activities (Athey, 1984; Bundy, 1991). TPBI's four domains capitalize on the aspects of development strengthened through play.

Theoretical Underpinnings of Play-Based Intervention

The theoretical work of many people supports play-based intervention. An in-depth analysis of the theories of these individuals is not attempted here, but a brief description of how aspects of different theories contribute to a play-based assessment and intervention approach is described.

Piagetian Theory   Piaget's theories of cognitive development and his theories related to development and learning are congruent with a play-based approach to intervention (Piaget, 1962). Piaget stressed that the child learns through interaction with the environment and people in the environment. He emphasized the child's role in regulating or driving his or her own learning and acknowledged that a child's world is qualitatively different from that of the adult. Although sensory perceptions may be similar to those of an adult, the child's interpretations and understandings of what he or she sees, hears, and touches may vary greatly from those of an adult. The importance of a child-centered approach to education is thus implied. The adult's role is one of observing and responding to the child's understanding of the world. Piaget considered self-initiated activity to be important, with the adult channeling exploration and thought regarding the actions pursued. He judged actions and explorations completed within meaningful contexts as more likely to be assimilated and adapted by the child (Ginsburg & Opper, 1988). Play, one of the most meaningful activities of the early years, is seen by Piaget to be a laboratory for learning.

Skill Theory   Kurt Fischer's *skill theory* (Fischer, 1980) builds upon Piaget's theories of cognitive development. Unlike Piaget's concept of stages, however, Fischer posits that the child learns through incremental acquisition of skills that build a base for learning. Skill combination, substitution, and intercoordination allow for the development of more efficient, generalized, and higher-order skills. Experimentation through play facilitates these transformations.

Dialectical Theory   Vygotsky is another theorist who argued the importance of the social environment to the developing child. He hypothesized the role of the child's private speech, or talking to self, in the development of language. Social interactions allow the child to hear language and acquire meanings associated with words. The social-cultural context is maximized in play. As Vygotsky (1962, 1978) has noted, when children are engaged in play, they are functioning at close to their optimum level. Communication in play with adults or more skilled peers, however, results in increased problem-solving and the advancement of representational skills.

Freudian Theory   Sigmund Freud (1973, 1974) was not a specialist in child development. Nevertheless, he was an early architect of the theory that development proceeds in a series of predictable phases and that early trauma can manifest itself in disturbances or deviations in development. In Freud's view, unconscious conflict is the mechanism that drives most aberrations in psychological functioning. Play assessment and intervention, however, are more directly derived from the work of his daughter, Anna Freud (1958, 1973). Her lifelong dedication to understanding the internal worlds of children led her to theories establishing the importance of play-based assessment in therapeutic, family, and educational milieus. Her methodology was observation in natural settings. From her observational data, she built theories of developmental delay and deviation that continue to influence educators, mental health professionals, and parents. She extolled the importance of play, recognizing that play is the child's natural medium and therefore the window into the child's psyche.

Psychosocial Theory   Erikson's theory emphasizes the psychosocial nature of development, focusing on the nature of the child's interrelationships. He accentuated the importance of the adult's responsiveness to the child and the encouragement of the child's autonomy and self-initiation. For Erikson, play serves as the initial informal stage for learning roles and social rules and for practicing the mores of the culture and society (Erikson, 1950).

Social Learning Theory   Albert Bandura's *social learning theory* (1977, 1986) highlights the importance of observational learning or modeling. Learning occurs both *enactively*, by actually performing an act, and *vicariously*, by observing someone else. By watching others, children acquire knowledge, understanding of rules, skills, strategies, beliefs, and attitudes. Children most readily imitate those who are warm and powerful and who possess desirable objects and characteristics. Modeling others' emotional responses is an important means through which a child comes to associate feelings with particular actions and events. Bandura also emphasized the significance of *triadic reciprocity*, the reciprocal interactions among behaviors, personal factors, and environmental variables.

Organizational Theory   Joseph Campos and his collaborators have identified an organizational theory (Barrett & Campos, 1987; Campos, Caplovitz, Lamb, Goldsmith, & Stenberg, 1983) of emotional development that regards cognitive and emotional development as interdependent. Emotional reactions can serve both as the consequence of learning and the foundation for the next learning experience. Emotions also help to organize behavior in social contexts, with the child's emotions regulating the behavior of parents and others and the emotions of parents and others having a reciprocal influence on the child's actions and reactions. Emotions also affect the development of self-awareness, sense of self, and self-regulation, all elements that are aroused in play.

Salient Responses Theory   Lewis and Starr (1979) proposed a model of human development that integrates developmental domains and addresses learning traits corresponding to developmental progress. The "salient attributes of response include: the quality, quantity, speed of acquisition, utilization, affective tone, generalizability, organizational properties, and intention in the use of information" (p. 657). Application of this theory to a play-based approach encourages the facilitation of development across these variables, thus expanding the intervention model from one of skills acquisition to one of increased developmental sophistication.

Philosophical Tenets of Play-Based Intervention

From the theoretical works of the individuals described above, a conceptual framework, or philosophy, can be articulated for a play-based approach to intervention. This play-based philosophy is guided by the following tenets:

1. Play-based intervention capitalizes on the key elements of the early years, including what is known about infant and early childhood development, how children interact with others, and activities children enjoy.
2. Play-based intervention responds to the developmental demands children face daily.
3. Play-based intervention is an enjoyable process for the child and family.
4. Play-based intervention is nonintrusive and comfortable for the family to implement consistently.
5. Play-based intervention is responsive to and respective of cultural, language, and familial differences.
6. Play-based intervention can be adapted across settings and disciplines.
7. Play-based intervention can be used to promote increasingly sophisticated developmental processes and skills as the child grows.

TPBI is responsive to and respective of cultural, language, and familial differences.

Play-Based Intervention Capitalizes on Key Elements of the Early Years   Any approach to early intervention should incorporate strategies that are shaped by the critical elements of the child's early years. What do we know about the young child? We know that the young child loves to interact with people, objects, and events in energetic and playful ways. We know that the young child loves to explore and engage his or her environment using all of the sensory systems. We know that as the young child gains mastery over various aspects of the environment, a great deal of energy is expended practicing new skills and exerting control over objects, people, and events. The early years are characterized by investigation, discovery, practice, struggle, failure, challenge, invention, mastery, imagination, and the full range of emotions that accompany these experiences.

Play-Based Intervention Responds to the Developmental Demands the Child Faces Daily   Every day of the young child's life presents new developmental challenges. How the child responds to each new challenge is influenced, in part, by how the family and others in the child's life react to these demands. Elements such as affect (i.e., emotion or feeling), degree of directiveness, expectations, and level and type of engagement have an impact on the child's responses (Mahoney & Powell, 1988). Whether the child's behaviors or actions are encouraged, reinforced, ignored, or obstructed also influences his or her subsequent responses (Norris & Hoffman, 1990). The young child's intervention program should address these response elements in a systematic way to promote his or her development.

Play-Based Intervention Is an Enjoyable Process for the Child and Family   Interactions and activities that involve strong emotions are retained longer in the memory (Barrett & Campos, 1987). Attaching a positive, rather than a negative, emotional significance is certainly preferable in early intervention. Consequently, an approach that incorporates play, which is by definition imbued with positive affect (Garvey, 1977), should encourage attention to and retention of skills gained in play. In the same way, involvement of the family in pleasurable intervention with play as a basis should motivate parent–child interactions and stimulate the retention of playful interaction skills.

Play-Based Intervention Is Nonintrusive and Comfortable for the Family To Implement   Approaches to intervention that feel intrusive, unmanageable, or unpleasant, or are difficult to incorporate into the family's daily life, are not as likely to be implemented on an ongoing basis as those that are relaxed and natural. Play and playful interactions with their children are parts of most parents' days. Most parents would like more time to play with their child and would appreciate assistance in learning how to facilitate development in play (Linder & Chitwood, 1984). As the family plays a critical role in the child's development (Bronfenbrenner, 1979, 1989), it is essential to identify intervention approaches that can easily be adopted by the family members.

Play-Based Intervention Is Responsive to and Respectful of Language and Familial Differences   Parents from all cultures enjoy playing with their children, although the amount of playful interaction and approach to play may differ. The amount of child-structured versus adult-structured play, the content of play, and the style of play, for example, may vary (Schwartzman, 1978). Infants, toddlers, and preschoolers are highly influenced by the values, beliefs, and traditions inherent in their families. Intervention personnel must be sensitive to the style of interaction, modes of play, and cultural content of play relevant for different families and specific family members. Intervention practices must be individualized to address families' concerns, priorities, and requirements (Lynch & Hanson, 1992).

Language is an aspect of culture that is critical to the child's cognitive and social development, as well as communication proficiency (Goldstein & Gallagher, 1992; Scales, Almy, Nicolopoulou, & Ervin-Tripp, 1991). Play-based intervention allows the child to follow play pursuits using whatever communication and language system is functional for the child. Although the child's play can be facilitated without the use of his or her primary language, conceptual development and social interactions can be encouraged best by using a common language. Involving bilingual professionals, interpreters, and/or parents or volunteers who are bilingual is recommended to maximize the benefits of play interactions (VanHoorn, Nourot, Scales, & Alward, 1993). However, even in the absence of such bilingual adults, play allows the adult to observe and follow the child's thinking, to join in interactive exchanges, and to model higher-level behaviors. In addition, play encourages children to use the full range of language skills available to them.

Play-Based Intervention Is Adaptable Across Settings and Disciplines   An approach that is to be transdisciplinary, or used by all members of the intervention team, must be flexible and adaptable (Bricker & Cripe, 1992). An approach that incorporates parents as members of the team must be based on strategies that can be used at home and in the community, as well as in other intervention settings (Spradlin & Siegel, 1982).

Play-Based Intervention Can Be Used To Promote Increasingly More Sophisticated Developmental Processes and Skills   One of the primary goals of early intervention is to foster the child's acquisition and use of developmental skills and processes (Linder, 1983). Strategies implemented in an early intervention program should be developmentally appropriate and further enhance the child's learning, application of knowledge or skills, or interaction with people, objects, and events in the environment.

More Evidence from Research for a Play-Based Approach to Intervention

The recent work of both behavioral and language researchers supports the use of play as a medium for intervention. While behavioral approaches have often used a series of unrelated and perhaps unfamiliar activities (Dyer & Peck, 1987) in a structured interaction directed and reinforced by the early interventionist, who frequently relied on unnatural reinforcers, current research is examining the use of more natural interactions that are directed by the child and responded to by the adult and that employ the use of internal and natural reinforcers.

Play-based interventions (Fewell & Vadasy, 1983; Smilansky & Shefatya, 1990; Van Hoorn et al., 1993) and more functional, activity-based approaches to intervention have been demonstrated (Bricker & Cripe, 1992). Bricker and Cripe recommend embedding intervention targets in routine, planned, or child-directed activities. They advocate using logical antecedents and consequences and developing functional and generalizable skills. Activity-based intervention encompasses all areas of development. Similarly, earlier studies have shown naturalistic training strategies to be effective with children who have autism or multiple disabilities, as well as children with less involved disabilities (Campbell & Stremel-Campbell, 1982; Koegel & Johnson, 1989; Rogers-Warren & Warren, 1980).

The natural, unstructured interactions between the adult and the child are reinforced through such approaches as mand-model (Rogers-Warren & Warren, 1980), time delay (Schwartz, Anderson, & Halle, 1989), and incidental teaching (Hart & Risley, 1975). Milieu language teaching (Hart & Rogers-Warren, 1978; Kaiser, Hendrickson, & Alpert, 1992) expands incidental teaching by requiring environmental manipulation, language assessment, and facilitation of the child's interaction with the environment. Milieu language training combines developmental theory and behavioral analysis learning principles, while still emphasizing child initiation. Responses to a child's language by the adult should be functional ("I like that book, too," rather than, "Good talking."). Generalization of language results from eliciting language throughout the day in all aspects of the child's environment.

The spontaneously occurring events, utterances, and communicative situations that arise in the context of play, daily routines, and instructional activities are the basis for naturalistic language therapy (Norris & Hoffman, 1990). Naturalistic therapy is viewed as a process involving cognitive, linguistic and nonlinguistic communications, and social development. Environments are established that are meaningful to the child, involve direct experience, provide opportunities to share information, and regulate the activities of self and others. Child-initiated activities are utilized as much as possible (Bricker, 1986; McLean & Snyder-McLean, 1978). The principles of "whole language" learning are based on this naturalistic approach.

Research has also demonstrated that the child's early interactions with parents and significant others is crucial to later development (MacDonald, 1989; Mahoney & Powell, 1984, 1988). This development is encouraged through approaches that build on a behavioral match between parent and child, that take advantage of the child's natural encounters in environments that provide motivating circumstances, and that require sensitivity and responsiveness on the adult's part.

THE TRANSDISCIPLINARY PROCESS

The transdisciplinary approach is ideally suited to integrating therapy into the natural events in a child's day. In the transdisciplinary approach, professionals seeing a child not only work together as a team but share knowledge about their respective disciplines among themselves. Professionals across many disciplines, including special education, early childhood special education, nursing, medicine, occupational therapy, physical therapy, and speech-language therapy have endorsed the transdisciplinary concept (Bennett, 1982; Campbell, 1987; Dunn, 1991; Garland, McGonigel, Frank, & Buck, 1989; Hutchison, 1987; Linder, 1990; Orelove & Sobsey, 1991; Rainforth, York, & Macdonald, 1992; Woodruff & McGonigel, 1988). Numerous professional organizations have written position papers supporting a collaborative and integrated model of service delivery. The American Speech-Language-Hearing Association (ASHA) Committee on Language Learning Disabilities (1991), the American Occupational Therapy Association (AOTA) (1989), the American Physical Therapy Association (APTA) (1990), and The Association for Persons with Severe Handicaps (TASH) (1986) have endorsed many of the principles of transdisciplinary practice. In addition, philosophical support, legal mandates and precedents, and evidence of "recommended practices" justify the use of a transdisciplinary approach. The following discussion lists alternative approaches to intervention, outlines the factors that led to the endorsement by many professionals of the transdisciplinary intervention approach, describes transdisciplinary team membership, explains the importance of role release, and highlights challenges that may accompany the transdisciplinary approach.

Alternative Approaches to Intervention

Unidisciplinary, multidisciplinary, and interdisciplinary staffing patterns all have been used in programs serving young children. A *unidisciplinary* approach involves the child being seen by those in a single discipline, usually for education or a specific therapy. The individuals seeing the child do not communicate with each other about their interventions. A *multidisciplinary team* approach consists of several team members from different disciplines working with the child independently. Communication among team members is limited to sharing individual results and recommendations in staff meetings. The child may then be seen by individual therapists independently, or recommendations may be given to the educator for implementation (Hart, 1977). Recommendations may be numerous and complicated by professional jargon and may provide contradictory views of the child's abilities, deficits, and intervention needs (Hart, 1977; Peterson, 1980). The *interdisciplinary team* approach includes more communication regarding program decision-making than the multidisciplinary team approach, but program implementation remains rooted to individual disciplines in isolated situations (Garland et al., 1989). Therapists provide direct therapy to children and are responsible for the outcomes in their intervention "area."

The Evolution to a Transdisciplinary Approach in Intervention

Several factors have influenced the move away from the unidisciplinary, multidisciplinary, and interdisciplinary models toward a transdisciplinary approach, characterized by sharing of information and skills across disciplines.

Emphasis on Functional Skills Assessment   There has been a move away from assessment of isolated skills and the use of tests that result in numbers and labels but no practical suggestions for teachers and families (York, Rainforth, & Giangreco, 1990). These tests have traditionally been conducted by individual team members, representing specific disciplines. The search for functional, practical, integrated assessment approaches has resulted in a shift to assessing children in less restricted, functional settings involving collaborative efforts of professionals and families (Linder, 1993). The natural corollary is a desire for more integrated, functional programming for children.

Greater Family Involvement   The involvement of families in more meaningful ways in assessment, program planning, implementation, and evaluation has resulted in parents desiring more family-focused, functional assessments and intervention plans. With the implementation of PL 94-142, the Education for All Handicapped Children Act of 1975, parents gained the right to review, contribute to, and approve of their child's individualized education program (IEP). PL 99-457, the Education of the Handicapped Act Amendments of 1986, expanded the parents' rights and roles. Part H, which pertains to services for infants and toddlers, requires the development of an individualized family service plan (IFSP) and gives parents a substantial amount of control over decision-making regarding the program for their child and family. PL 101-476, the Education of the Handicapped Act Amendments of 1990, changed the name of this legislation to the Individuals with Disabilities Education Act (IDEA) and furthers the mandates for meaningful parent involvement and special education and related services in least restrictive environments.

Inclusive Education Opportunities   The increased push toward inclusion of all children with disabilities into regular programs, which resulted from IDEA, and the consequent reduction in centralized therapy services, has necessitated a look at classroom-based intervention. Related services, as defined in the law, are to be provided "as may be required to assist a handicapped child to benefit from special education . . . " (PL 94-142, 20 U.S.C. §1401[17], 1975). The emphasis on related services supporting education has been interpreted to imply that therapies should be provided in such a way that the child's involvement in educational programs is enhanced. Direct, isolated therapy does not necessarily promote success in the education program (Rainforth et al., 1992). In addition, direct therapy is often not practical in inclusive settings due to limitations of staffing patterns and difficult logistics (Orelove & Sobsey, 1991; Rainforth et al., 1992).

Benefits of Integrated Therapy Approach   Professionals are now recognizing the benefits of integrating therapy into the various activities of the child's day, whether at home or at school. An integrated therapy approach allows the interrelated needs of children to be addressed. Each area of development has a direct impact on the others. For instance, motor skills affect the child's ability to communicate and to express cognitive understandings; cognitive skills affect the language the child understands and ideas that can be communicated, as well as the child's perception and demonstration of social skills; social skills, in turn, influence the child's acquisition of cognitive abilities, interaction and communication with others, and demonstration of interactive motor skills. By integrating all areas into the various contexts of the child's day, generalization of skills in functional settings is encouraged, therapy does not have to "compete" with education programming, and the efficiency and effectiveness of intervention are enhanced (Rainforth et al., 1992).

Combining Strengths and Creativity   Problem-solving, follow-through, and support are enhanced by a transdisciplinary approach that includes the parent as part of the team. With several minds working together to elicit ideas that promote learning and development across various environments, the opportunities for generating creative, cross-disciplinary activities are amplified. With all team members working to create, monitor, and evaluate the program, the implementation of a holistic intervention program is more likely to occur. In addition, the team members act as supports to each other to ensure realization of the intervention plan.

Transdisciplinary Team Membership

Membership of the transdisciplinary team varies depending on the needs of the children being served but some general characteristics can be described. A *core team* consists of the people who are responsible for the development and implementation of the individual child and family's intervention plan. The core team might consist of family members, an educator (general and/or special educator) or developmental specialist (depending on the child's age), a communication specialist, and an occupational therapist. For children requiring additional services, the core team might consist of the above, and one or more of the following: a physical therapist, a nurse, a vision or hearing specialist, and a teaching assistant (Giangreco & Eichinger, 1990). A social worker or services coordinator might also be part of the core team. Membership of the core team might change as the child's needs change.

Orelove and Sobsey (1991) also discuss the *support team*, which is used for students who may need occasional consultation from some of the above personnel. The core team meets on a regular basis to plan and evaluate the program for a given child, while support team members may meet with the team on an as-needed basis. As mentioned previously, the core team must convene on a regular basis, as meeting time is crucial to ongoing assessment, planning, monitoring, problem-solving, training, and team support. This becomes more difficult as team members are spread out across numerous programs and buildings, but should remain a priority.

The Importance of Role Release

The transdisciplinary team model implies integration of therapy to support development and education. Integrated therapy requires each member of the team to be knowledgeable about other areas as well. Role release is thus seen as a major characteristic of the transdisciplinary approach. Role release is the process of transferring information and skills from one discipline to another. Each discipline has a body of knowledge and skills that is traditionally viewed as its exclusive domain. Preservice training has typically reinforced the application of the domain-specific knowledge and skills in isolated or direct therapy approaches. A transdisciplinary model, however, emphasizes the implementation of a holistic approach, with representatives of all disciplines integrating all domains of intervention. In order to achieve this goal, it is necessary for each team member to be knowledgeable enough about the other disciplines to be able to follow through effectively on program recommendations. Many team members who are unfamiliar with the transdisciplinary team approach feel threatened by role release and hesitant about allowing other team members to assume what they view as their responsibilities. It is important to recognize that role release does not imply surrendering responsibilities. Ongoing management and consultation are essential to make indirect therapy effective. Role release as defined by Lyon and Lyon (1980) involves sharing general information about concepts and practices, more specific informational skills related to strategies and approaches, and performance competencies, or teaching distinctive practices and methods to other team members. Woodruff and McGonigel (1988) call the process of moving into a transdisciplinary mode and crossing disciplinary boundaries *role transition*. The transition process involves several steps, which in addition to role release, include role extension, role enrichment, role expansion, role exchange, and role support (Garland et al., 1989).

Role Extension   In order to most effectively teach each other a specific content or skill area, it is necessary for each team member to be well-versed in his or her own area of expertise. Self-directed study or staff development efforts may help various team members increase the depth and breadth of their understanding of theoretical, practical, or clinical knowledge. Attending workshops or conferences also may assist team members in acquiring new skills, which then may be shared with others. For instance, a teacher attended a workshop on the use of computer games in the classroom. She then worked with the speech-language and occupational therapists to demonstrate the use of the computer and identified the skills that she intended to target on the computer games. The team then worked together to discuss individual children and communication and language and sensorimotor skills that could be incorporated into the games. Adaptations that were needed for specific children were then solved as a team.

Role Enrichment   In order to work effectively as a transdisciplinary team, members need to develop a general awareness of and understanding of the terminology employed by various disciplines. Whenever possible discipline-specific jargon should be eliminated; however, at times, a one-word term is easier to use than a paragraph of explanation. The more parents and other team members become familiar with the terminology related to health, education, and therapies, the more comfortable all will be in participating in transdisciplinary team discussions. Role enrichment takes place in team discussions as team members discuss their observations and interactions with individual children. Explanations can be given and terms explained as needed. Team members and families need to feel comfortable asking questions and asking for clarification about terms or recommended strategies. Team members can help parents to feel less threatened by modeling the process.

For instance, in a discussion with Tim's parents after a TPBA, the occupational therapist noted that Tim seemed to exhibit some "gravitational insecurity" as he moved around the motor area. The speech-language therapist asked for an explanation of gravitational insecurity, and the parent commented, "I'm glad you asked that. I don't know what that is either." The occupational therapist then described Tim's exaggerated fear responses to movement when on unstable or suspended equipment and indicated that this fear appeared to be restricting his exploration and movement in the environment. The teacher then indicated that she noticed that his fear of movement seemed also to be affecting his social interactions, as Tim avoided motor equipment and thus the other children did not seek to play with him on the outdoor play equipment. Tim's parent's were intrigued by this new information because they were concerned about Tim's fears and lack of interactions with other children. They asked for more information about gravitational insecurity. The occupational therapist promised to provide an article for each team member.

In this example, each of the team members, including the parents, gained new information related to a specific discipline. However, the information clearly had implications for other disciplines and many environments in Tim's life. By explaining the terminology and then seeking to find information that was appropriate for the team, the occupational therapist was practicing role extension.

Role Expansion   As team members become more versed in other disciplines, they begin to feel more comfortable offering observations and making recommendations in areas other than that of their specialization. Parent team members gain more confidence in offering suggestions related to the child's home and community environments. Through ongoing in-service training, participation in team assessments, consultation with team members, and team planning, each team member continues to gain information and thus confidence in his or her ability to provide input into all areas of programming.

During a team planning session for the preschool program, the teacher commented that Jeremy seemed to be able to play with small toys and manipulate them with more control when he was seated in a chair with his feet on the floor. She noted that when he sat on the floor to play, he appeared to be hunched over and seemed to use his arms to support himself, thus restricting his manipulative skills. The occupational therapist commented that the teacher's observations were accurate and that her solution of providing stable seating was a good one. She then added a few suggestions for increasing his stability in sitting and at the shoulders to further improve his fine motor control.

Role Exchange   As team members begin to understand the theory and strategies of a given discipline, observation and guidance are important. Team members can practice and receive feedback as they begin to implement new methods. The presence of the team member who is conducting the training is a crucial factor. Often what sounds simple in a discussion or team meeting proves to be more complex when implemented.

Mr. and Mrs. Jones had discussed with the physical therapist during the staff meeting the idea of positioning Jason to break up his high tone, but both felt uncertain about whether they were positioning him in the best way. The physical therapist made a visit to the home and discussed the daily routine with the parents. They repeated several routines, including feeding, bathing, and playing, and both parents practiced the positioning techniques with Jason with guidance from the physical therapist. The parents commented that although it had sounded hard at first, meeting Jason's needs was actually easier when he was more relaxed and "not so stiff."

Role Support   A critical aspect of successful transdisciplinary teaming is the ongoing support that each team member provides to the others. Through encouragement, assistance, and continued input, team members strengthen their skills, the team process, and program outcomes.

Kaducia's preschool teacher integrated the speech-language pathologist's suggestions for increasing Kaducia's use of labels for objects. She used self-talk and parallel talk (see Chapter 5) and arranged the environment so that Kaducia needed to request desired objects. The speech-language pathologist visited the classroom each week, interacting with individual children and providing support to the teacher on communication issues. During the team planning meeting, the speech-language pathologist noted that Kaducia was spontaneously using three new words. As the team planned for the next week, the speech-language pathologist identified words associated with the theme that she thought Kaducia might be motivated to use. The teacher indicated that those labels could be easily integrated into several play activities throughout the week. Although the teacher felt confident about integrating language into the curriculum, she appreciated the objective observations, suggestions, and support for problem-solving with Kaducia and other children.

All of the above examples demonstrate various types of support. Through provision of the information, reinforcement of successful interventions, demonstration of techniques, and joint problem-solving, the transdisciplinary team can maintain a dynamic support system.

Anticipating the Challenges in a Transdisciplinary Approach

In many cases, implementing a transdisciplinary model involves making significant changes in the existing program. Changes in staffing patterns, schedules, interrelationships, processes, or procedures can lead to feelings of unrest. Knowledge of the obstacles to implementation of a transdisciplinary team can help staff to anticipate, recognize, and address these obstacles as they arise. Orelove and Sobsey (1991) describe the challenges involved in implementing a transdisciplinary team as falling into the following three categories: philosophical and professional, interpersonal, and administrative. Orelove and Sobsey (1991) include in their last category ethical and legal challenges. For the purposes of this volume, ethical and legal challenges are discussed as a separate category.

Philosophical and Professional Challenges   Differences in philosophical orientation usually derive from training practices that may emphasize a medical model of treatment, a functional approach to intervention, or conflicting treatment methods. It takes time and much discussion for teams to be able to meld their various backgrounds, training experiences, and philosophies into a unified approach. Team members cannot be expected to give up "overnight" those approaches that have been ingrained over time. As team members gain knowledge and experience across disciplines, the new knowledge must be integrated with former learning. The author has observed that for many, the process must include a gradual shift as the benefits of the transdisciplinary indirect therapy process are discovered. As with children, the Piagetian process of equilibration, or balancing of old and new information, is accomplished best by active engagement and discovery rather than through an assertive, didactic approach.

Interpersonal Challenges   In addition to philosophical differences, personal issues such as fear may also be an obstacle (Orelove & Sobsey, 1991). Team members may fear loss of status within the organization, with team members, or with parents. What typically occurs, however, is an enhanced status. As team members gain more information about various disciplines, they gain a respect for the expertise and knowledge of individuals on the team. The old adage "The more you know, the more you know you don't know" holds true. As team members gain greater understanding of the complexities of children, families, and intervention strategies, they gain an increased awareness of the need for ongoing support from the experts to address adequately these enigmatic and complicated concerns.

Another issue frequently mentioned is the insecurity many team members feel when called upon to share their knowledge and expertise with others. For experienced staff members who have functioned undaunted and without being questioned for years, the transdisciplinary process may pose a threat to their hegemony. Exposing what one knows to others opens the possibility of disagreement, contradiction, or confrontation. For young, inexperienced staff members who are not yet confident of their knowledge and skills, the idea of training others may feel threatening as well. Many of the anxieties, of experienced and inexperienced alike, diminish as the staff recognize that their ideas are respected and a sense of trust is developed.

Some apprehension may also be present with regard to roles and responsibilities. People who have been comfortable in traditional roles may resist the change to a model when roles seem more obscure. The roles and responsibilities of each team member need to be defined as clearly as possible with regard not only to children and families, but to other team members as well.

Administrative Challenges   Orelove and Sobsey (1991) identify administrative concerns as another important factor in the success of a transdisciplinary approach. Administrators need to understand the transdisciplinary philosophy and be prepared to support teams and provide necessary mechanisms to enable teams to function successfully. Administrators need to understand that a transdisciplinary approach does *not* mean that fewer therapists will be needed because teachers will now be meeting children's needs across all areas. For a transdisciplinary team to function effectively, schedules must be arranged so that all team members can spend time in the classroom, in consultation with staff and parents, in team assessments, in team planning meetings, and in formal and informal inservice training.

Administrators must provide leadership to the teams, assist the teams in joint goal-setting, model team problem-solving, and encourage the learning process through numerous alternative means. The administrator can also act to mediate conflicts as they arise, as they surely will. Administrators also need to be able to support the team by confronting team members who are resisting or sabotaging the transdisciplinary effort. People who cannot adapt to the shift to an integrated process should seek employment in a different type of setting. Change takes time, however, and administrators and staff need to allow sufficient time for the processes and procedures to evolve.

Ethical and Legal Challenges   Ethical and legal concerns are another area of challenge. Many professionals and administrators are concerned about the liability issues related to integrated therapy. Certain states have laws governing the practice of physical therapy, occupational therapy, and speech-language therapy designating who can provide therapy. Rainforth et al. (1992) recommend that for agencies using an integrated therapy or transdisciplinary approach:

> It is appropriate to say that a teacher (or other "nontherapist") is teaching motor skills, or reinforcing the physical therapy program, but inaccurate to communicate that a teacher is providing physical therapy services. By definition, only the activities performed directly by the physical therapist are considered physical therapy. (p. 14)

Another ethical issue is the need for adequate supervision to ensure that recommended procedures are adequately carried out by other team members. This is an administrative concern requiring that each team member has these supervisory responsibilities as part of his or her job description as well as the time to consult and provide guidance and feedback. The importance of this issue should not be overlooked, as negligence in this regard may defeat the intent of the process.

Certainly, there are health, medical, and therapeutic procedures that necessitate the use of a specialist. These procedures are usually dictated by state law. The concept of transdisciplinary intervention is a relatively new approach and legislation and policies may not always be aligned with current "recommended practices."

CONCLUSION

The play-based intervention process is a theoretically and philosophically sound, research-based, practical approach to working with infants, toddlers, preschoolers, kindergartners and their families. The transdisciplinary process, when fully implemented, also provides a more effective and efficient means of working with children. In combination, the transdisciplinary play-based intervention approach combines state-of-the-art techniques for serving young children with special needs and their families.

REFERENCES

Almy, M., Monighan, P., Scales, B., & Van Hoorn, J. (1984). Recent research on play: The teacher's perspective. In L.G. Katz (Ed.), *Current topics in early childhood education* (Vol. 5, pp. 1–25). Norwood, NJ: Ablex.

American Occupational Therapy Association. (1989). *Guidelines for occupational therapy services in the public schools* (2nd ed.). Rockville, MD: Author.

American Physical Therapy Association. (1990). *Physical therapy practice in educational environments.* Alexandria, VA: Author.

American Speech-Language-Hearing Association, Committee on Language Learning Disorders. (1991). A model for collaborative service delivery for students with language–learning disorders in the public schools. *Asha, 3*(33). Supple.

Athey, I. (1984). Contributions of play to development. In T.D. Yawkey & A.D. Pellegrini (Eds.), *Child's play: Developmental and applied* (pp. 9–28). Hillsdale, NJ: Lawrence Erlbaum Associates.

Bandura, A. (1977). *Social learning theory.* Englewood Cliffs, NJ: Prentice Hall.

Bandura, A. (1986). *Social foundations of thought and action: A social cognitive theory.* Englewood Cliffs, NJ: Prentice Hall.

Barrett, K.C., & Campos, J.J. (1987). Perspectives on emotional development: II. A functionalist approach to emotion. In J.D. Osofsky (Ed.), *Handbook of infant development* (pp. 1101–1149). New York: John Wiley & Sons.

Bennett, F.C. (1982). The pediatrician and the interdisciplinary process. *Exceptional Children, 48*(4), 306–314.

Bettelheim, B. (1987). The importance of play. *Atlantic Monthly, 259*(3), 35–46.

Bricker, D.D. (1986). *Early education of at-risk and handicapped infants, toddlers, and preschool children.* Glenview, IL: Scott, Foresman.

Bricker, D., & Cripe, J.J.W. (1992). *An activity-based approach to early intervention*. Baltimore: Paul H. Brookes Publishing Co.

Bronfenbrenner, U. (1979). Toward an experimental ecology of human development. *American Psychologist, 32*, 513–531.

Bronfenbrenner, U. (1989). Ecological systems theory. In R. Vasta (Ed.), *Annals of child development* (Vol. 6, pp. 187–251). Greenwich, CT: JAI Press.

Bundy, A.C. (1991). Play theory and sensory integration. In A.G. Fisher, E.A. Murray, & A.C. Bundy (Eds.), *Sensory integration: Theory and practice* (pp. 46–86). Philadelphia: F.A. Davis.

Burns, S.M., & Brainerd, C.J. (1979). Effects of constructive and dramatic play on perspective taking in very young children. *Developmental Psychology, 15*, 512–521.

Campbell, C.R., & Stremel-Campbell, K. (1982). Programming "loose training" as a strategy to facilitate language generalization. *Journal of Applied Behavior Analysis, 15*, 295–301.

Campbell, P.H. (1987). The integrated programming team: an approach for coordinating professionals of various disciplines in programs for students with severe and multiple handicaps. *Journal of The Association for Persons with Severe Handicaps, 12*(2), 107–116.

Campos, J.J., Caplovitz, K.B., Lamb, M.E., Goldsmith, H.H., & Stenberg, C. (1983). Socioemotional development. In M.M. Haith & J.J. Campos (Eds.), *Handbook of child psychology: Volume 2. Infancy and developmental psychobiology* (4th ed.) (pp. 783–915). New York: John Wiley & Sons.

Connolly, J.A., & Doyle, A. (1984). Relation of social fantasy play to social competence in preschoolers. *Developmental Psychology, 20*, 797–806.

Curry, N.E., & Arnaud, S.H. (1984). Play in developmental preschool settings. In T.D. Yawkey & A.D. Pellegrini (Eds.), *Child's play: Developmental and applied* (pp. 273–290). Hillsdale, NJ: Lawrence Erlbaum Associates.

Dunn, W. (1991). Integrated related services. In L.H. Meyer, C.A. Peck, & L. Brown (Eds.), *Critical issues in the lives of people with severe disabilities* (pp. 353–377). Baltimore: Paul H. Brookes Publishing Co.

Dyer, K., & Peck, C. (1987). Current perspectives on social/communication curricula for students with autism and severe handicaps. *Education and Treatment of Children, 10*(4), 330–351.

Education for All Handicapped Children Act of 1975, PL 94-142. (August 23, 1977). Title 20, U.S.C. 1401 et seq: *U.S. Statutes at Large, 89*, 773–796.

Education of the Handicapped Act Amendments of 1986, PL 99-457. (October 8, 1986). Title 20, U.S.C. 1400 et seq: *U.S. Statutes at Large, 100*, 1145–1177.

Erikson, E.H. (1950). *Childhood and society*. New York: Norton.

Fewell, R.R., & Vadasy, P.F. (1983). *Learning through play*. Allen, TX: Developmental Learning Materials.

Fischer, K.W. (1980). A theory of cognitive development: The control and construction of hierarchical skills. *Psychological Review, 87*, 477–531.

Freud, A. (1958). Child observation and prediction of development: A memorial lecture in honor of Ernst Kris. *Psychoanalytic Study of the Child, 13*, 97–98.

Freud, A. (1973). *The writings of Anna Freud, Vol. 7. Normality and pathology in childhood: Assessment of development*. New York: International Universities Press.

Freud, S. (1973). *An outline of psychoanalysis*. London: Hogarth. (Original work published in 1938).

Freud, S. (1974). *The ego and the id*. London: Hogarth. (Original work published in 1923).

Garland, C., McGonigel, M., Frank, A., & Buck, D. (1989). *The transdisciplinary model of service delivery*. Lightfoot, VA: Child Development Resources.

Garvey, C. (1977). *Play*. Cambridge, MA: Harvard University Press.

Giangreco, M., & Eichinger, J. (1990). *Related services and the transdisciplinary approach: Parent training module*. Seattle, WA: The Association for Persons with Severe Handicaps, TASH—Technical Assistance for Services to Children with Deaf-Blindness.

Ginsburg, H.P., & Opper, S. (1988). *Piaget's theory of intellectual development*. Englewood Cliffs, NJ: Prentice Hall.

Goldstein, H., & Gallagher, T.M. (1992). Strategies for promoting the social-communicative competence of young children with specific language impairment. In S.L. Odom, S.R. McConnell, & M.A. McEvoy (Eds.), *Social competence of young children with disabilities: Issues and strategies for intervention* (pp. 189–213). Baltimore: Paul H. Brookes Publishing Co.

Gottfried, A.W. (1985). Introduction. In C.C. Brown & A.W. Gottfried (Eds.), *Play interactions: The role of toys and parental involvement in children's development.* Skillman, NJ: Johnson & Johnson Baby Products.

Hart, V. (1977). The use of many disciplines with the severely and profoundly handicapped. In E. Sontag, J. Smith, & N. Certo (Eds.), *Educational programming for the severely and profoundly handicapped* (pp. 391–396). Reston, VA: Council for Exceptional Children.

Hart, B., & Risley, T. (1975). Incidental teaching of language in the preschool. *Journal of Applied Behavioral Analysis, 8,* 411–420.

Hart, B., & Rogers-Warren, A. (1978). A milieu approach to teaching language. In R. Schiefelbusch (Ed.), *Language intervention strategies.* Baltimore: University Park Press.

Heath, S.B., & Mangiola, L. (1991). *Children of promise: Literate activity in linguistically and culturally diverse classrooms.* Washington, DC: National Education Association.

Hohmann, M., Banet, B., & Weikart, D.P. (1979). *Young children in action.* Ypsilanti, MI: High Scope Educational Research Foundation.

Hutchison, D.J. (1987). The transdisciplinary approach. In J.B. Curry & K.K. Peppe (Eds.), *Mental retardation: Nursing approaches to care* (pp. 65–74). St, Louis: C.V. Mosby.

Individuals with Disabilities Education Act of 1990 (IDEA), PL 101-476. (October 30, 1990). Title 20, U.S.C. 1400 et seq: *U.S. Statutes at Large, 104,* 1103–1151.

Individuals with Disabilities Education Act Amendments of 1991, PL 102-119. (October 7, 1991). Title 20, U.S.C. 1400 et seq: *U.S. Statutes at Large, 105,* 587–608.

Johnson, J.E., Ershler, J., & Lawton, J. (1982). Intellective correlates of preschoolers' spontaneous play. *Journal of General Psychology, 106,* 115–122.

Kaiser, A., Hendrickson, J., & Alpert, K. (1992). Milieu language teaching: A second look. In R. Gable (Ed.), *Advances in mental retardation and developmental disabilities* (Vol. 4, pp. 63–92). London: Jessica Kingsley.

Koegel, R.L., & Johnson, J. (1989). Motivating language use in autistic children. In G. Dawson (Ed.), *Autism: New perspectives on diagnosis, nature and treatment.* New York: Guilford Press.

Lewis, M., & Starr, M.D. (1979). Developmental continuity. In J.D. Osofsky (Ed.), *Handbook of infant development.* New York: John Wiley & Sons.

Linder, T.W. (1983). *Early childhood special education: Program development and administration.* Baltimore: Paul H. Brookes Publishing Co.

Linder, T.W. (1993). *Transdisciplinary play-based assessment: A functional approach to working with young children* (rev. ed.). Baltimore: Paul H. Brookes Publishing Co.

Linder, T., & Chitwood, D. (1984). The needs of fathers of handicapped preschoolers. *Journal of the Division of Early Childhood, 8,* 133–139.

Lynch, E.W., & Hanson, M.J. (1992). *Developing cross-cultural competence: A guide for working with young children and their families.* Baltimore: Paul H. Brookes Publishing Co.

Lyon, S., & Lyon, G. (1980). Team functioning and staff development: A role release approach to providing integrated education services for severely handicapped students. *Journal of The Association for the Severely Handicapped, 5*(3), 250–263.

MacDonald, J. (1989). *Becoming partners with children.* San Antonio, TX: Special Press.

Mahoney, G., & Powell, A. (1984). *The transactional intervention program.* Woodhaven, MI: Woodhaven School District.

Mahoney, G., & Powell, A. (1988). Modifying parent–child interaction: Enhancing the development of handicapped children. *Journal of Special Education, 22,* 82–96.

McLean, J.E., & Snyder-McLean, L.K. (1978). *A transactional approach to early language training: Derivation of a model system.* Columbus, OH: Charles E. Merrill.

Mead, M. (1975). *Growing up in New Guinea.* New York: William Morrow & Co.

Morgan, G.A., & Harmon, R.J. (1984). Developmental transformations in mastery motivation. In R.N. Emde & R.J. Harmon (Eds.), *Continuities and discontinuities in development.* New York: Plenum.

Musselwhite, C.R. (1986). *Adaptive play for special needs children: Strategies to enhance communication and learning.* San Diego, CA: College-Hill Press.

Neumann, E.A. (1971). *The elements of play.* New York: MSS Information.

Nicholich, L.M. (1977). Beyond sensorimotor intelligence: assessment of symbolic maturity through analysis of pretend play. *Merrill-Palmer Quarterly, 23,* 89–99.

Norris, J.A., & Hoffman, P.R. (1990). Language intervention within naturalistic environments. *Language, speech, and hearing services in school, 21,* 72–84.

Orelove, F.P., & Sobsey, D. (1991). *Educating children with multiple disabilities: A transdisciplinary approach* (2nd ed.). Baltimore: Paul H. Brookes Publishing Co.

Pellegrini, A. (1981). Speech play and language development in young children. *Journal of Research and Development in Education, 14,* 73–80.

Pellegrini, A.D. (1984). The effects of exploration and play on young children's associative fluency: A review and extension in training studies. In T.D. Yawkey & A.D. Pellegrini (Eds.), *Child's play: Developmental and applied* (pp. 237–253). Hillsdale, NJ: Lawrence Erlbaum Associates.

Pepler, D.J., & Ross, H.S. (1981). The effects of play on convergent and divergent problem-solving. *Child Development, 52,* 1202–1210.

Peterson, C. (1980). Support services. In B. Wilcox & R. York (Eds.), *Quality education for the severely handicapped: The federal investment* (pp. 136–163). Washington, DC: U.S. Office of Special Education and Rehabilitative Services.

Piaget, J. (1962). *Play, dreams, and imitation in childhood.* New York: Norton.

Rainforth, B., York, J., & Macdonald, C. (1992). *Collaborative teams for students with severe disabilities: Integrating therapy and educational services.* Baltimore: Paul H. Brookes Publishing Co.

Rentzel, D.R., & Hollingsworth, P.M. (1988). Whole language and the practitioner. *Academic Therapy, 23,* 405–416.

Rogers-Warren, A., & Warren, S. (1980). Mands for verbalization: Facilitating the display of newly trained language in children. *Behavior Modification, 4,* 361–382.

Rubin, K.H., Fein, G.G., & Vandenberg, B. (1983). Play. In P.H. Mussen (Ed.), *Handbook of child psychology: Volume 4. Socialization, personality, and social development* (4th ed.) (pp. 693–774). New York: John Wiley & Sons.

Rubin, K., & Maioni, T. (1975). Play preference and its relation to egocentrism, popularity, and classification skills in preschoolers. *Merrill-Palmer Quarterly, 21,* 171–179.

Saltz, E., & Johnson, J. (1974). Training for thematic-fantasy play in culturally disadvantaged preschoolers: Preliminary results. *Journal of Educational Psychology, 66,* 623–630.

Scales, B., Almy, M., Nicolopoulou, A., & Ervin-Tripp, S. (1991). *Play and the social context of development in early care and education. Part II: Language, literacy, and the social worlds of children* (pp. 75–86). New York: Teachers College Press.

Schwartz, I.S., Anderson, S.R., & Halle, J.W. (1989). A time-delay procedure: An analysis of teacher training techniques. *Journal of The Association for Persons with Severe Handicaps, 14,* 48–57.

Schwartzman, H.B. (1978). Child-structured play: A cross-cultural perspective. In C.C. Brown & A.W. Gottfried (Eds.), *Play interactions: The role of toys and parental involvement in children's development.* Skillman, NJ: Johnson & Johnson Baby Products Co.

Sharp, E. (1970). *Thinking is child's play.* New York: E.P. Dutton.

Sigel, I.E. (1993). Educating the young thinker: A distancing model of preschool education. In J.L. Roopnarine & J.E. Johnson (Eds.), *Approaches to early childhood education* (pp. 237–252). Columbus, OH: Merrill/Macmillan.

Smilansky, S. (1968). *The effects of sociodramatic play on disadvantaged preschool children.* New York: John Wiley & Sons.

Smilansky, S., & Shefatya, L. (1990). *Facilitating play: A medium for promoting cognitive, socio-emotional, and academic development in young children.* Gaithersburg, MD: Psychosocial & Educational Publications.

Spradlin, J.E., & Siegel, G.M. (1982). Language training in natural and clinical environments. *Journal of Speech and Hearing Disorders, 47,* 2–6.

The Association for Persons with Severe Handicaps. (1986). *Position statement on the provision of related services.* Seattle, WA: Author.

Van Hoorn, J., Nourot, P., Scales, B., & Alward, K. (1993). *Play at the center of the curriculum.* New York: Merrill.

Vygotsky, L. (1962). *Thought and language.* Cambridge, MA: MIT Press.

Vygotsky, L. (1967). Play and its role in the mental development of the child. *Soviet Psychology, 12,* 62–76.

Vygotsky, L. (1978). *Mind in society: The development of higher psychological processes.* Cambridge, MA: Harvard University Press.

Woodruff, G., & McGonigel, M.J. (1988). Early intervention team approaches: The transdisciplinary model. In J.B. Jordan, J.J. Gallagher, P.L. Hutinger, & M.B. Karnes (Eds.), *Early childhood special education: Birth to three* (pp. 164–181). Reston, VA: Council for Exceptional Children.

Yawkey, T.D., Jones, K.C., & Hrncir, E.J. (1979). *The effects of imaginative play and sex differences on mathematics, playfulness, imaginativeness, creativity, and reading capacity in 5-year-old children.* Paper presented at the annual meeting of the North Eastern Educational Research Association,

York, J., Rainforth, B., & Giangreco, M.F. (1990). Transdisciplinary teamwork and integrated therapy: Clarifying the misconceptions. *Pediatric Physical Therapy, 2*(2), 73–79.

5

Conducting the TPBI Process

The TPBI process allows an intervention team to identify what the child is ready for (i.e., determine the child's strengths and needs), set priorities for intervention that focus on practical skills (i.e., functional goals) appropriate to the child's environment (i.e., an ecological approach), develop activity-based curriculum plans, and perform ongoing evaluation. At the core of the transdisciplinary play-based intervention process is the TPBI Planner, which identifies playful and pleasurable activities that correspond to the Observation Guidelines and developmental levels in TPBA (Linder, 1993). By careful selection of activities across the four domains (cognitive, social-emotional, communication and language, and sensorimotor) that match team-generated goals and objectives for the child, a framework for a holistic IFSP or IEP is developed. The TPBI allows enough flexibility to implement individual IFSPs in group or classroom settings by integrating methods, materials, and activities into centers or theme-based play activities. The team is assisted by the Team Ideas for Play (TIP) Sheet, which is developed collaboratively throughout the TPBI planning meetings. The following sections describe each phase of the process, which can be depicted graphically as a series of interlocking components (Figure 1).

THE ESSENTIAL COMPONENTS

Transdisciplinary play-based intervention consists of several essential components, the use of which guides the transdisciplinary team through the process for individual children and their families. These components include the TPBI Planner (see Chapters 8–11), which is divided into the four domains mentioned above, and three worksheets, which are used to plan intervention activities, evaluate the child's progress, and develop thematic programming.

The team, which consists of professional staff and parents or caregivers, is jointly involved in the planning process. The TPBI Planner can be used by both parents and professionals to derive ideas for facilitating development. Home planning worksheets are to be completed by professionals and parents working together. Professionals should complete school planning forms, with parents providing input whenever possible. Professionals and parents together should decide who will complete evaluation worksheets.

The TPBI Planner

The TPBI Planner is divided into four domains: 1) cognitive, 2) social-emotional, 3) communication and language, and 4) sensorimotor. These domains follow the Observation Guidelines used

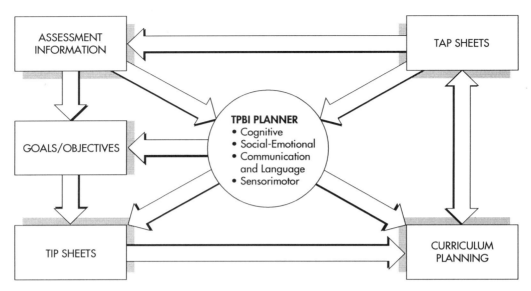

Figure 1.   The TPBI process can be depicted as a series of interlocking components.

to conduct transdisciplinary play-based assessment. Arranged by developmental levels, the guidelines are divided into clusters of skills for which specific information is provided.

- **Observation Guidelines Outline**
  A shaded box reproduces a portion of the Observation Guidelines that can be targeted as a unit for discussion of appropriate intervention strategies.

The parent's input in the TPBI process is critical.

- **Intervention Implications**
  The intervention implications sections of the curriculum provide a general discussion of cross-disciplinary information relevant to development in the skill areas being discussed. These discussions serve as a bridge from the TPBA Observation Guidelines, which have been used to identify the child's present level of functioning, to specific recommendations for interaction, and as an explanation of the developmental significance of the discrete actions targeted for assessment.
- **Developmental Level**
  Beneath each discussion of intervention implications, one or more developmental levels is dually identified by a functional action or behavior and a typical chronological age equivalent. Age ranges are included to provide a frame of reference, but are not intended to be used to "pigeon-hole," or label, children.
- **Intervention Guidelines**
  The team can select, modify, or create individualized activities for the child based on the suggestions offered in the intervention guidelines discussions. These can be translated directly into goals and objectives for the mandated IFSP or IEP.
- **Play Materials and Opportunities**
  Where relevant, intervention guidelines are followed by lists of play materials and times and places to embed the guidelines into the child's day. Of course, the team is encouraged to brainstorm to create activities based on the individual child's interests, the family's preferences, and available materials and opportunities.
- **Examples**
  Interspersed throughout the domains are stories that demonstrate how to implement guidelines and recommendations. These examples show a range of ages, developmental levels, abilities, cultures, and family situations. They underscore the flexibility and adaptability of the TPBI process.

The emphasis on play and fun activities at the heart of the TPBI Planner is designed to motivate children and engage families in nonintrusive ways that are a significant departure from many intervention programs for children with disabilities. Thus, the families and children do not feel that they are engrossed in therapy, yet the curriculum is rich with functional and effective intervention techniques.

Team Ideas for Play (TIP) Sheet

Intervention guidelines are matched to family goals and objectives and organized into a program plan, which is recorded on the Team Ideas for Play (TIP) Sheet (Figure 2) and any other forms that may be required by state or local agencies. In some cases, TIP Sheets may supplant existing planning forms. In other instances, TIP Sheets may supplement required information. The TIP Sheet is also used for ongoing evaluation as described below. The evaluation process is referred to as *Team Assessment of Play (TAP)*. Each worksheet, therefore, has two titles at the top. When beginning to work on a TIP Sheet or a TAP Sheet, the appropriate title should be circled. A TIP Sheet is completed for the settings in which the child spends his or her day, typically home and school. When a TIP Sheet is finished, the following components are recorded:

- **Identifying Information**
  Identifying information, which includes the child's name, date of birth, and age, the current date, and the location for intervention (e.g., home, school), is entered at the top of the TIP Sheet.
- **Family Goals**
  Specific family goals, which are identified during the program planning meetings, are expressed below the identifying information. These goals are written in the family's own words.

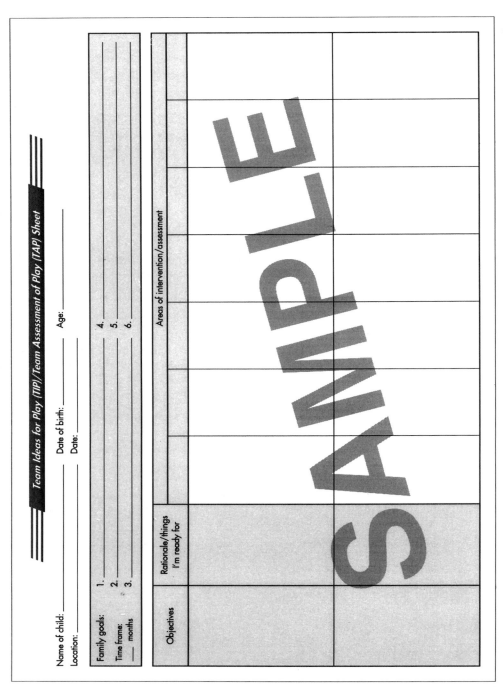

Team Ideas for Play (TIP)/Team Assessment of Play (TAP) Sheet

Name of child: _____ Date of birth: _____ Age: _____

Location: _____ Date: _____

Family goals:
1.
2.
3.
4.
5.
6.

Areas of intervention/assessment

Objectives	Rationale/things I'm ready for								

Figure 2. The first page of the Team Ideas for Play (TIP) Sheet. The second and third pages of this form provide additional grid space like that shown here. These grids are used to record suggestions for intervention in all areas of the child's life. Identifying information and the family's goals for the child are written above the matrix on the first page. Prioritized objectives are written on the vertical axis. The "Rationale/things I'm ready for" column re-phrases the objectives in terms of why they have been selected for the child and how they will help the child. The key periods in the child's day are written on the horizontal axis of the matrix. The names and roles of each team member in relation to the child are entered at the bottom of the last page of the form (see Figure 3). With the exception of the "Location" entry in the identifying information, these entries are the same for both home and center/school TIP Sheets. It is at this point that the form is photocopied for use as a Team Assessment of Play (TAP) Sheet.

- **Prioritized Objectives**
  Written to take into account family goals and the opinions of the various professionals on the team, prioritized objectives are placed on the vertical axis of the TIP Sheet. The time frame for evaluation of objectives can be based on federal and state mandates. However, it is recommended that updates be scheduled at least quarterly. Depending on the child or the wishes of the family, observations can be increased and objectives modified on a more frequent basis.
- **Rationale/Things I'm Ready For**
  The column entitled "Rationale/things I'm ready for" appears immediately adjacent to the objectives column and features the objectives rephrased in language that eliminates discipline-specific terminology and describes the reasons for the objectives.
  The title *Things I'm ready for* is used as a *positive* way of denoting the reasons for specific objectives. *Needs* and *concerns*, terms used frequently in the early childhood special education field, connote a problem and make a negative statement about the child. Here, *ready* has a very different meaning from *readiness*, which has come to mean a set of skills a child must have *before* he or she is prepared to learn. This view is ludicrous, as all children are ready to learn something. The job of parents and professionals is to determine *what* the child is ready to learn or *which* skills the child is ready to acquire.
- **Environments**
  The environments section of the TIP Sheet is a list of the key periods in the child's day. These are entered on the form's horizontal axis. After this portion of the form is completed, the form is photocopied and put aside to be used as a TAP Sheet later (see below).
- **The TPBI Planner Activities**
  The rest of the TIP Sheet is completed by entering activities that match objectives to environments. The layout of the TIP Sheet ensures that no opportunities are overlooked, as its gridlike format ensures the selection of an activity, where appropriate, for each objective in each setting.

Of the following five areas on the second part of the TIP Sheet (Figure 3), the first three provide suggestions across objectives that will help the child succeed in all activities:

- **Preparations**
  The preparations section of the TIP Sheet is used to record recommendations for facilitating the intervention activities (e.g., information on positioning for a child, suggestions for relaxing a child to decrease tone before an activity).
- **Cues and Prompts**
  The cues and prompts section of the TIP Sheet lists strategies to encourage the child to engage in the selected activities and to interact with others. For instance, if a child takes 10–15 seconds to consider what he or she sees or hears, a recommendation might be made to provide wait time before expecting a response.
- **Adaptations**
  Modifications of toys or equipment and alternative environmental arrangements are entered in the adaptations portion of the TIP Sheet. This is an appropriate place to consider the child's sensorimotor impairment or physical limitations. For example, adding Velcro straps, weighting objects, or adding switches might be recommended.
- **Evaluation Schedule**
  In addition to mandated yearly reviews, it is recommended that observational updates take place monthly for young infants, every other month for toddlers, and quarterly for preschoolers. The observational updates may be conducted by individual team members, the whole team, and/or the parents. The choice of observers may vary from month to month, depending on progress and the desires of the family. At the original staffing, the evaluation

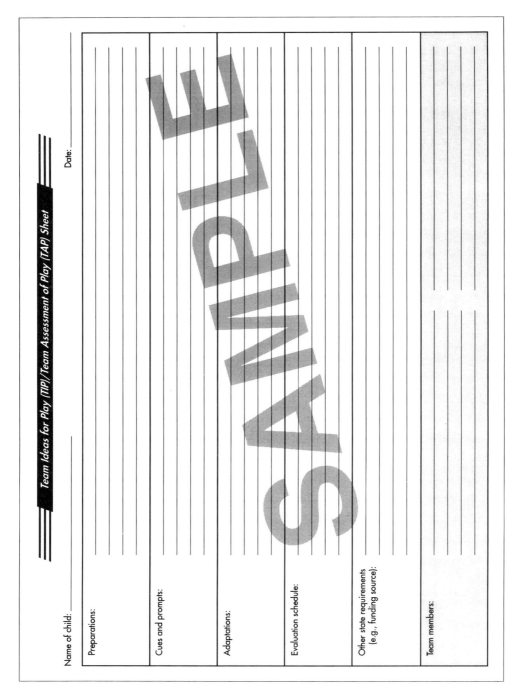

Figure 3. The final page of the TIP Sheet. This page provides suggestions to be incorporated into all of the child's activities.

time frame can be determined and the observers selected. This then can be modified as needed.

- **Other State Requirements**

  As a result of the requirements, particularly in Part H, for interagency coordination, there may be a need to document various aspects related to intervention, such as the resources or funding sources that will be used to pay for intervention services. Such entries can be made in this section of the TIP Sheet.

- **Team Members**

  The names of the team members and their roles in relation to the child (e.g., parent, occupational therapist, teacher) are listed at the bottom of the TIP Sheet.

Team Assessment of Play (TAP) Sheet

To implement the evaluation schedule, the TIP Sheet is modified to create a TAP Sheet. This form is created from the photocopied TIP Sheet, which lists identifying information, family goals, objectives, "rationale/things I'm ready for" entries, environments, and the team members section of the form, but leaves empty the grid for informal assessment of a child's progress in reaching the identified objectives, and the preparations, cues and prompts, adaptations, evaluation schedule, and other state requirements portions of the form. TAP Sheets can be completed by any team member. Because TAP Sheets provide a means for monitoring and do not provide a full formal assessment, team members may want to rotate observation duties. This reinforces the transdisciplinary approach. Parents also should be involved in observations if they so desire. The decision about who completes the TAP Sheets can be made in team planning meetings. An individual from a specific discipline may be interested in observing the children; certain team members' skills may lend themselves well to the particular activities taking place in the classroom; or the observations may be made by parents and/or caregivers, in addition to selected team members or home visitors. The observation schedule is determined during the program meeting and recorded on the TIP Sheet. At subsequent team meetings, members compare their notes on the TAP Sheets for home and school and make modifications as necessary or appropriate to the IFSP or IEP. Parents differ in how involved they want to be in the monitoring activity. Some prefer to let the home visitor do the monitoring of progress, while others enjoy taking notes on their child's new skills as they emerge. As with other areas of parent participation, the degree of involvement in this aspect of the program should be determined by the family.

This completes the cyclical nature of the TPBI process. The new assessment information is discussed, objectives changed, the TPBI Planner consulted, and the process repeats.

Theme Sheets

Transdisciplinary play-based intervention can be incorporated into any curriculum, but a theme or storybook curriculum is recommended. Planning sheets (Figures 4 and 5) are included to assist team members in generating activities that will incorporate intervention ideas across all areas of development. At the top of each planning sheet a space is provided to identify the theme for the planning period. On the preschool/kindergarten planning sheet, this is followed by a space to name the primary book being used as a stimulus for theme activities. The date for implementation is also provided at the top of the page. Two forms are provided—one for infant/toddler planning and one for preschool/kindergarten planning.

The body of the planning sheet lists the days of the week across the horizontal axis and the types of centers down the vertical axis. If desired, alternative labels (i.e., group time, outdoor time) also could be used. As many centers as needed may be incorporated into the form. The team develops a planning sheet by brainstorming various activities, materials, and play oppor-

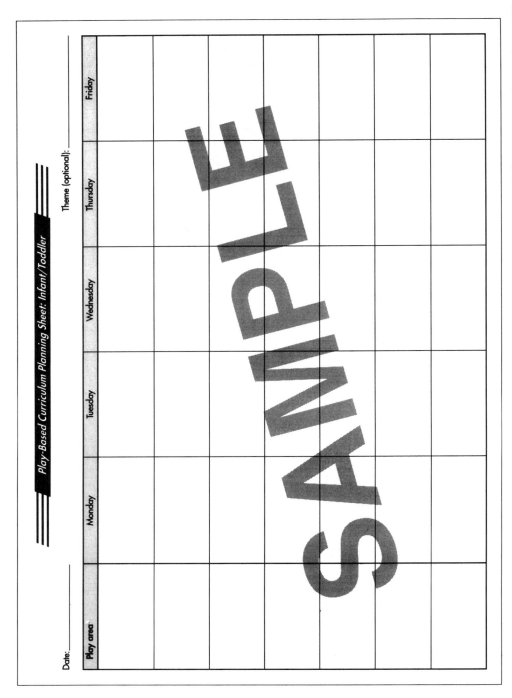

Figure 4. The Play-Based Curriculum Planning Sheet: Infant/Toddler. This form is used to record curriculum planning ideas for each day that a program meets. The group lists available play areas on the vertical axis and enters specific intervention ideas in the grid.

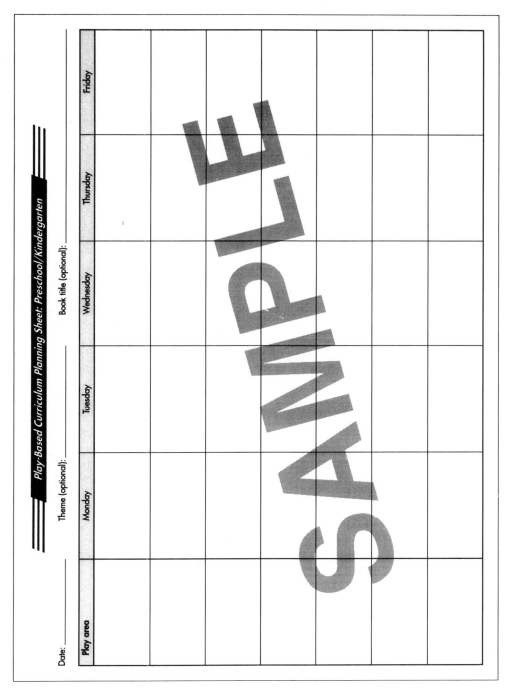

Figure 5. The Play-Based Curriculum Planning Sheet: Preschool/Kindergarten. This form is used in the same manner as its infant/toddler counterpart, but a second page of grid space is provided as more play areas tend to be relevant to older children.

51

tunities that can be integrated into the centers throughout the week. Individual child objectives are then addressed within these play alternatives. Observation of the child within these activities also enables staff to complete the TAP Sheets. Theme planning sheets thus provide the group planning basis into which individual planning is integrated.

THE IMPLEMENTATION PROCESS

For the purpose of clarification, the TPBI process is described in six phases or steps:

Phase I: Review available assessment data
Phase II: Generate family goals and program plan objectives
Phase III: Complete TIP Sheets
Phase IV: Integrate children's individual TIP Sheets into center's daily programming
Phase V: Implement intervention
Phase VI: Conduct ongoing evaluation

In the following discussion, each of the phases is illustrated using a case study based on Angela, a 24-month-old child with Down syndrome.

Phase I: Review Available Assessment Data

Program planning, which includes the first three phases of TPBI, may be done, if time allows, during the staffing process. However, often this is not possible due to time constraints, and it is recommended that another meeting be set to develop TIP Sheets for home and school. Home TIP Sheets also can be done informally in a home visit. The planning meeting usually requires about an hour and should involve all parties who will be actively involved in the child's program.

Many children have parents who work full- or part-time. These children often spend a portion of each day in family child care or other types of child care. If the child for whom intervention is being planned spends a significant portion of the day in child care, provisions should be made to involve the child care provider in the program implementation. Depending on the family's wishes, a child care worker (or extended family member) may be included in the planning meeting, or a team member may wish to create options for including play intervention ideas into the child care time. A TIP Sheet may also be developed for the child care provider. When program planning is in a follow-up meeting, the team or home visitor should review the assessment data gathered previously before beginning program planning. If the team has conducted a TPBA, this process will have ended with the writing of a report that includes developmental history, observations of the child's performance on the TPBA across domains, and recommendations with regard to intervention. Also available to the team are the TPBA summary sheets completed for the four domains. Any other available assessment data also should be used. These might include a developmental inventory completed by the parents prior to the TPBA session (see Linder, 1993), informal observations from the TPBA worksheets, and results from any other assessment instruments that have been administered. (Different states and localities may require the use of standardized instruments, parent needs inventories, or other specific tools.) Review of this information should then lead to the logical step of determining what the child is ready for in an intervention program. Ultimately, the outcome of this meeting and the subsequent steps of the TPBI process will be the development and ongoing monitoring of an IFSP (or IEP) for the child and family.

The family who has participated in the TPBA remains actively involved in decision-making and planning the child's IFSP or IEP. If specific concerns are identified from the review of the assessment data discussed above, the TPBA videotape may be viewed again to focus on learning style and communication strategies and to help identify priorities.

Angela G. is the second child of Richard and Mary G. Angela's brother Sean is 5 years old. Mr. G. is a plumber, and Mrs. G. is a homemaker. Angela has had heart surgery to correct a mitral valve defect and is currently healthy. Angela has been enrolled in an infant program since she was 1 month old. She has received a home visit once a week from a developmental specialist. As Angela is now 2 years old, she was evaluated for possible placement in the center-based toddler program, which meets twice a week in parent–child play groups. Mrs. G. also would like home visits to continue on an every-other-week basis as these visits have provided a great deal of support to the family.

Angela's TPBA revealed a pleasant, easily adaptable little girl. Angela primarily used vocalization and pointing to communicate. She used a few single words, including "ma," "da," and "ba" (for bottle). Angela also signs an approximation of "more." The frequency of her use of words was limited to four to five in an hour. She preferred to point to objects and vocalize "da," (which Mrs. G. interprets as "that"). Angela would initiate a comment or play interaction, but did not continue through more than one or two turns before losing interest. Angela was motivated by cause-and-effect toys and played longest when someone facilitated her play by imitating her and modeling an action. She primarily banged and waved objects. Angela was able to sit unsupported and play with objects; however, lack of strength, low tone, and unsophisticated fine motor skills made toy manipulation (and signing) difficult. Angela sat primarily with her legs straight out and spread wide with toys in the middle between her legs. She showed limited ability to rotate her body from side to side. Angela crawled or rolled to get from one place to another. She pulled to stand, but was not yet venturing to move in that position. She also demonstrated aversion to various textures, such as rough or sticky substances, although she enjoyed holding, rocking, and deep touch such as that given in a massage.

Phase II: Generate Family Goals and Program Plan Objectives

After all available assessment data have been reviewed, the team is ready to generate family goals and program plan objectives. By now, because the parents have been active participants in the TPBA process, the team members may have some idea of what the parents have in mind as goals for their child. The various professionals on the team also may have ideas for goals based on their specific areas of expertise and their observations of the child. It is, however, important that family members voice the goals they have chosen before other objectives are discussed. This is important because there should be a clear relationship between family goals and the order in which objectives are prioritized on the TIP Sheets.

As the team is still in a discussion phase of intervention planning, it is recommended that separate sheets of paper be used to take notes regarding this preliminary planning before moving to the TIP Sheets. One member of the team should be designated to take notes. He or she will generate both the list of family goals and prioritized objectives.

To begin the discussion, the team may want to look back over the strengths and things I'm ready for (originally, needs) columns of the TPBA Summary Sheets. The parents are then asked to identify the skills they would like to see their child develop. These skills are noted in order of importance to the family, who should consider their lifestyle, daily routines involving the child, and their interests.

Mr. and Mrs. G. voiced concern that at 2 years of age, Angela was using words only occasionally. They wanted her to talk more often. Mrs. G. said Angela demands her attention all of the time. She would like to see her be able to play alone for longer periods of time. They also wanted Angela to begin walking soon, as this would increase her independence and free Mrs. G. from having to carry her everywhere. The speech-language and occupational therapists agreed that these were areas in which Angela was ready for higher-level skills. They discussed what they had observed in the TPBA and related these observations to what Mr. and Mrs. G. had seen at home. Mr. and Mrs. G. identified the following as their goals for Angela:

1. *Use words to communicate.*
2. *Play in more ways with toys.*
3. *Walk alone.*

As the family offers their ideas, the other team members should supplement the discussion with their observations and recommendations. If clarification or reminders are needed at any point during the discussion, the team can review relevant portions of the TPBA videotape. From the family's goals and the other team members' recommendations, specific objectives for the child are developed. The team leader should be certain that the team keeps in mind an appropriate time frame for which these objectives should be aimed. Typically, a 6- to 12-month planning period is used. However, it is recommended that a shorter interval be used, especially for young infants, whose development may change rapidly. In order to keep the program responsive to the child's changing needs, reviews and updates should be completed monthly for infants, every other month for toddlers, and quarterly for preschoolers. After 8–10 objectives have been listed on the note-taking member's sheet, the team should select the items that are most important, being sure to refer to the family goals listed previously, and rank them in order of importance. It is not necessary to have written objectives for every identified need on the TPBA Summary Sheet, and parents may want to focus on fewer objectives on their own TIP Sheets. As described below, other portions of the TIP Sheets allow team members to plan strategies to build strengths and skills. The team is now ready to proceed to the TIP Sheet.

Phase III: Complete TIP Sheets

When the team has prioritized its objectives for the child, it should obtain one blank TIP Sheet for each setting in which the child spends time daily (e.g., home, school). On each TIP Sheet, the note-taking team member should complete six portions of the form. First, the identifying information, including the child's name, date of birth, and age, the current date, and the location for intervention, should be entered at the top of each form. Second, the names and roles of each team member should be filled in at the bottom of each TIP Sheet. Third, the family's goals should be transferred in order *and in their own words* to the forms. Using the same language the family selected eliminates jargon and enables the parents to know that their concerns are important. Fourth, the prioritized objectives should be entered in the first column of each TIP Sheet. These objectives are stated in behavioral terminology to allow for objective measurement of learning and to establish agreement regarding what is or is not occurring (Popovich, 1981). Fifth, for ease of implementation, the objectives are reworded in terms of why the objective has been selected and why it will help the child, and entered in the column labeled "Rationale/Things I'm ready for." This column provides anyone reading the TIP Sheet with a brief description of current behaviors and reasons for the program being planned for the child. Sixth, concentrating first on the Home TIP Sheet, and then on the School TIP Sheet, the family and other team members identify key periods in the child's day with the family. These are written across the horizontal axis of the TIP Sheet. The School TIP Sheet may be completed in a subsequent meeting not attended by the parents if time is a factor; however, it is helpful for the family to see how the various therapies and education techniques are integrated in the classroom.

The team should now pause while photocopies of each TIP Sheet are made. These photocopies are put aside to be used later as TAP Sheets.

When the meeting resumes, the team continues to work on the TIP Sheets. After discussing the child's objectives further, the team generates ideas for play and pleasurable interactions that will address the child's needs and fit into his or her regular routine. The TPBI Planner provides a wealth of ideas and an authoritative source of activities and opportunities to be matched to the skills and developmental levels related to the TPBA Observation Guidelines. The format of the Planner as described on pages 43–45 makes it easy to match assessment results to intervention guidelines. The need listed on the TPBA Summary Sheet that has been formulated as an objective is matched to an Observation Guidelines category. Finding the corresponding category in the TPBI Planner brings the team to the associated list of intervention guidelines and play materials and opportunities.

Professionals already familiar with the Planner will be able to offer recommendations immediately. In other situations, team members may want to have prepared in advance of the team meeting. Particular sections of the TPBI Planner can be referred to during the meeting and discussed with team members not familiar with the Planner.

On Angela's TIP Sheet for home (Figure 6), the team member filled in the grid with words that could be used during mealtimes to increase word approximations. The team member also wrote how the parents could use wait time to increase the frequency of Angela's vocalizations and to approximate words to communicate different needs or intents. The team did the same for other areas of the day. Angela's parents were especially helpful in identifying words to motivate Angela during different activities. The team emphasized keeping interactions fun, drawing on Angela's interests, and following her cues and agenda to motivate her to use more verbalizations.

Problem-solving in the cognitive domain and fine motor skills in the sensorimotor domain were combined into one cross-disciplinary objective. Again, the family helped by identifying specific toys and materials in their house that would be fun for Angela to play with. The rest of the team also generated play activity suggestions that would encourage Angela to use her forefinger and thumb or require varied actions of the hand, wrist, and fingers.

As each objective was discussed, the team also talked about the interrelationships among the various areas. For example, if Angela was playing with a pop-up box and trying to move a lever to get the animal to pop up, language could be incorporated at the same time by naming the animal; saying "push," "pull," or "pop"; or making the animal's sound. Social interactions and the pragmatics of communication, addressed through a cross-disciplinary objective related to turn-taking, could also be incorporated by interjecting a turn for Mom, Dad, or sibling. This type of integrated discussion helped Angela's family to see how the transdisciplinary process works and how integrating therapy into everyday play activities builds the foundations for all of the areas of Angela's development. During the discussion, the team referred to observations made during the TPBA and to the TPBI Planner; the family talked about typical interactions, activities, and issues related to Angela's family life; and problem-solving took place.

After the grid is completed, other aspects related to learning, including preparations, cues and prompts, and adaptations, are incorporated into the TIP Sheet. These sections allow areas of need not addressed by specific objectives to be targeted for intervention. The following is a representative list of questions to be considered for each child as the team completes the TIP Sheet. The team will want to individualize according to the child's needs.

- Will certain positioning techniques be needed to ensure that the child can perform at an optimal level?
- Are adaptive devices needed?
- Are techniques needed to normalize the child's tone prior to an activity?
- Does the child need help making transitions from one activity to another?
- What level of physical, verbal, and/or visual prompts does the child need?
- What interactive patterns enhance behaviors?
- What specific progress probes should be assessed?

Team Ideas for Play (TIP)/Team Assessment of Play (TAP) Sheet

Name of child: Angela G. Date of birth: 1-15-90 Age: 2 years

Location: Home Date: 1-20-92

Family goals:
1. Use words to communicate
2. Play in more ways with toys
3. Walk alone

4.
5.
6.

Time frame: 6 months

Areas of intervention/assessment

Objectives	Rationale/things I'm ready for	Eating	Bathing/Dressing	Playtime with Mom	Playtime outdoors	Chores	Afternoon/Siblings Evening/Dad	Bedtime
1. Angela will spontaneously use 1-2 words to communicate: • A request for objects • A request for action • A comment • A protest • A greeting to family in 75% of her utterances.	Angela uses gestures and vocalizations to communicate her intents. She is ready to use words and word approximations. Gestures and "na" to have. been very effective for her so she'll probably want to stick to that.	• Label food • "Eat" • "Good" • "more" • "spoon" • "cup" • "All done" • "milk" • "Juice"	• "Bubbles" • "out" • "Wash" • "Dry" • "push" • "Pour" • "cup" "spoon" • Name body parts on self/doll • name pieces of clothing	• "In," "out" • "Up," "down" • Wait for Angela to request • "Read" her gestures as words • words that use "front" of lips and teeth (e.g., baby bottle, Daddy, doggie, more, bye easier)	• "push," "pull" • "swing," "go" • "sand," "jump"	• Angela helps with washing her dishes • "wash," "cup" • "spoon" • "hot" water, • "cold" water.	• Rough and tumble-"up" • "down" • Label actions with toys — "push," etc.	• "Rock-rock" • "Night-night" • "Baby" • "Bear" • "cover" • "kiss" • "Light"
2. Angela will increase her rate of word approximations to 10 per hour.	Angela uses her few words infrequently. The sooner she approximates a word, the sooner she'll try real words.	Make a game of "more." Wait-for word approximation. Ask, "Which do you want?"	Play noise games with tub toys. Label tub objects		Wait for a request to push.	Wait for request. "Help" with clothes "out" of dryer, "in" basket.	• "Ball" • "Truck" • make noises	

Figure 6. The first three pages of a completed home TIP Sheet for Angela G.

Team Ideas for Play (TIP)/Team Assessment of Play (TAP) Sheet

Name of child: Angela 6. Date: 1-20-92

Objectives	Rationale/things I'm ready for	Areas of intervention/assessment						
		Eating	Bathing/dressing	Playtime with Mom	Playtime outdoors	Chores	Afternoon/Siblings Evening/Dad	Bedtime
3. Angela will take turns with family members in an activity through three turns.	Turns are important for language and social interactions. Angela is ready to pay more attention and interact with a play partner.	Take turns with having a bite — Angela, Mom, Angela. Same with a drink.	Dump and fill. Angela wash, Mom wash. Make game out of dressing.	Imitate Angela. Repeat her actions. Add words to actions (e.g., "put in," "stack blocks").	Take turns dumping sand.	Take turns washing and drying dishes, taking out clothes.	Ball play—"push," "roll." Wait for Angela to push.	• Take turns rocking "baby." • Take turns kissing
4. Angela will demonstrate improved problem-solving ability as demonstrated by her ability to: • push • pull • turn with her thumb and forefinger.	Angela uses her hand to manipulate objects. She is ready to move beyond banging and shaking to using her hands and fingers for more complex problem-solving. This will help her see how she can control her environment.	Let Angela dump Cheerios out and put them in a small bottle. Open jar lid to get food. Hide crackers in small box.	• Use tub toys and kitchen objects in water. • Open plastic containers, dump, and fill. • Put small toys in containers to find and get out. • Use tub toys with activating mechanisms	Use same toys, but emphasize turn-taking and adding one more action		Push knob on washer/dryer. Turn handle of faucet (cold).	• Imitate Angela's actions with toys; then wait. • Use toys that require putting things "in" and "out," turning or pushing	Turn lights off and on.
5. Angela will demonstrate an ability to relate object functionally as demonstrated by her ability to combine objects in play.	Angela is currently playing primarily with one toy at a time. She is ready to begin combining toys. This will help her to see how various things can go together, which will help her develop concepts and language.	Practice stirring with spoon in cup or bowl. Help pour cereal in bowl.	• Put soap on washcloth. • Put objects in containers • Wash doll with cloth • Put soap on doll's hair • Dry doll	Begin doll play. Use doll and bottle or doll and blanket. Start pretend play with dishes.		Give Angela pan of water and her own dishes to wash and dry.	Stack blocks and knock down	• Cover baby and bear • Give baby a bottle

(continued)

Figure 6. (continued)

Team Ideas for Play (TIP)/Team Assessment of Play (TAP) Sheet

Name of child: __Angela G.__   Date: __1-20-92__

Objectives	Rationale/things I'm ready for	Eating	Bathing/dressing	Playtime with Mom	Playtime outdoors	Chores	Afternoon/Evening (Dad)	Bedtime
				Areas of intervention/assessment				
6. Angela will demonstrate an ability to rotate her body so she can shift her weight and eventually walk.	Angela needs to be able to rotate her body so she can shift her weight and eventually walk.		• Hide toys under bubbles around tub • Look for objects she likes	Place objects in front, then move to side when she is motivated.		Place objects to either side of Angela so she must turn her body.	Place objects to either side of Angela so she must turn her body.	
7. Angela will demonstrate increased stability, as demonstrated by her ability to cruise around furniture.	Angela is ready to support more weight on her hips in preparation for walking.	Place cheerios or snack crackers around coffee table.		Play in standing at low table to build stability.			Place desired toys around coffee table or furniture.	
8. Angela will initiate play with different textures.	Angela is hesitant to touch things that have a different texture. She is ready to slowly be exposed to many different textures. This will encourage her to explore and discover and will help her to understand new experiences — soft, rough, smooth, squishy, and so forth.	Try different food textures. Let her finger feed part of the time so she explores the "feel."	• Sponges • Bubbles • Soap • Rough and soft washcloth • Bath "foam" • Rub with towel and lotion		• Play in sand and water • Rocks • Mud	Angela helps with cooking. Use cookie dough, top of cooked noodles, or vegetables.	• Rough and tumble tickle • Bristle Blocks	• Lotion • Wash face and hands

Team Ideas for Play (TIP)/Team Assessment of Play (TAP) Sheet

Name of child: Angela G.   Date: 1-20-92

Preparations:
1. Ensure that Angela is in a stable position on small chair.
2. Allow her to play standing or kneel standing for play to build hip stability.

Cues and prompts:
1. To encourage Angela to explore buttons, levers, and so forth, putting a different color or texture on the control mechanism might give her a clue.
2. Prompt Angela to respond by looking expectant and waiting.
3. Reinforce word approximations by repeating words you think Angela said and giving her what she requested.

Adaptations:
Although switches are not needed because of motoric limitations, the use of switch-activated toys with simple pads may get Angela interested in making things happen. You can then shift to more complex mechanisms. Lights and sounds may also help motivate her (bigger effects). Try checking out switch-activated toys from the lending library.

Evaluation schedule:
Use Team Assessment of Play (TAP) sheets weekly in school. Use TAP sheet monthly at home. Retest on TPBA in June.

Other state requirements (e.g., funding source):
Funding sources: Infant development class — Denver Options
Speech-language therapy — Medicaid

Team members:

Figure 7.   The last page of Angela G.'s TIP Sheet.

59

Other considerations for Angela (Figure 7) included positioning her to ensure and develop stability. Suggestions for using visual and physical cues and verbal reinforcement were listed. Adaptations for toys were suggested to motivate Angela to use higher-level actions on objects. The team suggested checking out some switch-activated toys from the toy-lending library to see how Angela liked them. The team identified Denver Options as the funding source for infant development classes and Medicaid as the source for speech-language therapy. These were recorded in the other state requirements portion of the form.

The portion of the TIP Sheet completed last is the evaluation schedule. Here the team agrees upon how frequently ongoing assessment at home and school will be conducted. *For Angela, it was decided that assessment of progress would be done by doing monthly observational checks and conducting another TPBA in 6 months.* Guidelines and recommendations for using TIP Sheets to implement the TPBI process are included on pages 45–49.

Phase IV: Integrate Children's Individual TIP Sheets into Center's Daily Programming

Crucial to the implementation of TPBI is the successful infusion of individual TIP Sheet planning into the child's group learning environment (e.g., infant or toddler program, preschool, kindergarten). This implementation process must be carried out in the context of the broader classroom activities planned for the children. This phase is discussed in Chapter 7.

In Angela's toddler program, the room is arranged with numerous centers around the room. A sensory center with tactile materials and toys (e.g., sand, shovels, jars) is in one corner. A sensorimotor area with climbing equipment and swings is in another area. Manipulatives and cause-and-effect toys are on the floor near a block area with different types of blocks. A music and book area has a tape recorder and various infant and toddler books. The children also have a snacktime. Angela's team discussed with Mr. and Mrs. G. how they would address the same objectives as they were addressing at home within the play groups conducted at the center.

For the first objective, increasing Angela's spontaneous use of words, the teacher, parents, and therapists discussed various words that could be incorporated into each of the centers (e.g., labeling objects on the sensory table; waiting for Angela to request a "push" on the swing in the sensorimotor area; using "in" and "on" in the block and boxes area; labeling her favorite toys and actions, such as "go," when she is playing on the floor or at the table; naming body parts and pictures in books in the book and music center; using such words as "more" and "eat" at snacktime). On the school TIP Sheet (Figure 8), these and other ideas were written in each of the boxes corresponding to the objective and each of the centers.

The same procedures were conducted for each of the other objectives. At times, the same suggestions applied across various centers, so rather than write the same ideas over, the notation was made to see ideas in another column. After completing the TIP Sheet, Angela's father commented that he never realized how therapy could be incorporated into "every minute of the day." Mrs. G. commented that she picks up a lot of ideas from other parents in the play groups and then uses them with Angela. As the team ended its conference, Mrs. G. commented that completing the TIP Sheet had given her renewed enthusiasm and she was anxious to try the ideas they had generated. Mr. G. agreed and thanked the team for its efforts on Angela's behalf.

Phase V: Implement Intervention

Given the dynamic nature and flexibility of TPBI, an explicit set of steps for implementation cannot and should not be provided here. Instead, working in a transdisciplinary fashion, the team members collaborate to incorporate activities from the TPBI Planner into the child's day. After completing the child's TIP Sheets, the team members plan to expand the child's play by determining at what level to participate in the play to facilitate interaction with objects, events,

Team Ideas for Play (TIP)/Team Assessment of Play (TAP) Sheet

Name of child: __Angela G.__   Date of birth: __1-15-90__   Age: __2 Years__

Location: __School__   Date: __1-20-92__

Family goals:
1. Use words to communicate
2. Play in more ways with toys
3. Walk alone
4.
5.
6.

Time frame: __6 months__

Areas of intervention/assessment

Objectives	Rationale/things I'm ready for	Sensory Center	Sensorimotor Center	Block/Box Area	Floor play area	Table play area	Books/music center	Snacktime
1. Angela will spontaneously use 1-2 words to communicate: • A request for objects • A request for action • A comment • A protest • A greeting to family in 75% of her utterances.	Angela uses gestures and vocalizations to communicate her intentions. She is ready to use words and word approximations. Gestures and "na" have been very effective for her, so she'll probably want to stick to that.	• Label sights, sounds, textures and objects. • Assign words to her protests. • Comment on actions.	• Up, down, in, through • Swing • Wait for request for more	• In, on, bang, down • Comment on Angela's actions	• Cause-and-effect toys "go" • Baby doll • Label toys and actions	• Place some floor toys on table to get Angela to stand at the table.	• Animals • Body parts • Music and movement with sounds	• Label food • "more" • "Eat" • "Juice"
2. Angela will increase her rate of word approximations to 10 per hour.	Angela uses few words infrequently. The sooner she approximates a word, the sooner she'll try real words.	• Assign meaning to approximations. • Use wait-time before responding to gestures or vocalizations.	• Assign meaning to approximations. • Use wait-time before responding to gestures or vocalizations.	• Assign meaning to approximations. • Use wait-time before responding to gestures or vocalizations.	• Assign meaning to approximations. • Use wait-time before responding to gestures or vocalizations.	• Assign meaning to approximations. • Use wait-time before responding to gestures or vocalizations.	• Wait-time when looking at pictures.	• Omit Angela's cup or juice.

(continued)

Figure 8.   The grid portion of Angela G.'s school TIP Sheet. The other considerations mentioned and recorded on the final page of her home TIP Sheet are applicable at school as well.

Figure 8. (continued)

Name of child: __Angela G.__   Date: __1-20-92__

Objectives	Rationale/Things I'm ready for	Areas of intervention/assessment						
		Sensory Center	Sensorimotor Center	Block/Box area	Floor Play area	Table Play Area	Books/Music Center	Snacktime
3. Angela will take turns with family members in an activity through three turns.	Turns are important for language and social interactions. Angela is ready to pay more attention and interact with a play partner.	Take turns with peer. Have peer imitate Angela.	• Follow peers through actions • Repeat through three turns on activities Angela likes.	• Take turns with mom + facilitator • In and out of boxes, stacking. • Take turns putting blocks in boxes.	• Take turns with Mom or facilitator activating toys. • Use duplicate toys	• Take turns with Mom or facilitator activating toys • Use duplicate toys	Take turns with peers in music.	Give crackers to peers.
4. Angela will demonstrate improved problem-solving ability as demonstrated by her ability to: • Push • Pull • Turn with her thumb and forefinger.	Angela uses her hand hand to manipulate objects. She is ready to move beyond banging and shaking to using her hands and fingers to more complex problem-solving. This will help her see how she can control her environment.	• Light board on and off. • Put materials into bottles or holes.	Incorporate gross motor problem-solving with pushing, pulling, and turning.	Use 1-inch cube blocks, in and out.	• Toys with mechanisms. • Pop-up boxes • Switch-activated toys	• Toys with mechanisms • Pop-up boxes • Switch-activated toys	Punch button on sound books. Tape recorder, or music box.	Open jar lids. Use fingerfoods (raisins).
5. Angela will demonstrate an ability to relate objects functionally as demonstrated by her ability to combine objects at play.	Angela is currently playing primarily with one toy at a time. She is ready to begin combining toys. This will help her to see how various things can go together, which will help her to develop concepts and language.	• Sponges and water. • Xylophone and stick • Water Table and toys • Sand, shovels, or buckets	Throw balls into containers; roll down side.	Combine blocks, boxes, and containers.	Doll play. Relate cup, bottle, and blanket.	Put things in and take them out.	Use instruments: • Drum and stick • Xylophone • sticks	Use spoons and forks. Stir in bowl.

62

Name of child: __Angela G.__   Date: __1-20-92__

Objectives	Rationale/things I'm ready for	Sensory Center	Sensorimotor Center	Block/Box area	Floor Play area	Table Play area	Books/music center	Snacktime
					Areas of intervention/assessment			
6. Angela will demonstrate an ability to rotate her body to either side to obtain a toy.	Angela needs to be able to rotate her body so she can shift her weight and eventually walk.	Place objects on sides as well as center.	Place objects on sides as well as center.	Place objects on sides as well as center.	Place objects on sides as well as center.	Place objects on sides as well as center.	"Dance" to music while sitting; move side to side.	Hand snack to peer next to her.
7. Angela will demonstrate increased stability as demonstrated by her ability to cruise around furniture.	Angela is ready to support more weight on her hips in preparation for walking.	Occasionally place objects at levels requiring kneel stand or stand.	Occasionally place objects at levels requiring kneel stand or stand.	Occasionally place objects at levels requiring kneel stand or stand.	Occasionally place objects at levels requiring kneel stand or stand.	Place objects that Angela wants around the table so she needs to move to get them.	Play music while at play table to encourage weight shift and movement.	Occasionally stand for snack—have her cruise to get her snack before sitting.
8. Angela will initiate play with different textures.	Angela is hesitant to touch things that have a different texture. She is ready to stably be exposed to many different textures. This will encourage her to explore and discover and will help her understand how to interpret new textures—soft, rough, smooth.	• Change materials in water table frequently. • Use foam, clay, cotton, etc. in activities. • Expose a little at a time.	Include play pool with shredded paper, packing peanuts, or sand (sand box).	Hide blocks in tissue or cotton when Angela is motivated to find.	Add textures to mechanisms.	Add textures to mechanisms.	Use different materials with sticks and music— sandpaper, tin pans, and so forth. move to music with hands in foam.	Vary textures.

and people, by preparing the environment accordingly, and by incorporating child-initiated activities.

Determining the Level of Intervention   The adults must decide what level of intervention (i.e., when and how to intervene) is needed for the child. This decision requires continual observation of the child. A general rule is that the adult should avoid interrupting the child's play when active exploration and experimentation are taking place. Similarly, the adult should intervene only when facilitation can be done unobtrusively and without disrupting the flow of play. If, however, the child is not playing at all, is exhibiting low levels of play, or is repeating the same play behaviors in a perseverative fashion, the adult can intervene to stimulate or modify the child's play behaviors. The adult may model a new behavior, introduce new materials, or demonstrate an extension of the child's current activity. The language strategies described on pages 64–65 also foster higher levels of interaction, communication, and play.

Preparing the Environment   Peters, Neisworth, and Yawkey (1985) describe the teacher as incorporating *free discovery* by making materials available and then allowing the child to choose materials and discover and learn independently; *prompted discovery*, in which the teacher makes only specific materials available; and *directed discovery*, in which the teacher guides the child's observations, asks questions, and poses problems. The latter is a more controlling intervention and is probably more appropriate with higher-functioning preschool children, although not as a primary approach.

Enhancing Adult–Child Interactions   After the intervention environment is established and the child's role within the environment is confirmed, the role of the adult in interaction with the child becomes central. The facilitation strategies employed by adults in the child's life stimulate exploration, problem-solving, and other cognitive abilities, communication and language skills, sensorimotor development, and social competence.

Numerous studies have been conducted to ascertain the importance of adult–child interactions. A study by Stallings (1975) found that although one-to-one interaction increased the child's task persistence, the type of interaction with the child was a critical factor. Verbally responsive, nondidactic teaching resulted in task persistence, independence, verbalization, cooperation, and self-esteem in children. Fagot (1973) and Hamilton and Gordon (1978) also found that the use of less directive, more responsive teaching, with less criticism and more supportive suggesting, resulted in higher task persistence and performance.

Increasing a child's communicative and interactive competence is a focus for early intervention and preschool programs (Miller, 1989; Roberts, Bailey, & Nychka, 1991; Warren & Kaiser, 1986). Strategies that adults can use to promote communication should be an integral part of intervention implementation. The following strategies are derived from the literature regarding interaction and communication, the INREAL approach (Weiss, 1981), and a study by Roberts et al. (1991). These strategies have been found to be a successful aspect of the TPBI model, as they promote higher-level behaviors across all developmental domains. Chapters 8–11 reexamine and give examples of how these strategies can be incorporated into the child's daily routine and intervention program.

Child-Initiated Activities   As much as possible, the child should be allowed to select and lead play activities. Eye-pointing or blinking can be used to allow the child with severe impairments to make choices. With very young infants or with children who are highly distractible, choices may need to be limited, but it is still desirable to give the child control over choices. Within preschool and kindergarten classrooms, where some small group play activities may be planned, the child can be allowed to make choices within the activity.

Engagement   Engagement refers to capturing the child's attention or drawing the child into interaction with a person or objects in the environment. Interest in the environment is a critical element of engagement. If the child is interested in toys, materials, movements, behaviors, or personal communication, interaction with the environment is more likely to occur. Determining what engages the child and then using that information to form an interactive relationship is a key to successful intervention (Argyle & Ingham, 1972; Bruner, 1983; Garvey, 1984; Halle, 1984; Warren & Rogers-Warren, 1985). Research has shown that the children of mothers who follow their child's attentional lead have more sophisticated language than the children of mothers who direct their child's focus of attention and communicate about topics of their own interest (Tomasello & Farrar, 1986; Yoder & Kaiser, 1989). Attending to the child's focus also results in longer "conversations," turn-taking, and the acquisition of new vocabulary (Tomasello & Todd, 1983; Valdez-Manchaca & Whitehurst, 1988). In TPBI, following the child's attentional lead is fundamental to the process.

Responsiveness   After the child is engaged in play or interaction, responsiveness to the child's cues becomes important. Mothers of children with disabilities have been shown to be more directive, changing topics and activities more frequently than mothers of children without disabilities (Breiner & Forehand, 1982; Mahoney & Powell, 1988; McDonald & Pein, 1982; Peterson & Sherrod, 1982). Responsiveness, or the degree, timing, and sensitivity of the adult's response to the child, is a critical factor in successful interactions (Coggins & Carpenter, 1981; Girolametto, Greenberg, & Manolson, 1986; Mahoney & Powell, 1988; McDade & Varnedoe, 1987).

The child may communicate with a look, movement, gesture, vocalization, verbalization, or specific behavior. The adult must interpret and respond to these cues or communicative intents with the appropriate level, degree of intensity, and synchronicity of reaction. Staying with the child's agenda gives continuity to the interaction, while responding to the child's cues and interpreting those cues as having meaning teaches the child about give-and-take in communication (Tomasello & Farrar, 1986; Valdez-Manchaca & Whitehurst, 1988). When the adult uses commands, asks questions, and shifts the child's focus to toys or topics of interest to the adult, the flow of play, maintenance of turn-taking, and child's interest level are jeopardized (Cross, 1984; Mahoney & Powell, 1988; McDonald & Pein, 1982).

Early interventionists must increase their awareness and interpretation of children's cues and match their language and pace to that of the child. They can then assist parents in becoming more responsive and less directive as well (Girolametto et al., 1986).

Responsiveness is also important for behavior management. Often, children who have difficulty communicating use socially undesirable actions as a means of accomplishing goals. Instead of interpreting the undesirable actions as behaviors to be modified or eliminated, the adult should read these actions as attempts to communicate. Reading the child's behaviors as carrying a communicative intent can lead to the adult helping the child to replace negative actions with other more positive ways of achieving a goal (Donnellan, Mirenda, Mesaros, & Fassbender, 1984). For instance, if the child hits other children to acquire toys, the adult can interpret this as an attempt to communicate the desire for the toys. The adult can then help the child to use a gesture, a word, or a phrase to accomplish the same end.

Wait Time   Many children with disabilities have longer response times than children without disabilities (Mahoney & Powell, 1988). Pausing after speaking or acting on an object and giving the child a nonverbal cue that a response is expected can increase the number of turns the child takes, thereby increasing play and communicative interactions. Lack of wait time on the adult's part results in the adult dominating the interactions. A wait time of 5 seconds has been found to increase the responsiveness of children with disabilities (Lee, O'Shea, & Dykes, 1987), but some children may require more time. The optimal wait time for an individual child may be determined through observation and experimentation.

Language Strategies   A variety of language strategies are recommended in the literature to increase children's communication efforts. These techniques, as discussed here and in Chapter 10, are used in combination, as is appropriate for a given child.

- **Mirroring**
  Mirroring is imitation of the child's actions or restatement of the child's sounds or utterances. Mirroring lets the child know that the adult is paying attention and understands the child's actions or intentions (Weiss, 1981). Imitation of the child also leads to turn-taking, as the child frequently repeats the action or sound in order to get the adult to repeat the imitation. Thus, mirroring promotes not only language, but also social interaction.

- **Commenting**
  Commenting on what the child is doing or describing the play event (also called *parallel talk*) promotes language acquisition and stimulates spontaneous language use (Fey, 1986; Girola-metto et al., 1986; MacDonald & Gillette, 1986). Commenting has the effect of keeping the adult focused on the child's activity as well as providing a model for the child of language associated with the activity of interest. Commenting should be done at the child's develop-mental level. For instance, for a child who is just beginning to use two-word phrases, the adult would not want to provide a long commentary on the child's actions. Rather, short phrases are appropriate (e.g., "Big ball. Amy's pushing the ball.").

- **Self-Talk**
  Self-talk, or talking about ones own actions, is also an effective language technique to prompt child communication (Weiss, 1981). This approach is well matched to the mirroring strategy and to parallel play. The adult comments on what he or she is doing, thus influenc-ing the child to attend to the adult's actions and comment or gesture to keep the interaction going. Again, the comments should be kept at the child's level.

- **Expansions**
  Another language facilitation technique is using expansions, or restating the child's utter-ance and adding new sounds, words, or ideas. For instance, if the child says, "Truck' while showing it to the adult, the adult might respond, "Yes. Blue truck." Expansions, like mirror-ing and commenting, confirm for the child that the message was understood. Expansions also provide a model for the child of the added language elements (Chapman, 1988). Re-search has demonstrated that parents who use expansions have children who learn to talk more quickly (Sherer & Olswang, 1984; Snow, 1984). This technique appears to be most effective when a child is producing two- and three-word utterances (Chapman & Miller, 1983). The adult needs to keep in mind the child's developmental level and use expansions in line with the child's ability level.

- **Modeling and Prompting**
  Modeling of sounds, words, or language structures also can be introduced into play. Labeling words, actions, or events can be part of any of the above strategies. In addition, prompting of responses has been shown to increase the number of utterances and vocabulary, the fre-quency of initiations and responses, and the structural complexity of speech (Hart & Risley, 1982; Warren, McQuarter, & Rogers-Warren, 1984; Warren & Rogers-Warren, 1985). The authors recommend the use of situation-specific and child-appropriate prompts in inciden-tal teaching and a systematic fading of the prompts.

- **Open-Ended Questions**
  Avoidance of closed questions is another language strategy. Adults ask children too many questions that have obvious one-word responses. The use of open-ended questions results in longer, more meaningful utterances. For instance, instead of asking, "Should we use this paper for a roof?", which requires only a "yes" or "no" response, the adult might ask, "What else could we use for a roof?" or, "What do you think would happen if we used this paper for a roof?" The latter two questions require the child to think and respond with a more complex response.

For Angela, the team presented toys and play opportunities that were at her developmental level and required her to use evolving skills, such as switch-activated toys and toys that require pushing, pulling, and turning (e.g., Busy Boxes, lids and doors, toy cars) in the floor play area. They prepared the environment by modifying toys to encourage her to use her fingers and push. For instance, the occupational therapist placed a tissue under the lid of a slot box and demonstrated poking her fingers and objects through the tissue into the slot. The team added various textures at the table area, such as wet sponges for dabbing, soft clay mixtures for squeezing, and beans, oatmeal, and birdseed for fingering. In each of the play centers, the team members would wait for Angela to initiate play or interaction. Adult–child interaction was consciously addressed. In each of the play centers, the team members responded enthusiastically to each effort, commenting on the object or action performed. They then would wait for her to vocalize or verbalize and would imitate her sounds. They incorporated noises into the play as frequently as possible to stimulate Angela's sound production. In order to develop hip stability, the team also gave Angela numerous opportunities to stand to play. Using toy cars and other motivating objects, they would then move the objects around the table, encouraging Angela to pursue the object.

Angela's mother was always present in the play session, and because she had been part of the planning process, she understood the purpose of each of the modifications and techniques that was being employed. She was adept at adding new modifications to interest Angela and encourage her to use her fingers in new ways. As they played, Mrs. G. commented to the team on the changes she was seeing in Angela, the new words Angela was using, or the novel actions Angela was performing. In this way, an ongoing dialogue was maintained and the informal assessment was sustained.

The strategies discussed above are not as easy to implement as they sound. Most early intervention professionals have been trained to be directive, to ask closed questions, and to guide children's actions and language. It takes time and effort to modify these teacher and therapist behaviors. The videotapes made during the TPBA or periodically during intervention provide a mechanism for self-appraisal of facilitative techniques. Figure 9 is a rating scale that can be used in formal training related to facilitation techniques for self-evaluation. If rating feels uncomfortable, team members may use the comment section only to discuss the effectiveness of various strategies. Comments such as "I wonder how Angela would have responded if you had . . . " or "Next time, you might try . . . " are less intimidating than negative ones. For formal training situations, however, the scale can be useful in identifying strengths and weaknesses in facilitation.

Phase VI: Conduct Ongoing Evaluation

After the child's intervention plan has been implemented based on the completed TIP Sheets for each environment, ongoing program monitoring is important. As mentioned previously, the family and other team members determine how often additional progress observations should be conducted. Observations of the child at home and center or school give the team an idea of whether new skills are generalizing across environments. Some families, however, feel uncomfortable with home visits and/or do not want to be involved in data collection. If this is the case, the team may have to rely on center-based observations and ask the parents questions directed at ascertaining which skills are being used at home, with whom, and in what contexts.

Transdisciplinary play-based assessment offers both informal and formal means of evaluating a child's progress. For example, the end of the child's day at a child care center or preschool provides an opportunity for team members to share anecdotal information with parents or caregivers about the day's activities and the activities planned for the next day. Conversation with parents or caregivers at the end of the day also allows the team to share with parents activities they can do at home. Sunshine notes are sent home with messages about something special the child did at school that day. This enables the parents to talk to their child and bring up words to

Facilitation Strategies Evaluation Checklist

Directions: *Check the box that most adequately reflects the level of skill demonstrated in facilitation.*

	Could be better	Good	Excellent
1. Environment promotes play through appropriate toys (e.g., variety, number, level) Comments:	[ ]	[ ]	[ ]
2. Facilitator follows the child's lead in selecting play materials Comments:	[ ]	[ ]	[ ]
3. Facilitator imitates the child when appropriate Comments:	[ ]	[ ]	[ ]
4. Faciltator reads the child's cues and responds Comments:	[ ]	[ ]	[ ]
5. Facilitator adapts mode of communication and the necessary level of sensory input Comments:	[ ]	[ ]	[ ]
6. Facilitator waits for the child to play before initiating new activities or modeling behaviors Comments:	[ ]	[ ]	[ ]
7. Facilitator observes child's optimal behaviors and builds on strengths Comments:	[ ]	[ ]	[ ]
8. Facilitator uses aspects of play that are motivating to the child to regulate attention Comments:	[ ]	[ ]	[ ]

(continued)

Figure 9.   A rating scale for self-evaluation of facilitation technique use. This form can be used formally or informally.

Figure 9.   (*continued*)

	Could be better	Good	Excellent
9. Facilitator responds to the child's initiations Comments:	[ ]	[ ]	[ ]
10. Facilitator uses parallel play Comments:	[ ]	[ ]	[ ]
11. Facilitator emphasizes turn-taking Comments:	[ ]	[ ]	[ ]
12. Facilitator models slightly higher-level behaviors for the child Comments:	[ ]	[ ]	[ ]
13. Facilitator encourages exploration and creative use of objects Comments:	[ ]	[ ]	[ ]
14. Facilitator uses the following language strategies:			
• Mirroring (i.e., reflecting nonverbal expression)	[ ]	[ ]	[ ]
• Parallel talk (i.e., talking about child's actions)	[ ]	[ ]	[ ]
• Self-talk (i.e., commenting on own actions)	[ ]	[ ]	[ ]
• Imitation (i.e., repeating child)	[ ]	[ ]	[ ]
• Elaboration (i.e., adding new information to what the child has said)	[ ]	[ ]	[ ]
• Corroborating (i.e., saying correctly what child has said in error)	[ ]	[ ]	[ ]
• Expanding (i.e., building on the child's words)	[ ]	[ ]	[ ]
• Modeling (i.e., conversing without using the child's words)	[ ]	[ ]	[ ]
• Open-ended questions (i.e., requiring more than a one-word response) Comments:	[ ]	[ ]	[ ]
15. Facilitator modifies play to match child's capabilities Comments:	[ ]	[ ]	[ ]
16. Facilitator responds to the child's affect Comments:	[ ]	[ ]	[ ]
17. Child appears to enjoy the play interactions Comments:	[ ]	[ ]	[ ]

remind them of what happened. Even children without disabilities are noted for answering, "Nothing," when asked, "What did you do at school today?" Sunshine notes help fill in the gap and prompt discussion with the child about the day.

For center-based programs, TIP and TAP Sheets for every child can be kept in a classroom notebook. On selected days, team members responsible for implementing the child's TIP Sheet observe and record the child's behaviors. Observers can watch selected children in a group or one child as he or she moves from center to center. Videotapes also can be made for an ongoing record. The observer watches the child and writes the highest levels of performance or actual accounts of behaviors in the box corresponding to the center and objective on the matrix. The degree of specificity needed (actual counts or sample behaviors) can be determined by the team and agency. In this way, by using a sampling procedure, the team member can note the child's skills across the day. By completing TAP Sheets with this information, the team is able to monitor child progress and evaluate the effectiveness of various centers, materials, and techniques. If children are not selecting certain areas, are showing lower levels of behavior, or are not consistent in their interactions and actions, the team should modify the environment or its facilitation.

The information obtained from the TAP Sheets is shared with parents informally and discussed at team meetings. Children's objectives are modified at this time or, if needed, changes are made in the program or intervention techniques used with the child. Notes, telephone calls, and informal meetings between parents and/or caregivers are necessary to keep communication open and discussions about the child's progress part of an ongoing process. Figure 10 illustrates a TAP Sheet completed by Angela's mother after 2 months. Using TAP Sheets enables the team to maintain a continuous cycle of assessment and program planning. This cycle ensures a process that is dynamic and ever-changing.

CONCLUSION

The TPBI process, like its predecessor, TPBA, provides a method for interacting with the child in a holistic approach with the inclusion of the parent throughout the process. The six-phase model described in this chapter is meant to provide a framework for developing cross-disciplinary, functional program plans that help children to generalize skills across settings, materials, and people. The process is cyclical and allows ongoing evaluation and modification of program objectives and intervention strategies.

REFERENCES

Argyle, M., & Ingham, R. (1972). Gaze, mutual gaze, and proximity. *Semiotics, 4,* 32–49.

Breiner, J., & Forehand, R. (1982). Mother–child interactions: A comparison of a clinic-referred developmentally delayed group and two nondelayed groups. *Applied Research in Mental Retardation, 3,* 175–183.

Bruner, J. (1983). *Children's talk: Learning to use language.* New York: Norton.

Chapman, R.S. (1988). Language acquisition in the child. In N.J. Lass, L.V. McReynolds, J.L. Northern, & D.E. Yoder (Eds.), *Handbook of speech-language pathology and audiology* (pp. 309–353). Toronto, Ontario, Canada: B.C. Decker.

Chapman, R.S., & Miller, J.F. (1983). Early stages of discourse, comprehension, and production: Implications for assessment and intervention. In R.M. Golinkoff (Ed.), *The transition from prelinguistic to linguistic communication* (pp. 219–233). Hillsdale, NJ: Lawrence Erlbaum Associates.

Coggins, T.E., & Carpenter, R.L. (1981). The communication intention inventory: a system for observing and coding children's early intentional communication. *Applied Psycholinguistics, 2,* 235–251.

Cross, T.G. (1984). Habilitating the language-impaired child: ideas from studies of parent–child interaction. *Topics in Language Disorders, 4,* 1–14.

Team Ideas for Play (TIP)/Team Assessment of Play (TAP) Sheet

Name of child: __Angela G.__ Date of birth: __1-15-90__ Age: __2 years, 1 month__

Location: __Home (by Mother)__ Date: __2-25-92__

Family goals:
1. Use words to communicate
2. Play in more ways with toys
3. Walk alone
4.
5.
6.

Time frame: __6 months__

Objectives	Rationale/things I'm ready for	Areas of intervention/assessment						
		Eating	Bathing/dressing	Playtime with mom	Playtime outdoors	Chores	Afternoon/Siblings Evening/Dad	Bedtime
1. Angela will spontaneously use 1-2 words to communicate: • A request for objects • A request for action • A comment • A protest • A greeting to family in 75% of her utterances.	Angela uses gestures and vocalization to communicate her intents. She is ready to use words and word approximations. Gestures and "na" have been very effective for her, so she'll probably want to stick to that.	• mo (more) • ee (eat) • tried to say pea! (bee)	• ba (bath) • wa (water) • signs bubbles • mo (more) • baba (baby)	• baba (baby) • making noises - brm with car - moo for cow and cat	• mo (more) • ba (push)	• ba for push, vacuum and switch on light • Initiated ba for pushing button on dryer	• dee (T.V.) to Dad • mo for more tossing in the air • tried to say "stop that" when brother tickled her (da)	When pointing to pictures in book, said • ba (ball) • baba (baby) • moo (dog)
2. Angela will increase her rate of word approximations to 10 per hour.	Angela uses her few words infrequently. The sooner she approximates a word, the sooner she'll try real words.	up to 5-6	5-6	10-12 in repetition of me	10-12 (mostly "more")	5-6 repeats	8-10	

(continued)

Figure 10.   A TAP Sheet completed by Mrs. G. for Angela 2 months after intervention planning was implemented.

Figure 10. (continued)

Team Ideas for Play (TIP)/Team Assessment of Play (TAP) Sheet

Name of child: __Angela G.__   Date: __2-25-92__

Areas of intervention/assessment

Objectives	Rationale/things I'm ready for	Eating	Bathing/Dressing	Playtime with mom	Playtime outdoors	Chores	Afternoon/Evening/Dad	Bedtime
3. Angela will take turns with family members in an activity through three turns.	Turns are important for language and social interactions. Angela is ready to pay more attention and interact with a play partner.	She will take turns feeding Cheerios through 10 turns!	Took turns with bubbles through 5 turns.	Took turns with putting in blocks — 2 turns.	Filling sand in pail — took turns through 6.	We took turns putting clothes in washer. She's really catching on to this!	They aren't into turns. They just do things to her!	Will wait for me to point then she will.
4. Angela will demonstrate improved problem-solving ability as demonstrated by her ability to: • Push • Pull • Turn with her thumb and forefinger.	Angela uses her hand to manipulate objects. She is ready to move beyond banging and shaking to using her hands and fingers for more complex problem-solving. This will help her to see how she can control her environment.	She is putting Cheerios in a box and turning box over.	• Pulled up pants once on. • Turned faucet. • Poked bubbles.	• Likes to do paper games with me. • Pushes cars, gets animals out and puts them in barn. • Pushes animal pop-ups.	• Pushes cars in sand. • Pokes fingers in sand.	• Pushes buttons on washer and dryer (with help). • I love her hand vacuum.	• Dad and son have her push them on floor. • Dad is teaching her to use T.V. control. • Pushes ball.	
5. Angela will demonstrate an ability to relate objects functionally as demonstrated by her ability to combine objects in play.	Angela is currently playing primarily with one toy at a time. She is ready to begin combining toys. This will help her to see how things can go together, which will help her develop concepts and language.	We are using spoon to move food from one container to another.	• Combs hair. • Puts paste on tooth brush. • Puts soap on cloth. • Puts bubbles in jar.	• Likes putting things in (we're trying to dump out). • Likes banging on objects.	• Shoveling sand into bucket. • Putting objects in bucket.	• Puts clothes in washer (I give her cloth and tray dishes to wash).	• Puts hat on Dad's head and knocks it off.	

Team Ideas for Play (TIP)/Team Assessment of Play (TAP) Sheet

Name of child: __Angela G.__   Date: __2-25-93__

Objectives	Rationale/things I'm ready for	Areas of intervention/assessment						
		Eating	Bathing/dressing	Playtime with Mom	Playtime outdoors	Chores	Afternoon/Siblings/Evening/Dad	Bedtime
6. Angela will demonstrate an ability to rotate her body to either side to obtain a toy.	Angela needs to be able to rotate her body so she can shift her weight and eventually walk.	I have been putting food on sides of tray and Angela moves her body to get it.	I move boat around her and she moves to get it.	If I hold her and put objects to side(s) she'll rotate.	On slide, she rolls over and goes down on tummy.			
7. Angela will demonstrate an increased stability as demonstrated by her ability to cruise around furniture.	Angela is ready to support more weight on her hips in preparation for walking.	She loves chasing Cheerios around coffee table.	New game— I line up toys on tub. She cruises down and knocks them in water.	The coffee table is now a main play area. She'll move if I motivate her with toys.			Sean likes to set toys and food around coffee table. She'll do anything for Sean!	
8. Angela will initiate play with different textures.	Angela is hesitant to touch things that have a different texture. She is ready to study be exposed to many different textures. This will encourage her to explore and discover and will help her understand new concepts — soft, smooth, rough, squishy, and so forth.	I am letting her finger feed everything — even peanut butter.	Towels, soap, Ninja Turtle foam.	We've added different kinds of paper, panty hose, and shaving cream to playtime. She's hesitant with the shaving cream.		She's taking out warm clothes from the dryer.		I've gotten some "feely" books at the library. She's starting to like them.

Donnellan, A.M., Mirenda, P.L., Mesaros, R.A., & Fassbender, L.L. (1984). Analyzing the communicative functions of aberrant behavior. *Journal of The Association for Persons With Severe Handicaps, 9*, 201–212.

Fagot, B.I. (1973). Influence of teacher behavior in the preschool. *Developmental Psychology, 9*, 198–206.

Fey, M. (1986). *Language intervention with young children.* San Diego: College-Hill Press.

Garvey, C. (1984). *Children's talk.* Cambridge, MA: Harvard University Press.

Girolametto, L.E., Greenberg, J., & Manolson, H.A. (1986). Developing dialogue skills: the Hanen Early Language Parent Program. *Seminars in Speech and Language, 7*, 367–384.

Halle, J.W. (1984). Arranging the natural environment to occasion language: Giving severely language-delayed children reasons to communicate. *Seminars in Speech and Language, 5*, 185–197.

Hamilton, V.J., & Gordon, D.A. (1978). Teacher–child interactions in preschool and task persistence. *American Educational Research Journal, 15*, 459–466.

Hart, B., & Risley, T.R. (1982). *How to use incidental teaching for elaborating language.* Lawrence, Kansas: H. & H. Enterprises.

Lee, J., O'Shea, L.J., & Dykes, M.K. (1987). Teacher wait-time: Performance of developmentally delayed and nondelayed young children. *Education and Training in Mental Retardation, 22*, 155–163.

Linder, T.W. (1993). *Transdisciplinary play-based assessment: A functional approach to working with young children* (rev. ed.). Baltimore: Paul H. Brookes Publishing Co.

MacDonald, J.D., & Gillette, Y. (1986). Communicating with persons with severe handicaps: Roles of parents and professionals. *Journal of The Association for Persons with Severe Handicaps, 11*, 225–265.

Mahoney, G., & Powell, A. (1988). Modifying parent–child interaction: Enhancing the development of handicapped children. *The Journal of Special Education, 22*, 82–96.

McDade, H.L., & Varnedoe, D.R. (1987). Training parents to be language facilitators. *Topics in Language Disorders, 7*, 1930.

McDonald, L., & Pein, D. (1982). Mother's conversational behavior as a function of interactional intent. *Journal of Child Language, 9*, 337–358.

Miller, L. (1989). Classroom-based language intervention. *Language, Speech, and Hearing Services in the Schools, 20*, 153–159.

Morrison, G.S. (1988). *Education and development of infants, toddlers, and preschoolers.* Boston: Scott, Foresman.

Peters, D.L., Neisworth, J.T., & Yawkey, T.D. (1985). *Early childhood education: From theory to practice.* Monterey, CA: Brookes-Cole.

Peterson, G.A., & Sherrod, K.B. (1982). Relationship of maternal language to language development and language delay of children. *American Journal of Mental Deficiency, 86*, 391–398.

Popovich, D. (1981). *Effective educational and behavioral programming for severely and profoundly handicapped students: A manual for teachers and aides.* Baltimore: Paul H. Brookes Publishing Co.

Roberts, J.E., Bailey, D.B., Jr., & Nychka, H.B. (1991). Teacher's use of strategies to facilitate the communication of preschool children with disabilities. *Journal of Early Intervention, 15* (4), 358–376.

Sherer, N.J., & Olswang, L.B. (1984). Role of mothers' expansions in stimulating children's language production. *Journal of Speech and Hearing Research, 27*, 387–396.

Snow, C.E. (1984). Parent–child interaction in the development of communication ability. In R.L. Schiefelbusch & J. Pickar (Eds.), *The acquisition of communicative competence* (pp. 69–107). Baltimore: University Park Press.

Stallings, J. (1975). Implementation and child effects of teaching practices in follow-through classrooms. *Monograph of the Society for Research in Child Development, 40*, 7–8.

Tomasello, M., & Farrar, M.J. (1986). Joint attention and early language. *Child Development, 57*, 1454–1463.

Tomasello, M., & Todd, J. (1983). Joint attention and lexical acquisition style. *First Language, 4*, 197–212.

Valdez-Manchaca, M.C., & Whitehurst, G.J. (1988). The effects of incidental teaching on vocabulary acquisition by young children. *Child Development, 59*, 1451–1459.

Yoder, P.J., & Kaiser, A.P. (1989). Alternative explanations for the relationship between maternal verbal interaction style and child language development. *Journal of Child Language, 16*, 141–160.

Warren, S., & Kaiser, A. (1986). Incidental language teaching: A critical review. *Journal of Speech and Hearing Disorders, 51,* 291–299.

Warren, S., McQuarter, R., & Rogers-Warren, A. (1984). The effects of mands and models on the speech of unresponsive language-delayed preschool children. *Journal of Speech and Hearing Disorders, 49,* 43–52.

Warren, S., & Rogers-Warren, A. (1985). *Teaching functional language: Generalization and maintenance of language skills.* Baltimore: University Park Press.

Weiss, R. (1981). INREAL intervention for language handicapped and bilingual children. *Journal of the Division of Early Childhood, 4,* 40–51.

6

Materials and Equipment

As the previous chapter has
illustrated with its description of developing TIP Sheets for home and school, the TPBI process
can be implemented at home or in center-based programs. Center-based programs can encompass a
range of environments, from child care centers to infant intervention programs to preschools
and kindergartens. These primary types of environments are rich with play environments, from
book areas to the outdoor playground. This chapter describes the fundamentals of TPBI at home
or at the center, explores in more detail the many potential play environments available, and
closes with information about toys and materials appropriate for each of these settings. As demonstrated by the items and activities in the TPBI Planner, infants and young children seem to be
able to play in almost any environment, using whatever materials are at hand.

INTERVENTION SETTINGS

Home-Based Intervention

Home-based intervention has the advantage of taking place in the child's natural environment,
where people, toys, and setting are familar. The goals and objectives set for the child are likely to
be functional and immediately relevant (Linder, 1983; Shearer & Shearer, 1972). Play, which is
usually an inherent part of the child's day at home, is a natural vehicle for intervention. Rather
than setting aside time to "work" with the child, the parents and family members can implement
intervention within typical interactions.

The planning that is done with the family at the initial meeting provides the basis for TPBI.
Monitoring, support, and program modification to assist parents can take place during home
visits. The TIP Sheets can serve as a basis for discussion about the child's activities during the
week. The home visitor then plays with the child and parent while modeling facilitation techniques discussed in Chapter 5, consults on issues of concern to the family, and generates with
the family fresh ideas for play and interaction. New TIP Sheets can be developed, or current ones
modified, as the child advances functionally and developmentally.

Every home, regardless of the family's socioeconomic level, has materials that are appropriate for play. Even if no toys are available, there are items of daily living, such as pots and pans,
cardboard boxes, measuring spoons, funnels, and materials that can capture a child's attention
and interest. Household items can be used in their existing state or modified and made into
toylike items. Shoe boxes and toilet paper rolls can become castles, socks can become dolls or
puppets, and the tub can become a water playground.

Center-Based Intervention

Center-based options include infant programs, toddler programs, child care centers, and numerous types of preschool and kindergarten programs. Infant programs that are held in centers usually involve the parent and child meeting with professionals and, typically, other persons. Play groups, parent consultation, and sometimes classes for parents or parent support groups are part of the center program. Therapy can be provided on an individual basis or within the play groups. Toys and materials appropriate for different developmental levels are available along with specialized therapy equipment. Children are allowed to make choices, but depend on adults to provide the toys and place them so they are accessible to the infant. Emphasis in infant programs is frequently placed on helping parents to facilitate their child's development through improved interactions and the integration of therapeutic techniques into play and functional activities.

Infants with special needs may have a separate service delivery system or, in some cases, infants may be included in toddler intervention programs. This differs from child care centers, where most states require infants to be cared for in separate spaces from toddlers. Early intervention programs for toddlers frequently involve parents in play groups as well. Some programs, however, serve toddlers in preschool type environments without the presence of the parent. These programs typically meet fewer days a week than preschool programs. As with infant programs, therapists may be included in play groups or provide services separately.

The play environment for toddlers is frequently similar to that provided for infants, with a range of toys and materials to meet the needs of children across developmental levels. Toddler programs, however, often allow children to begin to use their newly developed mobility by wandering from play center to play center. Play centers are often arranged by type of play, including floor play, table play, sensory centers, and sensorimotor centers. Again, emphasis is placed on parent–child interaction and functional activities.

Preschool and kindergarten environments are distinguished by the absence of the parent. Most programs involve parents in the classroom on a voluntary basis. Preschool and kindergarten environments offer the child the opportunity to explore and discover without direction from the parent and to develop new attachments beyond the family. Peers become a central feature of these environments. Centers in preschools are frequently set up to encourage the child to engage in various types of activities. Centers typically include a house area, water table, art area, gross motor area, manipulatives area, and a block area. Other areas may be added depending on the program philosophy. Kindergartens may include these same centers plus science and math areas and a greater emphasis on literary activites and large group activities. Kindergarten programs are becoming more play-based due to increasing research support that emphasizes the importance of play and meaningful contexts to the learning of academic skills.

The structure of the day and amount of direction from the teaching staff vary from program to program, as does the level and type of involvement of the related services staff (Linder, 1983). Preschools and kindergartens in some states provide segregated services to children with special needs. However, there is a growing trend to provide interaction within regular preschool and kindergarten programs. In inclusionary classrooms, therapists may provide a consultative role, work as classroom team members, or provide support services outside of the classroom.

Parents are typically involved through home visits, conferences, and occasional visits to the classroom. In programs in which parents transport the child to and from school, the primary time for communication may be at drop-off and pick-up times.

Child care programs differ from early intervention programs in that the staff are usually not as highly trained and are hired to provide child care and education, rather than intervention to ameliorate deficits or delays. However, with the emphasis on inclusion, more early intervention programs are providing consultative services to child care programs that serve infants, toddlers, and preschoolers with special needs. Child care environments are also set up with toys and materials and centers that are motivating to the child. The consultative intervention staff can then come into these environments and discuss individual children with staff, demonstrate specific techniques, and provide support for implementation.

Recommended Play Environments

A child's ability to engage in optimal interactions and hence benefit from TPBI can be influenced by the physical arrangement of furniture, toys, and equipment in the home or center. Smith and Connolly (1972) found that spatial density, or the amount of space that is available per child after unusable space is deducted, has an impact on play patterns. They found that less than 25 square feet per child resulted in reduced gross motor play, increased aggression, and less group play.

Learning is promoted by environments that encourage the child to interact with toys, materials, and people (McEvoy, Fox, & Rosenberg, 1991; Nordquist & Twardosz, 1990). In a preschool classroom, the arrangement of the room into specific, well-defined areas is recommended (Bailey & Wolery, 1984; Hohmann, Banet, & Weikart, 1979; Vergeront, 1987). Division of the room into areas helps the child to focus on the materials in that zone. Small areas encourage cooperative interactions among children in that specific section of the room (Brown, Fox, & Brady, 1987) and result in smaller groupings and quieter interactions (Fitt, 1974; Sheehan & Day, 1975), as well as more focused play with the materials in the area (Fitt, 1974; Pollowy, 1974). Figure 1 is a floor plan of a preschool classroom that contains most of the centers listed below.

If related areas are placed in close proximity, interaction from one area to another is encouraged. Separation of conflicting areas, such as noisy and quiet areas, is a consideration, along with provision of partitions or dividers to delineate specific areas. Dividers should be low so as to allow children to view the room and make play choices (Van Hoorn, Nourot, Scales, & Alward, 1993). Common play centers for infants and/or toddlers include:

1. A sensorimotor area for movement play, with swings and objects the child needs to maneuver up, over, around, under, and through (e.g., cardboard boxes to climb into, barrels to crawl through, steps to crawl up, boats to ride in)
2. A sensory center for exploration of various sensory stimuli, including tactile media (e.g., containers of torn paper or packing peanuts, a water table or tub, sticky substances, lotion). Sensory centers may also contain toys and materials that stimulate other senses: music boxes, bells, and sound and music toys for auditory stimulation; taste experiences with bland, sweet, sour, salty, and thick and thin food textures; visual stimulation experiences with moving bright objects, lights, and contrasting backgrounds. Sensory centers can be adapted to the needs of children with varying sensory deficits, as well as provide needed sensory input and sensory play to children without sensory disabilities
3. A block area with different types of blocks (e.g., 1-inch cubes, foam blocks, large cardboard blocks) encourages infants, depending on their developmental level, to bang, combine, stack, put in containers, sort, and match
4. A floor play area, including manipulatives, cause-and-effect toys, dolls, dishes, telephones, trucks, and other early representational toys, promotes both cognitive and fine motor problem-solving as well as social interaction and communication with peers
5. A book area with picture books, tactile books, audiotapes with books, and storybooks invites children to identify pictures (and, thus, concepts), turn pages, learn the sequence of operating a tape recorder independently, and match auditory words to pictures

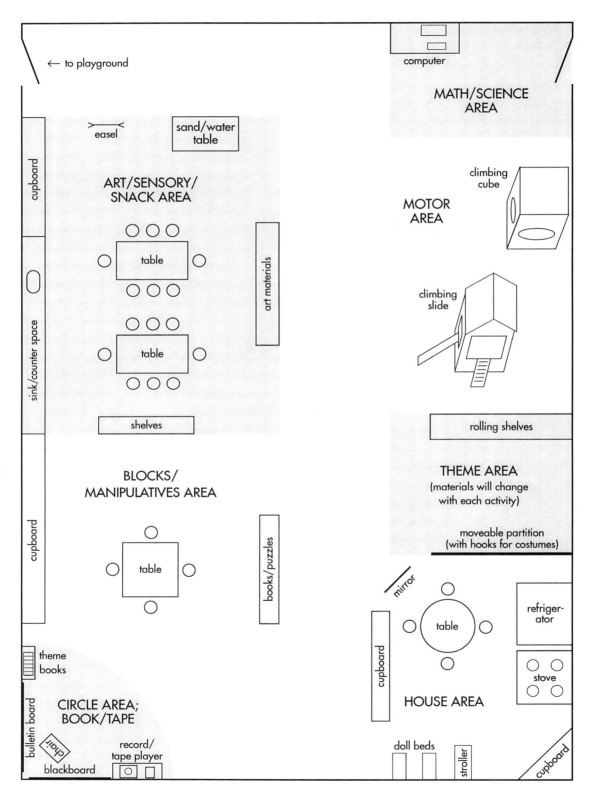

Figure 1. A typical preschool classroom.

6. A table area for coloring, puzzles, and any activities requiring the child to be seated in a stable, seated position provides another play center. (Snack is also considered a table activity.)

These and other infant centers can be interrelated and changed to meet the developmental and sensorimotor needs of the infant from birth to 3 years old. All of these areas can be adapted to include toys and materials for children with and without disabilities.

For the preschool child, the above areas are also appropriate, with modifications of toys and materials to match the child's developmental level. In addition, the following centers are often found in preschool settings:

1. An art area with paints, an easel, crayons, construction paper, Play-Doh, magazines, scissors, and pieces of fabric and other materials for cutting, gluing, drawing, shaping, and designing
2. A science and math area that includes a sand and water table, magnifying glasses, and various nature materials that can be compared, sorted, and studied (e.g., leaves, shells, rocks, animals, plants, insects)
3. A woodworking area with wood, hammers, screwdrivers, a vice, and numerous types of fasteners
4. A music area with record player or tape recorder, musical instruments, and rhythm devices, along with music culturally relevant to the children being served
5. A housekeeping area with stove, refrigerator, sink, and other household appliances and kitchen utensils, artificial food, a table and chairs, dress-up clothing, dolls, and beds. (The household area should reflect culturally relevant materials for the populations served. Parents can be asked if there are special cooking devices or foods used in their homes. These can then be purchased or donated to add to the household area.)

Providing a variety of areas that appeal to the sensory systems is important.

6. A theme area is an important adaptable center to encourage sociodramatic play. Depending on the theme or story being integrated into the class, the theme center changes. A doctor's office, zoo, pet store, grocery store, beauty shop, and shoe store are common theme areas, but a preschool using a storybook curriculum might incorporate a jungle, a camping site, an airplane interior, or any other site relevant to the storybook unit. Pertinent props and materials are added to heighten the children's involvement in the role play. Incorporation of themes into the TPBI process is discussed in more detail in Chapter 7.

For the kindergarten child, the above centers are still relevant. The level of materials and range of themes can be expanded to match the child's growing understanding and broadening experiences. The math and science center becomes more important as the child can deal with more sophisticated comparisons and problem-solving. The tl .ne area can be based more on the children's own stories and can be supplemented with lite ry activities, such as dictation of stories and scripts, illustration of stories, and labeling of o' jects with written words instead of pictures. Children will be able to combine longer sequenc of ideas and actions, thus enabling the team to engage children in higher levels of play. Increased ability to see relationships also allows children to interrelate concepts and materials from one center to another. In the kindergarten setting, peer pairing, grouping of children, and learning through cooperation with others can be maximized. Play centers can help the teacher manage the larger number of children placed in kindergartens, while at the same time play centers capitalize on the interests and motivating forces for the child at this level.

Of course, outdoor play is as essential as the variety of play opportunities provided in the above-described indoor areas. Outdoor play should be incorporated into the child's total play environment and his or her intervention plan. All areas of development can be facilitated in a conducive outdoor play area. Outdoor play is also appropriate for home-based programs, as community parks are frequently well-designed and equipped.

Outdoor Play

Outdoor play encourages gross motor development, social interaction, rough-and-tumble play, and depending on the type of materials available, sociodramatic play. Traditional playgrounds, consisting of large open areas and isolated play equipment have been found to encourage primarily gross motor play and not to sustain children's attention for long periods (Campbell & Frost, 1985; Hayward, Rothenberg, & Beasley, 1974). Contemporary playgrounds, however, provide a more motivating environment for children. They commonly contain more than one type of surface for different kinds of play. A variety of equipment, including tires, ladders, climbing nets, tunnels, bridges, swings, slides, and enclosures or playhouses, are connected in unique ways. Several aspects of these outdoor play areas seem to stimulate children and lead to various forms of play. Positive features include linkages between pieces of equipment, which encourage children to move from one area to another; graduated complexity, which allows children varying levels of challenge; and flexibility, which enables children to use the equipment in more than one way (Johnson, Christie, & Yawkey, 1987). The addition of enclosures or playhouses encourages children to engage in dramatic play that can change from one day to the next.

MATERIALS AND EQUIPMENT

Arrangement of materials also influences play behavior. Materials and equipment should be easily accessible so the child can make choices independently. Having toys visible on shelves, rather than in boxes or closets, has been shown to increase the amount of time the child spends in actual play (Montes & Risley, 1975). The number of toys and materials available also influences the play behaviors of children, with an insufficient number of toys resulting in more anti-social acts. When children have to wait to have a "turn" to play, disruptions occur (Odom & Karnes, 1988). The number and arrangement of materials are, thus, important considerations.

Toys become tools in the intervention process. The type, number, and variety of toys and materials available should be modified depending on the goals for specific children. Having duplicate toys encourages imitation and parallel play, while having few toys and materials increases sharing and interaction (see Chapter 5) (Montes & Risley, 1975; Quilitch & Risley, 1973). Martin, Brady, and Williams (1991) found that the type of toys available (i.e., social toys or isolate toys) influences the social behaviors of preschool children. Therefore, inclusion of social toys (e.g., balls, wagons, housekeeping materials, dress-up clothes, puppets, games) increases social interaction. Isolate toys (e.g., puzzles, pegboards, Play-Doh) may be motivating and promote the development of fine motor and cognitive skills, but do not encourage peer interaction. Both social and isolate materials may be desired, depending on the goals for individual children. Materials that seem to capture the child's attention or have high "holding power" include blocks, sand, art materials, and dramatic play materials (Odom & Karnes, 1988). All of these materials can be used in a variety of ways.

Rubin (1977) found that certain materials encourage different cognitive levels of play. The same materials that promote social interaction (e.g., housekeeping props, costumes) also stimulate dramatic or representational play. Crayons, paper, and blocks encourage constructive play, while puzzles and balls encourage functional play. Shure (1963) also found that social interaction was influenced by the type of play area that was made available to children. Higher levels and more complex interactions were found in the doll play area, while the art area encouraged the lowest degree of social interaction. Many toys are easily adapted to varying levels of play. Blocks, for instance, may be used in functional, relational play by the infant who puts one block on top of the other; in constructive play by the child who builds a bridge; or in dramatic play by the child who builds a castle and then brings in knights and horses to joust.

Categories of Play Materials

Toys and play materials are placed into four categories by Johnson et al. (1987), who classify play materials by the general purpose or function of the materials.

Instructional Materials   Designed to teach specific skills and concepts, instructional materials are structured and outcome-oriented. Puzzles, stacking toys, pegboards, and stringing beads are examples of instructional materials designed to work on concepts such as shape and color recognition, matching, sequencing, and understanding one-to-one correspondence.

Real Materials   A second category of materials identified by Johnson et al. (1987) is real materials. This category includes materials that have specific, nonplay uses in the adult world (e.g., woodworking tools and wood, adult dress-up clothes, food, sand, mud, water, clay). Children like to use real materials because they have many uses and, in the case of woodworking materials and dress-up clothes, they allow children to imitate adults. Books and recordings also fall into this category. Art materials (e.g., paints, paper, markers) are considered real materials, although they also fit in the construction materials category (see below) when children use them to "construct" specific pieces of art.

Construction Materials   A third category is construction materials, which offer creative opportunities to children because there is no one "right" way to use them. Blocks, a primary type of construction material, come in all different shapes, sizes, colors, and materials and can be adapted for use with children with disabilities. Construction sets (e.g., Tinker Toys, Lincoln Logs, Legos) can also be used to build everything from buildings to astronauts.

Toys   The fourth, and last, category identified by Johnson et al. (1987) is toys, which are defined as "miniature replicas of objects in the child's physical environment" (p. 176). These include facsimiles of real objects (e.g., a house, a car repair garage) and fantasy objects and characters (e.g., Ninja Turtles). Many of the miniature replicas represent daily living items, types of transportation, and animate characters, including animals, people, and creatures.

Availability of developmentally appropriate materials from each of the above categories is recommended. Frequent rotation of materials is also advisable to maintain the children's interest and motivation (Nordquist & Twardosz, 1990).

Criteria for Selecting Toys

The following criteria have been used for the selection of toys (Musselwhite, 1986; National Association for the Education of Young Children [NAEYC], 1985; Williams, Briggs, & Williams, 1979). These criteria are referred to frequently in the TPBI Planner.

1.   Safety and durability are important features. Toys should be easily washed or sterilized, be free of sharp or small, easily dislodged pieces, and be made of sturdy materials. They should be painted with nontoxic, lead-free paint; be well-made with no splinters or pieces that pinch; and be shatter-proof. It should be remembered that toys that may be safe under typical conditions may not be safe around children who are extremely destructive, who mouth objects excessively, or who fall easily.

2.   Degree of realism and structure of materials are significant developmental concerns. Children who are developmentally young enjoy toys that are very realistic and with uses that are clearly evident by the object's structure. Developmentally higher-functioning children enjoy materials with less clearly defined uses that leave room for the imagination. As the child matures, his or her ability to represent objects and events in the environment increases, so that materials can be viewed in numerous ways and the child can devise elaborate functions for everyday materials.

3.   The reactive or responsive nature of the toys is another important feature. Toys that produce sound and/or sustain motion as a consequence of manipulation increase the child's control over the environment, maintain the child's attention, and teach causal relationships (Bambara, Spiegel-McGill, Shores, & Fox, 1984; Chance, 1979). For children with severe cognitive, sensory, or physical limitations, a toy that has a big result for little effort can provide a needed sense of mastery. Adaptive switches or other adaptive devices can make a toy react more easily.

Toys and materials that provide different types of sensory input appeal to children who need more intense stimulation. Newson and Hipgrave (1982) describe 50 characteristics that can be discovered by touching:

> hard, soft, cold, warm, wet, dry, furry, soggy, prickly, springy, powdery, hairy, smooth, rough, jagged, crumbly, holey, crackly, long, short, heavy, light, wobbly, mobile, firm, thin, thick, big, little, tall, short, bumpy, sticky, alive, flexible, stiff, round, hollow, flat, hinged, leaved, many-sided, many-parted, pourable, stirrable, silky, scratchy, spongy, velvety, slimy. (p. 73)

Incorporating objects that have these and other tactile properties can serve to captivate the child's attention, arouse curiosity, and stimulate play.

4.   The motivational characteristics of the toy are critical and vary from child to child. Aspects of toys and materials that influence a child's desire to play include sensory characteristics, developmental appropriateness, type of feedback the toy provides, degree of realism, and gender and cultural relevancy.

Little boys and little girls appear to have different play preferences, with girls playing more frequently and longer with dolls and art materials, and boys selecting blocks and wheeled vehicles (Johnson et al., 1987; Liss, 1981). While the adults in the child's environment do not have to encourage sex-stereotyped play, availability of a range of toys that may appeal to both sexes is important. For example, a 4-year-old boy may not demonstrate sustained attention for play in the dollhouse with the Mommy, Daddy, and baby figures, but may play for extended time with hero figures (e.g., Batman). Availability of both types of toys allows the child to make choices.

Cultural relevancy is also critical. Lunch boxes and hard hats may be more motivating sociodramatic play props in a mining town than a dress hat and briefcase. Having dolls, books, and materials that reflect ethnic backgrounds commensurate with the backgrounds of the children is another consideration.

5.   Age appropriateness is an issue, particularly for children with severe cognitive or physical delays. The concept of normalization for children with special needs dictates that the dignity of the individual is preserved if toys and materials made available to the child are relevant to his or her age, but adapted to meet cognitive, sensory, and physical needs.

6.   The therapeutic value of toys and materials is also a consideration. Selection of toys that can be used to stimulate cognitive, social-emotional, communication and language, and sensori-motor development is a critical aspect of play-based early intervention.

7.   Musselwhite (1986) suggests that examining the cost-effectiveness of toys and materials is also an issue in toy selection. Consideration of the number of children who will use and benefit from the toy; the cost of replacement of parts; the flexibility of the toy and its therapeutic value; and the priority of the skills acquired through play with the toy should be taken into account when selecting materials.

CONCLUSION

Regardless of the intervention setting (home or center) or the intervention level (infant, toddler, preschool, or kindergarten), play environments that promote development share certain important characteristics. Consideration of the space needed, the visibility of toys and materials, the developmental characteristics of play opportunities, and variations in toys and play possibilities are important aspects of the environment. Flexibility, sociability, variety, relevance, and safety are critical features of toys and materials. The toys, materials, and play opportunities available to the child are vital to successful intervention and thus deserve careful attention and planning.

REFERENCES

Bailey, D. B., & Wolery, M. (1984). *Teaching infants and preschoolers with handicaps.* Columbus, OH: Merrill.

Bambara, L.M., Spiegel-McGill, P., Shores, R.E., & Fox, J.J. (1984). *Journal of The Association for Persons with Severe Handicaps, 9,* 142–149.

Brown, W.H., Fox, J.J., & Brady, M.P. (1987). The effects of spatial density on the socially directed behavior of three- and four-year-old children during freeplay: An investigation of a setting factor. *Education and Treatment of Children, 10,* 247–258.

Campbell, S.D., & Frost, J.L. (1985). The effects of playground type on the cognitive and social behaviors of grade-two children. In J.L. Frost & S. Sunderlind (Eds.), *When children play* (pp. 81–88). Wheaton, MD: Association for Childhood Education International.

Chance, P. (1979). *Learning through play.* New York: Gardner Press.

Fitt, S. (1974). The individual and his environment. *School Review, 8,* 617–620.

Hart, B. & Risley, T.R. (1982). *How to use incidental teaching for elaborating language.* Lawrence, Kansas: H&H Enterprises.

Hayward, G., Rothenberg, M., & Beasley, R.R. (1974). Children's play and urban playground environments. *Environment and Behavior, 6,* 131–168.

Hohmann, M., Banet, B., & Weikart, D.P. (1979). *Young children in action.* Ypsilanti, MI: High Scope Educational Research Foundation.

Johnson, J.E., Christie, J.F., & Yawkey, T.D. (1987). *Play and early childhood development.* New York: Harper Collins Publishers.

Linder, T.W. (1983). *Early childhood special education: Program development and administration.* Baltimore: Paul H. Brookes Publishing Co.

Liss, M.B. (1981). Patterns of toy play: An analysis of sex differences. *Sex Roles, 7,* 1143–1150.

Martin, S.S., Brady, M.P., & Williams, R.E. (1991). Effects of toys on the social behavior of preschool children in integrated and nonintegrated groups: Investigation of a setting event. *Journal of Early Intervention, 15*(2), 153–161.

McEvoy, M.A., Fox, J.J., & Rosenberg, M.S. (1991). Organizing preschool environments: Suggestions for enhancing the development/learning of preschool children with handicaps. *Topics in Early Childhood Special Education, 11*(2), 18–28.

Montes, F., & Risley, T.R. (1975). Evaluating traditional day care practice: An empirical approach. *Child Care Quarterly, 4,* 208–215.

Musselwhite, C.M. (1986). *Adaptive play for special-needs children: Strategies to enhance communication and learning.* San Diego, CA: College-Hill Press.

National Association for the Education of Young Children (NAEYC). (1985). *Toys: Tools for learning.* Washington, DC: Author.

Newson, E., & Hipgrave, T. (1982). *Getting through to your handicapped child.* Cambridge: Cambridge University Press.

Nordquist, V.M., & Twardosz, S. (1990). Preventing behavior problems in early childhood special education classrooms through environmental organization. *Education and Treatment of Children, 13,* 274–287.

Odom, S.L., & Karnes, M.B. (Eds.). (1988). *Early intervention for infants and children with handicaps: An empirical base.* Baltimore: Paul H. Brookes Publishing Co.

Pollowy, A.M. (1974). The child in the physical environment: a design problem. In G. Coates (Ed.), *Alternative learning environments* (pp. 370–382). Stroudsburg, PA: Dowden, Hutchinson, & Ross.

Quilitch, H.R., & Risley, T.R. (1973). The effects of play materials on social play. *Journal of Applied Behavior Analysis, 6,* 573–578.

Rubin, K.H. (1977). The social and cognitive value of preschool toys and activities. *Canadian Journal of Behavioral Sciences, 9,* 382–385.

Shearer, M.S., & Shearer, D.E. (1972). The Portage project: A model for early childhood education. *Exceptional Children, 36,* 210–217.

Sheehan, R., & Day, D. (1975). Is open space just empty space? *Day Care and Early Education, 3,* 10–13.

Shure, M.B. (1963). The psychological ecology of the nursery school. *Child Development, 34,* 979–992.

Smith, P.K., & Connolly, K.J. (1972). Patterns of play and social interaction in preschool children. In N. Blurton-Jones (Ed.), *Ethnological studies of child behavior* (pp. 65–95). Cambridge, England: Cambridge University Press.

Van Hoorn, J., Nourot, P., Scales, B., & Alward, K. (1993). *Play at the center of the curriculum.* New York: Charles E. Merrill.

Vergeront, J. (1987). *Places and spaces for preschool and primary (indoors).* Washington, DC: National Association for the Education of Young Children.

Williams, B., Briggs, N., & Williams, R. (1979). Selecting, adapting, and understanding toys and recreation materials. In P. Wehman (Ed.), *Recreation programming for developmentally disabled persons* (pp. 15–36). Baltimore: University Park Press.

7

Integrating TPBI into the Curriculum

Transdisciplinary play-based intervention not only allows planning for individual children, but also for group learning experiences. Child care centers, preschools, and kindergartens are set up to provide learning opportunities in group settings. (Due to the need for ongoing planning and consequent time requirements, curriculum planning is typically done during team meetings and parents are not involved. Parent input, however, is valuable and should be considered if possible.) Planning daily experiences for the group and individuals within the group is an important task for the core team. Thematic program planning is particularly beneficial and easy to implement in preschool and kindergarten programs, but also can be offered in a modified form in infant and toddler programs.

CENTER-BASED INFANT AND TODDLER PROGRAMS

Early intervention programs for infants and toddlers may be separate or combined programs. Infant programs involve the parent and child in center-based activities, while toddler programs may or may not include the parent. Some centers offer programs for infants and toddlers together. Infant and/or toddler programs typically meet for 2 or 3 hours once or twice a week. The early intervention program concentrates on providing interactions and activities to promote development and remediate deficits and delays.

In contrast, the child care programs are offered daily and are responsible for the child for longer periods of time—as long as 10 hours a day. Child care programs provide more global, developmentally appropriate activities. Child care staff also supervise naptime, supply meals or snacks, and administer personal care. The parent is not present, and due to the amount of time the child spends in the setting, the child care provider assumes a parenting role.

Although toys and materials may differ in the various types of centers (with more specialized and modified toys for children with special needs and developmentally different toys in infant versus toddler programs), the setting and planning process can be the same for both groups and for children with and without special needs in segregated or inclusive programs. Planning involves using a planning sheet to structure activities across the hours that the center is open for each day of the week the program meets. Planning is done on a weekly basis in order to accommodate overall play activities and individualization within the group. The team also plans how each of its members will be involved—through team teaching, consultation, or other forms of support. Role release and role support are important here, as the teacher or child care provider may assume responsibility for implementing intervention, and therapists may be responsible for supporting the staff in using various strategies or techniques with individual children.

TPBI provides a planning sheet that can be adapted to accommodate varying formats (Figure 1). The days of the week are listed on the horizontal axis; the periods of the day or centers on the vertical axis. For infants and toddlers, themes are not as relevant and each center basically has its own theme (Figure 2):

- Sensory center: How do things feel, taste, smell, sound, and move?
- Sensorimotor center: How many ways can I move?
- Block/box center: How many ways can I use these?
- Floor play center: What can I make these things do?
- Table play center: How can I solve this problem?
- Book/music center: What are these things? How can I make my voice and body change?
- Snack: How can I feel, taste, and move what I eat?

As toddlers mature, themes may begin to be introduced. The theme of "Sesame Street," for example, can be incorporated into all of the centers. In the sensory area, Big Bird feathers, Barkley fur, and the other characters' coats and skins could be felt using puppets or different scraps of material; small "Sesame Street" characters could be washed or buried in the sand table. The sensorimotor area could include Oscar's garbage can from which to climb in and out. The blocks/box area could contain boxes of different sizes containing the various "Sesame Street" dolls or puppets. "Sesame Street" blocks also might be included. Floor play toys could include "Sesame Street" pop-up toys, miniatures, and action figures. Table play could include easy "Sesame Street" puzzles and Play-Doh with cookie cutters. There are many "Sesame Street" books and audiotapes that could be incorporated into the book/music center, and snack could be anything that any of the characters would like, such as berries for Big Bird or cookies for the Cookie Monster. (Real cookies cut at the table play center would be a special treat.)

Themes can range from traditional holiday motifs to doing a whole week of activities with a specific color. Themes can relate to a favorite character, such as Mickey Mouse, or an activity such as grocery shopping. Themes are most effective for toddlers when the theme and play activities are familiar to the child.

As the planning sheets are developed, it is good to refer to individual children's TIP Sheets so that ideas can be included to meet the needs of all of the children. The team also discusses how to pair or group children to maximize the benefit from each of the play situations. Special toys or modifications then can be added as needed. To further reinforce the importance of individualization, TIP Sheets can be posted on a bulletin board or kept in a notebook for easy reference. Usually, however, the team is able to keep each child's objectives in mind after only a few days of integrating them into the curriculum.

PRESCHOOL AND KINDERGARTEN PROGRAMS

The team process for planning preschool and kindergarten programs is similar to the one described above for infant and toddler programs. Depending on the format of the day, the implementation of TPBI varies. Some programs divide the day into activity-based segments, emphasizing language activities, motor activities, and so forth. Other programs are structured around individual activities, small-group activities, and large-group activities. Given preschool and kindergarten children's chronological ages and developmental levels (as opposed to those of children in infant and toddler programs), a thematic approach to programming is appropriate. Thematic programming is discussed below.

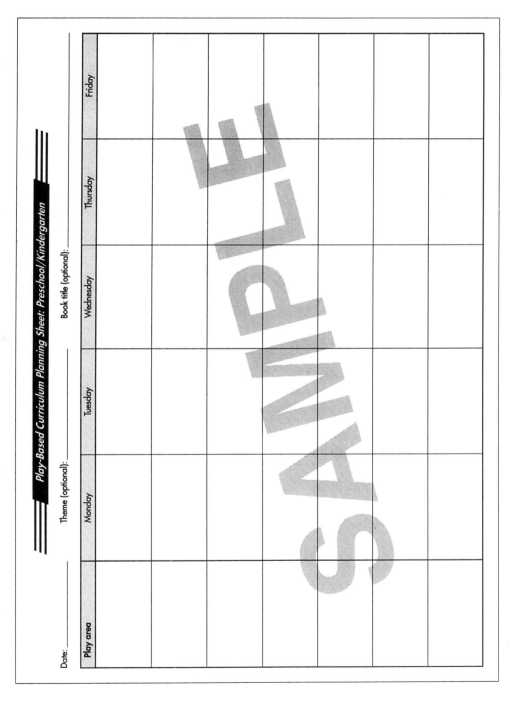

Figure 1. The Play-Based Curriculum Planning Sheet: Preschool/Kindergarten. Play areas are entered in the blanks of the vertical axis, and specific planning activities are entered for each area and day of the week that the program meets. A second sheet is provided in the original.

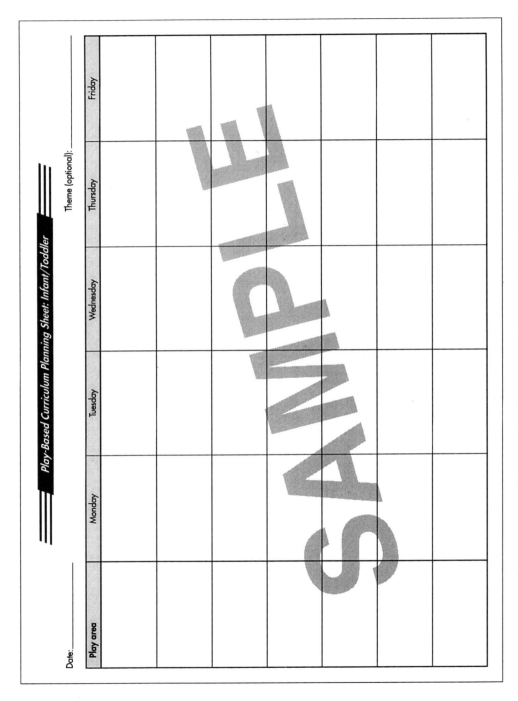

Figure 2.   The Play-Based Curriculum Planning Sheet: Infant/Toddler. Used like the Preschool/Kindergarten version. This form occupies one page because there are generally fewer play areas in infant/toddler programs.

90

THEMATIC PROGRAMMING

Themes provide a means for teachers to generate a series of play centers with props and materials that captivate and motivate children to learn. Theme areas encourage children to experiment spontaneously with a variety of roles and materials (Woodward, 1985). Storybook themes encourage "literate behaviors" that build the foundation for later literacy skills (Heath & Mangiola, 1991). Using themes provides a means for reinforcing concepts throughout a variety of play activities. If children's own interests are used as themes or their own stories are used as the basis for dramatic play, motivation is increased (Van Hoorn, Nourot, Scales, & Alward, 1993). For children with special needs and children who lack varied environmental experiences, themes can help them to structure and organize their play (Saltz & Johnson, 1974). It is important, however, for the team to offer only as much structure and guidance as is needed. Self-initiated play and self-generated sequences of action and problem-solving are preferred.

Prop boxes can be constructed containing key materials to be used in each thematic center (Isenberg & Jalongo, 1993), or materials can be compiled as a theme is designed. Involving children in the design and gathering or constructing of materials for specific themes is also recommended (Woodward, 1985). Very concrete materials should be included for children who need this level of representation to stimulate action; less defined or more abstract materials should be provided for children whose imagination is inspired by items with creative possibilities.

Because of its activity-based nature, TPBI naturally lends itself to thematic planning. Themes can be embedded into the daily schedule, which then can be extended for a week or

Having appropriate props and materials for each curriculum unit encourages child engagement.

more. Although the planning sheet permits the team to plot a week's activities, it is also necessary to structure a daily schedule. Such a schedule might look like the one shown in Figure 3. As the week's theme unfolds, team members add, modify, adapt, and build on the children's interests. Themes may be expanded and extended or move in an entirely new direction, as directed by the players. Toward the end of each theme, a TAP Sheet is completed for individual children. One of the team members moves around the room during the day and records anecdotal accounts of the children's behaviors. These notes might be examples of the highest levels of performance that a child has displayed or actual counts of behaviors. Although time does not permit an observational update of every child for every thematic unit, every child will be observed and observations recorded over time.

Storybook Planning

A storybook approach to planning themes has been found to be a particularly effective way of integrating play into each portion of the day (Jacobs, 1989; Tompkins & Hoskisson, 1991). This approach is useful for several reasons. First, children can relate to many of the themes in children's books. Social-emotional issues can be addressed through these themes, while still allowing the children to maintain some emotional distance from the topic (Bettelheim, 1987). Second, using a storybook theme provides opportunities for an infinite number of changes in play activities, props, materials, language, and interactions (Woodward, 1985). Thus, no one ever gets bored. Third, the use of storybooks on a continual basis, with the attendant repetition of words and actions over time, builds children's understanding of the attributes of books, including character, story sequence, and language (Donoghue, 1990; Kukla, 1987). Storybooks provide the basis for building literacy skills, a critical foundation for future academic success (Heath & Mangiola, 1991). Fourth, storybooks capitalize on children's imaginations, fostering dramatic play as a natural element in the classroom. Fifth, a storybook theme encourages the integration of skills from all developmental areas throughout the day. This approach is described below.

A different storybook is selected each week, or every 2 weeks if the children are extremely interested in a particular storybook theme. Storybooks should be selected on the basis of the action, simple plot, limited characters, and appealing dialogue. When possible, children should be involved in the selection of the story and the plan for its dramatization (Isenberg & Jalongo, 1993). Selection of storybooks that lend themselves to the development of other play centers is also important. Flexibility in planning is necessary, as some storybook themes will inspire great interest and need to be expanded. Extension of a theme has several advantages:

1.   The children have an opportunity to continue to practice the role-play scenarios and then modify or extend them by adding their own ideas.
2.   The children become familiar with the props and materials provided for the theme and begin to use them more creatively.
3.   Social interactions increase as the children become familiar with new roles.

9:00– 9:10	Children arrive, facilitated play
9:10– 9:25	Warm-up and story
9:25–10:15	Facilitated play in centers
10:15–10:40	Snacktime
10:40–11:10	Outdoor play/motor/science
11:10–11:45	Small group facilitated play
11:45–12:00	Closing, songs, discussion of day

Figure 3.   A sample daily schedule for a preschool program using thematic programming.

Play and other pleasurable activities are then developed to parallel the storybook theme and incorporate children's objectives. The play centers used and the order of the activities vary, depending on the theme. Figure 4 depicts a planning sheet for a week in which a theme was developed around *The Pet Show*, by Ezra Jack Keats (1972). The program's play centers are entered in the left column. Programs that use an approach to programming that does not revolve around play centers may substitute the segments of the day in this column.

The preschool that developed the play activities illustrated in Figure 4 is inclusive, integrating children with and without disabilities in a half-day program 4 days a week. One half-day is reserved for team planning, conducting transdisciplinary play-based assessments, making home visits, and participating in staff development activities. The week in which the children's activities were related to *The Pet Show* (Keats, 1972) is described below.

The pet show theme began on Monday. When they first arrived at school, the children played in centers of their choice. When all of the children were present, the teacher conducted a preparatory activity to get the children ready for the theme. She had brought her parakeet to school to greet the children and talked about the parakeet as a pet and then asked the children about their own pets. The storybook, *The Pet Show* (Keats, 1972), was then read to the children, after which they were free to play in any of the centers. Most of the centers were related to the theme in some way, as can be seen in Figure 4. The teacher and assistant facilitated the children's play at the various centers and helped them to make transitions to other areas when they were ready or when the adult felt that a change was needed. Because the pet show theme necessitated a field trip to a pet store in a local mall, the children role played their visit in small groups to prepare for the outing. They practiced walking with their partners, petted stuffed toys, and pretended to look, listen, and smell. Once in the actual store, the children were allowed to look at the animals, pet some of them, and examine the animals' toys, food, and other paraphernalia. The manager then had the children sit outside the store in the mall while she brought out different animals and equipment for them to see and touch. The trip stimulated language and understanding of concepts, encouraged social interactions, and generated abundant enthusiasm. Upon returning to school, the children had a snack of milk and animal crackers and talked about their field trip. They decided what to put in their pet store the next day. Children participated in the trip's activities and the discussions that followed at their own levels. For a few children, that meant petting an animal and taking in the sights and smells; for others, new words were added to their vocabularies; and some were able to retell the whole experience without missing a detail.

The next day, *The Pet Show* (Keats, 1972) was read again. Repeating the same story each day the theme was in use reinforced the concepts, helped the children begin to anticipate the next part of the story, and assisted them in seeing the relationship between the story and the play centers. After the story, the adults took the children around the room and showed them their choices of activities. The children were then free to choose a center in which to play. A group of children who had selected the theme area constructed a pet store. Plastic milk crates were used to set up "cages" in the store, and the children brought in stuffed animals from home. Parents contributed empty food boxes and bags, toys, leashes, and other items appropriate for use with pets. The children put these items on shelves and hung them on hooks. A toy cash register was put in place, and the store was open for business. The teacher remained in the area to facilitate play. Some children stayed in the pet store for an extended period, while others changed play centers more quickly. The teacher also helped children to make transitions—for instance, by suggesting that a sign was needed for the pet store and showing a child the art area and materials for making one. In other centers, the children expanded on other concepts and actions associated with the theme of pets. In the block area, the children set up large blocks to construct pedestals for their pets and built a large circle of blocks for a ring. They then pretended they were

Play-Based Curriculum Planning Sheet: Preschool/Kindergarten

Date: 2-17-92   Theme (optional): Pets   Book title (optional): The Pet Show (Keats, 1972)

Play area	Monday	Tuesday	Wednesday	Thursday	Friday
Theme area	Bring in props but set up on Tuesday.	Pet store—set up "cages" from crates, boxes, leash, register, pet food, and toys. Kids help arrange.	Bring stuffed animal from home. Put pets in store. Role play buying a pet.	Role play Scenario: 1) Get pet food and ribbons	Team planning time.
House area	Have props in house for pets	Add pets (stuffed), pet-feeding dishes, hamster, tub to wash pets, and pet beds.	Grooming materials to get ready for pet show.	2) Get pet ready	TPBA
Motor area	Practice movements in store (e.g., follow leader with partner to through room in practice.	Different-height boxes. Kids pretend to be pets at show.	Obstacle course. Take pet or peer through.	3) Show judges what pet can do; get ribbon.	
Blocks		Incorporate trucks for dog catcher; vet with unit blocks and Legos.	Build "arena" for pets with big blocks.	Same as Tuesday and Wednesday.	
Floor play		Mini-animals, Legos, to make cages. Tinker Toy cages.	Same, plus foam set.	Mini-animals, etc. Doctor kit to play vet.	
Sensory play	Have parakeet in room. Have mini-animals in sand table for free play when children arrive.	Water-table with miniature plastic toys to wash.	Sand table with buried dog biscuits and miniature dogs.	Wash old stuffed animals. Foam, soap, rinse, dry with dryer.	
Art area		Make sign for pet store. Use animal sponges to print pictures, play, easels, and colors.	Ribbon or string to make leashes and collars.	Popsicle sticks and glue for insect cages. Spiders from egg cartons and pipe cleaners.	

Figure 4.   The TPBI group planning sheet for a week with the pet show theme.

Play-Based Curriculum Planning Sheet: Preschool/Kindergarten

Date: 2-17-92   Theme (optional): __Pets__   Book title (optional): __The Pet Show (Keats, 1972)__

Play area	Monday	Tuesday	Wednesday	Thursday	Friday
Woodworking	None	Make toys, beds from wood strips.	Make cardboard box dog houses.	Same as Tuesday and Wednesday.	
Table play		Animal puzzles and drawing.	Beads for making collar—use pop-beads, stringing beads.	Animal Lotto and previous day's activities.	
Music area	Close with discussion about setting up pet store and pet show. Sing songs and finger-play like B-I-N-G-O.	Tapes of animal music. Move like different pets.	Movement like birds, snakes, or bugs.	Fingerplays with music.	
Book area	Read The Pet Show.	Book and tape of The Pet Show and stories about pets.	Book and tape of The Pet Show and stories about pets.	Book and tape of The Pet Show and stories about pets.	
Science	Talk about going to the pet store. What do the children think they'll see? What kind of pets? How do you take care of a pet? What makes a good pet?	Set up fish bowl. Choose things to put in it. Read about fish.	Big jars, leaves, or ant farm. Computer—animal counting game.	Talking parakeet—have kids teach new words. Computer games.	
Outdoors	Visit pet store. Owner will show pets, toys, food, and so forth.	"Escaped pet"—try to find him on the playground (hide stuffed animal).	Big jars outside to catch pet insects, ants for farm.	Bird watch—hike around playground.	
Snack	Milk and animal crackers. Review what they saw. "What do we need in our pet store?"	Granola	Sunflower seeds		

95

dogs and led one another around the "ring" to show. (This activity overflowed into the motor area as well.) One day, at the water table, they washed old stuffed animals with foam soap, rinsed them, and then put them out to dry in the sun. (The hair dryer was popular, but took too long.) They made ribbon leashes at the art table for their pets and attempted to build a cage in the woodworking area. Table play included putting animal puzzles together, making bead and string collars, and playing an animal lotto game.

The teacher and aide helped the children to interact with the materials at their own levels and stimulated cognitive, social-emotional, communication and language, and sensorimotor interactions that addressed the specific objectives on their TIP Sheets.

After 45 minutes to an hour of facilitated play in the centers, the children had a theme-related snack. Snacktime not only reinforces concepts, but is structured to address other objectives related to social-emotional, communication and language, and sensorimotor skills. The children are involved in everything from preparation to serving, eating, and cleaning up. During this particular week, the children ate granola (dog food) one day, sunflower seeds (bird food) another day, and lettuce and carrots (rabbit food) on still another day.

When weather permitted, snacktime was followed by outdoor play, which included motor play, science experiences, and sensory exploration. For instance, pets (stuffed animals) "escaped" and had to be found on the playground. While searching, the children climbed, ran, and crawled through and under many pieces of playground equipment. On days when the weather was inappropriate for outdoor play, the same type of motor play was done in the motor area inside.

Science activities also were part of the indoor and outdoor experiences. The teacher read about fish, and the children decided on things to put in the fishbowl for the goldfish they had purchased at the pet store. Outdoors, they captured bugs in their bug jars (most, unfortunately, came back squashed) and then analyzed them under a magnifying glass. An ant farm was begun and the children followed the ants' progress as tunnels were built. Another day, they made toilet-paper–roll binoculars and went on a birdwatch on the playground.

A more structured play activity followed the gross motor and science play. The children participated in small-group activities based on the play centers. For instance, one group in the pet theme made a doghouse out of a cardboard box; another sang animal songs and accompanied the music with movements; and others role-played a scenario of a pet show like the one in the storybook.

At the end of the day, there was time to come together and talk about the events of the day, sing songs, dance, do fingerplays, or read a final storybook. Closing time also allows the team and children time to talk about related things they can do at home and what they will do the next day or week. During closing time at the end of this week, the children and adults decided to extend the pet show theme for another week.

Ongoing Assessment Within the Storybook Curriculum   Toward the end of each theme, the team takes time to observe individual children and complete TAP Sheets. Children are selected for observation based on the time between observations or other indicators that might suggest that an update is needed. For instance, if a child has not seemed to make progress or has made very fast progress, the team might want to review and update the child's TIP Sheet. One of the team members, a teacher assistant, or the child's parent watches the child during the course of the day and records a sample of the child's behavior during play in each of the centers or play times.

Figure 5 is a TAP Sheet completed by the teacher assistant during the observation of Ahmad during the pet show storybook unit. When the team met to discuss these observations, it was determined that progress was being made on all of Ahmad's objectives. Ahmad was frequently using three-word sentences, so the team believed that this objective could be modified. A three- to four-word sentence was

Team Ideas for Play (TIP)/Team Assessment of Play (TAP) Sheet

Name of child: __Ahmad__ Date of birth: __4-1-88__ Age: __4 years__

Location: __Preschool__ Date: __5-5-92__

Family goals:
1. _____   4. _____
2. _____   5. _____
3. _____   6. _____

Time frame: ___ months

Areas of intervention/assessment

Objectives	Rationale/things I'm ready for	Sensory play	Gross motor play	Representational play	Manipulative play	Music/Books	Snacktime		
1. Ahmad will use 3-4 words in combination to initiate or maintain interaction with another.		• "Wash the dog." • "I want cup." • "you do it." Counted eight 3-4 word sentences in 10 minutes at water-table.	• "Don't push me." • "I pull it." Counted six 3-4 word sentences in 15 minutes	• "I want dog." • "Here's my money." Counted thirty 3-4 word sentences in 10 minutes.	Animal noises. Counted 3-4 word sentences in 10 minutes.	Didn't choose in centers. Did sing in imitation with class.	• "I like carrots." • "Art it here." Mostly 1-2 words.		
2. Ahmad will play a role in dramatic play and act out a sequence of 4-5 steps.		Put soap on dog, washed it, rinsed it, and dried it. Still mainly 2-3 steps, but doing more.	Chased other dogs, "caught one," brought to doghouse. T: "Does he need anything else?" A: "No."	Picked out dog and paid for it. Picked out food and paid for it. Got a leash and paid for it. Not in a linked sequence—separate.	Had animals run around and make noises. Went in house and ate from bowl.				

(continued)

Figure 5. A sample TAP Sheet.

Figure 5. (continued)

Team Ideas for Play (TIP)/Team Assessment of Play (TAP) Sheet

Name of child: __Ahmad__   Date: __5-5-92__

Objectives	Rationale/things I'm ready for	Areas of intervention/assessment					
		Sensory play	Gross motor play	Representational play	Manipulative play	Music/Books	Snacktime
3. Ahmad will persist in problem-solving on a task for 20 seconds.		Couldn't get top off jar—tried for 10 seconds, then gave to an adult. Persisted in rinsing soap out when adult painted out bubbles.	Looked for stuffed dog for 15 seconds, then got distracted. Persisted when "dog" was peel.	Couldn't get leash off hook, so cried. T: Pointed to stool. A: Got it and got leash. With facilitation persisted 20 seconds.	Played with table puzzles of animals.) Persisted 5-10 seconds on each piece. With adult cue, persisted 10-15 seconds.	Ahmad put tape in backwards, wouldn't go. Told T., "Broke." T and Ahmad to turn over. Turned over, pushed button. Smiled. Persisted 20 seconds with help.	Tried to peel carrots with scraper. Persisted 30 seconds with assistance.
4. Ahmad will use three new vocabulary words spontaneously in appropriate context each week.		Said, "Dog dirty." (after imitation). Later said spontaneously.	"Put on leash." (trying to get "dog" back to house.)	Got "cage" out.	Put string on dog (also good problem-solving)—said "leash." (He's really gotten into leashes.)	Labeled pictures in brochures from pet store: • "Dog food" • "leash" • house	Lettuce—in imitation. Carrots—spontaneously.
5. Ahmad will request information from adult or peer twice within an hour.		"Where's soap?"	None	With prompt from T.: "See if Tim knows where the dog food is." Ahmad to Tim, "Where's food?"	None	None	None

Team Ideas for Play (TIP)/Team Assessment of Play (TAP) Sheet

Name of child: __Ahmad__   Date: __5 - 5 - 92__

Objectives	Rationale/things I'm ready for	Sensory play	Gross motor play	Representational play	Manipulative play	Music/Books	Snacktime	
				Areas of intervention/assessment				
6. Ahmad will tolerate being above the ground (or being held suspended) for 1 minute.		None	Wouldn't climb up ladder to get stuffed animal. Put one foot up with T's assistance, got on first rail.	None	None	None	None	
7. Ahmad will relate concepts and group items that go together functionally in sets of 4-5 items.		Related soap, cup, towel, dog and hair dryer (towel and hair dryer with prompt).	Related leash and dog.	Dog food, dog, and leash were related spontaneously.	Animal, leash, and bowl.	Tape recorder, tape and book.	Carrot and peeler with prompt.	

still an appropriate objective, as he was still mostly using three words. The team modified the objective to increase his use of location words and adjectives as part of the three- to four-word sentences. The team also analyzed the objectives to see when skills were and were not being used. The team determined that Ahmad needed more facilitation in the manipulative play area to increase his verbalization. He was infrequently requesting information, so the speech-language therapist suggested "sabotaging" various areas by eliminating necessary items, putting unusual or unexpected things in the "wrong" places, and modeling by commenting on what he was doing with additional information. The occupational therapist noted that Ahmad had not participated in getting up on a box at the pet show and perhaps too few opportunities were being provided for him to work on moving his body through space and overcoming his anxiety about being off the ground. The team then brainstormed ideas for getting Ahmad motivated to climb, using his interest in dogs, leashes, and pets in general.

Other Thematic Approaches

The storybook curriculum should be distinguished from other thematic approaches. Some preschools and kindergartens have theme corners, which are used to act out specific scenarios (e.g., a grocery story, beauty shop, hospital, bank) using props associated with the particular concept. The theme corner is one option for play within the room and is not extended into other play areas (Isenberg & Jalongo, 1993). In the storybook curriculum described above, a theme corner is included but only as one aspect of integrating theme play throughout the curriculum. Dramatic play, which takes place in the theme corner, is only one type of play. The storybook curriculum extends concepts into all types of play, so that learning has a "spiraling" effect (Bruner, 1963). In other words, underlying concepts and processes are developed by repeated exposure in various ways, demonstrating different perspectives and meaningful experiences to the child.

Another approach to thematic play involves teacher-selected topics, such as seasons, holidays, or specific motifs, such as dinosaurs. In the teacher-directed thematic approach, the teacher integrates concepts believed to be important to the child. Activities are designed to elicit or reinforce these concepts. This differs from the storybook curriculum, in which the teacher may select the theme or storybook, but the children create their own experiences with the materials provided, and concepts or skills that are promoted are those that are relevant to a given child.

Play-generated curriculum and curriculum-generated play (Van Hoorn et al., 1993) are two additional thematic approaches that combine the interests of the teacher with those of the children. In the first, the teacher builds curricular themes based on the themes observed in the children's play. For instance, a child's interest in making tortillas in the house area might lead to a study of making different kinds of breads. In the latter approach, the teacher generates play activities based on his or her knowledge of children's interests and experiences. Both of these approaches are particularly sensitive to cultural differences. Attempts are made to integrate cultural diversity into art, music, literature, science, and mathematics experiences. Play-generated curriculum and curriculum-generated play are closely related to the techniques integrated into the storybook curriculum. It is also responsive to the interests and experiences of individual children if teachers select stories, props, and materials that are congruent with the backgrounds of children in the class.

CONCLUSION

The transdisciplinary play-based intervention approach incorporates programming for individual children into center-based programs (as well as home-based programs) for infants, toddlers, preschoolers, and kindergartners. The theme or storybook curriculum presented in this chapter can be used effectively with the preschool and kindergarten group, as it enables individual children's objectives to be integrated into all play centers within the room. Transdisciplinary planning and evaluation enable the team to develop and modify curricula as part of an ongoing process using TIP and Tap Sheets to guide intervention for individual children.

REFERENCES

Bettelheim, B. (1987). The importance of play. *Atlantic Monthly*, March, 35–36.

Bruner, J.S. (1963). *The process of education*. Cambridge, MA: Harvard University Press.

Donoghue, M. (1990). *The child and the English language arts* (5th ed.). Dubuque, IA: W.C. Brown.

Heath, S.B., & Mangiola, L. (1991). *Children of promise: Literate activity in linguistically and culturally diverse classrooms*. Washington, DC: National Education Association.

Isenberg, J.P., & Jalongo, M.R. (1993). *Creative expression and play in the early childhood curriculum*. New York: Merrill.

Jacobs, L.B. (1989). Dramatizing literature. *Teaching Pre-K-8, 19*(6), 26–29.

Keats, E.J. (1972). *The pet show*. New York: Macmillan.

Kukla, K. (1987). David Booth: Drama as a way of knowing. *Language Arts, 64*, 73–78.

Saltz, E., & Johnson, J. (1974). Teaching for thematic fantasy play in culturally disadvantaged children: Preliminary results. *Journal of Educational Psychology, 66*, 623–630.

Tompkins, G.E., & Hoskisson, K. (1991). *Language arts: Content and teaching strategies* (2nd ed.). Columbus, OH: Charles E. Merrill/Macmillan.

Van Hoorn, J., Nourot, P., Scales, B., & Alward, K. (1993). *Play at the center of the curriculum*. New York: Merrill.

Woodward, C. (1985). Guidelines for facilitating sociodramatic play. In J. Frost & S. Sunderlin (Eds.), *When children play* (pp. 291–295). Wheaton, MD: Association for Childhood Education International.

II

The TPBI Planner

As discussed in Chapter 5, the TPBI Planner is an important component of the transdisciplinary play-based intervention process. The intervention team is encouraged to become familiar with the suggestions and guidelines contained in the TPBI Planner before developing any child's intervention program. The TPBI Planner is also a useful resource to review periodically and to consult during the planning process.

WHAT IS THE TPBI PLANNER?

To facilitate use, the TPBI Planner, like the TPBA Observation Guidelines, is divided into four domains, or areas of development. Each domain is featured in a chapter here. Chapter 8 discusses cognitive development; Chapter 9, social-emotional development; Chapter 10, communication and language development; and Chapter 11, sensorimotor development. Each domain chapter is further broken down into units based on the *Observation Guidelines* used in the transdisciplinary play-based assessment process (Linder, 1993). Portions of these guidelines are reproduced in shaded boxes to open each discussion of a specific type of intervention strategies.

Following each set of Observation Guidelines is a discussion of *intervention implications* relevant to the skill areas being targeted. The intervention implications include cross-disciplinary information regarding the significance of certain abilities and development and descriptions of basic intervention principles.

Shown in unshaded boxes after the general discussions of intervention implications are specific *developmental levels* that are identified in two ways. The first is a statement of functional action. The second is a parenthetical notation of the action's typical chronological age equivalent. *Age ranges* are included to help users of the guidelines identify where to begin with intervention. Ages ranges are not meant as labels for children. A given child will probably demonstrate developmental variation across categories and domains. Behaviors observed are more salient indicators of what the child is ready for. Age ranges help the reader to find these behaviors.

Discussed after each developmental level, the *intervention guidelines* sections of the TPBI Planner recommend specific activities to do with children at the various developmental levels. It should be emphasized that these activities are only suggestions for intervention. The team is encouraged to modify the activities described and to create new activities that correspond to the child's specific interests, the family's goals for development, the play materials and opportunities available, and the family's lifestyle. Activities such as these will be written in the grid portion of the child's TIP Sheets (see Chapter 5).

Where relevant, *play materials and opportunities* are described following the discussion of intervention guidelines. Again, the items and opportunities listed here are suggestions and should be modified to reflect the individual child and family. It is important to note that in most cases the recommendations made in these discussions of play materials and opportunities do not require the acquisition of specific toys or equipment (see Chapter 6). On the contrary, the TPBI Planner encourages the use of routine household items as play materials and the incorporation of intervention activities into daily life.

One final element of each domain in the TPBI Planner are *examples* of transdisciplinary play-based intervention in action. These stories show how the intervention guidelines and recommendations in the TPBI Planner can be implemented for specific children.

HOW SHOULD THE TPBI PLANNER BE USED?

Although the activities and suggestions described in the TPBI Planner can be incorporated into any child's intervention program, the Planner is designed to be used following a transdisciplinary play-based assessment (Linder, 1993). The following discussion outlines how to use the TPBI Planner if a transdisciplinary play-based assessment has been conducted.

Following the child's assessment, the team will have available a Summary Sheet for each set of Observation Guidelines in the TPBA: cognitive, social-emotional, communication and language, and sensorimotor. The four domains in the TPBI Planner correspond to the four TPBA Observation Guidelines outlines. Therefore, the observation categories listed in the left column of each TPBA Summary Sheet correspond to the units of the Observation Guidelines used to introduce each new developmental objective in the TPBI Planner. By matching the Roman numerals by which each observation category is labeled in the outlines in *Transdisciplinary Play-Based Assessment* (Linder, 1993) to the Roman numerals in the shaded Observation Guidelines boxes in the TPBI Planner (the material contained in each of these boxes is actually a portion of the TPBA Observation Guidelines outlines), the team members can find their way to the strategies in which they are interested. By referring to the observation categories on the Summary Sheets and reading across to the strengths and things I'm ready for columns, the team determines which categories to target for intervention planning and then turns to the corresponding portions (introduced in the shaded boxes) in the TPBI Planner. After having located a specific portion of the Planner, the team is encouraged to read the discussion of intervention implications that follows the shaded box. The general discussion of intervention principles and developmental significance of actions is helpful regardless of the child's specific level. Then, the team should read the descriptions of the developmental levels found in the unshaded boxes in that section of the TPBI Planner. After having found the box that best matches the child's developmental level, the team should read the discussion of intervention guidelines and play materials and opportunities that follow. It is also recommended that the team members read the discussions of developmental levels immediately above and below the one that they have chosen, as it is difficult (and not recommended) to fit a child into a specific developmental level. If there is an example in that portion of the TPBI Planner, the team is encouraged to read it. The child described may prompt new insights into intervention for the child whose intervention is under consideration. When this review is complete, the team is ready to proceed with completing the grid portion of a child's TIP Sheet.

For additional information about the TPBI process, arranging play environments, choosing materials and equipment, and implementing thematic programming, readers are encouraged to review the preceding chapters in Part I.

REFERENCE

Linder, T.W. (1993). *Transdisciplinary play-based assessment: A functional approach to working with young children* (rev. ed.). Baltimore: Paul H. Brookes Publishing Co.

8

Facilitating Cognitive Development

Children with cognitive delays, or deficits in thinking skills, typically progress through the same play sequences as nondelayed children. However, children with cognitive delays demonstrate a more restricted repertoire of play skills, reduced language, less sophisticated dramatic play, more manipulation of toys and ritualistic play, and less organized play (Hulme & Lunzer, 1966; Li, 1981; Smilansky, 1968). Attention differences may also be demonstrated. Krakow and Kopp (1983) found that the child with developmental delays appeared to monitor the environment less, engage their mothers less in social play, and spend more time in unoccupied behavior than children without delays.

These differences reflected in children's play can have a substantial effect on their future development. The role of the parent in the child's play is particularly significant. Bruner (1982) describes the parent as providing a "scaffold" for the emerging skills of the child. In other words, as the child's skills emerge, the parent supports, encourages, and challenges the child. This scaffolding is of critical importance for the child with cognitive deficits, as the characteristics described above may mitigate the child playing with objects, exploring, and discovering things about the world independently.

Parents and early interventionists play the crucial role of facilitating higher levels of play. Using imitation of the child or "conspicuous affect and vocal marking" (Beckwith, 1985, p. 154) to capture the child's attention, the adult can then model playful interactions with objects, play materials, or people in the environment. The adult can structure the play in such a way that the child is encouraged to exercise higher-level strategies and stimulate the child to interact with the materials and people in the environment in creative ways (Christie, 1983; Dansky, 1980; Smith, Dalgleish, & Herzmark, 1981).

For children with or without disabilities, the environment, including play materials, people, and opportunities, is a key to successful facilitation of developmental progress. The ideas presented in this chapter are meant to promote children's comprehension of cause-and-effect relationships, spatial understandings, representational thinking, classification/discrimination abilities, and problem-solving. Attention preferences, imitative facility, and learning style are considered as well.

When integrated with ideas from other chapters, the ideas presented here result in a holistic approach to early intervention. As discussed in Chapter 4, the transdisciplinary approach to working with children is essential. One cannot adequately look at cognitive skills without considering the child's movement capability, communicative competence, and social proficiency, all of which allow the child to demonstrate what he or she knows. All of the ideas and suggestions in this chapter must, therefore, be considered along with the corresponding areas in other chapters that are appropriate for a given child.

The discussion begins with a general look at the areas of play in which the child engages and his or her attention preferences. The chapter then moves into more specific subcategories of the cognitive skills. It should be noted that preacademic skills are considered, although not as an isolated area. Rather, they are incorporated into classification/discrimination, one-to-one correspondence, sequencing abilities, and drawing skills among others. This is done purposefully, with the intent of showing the developmental progression in various areas leading to these abilities.

OBSERVATION GUIDELINES FOR
COGNITIVE DEVELOPMENT: CATEGORIES OF PLAY

I. Categories of Play
   A. What range of categories are observed in the child's play?
      1. Exploratory or sensorimotor play
      2. Relational or functional play
      3. Constructive play
      4. Dramatic or symbolic play
      5. Games-with-rules play
      6. Rough-and-tumble play
   B. Primary category in which the child engages

INTERVENTION IMPLICATIONS

The categories of play are, for the most part, listed in the observation guidelines hierarchically (i.e., they build on each other). As the child acquires new skills and abilities to relate objects and think in more abstract terms, lower-level abilities do not drop out, but are incorporated into play as needed (Rubin, Fein, & Vandenberg, 1983). For example, a 6-year-old who is capable of playing games with rules incorporates "rules," or expected behaviors, into his or her dramatic play. When constructing a model or elaborate block city, he or she also adds dramatic representation and relates blocks and objects functionally. When given an unfamiliar, challenging new toy, the child may revert to sensorimotor or exploratory play until the features and functions of the toy are established.

Encouraging Higher Levels of Play

A principle for intervention with the child in this area is to facilitate the category of play that is observed, but at the same time, encourage a higher level of play as well. The parent or early interventionist provides the scaffold for emerging skills (Bruner, 1982) by determining what is done with the child, when it is done, and the affect (i.e., feeling or emotion) with which it is done. For instance, if the child is stirring with a spoon in a cup, the parent or facilitator might model pretending to eat something from the cup with the spoon, at the same time smiling and saying, "Mmm." If the child imitates this behavior, the parent or facilitator usually smiles and comments on the child's action, "Yes, you're stirring." The adult uses "conspicuous affect and vocal marking" (Beckwith, 1985, p. 159) to get the child's attention and to comment on the child's play. To signal the end of the parent's turn and the beginning of the child's, repetitive verbalizations and pauses are used (Bruner, 1977). This is a natural interactive sequence that, in the example described, expedites early representational, or dramatic, play.

Establishing Prerequisite Skills

The facilitator must keep in mind that before modeling or encouraging higher-level behaviors, it is best to *confirm that the skills the child is demonstrating are firmly established and generalize to a variety of situations.* If for example, an infant is just beginning to exhibit exploratory play with objects, the facilitator should not try to encourage combining or relating objects. The child must be able to visually, tactually, auditorially, and in other ways explore and determine characteristics of objects sensorially before he or she can see how various characteristics could be related. The infant also needs the motor skills to be able to bring his or her hands to the midline or move objects together. In other words, one could model a higher-level activity and even have the child imitate some aspect of that behavior; however, prerequisite skills may be necessary. In addition, the higher-level play activity is more meaningful, and more easily integrated and generalized if the child understands *how* and *why* certain characteristics are associated. Mastery in play is facilitated by optimally challenging experiences (Harter, 1981; Morgan & Harmon, 1984).

   One role of the interventionist is to arrange the environment in such a way as to encourage the child's initiation of causal and goal-oriented play. Responsivity of play materials is, thus, important. *Modeling must build on what the child initiates and has a desire to master.* A child may be physically and verbally prompted to drop a cube in a cup, for example, but the concept of "putting things in" is more purposeful if the child has looked "in" many containers, felt the characteristics of containers, seen objects inside of containers, and has experienced dropping many items. Motivation to accomplish a goal comes partially from desiring to see an anticipated outcome and to control the actions that result in the outcome (Gottfried, 1985). The child begins to anticipate outcomes after being exposed to the action and outcome several times. Whether the child is shaking a rattle, pushing a button on a pop-up toy, feeding a doll, building a house, or winning a card game, the desired visual, auditory, physical, or mental outcome is more intrinsically motivating and meaningful to the child when he or she initiates the action and achieves the desired result.

Learning About Rules

Games with rules, such as card games and board games, require a higher level of conceptualization than rough-and-tumble play because they require the child to understand that some aspects of the game do not change. There are rules that allow one to "win." These types of game skills evolve as the child engages in a variety of social interactions involving organized, integrated sequences of action, or rules (Hughes, 1991; Ross & Kay, 1980). Small children have difficulty with fixed aspects of a game and like to change the rules to fit their needs. Rules are important as they teach children about roles, shared expectations, and standards (Berns, 1985; Piaget, 1932; Youniss, 1978).

   The idea of rules can begin to be incorporated into construction and representational play with older children. When building with blocks, "rules" about balance and construction can be jointly determined. For example, the facilitator can assist the child in experimenting with balancing different kinds of blocks and then making up a rule about balancing square and rectangular blocks in the center. When playing store, making up rules about taking turns or putting materials back in certain places also helps the child to understand the idea of having consistent expectations in specific situations.

Rough-and-tumble play, although listed in the highest age range, is not considered the most advanced form of cognitive play. It emerges later than the other categories of play, when the child has the motor skills and is socially interested in chasing, jumping, and tumbling group games (Garvey, 1977). While rough-and-tumble play almost implies the absence of rules in play, it actually sets a basis for learning social give-and-take. The combination of rough-and-tumble play and games with rules provides a balance for the child as the struggle to be wild and free competes with the need to be governed by rules.

DEVELOPMENTAL LEVEL

- Exploratory or sensorimotor play
  (0–24 months)

INTERVENTION GUIDELINES

Play with toys that have defined visual, auditory, and action characteristics. *Attend to the child's interests with the toy, even if the child's actions are not related to the intended function of the toy or object* (e.g., banging on a book). Model the typical use of the toy or object after the child has explored it in his or her own way, unless the child's exploration is harmful to him- or herself or the environment (e.g., mouthing a crayon or writing on the wall). If the child is engaging in harmful activities, immediate redirection and modeling of appropriate alternatives is necessary.

PLAY MATERIALS AND OPPORTUNITIES

Brightly colored objects and objects with sharply contrasting colors (e.g., black and white) are good for very young infants. Toys that involve action promote understanding of cause and effect. Start with toys that can be activated very simply, by moving the hand (e.g., rattles, mobiles, pop-up toys with activators that can be "swiped"). Gradually move to more complicated toys (e.g., pop-up toys requiring more difficult actions). For children with physical disabilities, toys can be adapted with easily activated switches. Toys that the child can put things "in" and "on" build the foundation for relational and later constructive play. To build the foundation for later representational play, introduce the child to dolls and simple objects that are used during his or her day (e.g., cups, diapers, washcloths) and allow him or her to explore them.

EXAMPLE

Twelve-month-old Jalisa S. was from a low-income, single-parent, African American family. Jalisa was a quiet baby who did not demand much attention and was consequently left in her crib much of the time. She was delayed in all areas of development and demonstrated hypotonia (low tone) in her lower extremities. Although her mother did not spend much time playing with Jalisa,

Ms. S. was fastidious in her care, making sure Jalisa was fed, changed, and dressed nicely. The team felt that beginning with activities that Jalisa and her mother performed on a regular basis would feel more comfortable to Ms. S. The team discussed Jalisa's caregiving times with her and looked at how they could incorporate play interactions.

Ms. S. reported that Jalisa did not like to have her diaper changed. She would squirm and cry, making the duty an ordeal for both mother and child. Together, the interventionists and Jalisa's mother generated several ways of incorporating play into diaper-changing time to make this activity more pleasurable for Jalisa and her mother. Jalisa's mother did not have many toys for her, but while talking to the team, she soon was able to come up with fun ways to entertain Jalisa while her diaper was being changed. Sometimes she would give Jalisa an extra diaper to shake and hide behind so they could play "peek"; sometimes she gave Jalisa a plastic jar with safety pins in it to shake; and occasionally, Jalisa was given a picture from a magazine to look at and crinkle and tear.

At the speech-language therapist's suggestion, Jalisa's mother started talking to Jalisa while she was changing her, imitating Jalisa's noises, commenting on her actions, and making funny sounds that made Jalisa laugh. While Jalisa's clothes were off, her mother could also play tickle games with Jalisa, thus giving her tactile input. At the end of the diapering, Jalisa's mother would turn her around so that Jalisa's feet were toward her and they would play a little kicking game. Jalisa would push against her mother's chest with her feet and Ms. S. would then lean over and kiss Jalisa's tummy. This turn-taking game was suggested by the occupational therapist as it encouraged Jalisa to push against resistance, which was beneficial for her low tone. The game also encouraged a give and take of eye gaze, sounds, and laughter that communicated the desire to continue the game. The sequence of play during diapering thus facilitated exploration through cognitive activities, communicative sounds, and motor movements. All of the games were fun and motivated Jalisa to interact with her environment.

Diapering soon became a playful interaction time for both mother and infant. Jalisa's mother was then anxious to discuss other "games" they could play together during specific times of the day. She became quite creative at using the materials found around the house and began to check toys out of the toy-lending library.

DEVELOPMENTAL LEVEL

- Relational or functional play (predominates from 15 to 21 months) (9–24 months)

INTERVENTION GUIDELINES

Put out "sets" of things that can be related for the child. Don't expect that he or she will search for a container to put blocks in or a spoon to go with a plate. If the child automatically relates objects, imitate the action and comment on the relationship (e.g., "You put it in the bowl; I put my Cheerio in, too."). If the child plays with the objects in exploratory ways, imitate his or her actions and then model using the toys or objects in a related or functional way (e.g., put the receiver of the toy telephone to your ear and say, "Hi.").

PLAY MATERIALS AND OPPORTUNITIES

Use simple toys that can be used functionally (e.g., drums, telephones, cars, balls). Everyday objects (e.g., pots, spoons, telephones, toothbrushes) also stimulate functional play. Toys that can be related spatially, by putting objects "in" (e.g., boxes, cans, bottles), "on" (e.g., blocks, dishes), or "together" (e.g., putting two objects together, putting a figure in a car) encourage combinatorial play and spatial awareness.

DEVELOPMENTAL LEVEL

- Constructive play (predominates from 36 months on)
  (24 months +)

INTERVENTION GUIDELINES

Construction, with the goal of building something, comes after the child can relate objects and has a mental image of the intended goal (e.g., building a tower, stringing a necklace). Construction fosters coordination and representational and creative thinking (Feeney & Magarick, 1984; Nicolopoulou, 1991; Reifel & Yeatman, 1991). If the child does not spontaneously construct, modeling can encourage the child to move from simply stacking blocks to constructing a simple house or fence. Use a theme that is of interest to the child based on a book that you have read together or a topic or character the child likes (e.g., building a sewer for the Ninja Turtles).

PLAY MATERIALS AND OPPORTUNITIES

There are many types of blocks on the market to meet the needs of almost every child. Large wooden blocks, varying sizes of Lego blocks, Duplo blocks, bristle blocks, and magnetic blocks are available. Tinker Toys, Lincoln Logs, bolt and screw assortments, and other commercially available sets are also good, depending on the child's ability level. Construction can also be done with beads, clay, sand and water, popsicle sticks, and other media. It is most important that the materials be able to be combined in many ways.

DEVELOPMENTAL LEVEL

- Representational/symbolic play
  (21–72 months)

INTERVENTION GUIDELINES

Dramatic play can be the richest arena for intervention, as it so fully engages the child (Isenberg & Jalongo, 1993; Van Hoorn, Nourot, Scales, & Alward, 1993). Opportunities for dramatizing scenarios, segments of stories, or whole imaginary tales are unlimited. With the younger child, emphasize role playing two- to three-step familiar sequences (e.g., feeding the baby) and progress to longer sequences. With the older child, add the interaction of characters. Use any everyday sequence or a story that is of interest to the child, or role play a fun activity (e.g., going camping). Build on the actions the child initiates and model an additional step in the sequence. Incorporate practice of functional, relational, and construction activities into dramatic play when possible, and model higher-level symbolic play and role differentiation. (See pp. 131–141 for recommendations for specific representational levels, and Chapter 10 for facilitating language.)

With the young child, everyday objects are best, especially when combined with actions the child performs on him- or herself. Dolls, bears, and other characters can be added as the child shifts actions to others. Miniature dolls and action characters become important as the child acquires the ability to assign roles to characters and act them out. Having props available is important, as props encourage the acting out of longer sequences and stimulate the imagination. Props can be actual items or replica items, or they can be created with the child, depending on his or her developmental level.

PLAY MATERIALS AND OPPORTUNITIES

- Rough-and-tumble play (predominates from 5 to 6 years)
  (36 months +)

DEVELOPMENTAL LEVEL

Pellegrini and Perlmutter (1988) describe rough-and-tumble play as "laughing, running, smiling, jumping, wrestling, play fighting, chasing, and fleeing" (p. 14). It is distinguished not by aggression, which results in separation, but by continued cooperative play. It, therefore, provides a means for social learning, as children take turns being the "victim" and "victimizer" (Smith & Boulton, 1990). Rule learning, invitation acceptance, turn-taking, situation interpretation, and cue reading are important social skills learned through rough-and-tumble play (Pellegrini, 1988). Such play may in fact help children to develop rules for social interaction.

Rough-and-tumble play provides an opportunity for children to practice motor skills, stimulate the vestibular system, and have high-intensity tactile input through social interaction. Most typical children of 5–6 years of age play run-and-chase games without adult assistance. This may not be the case for children with disabilities. The adult may need to initiate or be a partner in these types of activities. Roughhousing or rolling and tickling, running, hopping, climbing, and playing tag are all important to children. Although this type of play can take place between an adult and child, involvement with a group of children is more typical for the older child. *The facilitator should endeavor to initiate the fun and then withdraw from active participation if possible.* Many children with disabilities have been involved in structured therapy and intervention programs and, consequently, have infrequently experienced this type of free-for-all activity. Children who are not frequently sought out for this type of play also may interpret initiations as aggression. Teachers can help such children to read these cues as invitations to join in rough-and-tumble play. Adults or older peers can "coach" children in how to read cues and participate in nonaggressive rough-and-tumble play (Perlmutter, 1988).

INTERVENTION GUIDELINES

No toys are needed for rough-and-tumble play; however, children may incorporate dramatic play roles, such as cowboys, soldiers, or cops into their chase, in which case they may want the necessary props.

PLAY MATERIALS AND OPPORTUNITIES

- Games-with-rules play
  (60 months +)

DEVELOPMENTAL LEVEL

INTERVENTION GUIDELINES

Learning how to play games with rules is an important step for children. Games with rules promote physical coordination, develop language and social skills, and build concepts of cooperation and competition (Elkind, 1988). The child begins to seek out games with rules as he or she develops the idea of "winning," as roles within games are understood, and as conservation concepts (i.e., the notion that rules for a certain game remain the same from situation to situation) become consolidated (Piaget, 1962). Games should be challenging, but have a clear goal for the child. They should involve the child's fantasy or imagination and foster curiosity, which encourages the child to experiment with different approaches (Malone, 1983). Playing card games, such as Go Fish!; group games, such as "Tag"; and board games, such as Chutes and Ladders introduces children to many of these concepts. To facilitate readiness, the adult may choose to play simple games, like Hi-ho! Cherry-o! This game only requires the child to be able to count to four. The child learns the sequence of spinning, taking a turn, taking away or adding cherries from his or her tree, and being the first to get all of his or her cherries into the bucket. *The adult should be tolerant of the child's attempts to change the rules, explaining why a rule is needed.* Making up games and the rules to go with them is also fun and can help the child to appreciate the need for directives. Having children construct their own games also fosters understanding of rules and sequences, as well as cooperation (Berns, 1985). Using the term "rule" or "direction," as in "What do the rules say?", when the child forgets a procedure may serve as a reminder and allow the child to stay in control. Saying, "No, you can't do that!" makes the child feel that he or she has done something wrong and will not encourage problem-solving. Games with rules do not have to emphasize the competitive element. With adult support, children can develop cooperation and strategic thinking skills, understanding of how another person thinks and acts, and problem-solving skills tht encourage fair play. Winning should not be stressed; participation and doing one's best should (Hughes, 1991).

PLAY MATERIALS AND OPPORTUNITIES

Many excellent games with rules are available for young children. In addition to the ones mentioned previously, some other favorites include: Ants in the Pants; Blockhead; Perfection; various forms of Lotto, Bingo, and Dominoes; card games, such as Go Fish!; memory match games, such as Memory; and board games, such as Candyland and Uncle Wiggly.

Cards and pictures from magazines can also be used to make up games. Children love to color in squares on pieces of paper (game board) and paste on pictures. By making up rules for winning, adding dice and small toys for markers, they make their own games.

OBSERVATION GUIDELINES FOR COGNITIVE DEVELOPMENT: ATTENTION SPAN—ATTENTION PREFERENCES

II. **Attention Span**
   A. **Attention preferences**
      1. **What is the average length of time the child spends per activity?**
      2. **What activities engage the child for the longest time?**
         a. **Observation**
         b. **One of the categories listed in 1., A.**
      3. **What activities engage the child for the shortest time?**
      4. **Does the child demonstrate a sensory preference?**
         a. **Visual preference—the child attends longer to the visual features of objects or to objects that have strong visual features**
         b. **Auditory preference—the child attends longer to toys with auditory features**
         c. **Tactile preference—the child attends longer to toys that provide strong tactile input**
         d. **Vestibular preference—the child attends longer in activities that provide movement or vestibular input**

Fishbein (1976) defined attention processes as "those which underlie how we orient our sensory receptors to the environment, how we identify information, how we explore the environment, and how we select information for additional processing " (p. 208). Paying attention to relevant cues in the environment is essential for learning (Levine & Jordan, 1987). If the child does not attend to people, toys, and materials in his or her environment, the opportunities to gather information about the world are limited and the development of more sophisticated play skills is hindered (Beers & Wehman, 1985). Observation data related to attention in play provide guidance to facilitators and parents concerning the arrangement of the environment in such a way as to maximize the child's attention and learning.

INTERVENTION IMPLICATIONS

Selecting Activities

Begin the play session by focusing on activities that maintain the child's attention for the longest time and need the least amount of adult support. Arrange the environment to ensure that toys and materials will interest the child, peak the child's motivation, build rapport between the child and facilitator, and enable the facilitator to use minimal external prompting. In order to capture the child's attention, particular care must be paid to incorporating toys and materials that will engage the child's senses.

Using Information from Parents or Caregivers

Information gained from the child's parents will assist in planning the most stimulating play environment for a particular child. An infant with visual impairments, for instance, may not be motivated to do a manual search for toys or explore the immediate environment. He or she lacks the visual motivation natural to children with normal sight. Instead of seeking out toys and manipulating them, the child with visual impairments may sit passively until a toy is placed in his or her hands. Then, instead of using the toy functionally, the child may rub the toy on his cheek, lick it, or bite it. The parent may indicate that the child plays more in known, secure surroundings. This can be arranged by setting up a safe "nest," where the child can feel toys within reach. In addition, the proximity of materials may elicit more spontaneous play (Twardosz, Cataldo, & Risley, 1974). Toys that make noise with a light touch and that have interesting textures may also be appealing (Newson & Hipgrave, 1982). If the child sees light, a flashlight can be used to direct the child's attention to a toy.

Making Transitions Between Activities

Use the motivating aspect of one activity to help the child make a transition to activities that maintain his or her attention for less time. For example, if a preschool child selects and attends to the pegboards and puzzles first every morning and never chooses to play in the block area, the facilitator could move one of the puzzles into the block area and begin to play next to the child with blocks as the child plays with the puzzle. If the child is not enticed into the block activity, the facilitator could then stack the puzzle pieces and the blocks; or the facilitator could make the blocks into a "puzzle" and let the child place the "pieces" into the block puzzle.

Engaging the Child in Less Appealing Activities

Intersperse activities to which the child attends for less time between activities that hold his or her attention for a longer time. Activities that engage the child for the least amount of time demand more adult support through modeling, prompting, and reinforcement. Usually, the activities that command the least attention are those that are either difficult for the child or those that do not have strong motivating aspects. The adult needs to be creative to make these activities easier and more enticing for the child. Useful techniques include the following:

- Add something to the activity that captures the child's attention (e.g., a preferred toy, bright colors, sound, movement).
- Allow the child to experience success by building on skills he or she can demonstrate (even if the observed behavior is not the desired behavior).
- Model or prompt only the next increment or skill in the developmental progression.
- Reinforce the child's attempts with praise, hugs, or a primary reinforcer only when necessary (Beers & Wehman, 1985), as external reinforcers invite an external locus of control. The best reinforcers may be toys, play materials, and interactive games (Hopper & Wambold, 1978), which stimulate an internal locus of control and intrinsic motivation. Children can sustain attention on activities that are interesting and meaningful (Garreau & Kennedy, 1991).

Adapting the Environment
According to Sensory Preference

The child may demonstrate a sensory preference in activity selection. In other words, the child may be attracted to activities involving toys with certain visual, tactile, or auditory characteristics; activities involving movement; or some combination of sensory characteristics. The facilitator can use the child's sensory preferences to maintain attention by adapting the environment to incorporate the desired characteristics. For example, for the young infant who is attracted to sounds, bells or rattles can be added to objects (or even arms and legs). For the child with a visual impairment, the environment may be adapted by placing bright objects on black backgrounds. Movement and music can be incorporated into activities for the child who enjoys vestibular input. Assimilating varying textures into activities can attract the child who is intrigued by exploring tactile sensations. Materials that are soft, scratchy, squishy, or gooey can provide an incentive for some children to investigate and manipulate. (See pp. 82–85 for a more complete list of textures and materials that hold children's attention.)

OBSERVATION GUIDELINES FOR COGNITIVE DEVELOPMENT: ATTENTION SPAN—LOCUS OF CONTROL

B. Locus of control
 1. **Does the child select activities and stay with them without external prompting or reinforcement?**
 2. **What type of external support, direction, or reinforcement is needed in order for the child to maintain attention in an activity?**
    a. Verbal
    b. Physical
    c. Other
 3. **Distractibility—Do external stimuli interfere with an activity?**
    a. **Do visual stimuli (materials, toys, etc.) distract the child?**
    b. **Do auditory stimuli (bells, voices) distract the child?**
    c. **Do nearby activities distract the child?**
    d. **Do people in the room distract the child?**

INTERVENTION IMPLICATIONS

Locus of control relates to a person's perception of who controls the environment and causes events to occur in the world. A person who believes outcomes occur independently of how they behave attributes results to external control, while the person who believes that outcomes are contingent upon their behavior attributes results to internal control (Rotter, 1966). The child who has an internal locus of control is motivated to act on the environment and make things happen through self-initiation. The child who has an external locus of control relies more on others to initiate events and attributes effects to external causes. The amount of external control needed to motivate the child to attend to and have an impact on the environment has implications for intervention.

External Support and Reinforcement

After observing the child in play with the facilitator, a parent or caregiver, a peer, and, if possible and age appropriate, a group of other children, the team should have information about the amount and type of external support and reinforcement needed by the child to maintain attention on various activities. This information can be helpful in planning the child's program. Lack of spontaneous play is one characteristic frequently cited with regard to children with disabilities (Beers & Wehman, 1985). Lower-functioning children may not act on play materials without some form of cue, external supervision, or instruction.

Amount of External Support

The amount of external support needed varies from child to child. Simple imitation of the child's behavior may result in turn-taking; then modeling a new behavior or combining modeling with an instruction or self-talk about how an action is occurring may prompt imitation of the adult. Cuing the child, using verbal, gestural, or physical means, may assist the child to commence or continue a play activity (Hayden, McGuinness, & Dmitriev, 1976). Physical prompting may be necessary for children with severe disabilities, although gradual removal of physical prompts, or fading, should be accomplished as soon as the child understands and is physically able to play without the physical support (Whitman, Mercurio, & Caponigri, 1970).

Types of Reinforcement

The *type* of reinforcement the child needs is just as important as the amount of support or reinforcement required. An attempt should be made to move the child from primary or tangible reinforcers to social reinforcers (e.g., verbal praise, a hug, or adult attention), and then to having play materials and activities themselves serve as reinforcers. Concentrating on making activities self-motivating as described previously expedites this process. The goal is to help children to become less dependent on adult attention and reinforcement (Johnson, Christie, & Yawkey, 1987).

The child who performs best when in interaction with an adult needs more one-to-one intervention, while the child who is self-motivated and needs little external support is able to engage in activities without as much adult mediation. Children who interact well with peers, either leading or imitating in interaction, can play well in dyads or small groups. For the team members who are working with groups of children, this information can help in structuring dyad, group, individual, and self-directed activities. Team members can build the child's internal locus of control by reducing the amount of external support necessary and helping the child to see the outcome of his or her actions. The constant use of external reinforcement or adult direction can result in the child "performing" for adults and can reduce the child's ability to select and follow through on activities without adult supervision (Beers & Wehman, 1985; Williams, Brown, & Certo, 1975).

Distractibility

Distractibility is one factor that may hinder the child's ability to attend for long time periods, resulting in the need for increased adult support and direction (Thurman & Widerstrom, 1990). The child who is observed to be easily distracted by visual or auditory stimuli, by nearby activities, or by the mere presence of other adults or children may need environmental modifications. For example, the child who moves from one activity to another as he or she observes others playing or as he or she spots a different toy area may be able to practice skills and explore in a more focused way if the distractions are minimized. For this type of child, reducing the number of initial choices (but not eliminating choices) may be helpful. After a choice has been made, the other objects or activities can be removed to eliminate some of the distraction.

The use of low shelves that enable the child to see the whole room and move from area to area is recommended by many early childhood educators (Hohmann, Banet, & Weikert, 1979). Having objects and toys visible, labeled, and easily accessible to children is also recommended. For most children, this is an excellent approach, but some children need to make gradual transitions into environments with many choices. For highly distractible children, it may be necessary to reduce the distractions in one area of the room to enable one-to-one interaction (Nordquist, Twardosz, & McEvoy, 1991). The child can then be introduced to the more stimulating environment for varying lengths of time throughout the day.

DEVELOPMENTAL LEVELS

There are no age ranges for attention span listed in *Transdisciplinary Play-Based Assessment* (Linder, 1993). Research related to attention has demonstrated that infants between birth and 2 months of age do not show a preference for novel stimuli; they look longer at moving stimuli and stimuli high in black-and-white contrast. From 2 to 6 months of age, infants begin to show a preference for novel stimuli and attend more to patterned than unpatterned stimuli; more to faces than other patterns. By 6 months of age, infants can distinguish among colors and forms and can remember the orientation of familiar objects. Between the ages of 3 months and 1 year, the infant's ability to explore objects increases rapidly, with both attention and memory processes becoming more selective and guided by symbolic thought (Fishbein, 1984). Much of the research on attention has focused on infancy, with the research on older children limited to very specific attention processes. Age guidelines for attention and intervention are, therefore, not as helpful as examining the qualitative information obtained about the child's attention.

INTERVENTION GUIDELINES

Important qualitative aspects relevant to intervention include types of activities that *do* and *do not* engage the child's attention, the sequence of activities selected by the child, and the level of support needed to maintain the child's attention to various types of tasks. Cultural variations may also influence the child's attention preferences. As previously mentioned, children with specific disabilities may be drawn to specific sensory stimuli or need varying amounts of one-to-one support to maintain attention. The transdisciplinary intervention team should take these factors into consideration when planning the play environment.

PLAY MATERIALS AND OPPORTUNITIES

Chapter 6 concerns organizing the play environment and addresses in detail the types of play materials and opportunities that should be considered for maintaining the child's attention.

EXAMPLE

Juanita R. is a 15-month-old Mexican-American baby who is legally blind. Her mother spends much time holding her and talking softly to her. Juanita is never put on the floor to play because the Mexican culture from which her family came does not encourage babies to play on the floor. Mrs. R. holds Juanita or puts her on the couch or bed to play. Juanita is just beginning to walk but does not explore her environment motorically or search for toys with her hands. She waits for her mother to put something in front of her or in her hands. The team wants to respect Mrs. R.'s health concerns about having the infant on the floor, but also wants to encourage attention and exploration of the environment.

The intervention team discussed Juanita's interests with Mrs. R. and discovered that Juanita likes to stand at the window and stare out. She has a favorite squeak toy and likes to shake a tiny maraca. In the transdisciplinary play-based assessment, Juanita was enticed to explore objects by using a flashlight with an object. Among other activities, she enjoyed making bells fall in a coffee can, liked to shake or push noisemakers, and explored the feel of dried rice and beans in a pan.

To help Mrs. R. with play activities at home, the early interventionist showed Mrs. R. how to activate and sustain Juanita's attention to play materials. She showed her how the use of a black piece of cloth under the toys increased the contrast between the background and the materials, making the toys easier to see. Using a baby food jar with beans in it, she demonstrated how making a noise with the toy and then placing the toy close to Juanita encouraged her to reach for it. Then she moved the toy further away, still shaking it so that Juanita sustained attention and interest but had to search for the toy. The early interventionist helped Mrs. R. to take turns with Juanita. Juanita would shake or bang the toy and Mrs. R. would then imitate Juanita with another jar with beans in it.

Mrs. R. soon became adept at getting Juanita not only to search for an object while sitting on the bed, but also to pursue a toy around the coffee table. She even invented a game, putting pieces of tortilla around the edge of the coffee table so that Juanita would cruise around the table searching for the pieces of tortilla. She then noticed that Juanita started to walk to the coffee table and search even when she had not put out tortillas. The early interventionist suggested taking advantage of this association of the coffee table with desirable events. Mrs. R. began to put out a different toy on different parts of the table so that Juanita would have to explore to find the toy or "surprise." The coffee table was thus launched as the play table. It provided a limited, and thus secure and motivating, area for exploration; enabled Juanita to stand and walk with support; and stimulated investigation that could then be expanded and generalized to other parts of the house.

OBSERVATION GUIDELINES FOR
COGNITIVE DEVELOPMENT: EARLY OBJECT USE

III. Early Object Use
   A. Type and range of schemes
      1. What type and number of low-level schemes were observed (mouthing, banging, shaking, etc.)?
      2. What type and number of more complex adaptive schemes were observed (pushing, poking, pulling, throwing)?
      3. Does the child use a large number of schemes?
      4. How frequently does the child use the various schemes?
   B. Scheme use and generalization
      1. Which schemes does the child use spontaneously?
         a. Indiscriminate use of scheme with all objects (i.e., mouths all objects)
         b. Selective appropriate use of schemes (i.e., stirs with spoon)
         c. Generalization of schemes to similar objects (i.e., opens all things with doors, lids)
      2. Scheme use after modeling by facilitator
         a. What higher-level schemes can be instigated through modeling?
         b. What prompting is necessary (vocal, gestural)?
   C. Linking of schemes
      1. What behaviors demonstrate linking of schemes in a related sequence (filling a pitcher, pouring into a cup, then pretending to drink)?
      2. What events demonstrate linking of schemes in representational "script" play (child fixes dinner, serves it, washes dishes, and goes to bed)?

INTERVENTION IMPLICATIONS

The Piagetian concept of a schema is defined as a basic unit of knowledge, a mental structure that represents both the internal and external aspects of the child's world (Ginsburg & Opper, 1988). Piaget (1962) relates schemes to physical behaviors, mental images, or complex belief systems. With the young infant, physical behaviors or actions predominate, with a simultaneous development of mental imagery. *The goal for intervention is to increase the type and range of schemes used by the child in a functional manner.*

Developing Higher-Level Types and Ranges of Schemes

Early schemes of looking, grasping, and mouthing transition into more complex schemes as the child develops more differentiated fine motor skills along with goal-directed behaviors. The key to facilitation is to observe the child and see what schemes the child uses and what toys interest the child and then provide objects that allow the child to use the schemes within his or her repertoire and modify those schemes into higher-level behaviors. The facilitator encourages the child to practice a scheme or action by imitating the action the child is performing. He or she can help the child generalize the scheme by introducing new situations or objects where the scheme can be used. The facilitator can stimulate the use of new schemes by modeling, and, if the child does not imitate the action, by prompting or shaping the child.

Parents use this sequence of activities quite naturally. For example, the child may begin banging on the floor with his or her hand. The parent may then bang on the coffee table, inviting the child to do the same. The parent may then bang on a squeak toy, eliciting a noise with the action. If the child imitates the parent, he or she may then squeeze the squeak toy, demonstrating a new action. If the child does not imitate the behavior, the parent may physically assist the child through the action.

The same type of sequence is useful in intervention with the child with disabilities. The facilitator must be creative to think of the various ways the child's actions can be practiced in different situations. *The facilitator also should make sure that the schemes that are modeled are at only a slightly higher level than those the child exhibits.* An infant, for example, who is just banging and shaking is not ready to turn dials on a pop-up box.

DEVELOPMENTAL LEVEL

- Focus on action performed by objects (banging, shaking) (3–6 months)

INTERVENTION GUIDELINES

Observe what the infant is watching. When the infant moves, imitate the child's actions. Model different simple actions with toys that make interesting sights and sounds. Provide tactile materials for the child to explore, such as a wet sponge, soft stuffed animals, foam-rubber balls, and so forth. For children with visual impairments, the auditory, tactile, and spatial characteristics of objects must be emphasized so that the child can find the objects. If the child cannot see a model, physical prompting is appropriate and can be eliminated as the child begins to use appropriate actions with objects spontaneously. The child with physical impairments may also need additional assistance if actions are not able to be performed independently. Bells or other types of noisemakers also can be attached to ankles or wrists for a few minutes at a time so that the child can cause the bells to jangle when movements are made. The child then learns to associate his or her movements with a desired result. It is important to attach objects for only a few minutes, as the child satiates to the sound, and the intent of having the child initiate and repeat actions in order to gain a pleasurable response is lost.

PLAY MATERIALS AND OPPORTUNITIES

Bright or shiny objects or materials, noisy toys such as rattles, and objects that move attract the child's interest. Fancy toys are not necessary. The child may be just as intrigued with a shiny piece of foil paper as with a sophisticated toy. In fact, the foil paper probably has more uses. The child can scratch it, wad it up, wave it, and bang on it, among other things. Mobiles and other toys that can be swiped, jabbed, or slapped are also fun and can be either purchased or made. Homemade mobiles have the advantage of being less expensive and easy to modify so that the infant has a new challenge occasionally. Mobiles can be made from soft materials (e.g., cloth, yarn), shiny materials (e.g., aluminum pie pans), hard materials (e.g., decorated clothespins), or sound-producing materials (e.g., jingle bells).

DEVELOPMENTAL LEVEL

> - Begins to explore characteristics of objects
> - Range of schemes expands (e.g., pulling, turning, poking, tearing) (6–9 months)

INTERVENTION GUIDELINES

The infant's fine motor skills develop in tandem with cognitive skills in the typically developing baby. This may not be true of the child with disabilities. Depending on the child's abilities, different types of playthings are needed. Provide a range of materials to allow the infant to try new actions. The infant at this level attempts to pull levers or handles, turn lids, poke his or her fingers into holes, and figure out how to get an observed effect to occur again. *Allow the child to explore the toys or materials before demonstrating the actions that can be performed.* Let the child attempt actions without assistance to encourage problem-solving. *Assist only after a sufficient wait time.* For the child with visual or motor impairments, use toys that have large, easily moveable pieces.

PLAY MATERIALS AND OPPORTUNITIES

Objects that move, make sound, or have an interesting texture or smell encourage exploration. Again, foil, tissue, or cellophane paper may incite exuberant actions. In addition, toys that have moving parts (e.g., clear plastic balls with spinners inside) stimulate the child to examine and experiment with toys in order to create a desired action. The Pat Mat, with water and "swimming" fish inside, is also fun for infants to create waves and sloshing noises. Musical toys or cause-and-effect toys with handles the child pulls to create music or dancing characters are also fascinating.

DEVELOPMENTAL LEVEL

> - Begins to combine objects in relational play (e.g., objects in a container) (8–9 months)

INTERVENTION GUIDELINES

Adults should provide objects that can be combined and model appropriate actions. The child is now beginning to see how specific characteristics of objects can be related to the characteristics of other objects (e.g., a spoon makes a noise when pounded on a table, two blocks can be banged together, an object can be dropped into a can). This is significant as it demonstrates not only that the child is seeing the effect of his or her actions, but also that by exploring and combining objects in his or her environment, even more interesting effects can be realized. Pots and pans with spoons are a favorite. For children whose motor skills do not allow them to use their hands in such controlled motions, the adult can use larger objects or assist in the movement, so the child can experience the pleasure of making noise and causing things to happen. The child might be seated in a highchair with a large wooden spoon to bang on the tray table or placed on his or her side, lying so that his or her hands may be brought together at midline with a toy in each.

PLAY MATERIALS AND OPPORTUNITIES

Any small items that the child can hold in his or her hands to combine are fun: blocks, spoons, the Johnson & Johnson clear plastic spinning balls and plastic container, and other types of containers into which objects can be dropped. Musical instruments that require banging are also enticing.

DEVELOPMENTAL LEVEL

- Begins to see the relation between complex actions and consequences (opening doors, putting on lids)
- Differential use of schemes according to the toy played with, functional use of toys (e.g., pushes cars, throws balls)
    (9–12 months)

INTERVENTION GUIDELINES

Learning about Cause and Effect

Provide cause-and-effect toys (i.e., toys that allow the child to see something happen when an action is performed). For the child with visual or motor difficulties, the toy may need to be modified. A large switch may be attached to most battery-operated toys to enable the child to activate the toy with only light pressure on the switch pad. Infants with visual impairments may learn cause-and-effect relationships more quickly if sound and movement are the results of their efforts. For instance, rattles or noisemakers may be added to mobiles so the child can reach or kick. Pop-up toys may be modified to add a tactile and visual element to the buttons and knobs, so the child can more easily recognize the activating devices. *Adjust the type and amount of sensory input the child receives from a toy to match the level that brings the child the most pleasure.* For instance, a jack-in-the-box that pops up with a bang when a button is pushed may startle some infants and discourage their exploration of the toy. Other infants find this intense stimulation humorous.

Discovering Functional Uses of Objects

Infants discover the functional use of objects through exploration and use of toys and materials that have a specific purpose (e.g, spoons, cups, combs, everyday articles). The young infant is just beginning to associate objects with functions. A spoon or cup acquires a specific meaning and use. Everyday objects, such as diapers, washcloths, and telephones, are associated with certain parts of the body and specific actions. *Allowing the child to explore and manipulate objects as they are being used functionally is important.* For example, when washing the child's face, the parent or caregiver can let the child play with the cloth, touch it to his or her face, and play peekaboo. Such investigation encourages the child to develop early scheme and classification differentiations (i.e., which actions work with which objects, which objects are used for which purposes).

PLAY MATERIALS AND OPPORTUNITIES

Toys that have moving parts or are easily activated are appropriate for a child at this level. Toys with lids or doors that open, toys that produce sounds when squeezed or hit, and cloth books with pages that turn provide means for the

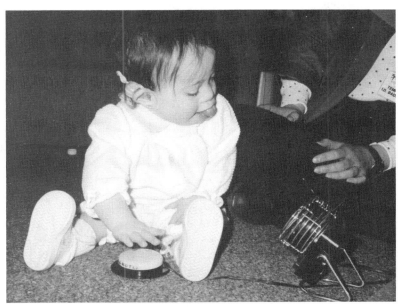

Switch-activated toys can be used to elicit cause-and-effect responses.

infant to begin to see the relationship between actions and consequences. Different types of "busy boxes," activity centers, or shape sorters requiring various actions are also absorbing.

All objects that have functional uses can also be explored. Objects that are part of the child's everyday life are most meaningful to him or her. Other toys, such as balls, plastic hammers, and plastic pots with lids, are fun for cause-and-effect play and also teach the child the functional use of objects.

• Acts on objects with a variety of schemes   (12 months +)

DEVELOPMENTAL LEVEL

INTERVENTION GUIDELINES

As the child develops a range of actions, he or she also learns how these actions can be used on different objects. The child can differentiate and apply different schemes to different objects, explore objects to determine their effects, and use multiple actions on a given object. The parent, caregiver, or early interventionist may demonstrate how toys and materials can be used in many ways. A pencil can mark on paper, make noise against the side of a glass, or be dropped into a container. Paper can be folded, torn, crumpled, or marked. A sponge (wet or dry) may be wiped on the face, squeezed, waved, pressed, and poked.

After observing the child's spontaneous explorations, the adult can model a new action with the object, material, or toy. For the child who repeats primarily one scheme, such as dropping or throwing, the adult may help the child to revise his or her actions by adding another element, such as a receptacle, so the child is dropping or throwing an object "into" a contained space. (See discussion of Imitation on pp. 140–151.) If the child is dropping a spoon off his or her highchair, an empty cup could be added to the tray, and stirring in the cup could be modeled. At the changing table, the infant can play with a cloth diaper. Mother can play peekaboo, wrap an object in the diaper for the baby to find, wrap the diaper on a doll, or just let the infant wave and shake the diaper. *The ability to use multiple actions on objects is an important element of problem-solving and should be encouraged through modeling and orchestration of the environment to require the use of diverse actions by the child.*

PLAY MATERIALS AND OPPORTUNITIES

Although any toy, material, or object can be used in multiple ways, certain toys lend themselves to multiple uses in more obvious ways. Toys that have parts that move in different ways (e.g., pop-up boxes that are activated through turning, sliding, pressing) encourage multiple approaches to use. Toys with doors, slides, wheels, lids, handles, openings, levers, and other operational devices are fun for children to explore and manipulate. However, it is important to keep in mind that multiple actions can be incorporated into any play activity. For instance, if the child is dropping blocks into a container, simply placing a piece of paper over the top of the container changes the actions required of the child. The child may drop a block onto the paper and see what happens, may remove the paper to continue the dropping game, may remove the paper and then replace it in imitation of the adult, or may start to play with the paper instead. In any case, the child has elaborated on the simple scheme of dropping.

DEVELOPMENTAL LEVEL

> - Links schemes in simple combinations (puts person in car and pushes car)
>
>   (12–15 months)

INTERVENTION GUIDELINES

The ability to link schemes is an important step for the child, indicating a burgeoning ability to link ideas and express them through related actions. Linking of ideas is related to language development as well as to cognitive development, as the child begins to express the ideas demonstrated through actions. The adult can assist the child who does not yet connect actions by modeling a two-step sequence of play for the child (e.g., stirring in cup, then drinking; stacking blocks, then knocking down). The infant benefits from both repetition of the same action, or practicing, and combining simple actions, or extending the idea sequence related to an object. As the adult observes the infant practicing an action, a logical "next step" can be added to the play. For example, if the child is holding his or her baby doll, the adult might model kissing the baby or holding a bottle to the baby's mouth. In the tub, if the child is playing with a toy boat, the parent might give the child a miniature doll or object to put in the boat and push around the tub. *It is then important to let the child repeat this sequence in practice play without interjecting another activity or step.*

PLAY MATERIALS AND OPPORTUNITIES

Linking of actions can be encouraged with any toys and materials. Fun centers with doors, chutes, spinners, slots, and so forth stimulate the child to follow a sequence of actions. Items and opportunities suggested on page 155 are also appropriate for children at this developmental level.

• Links multischeme combinations into a meaningful sequence (puts paste on toothbrush, puts cap on tube, brushes baby's teeth) (24–36 months)

The child at this level can think about a longer sequence of actions. If fine motor skills have developed at a commensurate level, the child is able to chain actions together with a variety of sophisticated schemes. The child is also able to engage in representational play with dolls, trucks, telephones, plastic animals, and so forth. *The adult may facilitate the child's expansion of ideas and linking of schemes by providing materials that require a sequence of actions.* For instance, if the child is holding a baby doll and the parent hands him or her a comb, the child is encouraged to comb the baby's hair, a simple, one-step action. However, if curlers, a brush, ribbons, and a hat are laid out, the child is motivated to relate some or all of these objects to the doll, requiring a sequence of ideas and actions related to fixing the doll's hair. If the child does not spontaneously use the materials, the adult might also play with a doll and model a sequence of events. While playing with the child in the tub, for instance, the mother might say, "My baby's hair is dirty," modeling putting shampoo on the doll's hair, washing it, and rinsing it with a cup of water. The child will inevitably want to repeat this sequence (particularly the part with the shampoo!), and additional steps of washing the doll and drying it can be added if the child is ready. When a sequence like this is modeled once or twice, the child frequently initiates the sequence spontaneously at the next opportunity.

Linking of ideas and actions is particularly important for children with disabilities, as this is frequently a limitation of their play. *The adult must observe the number and type of actions the child sequences in a given situation and add another step to the sequence.* This should be done across all of the child's play activities, whether playing with manipulatives (e.g., clay, puzzles), blocks, dolls, or gross motor equipment. Lengthening the child's idea progressions is relevant to language production and problem-solving skills such as analyzing, synthesizing, and planning. *The adult can also use language to encourage the lengthening of idea and action sequences.* For example, the adult could say, "Your baby looks cold. What can we do to warm her up?" (have a blanket and jacket visible) or, "I have a cookie cutter. Do you want to use it with your clay?"

Materials and opportunities suggested on page 135 are appropriate, with the addition of common everyday sequences. Eating, bathing, and dressing incorporate sequences the child can be involved in directing, both on him- or herself and on dolls.

EXAMPLE

Derrick G., a 4-year-old, was enrolled in a preschool program that integrated children with developmental delays. Derrick was capable of playing with the same toys as the other children, but his play was limited to repetition of one- to two-step sequences. While other children were acting out complex sequences in the house or other play areas, Derrick observed and imitated a segment of what he saw the other children do (e.g., stirring in a pot, pushing a truck, stacking blocks). He did not vary his actions on objects or extend his play sequences beyond two steps. Derrick's language was limited to one- to two-word sentences as well. Motorically, Derrick was capable of adaptive movement throughout the preschool room, although low tone and delayed movement patterns influenced the accuracy and fluidity of his movements. Derrick's fine motor skills were also influenced by his low tone, requiring deliberative effort and extra support on wrists or elbows. The team felt that he had the basic cognitive and motor skills to extend his play sequences to three or four steps.

The team then examined how they could incorporate sequence extensions into the various aspects of their play curriculum. The day began with a variety of centers with tactile fine and gross motor experiences. Children moved from center to center as they wished, with the adults facilitating their play at each area. The theme for the week was "exploring," with the book *Henry the Explorer* by Mark Taylor (1966) as the basis for setting up play centers. Footprints around the room led to different play centers. In the sand table, "treasures" were hidden for the children to excavate. An art area had materials to draw, play with clay, cut out pictures of animals, and make telescopes out of paper towel rolls. An obstacle course was set up so the children could climb a "mountain" with a rope, slide down a sliding board, cross a "river" of large blocks, and crawl through a "cave" and under a hanging jungle of crêpe paper. A representational playtime was next in the play schedule. Children could choose to play in the traditional house area; a play area that was set up with jungle animals, a tent, and props; or an area with miniature plastic animals and dolls. Following these activities, the morning ended with the children choosing from quiet endeavors, such as listening to an adventure story that was on tape or read by the teacher, playing games at the computer, or doing various table activities.

The team discussed extending Derrick's play sequences during each of these times of the morning. At the same time, the speech-language therapist made recommendations about incorporating labels, action words, and descriptions into the play and encouraging Derrick to expand the pragmatic elements of communication to include providing information to a peer and commenting on his actions. Turn-taking with peers was also desired, and suggestions were made about integrating peers into Derrick's play activities.

At the "treasure" table, various digging tools were provided. The teacher added a small pail of water so the "treasures" could be washed, a towel to dry them off, and a box in which to put the treasure. Derrick was excited about digging up a ring from the sand and continued to dig. The teacher commented that the ring looked dirty and maybe it needed to be washed. Derrick put the ring in the bucket and started to put it back in the sand when the teacher handed him a towel. When Derrick said, "Clean," his teacher commented, "Yes, it is clean. Let's dry it and put it in a special box." As he dried it, she held up the small box. Derrick put the ring in the box. After digging up another treasure, he spontaneously washed the item. He needed to have the teacher hand him the towel to remind him of the next step, but then looked for a box in which to put it. The teacher then asked a peer to help in the archeology dig. The teacher asked Derrick to help the peer. Derrick held up the bucket and said "Wash" after the peer found a plastic hat in the sand. He then gave the peer the box in which to put the hat.

After digging, washing, drying, and boxing (in varying sequences) for several more minutes, Derrick then followed the peer to the obstacle course. He started to follow him up the rope, but found it too difficult to coordinate his movements to pull himself up, so he stood and watched the peer instead. The aide came over and said, "Derrick, I need help. Hold on to my waist." She put his arms around her waist and hauled herself up with Derrick holding on. When they reached the top, the aide waited for Derrick to initiate another action. He finally decided to go down the sliding board. The aide followed, pointed to a peer, and said, "Eric is going across the river. I'm going to follow him." Derrick followed the aide, who was following Eric. The aide then moved to the side and pointed to the peer, and Derrick continued in his trail. Later, he returned to the rope climb and with assistance Derrick was again able to mount the hill. This time when he reached the top, he immediately went down the slide and then began to step on the blocks to cross the "river."

In the jungle camp, Derrick crawled in and out of the sleeping bag, came out of the tent, watched his peers for a while, went back into the tent and sleeping bag, came out, and cooked some food over the "fire." The teacher joined Derrick at the fire and said, "I'm hungry. Let's find something to cook." They took a can-opener out of a back pack and an empty can of corn. The teacher fastened the can-opener onto the side of the can and said, "I could use some help getting this open." She handed it to Derrick, who struggled to turn the handle. "That's good. Let's pour it in the pan." Derrick pretended to pour the corn into the pan, took a spoon, and stirred it around in the pan. The teacher handed him two plates and said, "Let's eat." Derrick stared at the plates for a minute, then pretended to put some corn on each one. The teacher then said, "Josh, are you hungry? Derrick is a good cook." As Josh came over to join them, the teacher took another can out of the bag and set it on the floor. She then moved away as Derrick again "opened" the can, poured it into the pan, stirred it, and served it to Josh.

The team was able to incorporate longer scheme sequences into each play activity that Derrick selected. By problem-solving as a team, they were able to integrate other developmental needs as well. Derrick was able, with modeling and encouragement, to extend his sequences to three to four steps. Although this did not occur spontaneously, with continued efforts of a similar nature, Derrick's play sequences will lengthen without rehearsal.

DEVELOPMENTAL LEVEL

- Links schemes into complex script
  (36–42 months)

INTERVENTION GUIDELINES

Once the child is capable of linking schemes in complex scripts, he or she can connect those sequences of actions into a "story" with a simple beginning, middle, and end. Role playing stories from favorite books or sequences from known activities (e.g., going to the grocery store) allows the child to put a series of events together in a meaningful progression. The adult may need to model a chain of events or prompt the child by asking, "What happens next?" In a pre-school class, a series of scenarios can be enacted with a simple script. After the children have role played the scenario several times, they will be able to enact key scenes spontaneously with their own creative interpretations, modifications, and language. (See also the discussions of Imitation on pp. 140–151 and Symbolic Representational play on pp. 131–140.)

Ordering Events from Books

Reading books to children is not only pleasurable, but also encourages children to think about the events in stories in order. Having the child retell stories in their own words or "read" books to an adult is also a good way of helping children to recall a series of events. Talking about the child's day and what is going to happen next also encourages the child to think about events in time.

PLAY MATERIALS AND OPPORTUNITIES

Props are essential for dramatic story play. Clothing items that can be used for costumes (e.g., hats, capes, scarves, belts, jackets, shoes, purses), lunch boxes, as well as specific props for scenes in distinct settings, can be used. Cardboard boxes can be used for multiple purposes, as can sticks, blocks, scarves, tables, chairs, wheels, and levers. Household items, such as paper towel rolls, plastic bowls, tools, and stepladders can serve multiple purposes in play.

Books

Books are a source of many story lines and can serve as inspiration for scripts and props. Choose books with simple plots that can be broken down into uncomplicated sequences of action.

OBSERVATION GUIDELINES FOR COGNITIVE DEVELOPMENT: SYMBOLIC AND REPRESENTATIONAL PLAY

IV. Symbolic and Representational Play
   A. Symbolic object use
      1. To what degree is the child capable of abstracting a concept—or using one object to represent another?
         a. Real objects needed for activity
         b. Realistic object may substitute for real object
         c. Unrealistic item may be substituted for real object
         d. Can pretend an object exists without a prop
   B. Symbolic play roles
      1. What roles is the child capable of assuming in representational play?
      2. Toward whom or what are the child's pretend actions directed?
         a. Self
         b. Object or toy (baby doll)
         c. Another adult
      3. How does the child demonstrate understanding of behaviors important to specific roles that he or she assumes (gas station attendant pumping gas with hose)?
      4. To what degree can the child direct the play scenario without being a player or role taker (has toy soldiers fighting, etc.)?
      5. When the child is directing actors (person, doll, puppet, or symbolic substitute for actor) in scenarios, how does he or she indicate understanding of the behaviors of the actors (has store clerk doll act out stocking the shelves, checking out groceries)?
      6. What level of role interaction is demonstrated in the child's play (having doll assume more than one role at a time, such as mother and wife)?

INTERVENTION IMPLICATIONS

Representational, or dramatic, play becomes an increasingly rich arena for intervention as the child matures. By responding to the child's initiations, the facilitator has an opportunity to build on the child's skills, expanding cognitive and language concepts inherent in the child's play. Again, the adult's role is one of facilitation through arrangement of the environment, stimulation of play sequences, and motivation of language production.

For the young child who is just beginning to represent activities in his or her world, the environment should include objects that are real or very similar to the real life objects. For the older child, however, realistic objects may inhibit the imagination (Musselwhite, 1986). The adult should provide, suggest, or help the child who is ready for more symbolic play to find or make props and materials that are developmentally and culturally relevant to the child's play interests.

Development in Other Areas

Within the context of representational play, many other areas of cognitive, social-emotional, communication and language, and sensorimotor development can be fostered. Within the cognitive area, scheme use and generalization, problem-solving, discrimination/classification, one-to-one correspondence, and sequencing skills can be stimulated. Language content, form, and usage (Bloom & Lahey, 1978) can also be advanced during representational play. As the adult observes the child's play, elaborations and extensions of these cognitive and language areas can be incorporated.

Promotion of Social Interaction

The social opportunities presented in dramatic play are infinite. Depending on their developmental level, children may observe, play parallel to, or engage other children in play activities. Proximity does not guarantee interaction among children (Brophy & Stone-Zukowski, 1984; Gresham, 1981; MacDonald & Gillette, 1984). The types of toys and materials needed for representational play *do* seem to promote social interaction, both in inclusive and noninclusive preschool settings, with inclusive settings showing the highest degree of social interaction (Martin, Brady, & Williams, 1991).

The adult promotes social interactions at the child's level by providing toys and materials that prompt social interaction (i.e., those that are most interesting when two or more children are involved) (e.g., telephones); by using language to arouse interest in the peer (e.g., "James needs a stop sign on his road"); by establishing a joint referent and encouraging turn-taking; or by structuring situations so that interactions occur within the representational play (e.g., "Who wants to be the cashier and who wants to be the shopper?")

Expression of Emotional Concerns

For the child with emotional concerns, dramatic or representational play may provide a safe arena for expression of emotional issues, which may then be responded to by the facilitator or therapist. The adult then plays the role of responding to, interpreting, and assisting the child in gaining mastery over the feelings that are interfering with daily functioning. (See Chapter 9 for more information on intervention related to social-emotional development.)

Modification of the Environment To Accommodate Sensorimotor Impairments

For children with visual or motor difficulties, representational play may be more difficult, as sensory limitations may prohibit spontaneous involvement. For these children, adaptations may be needed to enable the child to interact with toys, materials, and peers. Positioning equipment, adaptive switches, sensory adjustments, size, color, or other enhancements or alterations may be needed.

DEVELOPMENTAL LEVEL

- Simple pretend play directed toward self (eating, sleeping) (12–16 months)

INTERVENTION GUIDELINES

Provide the child with simple household objects and materials. The parent or facilitator can model the use of the objects or materials. For example, during bathtime, the parent can have two washcloths, giving one to the infant and keeping one for him- or herself. The parent can pretend to wash his or her face, hands, and body. When taking clothes out of the dryer, the parent can hand the child a washcloth to see if he or she pretends to wash his or her face. The parent can also give the child a comb when combing his or her own hair. The same is true of other events during the day. Brushing teeth, reading a book, and fixing dinner (give the child a pan and spoon) provide opportunities for the child to observe an action and then perform that action or some aspect of the action. *The facilitator's role is to create the opportunity for an everyday activity to become a "game," where the activity is initiated by the child or modeled for the child so that the activity will be imitated.* Keeping a small box full of simple objects (e.g., toothbrush, comb, washcloth, bottle) that is easily accessible to the child encourages the child to explore the use of these objects independently.

Any objects that are found around the house that the child uses or sees being used by others can stimulate early representational play. Cups, spoons, bowls, pans, blankets, pillows, washcloths, combs, brushes, and so forth encourage pretend play. Real objects rather than facsimiles are best at this developmental level.

PLAY MATERIALS AND OPPORTUNITIES

DEVELOPMENTAL LEVEL

- Can focus pretend play on animate and inanimate objects and others
- Combines simple schemes in acting out familiar activity
  (12–18 months)

Use of toys that promote both problem-solving and peer interaction is recommended.

INTERVENTION GUIDELINES

Again, props are important, but now the child is able to focus an activity on another person or character. The same activities that the child was performing on him- or herself are now able to be performed on others. The parent or facilitator provides the props, watches what the child does with the props, and follows the child's lead. After imitating the child, the parent or facilitator can then model performing an additional activity with the doll. For example, if the child has put a spoon to the doll's mouth, the parent might also feed the baby (with a second spoon) or a second baby. After the child repeats the feeding activity several times, the facilitator could introduce a bowl to dip the spoon into before feeding the baby or a cup to give the baby a drink. By adding a bowl to the spoon, the child is adding one scheme to the activity; by adding a cup, with the other hand, a different scheme is being substituted, and the concept of "feeding" is being expanded to include a new action. Both types of expansions enable the child to see and experience a higher level of thinking and performing. *The props should be familiar to the child and the actions performed on the dolls or characters should be simple so the child can more easily relate objects and use them functionally.*

PLAY MATERIALS AND OPPORTUNITIES

Dolls and stuffed animals are now incorporated into play, along with a variety of objects used daily. These include soap, washcloths, toothbrushes, toothpaste, bowls, spoons, pillows, and blankets.

DEVELOPMENTAL LEVEL

- Increased use of nonrealistic objects in pretending (similar to real)
- Can have inanimate objects perform actions (doll washes self)
    (18–24 months)

INTERVENTION GUIDELINES

As the child becomes more immersed in representational play, the facilitator will find opportunities to substitute nonrealistic, but similar, objects for their realistic counterparts. For example, if the child is stirring with a spoon, the facilitator might substitute a pencil to stir with in his or her own bowl. The pencil may then be offered to the child to see if he or she wants to use it as a substitute. The same might be done with a napkin for a doll blanket or a block for a plastic hot dog. *The facilitator should begin substituting with an object that is similar in shape to the more realistic prop.* If the child is engrossed in the play and observes the facilitator using the object within a play context, he or she is better able to relate the two objects and make the transition from use of real to unreal objects within his or her imagination.

DEVELOPMENTAL LEVEL

- Can use more abstract representation of object in play
- Uses multischeme combinations (feed doll with bottle, pat it on the back, put it to bed)
    (24–36 months)

The child can now use objects that do not look similar to the real object. A banana can substitute for a telephone or a piece of paper can be a lid for a pot. The facilitator can foster imaginative thinking by substituting unlike objects for necessary props in the scenario. With a 24-month-old, this ploy is best done only once or twice within a sequence. A block may be substituted for a baby bottle and later a book may become a pillow. One of the objects related in play should remain realistic. For example, it is demanding a great deal to expect a 24-month-old to substitute a pillow wrapped in a blanket for a doll and a block for a bottle at the same time.

As the child gets older and becomes more familiar with dramatic play and the use of props, the facilitator can incorporate problem-solving into the play. By removing one of the necessary props before play begins, the facilitator can set the stage for the child to try to determine what else could be used for a spoon, plate, towel, and so forth.

Modeling Scenario Sequences

Modeling of scenario sequences is another important facilitation technique. The team may incorporate a variety of cognitive, language and communication, sensorimotor, and social-emotional skills into play sequences. There are two primary ways of building scenarios. One is to use the scenarios initiated by the child and model additional creative pieces to lengthen the type and number of events linked together. If, for example, the child is playing a superhero and is "flying" around in a cape, the facilitator can add a person who needs to be rescued from a high place (on a chair) or can be the "bad guy" and get captured. The idea is to add a new element to the play scenario. The child typically continues to add this new piece to future role enactments.

The second type of scenario building is done first by the facilitator. The facilitator may role play baking a cake, getting groceries, putting gas in the car, or another common sequence. For the younger child, the steps of the sequence must be familiar and limited to two to three steps. The older child can handle longer, more imaginary sequences associated with activities he or she has seen or experienced and stories he or she has heard.

Props and materials for the child's representational play are household items and commonly seen materials, such as cooking and cleaning utensils, rakes, mowers, shovels, grocery carts, baby paraphernalia, superhero or cultural hero props, and props from sequences of favorite activities or stories. Miniature kitchen sets and other household replicas, such as a washer and dryer, begin to hold interest for the child at this level. Having the props to go with the sets, such as dishes, pans, fake food, or clothing, is important.

INTERVENTION GUIDELINES

PLAY MATERIALS AND OPPORTUNITIES

DEVELOPMENTAL LEVEL

- Can use imaginary objects in play
- Acts out sequences with miniature dolls (in house, garage, airport, etc.)
      (36–42 months)

INTERVENTION GUIDELINES

Now, the child can also pretend without props. He or she can pretend to wear hats or coats, pretend to perform activities (e.g., shovel or wash) with only the actions, or even pretend that objects are different sizes or colors. The facilitator can assist by modeling or suggesting an action or pretending to do something with an imaginary object. The action or object should be familiar to the child. The actions can be inserted into the context of the dramatization of a play sequence initiated by the child or modeled by the adult.

Role Play

The child is also capable of role play with miniature dolls assuming various roles. The facilitator should give the child opportunities to act out sequences with miniature dolls. The sequences can be from known stories (e.g., *Hansel and Gretel*) or familiar activities (e.g., getting groceries, watching television, going to bed). *The miniatures used should be culturally and socially relevant to the child and able to be expanded to include settings and activities that may be new to the child*, such as the airport and flying. The child can use any scenario that he has seen (recently or through books, movies, and television). The facilitator can assume the character of one of the small figures and follow the child's lead in the action and interaction. As with the facilitator's role in representational play directed at self, others, and larger dolls, the child leads, with the facilitator extending the child's ideas through modeling actions and encouraging language.

PLAY MATERIALS AND OPPORTUNITIES

There are numerous miniature settings and characters on the market, from dollhouses and farms to grocery stores, beauty shops, garages, airports, zoos, space stations, and towns. In addition, scenes can be constructed from pictures pasted on shoe boxes, with miniature characters added from other settings. For instance, for the Native American child who lives on a reservation, pictures of a hogan, or native house, could be pasted on boxes with local plants and animals drawn on as well. Similar scenes can be constructed to fit any environment or cultural situation.

Superhero character dolls, such as the Ninja Turtles, Spiderman, Superman, the Ghostbusters, G.I. Joe, and other popular characters are frequently favorites of young children. If children relate more to these type of characters that they do to the mother, father, and baby characters in the dollhouse, the facilitator should incorporate these characters into the dramatic play alternatives.

EXAMPLE

Sammy C. was a 5-year-old who attended an inclusive preschool program. He came every day on the bus from the local Indian reservation where he lived with his mother, grandmother, uncle, and 3-year-old sister. Sammy, who had been diagnosed with cerebral palsy, used a wheelchair and had limited use of his hands. He spoke in sentences that were intelligible when the context was evident. He was able to predict events in a story and act out a part when involved in a role play with his peers. Due to his fine motor limitations, Sammy was unable to sequence a series of schemes in his role play. His team met to discuss how to encourage his development through higher-level play.

The occupational therapist, who consulted with the preschool, recommended incorporating role play with miniature characters. Velcro straps could be made to go around Sammy's hands and allow him to hold the figures. The teacher said she would check with Sammy's family to see if they had any objections to using miniature dolls in play. She said that she, Sammy, and some of the other children would make a diorama during one of the center times. Sammy could direct what was needed and the other children could cut, help him paste, and color on the box. The speech-language therapist recommended vocabulary that could be included and suggested trying to expand his sentence length by adding adjectives related to size and other comparisons and classifications. She suggested talking to the family about any special objects that could be included in the play. When the diorama was completed, it would be set up as a center, and Sammy and the children could play with it singly or in pairs. Social interaction was a strength for Sammy, and the others in the class enjoyed assisting him in his play.

When the plan was implemented, Sammy chose to make a scene of the area near his home. They needed a river, high plateaus, scrub brush, wild flowers, birds, the tribal center, and the homes around the village. Sammy chose to include a tribal healer and his family. They found figures from other play sets, and, with the help of several children, found pictures in magazines to cut out, and then colored several others. Sammy narrated what was needed, described the colors, sizes, and relationships among the various elements, and helped press the pictures onto the diorama. The teacher facilitated the process by commenting, suggesting, asking problem-solving questions, and supporting social interchange among the children. He and the other children were quite proud of their final product. The diorama was set up at a level to accommodate Sammy's wheelchair. Sammy was anxious to try the new play area. He had the tribal healer perform a ceremony in the village. The teacher directed one of the dolls, who was ill. She asked the healer to make her well. The healer placed a small amulet on the doll. Then everyone had a celebration. The teacher then invited another child to replace her at the diorama, and Sammy repeated the sequence with this new partner. As he coached the peer in the elements of the action, the teacher could hear Sammy repeating the "lines" from the story that she had used as well as his own.

DEVELOPMENTAL LEVEL

- Plans out pretend situations in advance, organizing who and what are needed for role play
- Events in play are sequenced into scenario that tells a story
  (36–48 months)

INTERVENTION GUIDELINES

The child at this dramatic play level has moved to being able to act out more than a sequence. He or she can now act out a whole story with a beginning, middle, and end. The child can participate in interaction with other children playing different roles. The child has a much broader repertoire of knowledge and experience to draw on and is, thus, able to actively plan and carry out a complex series of events. The facilitator can assist by helping to generate ideas for dramatic play, making props available, and assisting children in determining what they need to make or do to carry out their intended story. Children can not only act out known stories, but they can also make up simple stories of their own. The goal is to encourage the child to plan, problem-solve, and include a logical sequence in role-play events.

PLAY MATERIALS AND OPPORTUNITIES

Props now can include everyday objects plus more unconventional items found in stories. Objects can be used for multiple purposes. Sticks can be spoons or magic wands, a Slinky can be a worm or a tail, or a pan can be a treasure chest or a hat. Props can be made from paper, cloth, or any other junk materials, as children can now more fully use their imaginations.

DEVELOPMENTAL LEVEL

- Can make dolls carry out several activities or roles
- Creates imaginary characters
- Can direct actions of two dolls, making them interact within two roles
  (42 months +)

INTERVENTION GUIDELINES

Children typically play with toys in a repetitive way. Superhero characters are continuously made to fight, mom dolls feed baby dolls, and so forth. The facilitator can promote story development by suggesting or modeling a variation in the characters' activities with each other. The facilitator can suggest (through his or her doll), for instance, that the mom doll (who is taking care of the baby doll) has to go to work, thereby assigning her a new role. The Ninja Turtle dolls can be friends eating pizza together and warriors fighting the "bad guys." *By talking through the mouthpiece of different characters, the facilitator can influence the roles and activities of the different characters. The facilitator must keep in mind culturally relevant characters, actions, and language for each child.*

The child's imagination is now ready for creative productions. A child can remember, sequence, reorganize, vary roles, and problem-solve. All the facilitator must do is provide a character, a setting, or props (or build in the children's own characters and props) and then enlist children's ideas for a story. Group stories can be written and acted out, favorite stories can be updated and modified to fit in the children's ideas, and free-play can be enhanced by the mere addition of interesting settings or props.

PLAY MATERIALS AND OPPORTUNITIES

Materials and opportunities suggested above and on page 136 are appropriate for the child at this level. In addition, the child can now play with smaller figures. Playmobil has figures and settings for almost every type of occupation and event, including camping and an operating room. Lego also has various adventure figures, including ships with pirates and castles with knights.

DEVELOPMENTAL LEVEL

- Organizes other children and props for role play
- Can direct actions of three dolls, making them interact
  (60 months +)

Again, providing the opportunity to act out various types of stories is important. Having a "prop box" available with an assortment of articles for use in dramatic play allows children to create their own stories. The leaders in the group organize the roles and sequence of action. The facilitator can provide ancillary suggestions, support, and props. Children of this developmental level are frequently more engaged in dramatic play without the adult assuming a role in the action. Depending on the language, motor, and emotional needs of the child, however, the facilitator may need to participate in a more involved way.

Enacting Unfamiliar Stories

The dramatizations can now be expanded into unfamiliar stories. The facilitator can read a story to the group and then help the children to find the props and talk about what they are going to act out first, second, and so forth. Re-enacting stories after reading a story gives the children a basis upon which to build their actions and language.

Miniature Doll Play

In miniature doll play, make several characters available to the child to encourage the development of character interaction and dual role assumption. The facilitator may still need to suggest actions involving interaction of all three characters.

Select storybooks that have simple plots and key props, such as *The Three Bears*. Books with emotionally relevant themes are also important to enable children to think about and come to terms with their anxieties through play. Stories about conflict, illness, divorce, being lost, being loved, and fears about specific things can be enacted in story lines. With the children, select or make props that are appropriate for the role play.

The miniature action characters mentioned on page 136 are appropriate here as well.

- Can direct dolls, where each doll plays more than one role (father and doctor, daughter and patient)
  (72 months +)

Both in dramatic play with other children and in play with action characters, the child is beginning to understand that a person can play multiple roles. The child can role play a mother, wife, and worker with another child who is a father, husband, and worker. Within each role, the child uses different props, different tones of voice, and different actions to demonstrate his or her understanding.

The facilitator may be able to observe and support where needed. Children at this level usually prefer to play with another child rather than an adult. The adult may facilitate by helping to create situations for the characters to enact or props to stimulate the imagination. For children at this level, props that are less realistic and have more imaginative possibilities are best. Cardboard boxes, blocks, toilet paper tubes, and ropes invite creative uses.

PLAY MATERIALS AND OPPORTUNITIES   Materials and opportunities suggested on pages 136 and 138 are appropriate for the child at this developmental level as well.

OBSERVATION GUIDELINES FOR COGNITIVE DEVELOPMENT: IMITATION

V. Imitation
   A. Level of imitation
       1. Simple visible gestures (child can observe his or her imitative actions, such as clapping hands)
       2. Simple invisible gestures (child cannot observe his or her imitative actions, such as patting top of head)
       3. Single scheme imitations using objects
       4. Complex imitations—sequence of schemes using gestures or objects (see also symbolic play)
       5. Imitation of problem-solving approaches
       6. Imitation of dramatic play sequences
           a. Familiar
           b. Unfamiliar
       7. Imitation of drawing
           a. Within child's repertoire
           b. Novel
   B. Timing of imitation
       1. Are the majority of imitations immediate (right after the model)?
       2. Are the majority of imitations delayed (after several elapsed seconds)?
       3. What examples of deferred imitation are seen (imitation after a period of elapsed time, such as Mom washing dishes)?
           a. Are deferred imitations replicated within the appropriate context?
           b. What behaviors denote deferred imitation in inappropriate or non-meaningful contexts?
   C. Turn-taking
       1. What type of imitative sequences or turn-taking play takes place?
           a. Physical movement or tactile play (bouncing, tickling)
           b. Vocal imitative play (vocalizations, words, rhymes)
           c. Imitative turn-taking with objects
           d. Imitative turn-taking in representational play
           e. Imitative turn-taking in structured games
       2. Does the child modify the turn-taking game by changing some aspect of the behavior?
       3. Does the child repeat a modification made by another person in the turn-taking?

Infants readily copy the behavior of others. Even babies who are only days old have been noted to imitate facial gestures and head movements (Meltzoff & Moore, 1977, 1989). Common actions within the babies' repertoires are those first imitated. Within the first 2 years of life, imitative abilities undergo considerable refinement. As the infant develops increased fine motor competence, he or she can imitate increasingly complex and unfamiliar behaviors with less approximation and more exact movements (Kaye & Marcus, 1981). By the second year, memory and cognitive abilities have increased to enable the child to imitate actions observed hours or days previously. The development of proficiency in imitation expedites the acquisition of cognitive, social-emotional, communication and language, and sensorimotor skills.

In the transdisciplinary play-based assessment, it is important to watch what the child does spontaneously and build on that foundation. The same is true in intervention. *It is important that the facilitator not model or demonstrate too quickly. After the child has initiated an activity and the facilitator has given the child time to explore and practice skills, imitation, modeling, and turn-taking are appropriate.* The child acquires new physical and mental schemes through his or her own experimentation and through observation and imitation of others. As the actions imitated become internalized, they are able to be produced without a model.

Bandura's Model of Observational Learning

Bandura's model of observational learning (1977, 1989) involves four separate processes. These include the following: 1) attentional processes, 2) retentional processes, 3) production processes, and 4) motivational processes. Each process is described briefly here.

Attentional Processes

Attentional processes determine how closely the child regards the actions of the model. Attentional processes are influenced by the characteristics of the model (e.g., how much the child likes or identifies with the model), by how interesting the child finds the model's behaviors, by the child's level of arousal or excitement, and by the child's expectations of what the model will do.

Retentional Processes

Retentional processes determine how well the child will remember the model's behavior. Retentional processes are influenced by how well the child can code the behaviors observed in memory and how well the child can mentally or physically rehearse the model's actions.

Production Processes

Production processes determine how well the child can reproduce the model's behavior. Production processes are heavily influenced by the complexity of the model's behavior, the physical and developmental competence of the child, and the child's facility in modifying his or her behaviors to match more closely that of the model.

Motivational Processes

Motivational processes determine how stimulated the child is to imitate the model. A critical element here is how reinforcing the behavior is to either the model or the child. If a model seems to really enjoy the behavior or if the model is reinforced for the behavior (e.g., an observed peer who is praised for a behavior by the teacher), the child observing the model is more likely to repeat the behavior. The child is also more likely to imitate a model who is respected or admired or a model who performs an action that is valued or receives a desired reward.

Skill Development Through Imitation

Imitation is critical for skill development in every domain: cognitive, social-emotional, communication and language, and sensorimotor. Adults who interact with the child can utilize Bandura's processes to increase the likelihood of the child imitating desired behaviors. *Capturing the child's attention and excitement, keeping actions at the child's level of understanding, assisting the child in producing specific behaviors, and providing incentives to the child for imitation increase the probability of imitation.*

One goal for young children in this subcategory is to improve their ability to imitate a model, first in time proximity to the model and later in deferred imitation. For many children with disabilities, learning to approximate a model is a slow process, requiring both attention, thinking, and physical skills. Children may not observe the model, may have difficulty remembering what they have seen, may have difficulty translating what they see into action, or may not be motivated to imitate behavior. Analyzing which of the observational learning processes is problematic is important for planning intervention.

Imitation can also serve as the first step in learning to take turns, another important goal for young children. Whether with physical movement, vocalizations, or objects in play, the child can learn to initiate, wait and watch others, and take another turn through an imitative pattern. It is important for the adult to imitate the child's actions as well as expect the child to imitate the adult's actions. An action that begins as an imitation can quickly become a turn-taking game. Learning to take turns is critical to the development of communication and social skills and is a foundation of learning for the cognitive and motor areas as well.

The parent or facilitator's role is to gauge the level of schemes the child can imitate, pace the action to be imitated to meet the child's needs, and ensure that imitative turn-taking is part of the play. After an imitative pattern is established, modifications can be incorporated to assist the child in adding new schemes to his or her repertoire and making longer play sequences.

DEVELOPMENTAL LEVEL

- Imitates vocalizations and actions that are part of his or her repertoire (4–8 months)

The facilitator observes and imitates the child's gestures and vocalizations. If the sounds and gestures are imitated immediately after the child produces them, the probability that the child will repeat them is increased. If the facilitator or parent initiates the sound or gesture, the stimulus should be one from the child's repertoire. For instance, the parent might shake a rattle and make an "ah-ah" sound because the child has been observed to wave his or her arms and make that sound. Gestural imitation is obviously related to early object use, and the reader is referred to that section (see p. 121) for a review. In order to get the child to produce vocalizations that can then be imitated by the adult, several techniques may be tried. Pairing interesting sights with an interesting sound, such as a noisemaking toy or a parent's face with a vocalization, frequently stimulates vocalization. Moving the child (rocking, swaying, bouncing) and giving tactile input through massage, tickling, or touching will also often result in the child producing vocalizations.

INTERVENTION GUIDELINES

Gestural imitation involves using toys that require those early schemes, identified under early object use—rattles, noisemakers, and so forth (see p. 123). Vocal imitation is stimulated by interesting sights and sounds as well as movement. The sights in which the young infant are most interested include the human face (Fantz, 1961), sharp contrasts such as black and white (Banks & Ginsberg, 1985), bright objects, and, after 2–3 months, specific colors (Adams, 1987). The child enjoys toys that incorporate these characteristics as well as sound and/or movement. Mobiles, squeak toys, tops, and music makers with moving parts produce vocalizations and gestures.

PLAY MATERIALS AND OPPORTUNITIES

DEVELOPMENTAL LEVEL

> • Imitates actions he or she can see performed that are in his or her repertoire
>   (6–9 months)

The facilitator or parent can now initiate vocalizations and have the infant imitate them. The vocalizations and gestures, however, still should be ones that the facilitator has seen or heard the infant produce. Having the child in a quiet, alert, and happy state enables the child to focus and attend, resulting in more interaction and turn-taking with sounds and gestures. *Demonstrating excitement and enthusiasm helps to capture the child's attention.* Using toys that capitalize on the child's strengths or interests also spurs attention. For instance, using a toy that spins bright colors when moved may motivate a child with visual impairments to imitate pushing the toy. Physical prompting or having the child "feel" the action, either by placing his or her hand on the adult's or by moving the child's hand through an action, also may encourage imitation.

INTERVENTION GUIDELINES

Toys that have previously captured the child's attention and interest prompt interaction with that toy and encourage memory for previous schemes used with the toy. Introducing new toys and materials that are easy to grasp and manipulate and produce interesting effects and sounds permits the infant to generalize developing skills and explore and modify existing patterns into new

PLAY MATERIALS AND OPPORTUNITIES

ones. Use toys that require the simple schemes in the child's repertoire, such as grasping, patting, and waving. For children with motor impairments, toys may need to be modified by adding Velcro or a simple switchpad that can be activated with a pat. For children with visual impairments, using lighted objects or bright, shiny objects may help them to notice the action being performed on the object. Toys and materials with different textures encourage scratching, crumpling, poking, and touching.

DEVELOPMENTAL LEVEL

- Imitates sounds and gestures not part of his or her repertoire (8–12 months)

INTERVENTION GUIDELINES

The child's repertoire of sounds and gestures can be greatly expanded following this stage, as the infant has the physical and mental abilities to imitate actions and sounds not previously in his or her repertoire. Using turn-taking games and toys requiring more complex schemes, the facilitator can model higher-level gestures. The facilitator may play movement games to music, incorporate problem-solving toys, such as pop-up boxes with different actions required to open the lids or doors, and demonstrate the functional use of objects, such as balls, combs, and trucks.

For the child with motor impairments, positioning is important to allow the child to manipulate objects most easily. Sufficient support in sitting or side-lying is needed. Place toys within the child's optimal visual range and use modifications (e.g., enlarge the handle on a lid) to enable the child to experience success in imitating the adult.

Sound Games

Sound imitation is becoming refined, and, toward the end of this period, the infant begins to form his or her first words. The parent or facilitator may name the objects with which the child is playing or toward which he or she is pointing. Emphasize words with sounds made with the lips, such as *mama, baby, blanket, bottle,* or *ball*. Sound games using all of the sounds are also fun and can be incorporated into tactile play, bathtime, or along with music or movement.

The adult can also pair the imitation of sounds or words with the actions being performed. For instance, pushing a truck and making a "brrrr" sound or saying, "Go" encourages the child not only to imitate sounds and actions jointly, but also assists the child in seeing the cognitive relationship between sounds or words and specific referents (i.e., an object or action).

PLAY MATERIALS AND OPPORTUNITIES

Toys requiring more complex actions and relational or functional use, such as everyday practical objects (e.g., balls, cars, toys with parts that open and close, elements that spin or turn, toys that require use of the index finger for poking), are good for prompting gestural imitation. Most of these toys can be paired with sounds, such as "pop," "brrr," or words such as "hi," on a toy telephone. Toys that combine sound and action, such as toys that say an animal sound or word when a part is turned, facilitate both gestural and vocal imitation.

• Imitates unseen patterns composed of familiar actions
(9–12 months)

As noted previously, imitative abilities are seen in newborns. However, these imitations are of an involuntary nature. The intent and ability to imitate emerges gradually. The infant is first able to imitate actions that he or she can see being performed. Now, the schemes for various movements and gestures are well integrated and the infant can perform actions that he or she cannot see. Wiggling the nose and blinking the eyes are "invisible gestures" (Piaget, 1952). The child has to be able to do motor planning without the benefit of sight to guide the movement. The facilitator can interject facial expressions and other invisible gestures into play. Facial expressions are particularly important as they are so closely related to demonstration of affect.

No particular toys are needed for the child to use unseen gestures; however, they can be incorporated into play with many different toys. Simple facial expressions, for instance, can be modeled by pretending to go to sleep or cry.

EXAMPLE

Yohe T. was a 20-month-old Japanese-American baby with developmental delays, who was being seen in a home-based infant program. Yohe was observed to sit unsupported but in a very curved posture due to low tone. He could bang and wave toys. He made primarily vowel sounds, but was beginning to make "raspberries." Yohe had a few rattles and a mobile in his crib, but few toys. His mother was quiet and gentle with him and responded quickly every time he cried. She held him while she did housework or left him on a blanket in the living room, where he liked to watch the television. The team observed Yohe in a play-based assessment at their center and also in his home. When they met with Mrs. T. she indicated she was most concerned about Yohe's limited play skills, lack of language, and inability to walk.

The team discussed Mrs. T.'s day with her family and generated ideas that she and her husband could incorporate into daily activities. Yohe was beginning to make sounds with his lips, so the team suggested making "raspberries," "ba-ba," and "ma-ma" sounds at various play times, pairing them with a toy car, a bottle, and baby and mommy in the mirror. "Mmm" could be incorporated into feeding time. Any time Yohe made a noise, Mrs. M. would imitate the sound, while at the same time getting down on his level so he could see her face. The team talked about using exaggerated sounds, expressions, and gestures to capture his attention and encourage imitation. Mrs. T. was very soft-spoken and typically refrained from showing intense reactions, but she practiced with Yohe and became very excited when he repeated her imitation of him.

The same approach was incorporated into play. Mrs. T. got one of her rice-cooking baskets and several of Yohe's rattles. She modeled dropping the rattle into the basket. She then handed one to Yohe and he also dropped it in the basket and then looked for it. This game was repeated several times, and then the lid was put on the basket. This became a new game: putting the lid on the basket. The team and Mrs. T. tried to think of all the items in and around the house that Yohe could use to manipulate and imitate new actions. They found paper, foil, sponges, rice noodles, string, empty boxes, balls, shoelaces, Velcro closures, and various broken items with knobs and handles. The team also offered to bring a new toy each week from the toy-lending library, so that Yohe could experiment with other toys with doors, lids, handles, and so forth.

The turn-taking game with sounds and gestures was also carried out in the evening with Yohe's father. At the same time, Yohe was placed in various positions to help build his hip stability. After he was engaged with a toy or plaything, he tolerated kneel-standing or standing supported by a low table. He also was able to focus attention and gain better hand control when he was seated in a low chair at the coffee table. Although Yohe needed to acquire many more skills before he could walk and talk, his parents were encouraged by the progress he was making in sound production and his motivation to play with toys in new ways.

DEVELOPMENTAL LEVEL

- Imitates novel movements (12–15 months)

INTERVENTION GUIDELINES

If the child's gross motor, prehension, and manipulation skills have matured at the same rate as the child's cognitive skills, the child will now be able to use a range of actions. With the onset of walking, the child can now gain access to any toy or object within his view and reach. He or she imitates unfamiliar actions of adults. Imitations are now more exact, and the child attempts to replicate facial expressions as well as gestures. The adult can now entice the child to imitate complex actions and combinations of actions. The child can poke, turn, point, tear, squeeze, scratch, sniff, kiss, hug, pinch, throw, crawl, climb, and "run," to name just a few skills.

Creating Imitation Games

The adult can combine these and other actions into fun games. Kissing the baby and rocking it; tearing up paper and throwing it; crumpling wax paper and dropping it into the trash; throwing a ball and running to get it; pushing a finger into cookie dough; sniffing flowers in the garden; and crushing crackling dried leaves are just a few of the fun games infants will imitate.

Encouraging Vocal Imitation

The child at this level is probably also beginning to imitate unfamiliar sounds and familiar words. These new words and sounds can be combined with actions to encourage vocal imitation as well. Use exaggerated affect and gestures to catch the child's attention. When the infant imitates the action or sound, provide encouragement by showing enthusiasm and repeating the action. Not all actions are repeated immediately. The adult may see the child attempt to imitate an action that was performed earlier or even the day before. The child was thinking about and processing the actions or words and was not yet ready to produce them. Repeating the child's imitation and reinforcing his or her effort encourages the duplication of the behavior.

Appealing to the Sensory System

The challenge for the adult is to look at an object and determine what can be done with the object that would appeal to the child's sensory systems. What actions can be modeled that will make the child ponder how to make the same action in order to get a similar result? Infants will also imitate older siblings who are demonstrating interesting behaviors, so siblings can be brought into the imitation game as well.

PLAY MATERIALS AND OPPORTUNITIES

Any toy that has a part to push, poke, or turn is fun for the infant. As can be seen from the ideas listed above, no special toys are needed. Toys or materials that provide interesting feedback encourage the child to repeat an action that was just modeled. For children who lack strength or have difficulty with motor control, use objects that are very soft or pliable for squeezing, objects with rough texture to encourage opening the fingers, facial expressions the child can model, and sounds or words the child can imitate.

DEVELOPMENTAL LEVEL

- Immediate imitation of a model
  (12–18 months)

INTERVENTION GUIDELINES

As the child becomes more adept at imitating the adult model, the attempts become more rapid. This results from increasing memory and recall abilities and fine motor dexterity. The child can now mentally and physically formulate how to imitate the model. The lack of physical abilities may be particularly frustrating for a child who wants to imitate a model, but cannot get his or her body to cooperate with the mind. For these children, it is important to play games, make gestures, and provide toys and materials that can be manipulated by the child. It is also necessary to afford enough wait-time for the child to formulate a response. At times, the adult will want to demonstrate more complicated toys or actions because they will entertain or delight the child; but if the intent is to have the child imitate behaviors, the behaviors must be within the child's repertoire or range of abilities.

PLAY MATERIALS AND OPPORTUNITIES

Play materials and opportunities suggested on page 126 are appropriate for children at this developmental level as well.

DEVELOPMENTAL LEVEL

- Imitates drawing of a stroke
  (15–18 months)

**INTERVENTION
GUIDELINES**

The child at this level, when given a crayon, automatically scribbles. However, an adult model can stimulate the child to draw a straight-line stroke. This imitation is important to the child because it takes the child beyond the sensorimotor effort of scribbling into the realm of drawing with intent to create a specific mark. This type of imitation helps the child to see that the crayon marks can be controlled and made to go where one wants. Learning the relationship between the crayon, the paper, and the hand and arm is a significant discovery for the child. This control increases as the child's grasp becomes more refined and cognitive representational skills develop. For now it is enough to know that the hand can be made to direct the crayon.

Providing infants with crayons, markers, pencils, and so forth is not advocated in all cultures, but if the family does not object, exploring with various marking media is a joy to many children. *The adult should not try to dominate and lead the child's sensory exploration, but rather watch, comment, imitate, and occasionally catch the child's attention and make a straight mark on the paper.* Making a noise or saying "zip" or "wheee" also entices the child to imitate. Large fluid movements are still preferred by the child, and the adult should not attempt to shift the child into controlled strokes too quickly. It's still more fun to scribble! (See also the discussion of drawing on pp. 189–195.)

**PLAY MATERIALS
AND
OPPORTUNITIES**

For children who are not prone to putting everything in their mouths, drawing is not limited to certain utensils. For children who are still mouthing heavily, large crayons or washable magic markers are good. Children who are already emulating their parents or caregivers may seek out pencils and pens. Adult supervision is needed for drawing at this level, as there is no discrimination between the paper and the wall in terms of a usable surface. In fact, walls are probably preferred due to their lack of boundaries.

**DEVELOPMENTAL
LEVEL**

- Recognizes ways to activate toys in imitation of adult
- Deferred imitation
    (18–24 months)

**INTERVENTION
GUIDELINES**

Activation of Play Materials by Imitation

The child can now imitate complex gestures, actions, and words, and has memory of previous events that enables him or her to recreate previously witnessed actions and events. Cause-and-effect toys are particularly appealing, and the child will figure out how to activate mechanisms after observing the adult. This manipulative imitation, in combination with the memory of previous events, enables the child to expand his or her problem-solving abilities. The adult should present various types of objects, toys, and materials to the child that present a problem to be solved (e.g., a door to be unlocked, a mechanism to be activated, a switch to be turned) and demonstrate a solution. The child may need a cue, such as a gesture toward the activating device, or a verbal suggestion, such as, "Mommy turned it to make it go." Cues should be given only if the child does nothing spontaneously. For children with visual or motor impairments, a physical prompt may be needed.

Deferred Imitation

Deferred imitation can be encouraged by presenting the child with objects or toys that he or she has previously seen the adult use and the adult is *not* demonstrating. Instead, the adult waits to see if the child's memory for what occurred with the object is aroused. If the child does nothing, the adult can then model and let the child imitate current activities.

Wind-up toys, lock boxes, button-activated toys and machines, such as tape recorders and remote control devices, are motivating to almost any child. For children with motor deficits, toys with simple switches, or computer adaptations with buttons that, when pushed, create exciting visual images are not only motivating, but allow the child to begin to develop the control skills for using higher-level switches or computerized equipment at a later time.

PLAY MATERIALS AND OPPORTUNITIES

- Varies own imitation creatively from that of model
  (21–24 months)

DEVELOPMENTAL LEVEL

The child is now beginning to think about alternative actions by drawing from the memories of past experiences. He or she can imitate an action or words and then add modifications. Most children automatically vary their play after imitation of the adult for several turns, but some children with disabilities continue to repeat the same actions unless prompted to think of something else. The adult may stop, watch the child for a minute, and then ask, "What else could we do with the blocks?," or suggest, "I think the baby is full now. Does she need a blanket?" For children who perseverate in their play, the adult may need to offer a cue to assist them in modifying their action pattern. *The adult should refrain from modeling a new action, as this will not assist the child in thinking of a new pattern without an exemplar.*

INTERVENTION GUIDELINES

Whatever the child is playing with at a given time can be used. No special toys are needed.

PLAY MATERIALS AND OPPORTUNITIES

DEVELOPMENTAL LEVEL

- Imitates drawing of a face
  (See also the discussion of drawing on pp. 189–195)
  (27–30 months)

The child may move into imitation of drawing a face in stages. The child is first able to draw a circle and shortly thereafter begins to see the relationship of the shape to the human face. The circle may be drawn with scribbles inside, with the child giving some indication that the scribbles are eyes or hair. The adult may assist the child by drawing a circle next to the child's and slowly adding eyes and then waiting for the child to imitate. The adult can then add a mouth

INTERVENTION GUIDELINES

and wait for the child to add his or hers. This process can continue through as many features as the child can re-create and is motivated to draw. Most children like this game and will draw a circle and bring it to the adult to "fill in." Modeling, rather than completing the child's circle, encourages the child to draw the features independently. Very quickly, the child moves to deferred imitation or drawing without a model, but based on memory.

PLAY MATERIALS AND OPPORTUNITIES

Any drawing materials that fit in the child's hand for a secure grip are fine. Children usually prefer colors, but magic slates in black are just as appealing and can be erased many times. In a toddler program, having duplicate slates, one for the parent or teacher and one for the child, is preferable. Duplicate materials allow the child to have ownership and plenty of space.

DEVELOPMENTAL LEVEL

> • Demonstrates increasingly complex role imitation (See Symbolic and Representational Play)
> (36–60 months)

INTERVENTION GUIDELINES

During this time, the child begins to imitate roles seen in daily life or read about in books and re-creates scenes watched on television or in the movies. The adult can stimulate the role play of new characters, roles, and actions by engaging in role play and modeling new ideas. For instance, if the child has been role playing a superhero by jumping off beds and fighting evil monsters, the parent may join in the play and add a new element. If, for example, the friend has been injured and needs medical attention, the superhero has to shift into a new role of administering to the ailing friend. The child frequently adds these new elements to the play the next time this theme is enacted.

Miniature Doll Play

Later in this period, the child begins to play with miniature dolls, such as Playmobil characters, action figures, Lego characters, and so forth. The parent or adult can do the same type of modeling with the child in this play. The child will typically have the characters enact stereotypic roles and dialogues. The adult can modify the themes, language, actions, and outcomes through modeling. These changes are then incorporated into the child's play with peers and in future play with the adult. The adult should be willing to become involved in the play so that modeling of different types and higher levels of play can take place.

PLAY MATERIALS AND OPPORTUNITIES

Culturally relevant toys and props are important, along with props and toys that are motivating to the child due to peers, books, television, or movies. For instance, the child may have observed peers playing certain roles or may pick up roles and storylines from favorite books, television cartoons or programs, or movies. Although family dolls (dad, mom, and kids), and dollhouses are motivating to many young girls, research has shown that they do not have the same appeal to most boys (Johnson et al., 1987; Paley, 1984; Shapiro, 1990).

Boys tend to be more interested in various action figures. Costumes and props appeal to both sexes. Whether at home or in a preschool, having a variety of props and costumes made from old discards is a sure way to stimulate role play. The adult should be ready to don a costume and assume a role.

• Imitates scenes from different aspects of life; pieces together into new script
  (48–60 months)

DEVELOPMENTAL LEVEL

Between 4 and 5 years of age, the child typically begins to be able to tell a whole story through his or her play. The adult can help the child move into that phase by modeling a sequence with a beginning, middle, and end. Asking questions such as, "What do you think should happen next?" stimulates the child to think of a progression. Modeling a logical sequence also moves the child from enacting isolated events to a logical script. For instance, the teacher may have a small group of children role playing going to the movies. The initial sequence may involve getting ready, getting in the car, arriving at the movie, paying for tickets, and watching the movie. After role playing the sequence a number of times, the adult can model or suggest alternatives (e.g., having a flat tire, getting gas, stopping to pick up a friend). Children begin to incorporate their own creative modifications after they become familiar with the sequence. Storybook plots also make good role-play sequences. The adult's role is to model the key steps in the story and then let the children role play. The adult can intercede when the plot gets lost or when a new idea is needed to keep the story interesting.

INTERVENTION GUIDELINES

Make or find the necessary props for each story. In the above illustration, keys, a box for a car, hats, popcorn boxes, paper cups, and a sheet for a movie screen are a few of the props that will stimulate creative role play for the "going to the movie" script. Props are a key component, although children at this level can invent or use imaginary props as well.

PLAY MATERIALS AND OPPORTUNITIES

OBSERVATION GUIDELINES FOR COGNITIVE DEVELOPMENT: PROBLEM-SOLVING APPROACHES

VI.   **Problem-Solving Approaches**
   A.   **What interest does the child show in cause-and-effect objects and events?**
      1.   **Does the child use physical "procedures" or bodily movement to make events recur?**
      2.   **What behaviors were observed where the child uses the adult as an agent to make something recur?**
      3.   **What behaviors were observed where the child acted as the agent to make something recur?**
      4.   **What behaviors were observed where the child used an object as a tool to solve a problem?**
   B.   **What means does the child use to accomplish goals? How does he or she figure out challenging tasks?**
      1.   **Does the child use a repetitive approach, doing the same act over and over to cause something to happen (continually bangs box to get it open)?**
      2.   **What evidence was observed of trial-and-error problem-solving using alternative approaches to achieve a goal?**
      3.   **What evidence is observed of advance planning in problem-solving?**
         a.   **The child uses physical searching behaviors in selecting an approach**
         b.   **The child uses visual scanning to select an approach**
         c.   **The child uses verbal mediation (talking to self) or questioning of another to select a problem-solving approach**

INTERVENTION IMPLICATIONS

The child progresses in understanding "how things work" based upon physical actions to mental problem-solving. As this transition occurs, the role of the parent or facilitator shifts from encouraging action through physical performance, toys, and games to assisting with problem-solving by using language. The young infant learns that the parent can solve problems or make interesting events occur, then that his or her own actions cause fun things to happen, and finally that through experimentation, verbal guidance, and/or thinking, he or she can solve problems encountered daily (Piaget, 1936, 1962). Reasoning and problem-solving involve the child's mastery of the spatial environment (Anooshian & Siegel, 1985), memory of events and actions (Case, 1985; Mandler, 1984, 1988), and the development of procedures, or "rules," for acting on the environment (Siegler, 1981). As the child develops, he or she encodes information in the brain. Siegler (1991) defines encoding as, "identifying the most important features of objects and events and using the features to form internal representations" (p. 10). This representation in the brain guides subsequent problem-solving. After a skill has been practiced, it becomes more automatic, thus freeing cognitive processes for more advanced problem-solving. As new information is added to the child's store of information, new competencies are acquired, integrated with others, and gradually transformed into more efficient, generalized, higher-order skills. The child begins to form strategies and rules about how to solve problems (Fischer, 1980; Siegler, 1991). *The facilitator's role* in encouraging problem-solving is to make interesting events occur so that the child wants to make them happen again, to organize the environment so that spatial and causal relationships are observed and actions attempted, to allow the child to practice problem-solving skills, to help the child to integrate different skills, to use demonstration and language to assist the child in experimenting with alternative solutions, and to help the child think about and generate strategies and rules for problem-solving.

An important point for both parents and early interventionists is to allow the child time to accomplish tasks independently. It is easy to do things for a child who hesitates or does not appear to be able to perform a task. However, this only teaches the child that if one waits long enough, someone will do it, thus stifling the child's desire to solve problems independently. Allowing the child to choose and retrieve desired objects, even if the movements are slow and labored, builds the child's sense of efficacy. Experimentation, although ostensibly not leading to the desired outcome, is meaningful. Learning what does *not* work is as significant as learning what does work. *A balance is needed between experimentation, demonstration, and guidance.*

- Finds object after watching it disappear
- Uses movement as a means to attain an end
- Anticipates movement of objects in space
- Attends to environmental consequences of actions
- Repeats actions in order to repeat consequences
        (6–9 months)

The child is now beginning to show curiosity about the consequences of the actions of self and others. During this time, the child usually sits and later begins to crawl, allowing him or her better access to desired objects. *At this developmental level, the facilitator or parent should provide opportunities for the child to attend to movement, cause actions to happen, and use his or her body to attain desired goals.* This can be done by moving objects into, and then out of, the child's visual field so that the infant attempts to track and then move his or her body to try to locate the object. Objects that move, such as balls and push cars, are fascinating to watch and to try to retrieve. A spoonful of food can disappear under a highchair tray or behind a bowl. A tub toy can disappear under the water; a rattle under a diaper. The parent or facilitator may find numerous ways to stimulate the infant's curiosity and cause searching behavior.

Repetition

The infant is also finding out that movements that cause interesting things to happen can be repeated to make something happen again. Moving your body up and down makes Daddy bounce you on his knee again; hitting the mobile causes it to swing and make noise again; knocking the bowl off the table a second time causes food to fly everywhere, and Mommy howls and makes those funny faces again.

Cause-and-Effect Events

The parent or facilitator may capitalize on this early problem-solving to repeat events by finding ways to incorporate cause-and-effect events into the day. During diaper changing, a toy that has movement and sound when swiped can be placed within reach; mobiles can be lowered so that the child can hit them with feet or hands while lying in bed; games between parent and child involving movement, funny faces, or noises can be invented; splashing or moving floating objects in the water can be incorporated into bathtime. *The key is to have the child repeat an action that resulted in an effect the child found absorbing.* After the action–consequence is repeated numerous times, the child begins to understand that he or she caused the desired event to occur through his or her actions, forming the foundation for later, higher-level problem-solving.

PLAY MATERIALS AND OPPORTUNITIES

No specific toys are needed for action games, but household objects, baby paraphernalia, and toys can generate engaging cause-and-effect events. Objects related to actions with big effects, such as banging a spatula in water, kicking feet when bells are worn on shoes; and playing with toys that can be activated by a simple touch or movement (e.g., weighted roly-poly doll, balls with spinners inside), are good for stimulating early problem-solving.

DEVELOPMENTAL LEVEL

- Demonstrates tool use after demonstration
- Uses goal-directed behavior
- Performs an action in order to produce a result
  (9–12 months)

INTERVENTION GUIDELINES

Now, two key elements are developing in the child's repertoire. These are the ability to *comprehend* and *carry out* actions needed to achieve goals. The parent or facilitator can orchestrate situations that enable the child to perceive a goal and then determine how to accomplish it. The goal may involve any of the senses. The child may want to experience a tactile, vestibular, auditory, visual, or even olfactory result. For example, when the infant wants the parent to tickle him or her again (tactile), he or she may make body movements with the arms and legs and make sounds to indicate he or she wants the tickling action to be repeated. If the parent or facilitator waits for the movements and sounds before repeating the tickling, the child soon intensifies the movements and sounds to get the action repeated.

If the child sees the parent push a button or pull a string to get the doll's head to pop up or move its legs, the child will attempt the same action in order to see the same result. If the child sees the parent use a stick to push the button, that also will be tried. By observing various means of achieving a goal, the child begins to incorporate the idea of trial-and-error. Incorporating simple language will reinforce the cause-and-effect process: "Push" or "Pop." Exaggerated movements on the part of the adult also helps to capture the child's attention and to assist in helping the child see the relationship between actions leading to a goal.

Toys that have simple activation devices, such as buttons that can be pushed with a hand or finger, toys that move (e.g., cars, balls) or any action device that intrigues the child, are suitable. Cause-and-effect and problem-solving are not limited, however, to toys. All daily activities hold potential for problem-solving. Pulling off a sock during diaper changing, finding a Cheerio behind a plate, and changing the channel on the television control are motivating to the child (although the latter may be exasperating to the rest of the family). Playful activities need not be limited to the use of toys.

PLAY MATERIALS AND OPPORTUNITIES

- Uses an adult to achieve a goal
- Attempts to activate simple mechanisms
- Rotates and examines three-dimensional aspects of an object
- Uses nonsystematic trial-and-error problem-solving
      (12–15 months)

DEVELOPMENTAL LEVEL

Due to increasing fine motor and cognitive abilities, the infant now explores objects more carefully and uses some trial-and-error poking, pushing, and banging to activate toys. The parent is still seen as a primary, causal agent, however, and toys are handed to the parent to "make them go." The parent or facilitator can encourage the child to try to "make it go" without demonstrating or activating the toy too quickly. *Using a partial prompt or an approximation of the needed effort may be enough to stimulate the action needed.* The facilitator may also encourage the child to examine the objects, pointing out critical features, such as activating mechanisms, specific parts, and so forth. Depending on the child's needs, the parent or facilitator should adapt his or her level of support, providing tactile cues for infants with visual impairments, physical cues for children who have difficulty with fine motor skills, and visual cues for infants with hearing impairments.

INTERVENTION GUIDELINES

The child at this developmental level enjoys any toy or household device with an easily activated mechanism that can be pushed, pulled, or turned; toys or objects with levers, handles, knobs, lids, and doors that make something interesting occur; toys or containers the child can put things into and then dump; toys or materials where something disappears and reappears with the child's actions; and toys or items the child can take apart.

PLAY MATERIALS AND OPPORTUNITIES

DEVELOPMENTAL LEVEL

- Attends to shapes of things and uses appropriately
- Uses some foresight before acting
- Uses a tool to obtain a desired object
- Invents means to attain a goal through thought processes rather than just trial-and-error
- Operates a mechanical toy
- Can foresee effects or infer causes
      (18–21 months)

INTERVENTION GUIDELINES

The task for the parent or facilitator at this developmental level is to allow the child to confront challenging situations and intriguing toys. Both in everyday activities and in play, the child can be presented with opportunities to experience interesting effects resulting from his or her actions. For example, in the bath the parent could add bubble bath to the water and then blow bubbles; put bubbles in a bottle and try to get them out with a stick; hide objects under the bubbles; put wind-up water toys in the water to move through the bubbles; and use a washcloth, finger, or spoon to have the child put bubbles on his or her body parts.

In play, the parent or facilitator can set up toys or materials in such a way that the child has to use his body in various ways to retrieve toys. The child could use a stool to climb up to a toy shelf, crawl under a chair to chase a toy car, walk behind a table to get a ball, and so forth. This type of activity involves using both cognitive and gross motor skills to solve a problem. In the same way, objects can be placed at varying heights to encourage the child to use different body positions. Objects placed on the floor encourage sitting, while objects placed on a coffee table encourage standing. *Positioning is important, especially for children with motor difficulties.* If the position in which the child is playing requires too much effort to maintain, the child will not have maximum cognitive resources available for problem-solving. Providing supports so that the child is stable and comfortable in play allows the child's attention and energy to be focused on play.

Cognitive problem-solving is encouraged by placing tools near the problem to be solved and allowing the child to experiment before demonstration. A stick could be placed, for instance, near the bottle with raisins in it or near the sand and water wheel in the sandbox. If mechanized toys are placed near the child and the child does not initiate investigation, the adult can demonstrate the actions necessary to activate the toys. Receptive language is increasing rapidly at this level, and the child can comprehend many labels, action words, and simple location words. If the child's language comprehension is at the same level as cognitive development, the adult can encourage language and support problem-solving by labeling the objects and actions in play (e.g., "Where is the baby?" "Push the button on the top." "You found the block in the pan.") Keeping sentences short and emphasizing key words assist the child in relating the words and actions.

PLAY MATERIALS AND OPPORTUNITIES

Play materials and opportunities discussed on page 155 are also appropriate for the child at this developmental level.

DEVELOPMENTAL LEVEL

- Recognizes operations of many mechanisms
- Matches configurations, such as circle, square, triangle
- Manipulates objects into small openings
    (21–24 months)

The child can now operate many types of mechanisms without adult assistance. Toys with different activation devices are recommended, as described above. With supervision, home appliances with buttons and levers can now also be activated by the child. The toddler enjoys helping Mom or Dad with chores by turning on the vacuum cleaner, operating electric appliances, pushing down the toaster lever, turning on the washer or dryer, turning on and off the light switches, and so forth.

INTERVENTION GUIDELINES

Recognizing Attributes

In addition, the child's increasing abilities to recognize and differentiate similarities and differences enables him or her to do simple shape puzzles and sorting boxes. At home the child can play with putting lids on pans, cans, bottles, and boxes, putting letters in the mail slot and glasses on round coasters and so forth. These problem-solving activities encourage the child to pick out key attributes of objects, a necessary skill for later problem-solving (Gibson & Spelke, 1983). *The adult can assist by pointing out attributes.* For instance, when the child is putting lids on pans, the parent might trace the edges of the objects and say, "The lid is round, and the pan is round." Although the child may not comprehend the word "round" yet, the visual matching and motor tracing of the objects has accented a key feature of the objects. The parent may later see the child studying the lid or touching the edge of the pan.

Increased finger dexterity allows the child to manipulate small objects. Putting small objects in holes is a delight. Finding acceptable outlets for this game is a challenge. Raisins or Cheerios can be dropped through cardboard toilet paper rolls or dropped into old, washed medicine containers. This empty-and-fill process can become a turn-taking game with the adult. Adding a stick to the game increases the problem-solving potential.

In addition to mechanized toys and devices, the child can now begin to appreciate simple shape puzzles and boxes. Begin with circles, then add squares and triangles. Stacking things that are alike, such as books, or finding places to put things away will encourage matching. Problem-solving with shapes can be done with almost any toys or objects.

PLAY MATERIALS AND OPPORTUNITIES

• Discriminates sizes   (24–27 months)

DEVELOPMENTAL LEVEL

The intervention guidelines discussed on page 158 are also appropriate for this developmental level. In addition, the reader is referred to the discussion of Discrimination/Classification Skills on pages 164–177.

INTERVENTION GUIDELINES

The play materials and opportunities discussed as part of the Discrimination/Classification Skills on page 172 are also appropriate for children at this developmental level.

PLAY MATERIALS AND OPPORTUNITIES

DEVELOPMENTAL LEVEL

- Can build with blocks horizontally and vertically (24–30 months)

INTERVENTION GUIDELINES

Problem-solving relating to building with blocks begins as the child sees how the blocks can be combined in various ways to form interesting patterns. Later the child will attempt to build representational structures, but now the emphasis is on manipulating the blocks and relating like objects. Begin with large blocks that are the same shape and size and are easy to handle. When the child can build vertically and horizontally, add more challenging elements, such as smaller blocks, different sizes and shapes, and varying weights of blocks. Stacking them up and knocking them down is a favorite game, so lightweight blocks are safer for the toddler. Varying the type of blocks used can keep the child interested in blocks and building.

PLAY MATERIALS AND OPPORTUNITIES

Blocks are now made of every material from wood to foam-rubber and come in every size imaginable. Individual children are attracted to distinct characteristics, such as colors, pictures on the sides, size, texture, and so forth. Observations of preferences enables selection of blocks that appeal to a particular child. Popular blocks, such as Legos, now come in varying sizes, so that even the toddler can stack very tall towers. Bristle blocks and magnetic blocks also stick together and can assist the child with motor impairments in having the experience of building. However, some of these blocks are actually more difficult to use, as Bristle blocks require strength to push them together and magnetic blocks require manipulation to get the magnetic poles aligned. Small 1-inch cubes are also exacting for children, as they necessitate refined dexterity. Small blocks, however, appeal to infants who have not yet been motivated to stack tall towers (as they can hold them easily, bang them, put them in cans, and put them together) and to older children who enjoy the demands of the fine motor skills required.

DEVELOPMENTAL LEVEL

- Relates one experience to another, using logic and knowledge of previous experiences
- Can plan actions in his or her mind without acting them out
- Can relate one experience to another using "if . . . then" logic (27–30 months)

INTERVENTION GUIDELINES

Generalization

Transferring information learned from one experience to another similar experience is an important ability in the development of problem-solving skills. *The parent or facilitator can promote generalization by providing a variety of toys or materials that require the same or similar abilities of the child as those mastered on other toys or materials.* If, for example, the child has a favorite toy at home that requires turning a handle to operate, the parent or facilitator can present a different toy that is also operated with a turning crank or handle. Varying the appearance of the crank helps the child learn that all sorts of things that turn result in interesting phenomena. When the child is just learning to turn handles, it is best to present the one that has been mastered first, then the unfamiliar object with a handle. Soon the child will recognize a specific type of "handle" as something to turn, another as something to twist, and yet another as something to push or pull. When a new object is encountered, he or she will be able to try all of the possible actions systematically to make the object function as it should.

The more opportunities the child has to apply previously learned skills to new situations, the greater the foundation for problem-solving. The adult can assist the child by pointing out the similarities among objects and events, encouraging exploration and manipulation through modeling and verbal suggestion, and altering situations to create new challenges for the child. By playing "Let's see what happens if we do this," the child can experiment through play and build a cornerstone of logical reasoning.

PLAY MATERIALS AND OPPORTUNITIES

Use toys and materials in the child's environment, but add an element or variation; for instance, put tape over a button on a pop-up toy so the child has to figure out how to get access to the button; take the batteries out of a battery-operated toy; substitute the wrong size lid for a pan. Any toys and materials can provide situations for problem-solving. Those with mechanisms may be more motivating to the child. Provide similar toys and situations to promote generalization. Computer programs to promote problem-solving can start with a program like McGee (Lawrence Productions, Inc., 1989), which requires the child to explore and play with objects in a seven-room house.

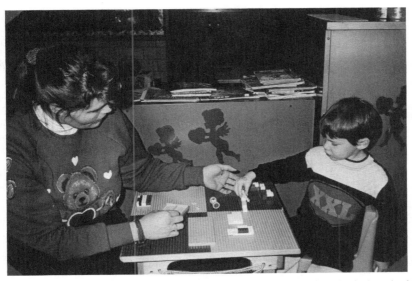

Blocks of varying sizes, shapes, and weights can be chosen according to the individual needs of the child.

DEVELOPMENTAL LEVEL

- Can build vertical block structure requiring balance and coordination (nine cubes)
- Can put graduated sizes in order
- Uses representational thinking in constructions
    (36–48 months)

INTERVENTION GUIDELINES

The child is now able to think about his or her constructions as more than interesting patterns or relationships. The child can visualize the blocks as a representation of an object or entity in the environment. He or she is also able to position and reposition blocks taking balance into consideration. Size relationships are also understood, allowing the child to make size relationships in constructions as well as in other forms of play.

Props

The facilitator should provide props (e.g., cars, people figures, animals) to assist the child in visualizing the block structures needed for certain scenarios. Props stimulate the child's imagination and move the child from simple tower, road, and fence structures to more elaborate buildings, bridges, and so forth. The facilitator can also model by building structures in parallel play with the child.

Understanding Spatial Relationships

The child develops a greater understanding of the spatial relationships of size and shape by incorporating various sequencing or matching activities into play. In the house area, for instance, different size pans, dishes, and glasses can be put out to be stacked and put in the cupboard. (For additional ideas, the reader is referred to the discussion of discrimination/classification skills on pp. 164–177.) The parent or facilitator should keep in mind the concepts the child is beginning to consider and make efforts to assimilate activities that address these concepts into the child's play.

Problem-solving skills are enhanced by asking open-ended questions, such as, "What could we use for a roof?" Providing situations that require a solution also enhances reasoning ability (e.g., "This door is too big for our house. We need to find the right size block."). At the same time, relational concepts, such as "smaller," "taller," and "heavier," can be addressed.

Adapting Problem-Solving Situations

Children should not be deprived of the experience of thinking about problems and experimenting with solutions just because they do not have the gross or fine motor competence to enable them to function independently. If the child is not capable of using adapted toys or materials, the adult can still allow the child to direct the action while the adult carries out the play directives. For the child with severe motor impairments, for instance, the adult may need to act out and construct while the child directs the action verbally, with his or her eyes, or with a pointer. The child should be encouraged to do as much of the thinking about a situation as possible, although others may try out the solution. Watching others play and solve problems is one way to learn, but observation of others' ideas is not as effective as experimenting with the child's own suggestions.

Social Problem-Solving

Social problem-solving also is needed as children of this developmental level begin to interact more in play. Giving children an opportunity to plan to prevent problems is important. "We only have one shovel. What do you think we should do to avoid a fight over who should get it?" When conflicts cannot be prevented, social problem-solving with adult support helps the child learn to generalize solutions to the next situation.

Blocks

Making a variety of types of blocks available is desirable and possible in the preschool classroom. The weight, texture, materials, size, and shape can be varied for different types of construction activities (e.g., large, cardboard blocks for life-size constructions, wooden blocks or Legos for miniature constructions, magnetic blocks for building animals and figures). Velcro can even be added to wooden blocks to aid the child with motor impairments.

Size-Sequenced Objects

Size sequencing is encouraged by playing with objects that come in varying sizes. Toys such as "nesting" cups are made for this purpose, but any size-sequenced objects, such as hats, bowls, and pans, can be fun to stack from large to small.

Figures and Props

As the child is now capable of representational thinking and dramatic play, figures and props can be added to construction activities. Problem-solving of the "if . . . then" mode can be incorporated with these play materials (e.g., if a stop sign is added to the block road, then a car is also needed).

PLAY MATERIALS AND OPPORTUNITIES

- Can construct complex structures with vertical, horizontal, and symmetrical aspects
- Can integrate spatial, cause-and-effect, and representational thinking into problem-solving
          (48–60 months)

DEVELOPMENTAL LEVEL

By now the child's thinking has progressed to the level of being able to think logically. He or she can see or deduce relationships between aspects of a situation, can use discrimination skills to evaluate and plan, and can relate objects in many different spatial configurations. At the same time, the child has developed

INTERVENTION GUIDELINES

representational skills that allow him or her to create unrefined real or imaginary representations in dramatic play, block play, and art play. The parent or facilitator can promote problem-solving by again using props and stimulating the ideas for play, but also by *omitting necessary objects so that a substitute must be found or created.* For example, if the child is acting out a story about a monster, the parent or facilitator could encourage the child to determine what he or she could use for a tail, teeth, spots, and so forth. (Having a "junk" box available with all kinds of odds and ends is useful.) The parent or facilitator can also ask questions or create situations that promote problem-solving (e.g., "What else could have happened to the dragon?", "What would have happened if the dragon had gotten sick and not come to the battle?").

Science Experimentation

Science is also an area ripe for experimentation and play at this age. Letting the child experiment with mountains of dirt and water "raining" on the dirt; building "roads" on sand, dirt, and rocks; and finding different ways to make things "go" are play for the child at the 4- to 5-year-old developmental level. The parent or facilitator's role is to set up the play environment; encourage experimentation; and model, question, and guide as needed. Peer interactions should be promoted at this point, with the adult stimulating ideas, concepts, actions, and problem-solving.

PLAY MATERIALS AND OPPORTUNITIES　Toys and playthings are limited only by the imagination of the parent or facilitator. The computer programs discussed under discrimination/classification, one-to-one correspondence, sequencing, and drawing are appropriate here as well.

EXAMPLE

Tony L. is a 6-year-old Philippine boy with profound hearing loss. His family immigrated from the Philippines when he was 4 years old. Tony lives with his mother, father, and younger sister, who is 3 years old. Both English and his native Philippine dialect are spoken in the home. As Tony's parents are both employed full time, Tony and his sister stay with his "comadre," or godmother, before and after school. His comadre acts as the intermediary with the school and is the person who communicates with the teachers concerning Tony's education. Tony is in a kindergarten class with typical peers, but receives individual speech-language therapy. His therapist is teaching his teacher and the whole class to sign. Tony is pairing his signing with speech, but, as the speech-language therapist does not know his native language, she is only working with him on simple words rather than fingerspelling. His mother, father, and comadre come to sign classes once a week, although they are hesitant to use sign as it draws attention to Tony's disability. They do not sign with Tony in public. Tony's mother believes that his hearing loss, a result of meningitis when he was an infant, is a punishment for her sins. Tony is taken regularly to see a faith healer. The family is quite close, and Tony cares lovingly for his younger sister.

　　In class, Tony is shy, preferring to watch others. He does not typically approach peers, although when others initiate an interaction, he responds with huge smiles. Learning to sign has been fun for the class and has made Tony the center of attention, which has caused him some embarrassment, but he has enjoyed his peers' resulting attempts at communication.

In a planning session with the speech-language therapist, the teacher indicated that she would like to see Tony begin to initiate more communication with his peers. Tony is bright, and his play is on approximately the same level as the rest of the class. Although Tony's language concepts are delayed, she thinks the class's primitive level of signing puts their communication on a more equal basis. The speech-language therapist suggested that perhaps involving Tony in problem-solving with his peers would encourage him to initiate questions and comments. Two different activities were discussed. The class developed a play about *The Lorax*, (Geisel, 1971), and Tony was the prop director. He needed to help the actors put together their costumes and get dressed. The class was also studying erosion. They have read stories together, watched an animated movie, and looked at pictures. Tony and two other peers helped to design an erosion center by finding containers that could be used to make different kinds of "rain," tools that can move dirt, and ways to build "hills" and "mountains."

Tony was a creative prop director. With each actor, he would look at the pictures in the book and then sort through the prop box to find the right costume. He would comment and sign, "This one?" and "Look good." If the actor disagreed, he always said, "Okay," and went along with their choice. With some assistance from the teacher, who asked questions such as, "What could we use to show that Alexandra is supposed to be a Swomee-Swan?", he was able to use feather dusters for Truffula Trees, bird feathers attached to a head band for Swomee-Swans, fur hats for Brown Bar-ba-loots, and the children's jackets for Thneeds. The teacher would facilitate by labeling the objects (The class made up signs for each of the strange names in the book.) and having Tony help the actors with their costumes. A "make-up artist" helped with the finishing touches. Tony was not only able to originate ideas for props, but he was able to direct his peers in wearing them. He laughed heartily at each of his creations, holding up a mirror for each to examine themselves.

In the beginning, the science center was just a water table filled with dirt. The speech-language therapist and three peers, including Tony, sat and examined pictures of a hilly farm and tried to decide how to create the scene in the dirt table. The children rummaged through a box of garden tools, trucks, and various containers. The speech-language therapist signed to Tony, "We need tools to make a hill." Tony sorted through the box and found a bucket and a shovel. The therapist labeled each object with words and signs, then said, "What should we do?" Tony signed, "Fill it and dump it upside down." Another peer took the toy road grater and said, "We could push it into hills." The therapist showed him how to sign this for Tony. Tony nodded and said, "Good idea." Each of the children chose a different way to make hills. They played for some time in the dirt, using different approaches, exchanging tools and comments. They then decided to make "rain" using a plastic watering can. They experimented with different kinds of rain, gentle and hard, and discussed what happened to the dirt when there was nothing to stop the rain from eroding it. They decided to dig up some grass from the yard and see if that made a difference. The therapist was able to integrate concepts, expedite problem-solving, and promote cooperative learning through play. The dirt center was popular, and the children returned to experiment every day for a week. They began to remember specific signs, had favorite tools, and each day added new elements to their landscape.

Each day Tony took home a list of new words they had used in class, with pictures of how the signs were made, so that he could discuss his day with his family.

OBSERVATION GUIDELINES FOR
COGNITIVE DEVELOPMENT: DISCRIMINATION/CLASSIFICATION

VII. Discrimination/Classification
  A. How does the child show knowledge of classification of concepts?
    1. What behaviors demonstrate combining related objects (spoon and plate)?
    2. What behaviors demonstrate combining like objects in sets (trucks all together)?
    3. What behaviors demonstrate spatial matching (stacking same size blocks or lining up like objects)?
    4. What behaviors demonstrate sorting or matching objects by color?
    5. What behaviors demonstrate sorting or matching objects by shape?
    6. What behaviors demonstrate sorting or matching objects by size (big, little)?
    7. What behaviors demonstrate that the child can sequence objects by size (nesting or stacking in order)?
    8. What behaviors demonstrate that the child can sort or match objects by functions (things that roll)?
    9. What behaviors demonstrate sorting or matching by a more complex functional relationship (stop signs on road in block area)
    10. What behaviors demonstrate that the child can identify objects by attributes?
      a. Single attributes
      b. Multiple attributes (big, blue square)
    11. What behaviors demonstrate that the child can match simple patterns or designs (puzzles, Lotto)?
    12. What behaviors demonstrate that the child can match more complex patterns or designs (parquetry blocks)?
    13. What behaviors demonstrate the child's ability to group or label objects within a classification or categorical system (e.g., an apple is a fruit, a poodle is a dog, a dog is an animal)?

**INTERVENTION
IMPLICATIONS**

Sensitivity to touch, postural orientation, taste, smell, and sound is present in the neonate. Within the first year of life, the vestibular system and vision become integrated, and sensitivity to pitch, loudness, and location of sound improves. Within the first 6 months of life, the infant's visual-perceptual abilities become highly refined. Differentiation of brightness and color, depth perception, pattern perception, and the perception of shape and object constancy (or recognition of objects as stable and unchanging) evolve (Berk, 1991). Intermodal coordination, or the ability to take in information from more than one sensory system at a time and perceive it as an integrated unit, also develops in early infancy (Spelke, 1987).

Differentiation Theory

Differentiation theory (Gibson, 1970; Gibson, 1979) is one perspective that accounts for the child's acquisition of discriminative skills. According to the Gibsons, the child actively searches for the invariant features in the environment, seeking order and stability in the complex world. As the child acquires more mature skill in perceiving and differentiating aspects of his or her environment and begins to assign meaning to what he or she perceives, the essence of cognitive development is generated (Salapatek & Cohen, 1987). With age, the features noticed and differentiated by the child become more subtle.

Discrimination/Classification Skills and Development

Discrimination/classification skills are closely related to academic success (Gibson & Spelke, 1983), self-esteem (Harter, 1990) and social acumen (Brooks-Gunn & Lewis, 1978). The ability to differentiate stimuli and then categorize those stimuli into meaningful sets lays the foundation for reading and writing skills as well as higher-level thinking skills. In the development of self-esteem, the child learns to differentiate a number of distinct self-evaluations. The ability to differentiate social stimuli is critical to social and emotional development. (Differentiation with regard to self and others is addressed in Chapter 9.)

Most parents and teachers spend a great deal of time on discrimination and classification of colors and shapes, but being able to discern and label differences is important for more than these two areas. Categorization of concepts goes beyond vocabulary to learning to think about the relationship between various concepts. Color, size, shape, function, and position in space or time are all means of classifying or thinking about the relationships among concepts. The parent or facilitator can promote discrimination/classification by setting up situations that enable the child to observe or experience specific phenomena, labeling the differential features, demonstrating likenesses and differences, and, for older children, asking questions that prompt thinking about the characteristics of objects, people, places, events, or ideas.

DEVELOPMENTAL LEVEL

- Growing sense of difference between self and mother and mothers and others
    (2–6 months)
- Differentiates primary caregiver from others
    (6–9 months)

INTERVENTION GUIDELINES

Although the infant recognizes the parent at an early age, even recognizing certain aspects of his or her mother at a few days of age (Stern, 1985), the onset of stranger anxiety demonstrates the infant's cognitive awareness of others as different from the parent. Having acquired the ability to differentiate the invariant features of the parent, the infant also associates specific feelings with the parent. Not all children go through this stage in the same way. Some react in distinct ways to the nonparent, but do not show distress; others demonstrate varying degrees of discomfort. The cognitive goal is *not* to have the child begin to cry when an adult other than the parent holds him or her, but to begin to differentiate among the other persons in his or her life. Exposure to other nurturing adults and children of both sexes is desirable. Parent–infant play groups can often assist the child in developing the beginnings of social cognition. Differentiation of the caregiver is noted here to emphasize that it is a cognitive, as well as social, milestone.

DEVELOPMENTAL LEVEL

> • Combines related objects
>   (9–12 months)

INTERVENTION GUIDELINES

At this developmental level, the infant recognizes characteristics of objects and makes associations between objects and actions. This requires both discrimination skills and denotes an early ability to classify. Objects that can be combined in some simple way can be placed before the child. If the child does not spontaneously combine them, the action can be demonstrated and turned into a turn-taking game with the adult. Banging two objects together at midline, putting a spoon on a plate, and putting items in a container are examples of relating objects. Even dropping the diaper in the diaper pail is a fun activity (for the child, if not for the parent) and demonstrates an understanding of the relationship between two objects.

Intermodal Learning

Because infants pick up intermodal, or cross-sensory, relationships rapidly (Spelke, 1987), the associations between various sensory aspects of objects are also distinguished. Using objects of differing sizes and shapes not only fosters the refinement of fine motor skills, but also encourages tactile discernment of characteristics of objects. Varying textures not only adds interest, but encourages comparison and differentiation of tactile materials. Auditory discrimination, an essential component of speech and language skills, is also important to incorporate into the child's play. By using toys and materials that produce different sounds, the child is soon able to identify specific toys or objects with distinctive sounds. The use of diverse sensory materials promotes intermodal learning and assists the child in developing more refined discriminatory abilities.

PLAY MATERIALS AND OPPORTUNITIES

Combinatorial Objects

Simple toys or objects that can be combined. Containers, sticks, and so forth are appropriate. The play materials and opportunities discussed regarding Early Object Use on page 124 are appropriate at this developmental level as well.

Objects with Specific Sensory Elements

Materials with discrete sensory aspects are also important. For example, balls of differing sizes and textures (some with bells or musicmakers inside), or toys that make noise when squeezed help the child learn the relationship between actions and resulting sensations. Using materials that provide varying textures in combinatorial play helps the child to discriminate tactile differences. For instance, the child could drop in and take out of a bin materials that are crunchy (e.g., potato chips), sticky (e.g., pieces of tape), scratchy (e.g., sand paper), or smooth (e.g., silk) (see p. 84 for a complete list of textures). Auditory discrimination can be encouraged by banging on a xylophone, cans of varying sizes, and boxes. Visual discrimination is enhanced by combining objects that are the same in one way but different in another (e.g., dropping in a pan blocks that are the same color but different in shape).

DEVELOPMENTAL LEVEL

- Begins to spontaneously cluster objects that share physical or functional similarities
- Matches objects with relational parts (round lid on tea pot)
  (15–18 months)

INTERVENTION GUIDELINES

Matching objects is an early form of one-to-one correspondence vital to the development of later mathematical, reading, and problem-solving abilities (Dawes, 1977). Giving the infant experiences with matching at this level encourages physical and cognitive manipulation of likenesses and differences.

Placing objects with similar physical or functional characteristics in close proximity and within reach of the infant encourages the child to match objects and experiment in play with toys that function in comparable ways. Putting a ball that rolls next to a car that rolls, placing a group of red and yellow blocks near a container, setting a lid near a pan and spoon, and putting several different toys with levers or moving handles adjacent to each other encourages the child to perceive similarities. During the day, the parent may find many opportunities to put related things within the infant's reach. A brush and comb, bowl and spoon, pans and lids, shirts and pants, toothbrush and toothpaste, and diaper and diaper pail can be incorporated in a playful way into the day. Every part of the day offers some learning opportunity for the child. *By making activities into playful games, the parent can underscore related concepts and extend play with objects that otherwise might be manipulated only momentarily.*

PLAY MATERIALS AND OPPORTUNITIES

The materials and opportunities suggested in the discussion of Early Object Use on pages 126–127 are appropriate at this developmental level as well.

DEVELOPMENTAL LEVEL

- Discriminates circle and square on form board
  (16–19 months)

INTERVENTION GUIDELINES

The ability to place a round or square object in a form board demonstrates the child's recognition of and ability to match simple shapes. The parent or facilitator does not have to sit with the child doing form board puzzles to foster this skill. In fact, the skill becomes more functional if it is learned using a variety of everyday objects or familiar toys. Putting tops on bottles and lids on boxes containing small objects is fun for a child and accomplishes the same goal. The parent can promote language at the same time by labeling the objects, "bottle," "cap," and "box." Pointing out things that are round or square and tracing them with the child's fingers while saying, "circle" or "square" gives the child tactile input and a verbal label. (The child is not expected to understand or use the words "circle" and "square" at this level, as abstract concepts are learned at a higher level. Using the label merely calls attention to the specific attribute of the object.) Discrimination of shape is enhanced by the combination of visual, tactile, and auditory input.

PLAY MATERIALS AND OPPORTUNITIES

Toys that have slots for different shapes are sometimes fun for the child at this level. Shape boxes are available that have different lids with a simple selection of holes in them, from all the same shape to simple circle, square, and triangle shapes to more complex shapes. Either the adult or the child can select a desired top. Alternative toys have different-shaped slots on the various sides of the toy.

Placing square blocks on top of each other is also a matching task. Simple shape puzzles can also be fun, but the child may tire of this quickly. Everyday objects can be just as effective and are usually more entertaining. Putting the stopper in and out of an old-style tub or pan with a drain plug is fun and motivating, particularly when the receptacle is filled with water. Putting the cap on the toothpaste tube or the top on a bottle of soda pop (preferably empty) is also great sport. Square plastic food containers with lids can serve the same purpose for the square shape. Putting objects, such as Cheerios or small jingle bells, in a box adds another relational element.

EXAMPLE

April M. was a 2½-year-old Caucasian child who was born 2 months prematurely. She was living in low-income housing with her mother, Mrs. M., who was unemployed. When April was 2 years old, she was taken from her mother as a result of child abuse. She lived in a foster care home for 3 months. Mrs. M. attended court-ordered parenting classes and received weekly visits from a developmental specialist, who monitored April's development and provided suggestions for encouraging April's development. The developmental specialist met with a support team, consisting of a social worker, a speech-language pathologist, and an occupational therapist, every other week to obtain input on the children she was seeing.

A transdisciplinary play-based assessment was done with April to update her evaluation and review her progress. She was found to be delayed in all areas and functioning in approximately the 12- to 20-month range, depending on the specific skill area. She had just begun to walk and could move around the apartment on her own, although she still occasionally fell. April was observed putting Corn Chex into a bottle using her thumb and the tip of her index finger and drawing a line with a crayon in the fisted position. April used one- and two-word phrases to communicate. She labeled objects, requested objects and actions, protested when she was unhappy with a situation, and commented on objects and actions. She was able to do what her mother requested as long as the direction was short and involved only one step. April was not yet interacting with peers and did not appear to enjoy interactions with her mother, although she was compliant and did what her mother suggested in their play. Mrs. M. indicated that she did not often play with April, but did watch cartoons with her. Mrs. M. said, "Now that April is finally walking, she is harder to entertain because she doesn't stay in one place." She said that April played by herself much of the time. In the cognitive area, April was observed to put lids on pots and put the circles in a puzzle. She had difficulty positioning the square piece in the puzzle, but knew where it went and persisted in trying to make it fit. She fed her baby doll, combed its hair, and did other simple actions with her doll and stuffed animals.

The team then met to discuss possible intervention approaches. They suggested helping April's mother to see the positive aspects of April's growing independence by having her "help" around the house. She could, for instance, find a pan and put a lid on it for Mommy, which would encourage her to use her walking skills, attach a label and action to an object, match shapes and things that go together, and follow a two-step instruction. Several other ideas were generated based on the developmental specialist's knowledge of Mrs. M.'s day. They generated ideas for bathtime using plastic containers and lids, combing April's and a doll's hair in front of the mirror, helping Mommy put her socks in a pile, and so forth.

When the developmental specialist met with Mrs. M. in her home, they watched the tape of April's TPBA and discussed what April was ready for developmentally. They then generated ideas of how these actions, concepts, language, and interactions could be incorporated into April's and Mrs. M.'s day in a playful way that would be fun for both of them.

The developmental specialist asked if Mrs. M. had any ideas about how they could show April that the things she was seeing on the cartoons and *Sesame Street* were the same as things she had in her home. Mrs. M. thought for a while, smiled, and said, "You know, there are a lot of things on TV that she sees here. Hats, clothes, cookies, beds, even Oscar's garbage can." They talked about the words April used and having Mrs. M. label April's play objects and actions.

When asked about their daily routine, Mrs. M. stated that April loved her bathtime. This led the developmental specialist into discussing tub play and ended up with Mrs. M. rummaging through the kitchen drawers and cupboards to find fun playthings for the tub. A funnel, a colander, a small pan and lid, a plastic cereal bowl, and a spoon were found. The developmental specialist talked about some of the team's ideas for incorporating fine motor and language skills into tub play, and Mrs. M. came up with several proposals of her own. She remarked that she was looking forward to trying out the tub games. Mrs. M. said that when she was a child, bathtime was not a time for play, but rather a hurried chore.

DEVELOPMENTAL LEVEL

- Matches objects by color, shape, and size
- Recognizes part/whole relationships (can identify parts and the objects with which they go)
- Discriminates size (can nest four boxes)
    (24–27 months)

INTERVENTION GUIDELINES

The child is now beginning to recognize and compare details of objects. Although he or she may not be able to name colors, shapes, and sizes yet, the ability to see likenesses and differences is emerging. Simultaneously, the child is gaining a greater understanding of part-to-whole relationships, demonstrating the ability to see a piece of an object, make an association, and remember the relationship of the pieces prior to separation. These skills are important to the child's growing understanding of concepts and set the foundation for reasoning and mathematical competence.

Matching Color, Shape, and Size

Experiences with matching influence the development of the child's reasoning capabilities. Finding things that are alike or go together in some way is fun for the child and can capitalize on the developing fine and gross motor skills. For example, when the clothes are being folded after being taken from the dryer, the child can find the socks that match. The child could also find clothes of the same color, big and little shirts, and tops and bottoms. It is best to start with just three items from which the child can choose, and, as he or she becomes more proficient, make the task more difficult.

Part/Whole Relationships

As toys are being put away, the child can help find missing pieces or the object with which the piece goes. For example, if a doll's shoe is found, the parent can ask the child, "Where does this go?" The child may say, "Baby," or may go and get the baby. The shoe can then be placed on the doll's foot to show the child he or she was correct. Having the child locate missing parts, such as the top to the cup, the spoon for the bowl, or the top to the pajamas, is a functional way to promote discrimination/classification skills and also encourage problem-solving.

Size Discrimination

Size discrimination can be approached in several functional ways: books can be put away so the big ones go together, then the middle-size ones, and then the small ones. Whenever several toys of different sizes, like balls, are out, the objects can be compared and labeled, as in, "Throw me the *big* ball." Boxes of different sizes that have lids can be saved. An earring box, a larger jewelry box, and a large gift box prompt the child to explore matching lids to boxes as well as nesting the boxes inside each other. Even various plastic bowls and empty cereal boxes can provide self-motivating entertainment for the young child. A box of jars, lids, and things to put inside jars may stimulate experimentation, although the child may not be accurate in sorting and matching when too many different sizes are available.

PLAY MATERIALS AND OPPORTUNITIES

Many toys that promote matching by color, shape, and size are commercially available. Shape sorters, nesting cups, blocks and other construction toys, and color-coded matching activities are easily found. As previously stated, many objects found around the house provide just as much stimulation and pleasure as materials purchased in stores. For children with visual impairments, tactile materials may be glued to various parts of toys to help them distinguish, for example, the top, an opening, or specific shape.

- Discriminates circle, square, and triangle
- Matches object to picture of the object
- Matches picture of object to another picture of the object
      (24–36 months)

The child at this level can not only match, he or she can now see differences and identify distinguishing characteristics, such as shape, with a label. The child's representational abilities are also developing, so that now pictures of objects found in books and magazines are perceived as real objects, fitting into the same classification system as the object itself. The child's rapidly expanding language system is also supporting his or her increasing proficiency in the classification of concepts. As similarities are noted in the environment, an adult attaches a label to the object or characteristic; repeated use of the label then reinforces the perception of the specific concept. Thus, concept development and language are simultaneously supported. *Identifying objects and characteristics of objects in the environment and helping the child to recognize and label them is the task of the parent or facilitator.*

Labeling Objects and Pictures

Reading books and identifying objects pictured is a natural activity for both parents and professionals. Adding an extra step of pairing real objects with the pictures or another picture of the same object helps the child to see that both the pictures and the objects have the same label. Early picture books contain pictures of familiar objects—ball, bottle, bear—that are easily matched to the real items. For children with visual impairments, tactile books are available to assist the child in making the connection between pictorial representation and object.

Signing Labels

For children with hearing impairments or cognitive delays, the use of sign language with pictures and objects reinforces the development of specific concepts. The visual cue that a sign provides enhances the auditory label. As the child begins to understand and identify familiar concepts, he or she is ready for the task of finding these and other objects in new books or magazines.

Generalization of Thought Schemes

Generalization of concepts, or thought schemes, is as important as the earlier generalization of motor schemes. *The parent and facilitator should take every opportunity to demonstrate, illustrate, and label objects, functions, parts, and charac-*

teristics of objects that have similar functions, appearance, parts, or characteristics. The following examples illustrate such opportunities:

- For the young child, use simple objects that are familiar to the child, such as real balls and pictures of balls, and talk about the characteristics of the balls (e.g., Balls are round. Balls roll. Balls come in varying sizes. Balls can be different colors or textures. Balls can be hard or soft). Compare the balls to other balls the child encounters or to pictures of balls in books.
- For the older child, use more complex objects, such as real cars and trucks and pictures of cars and trucks, and point out characteristics of cars and trucks (e.g., Cars and trucks make noises. People ride in cars and trucks. Cars and trucks have wheels, doors, and windows. Cars and trucks roll. Cars and trucks come in different colors and are made of different materials. There are many kinds of cars and trucks).

It is important for the child to be able to examine and perceive specific aspects of objects in his or her environment and be able to compare and relate these to other objects. This facility lays the foundation for higher-level reasoning skills. The adult's role is to assist the child in acquiring insight and understanding through exploration, making comparisons, and indicating associations and relationships.

PLAY MATERIALS AND OPPORTUNITIES

Materials for Learning Color, Shape, and Size

Abstract concepts such as color, shape, and size are incorporated into many preschool toys (e.g., shape boxes; puzzles; graduated, colored rings that stack on pegs; parquetry blocks; building blocks; pop beads; stringing beads).

Pictures

Picturebooks, magazines, newspaper advertisements, and junk mail flyers (for pizza, etc.) are all excellent sources of illustrations for real objects. The important thing to consider as the child matures is to go beyond the basic object label into descriptions and comparisons.

DEVELOPMENTAL LEVEL

- Matches objects that have the same function (comb and brush) (30–33 months)

INTERVENTION GUIDELINES

As in the previous section, the identification of functions of objects demonstrates the child's increasing ability to think about the abstract characteristics of objects. At this point functions are limited to those he or she can see—balls roll; people can ride in cars, trucks, buses, and trains; people can eat from forks and spoons. The role of the facilitator is to give the child the opportunity to perceive and label these functions and make comparisons.

Beginning with everyday objects (e.g., brush and comb, fork and spoon, coat and jacket), the parent or facilitator can point out the functions as the objects are used. For example, a parent or facilitator might say, "A comb takes the tangles out of your hair. What else could we use to make it pretty?" or "Yes, a brush takes the tangles out, too."

The items and opportunities suggested on page 135 are appropriate at this developmental level as well.

> • Can sort by one criterion (shape or color) without getting confused (36–48 months)

Sorting, or putting things that are somehow alike together, is a critical reasoning skill. The ability to decide whether and how things are alike is important for both mathematical and reading skills. Understanding sets and identifying letters and words comes after the child has established an understanding of matching and sorting. The child at this early level can concentrate on one characteristic of an object at a time. Earlier, if the child started to sort blocks by color, he or she might begin to sort by shape or size, losing track of the original intent of the task (Piaget, 1952). At this level, the child learns to concentrate, remember the task, and classify by one of the characteristics without getting confused.

To facilitate practice in a play context, the parent or facilitator can set up a situation that necessitates sorting. He or she might say, "What shall we build? A castle? O.K. What color should we make it? Red? Great idea. Let's find all of the red blocks" or, "I'd like to make my castle out of the big blocks. Could you help me find enough big ones?"

The parent or facilitator should refrain from setting up table tasks with puzzles or sorting tasks with required outcomes that have not been initiated by the child. Requiring a child to sit and do puzzles or sorting makes the motivation for the task external to the child. He or she may comply and attempt the activity but may not be focused on the problems and discriminations involved; instead he or she focuses on compliance and task completion to satisfy the adult.

Attributes are not limited to size and color. When the child puts toys away in various categories, such as hats, shoes, capes, dresses, or large and small dolls, he or she is sorting by attribute. In the classroom, playing games to find all of the children with shorts, all of the ones with blue eyes, or all of the tall children requires sorting by attribute. Play areas can be set up so the children can sort. Art areas can contain media for making thick and thin marks, dry or wet marks, and light and dark colors. The water table can contain objects that hold and pour water, objects that allow water to go through, soft and hard objects, and objects of different textures. *Through experimentation and with adult facilitation, the child discovers the characteristics of and labels attached to various attributes.* The same type of games can be played at home, with the child now able to help his or her mom put the clothes from the dryer into different piles according to the person who wears them, types of clothing, or size. Grocery shopping can involve the child in identifying vegetables, meats, cereals, soda in cans instead of bottles, and so forth.

The child also begins to experiment with discriminating sounds, letters, and numbers. This is a higher level of discrimination, however, and color, shape, size, and other visible attributes should be recognized first. Once the basic visible attributes are differentiated, the child begins to notice other attributes. The child may spontaneously generate his or her own discriminations, such as, "Hey,

Mom, box, blocks. Does that rhyme?" Build on the child's own initiations by making them into fun games. "That does rhyme! Let me see if I can think of a rhyme, too."

PLAY MATERIALS AND OPPORTUNITIES

Any toys or objects that have more than one attribute can be made into a game. For instance, in the fall, the adult can make a game out of having the child find all of the yellow leaves, while the adult finds the red ones. At a store, the child can help the parent find all the big coins to pay the clerk. As indicated, at school the teacher can incorporate sorting and classification into almost any activity, having children group themselves by hair color, height, or type of clothing; finding all the materials that can make marks on paper; or making up songs with words that rhyme.

Commercially available materials are also available. Attribute blocks consisting of five blocks of different shapes in three different colors and two sizes encourage the child to sort in different ways. Lotto games relating to colors, shapes, animal homes, types of transportation, and numerous other categories encourage the child to think about attributes and match objects. Numerous forms of dominoes are also on the market to match colors, shapes, zoo animals, and so forth. Stringing beads of different sizes and shapes are available for making necklaces or sequencing beads in a specific order. Many board games are also fun for the young child. Candyland, Alphabet Land, and other simple memory and matching games appeal to the very young child who is just learning about rules.

DEVELOPMENTAL LEVEL

- Can sort objects by size (large, medium, small)
- Can sort a group of objects in several different ways
- Can classify objects into categories (toys, food, animals)
- Matches or identifies basic symbols
- Identifies different coins
- Identifies left and right
- Can put together complex puzzle
- Can build elaborate symmetrical or asymmetrical block structures (48–60 months)

INTERVENTION GUIDELINES

Preacademics

Differentiation at this level lays the foundation for what is typically known as *preacademics*. The role of the parent or facilitator is to help the child make comparisons, see likenesses and differences, and perceive relationships.

Size Differentiation

Size differentiation is a form of classification. As the child develops the ability to discriminate sizes, he or she concurrently builds an understanding of "more," "less," and "the same," and the concept of ordering or seriation. All of these concepts are necessary for the child to be able to comprehend numbers.

Size differentiation can be incorporated into play. For instance, when the child arranges the blocks, dolls, pans, beds, and so forth in order of size, he or she is practicing size discrimination. Finding figures of the appropriate size for the cars and trucks allows the child to do size matching, or ordinal correspondence. (The child forms two series, and then matches them, placing together those that correspond.) If the classroom has numerous objects of varying sizes, the child experiments with placement by size.

Consideration of Multiple Attributes

The ability to focus on different attributes and group objects in more than one way is important for flexibility in thinking and assists the child in seeing how objects can be combined into different sets. This ability leads to an understanding of combinatorial logic in mathematics and reading. The child eventually learns that $3 + 2 = 5$; $1 + 4 = 5$; and $2 + 3 = 5$. In the same way, the child eventually learns that different combinations of letters make different words (e.g., hat, sat; owl, low; jump, jumps, jumping). Discriminating, classifying, and ordering are foundations for these tasks.

The child at this level understands sets, groupings, and attributes at a very concrete level. The child begins to develop one-to-one correspondence as he or she figures out problems in play; for example, how to make sure two children have the same number of blocks, finding enough aprons for the children at the water table; following a cooking recipe using pictures, and so forth. As previously discussed, matching or grouping by attributes can be incorporated into many aspects of play. Grouping can be done in the structures he or she builds in block play. Building a structure of all one color and then using blocks of the same size or shape to build a similar structure allows the child to see different means to an end. Building different structures with the same blocks demonstrates using similar means to different ends. *The adult's role is to observe the child's play, comment, question, and encourage the child to analyze and draw conclusions about what he or she has done.* For instance, if two children playing next to each other have each constructed a structure from blocks, the adult might encourage reasoning skills by giving them a ruler or stick to measure which structure is taller or wider. Asking, "How could we figure out which building used more blocks?" stimulates problem-solving and requires one-to-one correspondence, sequencing, and reasoning skills.

Categorization of Concepts

The child's classification of concepts is also developing rapidly as he or she puts new vocabulary into idea "compartments." For example, robins, ducks, chickens, and "things with feathers and wings" are birds. Labeling objects in different ways helps the child see that objects can have more than one label and that labels can fit into categories. Dump trucks, fire engines, and pick-ups are trucks, vehicles, and forms of transportation. Introducing these concepts during play, while reading books, or while noticing objects or events during the course of the day enables the child to enlarge his or her vocabulary and extend the underlying concept structure.

Identification of Symbols

In the eyes of parents, a major accomplishment comes when the child is able to identify letters and numbers. This signals mastery of preacademic skills necessary for reading and writing. Basic symbol identification is first signaled, however, in the child's ability to recognize other symbols in his or her environments: the stop sign on the corner, the McDonald's arches, certain brands of cereals or items in the store, the contents of a box by a symbol or word pattern, and different coins. Recognition of signs and symbols can be turned into a game. While driving down the road, shopping, watching TV, going up the elevator, looking at books, and so forth, playing the game of "let's see who can find . . . ," excites the child about identifying known patterns or symbols.

The pencil and paper, crayons and markers, blackboard, and easel are media for the child to attempt to draw symbols that represent letters, numbers, and pictures of people and objects. If allowed to play freely with these materials, the child experiments with writing letters or his or her name. Both drawing and writing require fine motor coordination and visual motor skills. Children who have difficulty with these skills, may still have the desire to experiment with symbols and lines using magnetic or felt letters and numbers and three-dimensional materials such as clay or sticks. See drawing, page 193.

Experimentation with Reading

Also at this level, the child develops spatial understanding of left and right and can thus imitate the movement of the eyes in reading from left to right and top to bottom. He or she also understands that the words on the page correspond to the picture on the page. Giving the child an opportunity to experiment with reading while playing school or "reading" the pictures to a peer or sibling is a nonthreatening, safe way for the child to practice prereading skills.

PLAY MATERIALS AND OPPORTUNITIES

Having numerous materials in the classroom that come in different sizes encourages size differentiation. Blocks and other construction sets in different sizes, shapes, and colors inspire investigation of arrangements, groupings, and designing structures of varying sizes. Plastic forms that stick to a surface come in all shapes and sizes and include many types of animals and objects that can be arranged by the child.

Children at this level are beginning to be more interested in structured games and playing with other children. They will, however, want to change the rules. Games such as Ants in the Pants, Candyland, Uncle Wiggly, Perfection, Cootie, the Oreo Cookie Factory game, and various memory matches and lottos require the child to discriminate and classify concepts.

DEVELOPMENTAL LEVEL

- Can identify objects that do not belong in a group
- Can identify abstract characteristics (living, as opposed to nonliving)
- Matches letters
- Discriminates and names letters
  (60–72 months)

INTERVENTION GUIDELINES

Sophisticated Concepts

The child's classification system is becoming more sophisticated. He or she can identify attributes that are not visible, but must be inferred through reasoning or judgment. He or she can identify such characteristics as "rude," "alive," and "handsome," and can mentally group characteristics of objects so that he or she can deduce which things belong in a group and which things do not. Concepts of time are also becoming more sophisticated, with hours, minutes, days, and months acquiring personal meaning.

In play, the parent or facilitator can assist this development by incorporating these more sophisticated concepts into the play sequences. When playing school, the parent can ask, "What month is it? How should we dress?" When playing house, the parent can say, "Please fix me something for dinner that's not too sweet."

Working with Letters

The child at this level can also discriminate, match, and name letters. He or she is experimenting with writing his or her name and other personally meaningful words. Familiar words may be recognized from television advertisements or favorite books. Pointing out and looking for certain letters or words can be a fun game as long as the child is motivated.

Books

PLAY MATERIALS AND OPPORTUNITIES

Spending time looking at books and being read to is critical for inspiring the child to want to learn to read. At this level the child enjoys all types of books and is able to follow a story by listening and not looking at pictures, although pictures are still desired. Reading should be incorporated into several times of the day, including time for the child to "read" alone.

Classification Games

Many classification games are of interest to the child at this level. Card games, such as Go Fish! and Lotto, are still fun for children and give the child an opportunity to practice discrimination and classification. In addition, the child can now play such games as Boggle Junior, Scrabble Junior, and more advanced computer games.

OBSERVATION GUIDELINES FOR
COGNITIVE DEVELOPMENT: ONE-TO-ONE CORRESPONDENCE

VIII. **One-to-One Correspondence**
    A. **How does the child demonstrate understanding of number concepts?**
       1. **How does the child demonstrate ability to count discrete objects using the correct number (can use corresponding number for separate objects, rational counting)?**
       2. **How high can the child count by rote?**
    B. **What concepts demonstrate the child's ability to compare quantities (big/little, one/many, more/less, equal/not equal)?**
    C. **What evidence is shown of understanding measurement concepts (heavy/light, full/empty, short/long, before/after, hot/cold)?**
    D. **Does the child demonstrate any understanding of conservation of number (changing the configuration doesn't change the number of items)?**
    E. **Does the child demonstrate one-to-one correspondence with words and pictures?**
       1. **Identifies pictures in books with the correct word or action**
       2. **Identifies words in print that correspond to pictures or common objects (labels on food cartons)**

INTERVENTION IMPLICATIONS

The ability to hold one concept in mind and match that concept to another is *one-to-one correspondence.* One-to-one correspondence is necessary for all math and science abilities and is also critical to the development of reading skills (Cohen & Gross, 1979). One-to-one correspondence derives from the child's classification, memory, comparison, and sequencing skills (Ginsburg & Opper, 1988).

The child acquires one-to-one correspondence through experience with counting real objects and matching those objects to a number. The child also acquires one-to-one correspondence by matching objects or pictures that are alike or correspond in some way. The child first learns that a word corresponds with an object, person or picture; then that specific words correspond with actions, feelings, and attributes. Eventually, the child learns that a specific number corresponds with a set number of objects, a specific unit of measurement corresponds with a specific amount, a written or spoken letter corresponds with a sound or sounds, and a certain sequence of letters corresponds with a word.

Experiences that Foster An Understanding of One-to-One Correspondence

The role of the adult in fostering the development of one-to-one correspondence is to provide experiences that allow the child to associate objects with corresponding labels, other objects, and numbers. In play, the child can find one fork for each plate, one blanket for each doll, and two shoes for each doll; build one garage for each car and one stall for each horse; put puzzle pieces in appropriate spaces, and pegs in each hole. The child moves from matching to searching for the right number of objects to place in each play situation. The child's concept of number is approximately equal to his or her developmental level; a child functioning at about the age of 1 year understands and is able to find one object, a child of 3 years is able to count (rational counting) three or four objects accurately. After age 4, the understanding of one-to-one correspondence grows rapidly and this rough rule of thumb no longer holds. *The adult can assist by helping the child to order his or her thoughts, pausing at each item as a number is assigned.* The same is true for sounds and letters. The adult can support the child's efforts to learn sounds and letters by helping the child to stop, look, and listen in reading and in games with sounds and letters.

DEVELOPMENTAL LEVEL

- Can count by rote to five
- Understands concept of one
- Can count two to three objects
  (24–36 months)

INTERVENTION GUIDELINES

During the course of the day, the child has many opportunities to count objects. *The important point is to take advantage of the opportunities and keep the counting at the child's level.* Although the child may be able to rote count to a higher level than he or she understands, counting the actual number that is meaningful to the child is best. When the child clearly has the concept of the number two, for instance, a third object can be added. Counting feet and hands in the tub and socks when the child gets dressed are natural counting opportunities. During play, the parent or facilitator can comment, "I have two babies. I need two bottles." This gives the child the opportunity to find the right number of objects, a higher-level task than having two bottles in front of you and asking the child to count them.

PLAY MATERIALS AND OPPORTUNITIES

No specific toys or play materials are required. The child can count any objects (or people) present in the room. At this developmental level, focusing on counting two or three objects with accuracy is sufficient, but the child generally attempts to count higher. He or she then loses the concept of one number corresponding to one object and begins to say numbers where there are no objects or to omit numbers in the counting process. These errors are a normal part of the learning process and allow the child to practice role counting while still integrating the meaning of numbers.

DEVELOPMENTAL LEVEL

- Can count up to five objects
  (36–48 months)

INTERVENTION GUIDELINES

In dramatic play, many situations can incorporate numbers. Playing post office and giving "mail" to each child, weighing the letters on a simple scale and putting "stamps" (labeled 1 cent so the child has to put on the right number of stamps, or 1, 2, 3, 4, and 5 cents, so the child has to identify the right number on "letters") gives the child opportunities to practice using numbers in a meaningful way. Set up a fruit stand with real apples, oranges, and bananas or a lemonade or juice stand and have the children purchase items with real pennies (up to five) or nickels.

PLAY MATERIALS AND OPPORTUNITIES

Playing games that require the knowledge of numbers promotes the development of number concepts. A game such as Hi-Ho! Cherry-o! requires the child to count up to four. Other games, such as Cootie, require the child to know up to the number six on the die or on a spinner. Playing card games, such as Go Fish!, adds the element of number recognition. For the younger child, removing the higher numbers makes the game less frustrating. Be prepared to play a "different" game than outlined by the rules, as the child at this level frequently changes the rules to accomplish his or her desired end. Scales that allow children to weigh and compare encourage one-to-one correspondence. Introductory computer programs, such as Counting Critters (MECC, 1985) and Math and Me (Davidson and Associates, Inc. 1987) also stimulate math skills.

DEVELOPMENTAL LEVEL

- Can count up to 10 objects
- Understands "more," "less," "same"
- Can count objects, enumerating each object once
- Identifies and names numbers
- Can match the number of items in a set to the correct number
- Understands concept of zero
      (48–60 months)

INTERVENTION GUIDELINES

Again, numbers can be incorporated into play. In dramatic play, making an elevator out of an old refrigerator box and playing "elevator operator" in a pretend store or apartment house is fun, particularly when kids dress for the part. Putting up children's actual address numbers on the playhouse; making up recipe cards with simple pictures and numbers for making play dough or muffins; playing shoe store with prices, pennies, and a cash register (with sizes on the shoes, of course); and playing farmer and planting a certain number of seeds, feeding each animal, and weighing the crop are just a few play ideas.

For the child with motor disabilities, many computer games involving numbers are available. Card games can be played with adaptive card holders and head pointers to show which card needs to be removed. For the child with visual impairments, braille numbers can be added to the materials or games. Structured games are still being modified by the child at this level, but he or she is acquiring a better sense of following prescribed directions.

PLAY MATERIALS AND OPPORTUNITIES

Almost any objects can be used in dramatic play situations. The key is to have 10 specific items for the child to count and situations where written numbers must be recognized. Situations that approximate real life or experiences read in books are more motivating to the child, so using real props is best if possible.

Any game that includes pieces that must be placed in specific places on a board or object incorporates one-to-one correspondence. All of the previously discussed games require the child to use counting or matching skills. In addition, computer games such as Easy Street (Mind Play, 1988) and Number Farm (DLM, 1984) develop early math skills.

EXAMPLE

Benjamin D., a 7½-year-old with Down syndrome, was integrated in a kindergarten class. During the TPBA, Benjamin had demonstrated that he had one-to-one correspondence of as many as five objects. He was able to point consistently to an object and say the correct number. He could identify the numbers one and two and was able to say which pile of blocks had more in it.

The team helped the teacher plan a unit on the zoo. Using Dr. Seuss's book *If I Ran the Zoo* (Geisel, 1950) as the storybook theme, they planned centers and play activities that incorporated all areas of development and included numbers in various ways. After reading the story, the class, which consisted of 28 children (five with disabilities), was able to choose from a variety of play centers. One center had popsicle sticks, glue, and various other materials for making small cages. Another center had wood, dowels, a hammer, nails, screws, glue, and materials for constructing larger cages. Yet another center had cardboard boxes of different sizes that could be colored, cut, and decorated to make unique cages.

Benjamin made his cage out of a cardboard box. He decorated it with pictures he cut from magazines. Using scissors was an activity recommended by the occupational therapist to assist Benjamin in refining his fine motor skills and using both hands together in a coordinated fashion. As a result of low muscle tone, the therapist had also advised the teacher to make sure Benjamin was seated in a stable chair with sides and to have both of his feet on the floor to provide more stability. Benjamin was able to turn the paper, cut out three pictures, glue them on his box, and count them.

The class then sorted the cages into categories of those that seemed to go together because they were alike in some way. Benjamin decided to place his box with the other cardboard boxes because they were "all big."

The cages were arranged around the room in increasingly larger sets, and the children labeled each set with the appropriate number. Benjamin was able to label the first five sets by standing next to each cage as he counted, but said the next set had seven cages. With a peer beside him they walked by each cage again, with the peer helping him to count to six.

1	2	3	4	5	6	7
X	XX	XXX	XXXX	XXXXX	XXXXXX	XXXXXXX

The following day, centers were arranged around the room with varying kinds of materials from which animals could be made. Different kinds of sensory materials were included to provide tactile input. Sandpaper, velvet, corduroy, fake fur, buttons, snaps, "googly" eyes, glue, and so forth were at one table. Pictures of animals that could be cut out of magazines were at another table; sticks, pipe cleaners, Tinker Toys, animal puzzle blocks, and Bristle blocks were at a different center; and construction materials and tools at yet another. The children could stay in one center and make a strange animal or move from center to center for different materials. After they had played with and experimented with the various materials, each had a distinctive rare animal. Each child named his unusual creature and placed it in or near his cage. The teacher wrote the animal's name on a card and taped it on the cage. Benjamin made a creature out of animal blocks and pipe cleaners and named it "Blackie," because that was his dog's name. When the teacher asked what kind of a strange animal it was, he said, "A dog." So Blackie, the strange dog, was placed in his cage beside the snizzles, jiffers, and whipples.

Motor centers were also set up. The occupational therapist took one group of volunteers "on safari" to the playground looking for a grunch. Another group followed the tracks of a spunkel around the room and through an obstacle course. A music center was arranged in one corner, and the children became animals moving to the music. A quiet center with tapes and copies of the book *If I Ran the Zoo* (Geisel, 1950) and other animal books was in the opposite corner.

The dramatic play area was set up as a jungle. Safari hats, ropes, hanging vines made from crêpe paper, a cave made from a refrigerator box, a wagon with a cardboard box for a cage, and various stuffed animals were hidden in the center. The children role played hunting and trapping animals.

In each of the areas, the staff facilitated language and communication, cognitive, social-emotional, and sensorimotor skills appropriate to the children. One-to-one correspondence was built into each of the activities so that matching related objects and counting were meaningful to the child. Although Benjamin's skills were at a lower developmental level than those of many of his classmates, the play centers contained materials that he could use, and the staff and his peers facilitated his movement into higher skill levels.

OBSERVATION GUIDELINES FOR
COGNITIVE DEVELOPMENT: SEQUENCING ABILITY

IX. **Sequencing Ability**
    A. **What behaviors demonstrate sequencing ability?**
        1. **Sequencing of schemes (See Linking of Schemes, III., C.)**
        2. **Sequencing (seriation) of concepts**
            a. **Number**
            b. **Size**
            c. **Sensory input (textures, smells, sounds)**
        3. **Sequencing of stories**
            a. **In dramatic play**
            b. **Through pictures in a book**
        4. **Sequencing of time**
            a. **In dramatic play**
            b. **In conversation**

INTERVENTION IMPLICATIONS

The sequencing of actions, as noted previously, develops as the child sees relationships between objects and events. The sequencing of concepts develops as the child is able to make comparisons between objects and events. The concept of number, for instance, derives from the child's understanding of one-to-one correspondence and a comparison of the number of units being measured. He or she perceives that two is one more object than one, that three is one more object than two, and so forth.

Ordering

Ordering, or seriation, is basic to number knowledge (Cohen & Gross, 1979). Concepts of more, less, and the same develop as the child begins to understand sequenced relationships. The ability to see three or more objects and put them in size order is also based on that sequential comparison. At first, the child only understands big and little, focusing on the largest and smallest items. As a more sophisticated understanding of relationships evolves, the child can make a sequence of comparisons, fitting each new object into a larger–smaller relationship until all items are in a graduated size sequence (Vast, Haith, & Miller, 1992). The ability to put other sensory stimuli into a graded sequence, such as sounds from soft to loud or textures from smooth to rough, requires comparing other types of sensory input and should also be promoted (Fewell & Vadasy, 1983). The adult's role is to provide opportunities for sequencing and to assist the child in making the comparisons. *By breaking tasks down into sets of comparisons of two objects at a time, the child can see the evolution of the longer sequence.*

Sequencing Stories

Sequencing of stories, or the ability to relate ideas in a logical order, also builds upon the child's sequencing of actions. As the child's memory for past actions increases, he or she becomes able to pick up a picturebook that has been read to him or her previously and retell the story. The child also becomes able to act out scenarios, and eventually stories, with increasingly longer sequences. The adult can encourage the child to add another event to the sequence or think about what will happen next in the story.

Sequencing Time

The sequencing of time also comes to be reflected in the child's dramatic play. Through conversation and observation of events, the child learns concepts related to before, during, and after; a second, a minute, and an hour; a day, a week, a month, and a year; spring, summer, winter, and fall; and other vague time concepts, such as "in a little while." Time concepts are highly influenced by cultural variables and how various groups measure time. People whose lives are scheduled around calendars and the clock, for work, appointments, and activities, relate to time concepts differently than those who do not work or whose lives are regulated by television shows, irregular, or seasonal events. Understanding time sequences can be enhanced by incorporating various concepts into play sequenc s. Using a timer in the house area to "cook the beans for 1 minute," referencir play activities with sequencing concepts (e.g., "After we clean up the water table area, we will play outside"), and relating events to a time sequence (e.g., "Let's talk about what we did yesterday") keeps time concepts relevant to children. Typical circle time activities involving preschoolers with calendar activities with number sequences up to 31, and day and month recall are not meaningful activities for a child with number concepts that are limited to a one-to-one correspondence of up to five. Such concepts, when presented, should incorporate ideas of significance to the child. "It's September. This month you will be 5 years old." Books, such as *Bear Child's Book of Hours* (Rockwell, 1987) also can help the child relate time to everyday events.

DEVELOPMENTAL LEVEL

- Understands big, little
  (36–42 months)

INTERVENTION GUIDELINES

The child's understanding of size begins with the gross comparisons of big and little. As the child develops concepts relating to abstract characteristics of objects, such as color, the concept of size also emerges. At this point, two objects can be compared and the larger one identified or labeled as "big." In play with the child, the parent or facilitator may comment, "I'm cooking lots of soup; I need the big pan," or "That baby's little; let's give her the little bottle."

Stories such as *Little Red Riding Hood* and *The Three Billy Goats Gruff* include characters of various sizes. Listening to the story and then acting out a scenario from the story gives the child a physical means of relating to the size sequence. Music and dance activities often provide opportunities for the child to "grow bigger," be "little" then "big," or be an "itsy-bitsy spider" or "little teapot."

Puzzles depicting objects of different sizes also allow the child to practice size differentiation in his or her play. The adult can use almost any situation in the playroom to make observations about size. The parent can also point out the difference in size between the child's old shoes and new shoes, Daddy's pants and the child's pants, and so forth.

PLAY MATERIALS AND OPPORTUNITIES

Puzzles, graduated cylinders or blocks, nesting cups, dolls and accompanying paraphernalia, bottles, boxes, and household materials that come in different sizes are recommended. Computer games such as The Playroom (Broderbund Software, 1989) develop the child's concept of time along with letters and numbers.

DEVELOPMENTAL LEVEL

- Understands questions about what is going to happen next
  (36–48 months)

INTERVENTION GUIDELINES

As indicated previously with regard to time, the child can remember and relate verbally and through actions the next expected event in a known series. The adult can encourage this ability by allowing the child to talk about what is going to happen in a favorite story before turning the page. Acting out familiar stories also allows the child to anticipate the next event in a story. When playing with cause-and-effect toys or toys for which particular outcomes are expected, the child can be engaged in problem-solving about what is going to happen. For instance, "What's going to happen when you put that big block on top of your tower?" Playing a character who causes events to occur can also prompt the child to create a logical next occurrence (e.g., "Oh, doctor, I feel terrible. I need some help.")

Storybooks are wonderful for helping the child to learn about sequences of events. Stories with predictable events, like *The 500 Hats of Bartholomew Cubbins* (Geisel, 1938), intriguing chains of events, such as those in the *Curious George* books by H.A. Ray, or simple sequences or relationships, as in *Whose Mouse Are You?* (Krauss, 1970), support learning about sequences. Predicting events in movies or television programs is another way to encourage thinking about what is going to happen next.

PLAY MATERIALS AND OPPORTUNITIES

DEVELOPMENTAL LEVEL

* Understands tall, short
   (36–52 months)

INTERVENTION GUIDELINES

The ability to label tall and short develops as the child focuses on the attribute of height and usually comes after the child understands the concepts of big and little. At this developmental level, understanding derives from the comparison of two objects, as the child is not able to focus on the relationship of more than two things at a time. Pointing out and labeling objects as tall or short or big or little helps the child to understand the concept label. Matching tall toys to other tall toys or materials is also important. For instance, the child might build a tall bridge for a tall truck to go under or find a short doll to fit in a short bed. Tall and short, of course, are most obviously relevant to children as they compare their own heights and see who is "tall" and who is "short."

PLAY MATERIALS AND OPPORTUNITIES

No special toys or materials are needed at this developmental level. The adult can use almost anything that comes in different sizes to make comparisons. Toys, such as puzzles, designed for the purpose of teaching size sequencing can be purchased. In addition, boxes or blocks of differing heights or dolls of different sizes also encourage comparison. Again, computer games are good for engaging the child in thinking about sequences.

EXAMPLE

Alisha P., a 5-year-old, was enrolled in a program for children with severe disabilities. She used a wheelchair and was unable to use her fingers, although she could move her arms and use her hands in a fisted position. Alisha had poor breath control and consequently her speech was very difficult to hear and understand. She did use one to two words to express herself. During the TPBA, it was noted that Alisha could use switches to activate toys and she was able to use a Muppet pad on the computer and was thus able to play some simple matching and counting games. In the house area, she was able to gesture toward toys, comment on the action, and direct the adult with words, eye gaze, and gesture.

The team who worked with Alisha and her family felt that sequencing of ideas and anticipation of events was an important intervention area for Alisha. In her school environment, the team would allow Alisha to direct the staff members as well as her peers in play and would encourage her to think of the next step in a given sequence. Using varying materials with small handles added, Alisha was able to make a simple picture. With a large piece of round paper on her tray, she could use her fist, which had been dipped in paint, to make eyes and ears. A triangle shape stamped a nose, and a long, thin rectangle with a handle was used for a mouth. A bookholder and pageturner were devised so that Alisha could look at books independently. A switch modification allowed Alisha to activate a tape recorder. In this way, she could listen to tapes of books and follow along in the book. Computer games were her favorite, and she frequently played with staff members or peers on the concept board. Alisha was also able to color pictures and make designs on the computer.

As a result of her motor difficulties, Alisha's play opportunities were limited within her home. Alisha watched television or toys and other objects were placed on the wheelchair tray. Alisha merely looked at most objects briefly or pushed them around her tray. She had no opportunity to sequence events. The social worker assisted the family in identifying resources for purchasing a computer and software appropriate for Alisha's needs. She also introduced the family to an agency in town that provided training to children with disabilities and their families on how to use computers and adaptive devices for computers and other toys. The teacher made home visits to help Alisha's older brother and younger sister see how they could use Alisha's eye gaze, gesture, and verbalizations in dramatic play, on game boards, and with switch-operated toys. A Velcro strap was made to go around her wrist and allowed her to attach small character dolls. The tape recorder in Alisha's home was modified to allow Alisha to activate it, and tapes were checked out from school so that she could enjoy a variety of music and book tapes. The television control was also adapted to enable Alisha to change the channel.

The team also problem-solved with the family and elicited suggestions regarding how to incorporate play sequences into Alisha's bathtime using easily activated tub toys, into outdoor play in the sandbox, and into her playtime with her father before bedtime.

DEVELOPMENTAL LEVEL

- Understands tallest, largest, shortest, smallest (42–52 months)

INTERVENTION GUIDELINES

The adult can incorporate comparisons into the child's play by labeling the parts, characters, or objects in the activities. For instance, in a race among small cars, the parent might comment, "My car is the smallest, but it's the fastest," or "Let's find the shortest animal and build it a house."

Many toys come in sets that are the same size. For instance, Playmobile characters are all the same height and fit into proportionally sized settings. Opportunities for size comparisons can be enhanced by mixing different sets of toys. The Ninja Turtle characters become "giants" when placed in a Playmobile setting. Matchbox cars, Hot Wheels, and Tonka trucks are all different sizes and can provide an opportunity for the child to discover and sequence size relationships. The adult can facilitate by commenting on or inquiring about the size characteristics. For instance, "You sure built a tall barn; let's see if the tallest animal will fit."

Many toys come in various sizes, including animals, dolls, cars, trucks, blocks, and so forth. Materials such as paper, boxes, containers, and other media (e.g., crayons, paintbrushes, sponges) come in various sizes. The adult role is to encourage the child to compare the size relationships.

PLAY MATERIALS AND OPPORTUNITIES

DEVELOPMENTAL LEVEL

- Counts objects in sequence with one-to-one correspondence
- Can put three pictures in a sequence to tell a story
- Knows sequence of reading book, from left to right and top to bottom
- Knows first, middle, and last
        (48–60 months)

INTERVENTION GUIDELINES

The child's increasing understanding of units or one-to-one correspondence has not only helped him or her to understand the concept of numbers, but also to understand that pictures correspond to the story on the page, that one spoken word corresponds to a written word on the page, and that, when put in order, words and pictures tell a story.

Acting Out Stories

During this time the child also develops the ability to act out a story with a beginning, middle, and end. For the child at this level, having him or her "read" or tell you a story and then act it out is great fun. At the same time, the adults can help facilitate problem-solving by having the child figure out what to use for props. For example, *Three Billy Goats Gruff* is fun to read and act out. The story incorporates size and age differences and repeats the plot so it is easy to remember what happened at each stage of the story. The child or children can figure out what to use for the bridge, how to make the troll look scary, and how to make themselves look small, medium, and large. Acting out known stories also gives the child a sense of safety and security, as they can control the actions.

The adult's role is to act as a catalyst for thinking about the story sequence and acting out short scenarios within the story. Props provide incentives and a reminder of important components of a story. Children with disabilities often have difficulty with lengthy sequences. By "scripting" or providing the action and words for a story sequence, the adult can facilitate the dramatization of specific aspects of the story. After the children have practiced a scenario several times, they then initiate and embellish the role play with their own language and story improvisations. Such story enactment also inspires the child to "read" the book. After enacting a story, the child may go back to the book, study the pictures, and match the words and actions used in the role play to the story in the book.

PLAY MATERIALS AND OPPORTUNITIES

Storybooks are important to the development of sequencing skills. Simple stories, with easily identifiable patterns or beginnings, middles, and ends are the best. A storybook such as *What Was That? A Funny Story About Night Noises* (Matthews, 1977) is fun to act out at home or school. Household materials can be used inventively for props. In addition, capes, hats, fake fur material, and other costume possibilities enhance the storytelling and role play. Miniature characters are also fun for the child at this level. By adding cars, airplanes, or a scene in the sand table or a shoe box, the child can build a story to enact.

Many computer games are available for developing the one-to-one correspondence skills necessary for reading. The Muppet Word Book (Sunburst Communications, 1986), Talking Tiles (Bright Star Technology, 1988), or Phonics Plus (Stone & Associates, 1988), for example, develop letter and word skills.

DEVELOPMENTAL LEVEL

- Can place objects in order from shortest to tallest, and smallest to largest
- Identifies first, last, middle
- Combines letters into words
    (60–72 months)

INTERVENTION GUIDELINES

Size Sequence

As noted previously, the child's opportunities to size sequence can be incorporated into play activities by providing various sizes of objects and materials. For example, instead of putting the same size paper in the drawing area, the adult can provide a series of increasingly larger pieces of paper. In this way, the child can draw his or her pictures in a size sequence, can make them into a sequencing puzzle, or can relate the differences to peers.

Reading

As the child's differentiation skills increase along with one-to-one correspondence, the ability to order objects and letters into meaningful sequences evolves. The child is more motivated to read the words that are most important in his or her life or in the story that is being read. Reading can be incorporated into play by labeling the toy areas and props in the dramatic play area. Making a label, "POLICE," for a hat the child likes to wear in dramatic play increases the child's interest in reading that word. Reading a story about the police reinforces the opportunity to recognize that familiar letter sequence.

First, Last, and Middle

Concepts of first, last, and middle can be assimilated into object play, storytelling, and dramatic play. Again, through commenting and inquiry, the adult advances the child's thinking about these concepts.

The materials and opportunities suggested on pages 139 and 177 are appropriate at this developmental level as well. In addition, more complex computer games are available, such as Treasure Mountain (The Learning Company, 1991), What Makes a Dinosaur Sore? (D.C Heath & Company, 1988), Stone Soup (William K. Bradford Publishing, 1989), and Reading and Me (Davidson & Associates, Inc., 1987).

PLAY MATERIALS AND OPPORTUNITIES

OBSERVATION GUIDELINES FOR COGNITIVE DEVELOPMENT: DRAWING ABILITY

X. **Drawing Ability**
    A. **What developmental level is represented in the child's drawing of lines and shapes?**
    B. **What developmental level is represented in the child's drawing of people or objects?**

Scribbling

INTERVENTION IMPLICATIONS

The evolution of drawing skills is similar across cultures and socioeconomic levels. Drawing, at the earliest stages, is a sensorimotor task, a cause-and-effect experiment of putting pencil to paper. The child delights in the kinesthetic movement that results in scribbles and zigzags that evolve into lines, arcs, and circles (DiLeo, 1977).

Preschematic Stage

As the child develops, drawing becomes another form of representation of the world as the child understands it. Althouse (1981) describes the phase after scribbling as the *preschematic stage*. The first representations are of faces, then the people and objects in his or her world. Figures may be spaced around the page with no obvious relationship. Children may paint or draw just to explore color, line, and design.

Schematic Stage

During the schematic stage (Althouse, 1981), the child's art is more organized and realistic. A baseline and sky may be drawn. An individual style evolves. Symbols that represent letters, words, numbers, and functions are also incorporated. The figures of the preschool child are unconsciously expressionistic, but gradually become more objective and impressionistic (DiLeo, 1977). Drawings come to reflect the personality, inner feelings, and cultural values of the child (Almy & Ganishi, 1979). *By observing and listening to what the child says about his or her picture, the adult can gain insights into the child's inner world.*

Experimentation and Adaptation with Media

Providing opportunities for the child to experiment with different forms of linear representation is also important. At the same time, it should be recognized that with the introduction of new media, the child's drawing may regress to a lower or exploratory level. Most children love to draw, color, and paint with different media. Drawing instruments can be adapted to be used by children with varying disabilities. Feathers, sticks, and fingers, in addition to the more typical pencils and crayons, can add a motivating factor as well. The parent or facilitator provides the materials, the model, and the encouragement for visual expression through drawing. A key principle is to allow experimentation and not direct or have specific expectations for the artistic result. Comments on the child's drawing can be descriptive, pointing out the specific aspects that are pleasing or unique (e.g., "I love the color you made." "You made lots of circles.").

Resistance to Changing Media or Other Experimentation

Some children may resist the use of different types of media, either because of sensitivity to different kinds of tactile input or due to cultural or familial reasons. For the child with tactile sensitivities, allowing the child to experiment at his or her own pace is important. Having an adult or peer model may entice the child to sample, test, and explore the material. If parents have objections about the use of certain materials, for fear of ruining clothes, smocks can be used. If other cultural considerations are causing the parents to object, perhaps a different, more acceptable, medium could be used.

Fine and Gross Motor Considerations

Drawing is highly influenced by the child's fine and gross motor abilities. As noted in the introduction to this chapter, muscle tone, strength, joint stability, flexion and extension patterns, and body symmetry influence the child's ability to use his or her hands with objects (Ehrhardt, 1982). Drawing skills are particularly influenced by these factors, as a significant degree of precision is required. Therefore, consultation with an occupational or physical therapist is recommended for children with motor impairments. *Considerations such as inhibiting abnormal reflexes, normalizing tone, providing joint stability, and positioning are important to enable the child to have has much visual-motor control as possible.*

DEVELOPMENTAL LEVEL

> - Imitates scribbling
>   (12–24 months)

INTERVENTION GUIDELINES

At this stage, the child's drawing is a sensory exploration experience and demonstrates the child's understanding of the relationship between the drawing tool and the marks on the paper. This perception coincides with increasing ability to discern cause-and-effect connections. The adult can promote this understanding by giving the child different tools and materials on which to mark. Even the hands and fingers can draw in finger paints and shaving cream or other materials that are nontoxic. The child's scribbles do not yet symbolize or represent anything in the world, so the adult can delight with the child in the purely kinesthetic movements of arm and hand, in fast and slow pace, with dark and bright colors, with staccato dots or fluid scribbles.

Pencils, pens, crayons, and markers are all fun with supervision. The child who is still mouthing must mark with safe materials and be watched carefully. Older children, too, need supervision to make sure they are not drawing on everything in sight. Paper is only one surface on which to draw. A plastic table top or place mat is easy to clean after a shaving cream drawing experience. Chalkboards or plastic surfaces that can be wiped clean are also good. Cardboard boxes provide several surfaces on which to mark and are fun for the child to crawl into when he or she tires of drawing.

PLAY MATERIALS AND OPPORTUNITIES

DEVELOPMENTAL LEVEL

- Imitates vertical strokes, horizontal lines, circular strokes (24–30 months)

INTERVENTION GUIDELINES

As the child develops more fine motor control and ability to imitate, he or she is able to make more controlled directional strokes. *The adult can model, wait for the child to draw, mark again, and wait; thus making drawing into a turn-taking game.* After the child has observed and practiced, the actions are repeated spontaneously. The circular motion and back-and-forth scribble predominate. Use of various marking tools and media generate ongoing interest and continued experimentation and practice.

PLAY MATERIALS AND OPPORTUNITIES

The materials described on pages 190–191 are appropriate, with the addition of media such as paints and chalks. Commercial products, such as Magic Slates, are also fun as they are "erasable" and the process can be repeated as often as desired. Use markers that are easy for the child to grasp and are not easily broken.

DEVELOPMENTAL LEVEL

- Imitates cross
- Draws lines, strokes, and arcs spontaneously
- Makes first spontaneous unrecognizable forms (30–36 months)

INTERVENTION GUIDELINES

The child's sensory exploration is now under more voluntary control. Movements are given direction. Intervention takes the form of showing the child how controlling the movement of the marker results in a definite line. The adult can now begin to draw recognizable circles and directional lines, modeling for the child. As the child imitates the different strokes, he or she is also engaging in a form of cognitive discrimination and matching. Pairing the movements with sounds, such as "zip" or "wheee," stimulates imitation of the hand movement as well as the sound. For the child with motor or visual impairments, physical movement of the arms and hands through space in arcs and lines may help the child to get the kinesthetic image of the motions needed to mark on the paper.

PLAY MATERIALS AND OPPORTUNITIES

Providing a variety of media and methods increases generalizability. In addition to the traditional drawing materials, the child can now draw in sand, use finger paints, draw in flour or oatmeal, draw lines on his or her face with face paint, and use most kinds of markers. The child should be given a choice of media sizes, with both drawing materials and paper varying in size, so the child can select the size that feels most comfortable for his or her purposes. The materials and opportunities discussed on pages 190–191 are also appropriate.

DEVELOPMENTAL LEVEL

> • Draws circle
> • Draws face of a person
>   (36–48 months)

INTERVENTION GUIDELINES

A major milestone occurs when the child draws with the intention to create a recognizable figure. The first representation is that of the human face, a significant feature in the child's life. Adults always exhibit copious enthusiasm when this first representational drawing is created. Of course, this unbridled excitement stimulates more drawing on the part of the child and language on the part of the adult, "Oh, look! I see his eyes and mouth. Where is his nose?" The adult labels the parts of the face and frequently attributes male or female characteristics or features, "That looks like Daddy." The child, who may not have had any particular face in mind when he or she drew the initial face, eventually learns that one can draw a specific face. *The adult's role is to observe, comment, embellish, model, and imitate the child.* The child frequently asks the adult to add other body parts to the face he or she has drawn. Ultimately, toward the end of this developmental level, the child adds to the face other features of the human body. Legs and/or arms begin to sprout from the head. *The adult should refrain from trying to get the child to draw an anatomically correct person with all the various features.* At this point, the key features of the adult are the head, arms, and legs. As the child acquires the ability to discriminate various body segments, these will be added.

PLAY MATERIALS AND OPPORTUNITIES

In addition to drawing with all of the media discussed previously, the new ability to create a face sparks in the child the desire to make faces in a variety of ways. Allowing the child to represent the face with Play-Doh, using yarn and raisins or buttons to make facial features and so forth, gives the child who cannot yet draw with precision more control over the representation he or she wishes to create. This type of representation also emphasizes different features of the face.

Children may also enjoy drawing with the computer. Color Me (Mindscape, Inc. 1986) is an easy drawing program, along with KidPix (Broderbund Software, 1991).

DEVELOPMENTAL LEVEL

> • Draws stick figure
> • Copies square, triangle, diamond
> • Copies diagonal and V strokes
> • Adds trunk and arms to person
> • Draws identifiable objects without model
> • Copies own name in large, irregular letters
> • Copies numbers unevenly
>   (48–60 months)

The child's figures are now becoming more complete, with a trunk and other body features such as fingers and hair being added. The child also attempts other objects in conjunction with or in addition to human figures. Hats or swords may be added to the figure. The child may attempt to draw a fish or other animal or familiar entities, such as a house or flower. Creativity is blossoming, with experimentation in color, lines, shapes, and figures. The child may be able to tell a story to accompany his or her drawing. *The adult can stimulate drawing through the use of stories, poems, nature, and music.* Reading a book or poem and drawing a picture (which also can be labeled with the child's dictated words), listening to music and picking colors that illustrate the sounds, and drawing or tracing items from nature (e.g., rocks, leaves) are means of stimulating the child's representation through drawing. Drawing allows the child to represent his or her play, family, and life activities. Depending on the child's level of language, the adult can facilitate communication about the drawing as well.

The same art materials are recommended as in previous levels. However, as a result of higher cognitive skills, the child can relate and represent a broader range of topics. Use of storybooks, dramatic play scenarios, and other play activities can serve to arouse images in the child's mind that can then be transferred to paper or other media. Sidewalk chalk or paint enables the child to transfer drawing to the outdoors where larger figures can be drawn using large muscle movements.

    Many good computer programs are also available for preschool-level children to experiment with drawing and coloring on the computer. The programs listed in the above age level are appropriate as well. In addition, Kid Works (Davidson & Associates, Inc., 1991) and Koala Pad Graphics Exhibitor (Koala Technologies, 1983) teach drawing skills.

- Copies rectangle
- Copies letters and numbers with more accuracy, but still has many errors
        (60–72 months)

Given a piece of paper and pencil, the child may choose to practice writing his or her newly learned letters and numbers or may choose to draw pictures of people and objects. Allowing the child's creativity to burgeon without too much adult interference is sometimes difficult. *Providing materials, ideas, and incentives enables the child to express his or her individual thoughts and feelings.* For drawing to remain a play activity for the child, *adult direction and expectations should be limited.* Given the opportunity to engage the media on his or her own terms, the child may sit for an extended period totally engrossed in the drawing that is materializing on the page. Given the opportunity, he or she may come back to a drawing and expand or change it over time.

    For the child with more severe motor impairments, the adults may need to provide adaptive instruments, such as computers or special markers to assist the child in drawing. The child with visual impairments may also need special supports, such as a black light to help him or her see. Expression and representation through clay or other three-dimensional media may be more pleasurable for the blind child. The child can also label or describe his or her drawing, and the adult can write down the child's descriptions on a different piece of paper. The child can then see the words that he has used to describe the picture and can choose whether to write some of the words. In this way, the practice of letter and number writing can be done in a fashion that is particularly relevant to the child's interests. Whole storybooks can be created if the child has the interest and motivation.

PLAY MATERIALS AND OPPORTUNITIES

In addition to the items previously mentioned in other age levels, having a place to store media so they are accessible to the child is also important. An art corner or center that is available at home and/or school prompts the child to think about drawing and may kindle the desire to draw.

Computer drawing programs enable the child to experiment with drawing using varying types of strokes, symbols, colors, and sequences. Computer drawing allows the child to experiment with many facets of drawing at the same time. The Treehouse (Broderbund Software, 1991), and Easy Color Paint 2.0 (MECC, 1991) are higher level programs. Adaptations are also available for many programs so that children with motor impairments can also enjoy the computer. Power pads, touch windows, light pens, Koala pads, joy sticks, and modified keyboards enable children of all ages and abilities to control the computer.

EXAMPLE

Charlie R., a 6-year-old from the Native American reservation, attended a kindergarten program in the public schools. Charlie had been raised primarily by his grandmother, as his mother and father were frequently in town at one of the local bars. There was evidence of neglect in Charlie's early years, but his grandmother was now providing a nurturing home for him. During the TPBA, Charlie demonstrated age-appropriate motor skills, but his language and social skills appeared delayed. Charlie demonstrated advanced cognitive understanding in his drawings, but he was so shy and withdrawn that he rarely spoke. When he did speak, his sentences were only four or five words long. He drew pictures of his life on the reservation with his extended family that included minute details of the people and the environment. He created incredibly detailed pictures of rockets going into space, complete with exterior and interior technicalities. He could watch a favorite television show and then draw specific scenes. Drawing was Charlie's passion and his primary means of self-expression. Clearly, he was a bright boy with emotional issues that were affecting his communicative and social interactions. The team felt that drawing might provide the means for expanding Charlie's social interactions and his communication skills.

The team planned a thematic play unit using *The Girl Who Loved Wild Horses* (Goble, 1978) as the storybook kick-off. They planned a variety of sensory, motor, art, and dramatic play centers using the Native American and horses theme. Planning included talking about the emotions of the little girl in the story and how the Native American's life is different now compared to the life of the girl in the story, building a tepee and making lassos and horse heads on sticks for the dramatic play area, using Playmobil figures in the manipulatives area, and putting a variety of media in the art center, including geometric shapes and stencils for creating Indian motifs, clay for making pots, and a small loom for making a "rug."

Charlie's grandmother came to class on several days and brought samples of Native American arts and crafts. Then she stayed to help facilitate in the art center. Charlie was proud to have his grandmother be the center of attention, and he stayed near her in the art center. When she suggested he draw a picture of the horses in the story, he obliged by drawing one of the scenes in the book of the little girl watching the horses. The teacher asked Charlie to describe what he had drawn and wrote down what he said on paper, then gave it to him to put with his picture.

The teacher set up the computer with the Color Me (Mindscape, Inc., 1986) software and began to create patterns of geometric shapes on the screen. She asked Charlie if he could help her. They took turns drawing and adding shapes and colors. The teacher suggested they print out patterns and put them up on the tepee. Charlie spent many minutes of each subsequent day at the computer.

The teacher asked Charlie if he could help another child learn to make designs on the computer, too, so Charlie sat and took turns with Missie at the computer, using a concept pad. Missie tried to do what Charlie did, then laughed when the design came out crooked. Charlie said, "That's O.K. Let's try again." When they had completed a design to Missie's satisfaction, they printed it out and taped it to the tepee. Then other children wanted to make designs, and Charlie became the tutor.

Each day, he drew another picture from the story and dictated the events in the picture to the teacher. The teacher commented on the feelings he was expressing and talked about how other kids and even she sometimes felt lonely or sad, too. At the end of the week, the teacher sat down next to Charlie as he was drawing and said, "You know Charlie, I think you have enough pictures and words to make a book. Let's see if we can put all of your pictures in order so they tell a story." Charlie easily arranged the pictures. The teacher asked if he wanted to make a cover for the book. Charlie drew an elaborate cover and the teacher helped him put it in a binder.

When Charlie turned the pages of the book and "read" his story the teacher taperecorded the reading. She then included the book and tape in the reading center for other children to see and listen. Charlie's eyes lit up when he went to the center and listened to himself reading the book. When another child came into the quiet corner and sat next to Charlie, he let her look at his book and listen to the tape.

In each of the play centers, the teacher tried to pair Charlie with another child. She also tried to elicit language from Charlie by asking him about the Native American culture and ways. His grandmother was helpful, as she reminded Charlie about certain aspects he had not mentioned.

At the end of the week, Charlie's grandmother asked if she could keep Charlie's book and tape. She said maybe she would have Charlie draw pictures of what was happening at school so he could tell her about them. She said

Charlie was always quiet at home, but that she had noticed during this week how he liked to talk about the pictures he made of the horses. She said he seemed to want to talk about his pictures, so maybe that was a way to "get him talkin'." The teacher and the rest of the team thought this was a great idea. Thus began the back-and-forth "communication pictures" that continued throughout the year. They served as a basis of communication for Charlie, his family, and his teachers.

ACKNOWLEDGMENTS

The age ranges provided in this chapter are based on recognized data and the work of the following researchers: for Early Object Use, Clark, Morgan, and Wilson-Vlotman (1984) and Kusmierek, Cunningham, Fox-Gleason, Hanson, and Lorenzini (1986); for Symbolic and Representational Skills, Fewell (1983), Nicholich (1977), Watson (1981), Watson and Fischer (1977), and Westby (1980); for Imitation Skills, Clark et al. (1984), Cohen and Gross (1979), and Kusmierek et al. (1986); for Problem-Solving Skills, Clark et al. (1984), Cohen and Gross (1979), and Kusmierek et al. (1986); for Discrimination/Classification Skills, Clark et al. (1984), Cohen and Gross (1979), and Kusmierek et al (1986); for One-to-One Correspondence, Cohen and Gross (1979); for Sequencing Abilities, Clark et al. (1984), Cohen and Gross (1979), and Kusmierek et al. (1986); and for Drawing Skills, Clark et al. (1984), Cohen and Gross (1979), and Kusmierek et al. (1986).

REFERENCES

Adams, R.J. (1987). An evaluation of color preference in early infancy. *Infant Behavior and Development, 10,* 143–150.

Almy, M., & Ganishi, C. (1979). *Ways of studying children.* New York: Teachers College Press.

Althouse, R. (1981). *The young child: Learning with understanding.* New York: Teachers College Press.

Anooshian, L.J., & Siegel, A.W. (1985). From cognitive to procedural mapping. In C.J. Brainerd & M. Pressley (Eds.), *Basic processes in memory development* (pp. 47–101). New York: Springer-Verlag.

Bandura, A. (1977). *Social learning theory.* Englewood Cliffs, NJ: Prentice Hall.

Bandura, A. (1989). Social cognitive theory. In R. Vasta (Ed.), *Annals of child development* (Vol. 6, pp. 1–60). Greenwich, CT: JAI Press.

Banks, M.S., & Ginsberg, A.P. (1985). Early visual preferences: A review and new theoretical treatment. In H.W. Reese (Ed.), *Advances in child development and behavior* (Vol. 19, pp. 207–246). New York: Academic Press.

Beckwith, L. (1985). Parent–child interaction and social-emotional development. In C.C. Brown & A.W. Gottfried (Eds.), *Play interactions: The role of toys and parental involvement in children's development* (pp. 152–159). Skilman, NJ: Johnson & Johnson Baby Products Co.

Beers, C.S., & Wehman, P. (1985). Play skill development. In N.H. Fallen & W. Umansky (Eds.), *Young children with special needs* (2nd ed.) (pp. 403–440). Columbus, OH: Charles E. Merrill.

Berk, L.E. (1991). *Child development* (2nd ed.). Newton, MA: Allyn & Bacon.

Berns, P.M. (1985). *Child, family, community.* New York: Holt, Rinehart, & Winston.

Bloom, L., & Lahey, M. (1978). *Language development and language disorders.* New York: John Wiley & Sons.

Brooks-Gunn, J., & Lewis, M. (1978). Early social knowledge: The development of knowledge about others. In H. McGurk (Ed.), *Issues in childhood social development* (pp. 79–106). London: Methuen.

Brophy, K., & Stone-Zukowski, D. (1984). Social play behavior of special needs and nonspecial needs toddlers. *Early Child Development and Care, 13,* 137–154.

Bruner, J.S. (1977). Early social interaction and language acquisition. In H.R. Schaffer (Ed.), *Studies in mother–infant interaction* (pp. 271–289). London: Academic Press.

Bruner, J.S. (1982). The organization of action and the nature of the adult–infant transaction. In E.Z.

Tronick (Ed.), *Social interchange in infancy: Affect, cognition, and communication* (pp. 23–25). Baltimore: University Park Press.

Case, R. (1985). *Intellectual development: A systematic reinterpretation.* New York: Academic Press.

Christie, J.F. (1983). The effects of play tutoring on young children's cognitive performance. *Journal of Educational Research, 76,* 326–330.

Clark, T.C., Morgan, E.C., & Wilson-Vlotman, A.L. (1984). *The SKI * HI curriculum: Early home programming for hearing impaired children.* Logan, UT: The SKI * HI Institute.

Cohen, M.A., & Gross, P.J. (1979). *The developmental resource: Behavioral sequences for assessment and program planning.* New York: Basic Books.

Dansky, J.L. (1980). Cognitive consequences of sociodramatic play and exploration training for economically disadvantaged preschoolers. *Journal of Child Psychology and Psychiatry, 20,* 47–58.

Dawes, C. (1977). *Early maths.* London: Longman Group.

DiLeo, J.H. (1977). *Child development: Analysis and synthesis.* New York: Brunner/Mazel.

Ehrhardt, R.P. (1982). *Developmental hand dysfunction: Theory assessment treatment.* Laurel, MD: Ramsco.

Elkind, D. (1988). Play. *Young Children, 43*(5), 2.

Fantz, R. (1961). The origin of form perception. *Scientific American, 204*(5), 66–72.

Feeney, S., & Magarick, M. (1984). Choosing good toys for young children. *Young Children, 40*(1), 21–25.

Fewell, R.R. (1983). New directions in the assessment of young handicapped children. In C.R. Reynolds & J.H. Clark (Eds.), *Assessment and programming for young children with low incidence handicaps* (pp. 1–41). New York: Plenum.

Fewell, R.R., & Vadasy, P.F. (1983). *Learning through play.* Allen, TX: Developmental Learning Materials.

Fischer, K.W. (1980). A theory of cognitive development: the control and construction of hierarchies of skills. *Psychology Review, 87,* 477–531.

Fishbein, H.D. (1976). *Evolution, development, and children's learning.* Pacific Palisades, CA: Goodyear Press.

Fishbein, H.D. (1984) *The psychology of infancy and childhood: Evolutionary and cross-cultural perspectives.* Hillsdale, NJ: Lawrence Erlbaum Associates.

Garreau, M., & Kennedy, C. (1991). Structure time and space to promote pursuit of learning in the primary grades. *Young Children, 64*(4), 46–51.

Geisel, T. (1938). *The 500 hats of Bartholomew Cubbins, by Dr. Seuss (pseudonym).* New York: Vanguard Press.

Garvey, C. (1977). *Play.* Cambridge, MA: Harvard University Press.

Geisel, T. (1950). *If I ran the zoo, by Dr. Seuss (pseudonym).* New York: Random House.

Geisel, T. (1971). *The lorax, by Dr. Seuss (pseudonym).* New York: Random House.

Gibson, E.J. (1970). The development of perception as an adaptive process. *American Scientist, 58,* 98–107.

Gibson, E.J., & Spelke, E.S. (1983). The development of perception. In J.H. Flavell & E.M. Markman (Eds.), *Handbook of child psychology: Volume 3. Cognitive development* (4th ed.) (pp. 1–76). New York: John Wiley & Sons.

Gibson, J.J. (1979). *The ecological approach to visual perception.* Boston: Houghton Mifflin.

Ginsburg, H.P., & Opper, S. (1988). *Piaget's theory of intellectual development: An introduction.* Englewood Cliffs, NJ: Prentice Hall.

Goble, P. (1978). *The girl who loved wild horses.* Bradbury Pub.

Gottfried, A.E. (1985). Intrinsic motivation for play. In C.C. Brown & A.W. Gottfried (Eds.), *Play interactions: The role of toys and parental involvement in children's development.* Skillman, NJ: Johnson & Johnson Baby Products Co.

Gresham, G.M. (1981). Social skills training with handicapped children: A review. *Review of Educational Research, 51,* 1.

Harter, S. (1981). A model of intrinsic motivation in children: individual differences and developmental change. In A. Collins (Ed.), *Minnesota symposium on child psychology* (Vol. 14, pp. 251–255). Hillsdale, NJ: Lawrence Erlbaum Associates.

Harter, S. (1990). Issues in the assessment of the self-concept of children and adolescents. In A. LaGreca (Ed.), *Through the eyes of a child* (pp. 292–325). Newton, MA: Allyn & Bacon.

Hayden, A., McGuinness, G., & Dmitriev, V. (1976). Early and continuous intervention strategies for severely handicapped infants and very young children. In N. Haring & L. Brown (Eds.), *Teaching the severely handicapped* (Vol. 1, pp. 239–275). New York: Grune & Stratton.

Hohmann, M., Banet, B., & Weikert, D.P. (1979). *Young children in action.* Ypsilanti, MI: High Scope Educational Research Foundation.

Hopper, C., & Wambold, C. (1978). Improving the independent play of severely mentally retarded children. *Education and Training of the Mentally Retarded, 13*(1), 42–46.

Hughes, F.P. (1991). *Children, play, and development.* Newton, MA: Allyn & Bacon.

Hulme, I., & Lunzer, E. (1966). Play, language, and reasoning in subnormal children. *Journal of Child Psychology and Psychiatry, 7,* 107–123.

Isenberg, J.P., & Jalongo, M.R. (1993). *Creative expression and play in the early childhood curriculum.* New York: Macmillan.

Johnson, J.E., Christie, J.F., & Yawkey, T.D. (1987). *Play and early childhood development.* Glenview, IL: HarperCollins.

Kaye, K., & Marcus, J. (1981). The sensory motor agenda. *Developmental Psychology, 17,* 258–265.

Krakow, J., & Kopp, C. (1983). The effect of developmental delay on sustained attention in young children. *Child Development, 54,* 1143–1155.

Kraus, R. (1970). *Who's mouse are you?* New York: Macmillan.

Kusmierek, A., Cunningham, K., Fox-Gleason, S., Hanson, M., & Lorenzini, D. (1986). *South metropolitan association birth to three transdisciplinary assessment guide.* Flossmoore, IL: South Metropolitan Association for Low-Incidence Handicapped.

Levine, M.D., & Jordan, N.C. (1987). Neurodevelopmental disfunctions: Their cumulative interactions and effects in middle childhood. In J.J. Gallagher & C.T. Ramey (Eds.), *The malleability of children* (pp. 141–154). Baltimore: Paul H. Brookes Publishing Co.

Li, A.K.F. (1981). Play and the mentally retarded. *Mental Retardation, 19,* 121–126.

Linder, T.W. (1993). *Transdisciplinary play-based assessment: A functional approach to working with young children* (rev. ed.). Baltimore: Paul H. Brookes Publishing Co.

MacDonald, J.D., & Gillette, Y. (1984). *Turn-taking with communications.* Columbus: Ohio State University.

Malone, T.W. (1983). Guidelines for designing educational computer programs. *Childhood Education, 59*(4), 241–247.

Mandler, J.M. (1984). *Stories, scripts, and scenes: Aspects of schema theory.* Hillsdale, NJ: Lawrence Erlbaum Associates.

Mandler, J.M. (1988). How to build a baby: On the development of an accessible representational system. *Cognitive Development, 3,* 113–136.

Martin, S.S., Brady, M.P., & Williams, R.E. (1991). Effects of toys on the social behavior of preschool children in integrated and nonintegrated groups: Investigation of a setting event. *Journal of Early Intervention, 15*(2), 153–161.

Matthews, G.B. (1977). *What was that? A funny story about night noises.* New York: Merrigold Press.

Meltzoff, A.N., & Moore, M.K. (1977). Imitation of facial and manual gestures by human neonates. *Science, 198,* 75–78.

Meltzoff, A.N., & Moore, M.K. (1989). Imitation in newborn infants: exploring the range of gestures imitated and the underlying mechanisms. *Developmental Psychology, 25,* 954–962.

Morgan, G.A., & Harmon, R.J. (1984). Developmental transformations in mastery motivation. In R.N. Emde & R.J. Harmon (Eds.), *Continuities and discontinuities in development* (pp. 263–291). New York: Plenum.

Musselwhite, C.R. (1986). *Adaptive play for special needs children: Strategies to enhance communication and learning.* San Diego, CA: College-Hill Press.

Newson, E., & Hipgrave, T. (1982). *Getting through to your handicapped child.* Cambridge, England: Cambridge University Press.

Nicholich, L.M. (1977). Beyond sensorimotor intelligence: assessment of symbolic maturity through analysis of pretend play. *Merrill-Palmer Quarterly, 16,* 136–141.

Nicolopoulou, A. (1991). Play, cognitive development and the social world: The research perspective. In B. Scales, M. Almy, A. Nicolopoulou, & S. Ervin-Tripp (Eds.), *The social context of play and development in early care and education* (pp. 129–142). New York: Teachers College Press.

Nordquist, V.M., Twardosz, S., & McEvoy, M.A. (1991). Effects of environmental reorganization in classrooms for children with autism. *Journal of Early Intervention, 15*(2), 135–152.

Paley, V. (1984). *Boys and girls: Superheroes in the doll corner.* Chicago: University of Chicago Press.

Pellegrini, A.D. (1988). Elementary school children's rough-and-tumble play and social competence. *Developmental Psychology, 24*(6), 802–806.

Pellegrini, A.D., & Perlmutter, J.C. (1988). Rough-and-tumble play on the elementary school playground. *Young Children, 43*(2), 14–17.

Piaget, J. (1932). *The moral judgment of the child.* Glencoe: Free Press.

Piaget, J. (1952). *The origins of intelligence in children.* New York: International Universities Press.

Reifel, S., & Yeatman, J. (1991). Action, talk, and thought in block play. In B. Scales, M. Almy, A. Nicolopoulou, & S. Ervin-Tripp (Eds.), *The social context of play and development in early care and education* (pp. 156–172). New York: Teachers College Press.

Rockwell, A. (1987). *Bear child's book of hours.* New York: Thomas Y. Crowell Junior Books.

Ross, H.S., & Kay, D.A. (1980). The origins of social games. In K. Rubin (Ed.), *New directions for child development* San Francisco: Jossey-Bass.

Rotter, J.B. (1966). Generalized expectancies for internal versus external control of reinforcement. *Psychological Monographs, 80,* (1, Whole No. 609).

Rubin, K.H., Fein, G.G., & Vandenberg, B. (1983). Play. In P.H. Mussen (Ed.), *Handbook of child psychology: Volume 4. Socialization, personality, and social development* (4th ed.) (pp. 693–774). New York: John Wiley & Sons.

Salapatek, P., & Cohen, L. (Eds.). (1987). *Handbook of infant perception: Volume 2. From perception to cognition.* Orlando, FL: Academic Press.

Shapiro, L. (1990, May 28). Guns and dolls. *Newsweek,* 56–65.

Siegler, R.S. (1981). Developmental sequences within and between concepts. *Monographs of the Society for Research in Child Development, 46*(189)(2, Serial No. 189).

Siegler, R.S. (1991). *Children's thinking* (2nd ed.). Englewood Cliffs, NJ: Prentice Hall.

Smilansky, S. (1968). *The effects of sociodramatic play on disadvantaged preschool children.* New York: John Wiley & Sons.

Smith, P.K., & Boulton, M. (1990). Rough-and tumble play dominance: Perception and behavior in children's encounters. *Human Development, 33,* 271–282.

Smith, P.K., Dalgleish, M., & Herzmark, G. (1981). A comparison of the effects of fantasy play tutoring and skills tutoring in nursery classes. *International Journal of Behavioral Development, 4,* 421–441.

Spelke, E.S. (1987). The development of intermodal perception. In P. Salapatek & L. Cohen (Eds.), *Handbook of infant perception: Volume 2. From perception to cognition* (pp. 233–273). Orlando, FL: Academic Press.

Stern, D. (1985). *The interpersonal world of the infant: A view from psychoanalysis and developmental psychology.* New York: Basic Books.

Taylor, M. (1966). *Henry the explorer.* New York: Atheneum.

Thurman, S.K., & Widerstrom, A.H. (1990). *Infants and young children with special needs: A developmental and ecological approach* (2nd ed.). Baltimore: Paul H. Brookes Publishing Co.

Twardosz, S., Cataldo, M., & Risley, T. (1974). An open environment design for infant and toddler day care. *Journal of Applied Behavior Analysis, 7,* 529–546.

Van Hoorn, J., Nourot, P., Scales, B., & Alward, K. (1993). *Play at the center of the curriculum.* New York: Macmillan.

Vast, R., Haith, M.M., & Miller, S.A. (1992). *Child psychology: The modern science.* New York: John Wiley & Sons.

Watson, M.W. (1981). The development of social roles: A sequence of social-cognitive development. In K. Fischer (Ed.), *Cognitive development: New directions for child development* (Vol. 12, pp. 33–42). San Francisco: Jossey-Bass, Inc.

Watson, M.W., & Fischer, K.W. (1977). A developmental sequence of agent use in late infancy. *Child Development, 48,* 828–836.

Westby, C.E. (1980). Assessment of cognitive and language abilities through play. *Language, Speech and Hearing Services in Schools, 11,* 154–168.

Whitman, T.L., Mercurio, V., & Caponigri, J. (1970). Development of social responses in severely retarded children. *Journal of Applied Behavior Analysis, 3,* 133–138.

Williams, W., Brown, L., & Certo, N. (1975). Basic components of instructional programs. *TIP: Theory into Practice,* 14(2), 123–136.

Youniss, J. (1978). The nature of social development: a conceptual discussion of cognition. In H. McGurk (Ed.), *Issues in childhood social development* (pp. 203–227). London: Methuen.

9

Facilitating Social-Emotional Development

Carol Lay and Toni W. Linder

Theories about the psycholog-
ical development of the infant and young child continue to be revised and expanded. Infant
research has influenced psychology, child development, and psychiatry, while altering earlier
formulations in psychoanalytic theory. The view of emotional development as mechanistic and
based upon specific stages that unfold in a particular order has been replaced with a biobe-
havioral model of development. This model is based on the belief that major periods of reorganization and integration occur during the first 2 years of life. Biological, cognitive, affective (i.e.,
pertaining to emotion or feeling), communicative, and social forces within and outside of the
infant emerge and interact, serving as the motivational force behind development. Theorists
such as Bowlby (1969, 1973, 1980), Emde (1985, 1988a, 1988b), Sander (1962), Spitz (1965),
and Stern (1977, 1984, 1985) base their work on childhood observations and convincingly demonstrate a developmental systems approach to emotional development. They have contributed
to the understanding of a developmental line of connectedness and autonomy as elements of the
child's development of "self" and "self and other." The psychoanalytic theory of sensual satisfaction as the organizer of emotional development has evolved into a theory that sees bonding, or
attachment, as the primary experience of infant development (Mahler, Pine, & Bergman, 1975).
From this develops an interdependence between "connectedness" and autonomy that is the
foundation of the child's sense of self and other. The evolution of this theory has occurred because of the integration of infant research with previously held understandings of psychological
development (Stern, 1985). The emergence of the importance of the infant's relationship with
the "other" is rooted in the earlier object relations theories about emotional development.
Whether "object" or "other" is used, both have to do with the development of interpersonal
relations, the beginning of which occurs with the infant's first human objects, usually his or her
parents.

Infant research indicates that babies are not psychologically unorganized beings possessing
few cognitive, language, and social competencies. Rather, we know that infants recognize, have
rudimentary memory, communicate, socialize, and quickly begin to distinguish between "self"
and "other." We have learned that babies also organize stimuli and develop internal organizing
responses for comfort and soothing. As we are able to understand and delineate more about the
elements of emotional development in young children, we become able to intervene more effec-

tively in areas of development that have met with delay or deviation. In this regard, play can be used effectively to aid children experiencing difficulties in some aspect of their emotional development.

As the child matures, play becomes increasingly critical to his or her evolving social competence (Linder, 1993). Children who possess social interaction skills tend to receive more attention from those around them, which may be especially important for the child with disabilities (Odom, McConnell, & McEvoy, 1992). Social competence is important in the development of a healthy sense of self as well as regard for the group and community. Without adequate social interaction skills, it is difficult for most children to feel liked and accepted, an important dimension of self-esteem. Regard for another person, for the group, or for the community depends in large part on the capacity for empathy. Empathy develops as an early affect in young children and allows older children to show concern and regard for others. Social competence has to do with the relationship between "self and other."

Odom et al. (1992) note that social competence is considered an important aspect of intellectual functioning (American Association on Mental Retardation, 1990; Gardner, 1987; Gardner & Hatch, 1989; Guilford & Hoepfner, 1971; Sternberg, 1985). Many measures of cognitive functioning now include assessment of a social competence domain. If social competence is viewed as a cognitively acquired or influenced skill, opportunities for teaching or facilitating social competence in educational settings can be designed. What many once thought was acquired or assimilated through acculturation is now regarded as an area of educational intervention.

Learning to play with other children does not come easily or naturally for some children. A child, for example, whose disability has impaired his or her opportunity for exploration of objects or the environment, may have difficulty moving into the more interactive world of playing with other children. The child with cognitive delays may not be able to match the play levels of age peers. Children with sensory impairments may struggle with how to initiate, maintain, or terminate play interactions with peers. Because most interactions are based on communication of one form or another, children with language delays or deficits may have difficulty with social play as well.

This chapter examines aspects related to social competence and emotional development in young children. Interventions related to temperament, motivation, parent–child and adult–child interactions, and emotional concerns, including fostering a sense of humor, peer interactions, and behavioral issues are addressed.

OBSERVATION GUIDELINES FOR SOCIAL-EMOTIONAL DEVELOPMENT: TEMPERAMENT—ACTIVITY LEVEL

I. Temperament
   A. Activity level
      1. How motorically active is the child during the session?
      2. Are there specific times during the session when the child is particularly active?
         a. Beginning, middle, or end
         b. During specific activities

INTERVENTION IMPLICATIONS   Temperament characteristics have been shown to be important factors in predisposing children to vulnerability or buffering them from stress. In combination with insensitive childrearing and a high degree of parental conflict, the child with a "difficult" temperament is more likely to demonstrate psychological adjustment problems (Thomas & Chess, 1977). For example, these children may have difficulties in their social interactional functioning. Sharing, reciprocity, and the ability to delay gratification may be impaired. Children with "difficult temperaments" may be difficult to comfort when distressed and may demand excessive amounts of attention. The match between the child's temperament, or "goodness of fit," plays a significant role in determining whether problems will arise. Studies have shown, however, that many aspects of temperament can be modified by experiences. Environmental supports, such as childrearing or educational practices, can influence the child's temperament (Chess & Thomas, 1984). In addition, family values and racial and ethnic differences influence the course of temperament modification (Fogel, Toda, & Kawaii, 1987; Plomin, 1989).

Activity Level

One aspect of temperament that appears to stay relatively stable over time is activity level (Riese, 1987). Activity level has to do with the child's general level of arousal as well as the child's engagement with a particular activity or toy. On a continuum, activity level may vary from inert and lethargic to wildly, diffusely hyperactive. In assessing activity level it is important to identify time of day, nature of activity or toy, and articulated expectation. An otherwise energetic toddler may shut down in the face of an activity that is boring or beyond his or her developmental grasp. Parents are usually aware of the child's typical activity level across various activities and can serve to confirm or refute what is being seen in assessment or in the classroom. The child who is expected to sit at a table and do worksheets may understandably exhibit more fidgety and "out of seat" behavior than he or she would at home in an unstructured play environment.

Family Expectations

The perceptions of the adults in the child's life with regard to what constitutes an over- or underactive child are important. The degree of tolerance and level of expectation for what a child should do varies from person to person and across cultures. Understanding the expectations of the family is an important consideration. If the family desires that their child's activity level be increased or decreased, the team can work with the family to provide supports for coping with the child's typical activity level, while at the same time working to modify this activity level to be more compatible with the family's needs.

EXAMPLE

Shanthu A., a tiny Asian Indian girl, was 4 years old and had been diagnosed with hemiplegia. She had difficulty with tasks involving fine motor skills on both sides of her body. Shanthu's temperament was very passive. She waited for someone else to initiate interactions, responded quietly and briefly, and let her parents do many things for her that she could have managed, although with difficulty. Discussions with her parents indicated that their family valued the quiet, passive child and liked keeping her dependent. They explained that in their culture, the family was supposed to care for each other, and when the children were older, they, in turn, would be expected to care for their parents. The team discussed with Shanthu's parents the value in having Shanthu be able to initiate interactions and become more independent with such skills as dressing and playing. While she still needed support with such things as someone reading to her and assisting when a task was too difficult, she did begin to initiate simple tasks. Because the family wanted Shanthu to be more passive, the team did not address increasing activity level or affective expression, but focused instead on increasing Shanthu's exploration, initiations with peers, and pleasurable interactions (with smiles). It was important to respect the values of the parents and not try to make Shanthu into the active class leader or encourage magnification of affect.

After family expectations have been considered, the next issue to address is whether the "problem" lies with the child or within the environment.

The Environment

When a child's activity level interferes with successful participation in appropriate activities, the adults should modify the environment in order to increase or decrease the child's activity level. Activity level can be thought of as the child's response in action or inaction to the various aspects of the environment. Evaluation of environmental factors is thus essential, for these factors often determine the child's behavioral response. Questions such as the following should be asked:

1.   How stimulating is the physical environment (e.g., colors, furniture, toys)? An environment may be either understimulating or overstimulating and result in changes in activity level. For example, some infants who have been prenatally exposed to drugs or alcohol may be easily overstimulated and consequently may need an environment with fewer toys and materials. Other children may become easily bored and need a constantly changing environment to hold their attention and to moderate their activity levels. Children who need a particular type of input (e.g., tactile) may move around in a neverending search for that specific sensory input. Some children may need an increased amount of movement or vestibular stimulation. They will find ways to give themselves this input through self-stimulation or constant movement. If the environment contains movement toys and means for the child to obtain vestibular input, the child can then alternate between these materials and those requiring more focused and restrained attention.

2.   Is the lighting in the environment bright, subdued, natural, or fluorescent? Individual children may be adversely affected by too much or too little light. For instance, a child with visual impairments may be drawn to the natural light emanating from a window. The child continuously moves to the source of light and rejects other activities. This need for visual stimulation may cause the child to appear to be highly active.

3.   What is the noise level of the environment? How much extraneous noise is present (e.g. sound of airplanes from nearby airport, sirens)? Auditory distractions may cause the child to be diverted and move to other activities. The sounds of children playing in other areas may be enough of a stimulus to cause the child to wander from area to area checking out the source of the interesting disturbance.

4.   What is the activity level of the adults in the child's environment? A high activity level on the part of parents or teachers can result in escalating the activity level of an already highly energetic child. Thoughtful moderation of adult activity levels can serve to help the child modify his or her level of animation.

Activity Selection

After the child's environment is addressed, consideration can be given to the design of specific activities that support the desired activity level. For example, for the exceedingly active child, introductory activities should seek to calm and focus the child. For the withdrawn or quiet child, introductory activities should stimulate and engage. Music, for instance, can set the initial tone for introductory activities, with either soft, slow rhythms or hard, rapid beats, depending on the desired result. Most children find storytelling time more calming than active motor games. The team can select activities to correspond to the behavioral mood or tone preferred for individual children.

Group Size

Group size can also be used to manage activity level. Children who have low activity levels can sometimes be stimulated by other children, as long as the size of the group does not overwhelm them. Smaller groups may be beneficial to more passive children as the adults can more easily facilitate activity of individual children. Children who are overly active may also benefit from a reduction of group size. The highly active young child may be sociable with peers, but may also become more involved in conflicts with less active counterparts. Smaller numbers may provide highly active children more opportunity for containment of behavior and enable the adults to monitor the child's activity.

Voice

Adult voice and behavior patterns also stimulate or subdue a child's activity level. A softer voice, for example, can be calming to an overly active child. An enthusiastic adult response can energize a child whose lethargy interferes with an optimal activity level. Increasing the intensity of the adult's intonation and affect can also assist in raising the child's level of reactivity. Adults can also model the movements and the tempo of movements in order to modulate the child's activity rates.

Visual Cues

Adults may find the use of cues helpful in managing activity levels. The teacher might raise her hand in a "slow" gesture, put a finger to the head to signal "stop and think," or use quick gestures to indicate an increase in speed of movement.

Role Playing

Role playing can be a useful technique for children as young as 2 years old. It can help them to step outside themselves and pretend new ways of behaving. The adult can identify affects or behavioral responses that would benefit the child to have in his or her repertoire. For the overactive child, role-playing vignettes can emphasize behavioral patterns that would help him or her learn to contain impulsive actions. The following are two examples of behaviors important for the highly active child to learn:

- Quiet: The idea of quiet and quieting can be taught through signals such as "shhhhh" and incorporated into songs and play. Quiet and noisy can be contrasted as behaviors, colors, sounds, animals, vehicles, and so forth. Role playing could include experimenting with very silly notions—"quiet" cheering sections or noisy libraries. Children should be encouraged in their play and discussions to determine where quiet is more appropriate than noisy and when noisy is just fine.

- Calm: Calm and calming are important concepts to address. Like quieting, the idea of calming suggests that the child learn what is useful to him or her in settling overactive behavior. Some children know, for example, that it is calming to curl up in a blanket to look out the window when the activity or noise level gets too high. The idea is to help children understand that they have some control over their behavior and that they can identify and respond to cues and strategies. Children are much more willing to do this if the problem to be solved is presented in the format of something fun, such as "slowing down the racing rabbit."

First, however, it is important to help the child identify when he or she is becoming overly active. The adult can facilitate by giving verbal cues and encouraging the child to verbalize the feelings associated with losing control. The child must learn to self-monitor by identifying both the feelings and the behaviors that indicate that the activity level is escalating. This will enable the child to then move to the next phase, that of using self-calming strategies, such as those identified above.

OBSERVATION
GUIDELINES FOR SOCIAL-EMOTIONAL
DEVELOPMENT: TEMPERAMENT—ADAPTABILITY

B. Adaptability
   1. What is the child's *initial* response to new stimuli (persons, situations, and toys)?
      a. Shy, timid, fearful, cautious
      b. Sociable, eager, willing
      c. Aggressive, bold, fearless
   2. How does the child demonstrate his or her interest or withdrawal?
      a. Smiling, verbalizing, touching
      b. Crying, moving away, seeking security
   3. How long does it take the child to adjust to new situations, persons, objects, and so forth?
   4. How does the child adjust to new or altered situations after an initially shy or fearful response?
      a. Self-initiation (slowly warms up, talks to self)
      b. Uses adult or parent as a base of security (needs encouragement and reinforcement to get involved)
      c. Continues to resist and stay uninvolved

Adaptability, another aspect of temperament identified by Thomas and Chess (1977), refers to the child's response and adjustment to new stimuli, including situations, circumstances, people, or changes in schedule or routine. The type and level of response to new situations has been shown to be relatively stable over time (Matheny, Wilson, & Nuss, 1984; McDevitt, 1986). Children vary in the manner in which they react to new environments and unfamiliar people, objects, and situations. Children who have difficulty with adaptation may appear rigid, insecure, anxious, or demanding. It is important to distinguish the child who is "slow to warm up" from the child who truly has difficulties with adaptation. For the child who is slow to adapt, reducing the pace of the new experience can help. Giving the child time to make transitions slowly into new situations by keeping a parent present or including him or her in initial activities assists the child who needs to separate slowly. Letting the child set the pace by initiating activities eases the anxiety of many children who find new situations difficult.

Transitions can be particularly difficult for children. Change produces anxiety for most young children, and especially for children whose self-confidence may be diminished by delays in their development or whose temperaments resist variations. The following suggestions may help ease transitional anxiety for children:

• Transitional objects can be helpful to the child entering a new program. The initial transition of entering the program may be eased if the child brings something special from home. Once in the class, the child may need to take a toy from one area or activity to another.

• The motivating aspects of a comfortable situation can be used in moving to the new. The facilitator might say, "Terri, you colored such a beautiful picture this morning. You might want to bring it to the story area to show your friends."

• The adult can make the new situation look appealing by demonstrating enthusiasm and modeling the shift in activity.

• The child's desire for mastery can be employed. "I saw you build a big house yesterday. Let's see if you can make an even bigger one."

• Looking at pictures of various parts of the child's life or day can assist the child in feeling more comfortable and secure. Pictures of the family members, the house, and pets may give the insecure child a substitute for the familiar when combined with a discussion of how home and school go together. The child can then look at the pictures any time to reestablish the connection. In the same way, pictures of activities in the classroom may help the child select and have control over the course of events. The child can make books about making changes and use it during transitions.

For all children, adaptation occurs most easily when a small number of changes is required at a given time. If, for example, a child is experiencing major changes within the family, it would be most beneficial if the education program remained constant. For example, 2½-year-old Emily had been highly adaptable to staff and scheduling changes in her preschool until the arrival of her baby brother. For several weeks after his birth, she regressed in her expressive language, toileting, and socialization every time she was faced with a change in her program routine. Keeping the routine constant helped Emily to adjust to the biggest change in her life first. When changes were needed, Emily's advice was sought about how to perform the new activity. She then initiated the new activity and led the rest of the group. The following are additional suggestions for preparing the child for a transition, and assisting him or her through new situations:

• *Verbal reassurance.* Anxiety is at the root of many of the difficulties children have with change. It is important for parents and facilitators to reassure children that change does not mean the important people will go away (e.g., "Mommy doesn't go away forever when she leaves," or, "Mrs. Conroy will be back tomorrow to play more games with you."). Identifying the source of alarm or fear is important in order for the adult to discuss these anxieties and then reassure the child.

• *Role playing.* Some emotions are incompatible with each other (i.e., they cannot coexist). The state of relaxation, for example, cannot coexist with anxiety. The feeling of bravery is incompatible with fear. Role playing the state that is incompatible with their "worry" can assist the child in gaining control of the situation. For example, for children whose adaptation is compromised by fearfulness, insecurity, timidity, or shyness, practicing "brave and bold" behaviors can be useful. Again, the development of short, simple role playing episodes can be effective. As children practice behaviors that are not consistent with their own, they should always be reassured and made to feel safe and protected. Children should not be asked to take risks that feel too great or too foreign.

OBSERVATION
GUIDELINES FOR SOCIAL-EMOTIONAL
DEVELOPMENT: TEMPERAMENT–REACTIVITY

C. Reactivity
1. How intense does the stimuli presented to the child need to be in order to evoke a discernible response?
2. What type of stimulation is needed to interest the child?
    a. Visual, vocal, tactile, combination
    b. Object, social
3. What level of affect and energy are displayed in response to persons, situations, or objects?
4. What response mode is commonly used?
5. What is the child's response to frustration?

INTERVENTION IMPLICATIONS

Reactivity to Stimulation

Reactivity, a third temperament characteristic, refers to the amount of stimulation needed in order to evoke a discernible response from the child and the intensity of the child's response to the stimulation. Reactivity to sensory input is also mentioned in Chapter 11. There is a distinct relationship between the two types of reactivity. Reactivity in temperament refers to the affective aspect of reaction to various types of sensory stimuli, while reactivity in the sensorimotor domain refers to the child's physical response to stimuli. The assessment determines which children need more intense stimuli and which need very little. Types and amounts of stimuli necessary to produce pleasurable interactions are also identified. *It is important to know the level of noise, tactile stimulation, visual stimulation, or other types of sensory input a child needs in order to perform optimally.* Light, for example, should be modified for the child with visual impairments. Children with tactile deficits, depending on the degree of sensitivity, may need reduced or more intense tactile input. Selection of toys that have characteristics that reflect the child's sensory preferences helps to hold the child's attention and increase interactions.

As discussed on page 205 in relation to activity level, modulation of timing, affect, voice, and movement by the adult can have a positive effect on the child's reactivity. Research on babies who were premature or experienced respiratory distress syndrome demonstrated that the "window" of response for these infants (i.e., the optimum level and amount of stimulation) is small (Field, 1983). The adult works hard to capture the child's attention; then, because the child cannot handle a large amount of stimulation, the child becomes overstimulated and turns away or begins to cry. The intent of play-based intervention is to keep the approach a positive and pleasurable experience for the child and family. *Helping the family to read the child's cues and provide the optimal type and amount of input is a critical aspect of intervention.*

Emotional Reactivity

Emotional reactivity is another important issue. The level of emotional intensity expressed in response to environmental events differs greatly among children. Children who have intense negative responses evoke more negative communication and actions and therefore become embroiled in more disputes (Brody, Stoneman, & Burke, 1987; Stocker, Dunn, & Plomin, 1989). However, some children have low-intensity reactions to events, including emotionally charged aspects of their lives. Others demonstrate high levels of reactivity to emotionally significant stimuli (see discussion of Trauma on pages 251–255). Extremes of emotional reactivity, in either direction, may compromise positive interactions with others.

Physiological and Psychological Causes of Unusual Response Levels

When a child has unusually high or low response levels to stimuli, physiological causation should be addressed first. Children with severe psychiatric disorders (i.e., childhood schizophrenia, pervasive developmental disorders, autism) often experience incoming stimuli differently than typical children. Medical and physiological involvement in the child's reactivity must be understood before intervention is begun. The relationship of psychological processes is also important and is addressed on page 240. For instance, the child who has been physically or sexually abused may show an extreme aversion to touch or may exhibit the opposite, using physical interaction as a primary means of relating.

Frustration Tolerance and Expressing Feelings

The child who has low frustration tolerance may react adversely to the smallest failure. The adults can help the child by being warm and accepting, structuring play so the child can solve problems in small steps, and helping the child to verbalize his or her actions and feelings. For many children with disabilities, the inability to verbalize feelings causes intense emotional responses. Helping the child to come up with alternatives for expressing feelings, such as a shrug of the shoulders and saying, "Oh, well" and a pattern for trying again by saying, "Let's try one more time," can help to establish a more tolerant approach on the part of the child. The adult also needs to recognize and reinforce the child's efforts to modulate and express emotions.

Modification of the Child's Environment and Adults' Interaction Styles

By analyzing the sensory and emotional reactivity of the child, the team can determine how to modify the diverse aspects of the child's environment so that the child receives maximum benefit from interactions with persons, objects, and events in his or her life. Modifications of the types and amount of sensory input can be considered, including visual, auditory, tactile, thermal, olfactory, gustatory, and vestibular modes. Modifications of the adult's interaction style with the child may also be needed, including intensity, pace, and affect. Selection and alterations of toys and other play materials is another way to react to the child's responsivity differences.

Although modifying the child's temperament may not be the goal of intervention, most studies show that parent–child and teacher–child interactions can have a pronounced effect on temperamental changes. At the very least, the intervention staff can assist parents in adapting to and dealing with the individual temperament differences of their child. For activity level, adaptability, and reactivity, increasing the child's ability to verbalize needs and feelings can have a positive effect. The need to use actions instead of words may diminish; anxieties about changes can be expressed; and requests for environmental modifications can be made. Increasing communicative abilities can thus have a positive effect on behaviors associated with temperament. With consistency at home and school, many of the more difficult temperament characteristics can be dealt with more effectively and can be modified in a direction that will benefit the child's developmental progress.

EXAMPLE

Devon R., a 2½-year-old who had been prenatally exposed to drugs and alcohol, exhibited intense reactions in highly stimulating situations. He would concentrate and focus on a task when the setting was quiet, without a lot of distractions, but when peers or adults became involved, he would lose his concentration and begin to jump up and down, making strange noises. If the environment had too much noise and activity, he would cry uncontrollably. Devon was not yet ready for a play group situation. He needed a more controlled environment, where the materials and amount of human contact could be modified to meet his needs. His mother and the intervention team worked with Devon at home to develop ways of controlling the sensory input, while at the same time giving Devon ways to moderate his emotions. He needed to learn ways to comfort himself, to "turn off" when the stimulation was too intense, and to request adult assistance. Devon was given a special chair and blanket that he could go to when he needed to be alone. He learned to hold his bear and rock in his rocking chair when he needed to calm down. He was also encouraged to use words to help adults know when he was getting overstimulated. He learned to say, "I need quiet," which was a cue to the adult to assist Devon in changing his activity. As he increased his ability to control his responses, a peer was occasionally included in the play. The gradual shift enabled Devon to be able to enter preschool when he was 3, first 1 day a week and over time increasing to the full week.

OBSERVATION GUIDELINES FOR SOCIAL-EMOTIONAL DEVELOPMENT: MASTERY MOTIVATION

II. **Mastery Motivation**
   A. **Purposeful activity**
      1. **What behavior demonstrates purposeful activity?**
      2. **How does the child explore complex objects?**
   B. **Goal-directed behaviors**
      1. **What goal-directed behaviors are observed?**
      2. **How does the child respond to challenging objects or situations?**
         a. **Looking**
         b. **Exploring**
         c. **Appropriate use**
         d. **Persistent, task-directed**
      3. **How often does the child repeat successfully completed, challenging tasks?**
      4. **How persistent is the child in goal-directed behavior?**
         a. **With cause—effect toys**
         b. **With combinatorial tasks**
         c. **With means—end behavior**
      5. **Given a choice between an easy and more challenging task, which does the child select? (Examine if the child is over 3½ years old.)**
      6. **How does the child demonstrate self-initiation in problem-solving?**
         a. **How frequently is assistance requested?**
         b. **How does the child organize problem-solving?**

INTERVENTION IMPLICATIONS

Mastery motivation, the tendency to display initiative and persistence in goal-oriented behavior, is inextricably intertwined with competence as it deals with the child's desire to master and control the environment. The degree of persistence, approach to problem-solving, and effectiveness of efforts are aspects of mastery motivation that are observed in different ways in children of various ages. Interest and persistence are related to learning and cognitive functioning from the youngest infant through the school years (Berk, 1991). Some children who have fewer skills and abilities may do better than their more skilled counterparts because of mastery, or achievement, motivation (Dweck & Elliott, 1983). (Mastery motivation for children with disabilities is a critical facet of their functioning.)

Mastery of Emotions

Mastery is also a very adaptive way of dealing with anxiety. The ability to master what is worrisome or causing feelings of incompetence allows the child to regain inner control. Mastery motivation, therefore, relates to emotional development as well as cognitive development. (Mastery of emotions is addressed on p. 255.)

Success and Failure

In infancy, children receive satisfaction from engaging in play with toys and repeat actions to experience the same events again. They are not yet concerned about internally or externally imposed standards or their self-worth. This natural inclination towards mastery serves as the basis for achievement motivation (White, 1959). At approximately 3 years of age, children begin to appraise their successes and failures cognitively and develop a sense of expectancy about their abilities. These expectancies influence their persistence on tasks, with children who do not expect to succeed giving up easily and those who think they can accomplish the task persevering. Children younger than 6 years tend to have very high expectancies of success and view the "smart person" as one who expends more effort (Nicholls, 1978). It is not until children are able to reason about various attributes that they can come to a more complex understanding of the reasons for success and failure.

Persistence

Persistence, which is frequently viewed as a temperament trait, is an important component of mastery motivation. Persistence, in the form of teacher-perceived task orientation, has been found to correlate with IQ, grades in school, and teacher estimates of academic ability. Distractibility, avoidance of new situations, and lack of adaptability correlate with poor school performance (Keogh, 1985).

Learned Helplessness

As they grow older, some children acquire what Dweck and Elliott (1983) refer to as *learned helplessness* (Seligman, 1975) or an acquired belief that they cannot succeed at difficult tasks. These children begin to give up easily, have little confidence in themselves, and develop low expectancies of success (Diener & Dweck, 1978). Learned helplessness acts to sustain itself, with self-defeating attitudes leading children to select less challenging tasks and ultimately less challenging careers than they are capable of mastering. Thus, mastery motivation, an important aspect of the personality, can have a profound effect on long-term developmental outcomes.

Evaluative Messages from Adults

A child's perception of his or her abilities is partially derived from actual performance and how well it compares to that of peers, but it is also influenced by the evaluative messages that are given to the child by parents and teachers. Adults also seem to treat the successes and failures of girls and boys differently. Girls are credited for successes, but their ability is denigrated when they fail. Boys, however, are not blamed by adults for their failures (Dweck, Davidson, Nelson & Enna, 1978; Parsons, Adler, & Kaczala, 1982). The way adults react to a child's success or failure may, therefore, play an important role in the child's developing sense of mastery motivation.

Promotion of Mastery Motivation

Some children, as a result of their disabilities, have experienced very little sense of mastery. This is an area, however, that lends itself to intervention through play. The adult can create an environment with play activities and experiences in which the child begins to achieve mastery. Through the feedback the adult gives the child as well as through appropriate selection of play materials and activities, the child can be encouraged to focus, attend, problem-solve, persist, and complete a task successfully.

High-stimulus activities are useful in capturing a child's attention. Activities that are too stimulating, however, may work against a child sustaining his or her attention. Action that leads to success is basic to the development of achievement motivation. The child must feel the capacity to master and meet with success in order to feel competent. Activities, therefore, should not be too frustrating and should have an accessible solution. Children of very young ages delight in solving something (e.g., getting a lid off a jar, fitting a puzzle piece correctly, putting an object in a correctly shaped hole). Children persist in problem-solving efforts when encouragement is offered and their successes are acknowledged with accolades. Children tend to stay with tasks longer and show a higher degree of mastery motivation with toys that produce some kind of effect.

DEVELOPMENTAL LEVEL

- Demonstrates exploration and curiosity in investigation of complex object that is not too challenging cognitively or motorically
  (6 months +)

INTERVENTION GUIDELINES

At this developmental level, satisfaction is derived from exploration, manipulation, and discovery of what objects can do. The adult encourages mastery motivation by allowing the child to experiment with objects and discover the consequences of different actions.

PLAY MATERIALS AND OPPORTUNITIES

Toys that look interesting and make intriguing sounds upon child activation motivate exploration. For example, Johnson and Johnson spinning balls and rattles with moving parts will keep the child interested and encourage him or her to accomplish a goal.

DEVELOPMENTAL LEVEL

- Practices skill repeatedly and is successful on:
  1) cause-and-effect toys
  2) combinatorial tasks (putting pegs in holes)
  3) means–ends tasks requiring getting a toy from behind a barrier
     (9 months +)

INTERVENTION GUIDELINES

By 9 months of age, most infants demonstrate task-directed responses. Providing the child with rudimentary cause-and-effect games or toys encourages the child to effect a result in play. For example, batting at a toy can make it go around and around; pulling a string can produce music; pushing at an object can make the glitter inside jump around; and banging on a drum or pot produces loud noise. These are simple problems that the child discovers can be solved by his or her actions. The adult can increase persistence by altering the toy in some way after the child has demonstrated skill in operating it. For instance, raising the height of the toy the child is batting, so that extra effort is required; changing the handle on the string pull toy, so that a different grasp is needed; making the child move to retrieve the glitter objects hidden behind a box or putting them in a can; and changing the container the child is banging or tools with which the child is hitting, so that different sounds are produced. Showing an enthusiastic response to the child's efforts adds to his or her pleasure in accomplishment.

PLAY MATERIALS AND OPPORTUNITIES

The child is now able to make actions occur. Toys such as clowns whose arms and legs fly up when a string is pulled, music boxes with simple push buttons, and roly-poly toys that make sounds when pushed stimulate cause-and-effect understanding and motivate the child to repeat actions.

The infant at this developmental level also enjoys putting things "in." Putting blocks in an empty cereal box, pegs in holes, and Cheerios in Daddy's pocket are fun games. Throwing tub toys in the water before bathtime will bring squeals of delight.

Parents can also encourage the development of mastery motivation by allowing the child to repeat actions and activities innumerable times. The parent may tire of turning a light switch on and off, but the infant may persist for what seems like an "eternity." This repetition on the part of the child and patience on the part of the adult is critical, as the child thus learns a sense of control and mastery.

DEVELOPMENTAL LEVEL

- Smiles at mastery of self-generated goal
      (12 months +)
- Is persistent in completing multipart tasks:
  1) combinatorial tasks (form board, shape sorter)
  2) means–ends tasks (lock board, cash register)
      (15 months +)

The child's smile at accomplishments is an indication of the growing sense of mastery motivation. This sense of pleasure encourages further exploration. The adult should acknowledge the child's pleasure, "You did it! You put them all in the hole." Indicating what the child has done is important. General "cheering" may encourage the child to perform to get a response, while specific comments encourage the child to repeat specific problem-solving behaviors.

By 15 months, the child can work persistently at multipart tasks. Meeting with success is critical at all ages when helping children develop a sense of mastery and accomplishment. *The adult can help the child persist by modeling and encouraging continued effort.* Increasing the level of difficulty involved in play with various toys can be accomplished through adding parts that need to be combined, put together, or restructured in some way (e.g., getting the shapes out of the wrong box and putting them in the right one). Again, toys that encourage the child to make an action occur or feel good about finishing an effort promote problem-solving.

The child is becoming interested in multipart activities, so toys that require sequencing actions are appropriate. Simple shape boxes or toys that require the child to push, pull, or turn various knobs and levers promote problem-solving. Busy Boxes and pop-up toys that require numerous actions are suggested.

Mastery motivation can be encouraged in any activity in which the child tries to accomplish a goal. Whether it be trying to climb up on the couch or crawling onto a scooter toy, if the task is challenging and requires persistence to accomplish, the parent can support the child's efforts. Waiting, watching, and encouraging the child to accomplish a goal independently is important. If the adult assists too quickly, the child learns that adults are needed to achieve difficult ends, thus discouraging independence and mastery motivation.

> • Recognizes adult standards and corrects self
> (24 months +)

At this developmental level, the child looks at the adult to check out the adult's response to his or her actions. The adult has acquired powerful reinforcement status because the child now knows that there are right and wrong ways to do things. A danger inherent in this power is that the adult can become controlling, requiring the child to perform in set ways, thus inhibiting the child's initiative and creativity. In extreme cases, the child may come to fear doing anything without adult direction and approval. *The adult role is one of encouraging exploration and persistence without providing all of the answers.* Providing reinforcement without making the child dependent on that reinforcement is a difficult, but important, balance.

Encouraging the child to explore and try new things is difficult for many parents. However, as the child develops increasingly advanced fine and gross motor skills, it is important that challenges be provided. Climbing toys, push-and-pull toys (e.g., wagons and carts), and riding toys facilitate gross motor exploration.

Messy materials (e.g., shaving cream, fingerpaint, mud, sand) provide a challenge to both the child and the parent. Tolerance within appropriate boundaries of health and safety encourages the child to explore and learn rule expectations simultaneously.

DEVELOPMENTAL LEVEL

- Prefers challenging tasks when given a choice between relatively easy and difficult tasks
    (36 months +)

INTERVENTION GUIDELINES

From this developmental level on, children gain a perception of self based on how skilled they think they are and how skilled others tell them they are. *Their mastery motivation can be increased by providing choices, encouraging them to attempt slightly challenging tasks, and reinforcing them for their efforts. Reinforcement of effort rather than just outcome is important* (e.g., "I can see you really tried hard," "I know you can do it if you try a little harder"). These "effort" statements let the child know that the adult is as interested in persistence and effort as the final product. Watching other children and listening to them talk about how hard they tried can provide a role model for the child who lacks persistence. Helping children to accomplish one step at a time rather than seeing the whole effort as an unsurmountable task can also help. Seeing success as incremental can begin to be taught in the preschool years. Adults should replace negative comments and criticism, negative comparisons to peers, and unreasonably high expectations with supportive communication emphasizing the effort that the child makes. These procedures can enhance the child's judgments of his or her ability, increase task persistence, and improve the likelihood of success. Changing the child's mastery motivation generalizes over other areas as well and can have long-term implications (Dweck & Leggett, 1988).

PLAY MATERIALS AND OPPORTUNITIES

The key to encouraging mastery motivation is to arrange the environment so that challenging toys and materials are present. This depends, of course, on the child's abilities. Parents, however, make a mistake when they always provide toys the child can successfully manipulate or operate. Introducing new, higher-level materials or altering old materials to make them more challenging can stimulate the child to persist on a new task. For instance, removing the batteries from a toy car and letting the child figure out how to get them back in provides a problem-solving opportunity and encourages the child to see that it is the person, rather than the thing, who controls how the toy works.

EXAMPLE

Jesús S. was a 5-year-old with developmental delays who demonstrated a short attention span, only 3–4 actions in his play sequences, and a lack of goal-oriented activity. He exhibited no pride in accomplishment either through actions or words. The team and his parents decided to work on increasing the length of Jesús' play sequences by increasing his problem-solving and goal-directed play. The indirect effect was to increase his attention span. The team began with play activities that were most appealing to Jesús. He liked block play, but primarily stacked tall towers and knocked them down or built long chains of blocks. The teacher would sit next to Jesús and would build a tower or road like his. Then she modeled adding a block that needed to be carefully balanced or a tunnel on the "road." She then encouraged Jesús to do the same, saying, "I know you can do it if you try hard." Each step of progress was reinforced, "That was really hard, but you did it." Soon Jesús was initiating building more complex structures and running cars over the "roads." He would frequently yell, "Teacher, look, I made a road."

The success in the block area did not automatically generalize to other activities. The team used the same techniques in all of the play areas to increase Jesús' goal-directedness and his pleasure in accomplishment. His parents were also encouraged to reinforce his *effort* rather than the end result. As Jesús became more persistent in his efforts, his play sequences increased, his attention span increased, and peers began to engage him in associative play.

In the TPBA, questions regarding the child's characteristics in interaction are asked in terms of both the parent and the facilitator. The same questions are used to determine whether and how the child's interaction style differs. The implications for intervention are combined here, as the goal of positive, responsive, pleasurable interactions is the same.

OBSERVATION GUIDELINES FOR SOCIAL-EMOTIONAL DEVELOPMENT: SOCIAL INTERACTIONS WITH PARENT/FACILITATOR—CHARACTERISTICS OF CHILD IN INTERACTION

III./IV.　Social Interactions with Parent/Facilitator
　　A.　Characteristics of child in interaction with the parent/facilitator
　　　　1.　What level of affect is displayed by the child in interactions with the parent/facilitator? Does the child appear to find the interactions pleasurable?
　　　　2.　How does the child react to the emotions expressed by the parent/facilitator?
　　　　3.　How does the child react to vocal, tactile, or kinesthetic stimulation by the parent/facilitator?
　　　　4.　What type of cues does the child give the parent/facilitator (vocal, tactile, kinesthetic)? How easily are these cues interpreted?
　　　　5.　What percentage of the time is the child active versus inactive in the play time with the parent/facilitator? What amount of activity is directed toward interaction with the parent/facilitator?
　　　　6.　How frequently does the child initiate an interchange with the parent/facilitator?
　　　　7.　How many interactive behaviors is the child capable of maintaining?
　　　　8.　How does the child react to parental/facilitator requests, limit-setting, or control?

INTERVENTION
IMPLICATIONS

Affect

The affect displayed by the child is an indicator of whether he or she is enjoying the play. In addition, affect has an effect on the person with whom the child is engaging. A positive, enthusiastic affect is more likely to result in the adult becoming engaged in ongoing interaction. Children who show a low level of affect as a result of physical disabilities (e.g., low muscle tone), psychological reasons (e.g., sadness, depression), or medical reasons associated with an at-risk status may be less desirable to engage and more difficult to sustain in interaction (Emde, Katz, & Thorpe, 1978, Field, 1983). Developmental delays in areas associated with affect, such as vocalizations or verbalizations, may also be interpreted by the adult as less enthusiastic affect (Holdgrafer & Dunst, 1986). Increasing the child's level of affect and response cues can thus increase pleasure for both play partners.

Expression of Affect

Expression of affect is a cross-disciplinary issue, and input from all disciplines is needed. Increasing affective expression in the child can be addressed by the following:

1. Increasing the child's activity level (see pp. 202–206), which has a tendency to increase affective expression
2. Increasing mobility so that the child has an opportunity to gain access to toys, materials, people, and events that are most interesting and fun (see Chapter 11)
3. Selecting activities that increase or decrease facial muscle tone so that facial expressions are easier to make (see Chapter 11)
4. Demonstrating exaggerated affect so the child has a model for smiling and laughing
5. Increasing eye contact, gestures, vocalizations, verbalizations, and other forms of communication that allow the child to express interest and joy (see Chapter 10)

Affective Cues

The child's ability to read the adult's emotional affect and respond to emotional cues also influences the play interaction. The child who not only gives affective signals but responds to the signals of the play partner is more likely to sustain interaction (Brazelton, Tronick, Adamson, Als, & Wise, 1975). The child with disabilities may have fewer face-to-face interactions (Barrera & Vella, 1987; Hanzlik, 1990), making it more difficult to read the adult's cues. Increasing the child's attention to the adult thus may result in more responsive interactions. *Positioning the child in such a way that eye contact and observations of gestures and body language can be made is critical for all children. Getting down on the child's level also makes it easier for the child to attend to the adult's cues.*

Understanding Affective Cues and Responding Appropriately Increasing the child's response to the adult's emotional expressions demands that the child not only attend to the adult, but also be able to interpret the adult's affect and understand an appropriate response. These are both social and cognitive abilities. Attention can be increased by having the adult exaggerate affective responses, using gestures (a visual cue) to indicate salient features (e.g., pointing to the smiling mouth or to tears in the eyes) and vocalizing (an auditory cue) or verbalizing an affective expression. Understanding emotional expression and demonstration of appropriate response require the child to have reached a cognitive level in which behavioral causes and effects are understood. The adult can help the child reach a level of understanding by matching affective behavior with actions (e.g., patting the child on the back and handing him or her a tissue); commenting on the child's affect (e.g., "I can see you are really mad"); and pointing out the affect and actions of others (e.g., "Alex was so mad he needed to sit in his chair until he calmed down").

Selecting Cues Based on the Child's Preferences   The child's affective response is also influenced by the type of input the adult gives in the play interaction. He or she may respond differentially to vocal, tactile, or kinesthetic input. Assessment of the child's preferences assists the adults in selecting toys and other play materials and interaction patterns that are suited to the child. For instance, the child who responds to tactile input may be engaged in tickle games or play with tactile materials. Tactile cues may be given to enhance turn-taking or capture attention. Understanding child sensory preferences and the type of cues that are needed can be a key factor in establishing play routines that are mutually pleasurable.

Recognizing the Child's Feedback   In addition to discerning what type of input the child enjoys, being sensitive to the child's feedback system is also important. The child without disabilities gives a great deal of feedback and reinforcement to the adult when interactions are pleasurable. Laughter, talking, and excitement on the child's part make the adult want to continue the play. Children with disabilities may give subtle cues; slight movements of arms or legs, or even a grimace, may indicate enjoyment. The adults in the child's life need to learn these cues so that: 1) they will perceive when the child is having fun, when the child desires continued interaction, and when termination of interaction is preferred; and 2) they will receive feedback and reinforcement for interacting with the child. The child can also be encouraged to give more blatant cues. *The adult must let the child know that cues are being read.* Telling the child, "I saw your hand move. I think you like that. I'll do it again," may eventually increase the child's hand movement. Wait time is also important. If the adult waits 5–10 seconds before acting, the child may give a stronger cue to indicate a desire to continue.

Activity Level and Interaction

Children with disabilities have been shown to be less active in their play (Hanzlik & Stevenson, 1986; Walker, 1982). This reduced activity level can also have the effect of discouraging interaction or decreasing the number of toys with which the child plays, which, in turn, diminishes the variety interactions that take place. Increasing the child's mobility and range of movement can influence the activity level of play (see Chapter 11). Increasing the tempo of play may also have the effect of increasing activity level (see pp. 202–206).

Initiation of Interactive Play

Initiation of play is a critical component of interactions. Children at-risk and those with disabilities have been shown to initiate interactions with their parents less frequently than those who are not at-risk or do not have disabilities (Cunningham, Reuler, Blackwell, & Deck, 1981; Field, 1979, 1983; Hanson, 1984; Tannock, 1988). In order to attain a balance in interactive play, the child needs to initiate play approximately 50% of the time. *The adult can increase the child's initiations by observing and interpreting actions as an initiation, even if the child did not initially intend for the action to be a "turn."* By imitating the child, the adult captures the child's attention and takes another turn. The child frequently repeats the action to determine whether the adult will again copy the action. This action of repetition to get a response from the adult becomes an interactive action initiated to get a response from the adult. Variations can then be added to change the course of the game. Moving the child from a dependent responder to an active initiator may be a goal for intervention for many children.

Turn-Taking

Turn-taking is another critical process related to initiation. The child not only must be able to initiate but also sustain interaction through numerous turns. Children with disabilities have been shown to be less responsive, have fewer sustained interactions, and take fewer turns than their typical peers (Mahoney, Fors, & Wood, 1990; Maurer & Sherrod, 1987; Tannock, 1988). Turn-taking is viewed as an important skill for learning cognitive skills, carrying on a dialogue, and participating in social routines. The adults in the child's environment can increase turn-taking by making turn-taking a focus of intervention. *Through imitation, modeling, and modifying play actions, the adult stimulates the child to take another turn.* For the child who is uninterested in interaction, the adult may need to interject, "My turn," imitate the child's actions, and wait for the child to take another turn. After several repetitions, the child may begin to wait for the adult to have a turn, thus indicating that true turn-taking has begun. It is important to interject a note of caution. *Turn-taking is not required in every play activity. If the child is engrossed in exploration and problem-solving with an object, the adult's interruption may be intrusive and detrimental to the learning*

Turn-taking does not always happen spontaneously.

process. The adult should watch and determine whether the child is engaged in an activity that lends itself to turn-taking and whether turn-taking will limit the child's discovery operations. However, for children who play perseveratively and do *not* explore, turn-taking can enable the adult to modify actions and help the child to make a modification in his or her turn. Other children have delayed responses (Maurer & Sherrod, 1987) and need a longer time or a cue to react to their turn.

Directiveness

Many of the characteristics of children with disabilities described above, including low affect, decreased activity level, and lack of initiation and turn-taking, lead parents and facilitators to be more directive with these children. Research (Hanzlik, 1993) has shown that mothers of children with disabilities are more directive with their children and request more actions than mothers of children without disabilities. Although there is some disagreement in the literature about the effectiveness of being directive in promoting development, most authors agree that directives may not be negative if used when following the child's lead, in a supportive, rather than intrusive way. However, directiveness can decrease levels of independence and child initiation (Beckwith, 1976). The TPBA examines the way the child reacts to adult requests, directives, and limit-setting. For the child who acquiesces easily, does not take initiative, and waits for a directive, intervention can aim to change interaction patterns to promote more expression of the child's will. For the child who is locked in constant combat in a war of wills and who must always be in control, the intervention may shift to support the parent in creating a balance of power. The issues of balance in initiation and turn-taking are closely related to power and control.

EXAMPLE

Chantille J. was an 11-month-old African American infant with developmental delays. She and her mother, Rhonda J., lived in an inner-city, low-income housing project. Rhonda was unemployed, had a ninth-grade education, and had been reported previously for child abuse with her other two children. When observed, Chantille showed little emotional expression, made few vocalizations, and demonstrated infrequent gestures. Rhonda frequently became upset when she left Chantille in child care because Chantille did not cry when she left. She said, "She don't care. She's ignoring me." Actually, Chantille was giving her mother cues, but they were not as obvious as the cues given by many children. When her mother told her she was leaving, Chantille would look at her. When Rhonda said, "Wave goodbye to Mama," Chantille would lift her hand and pat the floor. Rhonda needed assistance in seeing how her child's communicative patterns were different from her other children. Because "goodbye" communication was so meaningful to her mother, the team worked with Chantille to vocalize and give a more intense wave for her mother. They also taped sessions of Chantille at play and watched them with Rhonda. They helped her to read Chantille's idiosyncratic cues and communications so that future interactions could feel more comfortable for both Chantille and her mother.

OBSERVATION GUIDELINES FOR SOCIAL-EMOTIONAL DEVELOPMENT: SOCIAL INTERACTIONS WITH PARENT— CHARACTERISTICS OF THE PARENT–CHILD INTERACTION

B.   Characteristics of the parent–child interaction
   1.   Describe the level of mutual involvement that is demonstrated.
      a.   To what degree is there continuity of content in the play?
      b.   To what degree is there synchrony of timing in the interactions?
      c.   To what degree is there similarity in the level of intensity in the interactions?
      d.   To what degree is there equality of turn-taking?
   2.   To what degree do the interactions demonstrate a sequence of behaviors with a beginning, middle, and end?
      a.   To what degree are themes repeated with variation or expansion?
      b.   To what degree do parents and child anticipate the actions of each other?
      c.   To what degree does the parent modify sequences to match the capabilities of the child?
   3.   How do the parent and child indicate their enjoyment of the interactions?

INTERVENTION IMPLICATIONS

Quality of Parent–Child Relationships

Whereas the previous section of this chapter focused on the characteristics of the child and the effects of those characteristics on adult (parent or facilitator)–child interaction, this section addresses play interactions between the parent and child. Research regarding parent–child interactions has shown that several aspects of the relationship are associated with positive child development outcomes both for children with and without disabilities (Ainsworth & Bell, 1973; Ainsworth, Blehar, Waters, & Wall, 1978; Clarke-Stewart, 1973; Mahoney, 1988, Mahoney, Finger, & Powell, 1985; Mahoney et al., 1990). Behaviors such as the parent's sensitivity to the child's cues, contingent responsiveness, and affection and warmth during interaction were found by these researchers to be significant factors in a positive parent–child relationship. Although numerous factors in the child's immediate and extended environment influence development (Bronfenbrenner, 1989), the quality of the parent–child relationship appears to be a key factor influencing cognitive, social-emotional, communication and language, and sensorimotor development (Bricker, 1986; Hanzlik, 1989; Holdgrafer & Dunst, 1986; Johnson, 1983). Hanzlik (1993) states that for long-term intervention goals to be most beneficial, the child's parents need the opportunity to focus on positive facilitation of the parent–child relationship.

Parental Interaction Variables

The literature regarding parent–child interactions has primarily been conducted with mothers, although studies have shown that the interactive patterns of mothers and fathers with their children with disabilities are similar (Levy-Schiff, 1986; Maurer & Sherrod, 1987). Observations from the TPBA, which is based on research from the literature, provide team members with information about the variables that are associated with positive parent–child relationships. One set of variables, those related to the child, have been discussed previously (see pp. 217–221). Variables related to the parent can also be addressed in intervention. Mutual involvement, affective synchrony (i.e., regulation of content, timing, and intensity of emotional expression), balance in turn-taking, matching the child's developmental level, sequencing interactions, and warmth and responsivity are important components of positive interaction (Brazelton et al., 1975; Mahoney & Powell, 1986). Mahoney and Powell (1988) have shown that maternal behavior that is child-oriented, sensitive, and less directive can result in increases in language and cognitive levels. Yet, parental interactions are complex and should be addressed individually, taking into consideration cultural expectations and values.

By using the TPBA videotape, the parents can see themselves on tape in interaction with their child. As anyone who has ever been taped as part of a training process knows, these tapes can be eye-opening and very instructive. If the facilitator is using a child-directed, responsive, less directive approach in facilitation, it may be possible to see differences in the child's initiation, turn-taking, affect, pragmatic communication, exploration, and cognitive level of functioning. The team can discuss with parents those techniques that appeared to result in increased performance on the child's part. Keeping the discussion focused on aspects of the child behavior that change as interactions change helps the team to discuss interactions without the parents feeling that their parenting skills are being judged. This is important if the partnership with the parents for the benefit of the child is to be maintained.

Intervention Techniques

Intervention techniques addressed in the literature are aimed at improving reciprocity between the parent and child at the child's developmental level and empowering the child to become more independent and interactive with others. The following techniques are derived from numerous sources (Dunst et al., 1987; Field, 1983; Girolametto, 1988; Hanzlik, 1989; MacDonald & Gillette, 1988; Mahoney & Powell, 1988) and adapted from a summary in Hanzlik (1993).

Positioning   Positioning is a very important aspect of interacting with children for several reasons. First, effective positioning can optimize opportunities for interaction. *The parent and child must be able to share eye contact, read facial expressions, and communicate directly with gestures and words.* This is particularly true for children with developmental delays and motor disabilities, and children with hearing impairments. Even for children with visual impairments, who may not be able to see the adult with whom they are playing, the face-to-face position allows the parent to read the child's cues better and enables the child to hear sounds and words without distortions.

Second, positioning may be necessary to maximize interactive opportunities. The child should be well supported so that efforts can be concentrated on the play interactions rather than on maintaining balance. Head control is important for eye contact and ability to focus on the task. Shoulder, arm, and hand stability give the child freedom to manipulate objects and gesture to the parent. Positioning can also break up negative patterns that inhibit more functional movements and interactions.

Third, appropriate positioning can decrease the need for the parent to hold the child. Being held restrains the child and is a form of control that usually diminishes opportunities for eye contact and makes the child more dependent on the parent. *Using positioning techniques or adaptive equipment allows the child to move away from the parent, thus facilitating separation and independent functioning on the part of the child.* In addition, as Hanzlik (1989) points out, moving the child from the "infant-like" position on the mother's lap or on the floor to an upright sitting or standing position can have the effect of making the child appear older and more competent. This perception of competence can have the effect of modifying the interaction patterns between the parent and child to a more mature style.

Child Initiation   After the child and parent are positioned in a way to optimize personal exchanges and object manipulations, other aspects of interaction can be addressed. *One key is to respond to the child's initiations.* If the child does not seek specific toys and materials independently, the adult can place two objects before the child. This allows the child to make a choice and initiate play. *Child initiation of play ensures selection of a play activity of interest to the child. If the child does not initiate play, the adult needs to provide sufficient wait time to allow the child to think about and act on the toys.* Five to ten seconds is usually sufficient, but some children require a longer processing time. After the child initiates an activity, the adult can interact in several ways: 1) watch and react affectively to the child's actions, 2) imitate the child's actions, 3) comment on the child's actions, and 4) play in parallel fashion next to the child. The adult may elect to interact in one or more of these ways, depending on the child's developmental level and responsivity. For the young infant who is not yet playing with toys, the interactions revolve around vocalizations, looking at the mother's face and objects that the mother holds up, and interactive movements and gestures. Again wait time is important to allow the infant to initiate interactions through sounds or movements. Turn-taking can take place with vocalizations, with the parent repeating the infant's sounds or adding new ones, or physical movement (e.g., the child may bounce up and down to get the parent to play "horse").

Turn-Taking   If the child does not spontaneously initiate interaction with the parent or objects, the parent can initiate the interaction by modeling vocalizations or actions. A short verbal or nonverbal turn is recommended. If the child still does not engage, the parent can verbally or physically prompt the child to act. The desired outcome is turn-taking, with the child and parent each responding in a contingent way to the other, anticipating actions, and seeking to continue the interactive chain. The parent can cue the child to take another turn by: 1) waiting for a response; 2) signaling to the child with a nod or gesture and look of expectancy; 3) commenting, such as "Amy's turn"; or 4) physically assisting the child to take another turn. This sequence of action is recommended as it moves from the least to the most intrusive and allows the child to remain in control. In other words, the parent should do nothing first, then gradually increase directiveness. A balance in turn-taking, with each partner initiating approximately half of the interactions, is desirable (Mahoney, 1988). The parent needs to keep his or her turn short so the child does not lose interest or forget the nature of the turn-taking game.

There is always the possibility that the activity selected by the adult does not interest the child in the least. *If the child is not responding to one type of play, the parent can shift to another activity.* A caution is in order here. Adults can easily get impatient or bored and shift activities quickly. *Enough time is needed to ascertain the child's level of interest before switching to new toys.* However, the parent's desire to have the child engage with a particular object can lead to prolonged attempts to get the child interested and result in frustration for both parties. Sensitivity to the child's cues helps the parent interpret the child's interests. For instance, focused attention, generalized body movement, smiling, or specific facial responses may indicate interest, while turning away, a blank stare, lack of response, or fidgeting may indicate a lack of interest. Individual children have idiosyncratic means of communicating their desires, and parents usually become adept at "reading" these cues.

For children who switch activities frequently without completing any one, the parent is caught in the bind of having to decide whether to "follow the child's lead" or become directive. Using turn-taking strategies can help the child on task, but the parent may also need to use supportive guidance to help the child desire to stay with an activity (e.g., "Oh, look. Here's another button," "How could we get that lid off?").

Careful observation of the cues the child is giving can assist the parent in anticipating the child's actions. Certain behaviors may indicate that the child is bored, angry, excited, and so forth. If the parent can learn to read cues and anticipate actions and respond more quickly, smoother interaction patterns can evolve.

Interactive Match   Mahoney (1988) identifies interactional matching as adjusting parental behavioral style to match the child's in the areas of pace, tempo, and complexity. Several of the previously discussed areas include strategies that also facilitate interactive matching: 1) following the child's lead in selection and use of toys, 2) maintaining conversation at the child's level, 3) keeping play behaviors at a complexity level compatible with the child's cognitive abilities, 4) pacing turn-taking to respond to the child's processing and action patterns, 5) imitation of the child's verbal and nonverbal behaviors, and 6) timing responses to match the child's needs.

Imitation   Imitation of the child's behavior, as indicated previously, is one way of capturing attention and taking a turn. Imitation helps the parent to focus on the child's movements and lets the child know that the adult is in tune with his or her actions. Imitation of both verbal and nonverbal behaviors helps the parent to act at the child's level and slows the pace to be in synchrony with the child. Modifications can be added as the child becomes involved in the turn-taking game. Imitation is important for both turn-taking and creating an interactive match.

Nondirectiveness   Many early intervention programs may have inadvertently encouraged directive approaches to "working with" children (Dunst & Trivette, 1988). Relationship-focused intervention (Affleck, McGrade, McQueeney, & Allen, 1982), however, takes a different stance, one of supporting parents to allow them to increase positive, pleasurable interactions. Directiveness and nondirectiveness refer to the amount of physical and verbal control the parent exerts over the child's activities and is another area to examine. Studies have shown that parents of children with disabilities are more directive than parents of children without disabilities (Barrera & Vella, 1987; Mahoney, 1988; Sharlin & Polansky, 1972). Whether this is problematic is controversial. Reducing physical control makes intuitive sense and is supported by research that shows that excessive physical contact or controlling behaviors decrease the infant's level of competence and degree of independence and may restrict exploratory behaviors (Beckwith, 1976; Sharlin & Polansky, 1972). The parent who always chooses the child's activities and has expectations about the way these activities should be done may reduce the child's initiative and limit his or her ability to make choices. Verbal control through directives and questions may have a negative impact on development if done in an intrusive way. Directives push the child to act in response to the parent's agenda (Hanzlik, 1993; Mahoney, 1988). The effects of directiveness are probably related to other variables including sensitivity, warmth in the parent, type of activity being directed, and other sociological variables. Looking at directiveness in isolation should not provide the focus for intervention. Having made this qualification, however, reducing the degree of directiveness can help the parent to understand alternative means of promoting their child's development. Nondirectiveness can be increased through a variety of techniques: 1) following the child's lead in selection of an activity or topic; 2) reducing the number of commands given to the child; 3) increasing the number of comments on the child's actions; 4) allowing time for the child to imitate, maintain, or change the subject of play or communication; 5) reducing the number of questions asked of the child, particularly closed questions requiring a set response and leading questions directing the child's course of thought; 6) mirroring the child's actions or words; 7) increasing positive comments, praise, and exclamations; and 8) providing adequate wait time for the child to initiate and maintain interaction.

Sequencing   Children typically repeat play activities innumerable times in acquiring mastery (Stein, Beebe, Jaffe, & Bennett, 1977; Stern, 1977, 1985). Children with disabilities, however, may not have the same degree of persistence. Encouraging parents to repeat activities numerous times can help promote mastery motivation in the child. Expansions and variations can then be added to increase skills. For older children, encouraging play through a meaningful sequence with a beginning, middle, and end allows more time for interaction and fosters persistence to completion of an activity.

Enjoyment   The affective expression of the parent is also important. Warmth and positive affect can mitigate many difficulties in parent–child interaction; while all of the parent–child strategies discussed above are less effective if the parent is bored, depressed, hostile, or indifferent. Pleasurable interactions for both the child and the parent should be the goal. Being able to play at the child's level, enter the child's world, and enjoy child's play is not easy for some adults. Many feel awkward and simply need "permission" to play, while others may need more support to get down on the child's level. Team members may want to: 1) model play interactions that are pleasurable, demonstrating positive affect; 2) help the parent select toys and materials that motivate the child and are fun for both partners; 3) using the videotapes, comment on how the child's affect and enjoyment are increased when the adult models positive affect and enthusiasm; and 4) become part of a play triad, where parent, child, and a professional play and have fun together.

EXAMPLE

Rhonda J., the mother in the example on page 221, had difficulty playing with her 11-month-old, Chantille. As a child, Rhonda had not had many toys, and her parents did not play with her often. When Rhonda played with Chantille, she chose the toys she liked and with which she wanted to play. She would frequently choose toys that were too difficult for Chantille and then direct her in how to use them. Rhonda would take Chantille's hand and manipulate the object for her. When Chantille tried to pull away to get another toy, Rhonda would pull her back and persist in getting Chantille to play with the toy she wanted. The play sessions frequently ended with Chantille in tears and Rhonda frustrated and angry.

The team used videotapes and modeling to help Rhonda see how follow-ing Chantille's lead and responding to her subtle cues would result in more pleasurable interactions. They demonstrated imitation and turn-taking and showed Rhonda that Chantille needed a slightly longer wait time in order to respond to Rhonda's words and actions. They talked about the type of toys and actions Chantille was "ready for" and saw on the videotapes how Chantille's vocalizations increased when an adult imitated her sounds or talked to her in one- to two-word phrases. Rhonda became enthusiastic as she began to see Chantille initiating more play with her and vocalizing more frequently. As Rhonda demonstrated more excited, positive affect, Chantille responded with more smiles. A positive interactive exchange gradually replaced the negative cycle that had begun in Chantille's infancy.

OBSERVATION GUIDELINES FOR SOCIAL-EMOTIONAL DEVELOPMENT: SOCIAL INTERACTIONS WITH PARENT—CHARACTERISTICS OF THE CHILD IN RELATION TO THE PARENT WHILE NOT IN DIRECT INTERACTION

C. Characteristics of the child in relation to the parent while not in direct interaction (i.e., while interacting with the play facilitator)

1. What type and amount of sensory cues does the child give to the parent in order to maintain emotional contact (visual "checking in," seeking physical contact, talking to the parent, or none)?
2. How much does the child seek proximity with the parent while playing with the facilitator?
3. Do the child's reactions to the parent change during the play session? What behaviors does the child exhibit when he or she is proud of an accomplishment, or when anxious or fatigued?
4. How does the child react to parental separation or absence? What type and amount of response is seen?
5. What mechanisms does the child use to cope with the parents' absence?
6. How does the child react to the parents' return?
7. How aware is the child of self and others?
   a. Identification of self and others
   b. Identification of emotions in self and others
   c. Use of pronouns (I, you, me, mine)
   d. Identification of gender
   e. Use of adjectives to label concrete (brown hair) or abstract (nice person) per-sonal characteristics

INTERVENTION IMPLICATIONS

The process of attachment, separation, and individuation influences the child's development of cognitive, social-emotional, communication and language, and sensorimotor skills (Ainsworth, 1973; Ainsworth et al., 1978; Horner, 1985; Mahler et al., 1975). The process of attachment, separation, and individuation influences the child's development of cognitive, social-emotional, communication and language, and sensorimotor skills (Ainsworth, 1973). In the course of normal psychological development, the infant begins the process by creating a secure emotional bond with the primary object, usually the mother. In the early stages of this bond, the infant's ability to distinguish self from non-self is limited—baby and mother are one. When infants receive adequate psychological care (e.g., comfort, soothing), the attachment to the primary object grows. The infant mirrors the object's smiles and responses, paving the way for recognition that self and others are separate. As the baby begins to recognize his or her own attributes, the roots of separation are taking hold. Cognitive development supports the early awareness of psychological separateness. If all goes well for the child, individuation leads to a well-defined sense of "self." Confident separations cannot occur for a child without secure attachments, nor can individuation be accomplished without successful attachments and separations.

The characteristics of the child, the characteristics of the parent, and the interactions between the parent and child, as discussed previously, have an impact on the child's developing sense of self and others and his or her consequent sense of security (Carlson, Cicchetti, Barnett, & Braunwald, 1989; Fonagy, Steele, Moran, Steele, & Higgitt, 1991). How the child acts when the parent is present but not directly interacting with him or her and how the child responds when the parent leaves the room and returns give clues to the child's degree and type of attachment.

The child's growing sense of self is related to attachment outcomes. Whether and how the child perceives self as different from others is reflected in the child's language and actions. Observations from the TPBA (Linder, 1993) can give insight into the child's sense of trust, security, and independence as well as his or her level of awareness and understanding of self and others. As indicated in the discussion of attachment in *Transdisciplinary Play-Based Assessment* (Linder, 1993), the observations of the child and parent in this brief session serve as a screening. If concerns are raised a more in-depth assessment is needed.

Difficulties with attachment, separation, and individuation may result from many causes. The roots of problems, however, are usually complex, with intertwining child and parental variables that are not easily addressed in an intervention program for the child. Some factors, such as the child's characteristics related to disability, may not be able to be modified; other characteristics, such as parental depression that affects attachment or the child's behavioral characteristics, may be treatable. Child abuse or neglect and parental addiction to drugs or alcohol also profoundly affect the child's sense of security and perception of self. Some of these issues may be dealt with through therapy or other support services to the family; others may be addressed, albeit superficially, through intervention programs with the child. The parent–child interaction patterns addressed on pages 217–227 are related to attachment, and intervention that incorporates these issues also has an affect on the attachment, separation, and individuation process. The strategies discussed on pages 217–227 are appropriate for parents and children across developmental levels. The following guidelines provide additional suggestions for children in specific phases of the attachment, separation, and individuation process.

- Shows active differentiation of strangers
    (6–8 months)
- Recognizes self in mirror
    (6–8 months)
- Shows special dependence on mother—wants food, attention, stimulation, and approval from her, even when others are available
- As long as child sees parent, he or she plays contentedly. As he or she leaves the room, child cries and tries to follow
    (7–8 months)
- Shows mild to severe anxiety at separation
    (8–10 months)

Identifying Problems in the Parent–Child Relationship

The age ranges listed in regard to this developmental level are influenced by how frequently the child has been exposed to people other than family members and the amount of attention paid to the child by the parent. In addition, a parent's emotional problems or the child's physical and mental deficits may influence the attachment–separation process. Giffin (1981) identifies early signs of problems in the relationship, including:

- For the parent—extreme anxiety about separation from the infant; disinterest in the infant; a flat unresponsive affect; unusual awkwardness in handling the infant; inappropriate timing in response to the infant; too clinging or too casual with the infant; lack of concern about safety precautions; and an inability to accept and accommodate to the child's stranger anxiety.
- For the child—failure to thrive unexplained by physical causes; inability to be comforted by mother; lack of smiling and joyful interaction with the parent; lack of stranger anxiety; lack of response to mother's soothing; inability to console self; and lack of curiosity about the environment.

If several of these patterns are observed, support for the attachment process may be needed. *The parent may need assistance in reading the child's cues and responding appropriately.* Very young mothers or mothers with emotional concerns may not be aware of the child's basic need for eating, sleeping, being held and talked to, and exploring the environment.

Ascertaining Support Needs

By observing parent–child interaction and listening to how the parent talks to and about the child, the intervention team can determine where support might be helpful. The techniques described on pages 217–227 can be used to help the parent learn how to *observe* the child, how and when to *react* to the child, and which *actions* to take to improve *interactions*. Observation, reaction, action, and interaction are basic areas that serve as the foundation for supportive intervention. Specific techniques, such as those described in the following example, should be determined based on the parent's and child's interaction patterns, the parent's request for assistance, and the child's special needs.

Most parents learn by observing what seems to result in positive changes for their child. The facilitator can also discuss how the child's individual characteristics contribute to the type of interaction the parent is experiencing.

If the parent has severe emotional problems or if extremely negative patterns of interaction are observed, additional community supports may be needed.

PLAY MATERIALS AND OPPORTUNITIES

No specific toys encourage parent–child interactions; rather any toys that are of interest to the child can facilitate the interaction process. Depending on the child's developmental level, captivating toys and materials can be used to establish a joint referent, to take turns, and to build a positive interaction. Every interaction provides an opportunity for responsiveness and positive interchange.

EXAMPLE

Roberta L., a teenage mother, never responded to her baby's cries because she "didn't want him to get spoiled." P.J. consequently learned not to cry and was left unattended in his crib for hours. His mother only fed him when she realized that she was hungry herself. P.J.'s primary sensory stimulation was the sound of the stereo playing rock music or the sound of the television in another room. When she did hold her son, Roberta held him facing away from her, giving him little eye contact and seldom communicating with him. P.J. seldom smiled, which increased his mother's feeling that he "doesn't like me." He showed no stranger anxiety, was apathetic, and displayed little affect. A vicious cycle of lack of attention and response on the part of first the parent and then the child was setting a pattern that would inevitably lead to delays and interactional problems for the child. When he was 8 months old, P.J. could not sit unsupported, seldom vocalized, and showed little interest in the environment.

Intervention focused on helping Roberta establish a routine with P.J., so that she would be able to anticipate when he needed to eat, sleep, and play. Positioning P.J. so that he and Roberta could see each other and communicate was encouraged. Roberta learned how to read P.J.'s signs of pleasure, which began as body movements and progressed to full-fledged smiles. The facilitator helped Roberta find toys and other play materials in her home that could be used to stimulate P.J. and provided much praise and encouragement for each of Roberta's efforts to engage her child in play. Gradually, Roberta became more sensitive to P.J.'s needs, and as P.J. became more responsive and their interactions more reinforcing, Roberta showed increased enjoyment and appreciation of her son.

- Shy period passes, eager to go out into the world
  (12–15 months)
- Distinguishes self from others
- Reacts sharply to separation from parent
- Reacts to emotions expressed by parent and others
  (12 months +)
- Uses mother for emotional "refueling"
  (12–15 months)

Exploration

At this development level, the child should be encouraged to explore. For children without motor impairments, this is a time for increasing motor exploration. The child who can physically move away from the parent to find new and interesting objects and people can experiment with separating from the parent while the parent is still in view. Playpens and baby seats may be very confining. The parent can place the child several feet away and allow the child to move back and forth between the toys and the security of the parent. The parent can also move to another room and maintain vocal contact with the child, so the child is aware that the parent is close and can come to find reassurance.

Exposure to Adults Other than Parents

Exposure to other adults is also important for the separation process. Letting others hold the child and talking to others while the child plays nearby lets the child know that the parent trusts these adults and is comfortable with them. *Because the child is now picking up on others' emotions, it is important for the parent not to appear stressed or upset when leaving the child.* This only communicates to the child that this event should be upsetting. When the parent does leave, communicating to the child that the parent will return is also important. Reassurance in a confident, yet sensitive, voice is meaningful to the child even at this stage.

Learning About Self

The child learns about self by discovering skills and discovering characteristics of self that are different from others. *Mirrors are a tool for exploration of self.* The child can study his or her own features compared to those of others. Putting colored paints or bells on fingers, toes, and other body parts also calls attention to the child's various parts and helps to increase understanding of the components of self. Infants investigate characteristics of others with all of their senses, by pulling on hair, sticking their fingers in adults' mouths or noses, feeling texture of the skin, smelling, tasting, and watching. *Allowing the child to engage in such analysis is an important part of their differentiation of self from other.* Some parents place rigid constraints on their child not to poke, pull, or be "annoying." Explaining how the child is learning about the parent can help the parent to guide the exploration in a gentle, informative way. "Yes, this is Mommy's hair. Feel it gently." Nibbling on the child's fingers and letting him or her nibble on the parent's in turn sets up a game of personal discovery.

PLAY MATERIALS AND OPPORTUNITIES

Toys serve as a connection between the parent and child. The child will frequently bring the parent a toy, show it, and return to play. The object serves as a means of reconnecting with the parent.

Meanwhile, the child is discovering how separate he or she is and is experimenting with being away from the parent. As motor skills develop, motor toys (e.g., riding toys) encourage movement away from the adult. Mirrors of all sizes allow the child to discover how he or she looks and how his or her appearance is different from others.

DEVELOPMENTAL LEVEL

- Moves away from parent as home base into widening world
- Brings toys to share with parent
  (15–18 months)

INTERVENTION GUIDELINES

As the child gains confidence, he or she begins to feel more comfortable being apart from the parent, toddling into another room, or playing quietly while the parent moves around the house. However, returning to "home base" and checking in is important. New discoveries are to be shared with the most important person, the parent. Language is also emerging at this time, allowing the parent an opportunity to label objects as the child proudly presents them, offering, but not releasing, the precious articles. For the child who is at this level emotionally, but lacks motor skills, the parent can perform the ritual of placing the object near the child or in the child's hands, raising the hands in offering, and commenting enthusiastically about the object. *The parent also needs to allow the child with motor deficits the opportunity to be free of adult holding and restraint.* Positioning the child and using switch-activated toys or easily activated devices, so that play can occur independent of the parent is critical to the separation process for the child with physical involvement. *The child who is always held and always has assistance to engage the environment may have a more difficult time separating and learning about independence and self-control.*

For any child, encouragement of exploration, parental support of independent efforts through environmental structuring, and reinforcement of separation efforts can influence the child's progress toward separation. For the child with disabilities, who may have been more dependent on the parent for many functions, the process may be more challenging. For the parent of the child with disabilities, who may view the child as needing more assistance and support than typical children, the process of separation may also result in conflicting feelings. The parent may need support from the intervention team to allow the child more independence.

PLAY MATERIALS AND OPPORTUNITIES

The parent may want to have play areas that are sometimes close and at other times more distant from him or her. More distant play areas allow the child an opportunity to practice moving away and coming back to the parent; closer play areas allow the child to concentrate on play activities with a sense of security and closeness to the parent.

Again, motor toys may encourage moving away from the parent. Ball games also allow separation and reconnection with the ball as a "connector." Parents can also help the child to practice separation by sending the child to find objects in another room. This can become a game, which is also helpful to the busy parent.

- Demands proximity of familiar adult
- Alternates between clinging and resistance to familiar adult
- Refers to self by name
- Conscious of own acts as they are related to adult approval or disapproval
      (18–24 months)
- Shy with strangers, especially adults; may hide against parent when introduced to strange adults
- Makes constant demands of parent's attention
- Clings tightly to parent in affection, fatigue, and fear
      (24–30 months)

Although the child is gaining skills and confidence and seeking stimulation outside the realm of the parent, he or she still needs to come back to the parent for reassurance, comfort, and encouragement. The child at this level "practices" being separated from the parent (Lyons-Ruth, 1991; Mahler et al., 1975). The child may gleefully run away from the parent and then wait to be chased and swept up in the parent's arms.

The child is at the same time acquiring a sense of his or her own will and ability to control the environment. Temper tantrums and expressions of strong feelings regarding desires are matched against the need to cling and be held and comforted. The child tests the adults' responses by purposefully performing an act that results in a sharp "No." As toilet-training commences toward the end of this phase, the child discovers a new realm for control and conflict with the parent. How the child and parent handle these power conflicts influences the future course of their parent–child relationship.

The parent whose expectations for independence and self-control are too high may set the child up for feelings of incompetence. The parent who uses strong punitive measures to keep power and control may be setting up ongoing power struggles by giving the message that the only way to "win" is through strong negative actions. At the same time, the punitive approach may reinforce in the child a feeling of inadequacy or being a "bad" child. However, the parent who lets the child be in total control of events or feels the child's disabilities give license for free reign may be inhibiting the child's development of an understanding of the boundaries for acceptable behavior and the development of self-control. The child is beginning to associate the emotions that are seen in the adult with their actions and the consequences of their actions. The adults response can help the child understand that there are acceptable and unacceptable behaviors.

At the same time, the child is dealing with increased expression of aggression and trying to deal with conflicting emotions. Adults can help the child verbalize, rather than act out, aggression. Modulation of affect leads to self-control. The parent might say, "I can see that you're mad at your sister, but you can't hit her with your toy." Verbalization or labeling of affect helps the child to develop an internal representation of affect, which contributes to the development of a sense of self (Katan, 1961; Novick, 1986).

The intervention team can provide support to parents who are struggling with the concerns of this period by helping parents to understand the developmental issues with which the child is struggling and by providing suggestions for behavior management. Modeling different communication and interaction patterns can also help the parent learn a new method for influencing the child's behavior.(Suggestions for behavior management are offered on pp. 265–270.)

PLAY MATERIALS AND OPPORTUNITIES

No specific toys are recommended, but "special" toys or materials (e.g., a doll, stuffed animal, blanket) may offer the child comfort when dealing with separation or control issues.

DEVELOPMENTAL LEVEL

- Recognizes self in photograph
- Understands needs of other persons
  (30–36 months)
- Can answer whether he or she is a boy or a girl
- Separates from parent without crying
- Joins other children in play
  (36–48 months)
- Can explore neighborhood unattended
- Strong sense of family and home, quotes parents as authorities
  (48–60 months)

INTERVENTION GUIDELINES

Developing a Growing Sense of Self

The child acquires a growing sense of self, first by understanding the concrete characteristics that are associated with how he or she looks compared to others and then by understanding more abstract qualities of emotions and personal characteristics of self and others (e.g., whether someone is "nice" or "mean") and discerning family differences (e.g., who has a mommy and no daddy, who has brothers and sisters). This comprehension helps the child to see who he or she is compared to others, to understand the distinctions of others, and to begin to perceive the unique needs of others. For example, the child relates differently to infants than children of his or her own age, seeking to assist the infant, but competing with age peers.

The adults in the child's environment can enhance this growing sense of self by helping the child to make comparisons and note differences in children. The young child engages in onlooker behavior, studying other children's actions. The adult can comment on the child being watched or what the child is doing. As the child moves into associative and then cooperative play, opportunities for description and comparisons increase. *Encouraging the child to re-*

spond to the needs expressed by others also helps the child develop empathy and prosocial behaviors. As in the younger ages, the opportunity to explore and increase both cognitive and social problem-solving skills enables the child to gain self-confidence and mastery. *An environment that supports investigation and discovery promotes self-initiative.*

Dealing with a New Environment

The child's memory of his or her home environment and parental returning leads to a sense of security, which, when paired with increased skills and confidence and expanded relationships that include other adults and peers, allows the child to easily separate from the parent. The child who has lived in a restricted environment and not had exposure to other adults and peers may find a transition to preschool to be difficult for a period, but if a secure parent–child relationship exists, the adjustment period should be brief. Children who have not formed secure attachments may also find this transition difficult, as they have no sense of a secure base to which they can return. They may have difficulty forming attachments to other adults and peers in the class. Children who have been abused may lack trust in others or, at the other extreme, may relate with indiscriminate affection toward adults in their new environment.

Preschool presents a new environment to which the child must adjust and new people to whom he or she must relate. This shift from home to school can be stressful for some children. Teachers can assist children and parents (separation may also be difficult for parents) with this process. *Transition objects, or objects that are special to the child, may be brought from home and provide a "connection" for the child.* Pictures of family members kept in a special book may also provide "emotional refueling." In some extreme cases, the parent may need to stay for a few minutes and gradually make an exit as the child becomes engaged in activities. *Prolonged goodbyes only exaggerate the emotional stress the child experiences. Having fun things to distract and engage the child is important.* Standing and watching the parent go is much more difficult than realizing the parent is gone while actively playing in a fun activity.

Helping Parents To Cope with Separation

For the parent who is having difficulty with separation, it is important to acknowledge his or her feelings and provide support by giving the parent detailed input on the child's day and what activities seemed to be pleasurable. Parents sometimes feel competition with the teacher for the child's affection, so exhibiting affection with the child or talking about how much the child seems to like the teacher may make the parent feel more uncomfortable. Rather, discussing the progress the child is making in becoming independent and relating the child's comments about the family and home may be more reassuring.

Forming Relationships with Adults Other than Parents

For children with emotional problems, the teacher may need to make special efforts to form a relationship. *Some children need to relate to one primary adult for a period of time, until an attachment is formed and a sense of a secure base allows the child to expand relationships to other adults and children.* The teacher may want to provide special times for individual attention and nurturance through rocking, storytelling, comforting, and special activities such as making personal books about the child. Facilitation of the child's play may be needed for a period of time.

Forming Relationships with Peers

Some children will form relationships with peers more easily than adults. Pairing the child with a peer who matches the child's developmental and temperamental needs may provide needed support for the child. Occasionally a child who is very withdrawn benefits from being paired with a child who is at a lower developmental level, so that he or she takes the initiative in directing and assisting the peer. The opposite may also be true. A child may respond to being placed with a child with a stronger, leader personality who can provide a role model and encourage the child to participate. Experimentation with peer pairing provides information to guide decisions regarding which peer is the best match.

The Individuation Process

Forming attachments while learning to separate from significant caregivers is essential for the individuation process. Working with parents and children on these developmental issues is an important and often difficult component of the early intervention process. When the child begins to function as a unique individual, he or she acquires an identity that is separate but still a part of the rest of

The development of cooperative play skills is an important goal for preschool children.

the family. An understanding of others, a developing self-concept, and external relationships allow the child to expand his or her world.

Materials that assist the child in feeling confident and secure will support the individuation process. Taking photographs or special objects from home to school, for instance, may give the child a sense of security. Toys and materials that promote interaction (see Chapter 6) help to build the child's confidence with others. The more comfortable the child feels in social play, the more likely it is that he or she is expanding his or her world to include more than family. Toys such as blocks, dramatic play materials, and "two-way" toys (e.g., balls) promote interaction and experimentation. Discovering new skills and abilities with new objects and materials also helps develop the child's concept of self.

PLAY MATERIALS AND OPPORTUNITIES

OBSERVATION GUIDELINES FOR SOCIAL-EMOTIONAL DEVELOPMENT: SOCIAL INTERACTIONS WITH FACILITATOR— CHARACTERISTICS OF THE FACILITATOR–CHILD INTERACTION

B. Characteristics of the facilitator–child interactions
1. In general, how does the child relate to the facilitator (e.g., oblivious, cautious, anxious, fearful, comfortable, affectionate)?
2. How do the facilitation techniques of matching the child's content, timing, and intensity affect the child's:
    a. Initiations of interactions or activities
    b. Turn-taking
    c. Affect
3. To what degree do repetition and expansion of themes affect the child's play?
    a. Length of sequences
    b. Quality and degree of communication
    c. Initiation of interaction on the part of the child
    d. Affect

The interaction between the child and facilitator may look very similar to or very different from that of the parent and child. Variables that may contribute to differences include the degree of attachment between parent and child, the child's disability, and interactional style variations. Based on the literature reviewed on pages 64–66, the techniques used by an effective facilitator should result in interactions that increase child initiation, turn-taking, and positive affect. Imitation and expansion of the child's play should also result in longer play sequences, increased attention and communication, and spontaneous initiations of play on the child's part. The analysis of the consequences of using these facilitation techniques helps the team to determine which methods are effective with each child. In addition, comparison of these same child behaviors when the parent was interacting using similar or dissimilar interaction approaches assists the team in determining which strategies are most effective with a specific child. The team may then use the tape to discuss with the parent

INTERVENTION IMPLICATIONS

which tactics seem most productive and practical for expanding the child's repertoire of skills.

Terry H. was a 3-year-old child who had been diagnosed with autism. Terry had only fleeting eye contact and a typical attention span of a few seconds on any one toy. He had repetitive behaviors of rocking back and forth, poking the floor, and waving his arms in the air. These behaviors were interjected into his play every few seconds. His play was limited to visual examination, waving and banging, with some tactile exploration. Although Terry could walk, he usually chose to scoot on his bottom or crawl. When he did walk, it was stiff-legged with a wide base of support.

During the TPBA, Mrs. H., Terry's mother, was observed to sit behind Terry, holding him on her lap. She physically moved his hands to manipulate an object, while telling him what to do. "Wave it like this." Terry would rock back and forth, look away, and make a protest sound. Mrs. H. reported that Terry initiated no interactions unless he wanted something to eat, then he would look at her and vocalize the same protest sound. The interaction patterns between Terry and his mother remained consistent throughout the observations. The play facilitator sat in front of Terry and imitated his behaviors. He would glance at her and repeat his movements. After a time, it became evident that Terry was watching and waiting for the facilitator to imitate him. Only once was she able to get him to imitate one of her actions. Terry also showed more focused attention after sensorimotor activities. Activities, particularly those involving vestibular stimulation, seemed to give his sytem needed input.

After observing the TPBA, the team decided that in the preschool room, Terry would need someone to facilitate his behaviors for part of the day. They chose one team member, the teacher assistant, who would try to form an attachment with Terry over time. Terry would begin his day with some form of sensorimotor activities with the assistant, either in the room, the sensorimotor area, or on the outdoor playground. In all activities with Terry, she would use the techniques of imitation, turn-taking, and responding to Terry's cues. She would try to increase his interaction time, attention, and length and variety of play schemes. At other times of the day, Terry would be integrated into the class, so other peers could model and interact with him. The assistant would remain close to facilitate and encourage interactions.

On the first day of class, after playing with Terry on the playground swings, the assistant got down on the floor with Terry and positioned herself so that she was in front of him. She watched him rock and poke the floor with his hands. Then she began to imitate him. Terry continued to rock and poke, but occasionally glanced at her. The assistant then stopped and watched. After a wait time, she repeated the actions again. The next time the assistant stopped, Terry stopped, too, and looked at her. He started to rock and poke again. She placed a colorful stick with streamers on the end near Terry. Terry picked it up and started to wave it. The assistant picked up another one and imitated Terry. He glanced at her again and stopped. She stopped. He waved and rocked. She imitated him. When Terry placed the stick down, the assistant replaced it with a hammer. Terry began to bang on the floor. The same imitative process was repeated with the assistant waiting and watching for a cue from Terry to repeat her behavior.

Terry was then seated in a stable chair with sides, so that his feet touched the ground. Toys were placed on a low table in front of him within easy reach. Over a period of time, he began to poke at, bang, or wave the toys. The assistant patiently watched and imitated. After several days of these play periods, Terry began to anticipate them and turn-taking began as he initiated a movement, looked at the assistant and waited for her to imitate him. Gradually, the assistant was able to include variations and new movements that Terry would imitate. He became more observant of the other children in the class and eventually would sit next to a peer and play with the same toys. Although he retained many of the repetitive behaviors, his eye-contact, turn-taking, vocalizations, and play explorations increased.

Children with autism, or what have been described as "autistic-like" tendencies, respond to the techniques described on pages 238–239. Careful observations and responsiveness on the part of the facilitator are critical.

OBSERVATION GUIDELINES FOR SOCIAL-EMOTIONAL DEVELOPMENT: CHARACTERISTICS OF DRAMATIC PLAY IN RELATION TO EMOTIONAL DEVELOPMENT

V. Characteristics of dramatic play in relation to emotional development
  A. Structure of play
    1. To what degree is there continuity and logical sequence versus fragmented thought presented in the child's play?
    2. To what degree is there a linkage or recognition of past, present, and future?
    3. To what extent does the child's play demonstrate rigid or inflexible thought patterns?
  B. Content of play
    1. What are the dominant themes of the child's play?
      a. Dependency
      b. Loss
      c. Power/control
      d. Fear/anxiety
      e. Self-image
    2. Does the child recognize the boundaries between reality and fantasy?
  C. Awareness of self and others in dramatic play
    1. Is the child capable of joint referencing or sharing joint "topics" of attention?
    2. Does the child have the ability to see another's point of view?
    3. Is the child able to incorporate the adult into the play with shared goals?
    4. Is the child capable of making judgments about the consequences of actions?
    5. Is the child capable of recognizing and labeling emotions?
    6. Is the child capable of expressing and modulating his or her emotions?
    7. To what extent does the child demonstrate impulse control?

INTERVENTION IMPLICATIONS

Emotional Issues and Intervention Through Play

Observations from the TPBA (Linder, 1990) give the team some initial impressions of the child's emotional stability and any internal conflicts that may be influencing his or her behavior. Children with obvious severe emotional problems may be referred for individual therapy outside of the classroom. Many children who are being seen in outside therapy are also enrolled in a preschool program. Persons who work in the educational environment therefore need to be able to deal with the child's emotional issues in school as well. Communication and consultation with the child's therapist is, therefore, advised. The therapist, with the permission of the family and child, may be able to shed light on persistent feelings or conflicts within the child that may make the child's behaviors in school more understandable. The team, in turn, may be able to share valuable information with the therapist about the child's activities in school that may prove beneficial to the child's treatment.

Many children with emotional problems are not in treatment outside of the classroom. During the TPBA observations, the emotional difficulties of some children are clearly evident. Others, with more subtle problems, may demonstrate emotional issues over time in the classroom. Whenever the difficulties are identified, the team should address them as part of intervention. If the intervention team does not include a child psychologist and it is working with a child with social-emotional concerns, team members may want to request that a child psychologist join the team. A psychologist is able to provide ongoing suggestions to the team on how to respond to the child in the classroom. He or she may also want to work individually with the child, either in the classroom or in individual play sessions. For children with deficits in other areas as well as the social-emotional area, the psychologist may be able to help the team evaluate the aspects of the child's behavior that may be related to emotional development as opposed to cognitive, communication and language, and sensorimotor concerns.

Intervention with children with emotional difficulties should have both a home and school component. Relationships are key to many emotional concerns and parents must be involved for effective intervention to take place. For children who are not yet in school, many of the issues addressed on pages 217–227 regarding parent–child interaction are relevant. In infant, toddler, and preschool intervention approaches, psychological and behavioral concerns are probably present, with behaviors acting as symptoms for deeper psychological issues. This discussion provides suggestions for dealing with both levels. Play is the natural medium for examining and working through the child's emotional world. For children, who do not have the sophisticated language or cognitive abilities to communicate the complexities of their inner world, toys are their words and play is their symbolic language of self-expression (Ginott, 1964). The child can act out feelings, attitudes, fears, anxieties, wishes, and conflicts with emotional distance and begin to understand and master his or her inner world. Discussion of intervention that concerns these issues is addressed first. Techniques for managing behaviors are addressed on pages 265–270.

Facilitating Self-Expression

The toys and materials found in most preschool classrooms are suitable for play with the child with emotional concerns. Certain of these materials lend themselves to self-expression and communication. Depending on the child's developmental level, different types of dolls, puppets, action figures, games, bulding materials, balls, cars and trucks, and dress-up clothes may generate emotional expression. In addition, materials that can be used in multiple ways, such as Play-Doh, sand and water, fingerpaints, and drawing materials of different types, may elicit expression of both emotions and perceptions. *Children's self-expression can be observed through the choices they make, the tangible and imaginary products they create, and the verbalizations they make related to their play.*

These observations can take place during the course of the child's play. Consultation with the psychologist, if he or she is unable to participate in the classroom, supports the team's efforts. *To avoid misjudgments, it is also important to obtain consultation from persons of the same social, racial, or ethnic group as the child to ascertain whether some of the behaviors observed relate to cultural diversity.*

Establishing Rapport and Trust   Establishing rapport and trust with the child is critical to successful intervention. Acting naturally, in an honest and straightforward manner, gives credibility to the relationship. At the same time, the adult should be able to get down to the child's level and play with the toys and materials in which the child is interested. (The facilitation strategies discussed in Chapter 5 and the communication strategies addressed in Chapter 10 are also appropriate for the person who is working with a child on social and emotional development.) *Limits do need to be set. The child cannot be allowed to hurt him- or herself, other children and adults, or destroy property.* Other than these few rules, the play with the child should be child-centered and child-directed.

Attaching Significance to Play

Perry and Landreth (1991) try to derive meaning from a child's play behaviors by examining the child's social inadequacy, discomfort, and use of fantasy play. The goal becomes moving the child toward more comprehensible play, more appropriate social interactions, less aggressiveness, more cohesive play, more positive affect and expression of positive statements about self, feelings, and worries, and a reduced expression of conflicts. Gaining self-control is also an issue. Loss of control is as frightening as feeling that one has too much power. Without limits, the child's world can feel chaotic and disorganized. Adults must provide these limits until the child develops internal limits that allow him or her to feel emotionally safe.

While the adult plays at the child's level, he or she is also monitoring and attempting to interpret the meaning attached to the child's play. Patterns begin to emerge as the child repeats various themes and actions. The child's thoughts and attitudes may be observed in many ways. The team should consider its observations in terms of themes, structure, and affective content.

Themes   The themes a child chooses during free play reveal something about his or her inner world. Themes with different toys and the actions that accompany the toys may reveal that the child is using play to be powerful and master aggressive drives or to do the opposite—imitate nurturance and caregiving. The child may be the brave, bold adventurous hero of the play constructions or the frightened and timid character needing rescue. Most children, regardless of the circumstances of their lives, play the roles of heroes. Children rarely play the roles of "bad guys" even if they are identified "problem children" or "troublemakers." Universally, children seem to use play as an opportunity to be the ego ideal that is within us all. A child who selects "bad guy" roles should be given a second look by skilled mental health professionals. Similarly, children whose themes suggest that they may be victims should be referred for further evaluation.

Themes in children's play are influenced by both developmental stage and life circumstances. Children younger than 2 years of age and children with poor attachment often have dependency themes in their play. Between 18 months and 2½ years, play reflects the use of power and control to accomplish independent strivings. Feelings of dependency are overriden by the child's desire to feel powerful. Age and developmental level of play may not always coincide. Children may exhibit a variety of themes reflective of concerns from different developmental levels. Often children re-enact themes from an earlier phase in an attempt to solve conflicts.

EXAMPLE

Alisa F. was facing her third major surgery in 2 years to correct congenital birth defects of her legs and back. For a month prior to the surgery her play contained themes of children being hurt. Her teacher became particularly concerned when Alisa cut the legs and arms off paper dolls. Without intruding into Alisa's play, her teacher commented that Alisa too might be worried about being cut. In reaction to her teacher's sensitive remark, Alisa blurted out, "What if they make a mistake and cut off my legs?" Having revealed her fear, parents, teachers, and health professionals could help to reassure Alisa about the outcome of her surgery. Later in that week, Alisa was found with her mutilated paper dolls, taping the legs and arms back on. This example illustrates a child's use of play to master fears and anxieties associated with a frightening experience.

Abuse   Children who have been or are being abused usually reveal aspects of the abuse in their play. Dolls are often mistreated in much the same way the child has been. Toys or dolls representing adults or authority figures are often punitive, harsh, and rough with the child characters. When playing with puppets, animal or human, the mistreated child often demonstrates aggressive and hostile interactions. It should also be remembered that these themes can be played out by children who have not been abused as well. Hostility in play can be a reflection of concern about aggression in others or even their own feelings of aggression. However, children whose play suggests or hints at mistreatment should be taken seriously and referred to appropriate professionals for further evaluation.

Loss   Children usually do not develop themes of loss in their play unless they are struggling emotionally with an important loss or fear of a loss. Obvious losses are experienced through the death of people or pets. Sometimes the loss of a pet is underestimated; children who have lost a beloved animal companion can be seen in their play attempting to come to terms with the loss. For several weeks after his dog was hit by a car, 6-year-old Sean C. named many characters in his play "Tipper." Sean could be found in the corner of the classroom playing, usually with animals, whispering to the animals that they must all look for Tipper. A big, old, mean animal had taken Tipper away, and they must all search for him and rescue him. Sean, a psychologicaly healthy child, worked on his reaction to the loss of his pet for only a few weeks and then resumed his regular hero/mastery play.

Death is not the only cause of significant loss experiences for children. Many children feel the arrival of a sibling as though they have lost something very important in their lives, and often they have—their mother's time and attention and their position in the family.

Poor Attachment   Poor attachment can also create chronic symptoms of loss in children. Cynthia N., a 5-year-old, was from an intact family, but had a difficult relationship with her mother. Not an easy child, Cynthia's mother resented the extraordinary efforts her child required and often wished she had not interrupted her career to become a parent. Cynthia often developed the theme of an orphaned child, lost in the woods, desert, mountains, or city. The child was always rescued, sometimes by animals and other times by kind humans, who took her off to safety and cared for her in a loving environment. This theme persisted in Cynthia's play for years and appeared to be her attempt to deal with her wish to have a mother who loved and cared for her.

Structure   The structure of a child's play reveals a great deal about the child's cognitive and psychological development and functioning. Well before children are capable of reciprocal play (e.g., cooperative play), the child is able to show continuity in solitary or parallel play. *The child whose play is action driven may need help in developing play sequences with a beginning, middle, and end.* Lack of cohesive play themes may indicate that the child is in a state of internal or environmental chaos and is having difficulty ordering his or her world.

Recognition of Rules   Recognition of rules is an important aspect of structure in play. Early examples of rules are turn-taking and sharing. The child who is insecure in his or her attachments may have particular difficulty sharing and taking turns. This child may benefit from playing roles that encourage the development of these social skills. As children become increasingly able to play while maintaining consideration for the other person, the introduction of simple board games is appropriate. Games of luck should proceed games of skill. Learning to tolerate losing is not easy for children, especially those vulnerable to injury of self-esteem. Adults may need to "soften" the win—lose ending of games until the child can tolerate not winning.

Fantasy and Make-Believe   Fantasy and make-believe are essential ingredients of play. In allowing the child to depart from reality, the child feels safer and more comfortable in working through issues that may be causing conflict. It is easier to deal with "mean Mommy" in dolls or by slamming cars together than to risk a direct confrontation with Mother.

Children with disabilities often miss out on many normal avenues to mastery. The child with cerebral palsy, for example, cannot experience mastery of gross motor accomplishments. The delight of hide-and-seek may be unavailable to this child. Through fantasy play, however, children can be given the opportunity to imagine that which they cannot experience. Although a less direct route to mastery, it is better to imagine than never to contemplate the sensation.

For children whose play lacks logic and continuity, who cannot put order to experience, or whose internal world appears to be fragmented or show loose mental associations, the question of reality testing should be raised. Determination should be made as to whether the child can distinguish between his or her thoughts and reality. If fantasy and reality are indistinguishable or confused, the child should be referred for a comprehensive psychiatric evaluation. For some children, structuring the play situation is sufficient to help them remain in the world of reality. Open-ended and free-form play situations are usually not very productive for this type of child and can lead to emotionally chaotic constructions that can be frightening to the child. Psychotic-like behavioral responses may even appear. Play with adults allows for more guidance in the play than peer play.

Role Playing and Story Completion   For the child whose play is disorganized and fragmented, the use of role playing and story completion can be helpful. For many of these children, if they operate within the parameters that define the role, plot, and character, they can add detail, embellish, and conclude. Reading a book and acting out the simple sequence, for example, allows the child a framework for dramatic play. Imagination and the child's inner thoughts refine the story. Puppets can also be used. The adult can begin a story with one character and let the child help to construct the ending.

Affective Content   Playing should be pleasurable, yet not all children appear "happy" when playing. This may be because children are "working" on issues, attempting to master new ideas, behaviors, or actions, or dealing with unpleasant circumstances in their play. Range of expression is important in interactions, as affect gives social cues to others. Although many young children can only express "happy" and "sad" as emotions they know, they can successfully demonstrate a range of appropriate emotional responses to people and situations. *For the child with a restricted affective range or inappropriate affect, role playing can be an effective strategy to teach new reactions.* Matching games in which the children match feelings on faces to situations can also be fun for a group of children.

Labeling Emotions   Children often have more difficulty describing their own emotional states than recognizing them in others. When children need assistance in labeling emotions, it is effective to begin by having them name emotions in others, using pictures, pantomime, and role playing. After they have words to label feelings, they are ready to produce expressions of the feelings. Although making faces is one way, the use of color or music can be creative ways for children to play with associations to emotional content. Drawing a picture while listening to "angry" music can give a child another mode of expression of affects. Conflicting emotions may also be revealed through expression of words and actions that are incompatible. For instance, the child may say that he or she feels happy and yet draw a picture that shows all angry or sad people or is full of angry motion and dark expressive colors.

One of the issues with many children with emotional problems is that they don't understand what they are feeling or why they feel the way they do. Kagan (1971) discusses the motivations for behavior as being rooted in resolution of uncertainty (as a result of discrepancy, inconsistency, and unpredictability), mastery (the wish to increase knowledge, skill, or talent), hostility (from imposition of a threat or frustration), and sexuality (related to sensory gratification). Children's behaviors often reflect their inner turmoil and inability to express or control their emotions. Their emotions also influence the decisions they make and the manner in which they solve both cognitive and social problems. Helping children to identify their feelings is the first step toward understanding them and learning to deal with them in more adaptive ways. Identifying sources of feelings and associating past events in the child's life with current feelings, thoughts, and behaviors may also help the child to move toward understanding (Dodds, 1987).

Fear and Anxiety   Feelings of fear and anxiety can be effectively addressed in play because of the safety of the pretend situation. When adults are aware that a child's functioning is compromised by fear and anxiety, play can be used to help the child master the fear. Naturally, children play out wishes and fears as well as their interpretation of the way they are treated in life. The child's interpretation of his or her disability is usually revealed in the child's play, whether it is through characters, theme, plot, or affects. The use of distancing, or displacement, can help the child be one step removed from what feels threatening. For instance, talking about what a doll or character is feeling in a particular situation is less threatening than talking about his or her own feelings. The adult can then make the association by saying, "Maybe you feel that way, too, sometimes."

First, it is important to clarify that the strategies recommended here are not meant to be substitutions for other types of counseling that the child may need outside of the classroom. Intrapsychic interpretations and therapeutic work may best take place with specialists trained in these methods. The techniques discussed here are not intended to turn teachers into psychotherapists. Rather, the intent is to provide suggestions to team members for increasing their understanding of the child's inner world and to give suggestions for supporting the child in understanding and dealing more adaptively with the issues affecting his or her life.

INTERVENTION GUIDELINES

It is also important to differentiate between children whose development is delayed in the social-emotional area and children who have deficits or disorders resulting from internal conflicts and disturbances. In a third group, are children who have both delays in development and emotional disorders. Identification and intervention are most difficult for these children. For the child with delays, the team addresses attachment, separation, and individuation issues (see pp. 229–237) and the development of social skills (see pp. 228–237). The child with emotional disturbances requires a different approach which is discussed here. The child with both delays and disorders requires a combined approach that addresses internal conflicts, but remains within the child's developmental framework. The discussion that follows contains elements that are appropriate for children in all three circumstances. The major emphasis, however, is on working with children whose primary concerns are related to emotional disturbance. The language used in these examples is appropriate for children whose cognitive and language development are the normal range. For children with delays, language must be simplified.

Facilitating Behaviors

Faust and Burns (1991) identify various therapeutic facilitation strategies used by therapists. Many of these techniques, called *facilitating behaviors*, have been recommended as appropriate facilitation strategies in other parts of this book.

However, their use with children with social and emotional concerns is further clarified in this section.

Reflecting Feelings

Working with a child who has social and emotional concerns requires the adult to address the child's internal emotional world. Dodds (1987) discusses two general approaches to moving to a feelings level with young children: 1) modeling feelings for the child, and 2) labeling the child's feelings and encouraging him or her to express them. As the adult and child are playing with clay, for example, the adult might comment, "It makes me feel good when I make something," or "When nobody wants to play with me, it makes me feel sad." The adult can also help the child label emotions by reflecting back to the child the emotions the child seems to be expressing (e.g., "You seem really mad today"). *Helping the child to recognize and acknowledge feelings is a critical aspect of intervention.* At the same time, reflection of feelings allows the child to see that the adult can handle, tolerate, and accept his or her feeling states.

The child does not have to have emotional disturbances to benefit from reflection of his or her emotional world. Many children encounter life experiences that are difficult to handle and affect their social and emotional functioning for a period of time. Being sensitive to these changes can allow the team to identify issues that are of concern to the child and offer support to enable the child to cope more effectively. For instance, a child who typically plays at a developmentally appropriate level and then regresses to earlier forms of play may be preoccupied with concerns that are preventing developmental progress. These apprehensions often have to do with safety or danger to his or her well-being.

EXAMPLE

Timmy Z., a 2½-year-old, aimlessly wandered around the periphery of the play setting, unable to engage in play alone or in a dyad. Timmy was usually able to play in an engaged manner, but he had become withdrawn and displayed a lack of interest and sadness in his demeanor. Timmy's mother had recently had a third lengthy hospitalization, and there was no father in the home. Timmy was being cared for by an elderly aunt, and his older brother was temporarily staying with family in another city. Using storytelling techniques, the facilitator observed themes of anticipatory grief; Timmy was expecting people to go away and not return. By using talking and playing with Timmy, the facilitator was able to help Timmy bring into his conscious awareness his fear that his mother and his brother would not come back. After Timmy's fear could be acknowledged, the adults in Timmy's life could provide consistent reassurance while acknowledging how scary it was to have Mommy away.

The work of Kagan and his colleagues (Kagan, 1988; Kagan, Resnick, & Gibbons, 1989; Kagan, Resnick, & Snidman, 1987) has shown that some children have shy temperaments. These children stand away from the play of others and watch. Only gradually do they become involved. Other children who act as onlookers are interested in playing, but are somewhat fearful of becoming engaged, often due to worries about competence.

EXAMPLE

Sara M., a child with congenital muscular dystrophy, was precociously verbal and successfully social until she was 2½ years old. At that time, Sara began to stand on the sideline of activities at her preschool. When asked to join in, she would drop her head and refuse the invitation. If left to herself, she would sit alone in the book corner and flip through books or rock her doll. The first hint of the cause of her distress was her explanation to her mother for not wanting to go to school, "When I fall, I can't get up—the other kids can." Understanding that Sara was probably developing a deeper recognition of her physical disabilities, her mother talked with Sara's teacher. They decided to structure classroom activities, particularly those with gross motor components, so that Sara could experience success rather than frustration and failure. Their shared objective was to stress Sara's competencies and encourage her participation in all activities. Sara quickly felt better about herself and moved from an onlooker stance to active participant. Her increased confidence, in combination with her strong verbal and intellectual capabilities, aided her in beginning to anticipate occasions when she would need extra assistance. Then she could ask for help rather than retreat from the activity.

Reflecting Behavior

Reflection of behavior, as opposed to a judgmental response, is another approach that can help the child to think about what he or she is doing. Commenting on the child's actions emphasizes specific actions or aspects of actions the child is performing. This process may elicit further comment from the child that lends insight to the meaning of the actions. For example, when one child was playing in the sand table burying Fisher-Price people, the adult commented, "You're putting all the people under the sand." "Yeah," the child responded, "They were bad."

Imitation

Imitation of the child is recommended many times in this volume. Imitating of the child with emotional issues can also result in turn-taking and initiation as indicated in previous chapters. However, *imitation should be used selectively*. Imitation of some children can help the adult get into the child's world. Imitation of other children may be seen as intrusive and threatening. Imitation of emotional responses can help the child identify feelings and acquire some sense of control. For example, upon entering the classroom and seeing others present, one little boy turned toward the wall and buried his fists in his eyes. He said, "I'm hiding." The adult came over and squatted next to him, imitated his behavior and said, "I'm hiding, too. Those people are scary." The two stood there for a few seconds, hiding in their fists. The adult then said, "I feel better. I'm coming out to play." The child responded, "O.K.," and followed the adult into the room. In this instance, the adult's imitation of the child acknowledged that the behavior was accepted and gave the child permission to get control of his emotions. The adult then modeled a statement of feelings that might have reflected how the child felt. This also let the child know that his feelings were all right. Modeling "coming out" gave the child a means for making a transition out of those feelings in an acceptable way.

Modeling

Modeling emotions or behaviors is another means of helping children attach appropriate affect or use adaptive problem-solving. Modeling gives the child an example of how one might feel or act under different circumstances. In the above example, the adult modeled both feelings and actions to assist the child in identifying and coping with his emotions. Modeling can help the child find a way to handle certain difficult situations. For example, one child who had extreme anxiety about failure, would fall apart whenever he attempted a task and failed. After he stacked up a tower of blocks that tumbled down, he kicked the blocks and cried. The adult who was sitting in the block area with the child, commented, "It makes you mad when things don't go right." She began to build a tower, too. When she got it very high and it fell, she said, "I hate it when that happens, but I'm going to try again and do it more slowly." By now, the child was absorbed in watching the adult's tower go up. As it got higher, the adult said, "I think if we're very careful we could get another one on top. Could you help me please, Jason?" When Jason brought over a block, they carefully positioned it on top. "Wow! That was hard, but we did it when we were careful." In this instance, the adult responded to Jason's feelings and why he was angry, modeled verbalization of feelings and problem-solving, including asking for assistance, and then modeled feelings of pride and commented on how success was achieved.

EXAMPLE

Sean A., who was diagnosed with pervasive developmental disorder as a 4-year old, and later, when 7, was diagnosed with bipolar disorder (more commonly known as manic depression), attended special programs for children with behavior disorders. As an infant, Sean was extraordinarily sensitive to touch, finding it aversive. He did not cuddle, was difficult to comfort, and appeared attached only to his mother.

Sean began psychotherapy when he was 4 years old. In the first several months of treatment, his play was characterized by explosive outbursts. Themes other than danger and lack of safety were rarely developed. Sean would begin a session with Army toys, puppets, or animals and, within a short time, the toys were being thrown around the room—not randomly, but because they were bombed or exploded. After months of playing out his fears about danger and some acknowledgment of the therapist's interpretation about Sean's fear of not being protected from danger, a shift occurred in Sean's play. For the next few weeks, Sean arranged the furniture in the office to make underground homes for squirrels and prairie dogs. The therapist's job was to crawl through the imaginary tunnels with Sean and to ensure that the animals' undergound home was safe. Together, they fought off animal and human predators and unrelentingly fought to keep the homes safe for the animals who lived there. Badgers, foxes, and hunters were all sent away through the bravery of Sean and his therapist. After the fears of safety had been resolved, at least at this stage of his development, Sean moved into a phase of therapy in which his play was organized around themes of mastery (i.e., being the biggest, the bravest, the strongest, the best). At this point, the work of therapy proceeded compatibly within the lines of normal development.

Interpreting Feelings and Behaviors

Interpretation of feelings and behaviors is an area that becomes touchy for adults in intervention programs without the specialized training for interpretation of sources of internal turmoil and conflict. *Understanding the reasons behind a child's attitudes, emotions, and behaviors may evolve over time.* However, in many instances, these reasons are complex and related to many variables in the child's life, and total comprehension may not be possible. In Sean A.'s case (see example above) the adult's simple interpretation of the child's anger is superficial, but probably accurate. Whether the child's anxiety about failure stems from extreme parental expectations earlier in the child's life or from other complex intrapsychic factors is not known. For the purposes of intervention in the classroom, adults would be "safer" to stick with more obvious interpretations and leave the more complicated analysis to professionals with more specialized training.

Over the course of time the team may become aware of the themes of the child's internal struggles. Issues related to dependency, loss, power and control, fear and anxiety, and self-image may recur over time. *The adults in the classroom setting can react to these issues as they arise in the child's play by responding in a warm, nurturing way, providing assurance to the child of the safety of the surroundings in the room, encouraging the child to take the initiative, and helping the child to develop coping mechanisms and problem-solving approaches.*

EXAMPLE

Rodney E., age 4, whose father was in prison and who lived in a chaotic home environment, had many emotional problems. Rodney typically wore an unhappy facial expression, was bossy and aggressive with other children, was quick to blame others for problems, and was emotionally labile. Although the team did not try to conduct a psychoanalysis of Rodney, they were aware that many of his conflicts related to loss, lack of control, and poor self-concept. They therefore problem-solved ways of helping Rodney deal with these issues in the classroom.

Rodney missed his father and felt this loss in two ways. His play showed themes of both abandonment and concern that Rodney was somehow at fault. Through play with police toys and dolls, the adults helped Rodney understand that when an *adult* does something bad they go to jail and this makes the person's children very sad and sometimes angry that the parent did something bad and had to go to jail. With the consent of Rodney's mother, Rodney made a book with pictures of his father and other family members in it. He sent pictures and "letters" dictated to his father from school. The team also provided Rodney with as much consistency and affection as they could, giving him a special playtime with the teacher each day.

The team felt that many of Rodney's bossy and aggressive behaviors were an attempt to have some control in his life. He may also have been modeling behaviors he had seen in his home. At some level, Rodney may have been identifying with his father. At one point, he said, "If I do bad things, will I have to go to jail?" Rodney's belligerent attempts to get attention and form relationships had the opposite effect. Other children avoided him. This reinforced his notions that he was somehow bad or unworthy. The team tried to model and to use other children to model prosocial behaviors for Rodney. They modeled feelings, "When someone tells me I'm stupid, it makes me feel very sad," and "I don't like to play with little boys who hit me." They modeled prosocial behaviors, "I'm going to give him a toy and see if he'll play with me." They responded to his modified efforts at interaction, "I see you are smiling. It feels good to play trucks with someone, doesn't it?" They also worked on identifying things that Rodney could do well, bringing them to the attention of Rodney, his mother, and his class.

The play interpretation made by the team may not have been as sophisticated as a therapist's, and the team may have even been inaccurate, but Rodney's behavior and affect did change for the better.

Rodney's socioeconomic status and lack of parental concern prohibited him from obtaining individual therapy. There are many children like Rodney, who have emotional concerns that may continue to escalate unless classroom teachers take an interest and learn how to deal more effectively with emotional and not just behavioral issues.

Channeling Approaches

Faust and Burns (1991) have also identified other strategies as channeling, or directing, the child in certain ways. The following are classified as *channeling approaches.*

Questioning

Questioning is one way to probe a child's thoughts and feelings. As suggested in other chapters, *closed questions should be avoided as they frequently lead the child in a certain direction and result in responses of one or two words.* Asking, "Does that make you sad?" may indicate to the child that the adult thinks it should make him or her sad, thereby shaping the "yes" and "no" answers also provide limited information. Open-ended questions, such as, "How do you think that baby feels," give the child an opportunity to reply in any fashion ("icky" is as appropriate as "mad") and with as much or as little information as he or she desires. Problem-solving questions are particularly important as they make the child think about alternatives. "What do you think might make the baby feel better?" lets the child ponder what actions result in making one feel better. Once brought to consciousness, this information can be used at a later time when a similar situation arises.

Sometimes, the child asks the adult questions. Depending on the question, whether it is a request for information or a question about the adult's feelings and actions, the adult may respond differently. Requests for information are usually easy enough to answer. Some questions, however, are best turned back to the child to see what answer is desired or needed. If the adult playing patient is asked by the child, "Are you going to die?", the adult might ask, "What should I say?" This allows the adult to see what the child is thinking about and in which direction the child wants to take the play.

Making Suggestions

Making suggestions to the child about what he or she could be thinking or feeling may help the child identify an elusive emotion. For instance, conflicting feelings are abstract and difficult for a child to describe. The adult might say, "I think you love your daddy and miss him, but you are also mad at him." This allows the child to acknowledge or deny the adult's suggestion. The adult may also offer a suggestion about a course of action that might be tried. "Seana looks like she needs help. You could ask her if you could hold the blocks for her."

Confrontation

Confronting the child is another approach that is sometimes useful to get the child to face certain issues. Confrontation usually presents information to the child about the consequences of a child's behaviors or feelings. "Mandy, I've noticed you always start to throw things when it's time to go home. I think you are worried about what is going to happen at home." *Confrontation must be done without anger and at a time when the adult thinks the child is emotionally capable of handling the information that is presented.*

Limit-Setting

Limit-setting is often needed for children with impulsive behavior or anger that is out of control. As mentioned previously, the child should not be allowed to hurt him- or herself, other children or adults, or toys and materials in the environment. Many children test adults to see how much they can get away with. All children need limits and many children do out-of-bounds actions in order to get the adult to place some limits on them. Stating, "I care about you and cannot allow you to hurt yourself," lets the child know that he or she is loved and at the same time states the limits of behavior. The adult can explain why people are not to be injured and things are not to be broken. Explaining that, "Other children also want to play with the toys," may not be a sufficient reason to the child, but it is important to give justifications for rules and limits.

Trauma

Trauma is a lasting emotional shock or injury caused by something outside of the realm of the normal human experience. Traumas can be inflicted by nature, accidents, humans, or machines. Natural disasters (e.g., fire, flood, tornado) and accidents (e.g., automobile, airplane) are causes of trauma. Child abuse traumatizes deeply and permanently. No child is prepared for trauma, and recovery from trauma is long and painful.

The Effects of Trauma

Children expect adults to keep them safe. Rules about safety are taught through adults' warnings, scoldings, and teachings. When a child is harmed, a breech in the implicit trust agreement between child and adult occurs—even if the adult could not have protected the child. This is true even if the child's caregivers were not part of the traumatic experience because the child was not protected by adults in general. Children who have experienced trauma present a special challenge to the adults who work with them. For most of these children, regardless of the nature of the trauma, a breakdown of trust has occurred. After such a breech of trust, symptoms of trauma often occur. The child may, for example, become noticeably fearful or may evidence fears in dreams or nightmares. It is not uncommon for the traumatized child to regress from a previously mastered level of functioning (e.g., episodes of daytime and/or nighttime enuresis in a previously toilet-trained child). Affective disturbances are not unusual; the child may be unusually withdrawn, sad, anxious, or angry.

Of serious concern to professionals who work with traumatized children is the extent to which normal developmental accomplishments are compromised. Trauma can, for example, damage the child's developing sense of autonomy and independence as well as create new difficulties regarding separation. An otherwise mastery-directed young child can become inhibited and fearful of risk-taking after exposure to traumatic experiences. Trauma can have vastly different outcomes depending upon the child's phase of development when the trauma occurs. Children who are younger than 36 months old are unable to explain their traumas (Terr, 1989). Although traumatized infants and toddlers do not remember the events they experienced in the typical way, they do demonstrate fears, post-traumatic play, reenactment, difficulties envisioning a future, and dreams or night terrors.

> Young traumatized children, in other words, tend not to remember with the clarity what children traumatized at older ages do, but they tend to fear, to reenact, and to omit or limit their projections for the future based upon "pictorial" and "feel" memories. (Terr, 1991, p. 14)

Terr (1991) identifies four common symptoms resulting from trauma:

1.   *Trauma-specific fears.* A child who has been in an automobile accident may develop a fear of cars or riding in cars. Traumatized by a tornado that devastated her town, a child may become fearful of wind or sounds associated with wind. Fears of the mundane (e.g., the dark, strangers, looming objects) may also derived from trauma.

2.   *Tendency to repeat.* The traumatized child may, through play, behavior, or creative attempts in later life repeat aspects of the trauma. It is not unusual for the traumatized child to repeatedly re-enact the same scenario in imaginary play. A child who was physically abused from infancy until he was removed from the home at 2½ years was observed in foster placement to incessantly crash his trucks together. After the smashing of trucks he would pull the imaginary drivers from their vehicles and shake them violently while saying, "Bad boy."

3.   *Tendency to re-perceive the trauma, particularly visually.* The ability to re-see the traumatic event is an important characteristic of almost all externally generated disorders of childhood. Even when the event was not at all visual, most visually re-perceive it.

> Even those who were infants or toddlers at the time of their ordeals and thus were unable to lay down, store, or retrieve full verbal memories of their traumas tend to play out, to draw, or to re-see highly visualized elements from their old experiences. (Terr, 1991, p. 12)

4. *Changed attitudes about people, life, and the future.* Children who have not been traumatized show almost limitless ideas about the future, whereas traumatized children reflect a limitation of future perspective, as if to say, "I won't guess what will happen to my life" or "One day at a time." From both single and repeated traumas, children may reflect distrust of adults. They may think, "You can't trust your teacher," or "Don't count on anyone to protect you."

> Traumatized children recognize profound vulnerability in all human beings, especially themselves. This shattering of what Lifton and Olson (1976) call "the shield of invincibility" and what Erikson (1950) terms "basic trust" and "autonomy" appears to characterize almost all event-engendered disorders of childhood. (Terr, 1991, p. 14)

Types of Trauma

Terr (1991) cautions those who work with children that trauma in childhood may lead to symptoms that are different from those associated with post-traumatic stress disorder (PTSD). Traumatized children may "blank out" periods of the day or may be particularly creative and alert, as though their minds are working overtime. In part, symptoms are determined by the type of trauma the child has experienced. Terr classifies traumas into three types:

1. *Type I traumas* are caused by single unanticipated events. Examples are natural disasters, automobile accidents, and a single incident of sexual assault. The victim of a single-blow trauma usually has a full, clear memory and is often able to provide a precise verbal account. Type I traumas do not appear to cause the massive denials, psychic numbing, self-anesthesia, or personality problems that characterize Type II traumas. Type I traumas also carry with them the tendency for retrospective mastery (i.e., rethinking and reworking the incident). Questions such as "How could the event have been handled?" or "What else could I have done?" are frequently asked.

2. *Type II traumas* are the result of a number of events. They come from repeated exposure to horrendous external events. For example, a girl who knows that every few nights her father will appear at her bedside and make sexual demands will begin to anticipate the event. Defenses and coping mechanisms will be employed to protect the psyche and preserve the self. These defensive strategies are different than those associated with Type I traumas. They include massive denial, repression, dissociation, self-anesthesia, self-hypnosis, identification with the aggressor, and aggression turned against the self. It is not infrequent for repeatedly abused children to develop character and personality problems. These children are frequently diagnosed with conduct disorders, attention deficit disorders, depression, or dissociative disorders.

3. *Crossover Type I–Type II trauma* occurs when a single psychological shock creates a series of long-standing adversities. A 5-year-old child who witnessed the murders of his parents and subsequently was placed in one unsuccessful foster home after another developed symptoms characteristic of a Type II trauma. Early intervention can be successful in ameliorating the further development of Type II symptoms.

Dealing with Trauma

The strategies for intervening with children with disturbances in their emotional development presented here are not inclusive, but when used in combination with the approaches discussed on pages 240–251 and in the following discussion, they can provide insight into children's emotions and behavior. As the child works through and relates emotions to behaviors, positive adaptations can occur.

For the child who has experienced trauma, play can be a window into the child's internal experience. Particularly for the child who is preschool age or younger, play is often undisguised, direct, and uncensored. In play, one can see the vividness and immediacy of the traumatic experience, as if it had occurred yesterday. Using play can help the traumatized child channel anger and aggression toward the appropriate source. The conflict, thereby, is brought out in the open.

Theorists and clinicians who specialize in post-traumatic stress disorders in children agree that the re-experiencing of the trauma in a safe environment is essential to recovery from the traumatic experience. The adults should not, however, expect children to use play to re-create and then re-experience the trauma without substantial preparation. It may take weeks or even months for the child to begin to use toys to re-enact the trauma. A child who is not comfortable doing so should not be forced, cajoled, or pressured. Such a child probably needs help from a professional who specializes in working with traumatized children.

Phases of Dealing with Trauma   Three phases are present in working through trauma successfully: 1) re-enactment, 2) working through, and 3) mastery.

Re-enactment   There has been controversy regarding re-enactment —whether it is therapeutic to allow the traumatized child to repeat such play or whether it is re-traumatizing. Clinician and writer Theodore Gaensbauer (1985) stated:

> My own sense is that enactment play is crucial and should not be discouraged by the therapist or the parents . . . the presence of re-enactment play, or any other symptom . . . is a reflection of unresolved feelings about the experience (i.e., that there is more psychological work to be done). The re-enactment play itself offers the crucial vehicle for helping the child to assimilate the experience.

Gaensbauer believes the role of the adult is to help the child identify the emotion associated with the play and bring the emotion to the surface. *Unless the child can be helped to identify and relive the experience with the original emotions, re-enactment play will not diminish or be helpful.* Specialists who work with traumatized children agree that re-enactment play must be taken outside of metaphoric play and interpreted concretely as a reality that occurred in the child's life.

Play therapy for the traumatized child can take place in a standard playroom or classroom. The nature of the specific trauma defines what toys should be present. Many traumatized children have contact with health care providers; puppets or dolls representing nurses and doctors are useful as is toy furniture and vehicles associated with hospitals. Animal toys and puppets are important, not only for the child who may have been injured by an animal, but because for some children re-enactment play using animals may feel safer than using human representations. Toys that can be used to express aggression and anger are also important.

Drawing can be useful in the re-enactment phase. Less dependent upon verbal skills, drawing may enable the child to "speak" fully of the event or even help the child remember details of the event. Drawing is particularly useful for children who were younger than 3 years old when traumatized.

Working Through   Although it is difficult to distinguish the working-through phase as distinct from re-enactment, this phase allows for innumerable repetitions of the trauma. Ideally, the child deals with guilt that the trauma happened because he or she did something wrong as well as anger that parent or adults did not protect him or her from the event(s). One of the authors worked with a 4-year-old girl who was riding her tricycle when she was hit by a car and dragged under the car for several hundred feet. For several months, cars, trucks, and airplanes crashed in the playroom. Drawings contained people and animals with red heads and blood spurting from their mouths, ears, eyes, and noses. In dollhouse play, a child doll would shake and scold the mommy and daddy doll for "being away and not taking care of their children." The psychologist's role was to label the emotions of the various characters, with particular emphasis on those feelings that might have described the child's affective experience of the accident and subsequent medical treatment, which involved substantial separation from the parents. Near the end of the working-through phase, this child condensed the seemingly disparate elements of the re-enactment play into one integrated story of a terrible accident. The beginning of the final phase of treatment, mastery, then began.

Mastery   Most children who have been severely traumatized need continued support in gaining mastery over the effects of traumatization. *Children can be helped to learn to manage and master the anxiety that will always be nearby when memories of the trauma occur. To do so, children need help learning to modulate their aggression.* Their aggression can be both an aid and an impediment to recovery from trauma. It is through aggression that a child can move away from a victimized posture. Through aggression, a child can "fight back" and learn to "be the boss" of his or her own feelings and thoughts. Aggression can help a child develop confidence and self-assertiveness even after having felt helpless and despairing. The play of a child working through to achieve mastery has a very different quality than re-enactment play. In the mastery phase, the child is often the dominant character, defeating monsters (emotional or symbolic, but trauma-related, demons). *Assisting the child in channeling aggression toward its source can help the child in getting the conflict out in the open.* Parents should be forewarned that as the child becomes freer to express aggression in the program there may be a concomitant increase in aggressiveness at home.

PLAY MATERIALS AND OPPORTUNITIES

Toys and materials that allow children to express their inner worlds symbolically encourage handling and mastering of anxieties. Dolls, puppets, and action figures of various sizes may symbolize authority figures or victims and weak or strong characters and may represent many emotions. Dress-up clothes and props are essential. Materials that are flexible and can be put together and easily taken apart (or "destroyed") (e.g., blocks; paper, scissors, and glue; sand and water; Play-Doh) are expressive media. Trucks and cars that can "crash" or rush victims to a hospital allow acceptable means of expressing desires and worries.

Art materials and crayons, paints, and markers of many colors allow the child to represent his or her world through another symbolic means. Toy animals, including mother and baby animals (or large and small animals), domestic animals and wild animals, and puppet animals are important toys for distancing self from the immediacy and power of feelings. If feelings can be expressed through a toy, the child feels safer.

Dollhouses with miniature figures and playhouses with child-size props are all important toys for enabling the child to depict family life. The structures and sequence of the child's play with these materials may also reveal much about the child's thought processes.

Games requiring the use of rules, whether group games, board games, or games with child-constructed rules, enable the child to learn to handle boundaries and the needs of others. Depending on the child's cognitive level, these games may or may not be competitive.

Books are valuable tools for self-exploration and comparison to others. Fables and fairy tales contain many symbolically important figures representing children's concerns. Many of today's books also handle very serious topics in realistic stories and pictures. Adults need to assess what the child is ready to hear and discuss—in other words, "how close to home" the story can be and still have the child be able to relate to the adults about the story.

Toys and materials may be selected that directly or indirectly relate to the child's issues. Having options available so that the child can make the choice is important.

OBSERVATION GUIDELINES FOR SOCIAL-EMOTIONAL DEVELOPMENT: HUMOR AND SOCIAL CONVENTIONS

VI. Humor and Social Conventions
  A. Does the child demonstrate a sense of humor with smiling or laughter directed at appropriate events in the environment?
    1. Physical events in the environment involving self and others
    2. Physical events in the environment involving objects
    3. Physical events in the environment involving others
    4. Verbal jokes from self, parent, adult, child
      a. Involving labeling ambiguities
      b. Involving conceptual ambiguities
  B. Does the child show awareness of socially acceptable behaviors in specific contexts?
    1. Greetings
    2. Sharing, helping, and so forth
    3. Behaviors around eating, toileting
    4. Respect for adult authority
  C. Does the child exhibit maladaptive or socially inappropriate behaviors?
    1. "Self-stimulating" or self-abusive behaviors
    2. Eccentric habits or rituals
    3. Unacceptable behaviors directed toward others

The expression of emotions of pleasure and the demonstration of a sense of humor are important in cognitive development and social awareness. Humor depends on cognitive surprise, incongruity, and discrepancy from the expected. Some theorists believe that humor is supportive of emotional development in that it is an instrument for releasing anxiety, relieving boredom, and expressing happiness (Wolfenstein, 1954). Humor can also help children master fears and apprehensions about unknown concepts, such as death or monsters.

The Development of Humor

Stages of humor development, as identified by McGhee (1977, 1979, 1984), provide an overview of the development of the sense of humor. Pleasure experienced in physical movement, touching, and games with the young child (and still with the older child) can be intensified to the degree that laughter ensues. As the child matures, physical events that are incongruous or unusual strike the child as funny. Gradually the child comes to understand more subtle incongruities, until by elementary age, the child can understand puns, or words with a double meaning. In many instances, what the child finds funny is only humorous to other children of the same age. Anyone who has ever listened to a group of 4-year-olds laughing hysterically after each one says the word "diarrhea" has puzzled over the progression that led to this being the peak of entertainment! Should an adult enter into this realm, the children would most certainly stop because they recognize that this is not humorous to adults. Yet, although adults may not fully understand or be able to enter the child's humor world, there are means by which the adult can stimulate the child's sense of humor. Intervention that incorporates humor must take into consideration the child's cognitive level to be successful.

Stimulating the Child's Sense of Humor

Children must first understand a concept at a "serious" level and then be confronted with that concept in an incongruous situation. A moderate level of cognitive challenge, or thinking effort, on the child's part, appears to make the event more humorous (McGhee, 1984). Thus, identifying the child's cognitive level of understanding enables the adult to set up humorous situations. (However, as pointed out in *Transdisciplinary Play-Based Assessment* [Linder, 1993], the reverse is also true. Identifying what the child finds humorous can provide insight into the child's cognitive level.)

Assisting the child with disabilities to perceive humorous situations enables the child to interact more fully with peers. Children who smile and laugh at the actions and words of other children are more likely to be included in this type of play. Every adult who has ever attempted to tell a joke knows how important it is to have a responsive audience. If no one laughs at a joke, the likelihood of repeating that joke is diminished. However, if someone does find a joke funny, that person will likely be sought out with another joke in the future.

Social Conventions

The same can be said of social conventions. Persons who use social conventions and who do not display strange or unusual behaviors are more socially acceptable. Helping children to demonstrate social conventions appropriate to their culture and the mainstream culture can help the child to function more successfully in social environments. Techniques presented in Chapter 9 assist children in gaining verbal social conventions, while the previous and subsequent sections are helpful in addressing social actions.

DEVELOPMENTAL LEVEL

- Child smiles, later laughs at physical games and anticipated actions of objects
    (4–12 months)

INTERVENTION GUIDELINES

The infant delights in looking at faces, movement, and games of surprise. The adult who smiles or laughs may get a similar response from the child. Games of surprise, such as peekaboo, or pat-a-cake may also delight the child in the latter part of the first year. Games like "horsey," in which the child is bounced around on an adult's knee or is tossed into the air are also fun. Toys that have surprise actions, such as pop-up boxes, may be humorous as well.

PLAY MATERIALS AND OPPORTUNITIES

Pop-up toys, jack-in-the-boxes, and wind-up toys that walk, flip, or wave delight children. The key is to find toys that do something unexpected. The other option is to perform actions with the child or on objects that are unexpected. The parent can have a toy pop out from under the child's high chair tray to eat the food, or the adult can push toys under the bubble bath that will pop up when released.

DEVELOPMENTAL LEVEL

- Child laughs at incongruous events (wearing a bowl as a hat)
    (12–18 months)
- Child laughs at events that deviate sharply from everyday experiences
    (12 months +)

INTERVENTION GUIDELINES

The child still laughs at many of the same games as mentioned previously. However, as the child's ability to represent actions increases, the extent to which he or she sees humor in the actions of objects and the funny use of objects increases as well. The child now sees the discrepancy in how things are used. Wearing a diaper on the head, shoes on the hands, and using a pillow for a blanket may seem funny as the child's understanding of the functional use of objects increases. The child also appreciates funny faces (in a familiar adult, not a stranger) and humorous actions, such as "walking funny." Toys that have surprise actions, such as wind-up toys, and toys with unexpected actions that the child or adult can cause to occur may also be humorous.

PLAY MATERIALS AND OPPORTUNITIES

The child at this level laughs at any silly adult performance. This is an opportunity to let your "sillies" out. Putting underwear on your head, waving a straw from between your teeth, or throwing a baby doll high in the air can result in gales of laughter. As in previous sections, toys or people that behave in unexpected ways provoke laughter.

- Child laughs at incongruous labeling of objects and events (calling a nose an ear)
        (18–24 months)
- Child laughs at combinations of incongruous events and use of words (milking a dog)
        (24–36 months)

As the child begins to acquire language and understand that the label applies to a given object, person, or event, he or she begins to laugh at mislabeling. The adult might say, "I'm going to blow my nose," and place the tissue on his or her ear. Calling macaroni "cereal" or the dog a horse may be very funny to a 2½-year-old. The ability to see humor in words demonstrates the child's growing ability to symbolize the world in new ways. The child can see humor in words in addition to objects. As action words are added to language usage, the child may find action incongruities, such as "combing an arm" or "milking a cat." Intense vestibular activity, such as swinging the child around in a circle, or tactile activities, such as tickling, may also cause the child to squeal with pleasure.

As the child acquires vocabulary, toys can be made to perform unusual actions or make unusual noises. This is also a time of great imitation, so adults need to be mindful of language. More than one parent has been embarrassed by repetition of exclamatory phrases (i.e., swear words) in front of relatives or religious figures.

- Child laughs at concrete, perceptually incongruent events, and distortions of familiar sights and sounds (rhyming and nonsense words)
        (36–60 months)

The child who is 3 years old and older is influenced by appearances. Visual inconsistencies are found humorous. A picture of a hippopotamus sitting in a tree looks funny to the child. He or she is influenced not so much by the situation's lack of logic but by its unusual appearance. Dr. Seuss's books are funny to the child at this level, both because he inserts unique looking characters and unexpected actions, and because he plays with the sounds and uses of words. Davids (1987) identified several different forms of humor observed in a nursery. Laughter at strange names or words, language regarding excretory interests, telling jokes or joking, and laughing at mistakes were observed at this level along with joy at bodily movement and excitement. Making funny sounds, making up words, or saying words that get shocked looks from parents may also send the child into gales of laughter. Performing actions that are inconsistent from what is expected, such as popping out and scaring someone or acting out silly events in dramatic play, are also funny. The child also attempts to tell jokes, although the punch lines may make no sense to anyone but the child.

Fantasy is also important as the context for humor. The child may laugh at the clown who has a big nose, but the adult who actually has a big nose may make the child feel uncomfortable. Fantasy allows the child to examine incongruities or discrepancies from the typical in a safe environment. The child at this level also introduces incongruous events into his or her play for the purpose of being humorous. For instance, the child may don a Slinky as a tail and prance around in front of his or her peers to make them laugh. The adult can model this behavior if it is not observed spontaneously. For example, the teacher playing with several children in the house area stated, "I think I'll cook an elephant for dinner!" The children then imitated this behavior, crying, "I'm going to cook a camel!" and "I'm going to cook a zebra!" Each exclamation was followed by uproarious laughter and an attempt to "top" the previous statement.

PLAY MATERIALS AND OPPORTUNITIES

Tolerance is an important word at this level, as children will play with words and objects not only for their own pleasure, but to test the adult's limits. The adult is well advised to join the game, switching the topic to more acceptable phrases if needed. The adult's dramatic abilities are also tested at this level. The parent may be called upon to be a horse to be ridden, a ghost to be "busted," or a magic lamp to be rubbed. The more exotic and bizarre the adult's performance, the more glee exhibited by the child.

DEVELOPMENTAL LEVEL

- Child laughs at multiple meanings of words
  (60–72 months)

INTERVENTION GUIDELINES

As the child gains a greater understanding of words and the multiple meanings of words, jokes take on new meaning. Knock-knock jokes with simple ambiguities are comprehended.

> Knock, knock.
> Who's there?
> Lettuce.
> Lettuce who?
> Let us out. It's cold in here!

Jokes that rely on a dual meaning of a word require a complex understanding of the language. Children's ability to understand this type of humor grows from kindergarten through preschool. Books such as *A Chocolate Moose for Dinner* (Gwynne, 1976) give the child an opportunity to think about the different meanings of words and the funny ways to picture words. Phrases such a "wing on a house," "airplane hangers," and "driving me up the wall" can be visualized and understood in different ways. Words become objects that can be manipulated; word plays, riddles, rhymes, and transformations of sounds, words, or phrases are used to create new effects or double meanings (Flake-Hobson, Robinson, & Skeen, 1983).

Children can also use humor at this stage to be cruel to other children. Early interventionists must be aware of this and intercede to help children understand how hurtful this type of humor can be to others. *Helping children to undertand what is funny and what is harmful can also enhance the development of empathy.*

Puns are just beginning to be understood at this level. Discussion of the dual meanings of words (e.g., "arms," "hold up") may help the child to see why a phrase is humorous.

    Parents can also begin to sensitize children to the hurtful nature of words. "Fatty," "Bozo," and "Ugly" may be new words that the child wants to use. The adult can assist the child in seeing when these words are funny and when they hurt someone's feelings.

PLAY MATERIALS AND OPPORTUNITIES

OBSERVATION GUIDELINES FOR SOCIAL-EMOTIONAL DEVELOPMENT: SOCIAL INTERACTIONS WITH PEERS

VIII.   Social Interactions with Peers

    A.   Interactions with peers in dyad

        1.   How does the child acknowledge the presence of a peer?

            a.   Ignoring, withdrawing, unaware

            b.   Looking at, watching

            c.   Touching, gesturing

            d.   Vocalizing toward, talking with the peer

        2.   What level of play does the child exhibit?

            a.   Unoccupied—not involved in play

            b.   Isolated—primarily plays alone, oblivious to others

            c.   Onlooker—primarily watches the other child

            d.   Parallel play—plays with same or similar toys, but not together

            e.   Associative play—plays with peer in common play setting

            f.   Cooperative play—engages other child in play with similar goals and expectations

            g.   Games with rules—engages in games with preestablished rules and roles

        3.   What role does the child play in the dyad?

            a.   Plays no role

            b.   Follows lead of other child

            c.   Initiates and directs play of the other

         4.   What types of prosocial behaviors does the child display?

            a.   Taking turns with a toy or object

            b.   Sharing toys, food, and so forth

            c.   Helping other child to accomplish a goal

            d.   Responding to feelings of other children

        5.   How does the child handle conflict?

            a.   Assertiveness versus acquiescence

            b.   Use of physical means

            c.   Use of verbal (positive/negative) means

        6.   How does the child's play with peers differ from his or her play with parent and facilitator?

            a.   Qualitatively

            b.   Quantitatively

(continued)

OBSERVATION
GUIDELINES FOR SOCIAL-EMOTIONAL
DEVELOPMENT: SOCIAL INTERACTIONS WITH PEERS

VIII.   Social Interactions with Peers (continued)

   B.   Interactions with peers in group (can be observed in classroom)

   1.   How aware is the child of being in a group experience?
      a.   Oblivious of the group
      b.   Watches others in group
      c.   Participates in group—imitates others or follows their lead
      d.   Participates in group—initiates group activities

   2.   How much adult support does the child need to be able to maintain group involvement?
      a.   Demands individual attention
      b.   Needs occasional reinforcement and encouragement
      c.   Waits for turn in group without adult support
      d.   Operates independently without awareness of group expectations

   3.   How do others in the group respond to him or her?

   4.   How much does the child seek social interaction? In what ways does he or she try to engage others?

   5.   During what type of activities does the child exhibit the most social interaction (turn-taking, imitation, verbal exchange)
      a.   Exploratory
      b.   Manipulative or constructive
      c.   Representational or dramatic play
      d.   Motor
      e.   Tactile/social

   6.   With whom does the child exhibit the most social interaction?

INTERVENTION IMPLICATIONS

Peer-Related Social Competence

Social competence in young children is a vital aspect of development. Guralnick (1990) defines peer-related social competence as "the ability of young children to successfully and appropriately select and carry out their interpersonal goals" (p. 4) given a specific setting, context, or culture. Social behavior during interaction builds the basis for social competence. Certainly, social interaction with parents and the child's emotional inner world (see pp. 217–256) play an important part in the development of social competence as the child grows. Social behaviors with peers become more important as the child's world expands to include others of approximately the same age or ability level.

The Role of Development in Peer-Related Social Competence

Social competence influences and is influenced by the child's developmental abilities in other areas. Cognitively, social skills enable the child to advance conceptual ability through interactions with others. Through observation, modeling, and discussion, the child acquires new skills and problem-solving approaches. At the same time, higher-level cognitive abilities allow the child to see another's perspective and use more advanced social problem-solving (Tudge & Rogoff, 1989).

Motor and Communication Skills   Social skills are also influenced by motor abilities. Early interactions with peers are enhanced by the child's ability to crawl, reach, touch, and grasp a peer. As development proceeds, motor activity become an important component of the social interchange, both through fine motor play and through gross motor explorations on sliding boards, in boxes, and with balls (DeStefano & Mueller, 1982). Conversely, social competence influences motor skills, as many of the activities that children choose, especially in the preschool years, are activities with motor components. Thus, practicing motor skills is encouraged.

Communication skills are closely intertwined with social skills. In fact, social competence may provide an arena for acquiring communication skills (Odom et al., 1992). Within the social communication context, the child must attend, initiate, respond, take turns, plan, and organize social behaviors and integrate them into social contexts (Beckman & Lieber, 1992). Competence in communication may enhance social interactions, while, at the same time, competent social interactions require at least minimal communicative competence.

The Effect of Disabilities on Social Competence   Children with disabilities have been documented as having delays or difficulties in social interactions (Krakow & Kopp, 1983; Mindes, 1982; Odom & McEvoy, 1988), including children with hearing impairments (Antia & Kreimeyer, 1992; Gregory, 1976; McKirdy, 1972), visual impairments (Fewell & Kaminiski, 1988; Rogers & Puchalski, 1984; Sandler & Wills, 1965; Skellenger, Hill, & Hill, 1992), language impairments (Goldstein & Gallagher, 1992; Lovell, Hoyle, & Sidall, 1968; Williams, 1980), motor deficits (Jennings, Connors, Stegman, Sankaranarayan, & Medolsohn, 1985; Mogford, 1977; Newson & Head, 1979), and psychiatric disorders (Strayer, 1980). The reciprocal effect of competence in this area on other areas and the long-term implications of social competence for success in later childhood, adolescence, and adulthood compel early interventionists to emphasize social development and competence as part of the curriculum.

A Model of Social Competence   Guralnick (1992) describes a model of social competence that may guide early intervention efforts. The foundation of the model is social/communication efforts, which are critical to social interaction. These social/communication skills rely on the organization, integration, and synthesis of cognitive, affective, communication and language, and sensorimotor abilities. As mentioned previously, all areas of *development* influence the acquisition of social competence. The integration of these areas and promotion of increased skills and abilities, particularly as they relate to social interactions is, therefore, fundamental to enhancing social competence. At the second level, the integration, organization, and sequencing of social/communication skills in the context of *social tasks* result in *social strategies* that enable the child to solve interpersonal problems. Social tasks, such as entering into another child's play, resolving various forms of conflict, and establishing friendships, require that children use certain strategies to be successful. Depending on the situation and characteristics of the social peers, children may be more or less insistent or intrusive, use threats, negotiate, compromise, offer suggestions, or use other strategies. *A focus on the complex processes that result in resolution of social problems should also be an element of early intervention.*

Hierarchy of Play Phases   The developmental aspects of social interaction also should be considered. Deficiencies that are commonly seen are play styles that occur out of phase (e.g., parallel play predominating in the play of a 5-year-old), play characterized by lack of social/communication skills, and interactions that lack effective and appropriate social behaviors. Parten (1932) identified a frequently used hierarchy of play phases through which children proceed and to which they may return. Children may be noninteractive in several phases: unoccupied, or not engaged in play; isolated, or playing alone; or an onlooker, watchful of others. Social interactions begin to be seen as the child plays parallel to another child, in proximity with similar toys, but not in interaction; in associative play with common toys and with communication; in cooperative play with joint play and common goals; and in games with rules.

Children with developmental delays commonly demonstrate play that is out of phase. When the facilitator observes this phenomenon in a child, he or she should be alerted to a potential delay or regression in this developmental line. An example of a child whose play is arrested at an inappropriate level might be the 5-year-old who plays only in a parallel fashion in a dyad and in whom the facilitator can observe no examples of more sophisticated play capacities. It is very important, however, to have a good history from parents and teachers as to the other times in a child's life in which more sophisticated play capacities, have been observed. This is particularly important in making a distinction between arrest in development, in which there have never been greater capacities and regression in development, in which neurological degeneration or internal conflicts may have created a return to an earlier form of play. *Thus, the analysis of peer interactions must take into consideration social competencies, developmental levels, and physiological and psychological factors.*

Strategies that Cross Developmental Levels

Strategies for intervention to promote social competency in children typically address: 1) environmental structuring, 2) child-specific interventions, and 3) peer-mediated interventions. The following discussion presents strategies from these three areas that are relevant across developmental levels. Discussion of strategies that are specific to developmental levels are then included.

Environmental Structuring   Environmental structuring consists of manipulating social and nonsocial aspects of the environment to promote social interaction. The physical environment, activities in the intervention space, the social composition of the group, and specific intervention techniques employed by adults in the environment are variables that may be modified to foster positive social skills. All team members should be involved in the planning of the environment in which children will interact with each other and adults. The environment may be modified as needed by analyzing these elements to determine which are effective and which are hindering the development of social skills. (Chapter 6 discusses the play environment in more detail.)

The Physical Environment   The environment consists of the space, the arrangement of the space to include objects and materials, the people in the space, and the atmosphere and interactions between and among the persons in the space. Selection of play materials that promote social interaction is critical. Toys that require a partner (e.g., balls); props that encourage sociodramatic play; blocks in combination with trucks and cars; and for older children, games (e.g., board games), encourage interaction. For each child, assessment of preferences and interests helps the team to design an environment that invites play. Having separate areas so that children can clearly identify the type of play that takes place there can help children make choices.

The Play Group   The composition of the play group is another environmental variable that affects social interaction. Not only the age of the peers, but the level of their development, type of disability, temperamental characteristics, and play styles have an impact on whether children choose to interact in play. Children with disabilities engage in primarily solitary or parallel play and are not selected by children at his or her level as playmates if intervention approaches are not implemented. Selecting peer dyads and groups that match play and temperament styles and choosing children who are slightly higher functioning than the child with disabilities encourages modeling and imitation. However, some children are more interactive with children who are younger or less capable. The implication is that *heterogeneous groupings offer children options for selecting children with whom they feel comfortable in interaction.* The opportunities for social interaction are also increased if the environment is one that rewards prosocial behaviors and interactive play.

Also significant is the determination of what type and how much group experience a child is ready for. Some children may function at a higher level socially when they are with one or two other children, but become more threatened and inhibited by the group. If a child is oblivious to the group or merely watches, it may benefit that child to spend more time with one-on-one intervention. Gradually increasing the size of the group in which the child plays may help the child attend and learn to imitate the appropriate actions of other children.

Conflict Resolution Through Child-Specific Interventions

All of the strategies described in this chapter should be individualized to meet the needs of each child. In addition to these techniques the adult often needs to deal with behaviors that are antisocial or are not acceptable. Table 1 identifies several commonly used approaches for managing behavior. The following discussion addresses, in more detail, the development of conflict management skills, which are intended to move the child from adult-management to self-management.

Tantrums or other intense emotional responses may result from many causes—out-of-control aggression, total frustration, or even panic. Understanding what set off the tantrum can help the adult talk to the child at a later time and work into higher-level forms of conflict resolution.

The goal in teaching children skills of conflict management is to give them the tools to initiate verbal problem-solving strategies. Adults can assist children in undertsanding and coping with the specific events in their current lives. In so doing, they will be giving children the social interactional tools that will carry them through years of growing up.

Teaching conflict management should be thought of as a hierarchy of skills. The assessment should determine if the child is developmentally ready to

Table 1.   Alternatives for managing behavior

Alternatives	Guidelines
	Anticipation
Reduce boredom	Anticipate problem times in the child's day. Provide one or two activities appropriate for the child's level. Reduce TV time and gradually increase time child can occupy self.
Restructure time	If the child has difficulty at the same time every day, change something about his or her or the parent's schedule.
Plan transitions	Make expectations clear. Do not halt activity abruptly. Provide advance notice of what is coming. Use rituals (something child likes). For example, reading a book before bedtime may signal that it is time to go to sleep.
Prepare the child	If an upcoming event is uncomfortable or new, explain what will happen, what the child is expected to do, and how the child may feel.
	Clear expectations
Work at the child's level	Physically get down at the child's level and use language the child can understand. If there is a question, ask the child to explain what has been said, rather than saying, "Do you understand?"
Phrase questions and comments appropriately	Ask yes–no questions (e.g., "Do you want to go to school?") only if you are willing to accept either answer. Instead one might comment, "It's time to go to school."
Provide limited choices	Give the child a limited number of choices to make it easier for him or her to select and to reduce conflict.
Use "when–then" rules	(Called "Grandma's rules.) "When you do . . . , then you can . . . " structures the expectations for the child
	Feelings
Listen actively	Listen to the child's feelings and reflect back both the content and feelings that you hear. This helps the child clarify what is happening, lets him or her know you understand, and encourages the child to problem-solve.
Send I-messages	Express how the child's behavior makes you feel and the effect of the behavior ("When you . . . , I feel . . . because . . . ").
	Increasing behaviors
Offer positive reinforcement	Positive reinforcement can be physical (e.g., hugs, smiles) or verbal (e.g., praise) or tangible (e.g., candy, a prize). Reinforce behaviors or traits that you like or acceptable substitutes for an unacceptable behavior. To increase a desired behavior, the reinforcement must be valued by the child.
Praise	The best praise is specific to the behavior, immediately follows the desired behavior, and is sincere. Praise should not be coupled with negative comments or warnings. If the frequency or intensity of praise is overwhelming, it can lose its effectiveness.

(continued)

Table 1.   *(continued)*

Alternatives	Guidelines
Use reinforcement schedules	Reinforce a desired behavior every time it occurs until it is learned. Then reduce the frequency of reinforcement. Intermittent reinforcement is most effective.

Teaching new behaviors

Alternatives	Guidelines
Model behaviors	Do exactly what you want your child to do in his or her presence. This is a powerful teaching tool. Children model what they see. They also model behaviors they see being reinforced.
Give simple instruction	Use language at the child's developmental level and accompany the words with gestures.
Use shaping	Shaping combines simple instruction and reinforcement. Break the desired behavior into the smallest of steps and then reinforce the accomplishment of each step.

Decreasing inappropriate behaviors

Alternatives	Guidelines
Apply extinction techniques	Ignore the inappropriate behavior entirely. This ensures that the behavior is not reinforced with attention.
Apply substitution techniques	Substitute some aspect of the undesirable behavior to make it desirable (e.g., location, tool).
Modify the environment	Behavior is influenced by the environment. Changing the environment can change behavior. Adding interesting things, going to a new environment, restricting activities or materials in an environment, or reorganizing an environment can encourage or discourage behaviors.
Choose consequences Natural consequences	Natural consequences are those that follow naturally from a behavior without adult intervention. Natural consequences teach a child to be responsible for his or her own behavior.
Logical consequences	Logical consequences are logically related (in an obvious manner) to the event, but determined by the adult. To be effective, the logical consequence must occur each time the behavior occurs.
Follow through	Offer choices and consequences that are possible and realistic and follow through consistently. Arrange the environment so that compliance is easy. For example, if dirty clothes need to be put in a hamper, place the hamper where the child removes his or her clothes.
Use time out	Time out removes the child from a reinforcing event for a short time. The time out period should be short enough to allow the child to return and practice the desired behavior. The child should be told what is happening and why and placed quietly in an uninteresting location. The time out should be timed with a clock or timer after the child is quiet. When the time is up, the child should be told he or she may return to the situation from which he or she was removed. Reinforce appropriate behavior immediately.

Adapted from Crary (1979).

benefit from verbal problem-solving interventions. In order for a child to benefit from this approach the child should have certain readiness capabilities, including the folowing:

1. The child must be able to listen to the adult speaking.
2. The child must have adequate receptive vocabulary so as to comprehend the adult.
3. The child must be able to sustain attention for at least 2 minutes and must have sufficient self-regulation of body.
4. The child should be able to recall a simple sequence of events.
5. The child's expressive abilities should be such that by using words and actions he or she can communicate basic interaction. It is understood that some amount of adult interpretation is necessary.
6. The child should have some minimal awareness of self, others, and events.
7. The child must have sufficient trust that the adult genuinely cares about helping.

Adult Mediation   In the most concrete application of verbal problem-solving, the adult is highly active in the arrival at a solution. Later, as children develop more sophisticated skills, they define the solution. The role of the adult with very young children or children who are developmentally unprepared to benefit from verbal interventions is more active.

1.   The facilitator can act as a Band-Aid. He or she briefly describes the conflict and fixes it (e.g., "Timmy, you wanted Scott's brownie and took it away from him. Scott, you were mad at Timmy and hit him. Timmy, I want you to tell Scott you are sorry you took his brownie. (Timmy does so.) Thank you. Now I will give you a new brownie, Scott."). At this level basic social responses are taught. These include: 1) apology (e.g., "I'm sorry"), 2) sympathy (e.g., "I'm sorry you feel bad," "I'm sorry I made you feel bad"), and 3) empathy ("I feel bad that you feel bad").

2.   The facilitator has the child or children describe what happened.

3.   The facilitator summarizes. In the beginning stages, the facilitator again serves as a Band-Aid and offers solution.

4.   For children who are not ready to become more active in the problem-solving, story narration and role-playing techniques can be effective. In story narration, the facilitator tells the incident as a story and has the child fill in the blanks (e.g., "And when Timmy grabbed the brownie _____?" As children become ready the facilitator adds options (e.g., "And what Timmy should have asked was _____," "Scott could have _____ when Timmy grabbed the brownie"). Role playing is particularly effective when the children switch roles and try to respond within the other person's perspective.

5.   By the time children are 6 years old, their conflict management skills should include the ability to describe events, explain their own personal experience, indicate expected behavior, offer alternatives to their behavior, and label and understand simple values in social situations (e.g., fair–unfair, helpful–unhelpful, right–wrong).

Groups settings can be optimal for teaching social skills. They lend themselves to a variety of exploratory and dramatic play opportunities. Furthermore, *problem-solving engaged in by children in their own group milieu has a much greater likelihood of having meaning and being generalized than do solutions that come from adults.* Group conflict resolution and problem-solving fosters conceptual organization, communication, socialization skills, values incorporation, and an awareness of group and individual progress.

The manner in which children handle conflict influences the perception of their socialization skills. Children who respond to conflict with aggression often are thought of as bullies. When a child's emotional response to conflict is limited to screaming, hitting, or kicking, he or she becomes less appealing to adults and other children. These children often become labeled and less welcome in social situations.

As children get older the ability to manage conflict becomes even more important. Aggressiveness in a 6-year-old is much more problematic than in a 2-year-old. Because conflict management involves problem-solving, it engages a child's cognitive, language and communication, and social-emotional capacities. Conflict management also has developmental parameters (i.e., skills based upon maturation as well as learning). Adults can be very helpful to children in learning skills of conflict management. For some children, teaching such skills becomes essential to their survival in the social arena.

Limit-setting, labeling, and physical removal are the three basic elements of conflict management for the very young child or the child who possesses limited language or cognitive capacity.

Limit-Setting It is the adult's responsibility to keep the child's environment safe. Limits can be set within the physical environment or verbally. For example, 4-year-old Toby was easily overwhelmed by too many stimuli. If surrounded by toys, he frequently regressed to throwing them. When, however, adults placed him in a quiet location with only one or two toys, he engaged in imaginary play, and for short time periods, Toby played cooperatively with another child. Consequently, in order to minimize the opportunity for conflict, environmental limitations were set.

By the time most children are 1 year old, they can respond to verbal limit-setting, such as "no," "you may not . . .," or statements that imply consequences (e.g., "when you do that, this will happen"). The most common error adults make is to talk too much. *Expectations and consequences should be communicated in short, concise statements.* This is not the time to encourage development of negotiation or mediation skills.

Labeling *It is difficult for children to manage conflict if they are unable to label the feelings attached to it.* Sometimes conflict seems to erupt because a child is overtaken by feelings. By labeling the emotion, the child may become more emotionally organized and more quickly able to contain affects and move into verbal reasoning. Comments such as, "Bobby is mad. Bobby feels like hitting," can help a child link affects with action. When children are able to label their feelings or even understand them at a receptive, if not expressive, level, they are ready to be taught alternatives. For example, 2-year-old Jenny had gone through an intense phase of hitting people when angry or frustrated. With consistent practice, Jenny was able to learn to substitute saying, "Doggone it, I'm mad," for hitting.

Physical Removal There are times when the only reasonable response to a conflict-laden situation is physical removal of the child. *Emotional and physical safety must be the foremost consideration.* If the conflict has gone beyond the point where verbal limit-setting of reasoning are impossible, removal is appropriate. Reasoning with a child in the heat or a tantrum should not be attempted because at that moment, the child is unable to listen. When the child is calmer, it is appropriate to talk about the incident with him or her, and to discuss alternatives for handling the situation in the future.

Physical removal, it should be remembered, is a form of isolation, which, regardless of the child's age, is a powerful tool. Isolation during highly stressful periods or panic reactions can be harmful, or even traumatic, for the child. Time outs should be used carefully and should not necessarily isolate the child from human contact. For children who have serious psychiatric disorders and children who are vulnerable to separation and loss, the use of physical removal or social isolation should be done very cautiously. For instance, Rosy had been in four foster homes by the time she was 5 years old. She was fearful, slow to engage, and seemingly unattached. Her tantrums were aggressive explosions that endangered the children around her. If isolated for a time out, she would rock and pull her hair. Most effective in helping her calm and reorganize was to be held in a comforting, but nonverbal, manner. She was usually able to settle and rejoin the group within 5 minutes.

Peer-Mediated Interventions   Peers can be instructed in how to communicate with, model for, share with, imitate, suggest, complement, and give affection to children with disabilities both inside of and outside of instructional settings. The team can then reinforce peers for their efforts and, over time, fade out the reinforcement (McConnell, McEvoy, & Odom, 1992).

Other strategies, such as teaching peers to use sign language or other augmentative systems, are crucial to increasing communication and interaction between peers and children with specific disorders (e.g., hearing impairments). *Peers can also be taught how to position themselves with regard to the child with disabilities so that eye contact and turn-taking can take place.* Peers can observe and learn how to take into consideration specific needs, such as tactile input for children with visual impairments. *Peers can also be shown how to adjust their pace and level of intensity in play* (e.g., by waiting longer for the child with disabilities to have a turn or to respond to communication).

Structured activities that encourage peer interaction are also effective in increasing social exchanges among children. One such activity, affection training, developed by Twardosz, Nordquist, Simon, and Botkin (1983) uses structures games and songs to encourage children to give affection to each other. These activities have been shown to increase general social interaction as well with certain children (McEvoy, Twardosz, & Bishop, 1990).

EXAMPLE

Chanda B. was a 4½-year-old with hearing and vision impairments. In her inclusive preschool classroom, she wore thick glasses and hearing aids. When unattended, Chanda primarily sat alone and rocked back and forth with her head cocked to one side to listen to the sounds in the room. The other children ignored her presence, playing around her. Chanda's cognitive and language skills were only slightly delayed, as she displayed an understanding of representational play, assuming a role, sequencing actions into scenarios, and using sentences effectively to communicate. Chanda did not, however, seek to engage in this type of play and would only demonstrate her play skills when facilitated by an adult. At the beginning of the year the team planned several strategies to increase Chanda's social interaction in play.

Entry into the play arena seemed to be difficult for Chanda; so the teacher assisted her by helping her find an unobtrusive means of entering the action.

The teacher squatted next to Chanda and described what the children were doing. "Chanda, Alex and Missy are playing house. Alex is eating dinner and Missy is putting away groceries. Missy is talking about what she is putting away. There are other toys in the house, too—a doll and doll bed, washing machine, and a telephone. What do you think you could do in the house?"

Chandra replied, "I want to play with the doll."

The teacher remarked, "That's a good idea. No one is playing with it right now. What do you think the baby needs?"

"She needs to eat," replied Chanda.

"Well, Missy has some food and so does Alex. How could you get them to share?" the teacher asked.

"I'll just tell them my baby is hungry," said Chanda.

The teacher pointed her in the direction of the doll, and Chanda entered the house area. She found the doll and held it for a minute, then turned to Missy and said, "My baby is hungry."

Missy turned around, looked at her, then said, "I'll get her a bottle."

The teacher had to assist Chanda in surveying the play situation and determining a way to enter the play that would not disrupt the play of others. Later Chanda was able to ask, "What are you doing? Is there something I could do, too?" Script-training was employed with simple three-part stories, as well. Chanda was given a role and after several practice sessions, the others in the group would re-enact the scenario. If Chanda did not see or hear the developing play, a peer would come and get her, shouting, "The bus, get on the bus!" If someone was missing, the scenario could not go forth as planned.

The team also trained the class to watch Chanda and see when she was unoccupied. If a child approached Chanda and asked her to play or kept her involved in interaction, the child was reinforced with a hug. The children were taught how to give Chanda tactile cues, how to position themselves so that she could see them and hear them better, and how to use several important signs in her hand, such as "play," "come," and "feel." They soon needed only minimal prompts, such as the teacher pointing to Chanda, for the children to approach her and draw her into their play.

The team also frequently incorporated affection training activities. During group, songs such as "If you're happy and you know it" were modified to, "If you're happy and you know it, give a hug." These songs and interaction games not only gave the children practice in giving affection, but encouraged them to touch each other and use prosocial sayings.

Within the first 6 weeks of school, Chanda was actively seeking to engage peers in interaction, and peers were monitoring her and luring her into their play. Her peers showed pride in her social activities and frequently brought her attempts to the attention of the teacher. "Look, Chanda's playing blocks with Chris!" or "Chanda asked me to play. Give her and me a hug."

**DEVELOPMENTAL
LEVEL**

- Infant-to-infant interactions increase
  (6–8 months)
- Responds differently to children and adults
  (9–12 months)
- Begins to prefer interactions with peers
  (12 months +)

**INTERVENTION
GUIDELINES**

During the last half of the first year, infants become interested in their peers. By this time, they can usually sit unsupported, reach for and handle objects, smile, and laugh. In proximity to a peer, the infant reaches for or crawls to the other infant and attempts to make physical contact with hands or mouth. Infants can distinguish between children and adults. Nine-month-olds give different reactions to children and other babies than they do to adults. Children seem to be innately attracted to other children, which may be the basis for early play. When most infants are experiencing stranger anxiety with adults, a different response is seen with other infants. It is as if the child is thinking, "Hey, a little person. This one's not so scary." *The opportunity to see and touch other infants is important.* Cognitively, the child is helped to differentiate between different types and sizes of people, and socially, the infant is encouraged to develop his or her first social communications with peers. At this point, objects are not needed for interaction, as the peer is an interesting new "object."

If the child does not show minimal interest in another child through attraction to the child or child's toys, the prerequisite basis may not yet be present or the child may need assistance in directing attention toward the peer. *If a child ignores, withdraws, or seems unaware of the other child, the adult can alter the environment to see if reactivity can be increased though novel stimuli.* For example, the adult might give the peer a toy the infant likes or put a funny hat on the peer. Social engagement should begin within a realm of comfort for the child (i.e., within a setting and with people with whom the child feels comfortable). Display of social interaction skills should not be expected for the young child with strangers. Although the infant may be interested in a strange infant, he or she is more likely to engage a child who is familiar.

More formal interactions can be initiated through pragmatic gestures and words. Verbal greetings such as "hi" are easily taught to many children because they are so enthusiastically reinforced by adults and other children. Demonstration of enthusiasm in modeling is helpful. Prompting a wave or gesture also cues the child to attend to the peer.

**PLAY MATERIALS
AND
OPPORTUNITIES**

Action toys become a focus of mutual interest. A toy that moves, makes noise, or requires a partner promotes observation and encourages the child to seek interaction with the infant playing with the toy.

- Contacts with peer center around an object
       (12–15 months)
- Simple actions and contingent responses between peers
       (15–18 months)
- Spends most group time in solitary activity, watching other children
- Interactive sequences become longer until role sharing and turn-taking are evident
       (18–24 months)
- Intense watchfulness of peer
- Child imitates peer
- Child watches, points at, takes toys of other child
       (24 months +)

After 1 year of age, objects become more significant in peer interaction. The child throws objects at other children, offers them (although he or she may not release them), and uses vocalizations or words. For example, standing before another peer, the infant may hold out a ball and say "ba." When interactions do take place, infants typically display simple act–react exchanges. More elaborate interchanges develop as the child matures. Between 1 and 2 years, if development is proceeding normally in the motor area, the infant becomes a toddler. This allows the child easier access to peers who may be in the room. Physical interchanges, such as pushing, are not uncommon; although pleasurable interactions are increasing as one child responds to another's initiations. The toddler at this level also likes to observe the peer's activities, although the majority of time is spent playing alone, rather than with the peer. One child may make a gesture or movement and the other may imitate the gesture or movement. Conflicts may arise as coveted toys are taken from the peer.

Adults may facilitate interaction of peers at this level by bringing the child's attention to a peer, such as by pointing out what the peer is doing (e.g., "Tara is in the box"). When the child goes to investigate, the adult can comment on what is happening. "She's got toys in the box." The toddler, barring language delays, is also communicating in one- to two-word phrases and will probably comment to the peer, making overtures to get in the box or to get the other child out of the box. For children who do have delays or disabilities and who may not automatically observe and engage a peer, the adult becomes the facilitator of interaction. *The adult can prompt the movement from simple act–react exchanges to longer turn-taking sequences by structuring a "turn," modeling or suggesting another action, or physically assisting the child. The less intrusive the adult's role, however, the more natural the peer play will be.*

At this level it is easy to disregard the importance of peer interaction for the child with disabilities, focusing instead on intervention in one-to-one interaction with the adult. *Social competence with peers, however, starts with these early first steps, and adults make a mistake when they ignore social interactions with a peer for the infant and toddler.* The child with visual impairments, for example, may not be able to observe and imitate the peer, which is an important milestone. The adult, however, can place the child very close to the peer so that touching is possible, facilitate tactile exploration of the peer, if not initiated by the child, and comment on what the peer is doing. The children should not be discouraged from physical exploration or "rough" play, unless one child is injuring the other. Using sound toys, the adult can facilitate imitation of the peer and turn-taking. For example, if the peer is hitting a xylophone, the child can be given another xylophone. If imitation does not occur spontaneously, the adult can physically prompt the child to hit the xylophone.

Positioning the child in such a way as to optimize observation and interaction is important. In addition, expanding the child's pragmatic communication abilities also enhances social interactions (see Chapter 10 for further suggestions on increasing communication skills).

PLAY MATERIALS AND OPPORTUNITIES

The best way to instigate social interaction among infants is to provide a toy that is mutually intriguing. Toys that move or perform an action or make noises are recommended. Social toys (e.g., balls, dolls) promote interaction as well. Duplicate toys encourage imitation and turn-taking. For example, if one drum and stick is available, infants may vie for the toys, whereas having two drums and sticks prompts the infants to observe and imitate each other.

As mobility increases, peers will begin to follow the movements of one another, imitating not only actions with toys, but also gross motor actions. Climbing, running, and scooting around on riders are fun activities that facilitate interaction.

DEVELOPMENTAL LEVEL

- Parallel, noninteractive play predominates (24–30 months)
- Aggression increases, then declines (but at no time exceeds positive or neutral interactions) (24–48 months)

INTERVENTION GUIDELINES

Playing in Proximity to Peers

Children at this level like to play in proximity to peers, but are primarily noninteractive with the toys and materials. The child still observes and make overtures to the peer, particularly when the peer's toy looks more interesting. Many preschool children with delays and disabilities remain at the parallel play stage without guidance from facilitators. The intervention team should assist the child in moving into interactions with a peer rather than just playing in proximity. *For the child whose play is arrested at this level of development, the best strategies for intervention include modeling and verbal explanation. This is the type of child for whom teaching play skills is imperative.* At the same time, exaggeration of emotions by the facilitator encourages expression of affect within the interaction.

Child Dyads

Adult participation is necessary in child dyads when the children have minimal play skills. Typically "tug-of-wars" with toys and proclamations of "mine, mine" dominate unless adults explain and demonstrate the tenets of sharing and taking turns. As can be seen from the example on page 270, the facilitator can either become part of the play, which is more intrusive, or comment from the "sidelines." Using a child who plays interactively, at an associative or cooperative level, is helpful as this child is also able to draw the child into the play by modeling and proposing a course of action. The facilitator can then work with both the child and the peer to increase social interactions.

Games of Pretend

Before associative and cooperative play develop, adults can influence the emergence of interactions in representational play. Games of pretend delight children and can range from momentary fantasy interactions (e.g., a pretend cookie or cup of tea) to more elaborate make-believe creations (e.g., playing house, camping, acting like animals). The content of play scenarios can reinforce cooperation and mutual problem-solving. Children, for example, "going on a bear hunt" or a pretend camping expedition must figure out how to cross the stream, gather wood, set up a tent, and build a campfire. Singing songs together can also illustrate the benefit of doing something together.

Aggression

Aggression in children is normal. Children struggle with how to get and give attention, share, and accomplish their goals. Their inability to see another's point of view or even *care* about another's point of view makes aggression the easiest way to solve problems. Aggression becomes an emotional, rather than a social, concern when the number of hostile interactions observed exceeds positive or neutral interactions. Resolution of conflicts is discussed on pages 265–270.

Antisocial Behavior

The bases for antisocial behavior are complex and multiple. Many times, however, the antisocial child demonstrates little concern for others because he or she has had the experience of feeling "unlovable." For antisocial children, it is difficult, therefore, to take turns, share, assist other children, or respond to others' feelings. For these children there can be safety and a sense of security in make-believe. Furthermore, in play, the antisocial child can often assume roles of heroism, helpfulness, and interpersonal relatedness, attributes lacking in normal, nonplay interactions (see also pp. 244–245).

PLAY MATERIALS AND OPPORTUNITIES

The same toys and opportunities described for the previous developmental level are appropriate here. Duplicate toys diminish aggressive acts. Play opportunities with sensory materials, such as a sand-and-water table with shovels and pails or boats and water devices, encourage parallel and associative play. Art materials (e.g., fingerpaints, stamp pads) also provide a means for playing close to one another in a noncompetitive spirit.

EXAMPLE

Juanita S., a 4-year-old, was playing beside Mary. Juanita was dressing her doll while Mary cooked in the kitchen. Juanita was unable to link her play with Mary's in any fashion. The facilitator intervened by encouraging Juanita to take her doll to Mary and suggest that the two feed the doll breakfast. The facilitator continued to help Juanita further her interaction with Mary by commenting and suggesting what might happen with the dolls. The facilitator then assisted Mary in taking over the facilitator role by reinforcing her efforts to engage Juanita. Mary involved Juanita in numerous scenarios in the house over the next several days, and eventually Juanita began to initiate interactions with Mary in play.

DEVELOPMENTAL LEVEL

- Plays well with two or three children in a group
- Associative play predominates
  - (30–36 months)
- Plays spontaneously with other children in complicated verbal communication
- Increased rough-and-tumble play
  - (36 months +)
- Begins cooperative play
- Group play replaces parallel play
  - (36–48 months)
- Prefers playing with other children to playing alone, unless engrossed in a project
  - (48 months +)
- Peer interactions characterized by talking, smiling, laughing, playing
- Begins group games with simple rules
- Shows concern and sympathy for others in group
  - (48–60 months)
- Understands rules of fair play
- Likes competitive games
  - (60–72 months)

INTERVENTION GUIDELINES

Dyad and Group Play

As the child develops the ability to concentrate on toys and interactions with peers at the same time, he or she moves into the arena of dyad and group play. With increasing ability to represent and dramatize events, there is a greater need to involve peers in the action. At the associate play level, children may be involved in play related to the same theme, playing with blocks, playing "police" or "firefighter," but not having organized scenarios with a common goal in their play. Instead, each child plays independently, pursuing his or her own unique ideas.

Playing Roles

For the child who stays on the periphery, playing no role and never initiating or directing the play of others, the opportunity to "play a role" that differs from his or her natural one can provide a new and valuable experience. The "onlooker" child may find it much easier to "captain his ship" through a raging storm or "lead her troops" through danger in a structured play setting than on a playground. *As children experiment with new roles, ones that are probably inherently uncomfortable, it is advisable for the facilitator to remain active in the play. Demonstrating turntaking, sharing, and role elaboration can provide a useful model for the child. By delighting in make-believe, the facilitator encourages the child to abandon the constraints of reality-based play and join in the theater of the imagination.*

Entry into Group Play

After the child develops a level of representational ability and the capability of linking play actions together, he or she has the basis for interactive dramatic play or other types of group play. Unfortunately, cognitive prerequisites are insufficient to ensure interaction. Not only are children with disabilities often delayed in their play levels and play skills, they are also deficient in the social task of gaining entry into group play. This is a critical skill, as otherwise the child is relegated to the sidelines and onlooker, isolated, or parallel play persists. *Intervention to assist the child in learning how to gain entry to group play is essential.* Putallaz and Wasserman (1990) found that approximately 50% of initial attempts by a preschool child to enter a group were rejected or ignored. The successful child must have both persistence and effective strategies for persuading the peers to allow another into the play. Dodge, Pettit, McClaskey, and Brown (1986) propose a social-cognitive process that enables a child to gain group entry:

1. The child perceives the social cues given by the peers, including affective expression, play themes, and voice tone. The facilitator may help children develop strategies to work through this process.
2. The child interprets those cues.
3. The child generates possible approaches to entering the group.
4. The child evaluates the various approaches and selects a strategy.
5. The child implements the strategy.

The adult who observes that a child is not joining a group or has unsuccessfully attempted to join a group can use these same processes with the child. Depending on the child's verbal level, language may need to be adjusted. *The adult might observe with the child and elicit or provide descriptions of what is going on in the peers' play, how the children are talking, and what affect they are expressing.* The adult would then talk about what those cues mean, what may happen next, and how the peers may react if the child joins them. Together, the child and adult can discuss ways to enter the play successfully. *Less intrusive entry tactics appear to be more effective* (e.g., just going up and joining in, going up and doing something similar, asking someone to join). After deciding what to do, the child can execute the plan. The adult can provide support and encouragement if the plan fails so the child will persist with a different approach. (See also the discussion of conflict resolution on pp. 265–270.)

Maintaining Interaction

Once in the group, the child may have difficulty maintaining interaction. Many children with disabilities lack the verbal abilities to carry on the complicated conversations of a 3- to 6-year-old. *The adult can assist here as well, by either being a member of the play group and facilitating the child's language or by providing occasional suggestions as an observer.* The adult can also help peers read the child's cues and interpret what the child is intending to communicate. This helps the peers to become more sensitive to the child's cues and prepares them for future interactions.

Teacher-mediated interventions that require reinforcement schedules are effective, but also time-consuming and they may not result in generalization. In addition, the presence of the adult may alter the play situation. Approaches, such as those discussed above, that allow the child to be involved in thinking about, planning, and evaluating the effectiveness of his or her efforts are also time-consuming, but they can be implemented as needed and probably result in more generalization to other situations.

For the child who requires extraordinary amounts of adult attention and reinforcement in order to be maintained in the group, the message may be clear—the child is not ready. If it is not possible to provide the child with a more beneficial adult–child ratio, a child "buddy" may ease the child's need for attention. Peer pairing is supported through research (McEvoy, Odom, & McConnell, 1992; Odom & Strain, 1984). *One or more peers can be trained to involve the child in various types of play activities.* Reinforcement of peers for successful inclusion of the child with disabilities or social immaturities can increase peer interactions (Strain & Kohler, 1988).

Script Training

Script training is another approach to increasing both language and social interaction in play. Goldstein, Wickstrom, Hoyson, Jamieson, and Odom (1988) found script training to be effective in teaching sociodramatic play skills. *Children are taught a simple dramatic script with three roles and corresponding behaviors. They are then allowed to enact the script with minimal intrusion from an adult.* Use of props, familiar settings, and common language is incorporated to make learning the scripts easier. After the script is learned, children add their own adaptations and creative touches. The script, however, provides a safe basis for children, as it takes the pressure off of getting a theme started, figuring out roles and interactions, and generating language. The children are then free to expand the social interactions within the safe structure.

Script training is used with the storybook curriculum outlined on pages 497–499. Using "The Three Bears" story theme, for example, the children were able to enact the various roles after several practice sessions. They then modified the play by changing what was cooked, who played what role, and when a fourth large bear was brought to school, they added Uncle George!

The use of a theme with numerous activities related to that theme also encourages interaction among children, as associations are drawn from one area to another and children return to certain areas to expand on activities.

After Zack had experimented independently with the potato paints, for instance, he was ready to "help" a peer who came to that center for the first time. Pointing to the fall leaves that were cut out and hung from streamers and on the mural, Zack showed Nadia how to hold the potato, dip it, and print with it.

As children move into associative cooperative play, props and materials that stimulate representational play are recommended. Props related to familiar persons and scenes (culturally relevant), favorite stories, or invented adventures (e.g., flying to the moon) stimulate interaction. Simple props such as boxes can be space ships, boats, or caves. Realistic props (e.g., hats) or imaginative props (e.g., a stick for a control mechanism) can be used depending on the child's cognitive abilities.

PLAY MATERIALS AND OPPORTUNITIES

Trucks, cars, various types of blocks, and miniature scenes (e.g., Playmobil sets) are toys that encourage interaction and communication among peers. However, any materials can provide opportunities for interaction with facilitation by an adult or another peer.

ACKNOWLEDGMENTS

The age ranges provided in this chapter are based on recognized data and the work of the following researchers: for Mastery Motivation, Kusmierek, Cunningham, Fox-Gleason, and Lorenzini (1985), Morgan and Harmon (1984); for Attachment, Separation, and Individuation, Cohen and Gross (1979), Emde, Gaensbauer, and Harmon (1981), and Foley and Hobin (1981); for Social Relations with Peers, Cohen and Gross (1979), Hartup (1978), and Mueller and Lucas (1975); and for Development of Humor, McGhee (1979).

REFERENCES

Affleck, G., McGrade, B.J., McQueeney, A.D., & Allen, D. (1982). Relationship-focused early intervention in developmental disabilities. *Exceptional Children, 3,* 259–261.

Ainsworth, M. (1973). The development of infant–mother attachment. *Child Development Research, 3,* 1–93.

Ainsworth, M., & Bell, S. (1973). Mother–infant interaction. *Child Development Research, 3,* 1–93.

Ainsworth, M.D., Blehar, M.C., Waters, E., & Wall, S. (1978). *Patterns of attachment.* Hillsdale, NJ: Lawrence Erlbaum Associates.

American Association on Mental Retardation. (1990). AAMR takes the lead in defining mental retardation. *AAMR News & Notes, 3*(6), 1.

Antia, S.D., & Kreimeyer, K.H. (1992). Social competence intervention for young children with hearing impairments. In S.L. Odom, S.R. McConnell, & M.A. McEvoy (Eds.), *Social competence of young children with disabilities: issues and strategies for intervention* (pp. 135–164). Baltimore: Paul H. Brookes Publishing Co.

Barrera, M., & Vella, D. (1987). Disabled and nondisabled infant's interactions with their mothers. *American Journal of Occupational Therapy, 55,* 168–172.

Beckman, P.J., & Lieber, J. (1992). Parent–child social relationships and peer social competence of preschool children with disabilities. In S.L. Odom, S.R. McConnell, & M.A. McEvoy (Eds.), *Social competence of young children with disabilities: Issues and strategies for intervention* (pp. 65–92). Baltimore: Paul H. Brookes Publishing Co.

Beckwith, L. (1976). Caregiver–infant interaction and development of the high-risk infant. In T. Tjossem (Ed.), *Intervention strategies for high-risk infants and young children* (pp. 119–139). Baltimore: University Park Press.

Berk, L. (1991). *Child development* (2nd ed.). Newton, MA: Allyn & Bacon.

Bowlby, J. (1969/1982). *Attachment*. New York: Basic Books.

Bowlby, J. (1973). *Separation*. New York: Basic Books.

Bowlby, J. (1980). *Loss*. New York: Basic Books.

Brazelton, T., Tronick, E., Adamson, L., Als, H., & Wise, S. (1975). Early infant–mother reciprocity. In *Parent–infant interaction, Ciba Foundation Symposium 33*. Amsterdam: Associated Scientific Publishers.

Bricker, D.D. (1986). *Early education of at-risk and handicapped infants, toddlers, and preschool children*. Glenview IL: Scott, Foresman.

Brody, G.H., Stoneman, Z., & Burke, M. (1987). Child temperaments, maternal differential behavior, and sibling relationships. *Developmental Psychology, 23*, 354–362.

Bronfenbrenner, U. (1989). In R. Vasta (Ed.), *Annals of child development* (Vol. 6, pp. 187–251). Greenwich, CT: JAI Press.

Carlson, V., Cicchetti, D., Barnett, D., & Braunwald, K. (1989). Disorganized/disoriented attachment relationships in maltreated infants. *Developmental Psychology, 25*, 525–531.

Chess, S., & Thomas, A. (1984). *Origins and evolution of behavior disorders*. New York: Brunner/Mazel.

Clarke-Stewart, K. (1973). Interactions between mothers and their young children: Characteristics and consequences. *Monographs of the Society for Research in Child Development, 38* (153), 6–7.

Cohen, M.A., & Gross, P.J. (1979). *The developmental resource: Behavioral sequences for assessment and planning* (Vol. 2). New York: Grune & Stratton.

Crary, E. (1979). *Without spanking as spoiling*. Seattle, WA: Parenting Press.

Cunningham, C., Reuler, E., Blackwell, J., & Deck, J. (1981). Behavioral and linguistic developments in the interactions of normal and retarded children with their mothers. *Child Development, 52*, 62–70.

Davids, J. (1987). Laughter in the nursery. *Bulletin Anna Freud Centre, 10*, 307–318.

DeStefano, C.T., & Mueller, E. (1982). Environmental determinants of peer social activity in 18-month-old males. *Infant Behavior and Development, 5*, 175–183.

Diener, C.I., & Dweck, C.S. (1978). An analysis of learned helplessness: Continuous changes in performance, strategy, and achievement cognitions following failure. *Journal of Personality and Social Psychology, 36*, 451–462.

Dodds, J.B. (1987). *Child psychotherapy primer: Suggestions for the beginning therapist*. New York: Human Sciences Press.

Dodge, K.A., Pettit, G.S., McClaskey, C.L., & Brown, M.M. (1986). Social competence in children. *Monographs of the Society for Research in Child Development, 51*(2, Serial No. 213).

Dunst, C., Lesko, J., Holbert, K., Wilson, L., Sharpe, K., & Liles, R. (1987). A systematic approach to infant intervention. *Topics in Early Childhood Special Education, 7*(2), 19–37.

Dunst, C., & Trivette, C. (1988). Determinants of parent and child interactive behavior. In K. Marfo (Ed.), (pp. 125–130). *Parent–child interaction and developmental disabilities* (pp. 3–31). New York: Praeger.

Dweck, C.S., Davidson, W., Nelson, S., & Enna, B. (1978). Sex differences in learned helplesssness III: An experimental analysis. *Developmental Psychology, 14*, 268–276.

Dweck, C.S., & Elliott, E.S. (1983). Achievement motivation. In E.M. Hetherington (Ed.), *Handbook of child psycholoyg: Vol. 4. Socialization, personality, and social development* (pp. 643–691). New York: John Wiley & Sons.

Dweck, C.S., & Leggett, E.L. (1988). A social-cognitive approach to motivation and personality. *Psychological Review, 95*, 256–273.

Emde, R.N. (1985). The affective self: Continuities and transformations from infancy. In J. Call, E. Galenson, & R.L. Tyson (Eds.), *Frontiers of infant psychiatry* (Vol. 2, pp. 38–54). New York: Basic Books.

Emde, R.N. (1988a). Development terminable and interminable I. *International Journal of Psychoanalysis, 69*, 23–42.

Emde, R.N. (1988b). Development terminable and interminable II. *International Journal of Psychoanalysis, 69*, 283–289.

Emde, R.N., Gaensbauer, T., & Harmon, R.J. (1981). Using our emotions: Some principles for appraising emotional development and intervention. In M. Lewis & L. Taft (Eds.), *Developmental disabilities in preschool children* (pp. 409–424). New York: Spectrum Publications, Medical and Scientific Books.

Emde, R., Katz, E., & Thorpe, J. (1978). Emotional expression in infancy II: Early deviations in Down's syndrome. In M. Lewis & L. Rosenblum (Eds.), *The development of affect* (pp. 351–360). New York: Plenum.

Erikson, E. (1950). *Childhood and society*. New York: Norton.

Faust, J., & Burns, W.J. (1991). Coding therapist and child interaction: Progress and outcome in play therapy. In C.E. Schaefer, K. Gatlin, & A. Sandgrund (Eds.) *Play diagnosis and assessment*. New York: John Wiley & Sons.

Fewell, R.R., & Kaminski, R. (1988). Play skills development and instruction for young children with handicaps. In S.L. Odom & M.B. Karnes (Eds.), *Early intervention for infants and children with handicaps: An empirical base* (pp. 145–158). Baltimore: Paul H. Brookes Publishing Co.

Field, T. (1979). Interaction patterns of high-risk and normal infants. In T. Field, A. Sostek, S. Goldberg, & H.H. Shuman (Eds.), *Infants born at-risk*. New York: Spectrum Publications.

Field, T. (1983). High-risk infants "have less fun" during early interactions. *Topics in Early Childhood Special Education, 3*, 77–87.

Flake-Hobson, C., Robinson, B.E., & Skeen, P. (1983). *Child development and relationships*. Reading, MA: Addison-Wesley.

Fogel, A., Toda, S., & Kawaii, M. (1987). Mother–infant face-to-face interaction in Japan and the United States: A laboratory comparison using 3-month-old-infants. *Developing Psychology, 24*, 398–406.

Foley, G., & Hobin, M. (1981). *The attachment-separation-individuation (A-S-I) scales* (Revised). Reading, PA: Family Centered Resource Project.

Fonagy, P., Steele, M., Moran, G., Steele, H., & Higgitt, A. (1991). Measuring the ghost in the nursery: A summary of the main findings of the Anna Freud Centre—University College London Parent-Child Study. *Bulletin Anna Freud Centre, 14*, 115–131.

Gaensbauer, T. (1985, September). *Case presentation of the treatment of a two-and-one-half-year-old boy who was bitten by a dog*. Paper presented at the meeting of the Colorado Child Psychiatric Council Annual Meeting, Denver, CO.

Gardner, H. (1987). Developing the spectrum of human intelligence. *Harvard Educational Review, 57*, 187–193.

Gardner, H., & Hatch, T. (1989). Multiple intelligences go to school. Educational implications of the theory of multiple intelligences. *Educational Researcher, 18*(8), 4–10.

Giffin, M. (1981). Assessing infant and toddler development. In B. Weissbourd & J. Musick (Eds.), *Infants: Their social environments* (p. 48–63). Washington, DC: National Association for the Education of Young Children.

Ginott, H.G. (1964). The theory and practice of "therapeutic intervention" in child treatment. In M.R. Haworth (Ed.), *Child psychotherapy* (pp. 125–130). New York: Basic Books.

Girolametto, L. (1988). Developing dialogue skills: The effects of a conversational model of language intervention. In D. Marfo (Ed.), *Parent–child interactions and developmental disabilities* (pp. 145–162). New York: Praeger.

Goldstein, H., & Gallagher, T.M. (1992). Strategies for promoting the social-communicative competence of young children with specific language impairment. In S.L. Odom, S.R. McConnell, & M.A. McEvoy (Eds.), *Social competence of young children with disabilities: Issues and strategies for intervention* (pp. 189–213). Baltimore: Paul H. Brookes Publishing Co.

Goldstein, H., Wickstrom, S., Hoyson, M., Jamieson, B., & Odom, S. (1988). Effects of sociodramatic play training on social and communicative interaction. *Education and Treatment of Children, 11*, 97–117.

Gregory, F. (1976). *The deaf child and his family*. London: Allen and Unwin.

Guilford, J.P., & Hoepfner, R. (1971). *The analysis of intelligence*. New York: McGraw-Hill.

Guralnick, M.J. (1990). Social competence and early intervention. *Journal of Early Intervention, 14*, 3–14.

Guralnick, M.J. (1992). A hierarchical model for understanding children's peer-related social competence. In S.L. Odom, S.R. McConnell, & M.A. McEvoy (Eds.), *Social competence of young children with disabilities: Issues and strategies for intervention* (pp. 37–64). Baltimore: Paul H. Brookes Publishing Co.

Gwynne, F. (1976). *A chocolate moose for dinner*. New York: Windmill Books.

Hanson, M.J. (1984). Parent–infant interaction. In M.J. Hanson (Ed.), *Atypical infant development* (pp. 179–206). Baltimore: University Park Press.

Hanzlik, J. (1989). Interactions between mothers and their infants with developmental disabilities: Analysis and review. *Physical and Occupational Therapy in Pediatrics, 9*(2), 33–51.

Hanzlik, J. (1990). Nonverbal interaction patterns of mothers and their infants with cerebral palsy. *Education and Training in Mental Retardation, 25,* 333–343.

Hanzlik, J. (1993). Parent–child relations: Interaction and intervention. In J. Case-Smith (Ed.) *Pediatric occupational therapy and early intervention.* Stoneham, MA: Andover Medical Publishers.

Hanzlik, J., & Stevenson, M. (1986). Interaction of mothers with their infants who are mentally retarded, retarded with cerebral palsy, or nonretarded. *American Journal of Mental Deficiency, 90,* 513–520.

Hartup, W.W. (1978). Children and their friends. In H. McGurk (Ed.), *Issues in childhood social development* (pp. 130–170). London: Methuen.

Holdgrafer, G., & Dunst, C. (1986). Communicative competence: From research to practice. *Topics in Early Childhood Special Education 6*(3), 1–22.

Horner, T. (1985). The psychic life of the young infant: Review and critique of the psychoanalytic concepts of symbiosis and infantile omnipotence. *American Journal Orthopsychiatry, 55,* 324–344.

Jennings, K.D., Connors, R.E., Stegman, C.E., Sankaranarayan, P., & Medolsohn, S. (1985). Mastery motivation in young preschoolers. *Journal of the Division of Early Childhood, 9*(2), 162–169.

Johnson, N.M. (1983). Assessment paradigms and atypical infants: An intervention perspective. In D.D. Bricker (Ed.), *Intervention with at-risk and handicapped infants* (pp. 129–138). Baltimore: University Park Press.

Kagan, J. (1971). *Understanding children: Behavior motives and thought.* San Diego: Harcourt Brace Jovanovich.

Kagan, J. (1988). Temperamental contributions to social behavior. *American Psychologist, 44,* 668–674.

Kagan, J., Resnick, J.S., & Gibbons, J. (1989). Inhibited and uninhibited types of children. *Child Development, 60,* 838–845.

Kagan, J., Resnick, J.S., & Snidman, N. (1987). The physiology and psychology of behavioral inhibition in children. *Child Development, 58,* 1459–1473.

Katan, A. (1961). Some thoughts about the role of verbalization in early childhood. *Psychoanalytic Study of the Child, 16,* 184–188.

Keogh, B. (1985). Temperament and schooling: Meaning of "goodness of fit?" In J.V. Lerner & R.M. Lerner (Eds.), *New directions for child development* (No. 31, pp. 89–108). San Francisco: Jossey-Bass.

Krakow, J., & Kopp, C. (1983). The effect of developmental delay on sustained attention in young children. *Child Development, 54,* 1143–1155.

Kusmierek, A., Cunningham, K., Fox-Gleason, M.,, & Lorenzini, D. (1985). *South Metropolitan Association birth to three transdisciplinary assessment guide.* Flassmoor, IL: South Metropolitan Association for Low-Incidence Handicapped.

Levy-Schiff, R. (1986). Mother–father–child interactions in families with a mentally retarded young child. *American Journal of Mental Deficiency, 91,* 141–149.

Lifton, R., & Olson, E. (1976). The human meaning of total disasters. *Psychiatry, 39,* 1–18.

Linder, T.W. (1990). *Transdisciplinary play-based assessment: A functional approach to working with young children.* Baltimore: Paul H. Brookes Publishing Co.

Lovell, K., Hoyle, H.W., & Siddall, M.C. (1968). A study of some aspects of the play and language of young children with delayed speech. *Journal of Child Psychology and Psychiatry, 9,* 41–50.

Lyons-Ruth K. (1991). Rapproachement or approachement: Mahler's theory reconsidered from the vantage point of recent research on early attachment relationships. *Psychoanalytic Psychology, 8,* 1–23.

MacDonald, J., & Gillette, Y. (1988). Communicating partners: A conversational model for building parent–child relationships with handicapped children. In K. Marfo (Ed.), *Parent–child interaction and developmental disabilities* (pp. 220–242). New York: Praeger.

Mahler, M., Pine, F., & Bergman, A. (1975). *The psychological birth of the infant.* New York: Basic Books.

Mahoney, G. (1988). Maternal communication style with mentally retarded children. *American Journal of Mental Retardation, 92,* 352–359.

Mahoney, G.J., Finger, J., & Powell, A. (1985). The relationship of maternal behavior style to the developmental status of mentally retarded infants. *American Journal of Mental Deficiency, 90,* 296–302.

Mahoney, G., Fors, S., & Wood, S. (1990). Maternal behavior revisited. *American Journal of Mental Retardation, 94,* 398–406.

Mahoney, G., & Powell, A. (1986). *The transactional intervention program: A child-centered approach to developmental intervention with young handicapped children.* Farmington, CT: Pediatric Research and Training Center.

Mahoney, G., & Powell, A. (1988). Modifying parent–child interaction: Enhancing the development of handicapped children. *The Journal of Special Education, 22,* 82–96.

Mattheny, A.P., Wilson, R.S., & Nuss, S.M. (1984). Toddler temperament: Stability across settings and over ages. *Child Development, 55,* 1157–1211.

Maurer, H., & Sherrod, K. (1987). Context of directives given to young children with Down syndrome and nonretarded children: Development over two years. *American Journal of Mental Deficiency, 91,* 579–590.

McConnell, S.R., McEvoy, M.A., & Odom, S.L. (1992). Implementation of social competence interventions in early childhood special education classrooms: Current practices and future directions. In S.L. Odom, S.R. McConnell, & M.A. McEvoy (Eds.), *Social competence of young children with disabilities: Issues and strategies for intervention* (pp. 277–306). Baltimore: Paul H. Brookes Publishing Co.

McDevitt, S. (1986). Continuity and discontinuity of temperament in infancy and early childhood: A psychometric perspective. In R. Plomin & J. Dunn (Eds.), *The study of temperament: Changes, continuities and challenges.* Hillsdale, NJ: Lawrence Erlbaum Associates.

McEvoy, M.A., Twardosz, S., & Bishop, N. (1990). Affection activities: Procedures for encouraging young children with handicaps to interact with their peers. *Education and Treatment of Children, 13,* 159–167.

McEvoy, M.A., Odom, S.L., & McConnell, S.R. (1992). Peer social competence intervention for young children with disabilities. In S.L. Odom, S.R. O'Connell, & M.A. McEvoy (Eds.), *Social competence of young children with disabilities: Issues and strategies for intervention* (pp. 113–133). Baltimore: Paul H. Brookes Publishing Co.

McGhee, P.E. (1977). A model of the origins and early development of incongruity-based humor. In A.J. Chapman & H.C. Foot (Eds.), *It's a funny thing, humor.* Oxford, England: Pergamon.

McGhee, P.E. (1979). *Humor: Its origins and development.* San Francisco: W.H. Freeman.

McGhee, P.E. (1984). Play, incongruity, and humor. In T.D. Yawkey & A.D. Pellegrini (Eds.), *Child's play: Developmental and applied* (pp. 219–236). Hillsdale, NJ: Lawrence Erlbaum Associates.

McKirdy, L.S. (1972). *Play and language in four- to five-year-old deaf and hearing children.* New Brunswick: Rutgers University. (ERIC Document Reproduction Service No. EC 113 220).

Mindes, G. (1982). Social and cognitive aspects of play in young handicapped children. *Topics in Early Childhood Special Education: Play and Development, 2*(3), 39–52.

Mogford, K. (1977). The play of handicapped children. In B. Tizard & D. Harvey (Eds.), *Biology of play* (pp. 70–184). Philadelphia: J.B. Lippincott.

Morgan, G.A., & Harmon, R.J. (1984). Developmental transformations in mastery motivation. In R.N. Emde & R.J. Harmon (Eds.), *Continuities and discontinuities in development.* New York: Plenum.

Mueller, E., & Lucas, T. (1975). A developmental analysis of peer interaction among toddlers. In M. Lewis & L.A. Rosenblum (Eds.), *Friendship and peer relations* (pp. 223–257). New York: John Wiley & Sons.

Newson, E., & Head, E. (1979). Play and play-things for handicapped children. In E. Newson & J. Newson (Eds.), *Toys and play-things in development and remediation.* New York: Penguin Books.

Nicholls, J.G. (1978). The development of concepts of effort and ability, perception of academic attainment, and the understanding that difficult tasks require more ability. *Child Development, 49,* 800–814.

Novick, K. (1986). Talking with toddlers. *Psychoanalytic Study of the Child, 41,* 277–286.

Odom, S.L., McConnell, S.R., & McEvoy, M.A. (1992). Peer-related social competence and its significance for young children with disabilities. In S.L. Odom, S.R. McConnell, & M.A. McEvoy (Eds.), *Social competence of young children with disabilities: Issues and strategies for intervention* (pp. 3–36). Baltimore: Paul H. Brookes Publishing Co.

Odom, S.L., & McEvoy, M.A. (1988). Integration of young children with handicaps and normally developing children. In S. Odom & M. Karnes (Eds.), *Early intervention for infants and children with handicaps: An empirical base* (pp. 241–267). Baltimore: Paul H. Brookes Publishing Co.

Odom, S.L., & Strain, P.S. (1984). Peer-mediated approaches to increasing children's social interactions. *American Journal of Orthopsychiatry, 54,* 544–557.

Parsons, J.E., Adler, T.F., & Kaczala, C.M. (1982). Socialization of achievement attitudes and beliefs: Parental influences. *Child Development, 53,* 310–321.

Parten, M.B. (1932). Social participation among preschool children. *Journal of Abnormal and Social Psychology, 27,* 243–269.

Perry, L., & Landreth, G. (1991). Diagnostic assessment of children's play therapy behavior. In C.E. Schaefer, K. Gitlin, & A. Sandgrund (Eds.), *Play diagnosis and assessment* (pp. 643–662). New York: John Wiley & Sons.

Plomin, R. (1989). Environment and genes: Determinants of behavior. *American Psychologist, 44,* 105–111.

Putallaz, M., & Wasserman, A. (1990). Child's entry behavior. In S.R. Asher & J.D. Doie (Eds.), *Peer rejection in childhood* (pp. 60–89). Cambridge: Cambridge University Press.

Riese, M.L. (1987). Temperament stability between the neonatal period and 24 months. *Developmental Psychology, 23,* 216–222.

Rogers, S.J., & Puchalski, C.B. (1984). Development of symbolic play in visually impaired infants. *Topics in Early Child Special Education, 3*(4), 57–64.

Sander, L. (1962). Issues in early mother–child interaction. *Journal of the American Society of Child Psychiatry, 1,* 141–146.

Sandler, A.M., & Wills, D.M. (1965). Preliminary notes on play in the blind child. *Journal of Child Psychology, 1,* 7–10.

Seligman, M. (1975). *Helplessness.* San Francisco: W. H. Freeman.

Sharlin, S., & Polansky, N. (1972). The process of infantilization. *American Journal of Orthopsychiatry, 42,* 92–102.

Skellenger, A.C., Hill, M.M., & Hill, E. (1992). The social functioning of children with visual impairments. In S.L. Odom, S.R. McConnell, & M.A. McEvoy (Eds.), *Social competence of young children with disabilities: Issues and strategies for intervention* (pp. 165–188). Baltimore: Paul H. Brookes Publishing Co.

Spitz, R. (1965). *The first year of life.* New York: International Universities Press.

Stein, D., Beebe, B., Jaffe, J., & Bennett, S. (1977). The infant's stimulus world during social interaction: A study of caregiver behaviors with particular reference to repetition and timing. In H. Schaffer (Ed.), *Studies in mother–infant interaction* (pp. 177–202). London: Academic Press.

Stern, D.N. (1977). *The first relationship: Infant and mother.* Cambridge, MA: Harvard University Press.

Stern, D.N. (1984). Affect attunement. In J. Call, E. Galenson, & R.L. Tyson (Eds.), *Frontiers of infant psychiatry* (Vol. 2, pp. 3–14). New York: Basic Books.

Stern, D.N. (1985). *The interpersonal world of the infant.* New York: Basic Books.

Sternberg, R.J. (1985). *Beyond IQ: A triarchic theory of human intelligence.* Cambridge, MA: Cambridge University Press.

Stocker, C., Dunn, J., & Plomin, R. (1989). Sibling relationships: Links with child temperament, maternal behavior, and family structure. *Child Development, 60,* 715–727.

Strain, P.S., & Kohler, F.W. (1988). Social skill intervention with young children with handicaps: Some new conceptualizations and directions. In S.L. Odom & M.B. Karnes (Eds.), *Early intervention for infants and children with handicaps: An empirical base* (pp. 129–143). Baltimore: Paul H. Brookes Publishing Co.

Strayer, F.F. (1980). Child ethology and the study of preschool social relations. In H. Foot, A. Chapman, & J. Smith (Eds.), *Friendship and social relations in children* (pp. 235–265). New York: John Wiley & Sons.

Tannock, R. (1988). Mothers directiveness in their interactions with their children with and without Down syndrome. *American Journal of Mental Retardation, 93,* 154–165.

Terr, L. (1988a). What happens to the memories of early childhood trauma? *Journal of the American academy of Child and Adolescent Psychiatry, 27,* 96–104.

Terr, L. (1988b). What happens to the early memories of trauma? A study of twenty children under age five at the time of documented traumatic events. *American Journal of Child and Adolescent Psychiatry, 27,* pp. 96–104.

Terr, L. (1989). Treating psychic trauma in children: A preliminary discussion, *Journal of Traumatic Stress, 2*(1), 3–19.

Terr, L. (1991). Childhood traumas: An outline and overview. *American Journal of Psychiatry, 148*(1), 10–20.

Thomas A., & Chess, S. (1977). *Temperament and development.* New York: Brunner/Mazel.

Thorndike, E.L. (1920). Intelligence and its uses. *Harper's Magazine, 140*, 227–235.

Tudge, J., & Rogoff, B. (1989). Peer influences on cognitive development: Piagetian and Vygotskian perspectives. In M. Bornstein & J. Bruner (Eds.), *Interaction in human development* (pp. 17–40). Hillsdale, NJ: Lawrence Erlbaum Associates.

Twardosz, S., Nordquist, V.M., Simon, R., & Botkin, D. (1983). The effect of group affection activities on the interaction of socially isolate children. *Analysis and Intervention in Developmental Disabilities, 13*, 311–338.

Walker, J. (1982). Social interaction and handicapped infants. In D.D. Bricker (Ed.), *Intervention with at-risk and handicapped infants: From research to practice* (pp. 217–232). Baltimore: University Park Press.

White, R.W. (1959). Motivation reconsidered: The concept of competence. *Psychological Review, 66*, 297–333.

Williams, R. (1980, February). *Symbolic play in young language handicapped and normal speaking children.* Paper presented at the International Conference on Piaget and the Helping Professions, Los Angeles.

Wolfenstein, M. (1954). *Children's humor: A psychological analysis.* New York: Free Press.

10

Facilitating Communication and Language Development

Sandy Patrick

Every time we teach a child something, we keep him from inventing it himself . . . That which we allow him to discover by himself . . . will remain with him.
Bev Bos

In teaching it is the method and not the content that is the message . . . the drawing out, not the pumping in.
Ashley Montague

Communication is the process of exchanging ideas, information, needs, and feelings. Words such as *communication, language,* and *speech* are often used interchangeably when describing the communication process, but each has a distinct and different meaning. *Communication* is a broad and general term that describes the process of exchanging information between at least two individuals; one individual must be the transmitter and the other the receiver. Before communication can occur, it must have some effect on the receiver. Communication can occur through verbal and nonverbal means. Speech and language are components of communication but describe specific processes. *Language* refers to a rule-governed system for representing concepts through symbols. Language can be either written, spoken, or signed. *Speech* specifically describes the motor movements that occur when an individual articulates the sound of a language and forms words.

Communication begins at birth when the infant cries and gazes at his or her parent or caregivers. In the early stages of communication, the infant conveys needs by vocal and gestural methods. Language and speech emerge when the child produces his or her first words. Efficient

Observation Guidelines for communication and language development from Dickson, K., Linder, T.W., & Hudson, P. (1993). Observation of communication and language development. In T.W. Linder, *Transdisciplinary play-based assessment: A functional approach to working with young children* (rev. ed.) (pp. 191–195). Baltimore: Paul H. Brookes Publishing Co.; reprinted by permission.

This chapter is dedicated to my parents, who practiced these beliefs; Jeanne, for tirelessly typing; my husband, who encouraged me; my friends and colleagues, who offered suggestions; the graduate students at University of Colorado, who helped me to see the unlimited dimensions of communication; and the parents and children who helped me learn.

speech-language and communication skills are critical for reading, writing, academic success, development of interpersonal relationships, and functional independence. The quality of one's life can be significantly affected if he or she does not have good communication skills. The foundation for speech-language and communication skills is established in the first 5 years of life (Lee, 1979). Approximately 5%–10% of the population present some type of communication disorder (Secord, 1989). With early identification and intervention, these communication problems can be minimized or eliminated. In this chapter, a communication and language intervention model is outlined and described.

LANGUAGE ACQUISITION

Before an intervention model can be described, one must understand how a child acquires language. Many research studies have tried to unravel this mystery, and many theories have flourished. Each theoretician has analyzed some component of communication (e.g., semantics, syntax, pragmatics, phonology, paralinguistics) in order to discover the key variables that result in language acquisition. Much more is known about the structure of language than about how it is acquired. Thus, educators have searched endlessly for the most efficacious intervention model.

During the 1940s and 1950s, linguists investigated structural aspects of language such as phonology and morphology and attempted to apply this knowledge to language learning (Shuy, 1984). In the 1960s, Chomsky looked at the role the child played in the learning process. He proposed that children learned language due to an innate ability to learn syntax. Skinner (1957) proposed the operant approach, which emphasized the key role environment and imitation play in the learning process. This approach suggests that language, like any other behavior, develops because it is reinforced. The role of the learner was de-emphasized. In the 1970s, sociolinguists, psycholinguists, and psychologists began to describe the communication process as a whole. All aspects of communication were viewed for both the form (i.e., phonology, syntax, morphology, semantics) and function (i.e., use of language) (Shuy, 1984).

From this research, it was proposed that the child is born with the ability to communicate and learn language but he or she must *reinvent* and discover language through a learning process. *Interaction* with language learning occurs in *naturalistic* and *meaningful contexts*. Communication and speech-language development evolve in an organized and definable pattern.

Behavioral Intervention Approach

A behavioral intervention approach has been one of the most widely used language models in clinical settings. Behaviorism evolved from a branch of psychology that analyzes how organisms learn. Learning theorists searched for scientific knowledge that would explain how all behavior, including language, is learned. According to Mowrer (1954) and Skinner (1957), language is learned or conditioned through association between a stimulus and the following response. According to these theorists, language is a set of associations between meaning and word, word and phoneme, statement and response (Owens, 1988). The strength of the stimulus–response association determines the probability of occurrence of a specified response. Language, which is the end result, represents chains or combinations of various stimulus–response sequences.

B. F. Skinner (1959), who was one of the most widely known psychologists associated with this theory, identified a number of laws that seemed to govern behavior. One of these laws explained how a behavior could be manipulated by the environment. Skinner identified the effects that consequences have on the rate of a behavior. When a desired event (e.g., food, social praise) follows an identified behavior (e.g., vocalizations), it increases the likelihood the behavior will occur in the future under similar circumstances. If an undesirable event (e.g., electric shock) follows a specified behavior, it decreases the chances for that behavior to occur in the future. As the behavior is repeated, learning occurs. Because speech and language are learned behaviors, these skills also could be acquired by implementing this model. Language is learned in response to the environment through the child's imitation of adult speech and reinforcement of his or her attempts.

One of the biggest shortcomings of a direct behavioral approach is the problem with generalization (i.e., children learn new linguistic behaviors in a highly structured setting but fail to transfer the newly learned skills to other situations and people) (Spradlin & Siegel, 1982).

By examining a traditional clinical therapy session, one can understand why language learned in this fashion does not transfer. For example, therapy usually includes one therapist and the child in a structured environment. The therapist determines which language structure will be learned and in which sequence. The linguistic forms that a child learns are acquired via a stimulus–response reinforcement paradigm and not acquired with normal discourse. Children are often required to repeat what has been said, name objects and events, describe flashcards, or ask contrived questions or requests (Spradlin & Siegel, 1982). Because the child has little control over the situation and limited opportunities to express his or her desires, needs, or intentions, the therapist must introduce primary reinforcement to encourage and motivate the learner and shape responses. For instance, a therapist may determine that the child needs to learn the meaning of various verb forms. The clinician presents various toys that perform action (e.g., bear that beats a drum, frog that jumps). If the child does not name the action spontaneously, the facilitator supplies the words and encourages the child to imitate the response (e.g., "Ernesto, you say 'Frog's jumping'"). The child is reinforced with social, token, or primary reinforcement and then encouraged to repeat the response several times because repetition is needed to learn a new behavior. During another session, the same materials are repeated but the clinician encourages the child to name the action spontaneously. The adult might prompt the child for the specific response (e.g., "Ernesto, what's the frog doing?") and decrease the frequency of reinforcement.

In this type of learning situation the adult initiates the interaction and maintains control within goal-oriented activities. Instruction is formal, direct, and systematic. Learning is motivated by the adult with external rewards (i.e., token, primary, social reinforcers). The child learns one small linguistic unit as the adult shapes the child's behavior. Therapy emphasizes acquisition of a linguistic form and not learning in general. Shuy (1984) describes this type of learning format as a "reductionist" approach because linguistic units are reduced to small parts in order to decrease the complexity of the task and facilitate learning. Children who learn with this model demonstrate difficulty generating the linguistic forms outside the clinical setting. A "constructionist" philosophy has affected education in general. "Constructionists" propose that children actively learn through self-discovery and exploration (Shuy, 1984). When learning occurs in naturalistic and meaningful settings, it is easier for the child to gather information because there are more clues to facilitate the process. Theoreticians and academicians have designed alternative remedial programs aimed at promoting language development in more naturalistic environments and with natural conversational discourse that is interactive (McLean & Snyder-McLean, 1978; Powell & Mahoney, 1986).

Naturalistic Intervention

Naturalistic intervention is based upon principles of *whole language* learning (Goodman, 1986; Norris & Hoffman, 1990; Winitz, 1983). Language is viewed as a process involving cognitive, semiotic (i.e., both linguistic and nonlinguistic communications), and social development (Norris & Hoffman, 1990). Through the integration of these three processes, children develop communication skills that express content, form, and use (i.e., semantics, syntax, pragmatics). With a whole language approach, the adult helps a child attend to meaningful aspects of the environment so that he or she develops an organized and adapted conceptualization of words. The child learns communication skills when his or her actions produce some desired effect on people within the social context. Through interaction, the child's utterances are expanded and refined to be more specific and conventional and to approximate the adult linguistic model (Norris & Hoffman, 1990).

INREAL (IN-ter-Reactive Learning) is a *naturalistic educational approach* that has been used with a variety of children with different disabilities and at different age levels (Weiss, 1981). The TPBI model incorporates the INREAL approach because it is a communication-based method of learning designed to be used in a classroom, clinic, or home environment. The INREAL approach facilitates general learning and oral and written language development and is based on the following principles:

- Language (oral and written) is a tool one learns to use by communicating. Language cannot be taught. Each person must reinvent language through meaningful social experiences. Learning language is a life-long endeavor.
- Becoming educated in American society occurs while learning and using language.
- Educators and parents must actively participate with children in the structure of natural conversation to support children's language learning.
- Educators and parents best support children's language learning when they are self-reflective about the intention of what they say and how it affects children (INREAL/Education Center, 1978).

The INREAL approach recognizes that children acquire language by interacting with their environment and through natural conversation. The facilitator's ability to interact and react to the child plays a key role in the intervention process. Children's acts, wants, reactions, and feelings must be clarified, restated, and reflected back to them at an appropriate linguistic level. Successful conversational interaction with children enables adults to support and expand children's learning. It is through communication, not correction, that children learn to talk. INREAL has identified seven conversational strategies that facilitate learning and communication. These strategies include the following:

1. S.O.U.L. (**s**ilence, **o**bservation, **u**nderstanding, **l**istening) is a key component for successful interaction with children. The adult must use "silence" to "observe" and "understand" the child's actions and verbal and nonverbal behaviors. Often, adults "talk to" children but not "with" them. By practicing S.O.U.L., the adult expresses to the child "I'm ready to listen and talk with you, and I will follow your lead." By using "silence" the adult *understands* the child's communicative efforts and can respond to him or her in a meaningful manner.
2. Mirroring is joining and reflecting the child's nonverbal expressive behaviors through genuine conversation. For example, if the child shakes his or her hand and the adult imitates the movement, the adult has "mirrored" the child. This technique helps the adult to establish a relationship with the child and begins a nonverbal conversation that includes turn-taking and responding.
3. Self-talk helps children associate words with actions and events. In self-talk, the adult talks about what he or she is doing, thinking, or feeling (e.g., "Mama picks you up").
4. Parallel talk—In parallel talk, the adult describes the child's actions, thoughts, or feelings (e.g., "You're happy," "You're jumping"). This technique also helps children associate words with actions and events.
5. Vocal/manual monitoring and reflecting (VMR) allows the child to know he or she has communicated and encourages more talking. With VMR the adult listens to what the child has said and then says it back conversationally. The adult can also correctly restate what the

child has said incorrectly (e.g., Child: "Da eep," Adult: "Dog sleep"; Child: "Bunny sleepin," Adult: "Bunny sleeping").

6. Expansion—With expansion, the adult listens to what the child says and responds by adding to the child's words and building on ideas (e.g., Child: "Mama, see the fire truck," Parent: "Yes, I see a fire truck. A big, red fire truck.").

7. Modeling—In modeling, the adult listens and converses without using the child's words and maintains or expands the child's topic through conversation. Because modeling is the way adults talk most of the time, it is easy to use it with children to the exclusion of other strategies. With young children, it is important to use the language they use when responding because using their words and then expanding on them helps children construct and develop their communication skills (e.g., Child: "Ball?" Parent: "We can play catch.").

All of these strategies allow adults to promote language development in children without the need for direct correction (Gardner, 1986; Heublein et al., 1991; Weiss, 1981).

Implementing the TPBI Model

Following the transdisciplinary play-based assessment, the team identifies the child's strengths and developmental needs and establishes goals to increase communication skills and play-based intervention can be implemented. Goals should be based on a normal developmental sequence (Schiefelbusch, 1978).

Communication goals should be implemented throughout the child's day and should be incorporated into play and routine activities such as mealtime and snacktime, bathing, hand washing, brushing teeth, dressing, and toileting. Children learn language throughout their daily activities.

Playtime should incorporate toys and materials that are developmentally and culturally appropriate and will increase skills in the areas of sensorimotor, social-emotional, communication and language, and cognitive development. For example, toys and events should be selected so they are culturally relevant to the child. A Ute tribe in southern Colorado constructed mobiles to put over their infants' beds that included pictures of symbols that were meaningful to the Native Americans and were also developmentally appropriate for cognitive and sensorimotor development (e.g., black and white pictures of a tepee, an eagle feather). They also selected tribal music to be used for children when they were fussy and needed to be calmed. For all children and especially children of color, it is important to provide a variety of crayons and paints to represent all skin tones and various colors of paper and play dough. The environment needs to include familiar pictures, toys, music, and books from many cultures (Sparks & the A.B.C. Task Force, 1989).

The facilitator should follow the child's lead and interests. This is a child-oriented approach (Fey, 1986) that includes three essential steps. The adult needs to wait for the child to initiate some behavior and to interpret behavior as meaningful and communicative even if that wasn't the child's intent, and to respond to the behavior in some communicative manner that will facilitate language development (INREAL strategies). The child is free to choose materials that suit his or her interests and are self-reinforcing, which means extrinsic (e.g., primary reinforcement) reinforcement is not necessary (Fey, 1986).

The adult's role is to establish a developmentally appropriate environment that matches the child's level of play (e.g., sensorimotor to imaginative play). After the environment has been organized, the adult needs to maintain the organization so that play remains thematic, coherent, and interactive (Norris & Hoffman, 1990). For instance, if a child plays with a toy conducive to a limited number of actions, the adult can help the child understand new relationships among objects by providing prompts and cues. If a child holds a baby doll and then throws it down because he or she has abandoned the toy due to limited knowledge of ways the toy can be manipulated, the adult can extend the child's understanding by focusing the child's attention on other objects. The adult might say, "Oh, here's a bottle," "The baby's hungry," or "Here's a diaper" and guide the child to feed or diaper the baby. While the child performs the behavior, the adult can describe the event so the child begins to associate the words with the actions and also learns how objects and actions can be related, extended, and organized into an event.

It is apparent that the adult must develop good observation skills (S.O.U.L.) and judge when the level of an activity is too abstract or complex or too simple. If an activity is above or below the child's age level he or she may exhibit a poor attention span or begin to "act out." The adult must modify the activity to meet the child's needs. Because the interventionist plays a key role in facilitating learning, he or she must consider the following variables:

1. Intervention is most effective when a child directs his or her own actions, and the facilitator unobtrusively directs the environment (Ayres, 1979).
2. Rapport between the facilitator and child will affect the outcome of intervention. The adult should treat the child as a conversational partner and a friend and facilitate learning through natural conversational interaction. It is important to show warmth and positive regard for the child and value his or her comments.
3. The adult should consider how eye contact, physical proximity, and positioning affect interaction and then modify these variables to enhance communication (Heublein et al., 1991). For example, when talking with a child, it is important to kneel or sit on the floor so the child and facilitator are at the same level. Eye contact with the child will begin the interaction by engaging him or her in a nonverbal conversation.
4. The facilitator and child should take turns and construct the sequential chain of a conversation (Heublein et al., 1991). The adult should avoid monopolizing the conversation and make sure the child takes 50% of the turns (Kaye & Charney, 1981). The facilitator should follow the child's lead and maintain or end a topic of conversation when it is appropriate. The use of *wait time* is a critical variable in the learning process and must be included in all conversational interaction with a child (Heublein et al., 1991). Rowe (1986) suggested that wait time should be a minimum of 3–4 seconds. Pausing, or waiting for the child to respond, gives the child time to process information. Adults often speak too quickly and interrupt a child's thinking, which interferes with their ability to express themselves.
5. To promote social relationships, it is important for a child to learn and use targeted communication skills in a variety of settings and with different conversational partners (e.g., parent, grandparents, brothers, sisters, teachers, neighbors, therapists friends) and small and large groups.
6. The interactor must be self-reflective and periodically videotape an interaction with the child and analyze the session (Heublein et al., 1991). The interactor should note the use of wait time, turn-taking, efficacy of an activity, and use of INREAL strategies. Although a nondirective intervention approach has been presented, the facilitator is urged to implement and evaluate different approaches that best meet the needs of a child and his or her family. All children are individuals with unique learning styles; consequently, the facilitator must be open to trying alternative approaches that might be more appropriate.

OBSERVATION GUIDELINES FOR COMMUNICATION AND LANGUAGE DEVELOPMENT: MODALITIES OF COMMUNICATION

A. What is the primary method of communication by the child?
  1. Eye gaze
  2. Gesture
  3. Physical manipulation
  4. Vocalization (nonspeech, e.g., grunts)
  5. Sign language
      a. Idiosyncratic
      b. Formal
  6. Verbalization
  7. Augmentation (e.g., symbol board)
B. What supplemental forms are used in communication?
C. What is the frequency of communication acts?

Communication Modalities Other Than Speech

INTERVENTION IMPLICATIONS

After a child has been observed interacting with a parent, facilitator, and a peer or group of peers, the team can determine the forms of communication the child uses and the frequency with which they occur. The modalities utilized depend on the disability and child's functioning level. For instance, a child with a hearing impairment who has not been exposed to a formal sign language system may develop an idiosyncratic or natural sign system to express basic needs and wants. A child with cerebral palsy who cannot use his or her arms or speak may indicate needs by using eye gaze. A child with a severe articulation problem may use physical manipulation and gestures to communicate. *An intervention principle for the child who uses modalities other than speech is to recognize and encourage the communication systems he or she utilizes to explore other available modalities, and to encourage development of higher-level communication skills* (e.g., oral communication, augmentative systems).

For the child with hearing impairments who has developed an idiosyncratic sign system, the team could recognize and formalize the sign system the child is using. This information could be shared with everyone who cares for and interacts with the child. Additional "sign vocabulary" that the child needs to communicate more effectively could be generated by the teacher, parent, and other team members. These signs could be added to the child's communication system and expand the child's skills. For the child with cerebral palsy who gazes toward desired objects, a communication board that includes pictures might be introduced. If the child cannot nod his or her head for "yes" or "no," an alternative "yes" or "no" system might be devised. For example, the child may indicate "yes" by closing his or her eyes and "no" by wrinkling the nose. For the child with a severe articulation problem, gestures and physical manipulation are acceptable, but, the child should be encouraged to vocalize when expressing wants. The child could be given a choice of items in a question (e.g., "Bobby, do you want milk or juice?"). The adult would accept the gesture and any vocalization (e.g., grunt). Gradually, the vocalizations could be developed to closer approximate the first sound of the word or a close approximation of the word.

In some instances, it may be necessary to help a primarily vocal child use supplemental nonvocal techniques when there is a communication breakdown (Musselwhite & St. Louis, 1982). For example, a child with a severe oral motor and speech disorder, such as dysarthria, might be intelligible only when a context is known. The child could be encouraged to use a nonvocal method, such as a communication board with pictures, to establish a context and increase the child's functional communication. Initially, the child could be encouraged to vocalize and point to the pictures, but as the child's speech intelligibility improves he or she could decrease use of the board and only use it as a back-up system.

Whenever planning to implement supplemental or augmentative communication systems, the team should make sure the child has the needed prerequisite or precursor skills before expecting him or her to develop higher-level communication skills. For instance, before a child can nod his or her head to indicate "yes" or "no," he or she must have a range of movement and head control. Before a child can use a picture board he or she must point or gaze at a named picture. Before a child can say words, he or she must demonstrate understanding of the words, communicate intention, and be able to vocalize. For a child to use a gestural sign system, he or she needs good fine motor abilities and appropriate cognitive abilities.

A key intervention principle is to increase the frequency of communication acts and help the child generalize the behavior to new situations. After observing the child with different individuals and situations, it becomes apparent that communication efforts occur more often in selected contexts. For instance, children often communicate during snacktime or with parents. Targeted behaviors that occur in selected situations can be identified, and the adult can increase the frequency of these acts. By increasing the frequency of the behavior, the child is given an opportunity to practice this skill repeatedly in a natural manner and master it. For example, if a nonverbal child occasionally requests more food by pointing toward a food item, the adult could use snacktime as an opportunity to increase the frequency of requesting and to expand the child's communication skills to a verbal level. When the child points to a desired food item to request "more," the adult could give the child the food and model the word "more." After repeated practice, the adult could model the word and then delay giving the child the item so the child has time to point and vocalize. When the child begins to request an item spontaneously by pointing and vocalizing, the adult could help the child generalize this behavior to other settings and with other people by involving the parents and asking them to use the same strategies (Harris, 1975).

In some cases, children attempt to communicate minimally. In these instances, the facilitator should observe the child closely and reward any communicative efforts. If the child is preverbal, the facilitator could help the child feel validated and acknowledged by mirroring or imitating the child's actions and engaging him or her in a nonverbal game. The facilitator could help the child to generalize interaction with others by involving the parent or teacher in the interaction and demonstrating the game.

Assessing Cognitive Skills with Piaget's Stages of Development

Before one can select an effective communication system or appropriate communicative modality system for a child, his or her thinking or cognitive skills must be assessed. For example one would not expect a child who is functioning at the 6-month developmental level to communicate by pointing and identifying pictures because a 6-month-old does not have the thinking skills necessary for completing this task. Children at this level are just beginning to realize that an object exists when it is not visible (e.g., child begins to search for a partially hidden toy). Because object permanence has not been established (i.e., a mental image of a three-dimensional object has not developed), it is unlikely the infant would ascribe meaning to a two-dimensional image that carries less information.

A child's cognitive abilities can be identified by comparing the child's skills to *sensorimotor stages* proposed by Jean Piaget (1951, 1952, 1954). Piaget, a philosopher and psychologist, proposed a theory of intellectual development and defined four different stages for normal cognitive development that includes the following:

- Stage 1—the sensorimotor stage (birth to approximately 2 years of age)
- Stage 2—the preoperational stage (2 years to approximately 6 or 7 years)
- Stage 3—the concrete operations stage (from approximately 7 to 11 years)
- Stage 4—the formal operations stage (adolescence)

Piaget proposed that these stages describe how children think and solve problems and reflect a normal developmental sequence. Because the focus of this section is the development of precursor cognitive skills that support symbolic thought (0–2 years of age), developmental norms are provided from substages of the sensorimotor period.

In addition to the child's cognitive skills, the facilitator must also consider the child's hearing, oral motor, fine, and gross motor abilities. By considering all of these variables, the team can select the most effective communication system for the child to use (e.g., gestures, vocalizations, eye gaze to objects, eye gaze to pictures, switch to access a computer.)

Piaget divided the sensorimotor stage into six different substages. These substages are used below as the developmental levels for modalities of communication. The descriptions of the developmental levels on pages 295–300 are adapted from Dunst (1981), Table 3, with permission.

DEVELOPMENTAL LEVEL

- Use of reflexes
    (0–1 months)

- *Vocal imitation:* Child cries when hears another infant crying (i.e., vocal contagion).
- *Gestural imitation:* Child does not appear to imitate movements.
- *Purposeful problem-solving:* Shows reflexive movements in response to external stimuli.

- *Object permanence*: Does not search for objects that vanish.
- *Causality*: Child does not appear to understand causal relationships.

INTERVENTION GUIDELINES

At this stage, the child shows reflexive reactions in response to the external world (e.g., sucks, grasps, tracks objects, cries). He or she does not search for objects that disappear, demonstrate an understanding of causal relationships, attempt to imitate movements, or exhibit intentional play behavior. *An intervention principle at this stage is to increase the child's level of awareness of people and objects by offering enticing toys he or she can hear, taste, and touch.* Through one-to-one interaction, the adult can help the child discover objects and learn about the world through all of the senses. When the adult interacts with the child, he or she must wait for the child to initiate interaction and respond to the child with INREAL strategies (e.g., mirroring, self-talk, parallel talk).

PLAY MATERIALS AND OPPORTUNITIES

Place the child in various positions (e.g., carried upright in the facilitator's arms, resting on his or her back, sidelying, placed on abdomen). Offer interesting visual experiences (e.g., black and white pictures and patterns, crib mirror, mobiles) and encourage visual tracking. Toys with auditory characteristics catch the infant's attention, (e.g., mobiles, music boxes, chime toys, bells). The child needs to hear voices and see faces and people talking. Vocalizations should be reinforced with smiles and a loving touch. Rattles should be placed in the child's hands so he or she will hear the sound and feel the object. Adults can mirror the infant's reflexive behaviors (e.g., infant protrudes his or her tongue and the adult imitates the behavior) to develop turn-taking. Interaction should be pleasurable and short in duration. Adults should follow the child's interests and present activities that engage him or her.

DEVELOPMENTAL LEVEL

- Primary circular reactions
  (1–4 months)

- *Vocal imitation*: Repeats sound just produced following adult imitation of the sound.
- *Gestural imitation*: Repeats movements just made following adult imitation of the action.
- *Purposeful problem-solving*: Coordinates two behavioral schemata (e.g., hand–mouth coordination).
- *Object permanence*: Attempts to maintain visual contact with objects moving outside the visual field.
- *Causality*: Shows signs of precausal understanding (e.g., places thumb in mouth to suck on it).

INTERVENTION GUIDELINES

At this stage, infants move their arms and legs and track objects visually. They accidentally hit objects with their hands or feet and repeat the movements. Late in this stage, infants begin to localize and react to external stimuli by turning toward a sound source. Vocalizations include cooing, gurgling, laughing, and crying.

Goals at this stage include increasing visual, auditory, and tactile awareness, turn-taking, spontaneous vocalizations, gestural and vocal imitation, and cause-and-effect relationships. Visual awareness helps the infant learn about objects and can be facilitated by presenting brightly colored and interesting toys. Toys can be moved on horizontal and vertical planes to increase tracking. Noisemakers (e.g., music boxes) can be placed in the child's visual field and moved slowly so the child will follow the objects with his or her eyes and begin to rotate the head to follow the sound source.

Rattles can be placed in the child's hands so that when he or she moves, the object will make a sound; this will encourage understanding of early cause-and-effect relationships. Toys can be placed by the infant's hands so he or she will accidentally bat or hit them. The adult can help the infant find his or her hand and get the hand into the mouth to facilitate early problem-solving. Infants repeat sounds and gestural movements if the adult imitates them; therefore, adults can observe the child's motor movements and vocalizations and imitate them. Interactions support and encourage turn-taking and increase vocalizations. Adults can facilitate the development of communication by also using *self-talk, parallel talk,* and *mirroring.*

PLAY MATERIALS AND OPPORTUNITIES

Present toys that are visually pleasing and produce sound (e.g., music boxes, bells, musical mobiles, chime toys, rattles of various shapes, colors, and sizes, crib mirrors, baby gyms). To help the child develop awareness of his hands or arms, a terrycloth bracelet with bells can be placed on the infant's wrists and ankles for short periods of time.

DEVELOPMENTAL LEVEL

- Secondary circular reactions
  (4–8 months)

- *Vocal imitation:* Imitates sounds already in his or her repertoire.
- *Gestural imitation:* Imitates simple gestures already in his or her repertoire, which are *visible* to him or her.
- *Purposeful problem-solving:* Repeats actions to maintain the reinforcing consequences produced by the action (e.g., try to make interesting sights last).
- *Object permanence:* Reinstates visual contact with objects (e.g., anticipate a moving object's terminal position, remove a cloth placed over his or her face, removes a partially hidden object).
- *Causality:* Uses "phenomenalistic procedures" (e.g., generalizes excitement) as a causal action to have an adult repeat an interesting spectacle).

INTERVENTION GUIDELINES

Goals at this level include *facilitating the development of cause and effect, object permanence, turn-taking, vocal and gestural imitations, and spontaneous vocalizations.* The infant follows falling objects, which indicates that he or she is beginning to understand relationships between the self and external events, and begins to experiment with objects (e.g., shaking, touching, smelling, tasting).

Young children are also beginning to develop object permanence and will search for a toy that is partially hidden. Adults can facilitate this skill by covering part of a toy, an object, or a face. Children will imitate sounds and gestures if they are *part of their repertoires*. The facilitator can imitate the child's action and then introduce a new movement and encourage the child to imitate it. For example, if the child pats a toy, the adult can imitate the movement, wait for the child to take another turn, and then pat hands and wait for the child to imitate the response. If the young child does not imitate the new action, the facilitator can mirror the child's actions. Adults can support development of communication skills by using *self-talk, parallel talk*, and *mirroring*.

PLAY MATERIALS AND OPPORTUNITIES

Play "fetch" with the child (e.g., adult picks up fallen objects repeatedly). Peekaboo can be played when changing the infant's diaper or during bathtime (e.g., a diaper or wash cloth can be draped over the child's face). A bottle, cookie, or music box can be partially hidden with a cloth, and the child can be encouraged to find it. Stand-up rattles can be placed on the child's high chair to encourage cause-and-effect awareness. Children enjoy looking at themselves in mirrors; this activity helps them to develop awareness of themselves and encourages vocalizations.

DEVELOPMENTAL LEVEL

- Coordination of secondary circular reactions
  (8–12 months)

- *Vocal imitation:* Imitates novel sounds but only ones similar to those he or she already produces.
- *Gestural imitation:* Imitates *invisible* movements made by self (e.g., sticking out the tongue) and novel movements composed of actions familiar to him or her.
- *Purposeful problem-solving:* Serializes two heretofore separate behaviors in goal-directed sequences (e.g., crawl or scoot to a toy, push a bowl aside to get a cookie).
- *Object permanence:* Secures objects *seen* hidden under or behind a single barrier.
- *Causality:* Touches an adult's hand to have the person instigate or continue an interesting game or action.

INTERVENTION GUIDELINES

At this point, the infant remembers objects exist even though they are out of sight. Memory is still not well developed so the child must see the object being hidden before he or she will search for it. Objects can be rotated and examined, which suggests that the infant is aware of three-dimensional attributes (e.g., size, shape, weight). Children use adults to help them start or to continue an interesting game. They may touch the adult's hand to request assistance. These behaviors suggest that the child is beginning to understand cause-and-effect relationships. With vocal imitation, the young child imitates novel sounds if they are similar to sounds in his or her repertoire; the same is true with gestural imitation as the child will imitate gestures if they are composed of familiar actions. Children begin to demonstrate appropriate social actions with objects (e.g., drink from a cup, hold a spoon). Adults can facilitate the development of verbal and nonverbal communication by using self-talk, parallel talk, and mirroring. Turn-taking skills develop when the adult engages in play with the child and demonstrates turn-taking.

Cause-and-effect toys are important at this time (e.g., busy boxes, pull toys, music boxes, adapted switch-activated toys). Adults can explore the toys with the child. In time, the child will learn how to manipulate the switches by themselves. Adults can help the child begin to develop functional gestures by modeling them (e.g., wave "hi," and "bye"; extend arms for "up"; extend open hand for "give me"). Functional use of objects can be modeled (e.g., comb hair, drink from a cup, eat with a spoon). Adults can introduce gestural games like pat-a-cake, "Piggy Went to Market," and "So Big."

PLAY MATERIALS AND OPPORTUNITIES

DEVELOPMENTAL LEVEL

- Tertiary circular reactions
  (12–18 months)

- *Vocal imitation:* Imitates novel sound patterns and words he or she has not previously heard.
- *Gestural imitation:* Imitates novel movements he or she cannot see self perform (i.e., *invisible* gestures) and has not previously performed.
- *Purposeful problem-solving:* Discovers "novel" means behavior needed to obtain a desired goal.
- *Object permanence:* Secures objects hidden through a series of *visible* displacements.
- *Causality:* Hands an object to an adult to have that person repeat or instigate a desired action.

Children at this level typically search for objects that vanish, which suggests development of object permanence; combine and relate objects; hand objects to an adult to request action; imitate novel sound patterns and words he or she has never heard; imitate novel movements he or she has never seen; begin to comprehend single words in context. Goals at this stage include increasing turn-taking, gestural and vocal imitation, spontaneous vocalizations, and comprehension skills.

INTERVENTION GUIDELINES

To help the child produce new words, the adult can watch the toddler's behavior and determine what he or she is saying. By watching for cues such as where the child is looking, pointing, or reaching, one can interpret their messages. When the child produces part of a word, the adult can repeat the corrected form. The toddler's comprehension skills can be expanded by labeling familiar pictures and objects. Adults can facilitate the child's communication skills by using self-talk, parallel talk, VMR modeling, and expansion.

Adults can help the child to develop natural gestures or formal sign language by modeling the response in a meaningful context. For example, when the child is eating, the adult could model the sign "eat" so the child would associate the sign with the event. When giving the child a cookie, the sign for "cookie" can be demonstrated. The signs should be used throughout the child's day and not just during therapy. *When considering an alternative communication system natural gestures, sign language, or augmentative devices, it is recommended that gestures and formal sign language be introduced when the child has a mental age of 12 months* (Musselwhite & St. Louis, 1982).

PLAY MATERIALS AND OPPORTUNITIES

Play hide-and-seek with familiar toys and objects (e.g., blanket, ball, music box, paper, dolls, spoon). Provide toys that can be related and will promote cause-and-effect and means–end thinking (e.g., water toys and water table, containers of different sizes and shapes with blocks, switch-activated toys, pots, pans, spoons). Let children help with simple household chores such as sweeping the floor or cleaning up spills. Read books and encourage picture identification.

DEVELOPMENTAL LEVEL

- Representation and foresight
  (18–24 months)

- *Vocal imitation:* Imitates complex verbalizations and reproduces previously heard sounds and words from memory; deferred imitation.
- *Gestural imitation:* Imitates complex motor movements; reproduces previously observed actions from memory; deferred imitation.
- *Purposeful problem-solving:* "Invents" means behavior, via internal thought processors, needed to obtain a desired goal.
- *Object permanence:* Recreates sequence of displacements to secure objects; secures objects hidden through a sequence of *invisible* displacements.
- *Causality:* Shows capacity to infer a cause, given only its effect, and foresee an effect, given a cause (e.g., sees a toy on a table and uses a chair or another person to obtain it).

INTERVENTION GUIDELINES

At this stage, object permanence has been established. The child knows that people and objects exist even if she or he can't see them. Thinking skills are expanding and the child demonstrates trial-and-error problem-solving. He or she recalls past events and exhibits deferred imitations (e.g., 22-month-old child lies down on the floor while pretending to talk on the telephone in imitation of teenage sister).

Symbolic play, which reveals the child's ability to represent objects or feelings and ideas, is present. Children can assume different roles and demonstrate pretend play with objects, which shows their understanding of other people or objects as separate from themselves.

In the area of comprehension, the child understands many words and follows two-step directions. Expressively, the child produces two- to three-word sentences. Goals at this stage include increasing turn-taking, spontaneous and imitative vocalizations and verbalizations, and comprehension. Children who cannot produce speech at this stage should be encouraged to communicate by pointing to objects or pictures or to use natural or formal sign systems.

PLAY MATERIALS AND OPPORTUNITIES

Children enjoy searching for toys that disappear in sand, drawers or pockets. At this stage they like symbolic play, so props are important (e.g., doll with bottle and blanket, tea set, broom, telephone, car, blocks). Cause-and-effect toys (e.g., computer games, switch-activated toys) are recommended.

Bobby S., a 5-year-old Native American, was injured in a car accident and experienced brain injury. Prior to the accident, his overall development was judged to be age-appropriate. He was attending preschool and was described to be a happy and outgoing child.

A TPBA (Linder, 1993) revealed that Bobby vocalized but his speech was unintelligible, and he presented severe oral motor problems that affected eating and speech. Bobby walked independently but presented slight muscle weakness on the left side of his body. Bobby's cognitive skills were a strength. He enjoyed playing with cars and trucks and would link multischemes into simple combinations. For example, Bobby would put a person in a car, drive the car, and add more people systematically. Bobby tried to fix the wheel of a broken car with a piece of tape. In the area of "discrimination/classification, Bobby completed a simple form board and matched a circle, square, and triangle. When looking at a picturebook, he pointed to named pictures (e.g., shoe, boy, dog eating). He demonstrated difficulty sorting blocks by color or size, did not stack blocks, and refused to draw. To communicate, Bobby used natural gestures and pointed and grunted. He followed simple two-step commands and answered "yes" or "no" questions. Bobby's grandmother, the child's primary caregiver, reported that Bobby was beginning to throw temper tantrums when she couldn't understand him.

The team felt a priority for intervention was to improve Bobby's communication skills. An oral-motor and speech program to increase Bobby's vocalizations and eating was implemented. It was determined that Bobby needed to vary the types of vocalizations he produced. Bobby's grandmother, his teacher, and the team's speech-language pathologist decided to encourage sound exploration during mealtime, when brushing Bobby's teeth, and with singing. (Bobby enjoys music.) Bobby discovered new sounds through these activities. The adults in his environment observed Bobby, imitated his sounds, and modeled new sounds in a playful, nurturing way. Because Bobby presented low tone in his lips, tongue, and cheeks, it was recommended that these muscles be stimulated and strengthened. For example, before eating, Bobby was given an ice popsicle. The cold stimulated his oral muscles. While eating the popsicle, his grandmother or other adults encouraged Bobby to imitate playful lip and tongue movements. Bobby was encouraged to smack his lips and lick around the mouth when eating. Bobby massaged and stimulated the oral muscles after eating by brushing his teeth and washing his face with a terry cloth washcloth. Bobby's grandmother agreed to bring some tribal music tapes to the preschool so Bobby could share his favorite music with his friends. The teacher planned to use tapes during circle time so all of the children could learn new songs.

A computerized augmentative device that produced a voice was also introduced. Bobby's grandmother and the rest of the team identified common phrases that were necessary for Bobby to communicate at home and at the preschool, and these phrases were programmed into the computer. Bobby was encouraged to communicate by gesturing, vocalizing, and pointing to the pictures on the computer. The occupational therapist suggested that everyone encourage him to activate the computer with his left hand and to use both hands for common activities (e.g., play ball, manipulate cars, wash his face, clap hands, perform finger plays, finger paint, wash dishes).

OBSERVATION GUIDELINES FOR COMMUNICATION AND LANGUAGE DEVELOPMENT: PRAGMATICS—CHILD'S PRAGMATIC STAGE OR LEVEL OF INTENT

II.   **Pragmatics**
  A.   **What pragmatic stage or level of intention is demonstrated by the child?**
    1.   **Perlocutionary stage—lack of specific intent on the part of the infant, but behaviors are interpreted by the parent or caregiver**
    2.   **Illocutionary stage—use of conventional gestures or vocalizations to communicate intentions**
    3.   **Locutionary stage—use of words to show intent**

INTERVENTION IMPLICATIONS

Pragmatics and Communicative Intent

Pragmatics can be defined as the social *use* of communication. Bates (1976) described pragmatics as the "rules" that determine the use of language in a context. Recent research has highlighted the importance of pragmatics, indicating that pragmatics represent an overall organizing principle of language because the need to communicate precedes the development of form and content (Bloom & Lahey 1978; Grice, 1975). Children first acquire cognitive–pragmatic behaviors and then move down the ladder of hierarchy to semantics and eventually grammatic and phonologic skills. *Communicative intent* is one aspect of pragmatics. Bates, Camaioni, and Volterra (1975) identified a three-stage, developmental progression for communicative intention. The sequence begins with the perlocutionary stage, proceeds through the illocutionary stage and ends with the locutionary stage.

The Perlocutionary Stage

The perlocutionary stage is usually observed until the child is approximately 8 months of age. During this time, infant's movements are primarily reflexive, and the primary caregiver must ascribe meaning to the infants' cries and nonverbal behaviors. For example, a parent can usually tell when a child is in pain, hungry, or needs his or her diaper changed because of the difference in the way the child cries.

The Illocutionary Stage

The illocutionary stage can be identified when the child begins to use nonverbal behaviors consistently in a purposeful manner to convey intentional communication. Gestural communication begins to emerge and the child exhibits many functional gestures. For example, when the child points to or brings the adult a toy, he or she is demonstrating that he or she wants to play with the toy. At this stage, the child deliberately tries to communicate needs and wants nonverbally. Children begin to use common objects and understand their purpose (e.g., cup, spoon).

The Locutionary Stage

When the young child begins to produce words, the locutionary stage can be identified. The child first uses words that are accompanied by gestures. Later, he or she uses words that are of a concrete nature and pertain to the environment and a situation's context. As the young child's cognitive and linguistic skills expand, words become less context-bound and the child can talk about events that occurred in the past.

Intervention Principles that Promote Communication

Respond to the Child

During all three stages, an important intervention principle is to respond to the child in a timely and thoughtful manner since the foundation for later communication begins at this point. Infants and children learn that their cries and actions have meaning. Thus, the process of communication begins to emerge when the adult begins to "react" to the child's behavior. Acknowledging a child's preverbal and verbal behaviors reinforces his or her efforts and increases the frequency of these acts. Research has shown that infants who have been abused and neglected stop crying because they have learned that their cries do not bring help from their caregivers. Ainsworth and Bell (1972) found that infants whose mothers were more attentive and responded promptly were developmentally advanced relative to infants of unresponsive mothers.

Observe Changes in the Child's Behavior

Adults should develop keen observation skills and begin to notice subtle changes in the child's movements and typical routine patterns that signal the child's needs (i.e., practice INREAL interaction strategy—S.O.U.L.). For example, when the infant cries, a parent must decide if the baby is ill, hungry, or needs a diaper change. The parents of a premature infant may watch for motor movements that signal overstimulation. When a toddler first begins to produce close approximations of words, the adult must rely on the situation's context to understand the child.

Ascribe Meaning Based on Context

The adult should ascribe meaning to the child's actions and words based on the context of the situation and respond in a meaningful manner. Although movements at the perlocutionary stage are of a reflexive nature, the adult must treat overt behaviors as communicative acts and name and label them. For example, when an infant squints his or her eyes in response to sitting in the sun, the adult can say, "Oh, that sun hurts your eyes. Let's move." (i.e., parallel talk). When the child exhibits a motor behavior, the facilitator can "mirror" or imitate the behavior. For instance, if the infant protrudes his or her tongue, the adult can imitate this movement and wait for the child to repeat the movement.

Create a Need for the Child To Communicate

Another intervention principle is for the adult to create a need for the child to communicate. For example, when the child presents skills that are characteristic of the illocutionary stage and points toward objects, the adult can begin to give the child choices (e.g., food, toys) and increase the child's opportunity to express communicative intention. When the child begins to produce words, the adult could continue to offer the child choices but encourage verbalizations. For instance, the adult could pour milk and water and wait for the child to request the items. Clinical experience has shown that caregivers often antici- pate the needs of children with disabilities and can hinder the development of communication skills (Froshl & Sprung, 1983).

Collaborate with the Child To Communicate

Intervention should aim toward "bumping" the child up to the next higher- level skill by modeling and by providing prompts and cues. The adult should become a collaborator with the child in communicating messages more effec- tively (Norris & Hoffman, 1990). The adult must be sure prerequisite skills have been mastered before this can occur. For example, when presenting a bottle, it is important for the adult to show the infant the bottle and say, "Bottle, bottle, You want your bottle." When the infant begins to reach with the arms and hands, the adult can hold the bottle, name it, and wait for the child to show gestural intention and reach for the bottle. When the child begins to point, the adult can place the bottle out of reach, hold the infant, and say, "Where's bot- tle?" The adult should encourage the infant to point or look toward the bottle and vocalize. The adult can imitate the child's gestures and vocalizations and reward him or her with the bottle. As the child begins to look toward the bottle, when he or she hears the word, the adult can decrease the number of cues and prompts and begin to say only the word and wait for the child to search the room and find the bottle. If the child does not respond, the adult can drop back to a lower level, providing prompts and cues by repeating the name and show- ing the object.

Decontextualize the Child's Use of Language

When the child begins to express wants and needs with words, the adult should help the child begin to understand the names of objects when they are not present. For example, the facilitator can hide toys and ask the child to find the missing toy or ask them to go into another room and bring back a diaper, shoes, or a toy. When the child's cognitive and linguistic skills have developed, the adult can encourage the child to talk about past events (e.g., trip to the zoo, visiting a relative, a birthday party). This step is critical for developing reading skills later. With reading, the child must rely totally on the words for meaning.

DEVELOPMENTAL LEVEL

- Perlocutionary stage
  (0–8 months) (approximate)

- *Characteristics:* Child cries, coos, makes movements; intention inferred by adult

Observe the child, interpret behavior, describe, and imitate actions and vocaliza- tions. It is important to watch the child for clues that might indicate how to approach him or her. For instance, facial expressions, body posture, and move- ment signal whether a child is ready to interact. Establish eye contact and smile. Greenspan (1990) describes this phase of development as *the engagement phase.* The child is just beginning to learn the rules for communication. *Ascribe mean- ing to reflexive behaviors.* For example, when the young infant grimaces in re- sponse to some new food and accidentally moves his or her head, mirror or imitate the child's actions and say, "Yuk" or, "No." Pause and wait for the child to imitate your actions or present the food again and elicit the same response. At first, it will be a game, but with repeated practice, the head shake and facial grimace will become meaningful to the child because the adult reacted to the behavior in a meaningful way. When a child begins to explore use of his or her hands he or she often accidentally isolates finger movements and appears to point. It is important to acknowledge this movement, imitate it, and then *add to the response by pointing to objects in the environment.* At first, the pointing is unin- tentional but, with repeated practice, the infant begins to associate meaning with behavior.

During the perlocutionary stage, common objects and toys that involve action, are visually appealing, make a sound, or have a different texture are recom- mended because the child is beginning to learn about the world and everything is new and novel. Toys should be relevant to the child. The child needs playtime with objects and one-to-one interaction with adults. Interaction should be short in duration and match the child's attention span. By respecting the baby's needs, the adult is conveying to the infant that his or her feelings and prefer- ences are important and that the human world is deeply gratifying (Greenspan, 1990).

Playtime should be geared toward increasing cognitive, social-emotional, communication and language, and sensorimotor skills. Toys that encourage visual tracking and reaching and grasping help the child develop motor skills that can be used for gestural communication (e.g., mobiles, keys, cup, bottle, spoon, blocks, rattles, balls, bubbles). Children should be encouraged to ex- plore toys with their mouths and face (e.g., fuzzy stuffed animals, hard and soft rattles, rubber toys) (Liebman, 1977). This tactile input results in increased oral awareness and control, which helps the development of vocalizations. Vestibu- lar stimulation (e.g., rocking, swinging) also increases vocalizations in some children (Ayres, 1979). When the child vocalizes, the facilitator can imitate these sounds. Interactive games might include bouncing an older infant on a knee and then waiting for him or her to use some natural gesture (e.g., wiggle body to indicate "more"). To develop object permanence, play peekaboo and put a washcloth over the infant's face so he or she will remove it or partially hide a toy under a washcloth and encourage him or her to find it.

To help develop precursor skills for literacy (i.e., reading, writing, and speaking), it is important for adults to show infants simple books and describe the pictures (Garton & Pratt, 1989). Infants at this stage do not understand words or pictures, but they begin to associate books with a pleasant experience of being held and loved. Suggested books might include *Looking at Animals* (Bruna, 1972), and *Say Goodnight* (Oxenbury, 1987).

DEVELOPMENTAL LEVEL

- Illocutionary stage
    (8–12 months)

- *Characteristics:* Emergence of intention to communicate; demonstrates understanding of objects' purpose; displays full range of gestures

INTERVENTION GUIDELINES

Primary goals for intervention during the illocutionary stage include increasing intentional communication, vocalizations and gestural communication, and functional use of objects. Interaction can occur while playing with a toy or during daily activities (e.g., changing diaper, eating, bathing). *The adult increases intentionality by observing the child's actions and then reacting by mirroring the child's behavior and describing the actions with parallel talk and self-talk.* For example, if the infant drops a block in a container, the adult can wait for the child to complete the turn and then join the interaction by dropping a block into the container (mirroring). The action can be described as "in" (self-talk) as the block is dropped. The adult takes a turn and then waits for the child to take a turn. When the child drops the block, the adult can describe the action again as "in" (parallel talk). The game can continue until the child ends it. The child and adult are both focused on the activity and although the child doesn't comprehend the words, the repetition of an action paired with a word facilitates comprehension. The adult has responded to the child's behavior and ascribed meaning to the act. *The adult can help the child acquire new gestures and vocalizations by modeling new behaviors.* For example, when food is "all gone," the parent can model the word with a gesture and repeat the behavior. After repeated demonstrations, the adult can occasionally physically direct the child through the gesture. Encouragement should be offered in a playful supportive manner and should not be demanding or critical. *Routine activities that occur daily are the best times to repeat any activity to increase intentional communication and to help the child learn the use of objects.* For instance, bathtime is an opportunity for a child to explore the use of objects and practice communicating. Encourage the baby to explore a washcloth, soap, bottles, a comb, and a diaper. When the baby tastes a soapy washcloth and makes a face, the adult can react to the facial expression with a frown and say, "yuk," and then smile. Children often find this a fun game and repeat the facial expression for the parent. When the child accidentally drops a bottle, the parent can say, "uh oh," and smile. The child usually repeats the action. The washcloth or diaper can be used to play peekaboo. At first, the child removes the cloth when it covers the face, but when the adult adds meaning to the interaction and initiates peekaboo, the child eventually integrates the event and initiates the game. *The adult must respond and interact with the child in a joyful manner and convey love and acceptance.*

PLAY MATERIALS AND OPPORTUNITIES

During the illocutionary stage, cause-and-effect toys and common objects should be selected to increase cognitive and communication and language skills (e.g., Busy Box, jack-in-the-box, squeezie books, balls, hammer and pegs, pots and pans, plastic pots with lids, dolls, stuffed toys, play telephones, dolls, pop-up toys). The child learns something happens when an action is performed and begins to know he or she has an effect on the environment.

Introduce motor activities with songs or rhymes (e.g., bounce the child on the adult's knees and sing "Pop, Goes the Weasel"; with the word "pop" lift the child up in the air). Other fun songs might include, pat-a-cake, and "Piggy Went to Market." When playing games the child enjoys, it is important for the adult to stop periodically and wait for the child to communicate that he or she wants the game to continue.

To facilitate the development of literacy, it is important that the child be exposed to books and reading at this stage. Children enjoy being held while the adult names the pictures. They also enjoy turning the pages and chewing or mouthing books.

- Locutionary stage
  (12+ months)

DEVELOPMENTAL LEVEL

- *Characteristics:* Words accompany or replace gestures to express communicative functions previously expressed in gestures alone or gestures plus vocalization

INTERVENTION GUIDELINES

The goal of intervention during the locutionary includes increasing intentional communication and the variety of vocalizations and word production. Cognitively, the child needs to play with objects that can be used in a variety of ways. For example, with block play, the facilitator could observe the child manipulating and exploring the blocks. If the child bangs two blocks together, the facilitator can imitate the action and wait for the child to take another turn. If the child bangs the blocks together again, the facilitator could model changing the action by banging the block against the child's and wait for the child to take a turn. If the child repeats the action, the adult could model the sound "boom boom" as the child bangs the blocks together. With this sequence the child is expanding the number of actions that can be used with the blocks and is also hearing a fun sound paired with the action. Clinical experience has shown that children enjoy and often imitate sounds that are paired with actions (e.g., saying "boom boom" each time some one steps on a stair, saying "uh oh" when something falls down, saying "boo" during peekaboo, pairing motor sounds with car movements, saying "zip ziiip" when zipping up a zipper; pairing sound with movement of a crayon). Vocalizations then can be shaped to approximate words. If the child says "boom" when the blocks fall, he or she has used the /b/ sound and can be encouraged to say the word "block." At this stage, *adults should describe their actions (self-talk) and the child's actions and wants (parallel talk), mirror the child's acts, reflect and restate the child's vocalizations or approximations of words (vocal monitoring/reflecting), model new words and gestures, and expand the child's comments through natural conversational interaction.* For example, if the child and adult are playing with a child or another adult, the adult could encourage the child to use gestures (e.g., "Let's wave and say 'bye-bye' to the baby," "Let's blow Daddy a kiss").

PLAY MATERIALS AND OPPORTUNITIES

Children need toys that can be explored and acted upon with a variety of schemes and can be used functionally (e.g., blocks, pots and pans, buckets and blocks, balls, cars, baby dolls and bottles, cups and spoons, Busy Boxes, toy telephones). Picturebooks that include animals, actions, and common objects are recommended.

To develop literacy (e.g., reading, writing, speaking skills), it is important the child have experiences looking at books, listening to 1-minute stories, and practice with crayons and paper and paints. Children need to observe others reading and writing. Children enjoy learning language with song. Give them many opportunities to repeat songs, finger plays, and interactive games. It is important for the adult to express joy when interacting with the child.

EXAMPLE

Ari A. is a 12-month-old Greek child with Down syndrome. Ari presents motor, speech-language, and cognitive skills that are characteristic of a 6- to 9-month old infant. He is beginning to sit independently and gets on all fours and rocks back and forth. He bites, pulls, bangs, and shakes toys. Ari does not demonstrate functional use of objects or demonstrate relational play. He imitates vocalizations and actions that are a part of his repertoire.

Ari presents perlocutionary level of intentionality. He smiles, cries, and vocalizes to express his needs, but intentionality is inferred by the adults in his environment.

The occupational therapist reported that Ari's overall muscle tone is hypotonic. He demonstrates a weak grasp and becomes fatigued quickly with motor activity. Ari holds his mouth in an open position with his tongue held in a forward manner. Drooling occurs during all activity.

The occupational therapist recommended that the family provide tactile stimulation to Ari's facial muscles to increase tone. The therapist demonstrated playing pat-a-cake on his cheeks and stroking his lips and tongue to increase muscle tone. She suggested that the parents introduce these playful activities before and during mealtime and bathtime. She also encouraged them to play with Ari on the floor and offer fun toys and activities that would motivate him to stay up on his knees for extended periods of time.

The speech-language therapist suggested that the family engage in playful interaction with toys and one-to-one interaction. It was recommended that Ari's parents talk to him throughout the day with short sentences (self-talk). The parent could describe his or her actions (e.g., "Mom's gonna get the bottle," "Dad's gonna sit you down"). When Ari plays with toys, it was suggested that his parents watch his actions and mirror them. For instance, if Ari picks up a rattle and shakes it, his mom or dad imitates him. Mr. and Mrs. A encouraged him to vocalize more often by rocking, tickling, and singing to him. When he vocalized, they could imitate his actions. They could use parallel talk and describe Ari's actions (e.g., "You're smiling," "You're shaking that toy"). To expand and increase his actions and vocalizations, Mr. and Mrs. A. imitate Ari's actions and then wait until after his turn. They then vary the action slightly so it is still a part of his repertoire. For instance, if Ari shook a rattle, a parent imitated the movement, waited for Ari to take a turn, and then varied the act. For example, a parent might drop a rattle and wait for him to imitate the new behavior. The same procedure could occur with vocalizations by imitating Ari. Ari's parents could also model intentional gestures for him (e.g., waving bye-bye, giving up a toy when cued with an open hand, raising his arms when a parent says "up," gesturing with arms, playing "So Big").

OBSERVATION GUIDELINES FOR COMMUNICATION AND LANGUAGE DEVELOPMENT: PRAGMATICS—IMPLIED MEANING, FUNCTIONS

B. **What meaning is implied by the child's gestures, vocalizations, and verbalizations?**
   1. **Seeking attention**
   2. **Requesting object**
   3. **Requesting action**
   4. **Requesting information**
   5. **Protesting**
   6. **Commenting on an object**
   7. **Greeting**
   8. **Answering**
   9. **Acknowledging other's speech**
   10. **Other**
C. **What functions does the child's communication fulfill?**
   1. **Instrumental (to satisfy needs or desires)**
   2. **Regulatory (to control the behavior of others)**
   3. **Interactional (to define or participate in social interchange)**
   4. **Personal (to express personal opinions or feelings)**
   5. **Imaginative (to engage in fantasy)**
   6. **Heuristic (to obtain information)**
   7. **Informative (to provide information)**

INTERVENTION IMPLICATIONS

The stage of "communicative intent" demonstrated by a child and the functions and meanings he or she expresses are interrelated. After the level of intentionality has been determined, the child's intended meaning can be identified. As with intentionality, function or meaning also emerges in a developmental sequence from prelinguistic to single words to multiword stages. At 9–12 months, the young child exhibits *requests* (instrumental) and *commands* (regulatory) through gestures and vocalizations (i.e., meaning is conveyed without words) (Westby, 1980). By 13–17 months, the child varies the types of meanings that are expressed and begins to use some words, and by 17–19 months, he or she uses a greater number of functions and more words. By 22 months, the child begins to use the same functions but expresses them with two-word combinations. As development proceeds, the child uses a variety of the functions and expresses ideas with more complex semantic and grammatical forms.

"When identifying the level of intent, function, or meaning of an utterance, gesture, or vocalization, descriptions of the child's behaviors and the context in which the behavior was observed must be included" (Dickson, Linder, & Hudson, 1993, p. 169) Descriptive information helps the team plan appropriate goals that will best meet the child's needs. For example, if a child appears to be verbal but his or her language usage is limited (e.g., uses intentions only to greet and protest), goals should include increasing the number of intentions by creating a need for communication. The facilitator could fail to give the child a cookie at snacktime or a crayon for art work. This would encourage the child to request objects. If during snacktime the child routinely gestures to indicate wants, the adult could wait to respond, which will prompt the child to vocalize to express what he or she wants.

Responding to Communicative Behavior

The adult should observe the child using S.O.U.L. (see pp. 290–291), understand the child's communicative intention, and respond to the communicative behavior. When an infant pulls the glasses from the adult's face, the adult should react by describing the child's action (parallel talk) (e.g., "Oh, you want my glasses"). When a child cries, a parent or caregiver might say, "Oh, Mama will feed you" (self-talk). When the child points at his or her nose, the parent might imitate this action (mirroring) and say "nose." When a child says "more" when requesting candy, the adult could say "more candy" (expansion).

Rearranging the Environment

Adults should also help the child to expand and increase the frequency of communicative acts and expand the range of communicative functions. Research has shown that children with language impairments may express a limited range of communicative functions. *The adult can facilitate the development of a variety of functions by organizing the environment in such a manner that it creates a need for the child to communicate.* Fey (1986) noted that setting up the environment to elicit a specific structure is not an easy task and requires practice and many "hit and miss efforts" (p. 206). Yet, the adult can change the environment so the child needs to communicate. For instance, the adult can encourage the nonverbal child to request more food by pausing between bites and waiting for the child to vocalize a request for the object. The adult might place a toy out of reach so the child must ask for help and request it (request object/instrumental). One could hide a toy in a container that is difficult to open so the child must ask the adult to "open it" (request for action/instrumental).

Advancing to a Higher Developmental Level

As with other areas of development, it is important to help the child move to the next developmental level. If a child does not show any communicative intention, but all movements are of a reflexive nature, the adult must ascribe meaning to the child's acts (e.g., parallel talk, self-talk, mirroring). Through the process, the child discovers that his or her acts are meaningful and moves to the next stage of development in which he or she demonstrates intentional communication with gestures. The gestures can be expanded to close approximations of words if the adult uses the same reactive strategies (e.g., self-talk, mirroring, parallel talk). At the verbal stage of intentionality, the child's single-word functions can be increased to two-word and multiword utterances by using vocal monitoring and reflecting, and modeling and expansion. For example, if a child points at a stuffed dog and says "dog," the adult responds to the child by *expanding* the utterance (request object) by saying, "Want the dog" and giving the child the toy. If the child hands the adult a jar and says, "oh, oh" to indicate "open the jar" (request action), the adult can say, "Open" (vocal monitoring and reflecting). If the child says, "Shoe?" while pointing to a shoe box (request information), the adult could say, "Shoes in box?" (expansion).

- Attention seeking
    (12–18 months)

- *Definitions:* Solicits attention to self or aspects of the environment: has no other intent.
- *Prelinguistic:* Child tugs on his or her mom's skirt.
- *One Word:* "Mommy" as she tugs on skirt.
- *Multiword:* "You know what?"

The adult must be aware of the child's early efforts to communicate and must acknowledge these acts appropriately; this says to the child, "you are important" and "you get attention when you speak or act." For example, if the child smiles, the parent can smile back. When the child vocalizes, the parent can respond by vocalizing back to the child. However, it is important that the adult not "overhelp" or "overpraise" a child and create dependence and passivity. Froschl and Sprung (1983) did an observational study of preschool children between the ages of 2½ and 5 years. They found that girls and children with disabilities are "overhelped" (i.e., their needs are anticipated and met so they never have to ask for help and do not learn how to do tasks independently). Boys, however, are encouraged to be independent. They are verbally and nonverbally encouraged to complete tasks without assistance. For intervention, the adult can select an activity and appear to ignore the child. The adult can sit a short distance from the child and focus on the activity. The adult needs to avoid looking at the child so he or she must vocalize or gesture to gain the adult's attention. *The key is to wait for the child to seek the adult's attention and then reward the child by responding immediately and with pleasure.*

It is important to respond to the child so that he or she feels motivated to initiate interaction.

- Request objects
    (13–17 months)

- *Definitions:* Demands desired tangible object: includes requesting consumable and nonconsumable objects.

- *Prelinguistic:* Child points to a dog he or she wants.
- *One Word:* "Dog."
- *Multiword:* "Give me dog."

INTERVENTION GUIDELINES

The adult should select toys and foods that appeal to each individual child. The adult can visually present the item and use the S.O.U.L. method (see pp. 290–291) and wait for the child to reach, point, or gaze at the item. The adult can also routinely offer the child a choice of two items (e.g., clothes, food, toys). This encourages the child to request a specific object. When the child points to indicate needs, the adult can label the desired item. When the child vocalizes names of objects, the adult can expand the utterance. For example, if the child says, "dog," the adult could say, "Give you the dog" or use parallel talk, "Give me the dog." The adult can also provide the child with a phonemic prompt when the child knows the word but cannot think of it at the moment (e.g., "Want the c ___ (cat)" (Norris & Hoffman, 1990).

PLAY MATERIALS AND OPPORTUNITIES

Select toys and foods that match each individual child's interests and level of play so he or she feels motivated to obtain the toy or food. It is also critical to select toys that will increase the child's sensorimotor abilities.

DEVELOPMENTAL LEVEL

- Request action
  (13–17 months)

- *Definitions:* Commands another to carry out an action: includes requesting assistance and other actions involving another person or between another person and an object.
- *Prelinguistic:* Child puts adult's hand on jar while looking at the adult.
- *One Word:* "Open," while giving jar to adult.
- *Multiword:* "Mama, open bottle."

INTERVENTION GUIDELINES

The adult must create a need for the child to communicate by providing "communicative enticers" (e.g., provide activities that will encourage *requesting*). It is important to *draw the child's attention to the event* and then *wait* for a response. When the child attempts to communicate the facilitator should *accept* the communicative modality the child utilizes and extend the child's knowledge with vocal monitoring and reflecting, modeling, or expansion. For example, if the child requests an object by pointing and grunting the adult can offer the object and label the referent. After repeated experiences, the child will begin to produce a close approximation of the word. If a child is also learning a sign language system, the adult should accept the natural gesture and model the formal sign for the referent. When the child acquires the name of the desired event, the adult can expand the communicative utterance by using expansion and modeling.

PLAY MATERIALS AND OPPORTUNITIES

Provide toys and activities that are appealing to the child and also require assistance from an adult (e.g., swinging on a swing, riding a mechanical horse at the grocery store, going down a high slide, opening a jar that contains a favorite toy or food, turning a knob on a musical instrument, riding a merry-go-round, playing ball, lifting the child up in the air and then putting him or her down and waiting for a signal to repeat the action, playing tickle games and waiting for the child to signal that he or she wants the action repeated, waiting for the child to bring his or her coat to the adult for assistance, blowing bubbles, taping a balloon out of the child's reach so he or she needs to ask for help reaching it). When the child gestures to indicate wants, the adult can provide words that describe the child's thoughts. For example, if the child puts the adult's hand on a jar while looking at the adult, the adult can say, "open" and open the jar. When the child uses gestures and words and says, "Open," the adult can expand the utterance by saying, "Open the bottle?" To further expand an older child's language and develop more abstract thought, the adult can use a *relational prompt* (Norris & Hoffman, 1990) or ask for clarification. A relational prompt indicates to the child that more information is needed and cues the child to the type of information that is necessary. For example, if the child says, "Open the jar, Mama," the adult may respond, "Open the jar *because* (relational/causal prompt)." The child then says, "Because the lid's broken," and the parent could expand the child's knowledge by saying, "Oh, the lid's *too tight.*"

DEVELOPMENTAL LEVEL

* Request information
    (24 months)

* *Definitions:* Finds out something about an object or event: includes "wh-" questions and other utterances having the intonation contour of an interrogative.
* *Prelinguistic:* Child points to shoe, and with intonation of question, says "Uh?"
* *One Word:* "Shoe" while pointing to shoe box.
* *Multiword:* "Where shoe?"

INTERVENTION GUIDELINES

The adult can present activities and then model the question form. At the prelinguistic level, the adult could say, "huh?" with a puzzled look when examining a new or novel toy or looking at a picture and asking a question with rising intonation (e.g., "Daddy" [where's daddy?]). By talking out loud, the adult has demonstrated how people think and has modeled a question form. When the child asks questions with a single word and rising intonation, the adult could model a two-word question form (e.g., "What's that?" "Where's _____?"). When children are practicing this skill, they frequently ask the adult "wh____" questions even though they know the answers. "Yes" or "no" questions are usually produced when children are 2 years of age; "where" and "who" questions usually emerge by 2½–3 years; "why" and "how" are present by 4–5 years; and "when" questions are the last to occur at 5–6 years.

PLAY MATERIALS AND OPPORTUNITIES

Lucas (1980) said that interventionists can act as "saboteurs" and omit critical items from the environment so the child needs to verbally interact (e.g., a child's chair might be removed, he or she might be given a cup with a hole in the bottom, a coat and shoes might be hidden, the adult may "forget" to give the child a snack or crayon). Photographs and picturebooks are also useful for eliciting "what," "where," and "who" questions. The adult can also help a child formulate "wh_____" questions by interacting with a third party. For instance, the adult might prompt the child to ask for something (e.g., "Let's ask Grandma 'Where's the cookies,'" "Ask Daddy 'where's the keys?'"). While playing with dolls or a puppy, the adult might prompt the child to ask the doll, "Where's the bottle?"

DEVELOPMENTAL LEVEL

- Protest
  (13–17 months)

- *Definitions:* Commands another to cease an undesired action: includes resisting another's action and rejection of object that is offered.
- *Prelinguistic:* Child pushes the adult's hand away when an undesired food item is offered.
- *One Word:* "No," in response.
- *Multiword:* "No peas, Mama."

INTERVENTION GUIDELINES

A child typically "protests" before intentionality emerges by responding with a natural gesture (e.g., moving away from something unpleasant, crying when disliking a position). At this early stage of development, the adult needs to respond and honor the child's wishes when possible. The adult also needs to model appropriate gestures and say "No." When the child says "No," the adult needs to expand the child's response by adding "No more _____."

PLAY MATERIALS AND OPPORTUNITIES

Toys and activities should be selected based on the child's individual dislikes. Communication and language skills should be learned in meaningful situations. When a child turns his or her head away from food, the adult can model the word and gesture for "no." If the child dislikes a particular food, the adult could give the child choices and present the undesirable item so the child can refuse it.

DEVELOPMENTAL LEVEL

- Comment on object
  (13–17 months)

- *Definitions:* Directs another's attention to an object: pointing, showing, describing, informing, and interactive labeling.
- *Prelinguistic:* Child holds up toy car toward the adult and smiles while looking at the adult.
- *One Word:* "Car," said while pointing.
- *Multiword:* "My car."

INTERVENTION GUIDELINES

The adult can increase the child's level of intentionality by requesting an object, naming it, and then returning it to the child. This game progresses to the child spontaneously bringing the adult a toy. The adult can also model pointing to objects and naming them or naming objects that the child looks at, points to, or explores. A "cloze" prompting strategy can also be used (Norris & Hoffman, 1990). The adult pauses so that the child can supply needed information. "Here's a _____. There's a _____." "Gestural and pantomime" prompts can be provided. (Norris & Hoffman, 1990). These prompts provide the child with nonlinguistic cues to prompt ideas that need to be expressed. For example, the adult could point to items: "We need a (brush) to fix your (hair)."

The adult and child can point at body parts and play the "beep-beep" game with the nose (i.e., push the child's nose and say "beep beep, nose") or "I'm gonna get your nose, tummy" and so forth. During bathtime, the adult can introduce a terry cloth puppet and tickle the child's nose and name it. The child can be encouraged to reciprocate and use the puppet to find and name his or her mother's body parts. The adult can name toys when they are removed or returned to a toybox, or when they are on a shelf, or name and label toys as the child manipulates them (e.g., "ball," "car," "baby"). A "feely box" is a good way to increase labeling and naming. Books also encourage naming and labeling. A child first identifies things in his or her environment and the adult should name clothes, household items, outdoor items, and furniture before emphasizing adjectives and adverbs.

PLAY MATERIALS AND OPPORTUNITIES

- Comment on action
  (12–18 months)

DEVELOPMENTAL LEVEL

- *Definitions:* Calls listener's attention to the movement of some object or action of others or self.
- *Prelinguistic:* Laughs and looks at adult while adult falls down.
- *One Word:* "Down" as adult falls.
- *Multiword:* "Bobbie fall down."

The adult can respond to the child's actions in a nurturing way (i.e., smile, laugh, imitate the child's actions). For instance, when the child knocks blocks down, the adult can smile and imitate the actions, say, "uh oh," and then stack the blocks so the child can repeat the action. When the child produces single words, the adult can expand the child's utterances by using the child's words. For example, the child may say, "Down" when the blocks fall, and the adult can say, "Fall down."

INTERVENTION GUIDELINES

At this developmental level, toys that have moving parts and can be manipulated are ideal. For example, wind-up toys are motivating and entertaining (e.g., a fish that swims, a jumping frog, a moving car). Balls, cars, jack-in-a-boxes, Busy Boxes, pop-up toys, and blocks offer a variety of actions. Action games help the child discover movement through self-discovery (e.g., Ring-around-the-rosy, London bridge is falling down). Songs and fingerplays help the child watch others pair words and actions together (e.g., Wheels on the bus, pat-a-cake). The adult can model describing a peer's movements when children are interacting together in a group. Art activities encourage exploration and the

PLAY MATERIALS AND OPPORTUNITIES

discovery of actions (e.g., coloring with crayons, painting with brushes and fingers, gluing paper).

DEVELOPMENTAL LEVEL

- Greeting
    (13–17 months)

- *Definitions:* Communicates salutation and offers conversation rituals: "hi," "bye," "please," and "thank you."
- *Prelinguistic:* Child waves as mother leaves.
- *One Word:* "Bye."
- *Multiword:* "Bye, Mom."

INTERVENTION GUIDELINES

The child initially learns these responses when he or she observes and hears others say the words in the appropriate contexts. The adult can model the behavior (e.g., waving, saying please and thank-you for the child when it is appropriate). When the child produces single words such as "bye" and "hi," the adult can expand the utterances and add additional words to increase the length of the child's utterance. The adult can not force the child to learn or imitate the words, but if the behavior is modeled repeatedly in a natural conversational manner, clinical experience has shown that children typically begin to use the constructions.

PLAY MATERIALS AND OPPORTUNITIES

Salutations and conversational rituals should occur during daily routine activities (e.g., snack/mealtime [please, thank-you]). When leaving or entering a room, the child can greet toys, pets, and people. "Hi" and "bye" can be modeled when putting toys away or when watching a toy disappear (e.g., jack-in-the-box, a toy hidden in Styrofoam "peanuts," sand, beans).

DEVELOPMENTAL LEVEL

- Answering
    (9–18 months)

- *Definitions:* Responds to request for information.
- *Prelinguistic:* Child points to his or her nose to answer the question, "Where's your nose?"
- *One Word:* Child says "nose" in response to "where's your nose?"
- *Multiword:* "Here my nose."

INTERVENTION GUIDELINES

The adult must begin turn-taking by observing the child and responding to the child's actions in a meaningful way. For example, when the child points to or touches an object, the adult can name and label it. After many repetitions, the child will comprehend the name of a referent when he or she hears it. The adult can play an interactive game (e.g., "Where's your tummy?"). If the child does not respond, the adult can show the child the object and name it. As the child begins to produce words, the same games can be played. Cuing and prompting strategies can also be used. For example, the adults can point to body parts and say, "Is this Mama's nose?"

Books, wind-up toys, jack-in-the boxes, balls, blocks, dolls, trucks, and cars are appropriate at this developmental level.

> - Acknowledgment of other's speech
>   (9–18 months)

- *Definitions*: Acts on utterances used to indicate that the other's utterance was received, not in response to a question; includes repetition of an utterance.
- *Prelinguistic*: Child acknowledges another's speech by turning head and smiling.
- *One Word*: Child says "yea" when favorite song is mentioned.
- *Multiword*: "My song."

The adult can demonstrate this function by responding to the infant's vocalizations. When the infant vocalizes, the adult can look at the child and smile. When the child vocalizes, the adult can look at the child and wait for the child to finish. The child's vocalizations can be treated as a conversation. For example, when the infant vocalizes the adult can nod his or her head and say, "Yes, is that so? Well, tell me more." This same type of respect and acknowledgment must be demonstrated for the child from the preverbal to the verbal stage. When the child begins to produce close approximations of words, vocal monitoring and reflecting can be used as a technique to acknowledge the child's utterances. When playing with peers, the adult can model acknowledging others' speech. For example, a child may say to a peer, "Eddie, see my balloon." If the child does not respond, the adult might prompt the child, "Eddie, Hannah's talking to you." This gives the child another opportunity to respond. If Eddie does not respond, the adult can model the correct behavior.

EXAMPLE

Jesús M. is a 3-year-old child with speech-language, cognitive, and motor delays. Jesús is the only boy in a family of four girls. His mother and father are migrant workers who recently came to the United States from Mexico. Both parents are learning English and are very proud of their newly learned skills, but would like their children to learn Spanish before English.

Jesús uses a combination of gestures and vocalizations to express intentions, demonstrating communication at the illocutionary stage. During the session, he used a limited number of functions and meanings. He requested a car by grunting and pointing (instrumental function/requesting an object), shook his head "no" when refusing a peanut butter sandwich (regulatory function/protesting), and greeted his family by waving "hi."

In the area of cognition, Jesús demonstrated exploratory/sensorimotor play and enjoyed toys that could be manipulated (e.g., bucket and blocks, car, Busy Box). He usually demonstrated a limited number of schemes per object and did not link schemes (e.g., dumped and filled a bucket but refused to stack blocks, pushed a car but would not put a person in a car, perseverated on moving one lever on the Busy Box, and minimally demonstrated functional use of common objects such as a wash cloth and Kleenex).

Jesús' social-emotional skills were characterized by extreme shyness. He avoided interacting with the facilitator and other children, tended to stay close to his mother, and avoided new situations. His mother reported that Jesús is cared for by his 12-year-old sister. She reportedly anticipates Jesús' needs and looks after him. Due to his shyness, he plays with few children.

The occupational therapist reported that Jesús' fine motor skills were delayed due to overall low tone. His strength and endurance were below his age level. He tended to avoid movement such as swinging on a swing or riding a merry-go-round. Mrs. M. reported that Jesús is particular about food and does not like sticky foods such as honey or peanut butter to touch his fingers.

It was determined that Jesús would be placed in a bilingual preschool setting where he could receive occupational and speech-language intervention and have an opportunity to increase his social and cognitive skills by participating in a classroom setting. Jesús' family agreed to interact with Jesús in Spanish, and his sister said she would read him bedtime stories in Spanish. Both Mrs. M. and Jesús' sister agreed to read a story to the children in the preschool in Spanish. Since Jesús' parents indicated they wanted Jesús to learn Spanish before English, it was decided that all bilingual adults would speak to Jesús in Spanish. In the preschool, he would be exposed to both English and Spanish speakers.

Speech-language goals included increasing the number of communicative intentions Jesús uses and expanding his vocalizations to closer approximations of words. The speech-language therapist recommended increasing Jesús' use of a variety of sounds through vocal play during mealtime and play. The occupational therapist recommended increasing muscle tone in his mouth and upper body and decreasing his tactile defensiveness. The teacher suggested Jesús' level of play be expanded so he will demonstrate a greater number of schemes and begin to link them.

The speech-language therapist, occupational therapist, teacher, and parent agreed to increase communicative intentions by encouraging Jesús to use a greater number of intentions (e.g., attention seeking, requesting action, commenting, answering), rather than anticipating his needs. Objects and actions would be presented, and the adult would wait for Jesús to initiate interaction.

Jesús' mother reported that Jesús wants to "help" around the house but she did not want him to get messy. The team discussed how the parent could encourage Jesús to "help" with daily activities. The occupational therapist highlighted how cooking tortillas could help decrease tactile defensiveness by exposing Jesús to different textures (e.g., sticky materials, dry flour) and that the patting, pounding, and rolling could help increase muscle strength and endurance. The teacher noted how learning functional tasks could increase Jesús' thinking skills and ability to associate and relate tasks into a scheme. The speech-language therapist said the cooking activity could be motivating for Jesús and that the parent could model "funny sounds" with actions and increase Jesús' exploration of a variety of sounds. For example, when patting the tortilla, the parent could model "pat, pat, pat" or taste the warm tortilla and say, "mmm." The speech-language therapist also described turn-taking, the importance of understanding Jesús' nonverbal communicative intentions, and various communicative strategies to use during the activity (e.g., mirroring, parallel talk, self-talk, reflecting).

OBSERVATION GUIDELINES FOR COMMUNICATION AND LANGUAGE DEVELOPMENT: PRAGMATICS—DISCOURSE SKILLS

D. **What discourse skills does the child demonstrate (typically and optionally)?**
    1. **Attending to speaker**
    2. **Initiating conversation**
    3. **Turn-taking**
    4. **Maintaining a topic**
    5. **Volunteering/changing a topic**
    6. **Responding to requests for clarification**
    7. **Questioning**

INTERVENTION IMPLICATIONS

Discourse is another area of pragmatics. Discourse describes the child's ability to act as a conversational partner. Components of discourse include attending to the speaker, initiating conversation, turn-taking, maintaining a topic, changing a topic, and responding to requests for clarification and questions. These conversational skills emerge in a developmental sequence. Despite the fact that discourse appears to require verbalizations, preverbal children demonstrate readiness skills for later conversational abilities (Dickson, Linder, & Hudson, 1993).

Early Discourse Skills

An infant demonstrates early discourse with his or her parent nonverbally with mutual eye gaze, vocal imitation, alternating vocalizations, and physical interchanges (Argyle & Ingram, 1972; Bruner, 1977; Stern, Jaffe, Beebe, & Bennet, 1975). As the child acquires words, discourse skills become more complex as he or she learns techniques to maintain and extend a topic of conversation. Techniques that children commonly use include the following: 1) revisions (focus operations and substitutions), 2) clarifications, 3) extensions, and 4) questioning. Revisions occur when the child repeats part of an utterance that he or she has just heard. For example, the adult says, "Let's go bye-bye," and the child says, "Bye-bye" (focus operation). Another type of "revision" includes a *substitution*. In this case, the adult makes a statement and the child changes the utterances; for example, if the adult says, "Bobby, get your coat" and the child says, "My coat." (Keenan, 1975).

Children use *clarification* to ask for repetition or additional information. With this strategy, children frequently ask, "What?" to keep interacting with the adult. *Extensions* are used when the child adds information to an utterance. For example, the adult may say, "Here's a tractor," and the child may say, "Red tractor." *Questioning* occurs when the child asks one question after another before the adult can respond. Excessive questioning by an adult or child can limit dialogue.

As discourse skills begin to emerge, the child learns appropriate use of different strategies and learns the rules for turn-taking. The child learns when to take a turn, how to take a turn, how long a turn should take, and when to not take a turn.

Higher-Level Discourse Skills

In addition to learning rules governing turn-taking and incorporating rules for maintaining a topic, a child must also begin to understand "role-taking" (Linder, 1993). Role-taking is a higher-level discourse skill. The child learns to monitor the listener and determine what is being understood. For example, the child must be able to modify his or her language when speaking with an adult versus a younger child. Research has shown that 4-year-old children use shorter simpler sentences when they talk with 2-year-old children (Gordon & Ervin-Tripp, 1984; Leonard, Bolders, & Miller, 1976). In addition to monitoring the listener, the child must also begin to self-monitor and determine what aspects of the conversation are being understood. This is often a difficult skill for children with language impairments and learning disabilities to learn.

Addressing Discourse Skills and Setting Goals

After a TPBA, the team can describe the child's discourse skills. Specific discourse components that should be addressed include the following: 1) whether a child initiates or responds to interaction; 2) describing the strategies a child uses to maintain conversation (e.g., clarification, revisions); 3) prelinguistic and linguistic behaviors that the child uses for turn-taking (e.g., request for information, request for actions, request for objects, acknowledgment); 4) the number of turns per topic; and 5) role-taking. The data can be used to determine the appropriateness of the child's communication skills and the child's desire to participate in a given interaction.

Intervention should emphasize developing discourse skills in a developmental sequence within natural conversational interaction. Specific goals vary with each child but there are some guidelines and principles that address conversational discourse that were proposed by Fey (1986). Fey stated that traditionally children with language impairments are diagnosed and described in terms of their ability to use and understand lexical and grammatical forms. Children are then described as presenting expressive language delays, receptive/expressive delays, or vocabulary or grammatical deficits. He proposed an alternative way to describe the abilities of children with language impairments based on their *social-conversational abilities.* He included suggestions for intervention for each particular style. The four types of conversationalists, according to Fey (1986), include: 1) active conversationalists, 2) passive conversationalists, 3) inactive conversationalists, and 4) verbal noncommunicators. The following subsections draw heavily on the work of Fey (1986) with the author's permission. Below, each conversationalist type is described and goals for intervention are recommended. Fey (1986) stressed the importance of using the intervention guidelines when they seemed to fit a child. Clinical experience has shown that there are always children who cannot be classified, or fit into expected profiles.

Active Conversationalists

Active conversationalists include children who exhibit "high levels of activity both as initiators of conversation and as respondents to the initiatives of their conversational partners" (Fey, 1986, p. 80). According to Fey (1986), these children realize that social conversational interaction is reciprocal and they demonstrate both interest in those with whom they are talking and a willingness to convey information. However, active conversationalists may have impairments of language forms (e.g., comprehension, expression); even in these cases, active conversationalists are usually able to communicate effectively. These children also may have pragmatic impairments. They may have trouble requesting information or exchanging words and phrases in conversation. "For example, they may use imperative forms and need statements (e.g., "I need a drink") but fail to make use of interrogatives to express requests for action (e.g., "Can I have a drink?" or "Where's my juice?")" (Fey, 1986, p. 81).

A goal recommended by Fey (1986) for the active conversationalist includes facilitating *"new content–form interactions to perform available conversational acts"* (p. 83). This may occur when the child asks "yes" or "no" questions, but does not include the auxiliary "do" in questions (i.e., the child asks, "Want a drink of water?" instead of "Do you want a drink of water?") (Fey, 1986).

Passive Conversationalists

It is important to help passive conversationalists, who respond to conversational discourse but infrequently initiate a conversational act, to become more active (Fey, 1986). It will be nearly impossible for children to acquire language if they do not take advantage of the opportunity to play and converse with others.

As Fey (1986) suggests, a goal for these children is to *"increase the frequency of use of available assertive conversational acts in a variety of social contexts"* (p. 88). For example, most children show some context in which they are likely to initiate conversation (e.g., a particular routine such as snacktime, with a specific person). Intervention can be implemented in that context by having the adult watch the child and encourage the child by providing prompts. Another goal Fey (1986) recommends is to *"increase the child's repertoire of assertive conversational acts, using existing forms, when possible"* (p. 88). This may entail encouraging the child to ask for clarification of deliberately vague statements the adult makes.

The adult's role in intervention for the child who is a passive conversationalist is to facilitate linguistic forms that will help the child to initiate conversational acts. One basic rule is that the adult should ask fewer questions and create scenarios in which the child must ask or request.

Inactive Conversationalists

Fey (1986) suggests that for an inactive conversationalist (i.e., a child who does not initiate or respond to communicative acts but often demonstrates the capability in selected contexts), a goal is to *"increase the child's rate of positive social bids (verbal and nonverbal) in a variety of social contexts"* (p. 93). Intervention emphasizes encouraging any attempt at social interaction. One *"specific goal might include increasing the rate of positive social responses to partners (e.g., smiling, sharing, associative and cooperative play)"* (Fey, 1986, p. 93). If the general frequency of socially directed behaviors and appropriate assertive and responsive behaviors is increasing, then specific acts or linguistic forms should be de-emphasized. However, because such requests are very beneficial, it may be productive to facilitate use of them.

Verbal Noncommunicators

According to Fey (1986), verbal noncommunicators are "children who are capable of assuming the role of initiator of conversations and conversational topics, but who fail to accommodate their own language to the needs of their partners" (p. 94). These children are usually very verbal, with a broad repertoire of conversational acts. The semantic–syntactic relationships that they employ may be similar to those indicative of normal language skills. These children's weaknesses are evidenced by their high rates of utterances that are only tangentially related, or are completely unrelated, to their own prior utterances or their partner's utterances. These children also often have difficulty initiating conversations on appropriate topics and sustaining exchanges concerning topics that have already been established.

A goal for the verbal noncommunicator includes attempting to *"increase the relatedness of the child's responses to the assertive acts (e.g., requestives, assertives, performances) of the partner"* (Fey, 1986, p. 97). Because these children produce divergent speech and have difficulty planning utterances that relate to prior utterances, questions and other requestives that place constraints on the way the child can respond are suitable.

Another goal for the verbal noncommunicator is to *"facilitate the child's production of sequences of utterances that are topically related to one another"* (Fey, 1986, p. 97). These children could speak in highly contrived patterns because they have comprehension problems. The adult must tailor conversation carefully to match the child's linguistic abilities. After the adult matches the child's comprehension level, this may increase the number of utterances regarding one topic.

Another goal for the verbal noncommunicator might include attempts to *"encourage the child to establish referents in a clear and unambiguous fashion"* (Fey, 1986, p. 97). Because the verbal noncommunicator fails to take the listener's perspective into consideration when planning utterances, he or she may tend to use too many pronouns and nonspecific nominals (e.g., "thing," "stuff") for which reference has not been established. More explicit language could be encouraged; for example, the adult could ask the child to specify the referents that he or she uses. (If the child says, "I don't like that stuff," the adult could ask, "What stuff?" The child would then clarify by saying, "The snow.")

Generalizing New Language Forms

Spradlin and Siegel (1982) noted that children often fail to generalize new language forms outside a clinical setting. They feel the reason for this phenomenon is that early interventionists rarely help a child decontextualize conversational discourse (i.e., talk about things not present in the immediate context). Intervention goals should include opportunities for the child to talk about events that are divorced from the immediate context.

At 2½ or 3 years of age most children talk about what is directly related to the immediate, perceptible context (Fey, 1986). As cognitive and linguistic skills develop, children become increasingly capable of talking about objects, events, and relations away from the speaking context. Words gradually become less context-bound during the preschool years. Bates, Benigni, Bretherton,

Camaioni, and Volterra (1977) stated that true decontextualization is seen when the child begins to read words.

A method for providing such opportunities is to sit down and talk with the child with few or no props. The adult can initiate a conversation about a topic that interests a child (Fey, 1986).

DEVELOPMENTAL LEVEL

- Initiates a topic by combination of glances, vocalizations
- Maintains one or two turns
- One-half utterances on topic, extended topic maintenance in routines
    (By 1 year)

- *Content*: Limited to topics that are physically present

INTERVENTION GUIDELINES

At this stage, the child usually initiates interactions with eye gaze, vocalizations, and gestures. The child has few expressive words and a short attention span so he or she can maintain a topic for one or two turns. For example, the 1-year-old may point at a toy and say "ba" (ball) and then drop it and explore another object. During diaper-changing, the child might pinch his or her nostrils and say, "poo." If the parent smiles and acknowledges the behavior and waits for the child to take another turn, the child may repeat the behavior again. The parent and child are engaged in a *child-initiated conversation*. The child initiates the topic, and the parent supports the child by responding and taking turns. *If the parent does not acknowledge the child's behavior, the child probably will not repeat the act and a conversation will not occur.*

Guidelines for increasing discourse include the following: *observe and watch the child, interpret the behavior, and react to it in a meaningful manner.* When an infant gazes at the adult, he or she can return the gaze and reinforce the child with a smile. When the child turns away, he or she has ended the nonverbal conversation. The adult needs to respect the child's feelings and moods and not try to force continued interaction. Small children have short attention spans, and "baby conversations" are shorter *in duration* than "adult conversations." In order for interaction to be successful, it is important that the adult be sensitive to the child's moods, interests, and cues (Powell & Mahoney, 1986).

An adult can increase the number of turns per conversational topic by following the child's lead and imitating (i.e., mirroring), reflecting, expanding, and modeling behavior. For the preverbal child, the topics of conversation are nonverbal. "Baby conversations" can begin with a newborn. When the child sticks out his or her tongue, the adult can respond in kind and mirror the behavior. The adult must use wait time and give the child time to respond again. Again, it is important to stress that the adult must be sensitive to the child's mood, watch the child's cues, and end the interaction when the child has had enough. Sometimes adults do not watch for cues from the child and overstimulate him or her, causing the child to fuss and cry.

As motor skills increase, the child begins to manipulate objects and a conversation can occur with toys. For example, if a child holds a rattle in his or her hand and shakes it, the adult can pick up a rattle and mimic the movement and wait for the child to take another turn. To increase a variety of actions and to expand the conversation, the adult can vary the activity slightly (e.g., extend the rattle and tap the child's rattle). The adult has remained on the child's topic but has attempted to expand it by demonstrating a new behavior. If a toddler picks up a comb, turns it over, and explores it, the adult can mirror the actions and demonstrate functional use. When the child tries the new behavior, the adult must acknowledge the child with a smile.

With vocalizations, the adult follows the same procedure. For instance, if a child squeals when splashing the water in the bathtub, the adult could smile, imitate the motor movement and vocalization, and wait for the child to respond. If the child repeats the action, the adult could take another turn and mimic the child's vocalization, adding a new word (e.g., "splash") to the turn.

PLAY MATERIALS AND OPPORTUNITIES

Toys and play materials should include common objects (e.g., comb, washcloth, cup, spoon, pots and pans), because children at this developmental level are developing cognitive skills by discovering the functional use of items. They also need toys that encourage problem solving (e.g., cause-and-effect toys, Busy Boxes, pop-up toys). The adult provides the toys, watches the child explore and manipulate them, and then joins the child's play and engages in nonverbal and/or verbal discourse.

DEVELOPMENTAL LEVEL

- Can introduce topic in short dialogue of a few turns
- Adult scaffolds or structures conversation (gives child choices)
- Repetition used to remain on topic
  (2–3 years)

- *Content:* Topic does not have to be physically present; uses attention-getting words, rising intonation (*move, what, mine*); provides descriptive detail; can comprehend and use "I," "you," "he," and polite form "please"; responds to partner.

INTERVENTION GUIDELINES

At this developmental level, the adult's role is to provide toys and activities that will motivate the child to interact with objects and people. *Intervention should emphasize increasing initiation of conversation, increase number of turns per topic, increase a variety of pragmatic functions/meanings, and facilitate development of grammatical and semantic forms.* Discourse can be increased through natural conversational interaction. The adult waits for the child to select an activity and topic of conversation and then joins the child in interaction. The adult uses reactive INREAL strategies to increase language (see pp. 290–291). For example, if the child hears a dog barking, stops playing, and says, "dog," the adult might say, "Dog barking" (i.e., expansion). If the child repeats the word "Dog," the adult could take the child to the window and point to the dog and say, "Dog barking" (i.e., expansion) or "Woof woof." If the child says, "Dog oo oo," the adult could say "Dog woof woof" (i.e., vocal monitoring and reflecting).

For an older child, the parent and child could interact while reading a bedtime story. If the child points to and names pictures, the adult could expand the child's knowledge through conversational interaction. When the child points to a bumblebee and says, "That *fly's* flying," the parent could respond, "That bumblebee is flying. He's flying to the flower." If the child asks, "He bite me?," the parent could respond, "No, he won't bite. He stings." Through the interactive sequence, the adult supports the child, initiating a conversation and increasing the number of turns (i.e., maintaining a topic), facilitates development of longer phrases, and provides vocabulary enrichment.

The adult functions as a collaborator with the child, assisting the child to communicate a more effective message. This collaborative process is referred to as *scaffolding.* (The information in this section is adapted, with permission, from Norris & Hoffman, 1990, and the American Speech-Language-Hearing Association.) Scaffolding includes verbal and nonverbal prompts or assistance the adult provides so the child can communicate. Norris and Hoffman (1990) provide the following communication strategies adults can utilize with children to help them communicate and develop social skills:

1. *Cloze procedures* essentially consist of filling in the blanks for the child. The adult pauses and encourages the child to supply the needed words (e.g., "Baby, I will _____ your _____ so it will look _____.").

2. *Gestures and pantomimes* are used to prompt the child with nonlinguistic cues to help the child to develop an idea (e.g., "Baby, we need the _____ [point to brush] so that we can _____ [make brushing motions] your _____ [touch the baby's hair]").

3. *Relational terms* are prompts that require the child to provide specific information. For example, an *additive prompt* would signal that more information needs to be added. The facilitator would say "and . . ." A *temporal prompt* indicates that time elements need to be included. The adult provides the prompt and waits for the child to respond. For example, the facilitator could say, "But first _____," "After _____," "Next _____," or "When _____." *Causal prompts* are indicated with cues such as, "Because _____," "So _____," or "Since _____." "But _____," "Except _____," and "However _____" are prompts used to illicit *adversative* information.

4. *Preparatory sets* provide the child with information about a concept that must be expressed or a communication act that must be performed. This generally occurs in the context of the adult pointing out what is new and relevant (e.g., "You need to ask the baby how she feels.", "You can't just take the toy. You have to ask for it.").

5. *Comprehension questions* ask for information for different levels of understanding. Questions might include, "What will happen?", "What should we do?", and "Why didn't it happen?"

6. *Summarization evaluation questions* encourage the child to restate information about an event and therefore provide a second opportunity to communicate the message (e.g., "What did you ask Bobby Sittingbear?", "Tell Bobby what you saw at the zoo").

7. *Binary choices* provide the child with alternative utterances (e.g., "You can ask her nicely—I want the bottle—or make her give it to you—Give me the bottle.").

8. *Turn-taking cues* are indicators that more information is needed. These types of cues might include repeating the child's utterance with an expectant pause ("I want the _____.").
9. *Phonemic cues* include providing an initial sound or syllable for a targeted word (e.g., "Tell Mario, 'I need the b____.'").

As the child's linguistic and cognitive skills begin to increase, it is important to talk about events that are not in the immediate environment (i.e., decrease contextual cues). The adult can talk about events before and after they occur. For instance, before going on a visit to see a grandparent, the adult could periodically talk about the event (e.g., "Gonna see Grandma."). If the child repeats, "Grandma," the adult can say, "See Grandma." After the event, the adult recalls the event by asking simple questions and modeling responses. Photographs and keepsakes brought back from the trip could be used as conversational props. In this example, the adult might show the child a photograph and say, "Here's Grandma." If the child fails to take a turn, the adult could say, "Here's Grandma's house?" If the child says, "Grandma?" the adult could say, "Grandma's home."

PLAY MATERIALS AND OPPORTUNITIES

Toys that are open-ended (i.e., can be used in many ways) are recommended as they facilitate many opportunities for language development. For example, Play-Doh can be used in many different ways, allowing the child to be creative and offering an opportunity for learning new concepts (e.g., squeeze, pound, roll, pat, cut, name colors, count). Playing with cardboard boxes is a joyous experience for children. They learn about their bodies in relationship to space, and it promotes interaction and linguistic development (i.e., especially an understanding of prepositions). Waterplay and sandplay promote interaction with other children and adults. Clinical experience has revealed that even passive children tend to engage when bubbles are introduced. Special events are great for developing conversational topics (e.g., birthday party, Christmas, trip to the zoo, shopping, doctor visit). Storybooks provide new information, which prompts conversation. Books such as Eric Carle's (1969) *The Very Hungry Caterpillar* or Bill Martin's (1967) *Brown Bear, Brown Bear, What Do You See?* work well at this stage. Children need opportunities to explore a variety of arts and crafts materials (e.g., crayons, markers, paints, paper, scissors).

DEVELOPMENTAL LEVEL

> - Can engage in dialogue beyond a few turns
> - More aware of social aspects of discourse
> - Acknowledges partner's turn, can determine how much information listener needs
>   (3–4 years)

- *Content*: Action is a common topic; verbs "go" and "do" predominate; uses direct requests (*May I, Could you*)

INTERVENTION GUIDELINES

The facilitator's role is to provide an opportunity for the child to talk about an event. The facilitator can then prompt the child with questions. For instance, comprehension questions can be used to ask for information for different levels of understanding (Norris & Hoffman, 1990). Questions should be stated so the child needs to provide more than one-word answers (e.g., "What will happen next?", "What should we do?", "Why didn't it happen?", "I wonder what he'll do?"). Summarization evaluation questions encourage the child to restate information about an event and therefore provide a second opportunity to communicate the message (Norris & Hoffman, 1990) (e.g., "What did you ask Bobby Sittingbear?", "Tell Bobby what you saw at the zoo."). At this level, children have learned many words and speak in longer sentences. They need to refine their discourse skills by respecting turn-taking, increasing the number of turns per topic, and self-monitoring their verbal expressions and their partners' comments to make sure they are being understood.

The adult can identify skills that are problematic and give the child feedback during conversational discourse. *The key is to provide feedback in a nonpunitive and nonjudgmental manner because the child is learning and needs practice gaining these skills. The adult must monitor his or her intonation and make sure it does not sound like the child is being punished for bad behavior.* Feedback provided in a negative manner discourages the child from talking. For example, when a child interrupts, the adult might say, "Wait, it's my turn" and then proceed with the interaction. The adult could also prompt discourse by reminding the child, "It's your turn now."

PLAY MATERIALS AND OPPORTUNITIES

Children at this level know many words, can speak in long sentences, and know a great deal about their world. At this time, they need exposure to their community and new experiences. Children usually talk if they have experiences to share and someone who is interested in listening. Outings to the zoo, bakery, grocery store, library, park, friends' and relatives' homes, police station, fire station, and swimming pool encourage conversational discourse. Since action is a common topic, give children activities that provide this interest (e.g., make cookies, pop popcorn, make pudding, paint and draw, read books). Talk about what will happen before an activity occurs and then recap the event when it is over. Providing momentos from a trip sparks conversations (e.g., pictures, toys).

DEVELOPMENTAL LEVEL

- Modifies language when talking to younger child
- Increased awareness of listener's role and understanding
        (4–5 years)

- Content: Discusses state, feelings, emotions, attitudes; verbs "be" and "do" predominate.

INTERVENTION GUIDELINES

Children at this developmental level need opportunities to use conversational discourse while assuming different roles. The adult can plan activities that meet the individual child's specific needs and then increase the child's skills by modeling appropriate behavior. During activities, the adult needs to find opportunities for discussion regarding feelings, emotions, and attitudes. Storybooks are an excellent vehicle for promoting these discussions (McCord, 1993). The adult can prompt or cue the child by questioning (e.g., "I wonder how this little boy feels"). Preparatory sets are appropriate (e.g., "You need to ask the baby how she feels.", "You can't just take the toy. You have to ask for it." (Norris & Hoffman, 1990). When the adult observes two children fighting, verbal prompts and modeling may be necessary to help the children negotiate (e.g., "Ari, that made Dominique sad when you tore her picture. What do you want to tell her?").

PLAY MATERIALS AND OPPORTUNITIES

Storybooks are excellent for this level of development. Children also need opportunities to engage in role-playing activities so puppets, dolls, and dress-up play are especially beneficial. Themes in the story book can be incorporated into imaginary play (McCord, 1993). Children enjoy constructing and writing books about a past event or some aspect of their personal lives (e.g., a pet, a visit to Grandma's, a new baby brother).

DEVELOPMENTAL LEVEL

- Can sustain topic through a dozen turns
- Conversation much like adults'
  (5–6 years)

- *Content:* Uses most varieties of English sentences.

INTERVENTION GUIDELINES

Children at this developmental level have finely tuned their conversational skills. The emphasis of intervention is to increase higher-level semantic and grammatical forms. Adults can help children develop higher-level skills by expanding or adding to the child's knowledge base with natural conversation. It is important to use topics that interest each child (e.g., dinosaurs, turtles, themes from movies).

PLAY MATERIALS AND OPPORTUNITIES

The suggestions provided on pages 372–373 are also appropriate for children at this developmental level.

OBSERVATION GUIDELINES FOR COMMUNICATION AND LANGUAGE DEVELOPMENT: PRAGMATICS—ECHOLALIA

E. Does the child demonstrate echolalia in communication?
1. Timing
   a. Immediate
   b. Delayed
2. Echolalia
   a. Exact
   b. Mitigated (changed)
3. Function
   a. To continue interaction
   b. To demonstrate comprehension
4. Degree of pragmatic success

Echolalia is defined as "the immediate or delayed repetition of a word or group of words just spoken by another person" (Linder, 1993, p. 159). As a child learns language, it is not uncommon for him or her to say a word that is not understood; this type of communication is a form of echoing what was previously heard and may be regarded as nonpropositional or nonmeaningful language (Weiss & Lillywhite, 1981). In normal development, a young child uses imitation for a variety of purposes. Imitation is used as a technique to practice new words and constructions and to understand their use (Clark, 1973). McDonald and Gillette (1982) found that imitation is also utilized by the child to take a turn and maintain interaction. Research has identified two different forms of echolalia—immediate and delayed (Prizant & Duchan, 1981). Children may use both forms as techniques to continue interaction. The echoed response acts as a "place holder" and gives the child time to hold his or her place in the conversation and also have time to process the meaning of the utterance.

Echolalia may be an exact replication or it can be mitigated. *Mitigated* means that the utterance is repeated with minor changes from the original form (e.g., the adult tells a 16-month-old child "I love you" and the child repeats "love.").

After the TPBA, the team determines whether the child uses echolalia and identifies the function it serves in his or her overall communication repertoire.

An intervention principle is to reinforce the child's desire to communicate and facilitate development of higher-level skills. If a child echoes words because he or she is increasing language abilities, emphasis should be placed on continuing to increase comprehension and verbal expression. With excessive echolalia that does not appear to follow a normal developmental progression, the adult can begin to implement strategies that facilitate spontaneous language. For example, the adult could give the child choices (e.g., "Bobby, do you want a cookie or cake?"). A cloze procedure can also be used. For instance, the adult might say, "I'm washing the baby's _____."

EXAMPLE

Eddie Ray B. is a 6-year-old child who has been in and out of foster homes due to abuse and neglect since he was 18 months old. He has been diagnosed with attention deficit hyperactivity disorder and language and cognitive delays. It was reported that Eddie Ray's mother used both drugs and alcohol when she was pregnant.

Eddie Ray appears to be a healthy, well-nourished child with a pleasant smile. His motor skills are at age level. In the area of cognition, he demonstrates difficulty classifying and organizing objects (e.g., food, toys, animals), counting 10 objects, and sequencing and telling a story.

Conversationally, Eddie Ray initiates and ends conversations. He is quite verbal and uses sentences that are syntactically complete. Yet, the facilitator noted that whether Eddie Ray produced responses or initiations, his utterances were rarely appropriate to what she had said previously. He did not follow a theme in any coherent manner, and he seemed basically disinterested in the content of the facilitator's verbalization.

The team felt that Eddie Ray's discourse skills were related to his cognitive skills. It was decided that activities would be planned to include Eddie Ray's interests and help him begin to organize the world around him.

The foster parent reported that Eddie Ray is interested in Ninja Turtles and Batman and enjoys helping around the house. The foster parent agreed to have Eddie Ray help her with such tasks as setting the table, putting the dishes away, sorting and folding laundry, and buying and putting away groceries. The teacher said she would provide Ninja Turtle and Batman props so Eddie Ray could engage in imaginative play. Team members agreed to engage in imaginative play with Eddie Ray and his peers. The goal for interaction would be to help Eddie stay on topic for two to three turns. When he produced tangential remarks, it was recommended the adult ask Eddie Ray questions to clarify his meaning and then model a response that pertained to the topic.

The speech-language specialist recommended that Eddie Ray learn nursery rhymes and songs and read storybooks. Props on a flannel board, pictures, or real objects could be used to help him recall the sequence and retell the story. The therapist also encourage the foster family to play simple board games with Eddie Ray. The game would facilitate turn-taking, staying on topic, and developing organizational skills and problem-solving.

OBSERVATION GUIDELINES FOR COMMUNICATION AND LANGUAGE DEVELOPMENT: PHONOLOGY: SOUND PRODUCTION PATTERNS

I. Phonology: Sound Production Patterns
  A. What phonemes or speech sounds are produced by the child?
    1. Preverbal sounds
    2. Speech sounds
    3. Babbling—constant vowel combinations
    4. Jargon—speech sounds combined into patterns with cultural intonations
    5. Words
  B. Phonological processes or errors
    1. Deletions
       a. Consonants
       b. Syllables
       c. Sounds
    2. Assimilation (one sound becomes similar to another in the same word)
    3. Substitutions
       a. Initial sounds
       b. Final sounds
       c. For liquids, /l/ and /r/
       d. Vowels
  C. Intelligibility level—percentage of verbalizations understood
    1. In known context
    2. In unknown context
    3. By familiar person or family member
    4. Appropriateness of intonation
    5. Dysfluencies or stuttering

Articulation and Phonology

Stages of Sound System Development

> *Speech* describes the motor movements that occur when an individual articulates the sound of a language and forms words. *Phonology* is the study of linguistic rules governing the sound system of language including speech sounds, speech sound production and the combination of sounds into meaningful utterances. (Creaghead & Newman, 1989, p. 9).

The sound system begins to emerge at birth. By 8 years of age, most children have mastered all of the phonemes of English and produce clear and intelligible speech. The sound system evolves in an organized and systematic fashion and follows a developmental sequence. An articulation test profile is shown in Table 1.

At birth, the infant begins to experiment with motor movements and produces a variety of speech-like and non–speech-like sounds. This stage of development is often referred to as the *preverbal stage*. It begins at birth and ends when the first true words appear.

Infants exhibit several different sound patterns during the preverbal stage. During the first few months of life, the infant produces vowels (e.g., a, e, o, u) and throaty gurgles often referred to as *cooing*. *Babbling*, which includes strings of syllables produced in a singsong fashion, begins to appear at 6–8 months. By

Table 1. Articulation Test Profile*

Articulation Behaviors			
t- n- -n k- g- p- -p b-	m- -m h- au u æ (c<u>a</u>t) ɔ (f<u>a</u>ll) ə (sof<u>a</u>) ai	ɛ (s<u>e</u>nt) a (f<u>a</u>ther) i (f<u>ee</u>t) e (vac<u>a</u>tion) ʌ (<u>u</u>p) ʊ (b<u>oo</u>t) o (<u>o</u>bey) ɪ (b<u>i</u>n) oi (o<u>i</u>l)	
-s d- -d	-k f- -f	-ŋ (n<u>g</u>) i- (<u>y</u>ell)	
-t -r	-b w-	ɝ (bi<u>r</u>d)	
s- -l	-g	ɚ (crack<u>er</u>s)	
-'ʃ(di<u>sh</u>) l-	bl- r- br-	tr- -v	
ʃ-(<u>sh</u>oe) t-	-tʃ(<u>ch</u>oke) fl-		
sp- st-	kl- ð- (<u>th</u>eir)	-ð (smoo<u>th</u>) -ʒ (mea<u>s</u>ure)	
z- -z	θ- (<u>th</u>umb) -θ (ba<u>th</u>)	hw- (<u>wh</u>at) ju	-ʤ (bu<u>dge</u>) ʤ- (<u>j</u>oy)

Adapted with permission from Pendergast, K., Dickey, S.E., Selman, J.W., & Soder A. (1969). *Photo articulation test*. Austin, TX: PRO-ED.

*Symbols are from the international phonetic alphabet. Examples are provided for unusual sounds. The hyphen indicates the position of the word.

10–18 months, infants and toddlers sound like foreign language speakers because they produce *jargon*; this speech pattern includes productions of non-reduplicated syllables and "adult-like" intonation (Bernthal & Bankson, 1981; Eisenberg, Murkoff, & Hathaway, 1989; Weiss & Lillywhite, 1981). With the advent of the first recognizable word, which occurs between 11 and 13 months, the preverbal stage ends and the linguistic stage appears.

First words that emerge in a toddler's speech usually include productions of single syllables, which are formed by combining vowels with early developing consonants such as p, b, m, n, or h. Words that are often produced include "mama," "hi," and "bye." As motor skills develop and mature, the child learns to coordinate movements of the articulators and produces longer speech units (e.g., multisyllabic words), which incorporate later developing sounds like "r," "l," and "s." Figure 1 illustrates the average age and upper age estimates for consonant production. The developmental and age levels illustrated in this figure are used on pages 335–336 to present intervention guidelines and opportunities.

During the linguistic stage, children learn how to coordinate their articulators to produce sound and experiment with different ways of combining sounds into meaningful units. When the child has acquired approximately 25 words, he or she demonstrates an emerging phonological system or an understanding of how sounds that are heard in the environment are combined to form words (Hodson, 1991). As the child begins to create words, he or she produces phonological errors. During the learning process, the child substitutes known sound patterns for others not yet mastered or may omit or alter complex sounds. These errors occur because the child is attempting to learn words by interpreting and simplifying the adult patterns he or she hears.

Ingram (1976) described and identified common phonological errors produced by children, which included *deletions, assimilations,* and *substitutions.* Deletions occur when sounds are omitted in words. In some cases, sounds are omitted when they occur at the end of words (e.g., "da" for "dog"), within a consonant cluster (e.g., "tov" for "stove"), within a word ("winow" for "window"), or when unstressed syllables are deleted (e.g., "nana" for "banana"). Assimilation errors are noted when one sound in a word becomes similar to another sound in the word. For instance, an end sound may become like the beginning sound (e.g., "dod" for "dog"), a front sound may become like the end sound (e.g., "tat" for "cat"), or one syllable sounds like another (e.g., "baba" for "bottle"). The third category of phonological errors are substitutions. Errors might include: substitution of initial sounds (e.g., "bish" for "fish"), substitution of final sounds (e.g., "jumpin" for "jumping"), substitution of /l/ and /r/ with /j/ or /w/ (e.g., "wed" for "red"), and substitution of vowel sounds (e.g., "fawa" for "flower"). Dyson and Paden (1983) found that phonological process errors are common in the speech of children younger than 2 years of age and begin to disappear between the ages of 3 and 4 years. Hodson (1991) provides data regarding other phonological processes exhibited by children. Due to the complex nature of speech development, children often present difficulty articulating specific *speech sounds* or learning the *rules* for combining sounds. Both variables must be considered when planning an intervention program.

Intelligibility Level

When toddlers initially begin to speak, they misarticulate sounds and delete parts of words. Consequently, their speech is difficult to understand unless

AGE LEVEL

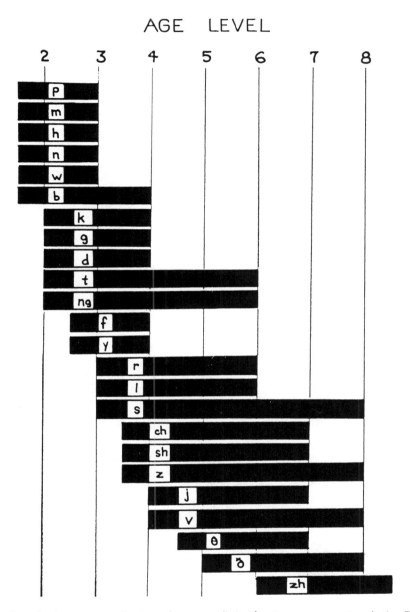

Figure 1.   Average age estimates and upper age limits of customary consonant production. The solid bars indicate when a sound begins at the median age of customary articulation. It stops at an age level when 90% of children are producing the sound. (From Sander, E.K. [1972]. When are speech sounds learned? *Journal of Speech and Hearing Disorders, 37,* 62; reprinted by permission.)

there are contextual cues (i.e., the listener knows that the utterance "da" means "dog" because the child uses the sound combination when the dog is present). Family members quickly learn a child's speech system and interpret for strangers. As additional sounds are mastered and fewer phonological errors oc- cur, the child's speech becomes more intelligible and fewer contextual cues are needed to interpret their speech message and an unfamiliar listener will comprehend their comments. As the child matures and acquires the speech sound system of language, his or her speech becomes more like the adult model.

Other factors can also affect intelligibility. For example, intelligibility decreases if a child speaks with a rapid speech rate, produces a soft, weak voice, or has unusual nasal resonance (i.e., speech sounds denasal or child sounds hypernasal).

Assessing the Child's Sound System

A child's speech is evaluated by recording errors that are noted during the play session. *The team should determine age-level and above age-level speech sounds that are present in the child's speech and identify where the child produces the sounds.* For example, a child might produce the consonant "b" when it occurs in the first position of words but omit the phoneme in the middle or ends of words (e.g., "ba"/ball, "wait"/rabbit, "Ba"/Bob). *Below, at, and above age-level speech sounds that do not appear or are misarticulated should be identified.* For example, "s" may occur but be distorted because the child lisps.

Speech errors should be analyzed for patterns to determine phonological processes that are being used by the child. Analysis of errors could reveal that the child omits all sounds that occur at the ends of words or that consonants are omitted when they appear in a sequence (e.g., t/st, b/bl, d/dl). This information can be used when planning intervention because the child's speech could be improved by planning speech activities that would help the child discover new phonological patterns.

Overall speech intelligibility must be calculated. A spontaneous language sample that includes 50–100 utterances can be used for this analysis. The total number of words or syllables spoken can be calculated. Words that are not understood and words that can be understood only with contextual cues are counted. By dividing intelligible words by the total number of words spoken and then multiplying by 100, one can find an intelligibility rating. *When a child's speech intelligibility is judged to be significantly below age level and errors cannot be evaluated because of low intelligibility, further formal testing is warranted.* The speech-language pathologist can administer formal articulation or phonological tests and determine the severity of the problem and recommend an individualized plan.

Through observation and interaction the facilitator will determine if the child can imitate age-level sounds that are inaccurately produced or did not occur in his or her sound repertoire. Imitative productions should assess the child's ability to produce the error sounds both in isolation and in words. This information is necessary for planning intervention because sounds that are easily produced would be taught before sounds that cannot be produced.

If a child presents difficulty in this area, a hearing problem must be ruled out before intervention can occur because a child learns the sound system by hearing speech. A referral should be made to a physician or an audiologist to assess hearing acuity.

Production of the speech sounds of language is a motor act (i.e., consonants and vowels are formed by the articulators such as the lips, tongue, jaw and palate). *Precise articulation cannot occur unless functioning of the oral mechanism is satisfactory. A complete assessment of oral motor abilities must be completed before intervention can proceed.* For instance, a child who omits "t," "d," "n," and "l" sounds and cannot elevate the tongue tip may have an organic problem (e.g., ankyloglossia), which would require medical management before intervention would be beneficial. A child who cannot imitate selected lip, tongue, or jaw movements could present a motor speech disorder (e.g., apraxia).

Because phonological development is a part of language development, the child's overall language abilities must be compared to·the child's articulation skills and phonological system before intervention can occur. For instance, a child who is 3 years old, produces unintelligible speech, and presents receptive and expressive language and cognitive skills that are characteristic of an 11-month-old probably does not present a speech delay but presents a language delay. For a child who is 3 years old and presents unintelligible speech and receptive language and cognitive skills that are at the 3-year level presents a phonological and possible expressive language impairment. Intervention for each of these cases is quite different. For the first child, if there were no oral motor deficits, intervention would emphasize increasing cognitive and receptive and expressive language skills. In the second case, intervention would emphasize increasing the child's speech intelligibility by increasing correct production of speech sounds, decreasing usage of specified phonological processes (e.g., deletions, substitutions, assimilation errors), and increasing expressive language skills.

Facilitating Intervention

After the child's speech pattern has been thoroughly assessed, an intervention plan can be developed. *General goals for intervention include increasing accurate speech/sound production, decreasing use of phonological processes, and increasing speech intelligibility.* How these goals are achieved varies depending upon the need of each individual child. For a child who misarticulates a few below age-level speech sounds and presents slightly decreased intelligibility, a traditional articulation approach that emphasizes teaching 1–2 sounds at a time in a developmental hierarchy (e.g., isolation, syllables, words, phrases, sentences, conversation) is recommended. The following factors must be considered when selecting a target sound or sounds for intervention:

1. Consider the chronological age of the child and select target speech sounds that are developmentally appropriate for the child. Consonants such as "p," "b," "m," "w," "t," "d," "n," "k," "g," and "h" can be expected to develop before 3 years of age. Children younger than 4 years of age cannot be expected to have acquired "th," "z," "v," "sh," "zh," "ch," or "j" (Creaghead & Newman, 1989).
2. Sounds that are more visible are easier to acquire than sounds that cannot be seen. For example, "p," "b," and "m" are produced with the lips and are more visible than the consonant "r."
3. Targeting speech sounds that occur more frequently has a greater effect on speech intelligibility. Table 2 lists the 24 consonants and 14 vowels of American speech in order of frequency of occurrence.
4. Sounds that are easier for the child to imitate will be acquired before sounds that the child cannot produce. For instance, if a child can imitate the "k" sound but not the "s" phoneme, the "k" sound would be targeted.
5. It is advisable to select speech sounds that the child produces in some context or just slightly misarticulates as these productions are easier to

Table 2.   Occurrence of phonemes in general American dialect

Rank by frequency	Phoneme	Rank by frequency	Phoneme
Consonants		Vowels	
1	/t/	1	/ə/ (sofa)
2	/n/ (nose)	2	/I/ (bin)
3	/s/ (see)	3	/i/ (feet)
4	/d/ (dog)	4	/a/ (father)
5	/r/ (rabbit)	5	/æ/ (cat)
6	/l/ (look)	6	/ɛ/ (sent)
7	/k/ (cat)	7	/ɔ/ (fall)
8	/z/ (zebra)	8	/ɝ/ (bird)
9	/w/ (window)	9	/ɚ/ (crackers)
10	/m/ (mine)	10	/u/ (blue)
11	/ð/ ("th" voiced-the)	11	/e/ (vacation)
12	/h/ (hot)	12	/ʊ/ (boot)
13	/b/ (boy)	13	/ʌ/ (up)
14	/v/ (vacuum)	14	/o/ (open)
15	/p/ (peas)		
16	/g/ (go)		
17	/f/ (fox)		
18	/ŋ/ (ring)		
19	/j/ (yellow)		
20	/ʃ/ (she)		
21	/tʃ/ chew		
22	/θ/ th (voiceless throw)		
23	/dz/ (jump)		
24	/z/ (treasure)		

Adapted from Weiss, C.E., & Lillywhite, H. (1981). *Communicative disorders: Prevention and early intervention*. St. Louis, MO: C.V. Mosby.

generalize and modify. For instance, if a child omits "t" in initial positions of words but produces them in final positions, this sound could be targeted. Speech sounds that are slightly distorted can be acquired before a speech sound that does not occur in the child's sound repertoire. For example, if a child lisps when producing the "s" phoneme, one would help the child modify this production rather than introducing a new sound that does not appear in the child's phonetic inventory. *When a child produces at least 25 words, his or her speech contains multiple articulation errors, and speech intelligibility is severely impaired, a phonological approach is usually recommended.* A child's phonological system must be evaluated with a formal test instrument (e.g., Hodson, 1991; Khan & Lewis, 1986) and specific processes identified for remediation.

With a phonological approach, specific phonemes are not targeted but the phonological processes that the child uses are suppressed by teaching new patterns. For example, if the child omits all final sounds of words, he or she would learn a new speech pattern and would be encouraged to produce sounds at the endings of words. To accomplish this goal, the interventionist would select *practice words that include sounds the child can articulate.* For example, if the child can produce the "t" sound, practice words could include this sound at the beginning of words. Practice words that contain new patterns would be introduced during play. While playing with Play-Doh, the interventionist could model the words "pat, pat," "beat," and "hit" to emphasize the new pattern.

In addition to articulation and phonological processes, one must consider other factors that affect speech intelligibility. For example, all variables that contribute to decreased speech intelligibility must be addressed. Perhaps the child produces all age-appropriate phonemes and processes, yet speech intelligibility is poor. The child may present a fast rate of speech and a soft voice, which means his or her speech seems to be slurred and mumbled. Intervention goals would include decreasing the speech rate and increasing vocal loudness to increase speech intelligibility. If a child's speech seems to be affected by decreased nasal resonance or excessive nasality (e.g., excessive nasality could indicate velopharyngeal insufficiency such as a cleft palate disorder; decreased nasality could indicate blockage of the nasal passages), a medical consultation would be necessary before intervention could proceed.

After targeted speech sounds, phonological processes, and intelligibility factors have been identified, intervention can proceed. As with all other aspects of communication, these targeted skills will be acquired in meaningful social and communicative contexts. The child will practice speech sounds and phonological patterns in prosocial communicative activities in which correct responses are reinforced by natural consequences (Low, Newman, & Ravsten, 1989). For a child who is learning the "f" sound, this phoneme would be emphasized throughout daily activities and he or she would be encouraged to name toys or request items with the target sound. When the child requests a "firetruck," he or she can be reinforced by receiving the toy.

Psycholinguistic research in the 1970s highlighted the importance of children learning language in functional contexts. Since phonology deals with the units that make up a language, it is apparent phonology needs to develop in meaningful functional contexts as well. *A child can learn new speech patterns during play and daily activities.* Targeted sounds and phonological processes that the child needs to learn can be incorporated into functional vocabulary that the child will use frequently. For a child who deletes final sounds of words and can repeat early developing sounds (e.g., "m," "n," "p"), words that contain these sounds could be introduced such as "mine," "mom," and "pop."

To facilitate speech sound development, the early interventionist must consider the following. A child will learn speech sounds through all of the senses. By implementing the following strategies, an adult can help the child to recognize auditory characteristics of target sounds or sounds in specific positions of words by highlighting or drawing attention to these sounds: 1) emphasize the sound by saying it louder (e.g., "*cat*," "*pop*"); 2) slow speech down and emphasize all of the sounds (e.g., "di . . . no . . . saur"); and 3) repeat the sound several times "*c-c-cat.*" A combination of all of these techniques helps the child learn the targeted processes.

In addition to acquiring speech sounds through hearing, the child also learns characteristics of sounds through vision and touch. To help a child learn sounds, provide visual and tactile cues. For instance, *when talking with a child, get down on his or her level so he or she can see the position of the lips, tongue, and jaw.* In addition to providing visual cues with the articulators, supplemental visual cues can also be used. A specific hand gesture can be paired with the production of a sound and can provide the child an additional cue and draw attention to a sound. For example, if a child is a learning the "b," sound in the initial positions of words, the adult could produce a hand sign (e.g., "b" sign of

SEE II sign language), each time a word containing the "b" sound is produced. Gestures could be determined by the team and *could be* selected from SEE II sign language or arbitrarily developed.

An adult also could provide tactile input to emphasize the characteristic of a sound. This occurs naturally with infants because, as they are cradled and held, they feel the vibration of sound. As infants start to reach for objects, they begin to touch and explore the caregiver's mouth and face. For the older child, the adult can encourage the child to learn about the characteristics of sounds by touching the nose, lips, and throat. For instance, when the adult produces the "p" sound, he or she could place the child's hand in front of his or her mouth. The child would feel the air that is released from the lips and learn the characteristics of voiceless sounds. The throat could be touched when voiced sounds are produced such as "g," "b," and "d." The nose could be touched for nasal sounds, such as "m," "n," and "ing."

Children acquire the sound system by interacting with their caregivers' and environment. Research has shown that when mothers talked less to their infants, the infants also tended to vocalize less often (Ramey, Sparling, & Wasik, 1981). Another study by Clarke-Stewart (1973) found that "the amount of verbal stimulation directed toward the child significantly influenced the child's intellectual development, particularly the ability to comprehend and express language" (p. 92). The adult needs to interact with infants and children and treat preverbal vocalizations as meaningful forms of communication. The adult can reward the infant's vocalizations with smiles, touch, and imitation of his or her sounds. As the infant matures, the adult can engage in communication games and imitate the child's preverbal sounds, encouraging the infant to imitate new sound sequences and approximations of words. When children are at the linguistic stage of development, the adult can accept and expect speech errors as the child practices and acquires new sounds and phonological patterns. The facilitator should avoid criticizing the child's incorrect responses and avoid saying things like, "no, that's the wrong way" and "now say it the right way." Other feedback can be more supportive and rewarding (e.g., "you said the word *cat* the new way"). When the child says a word incorrectly, it is better to just model the word the correct way. For instance, if a child says, "That's my *tat*, mom," the adult could say, "Yes, that is your *cat*. I like that *cat*."

Dysfluency and Stuttering

Dysfluent speech is a common speech pattern observed in young children. Dysfluent speech appears to occur when there is an interruption in the general flow of speech. Types of dysfluencies might include repetitions, pauses, interjections, revisions, or prolongations.

Repetitions may include repeating individual sounds or syllables. These usually occur at the beginning of words (e.g., "B-b-b baby is crying," "I-I-I go with you, Mom.") Other children may repeat more than one word in the phrase or sentence (e.g., "The boy, the boy is crying") (Dejoy, 1988).

Pauses may occur between words in a phrase (e.g., "The boy is . . . crying") (Dejoy, 1988). Pauses need to be evaluated in terms of how they interrupt the meaningful flow of speech. They may be disruptive if they last longer than 2 seconds.

Interjections include production of extra sounds, syllables, or words that do not add meaning to the utterance. They may sound like place holders, such as "uh," "um," or "I mean, ah, ah, you know" (Dejoy, 1988).

Revisions also may appear in the child's speech; the child revises what has been said. For instance, he or she may change pronunciation or grammar or add a word to an utterance (e.g., "Mom, I goed, Mom, I go school?", "Jerry eat take—Jerry eat cake") (Dejoy, 1988).

In some cases, a child may prolong sounds or syllables. A child may show a change in intonation or apparent tension in the facial muscles (e.g., "Mmmmy baby," "See the puuppy") (Dejoy, 1988).

When parents or teachers see or hear these patterns, they often become alarmed and believe the child is "stuttering." There are differences between "normal dysfluency" and "stuttering." Usually revisions, interjections, and word and phrase repetitions are observed in children's speech, while sound and syllable repetitions and sound prolongations are less common. If the dysfluent pattern appears to be beyond the range of normal, compared to other children of that age, it may indicate the child is indeed beginning to develop a stuttering pattern. One would be especially suspicious if a child appears to avoid or fear talking. Usually this is not the case. Normal dysfluency is common in the pre-school years. VanRiper (1978) noted that children who produced normal speech patterns had 45 dysfluencies per 1,000 words.

The etiology of normal dysfluency is not fully understood. Some researchers theorize that children are having difficulty learning how to coordinate breathing, articulation, and sound production to form words and sentences. In addition to learning new motor patterns, children are acquiring new vocabulary words, and grammar and are refining their ability to organize their thoughts. These skills take time to master and do require practice.

The etiology of stuttering is also a mystery and although research studies have abounded, the cause still is not known. Children who appear to produce early signs that may signal "stuttering" behavior should be referred for a speech evaluation.

The following suggestions can be introduced when working with children who present dysfluent speech patterns:

- If a child presents a dysfluent pattern, adults in the environment should focus on what the child has to say and disregard how they say it. Statements such as, "Ernesto, think before you speak," "Slow down," or "Take a deep breath" should be avoided.
- *The adult should model a calm, relaxed manner and give the child ample time to take a turn.*
- Monitor times when the child appears to be more dysfluent and consider the variables that may affect the pattern (e.g., parent is not listening when child talks, adults appear to be in a rush, child is upset). Modify the variables when possible. For example, get down on the child's level, establish eye contact, and give the child attention.
- If the pattern draws attention to the child's speech, the parents are con-

cerned, or the child appears to avoid talking or displays fear when speaking, he or she should be referred for a speech evaluation.

Multiculturalism

The United States is populated by people from many different racial and ethnic groups. American citizens often define themselves by their ancestral roots. It is common to hear the following statements, "I'm half Irish and Native American," "I'm German," "My dad's family was Italian," or "I'm a Mexican American." People in Japan, Norway, and Mexico would not make such statements because their cultures are more homogeneous.

Although the United States is multicultural, its institutions (e.g., schools, government, work settings, hospitals), do not always reflect that diversity. Most institutions reflect and represent the white European culture. Porter and Samovar (1976), defined culture as:

> The cumulative deposit of knowledge, experience, meaning, beliefs, values, attitudes, religions, concepts of self, the universe and self universe relationships, hierarchies of statues, role expectations, spatial relations, and time concepts acquired by a large group of people in the course of generations through individual and group striving. Culture manifests itself both in patterns of language and thought and in forms of activity and behavior. These patterns become models for common adaptive acts and styles of expressive behavior, which enable people to live in a society within a given geographical environment at a given state of technical development. (p. 7)

From this definition, one can see that culture forms the foundation for values and views of the world. Culture affects the development of language, cognition, perception, and feelings.

Conflict has arisen between different racial and ethnic groups in the United States because by representing the white European cultural beliefs and excluding other cultures, biases and prejudices toward nonwhites developed. For example, individuals who spoke Spanish, used nonstandard dialects or had brown or black skin were, at one time, viewed as deficient. African Americans and Mexican-American children who scored poorly on standardized tests were placed in special education classes. Their poor performance was attributed to lower intelligence rather than as a factor of culturally biased test instruments.

In an effort to change cultural biases and support diversity, a multicultural movement is sweeping the United States. From the federal government to the private sector, social reform is beginning to occur as institutions take measures to support cultural diversity. President Bill Clinton selected cabinet members from diverse groups. Educational curricula, from the preschool to the university level, have been revised to reflect the populations they serve. Private businesses offer in-services and workshops for employees to increase cultural sensitivity and competence. Educators and therapists must be aware of cultural differences and develop intervention practices that will support these differences. Research data suggest that, for minorities, the degree to which students' language and culture are incorporated into a school program is a predictor of academic success (Cummins, 1986).

Dialects and Accents

As one travels across the United States, it is apparent that the country is very diverse. From state to state, one sees differences in climate, geography, and the social economy. Individuals who reside in various geographical areas also speak differently. For instance, John F. Kennedy, who came from Boston, Massachusetts, spoke with a different dialect than did Jimmy Carter, who is from Georgia, or Bill Clinton, who is from Arkansas. All of these presidents spoke English but each used a different dialectical form of the language.

Language is a rule-governed system, and the rules of language use vary among groups of people. A dialect is a variation of a language that characterizes a group of people, and this rule-governed system deviates in some way from the ideal standard. In the United States, the ideal standard is "standard American English." This standard form is rarely used except in formal writing and the belief in a standard is almost a myth (Owens, 1988).

All language has structure and is used for the purpose of communication. The structure of a language is always changing in order to reflect changes in the culture. For instance, when a new technological invention appears, new words must be created to describe them (e.g., personal computer, microwave oven, video camcorder, videocassette recorder [VCR]). Spoken language is the primary mode of communication, and written language is a secondary form. Culture is conveyed by both oral and written forms but mostly by oral means; oral language changes very quickly (Brandes & Brewer, 1977). Written language remains constant for longer periods of time and is slow to change.

Dialects commonly appear in oral language. Each dialect can contain variations in many components of the language (e.g., lexicon, prosodic features, sound patterns, idioms, nonverbal cues, grammatical structures). Several factors influence a dialect, including the following: 1) geography, 2) socioeconomic level, 3) race and ethnicity, 4) situation or context, 5) peer group influences, and 6) first or second language learning (Owens, 1988). Individuals who live in various geographic areas use different dialects. For instance, a child reared in rural Appalachia uses different sound patterns, words, prosody, and syntactic structures than a child raised in an urban city in California. As far as socioeconomic level, children who live in lower socioeconomic homes appear to have a less-developed linguistic system when compared to their peers who come from middle- to upper–middle-class homes. Race and ethnicity contributes to differences heard in dialects. African American children who are raised in inner-city environments use a form of Black English, and Hispanic children reared in Spanish-speaking homes often speak English with an accent.

Skillful conversationalists vary the form of language they use according to the speaking situation. For instance, an African American who is a business executive may use a standard English form when presenting information to his colleagues in a boardroom meeting but may speak with an informal Black English dialect when conversing with friends at a barber shop or local bar.

Peer groups influence the way young people speak. For instance, youth in gangs develop a whole language system that enables them to communicate with one another and exclude those outside of the group. Teens are constantly coining new words and phrases. In the 1960s, words like "groovy," "cool," and "boss" were popular. In the 1980s, words and phrases such as "chill out," "rad," and "Hey, dude" were common. Individuals who are bilingual tend to produce a second language by imposing rules of the first language on a second. For instance, a Norwegian speaker might say, "Tursday" for "Thursday" and a Hispanic student might say, "watch" for "wash." Because the "th" sound does not occur in the Norwegian phonological system, Norwegians do not produce the sound when it occurs in another language. In Spanish, "sh" at the end of a word is pronounced as "ch" so this rule is transferred to English. Thus, the question of how intervention should address these problems arises.

Multicultural Education

American educators must accept the reality of multiculturalism and diversity in schools or fail to educate (Betances, 1991). Yet, another reality is that learning the English language is essential for survival. English has replaced German as the language of science and French as the language of diplomacy. The world's commerce largely takes place in English. English must be taught, required, strengthened, and perfected in our schools (Betances, 1991), but English, or a standard dialect, cannot be taught to the exclusion of other dialects or languages. To devalue a child's language or to believe standard English is a better system is to devalue the child and his or her culture and to reveal a naïveté concerning language (Barataz, 1969). Clinical experience has revealed that African American children who receive intervention in middle-class white environments adopt that dialect and find it difficult to relate with their peers or fit into their culture because they speak like white people. The system does not fully enhance or improve the communication skills of these children.

Although each dialect varies in some way from the "standard English" form, none are any better than another. All dialectal forms are tools used to communicate with members of one's speech community. Goodwin (1990) concluded from an in-depth study of African American children using a Black English dialect that the language of black children is not deficient, but is rather rich in meaning and thought.

Unfortunately, some individuals judge a person negatively because they speak with a particular dialect. Employment and educational opportunities may be affected by the use of a particular dialect. Most newscasters who appear on prime time television use a standard American English dialect. Ambitious communications majors who have dialects other than the standard take special classes to learn new speech patterns. Research has revealed that Black English speakers are granted shorter employment interviews, offered employment less frequently, and offered lower-paying positions than speakers of standard English (Owens, 1988). Children who enter school with dialects different from the one used at school may experience academic difficulties because the teachers may judge the child in terms of stereotypes associated with the dialect and treat the child as if he or she were inferior to peers (Owens, 1988).

Intervention must acknowledge, support, and affirm a child's native dialect by offering a "bi-dialectal approach" (Brandes & Brewer, 1977) or an *additive language learning environment* (Damico, 1992b) and equip the child to use two or more systems. Through dialogue, play, and modeling, the adult can help the child learn how to use each dialect in appropriate speaking situations. *The goal of intervention should be to build on what the child already knows by adding "standard American English"* to the child's home speech. The facilitator must convey to the child that the child's home speech is valued and an efficient means of communicating and that there are other language forms that are also useful. If the child is provided an opportunity to learn in a prejudice-free environment, his or her learning will be greatly enhanced, he or she will hear and produce more than one dialect, and the quality of his or her life will be enhanced by the newly acquired communication skills.

Bilingualism

The United States is a pluralistic and diverse society that includes children from many different cultures. Children acquire values, mores, and language within the culture in which they reside. When the language of the culture is not English, children appear to encounter academic difficulties when they enter school because they do not speak the mainstream language. Educational institutions have developed academic programs designed to teach non-English speakers English (e.g., submersion education, bilingual education). Research studies have flourished regarding the most efficacious method for teaching children English as a second language. Some of these methods appear to be better than others. It is beyond the scope of this discussion to discuss the details of formal educational approaches. The focus of information presented here is to explore ways to prepare infants and children for bilingualism.

The definition of bilingual proficiency suggests that the child or adult can read, write, and speak in two different languages; this process requires many years of learning (Collier, 1989). It has been assumed that children who are bilingual are at a disadvantage when learning a language and that their acquisition of one or both languages is delayed (Owens, 1988). However, selected research studies have disputed this belief. In fact, bilingual children who continue to develop cognitive skills in both languages during their elementary years frequently surpass their monolingual peers in areas of cognitive flexibility, verbal abilities, concept formation, divergent thinking skills, creativity, and diversity (Cummins, 1984; DeAvila & Duncan, 1980; Diaz, 1983; Hakuta, 1990). This is true for children with disabilities and children who are at risk as well (Damico, 1992a).

It is apparent that bilingualism enhances, rather than hinders, a child's development. Given these facts, one questions when a child should ideally begin to acquire a second language. Research studies have examined language development in children who acquired two languages *simultaneously* from birth and others who began a second language between the age of 3–5 (i.e., successive bilingual learners) (Collier, 1989). The *successive* bilingual learner typically acquires a first language at home and then learns the second language while interacting with peers. The simultaneous bilingual learner goes through a process similar to a monolingual learner. He or she initially mixes the two languages and then separates the two linguistic systems between the ages of 3–5. The rate and manner of language acquisition appears to be similar if the child is monolingual or bilingual (Padilla & Lindholm, 1976).

Successive bilingual learners also acquire both languages and are not at any disadvantage as long as they continue to develop cognitive skills in both languages throughout their elementary school years (Collier, 1989). However, for children who do not continue to develop their cognitive skills in their first language while they acquire a second language, there is actually lower proficiency in the second language and general cognitive and academic development (Collier, 1989). If a child does not develop age-appropriate skills in at least one of the two languages, neither language can serve as a base for cognitive growth (Cummins, 1989). A bilingual child with this profile could be at risk for lower intellectual and educational progress than a monolingual peer. *A key principle for intervention is to support the child's cognitive and language development in his or her primary language if he or she is a successive or simultaneous bilingual learner.* Children develop cognitive and language skills when activities are experientially based and when learning occurs while interacting with adults and other children in their primary language.

When children acquire a home language and then enter preschool or kindergarten, they may begin to learn a second language. As they acquire a second language, they frequently stop using their first language unless they are given environmental support and encouragement (Fillmore, 1991). In addition to effecting cognitive development, this loss of language can also have a detrimental sociological effect on the growth and development of a family. For example, some children lose their ability to communicate with their non–English speaking parents and relatives and then fail to learn valuable life skills. This loss of language and culture can lead to the disintegration of a family system, which is damaging to the development and well-being of the child. If a child develops a firm foundation in one language, this can have a positive effect on the child's general development. Skills that a child acquires in the first language can be generalized to a second language. *Because parents are the primary teachers, they should be encouraged to speak with their child in their native tongue.* When non-English parents are learning English, they may start speaking to their children in their second language. Children need good language models to acquire language, so parents should be encouraged to facilitate cognitive and linguistic growth through interaction with them in their primary language. Collier (1989) suggests that bilingual children need to continue developing cognitive skills in their primary language until they are 12 years of age. Cummins (1984b) recommends 7 years. Children can master the language for conversational purposes by age 5 but require higher-level language skills for reading a textbook, writing a composition, and thinking in abstract terms.

Research data suggest that the extent to which a student's language and culture are incorporated into a school program is a significant predictor of academic success (Cummins, 1989). *Therefore, it is important to plan an intervention program that will support a child's cognitive and academic development in his or her primary language and reinforce cultural identity. The following guidelines may be incorporated to create a language learning environment that will support young children:*

1. The interventionist must examine his or her cultural values and prejudices. One's prejudices can interfere with effective interaction with children and adults.
2. The intervention team should include pictures, objects, toys, books, signs, and foods that represent different cultures in activities and the environment (e.g., dolls that reflect different ethnic groups, various snack items, ethnic groups).

3. The children should be encouraged to use their primary language by providing opportunities to play with other children from their ethnic groups. Bilingual interpreters can be recruited from the community to assist with intervention.
4. Parents can be encouraged to assist in the classroom and with intervention.

DEVELOPMENTAL LEVEL

- Cry, burp, cough, sneeze, and hiccup
        (birth)
- Cooing and throaty gurgles
- Sounds such as a, e, o, and u are heard
        (1–3 months)
- May produce consonants such as k, g, or h
- Laughs out loud
        (2–4 months)

INTERVENTION GUIDELINES

The adult can hold the infant or provide face-to-face contact when the infant is seated in an infant seat or positioned in a supine position on a sofa, bed, or the floor. The infant should be comfortable so he or she should have a dry diaper and a full stomach for interaction to be successful. Observe and watch the infant. Imitate the infant's simple gestures and vocalizations. Reward vocalizations with smiles. Respect the infant's cues. For example, infants have short attention spans and may not enjoy the interaction for long periods of time. When the child fusses, try different positions and toys that please them. Avoid loud voices and rough games.

PLAY MATERIALS AND OPPORTUNITIES

Face-to-face interaction while holding the infant facilitates the development of sound awareness. Toys that have sound characteristics are also beneficial (e.g., musical toys, rattles). Touch the child's lips, tongue, and face in a playful manner to provide tactile input, increase awareness, and decrease sensitivity. Encourage the child to explore objects and hands with the mouth. This helps the child develop an increased awareness of the muscles responsible for speech.

**DEVELOPMENTAL
LEVEL**

- Squealing
    - (3–5 months)
- Two syllable, one-consonant sound strings are produced (a-ga, a-ba, a-da) repetitively
    - (3–6 months)
- Growling
- Yelling, not associated with distress
- Inhalation/exhalation sequences
- Variation in vocal pitch
- Consonants produced may include: b, m, w, d, n, r
    - (4–6 months)
- Makes a wet razzing sound
    - (6–7 months)
- Babbling begins to occur, for example, sing-song strings of conso-nants (da-da-da-da), and word-like double consonants (da-da, ma-ma, ba-ba)
    - (6–8 months)

**INTERVENTION
GUIDELINES**

Allow the infant to engage in vocal play when he or she awakes from a nap or when eating. The infant needs opportunities to experiment with sounds inde-pendently and during interaction.

   Talk to the infant in loving ways throughout the day. Cuddle and hold the infant close to the body. Play "communication games" in which the child vocal-izes and the adult waits until the child pauses and then imitates the sounds. Use a variety of facial expressions and hand gestures. Sing to the child and offer a variety of toys that produce sound. Monitor situations that elicit more vocaliza-tions (e.g., movement, a toy, face-to-face interaction) and repeat them.

**PLAY MATERIALS
AND
OPPORTUNITIES**

Put a Busy Box, toys, pictures, and mirrors inside the child's crib. Place pictures and toys by the changing table or over a carseat, stroller, or swing. Give the child safe toys with which to play, such as rattles and stuffed animals. Continue to encourage exploration of hands and toys.

**DEVELOPMENTAL
LEVEL**

- Says Mama or Dada indiscriminately
- May produce vc, cvc syllables occasionally
- Intonation patterns include rising pattern for "yes" or "no" questions and rising/falling of declarative sentences
    - (7–13 months)

**INTERVENTION
GUIDELINES**

Talk to the infant throughout the day. Direct his or her attention to sounds around the house (e.g., the telephone when it rings, an airplane, the television and radio). Pair sound with action. When blocks fall down, say "boom." Say "vroom" when moving toy cars. Show the child books with animals and cars, and produce simple sounds for them. Continue to imitate the child's responses and encourage him or her to make new sounds. Children seem to learn how to imitate from their experience of others imitating them (Powell & Mahoney, 1986). Encourage them to play games such as peekaboo and pat-a-cake. When the children do not imitate sounds or gestures, be patient and remember it will take a long time for them to learn new skills.

Use environmental sounds around the child. For example, point to an airplane and make the associated sound or make a ringing sound for the telephone. Show the child picturebooks with animals and make the appropriate animal sounds. Present a Busy Box and cause-and-effect toys that make sound.

MATERIALS AND OPPORTUNITIES

- Intelligibility: 25%–29% of words will be understood (1–2 years)

DEVELOPMENTAL LEVEL

Talk with the child throughout the day using short simple sentences. Name and label objects. Engage in "parallel talk" and describe what the child is doing. The adult can also engage in "self-talk" and describe what he or she is doing or feeling. Draw attention to sounds in the environment and imitate them (e.g., "The clock goes tick-tock," "The train goes toot-toot"). Speak at a slower rate, emphasizing developmental sounds, and repeat frequently. Read books that the child enjoys. Omit words and encourage the child to fill in key words. Introduce nursery rhymes, songs, and fingerplays that include developmental sounds (peekaboo, pat-a-cake, "pop goes the weasel," "So big"). Encourage the child to use both gestures and words. Play in front of a mirror. Expect and accept articulation errors. Children at this age commonly produce articulation

INTERVENTION GUIDELINES

Storytelling and books on tape lay a foundations for literacy.

errors (e.g., "ca" for cat). When this occurs, model the correct developmental sound in words. Provide visual, auditory, and tactile cues.

PLAY MATERIALS AND OPPORTUNITIES

At this developmental level, the following items are appropriate play materials: tape recorder with microphone, mirrors for mirror play, records and a record-player, books, musical instruments (e.g., whistles, harmonicas), bubbles, plastic animals, a train, a clock, toy cars, toy boats, bells, toy telephones, blocks, and any toy that has some type of sound properties that can be highlighted. Adults can find objects that contain the child's target sounds and play with the toys often.

DEVELOPMENTAL LEVEL

- Intelligibility: 50%–65% of words will be understood by 2 years and 70%–80% will be understood by 3 years
  (2–3 years)

INTERVENTION GUIDELINES

Adults can continue to increase the child's awareness by pointing out sounds in the environment and imitating the sounds. Read books that the child enjoys and highlight words that contain sounds with which the child has difficulty. Include fingerplays, songs, and nursery rhymes that contain this error sound. Increase the child's awareness and control of the oral muscles that are important for speech by blowing bubbles and whistles, inflating balloons, and playing with pinwheels. Play in front of a mirror and add face make-up. *Accept a child's articulation errors and model correct production of words.* For example, if the child says, "See the tat," the adult can say, "Yes, I see the cat. That cat is big." In this instance, the adult acknowledges the child's utterance and repeats the correct form of the word twice so the child hears the word more than once.

PLAY MATERIALS AND OPPORTUNITIES

Adults can take advantage of daily routine events to highlight target sounds in words. The parent or caregiver must be aware of a child's targeted sounds and phonological processes so that he or she can introduce them at home. If the child is working on the "p" sound, the parent or caregiver could sing the song "Pease Porridge Hot." While reading storybooks, the adult could point to and have the child name objects that start with the "p" sound. Perhaps the parent or caregiver and child could construct a scrapbook with "p" words. During play activities with Play-Doh, the adult could model making objects that start with the target sound. When cooking, the parent and child could make pudding or popcorn and listen to the "pa-pa" noise of the popping corn. When the child is working on the "b" sound, this sound could be emphasized when making **b**lack and **b**lue **b**lizzards (i.e., chocolate ice cream drink with blueberries on top) (Edwards, Magiuk, & Louko, 1991).

DEVELOPMENTAL LEVEL

- Intelligibility: 96%–100% of words will be understood by 4 years
  (3–4 years)

The adult should increase the child's awareness of sound by pointing out environmental sounds, listening to rhyming songs and nursery rhymes, and drawing the child's attention to specific words when reading a book or engaging in play. A child's oral motor skills can be developed by blowing bubbles, blowing paint with a straw, and playing musical instruments. Children enjoy playing with sounds and words and particularly enjoy changing words. The adult and child can play silly word games and change nursery rhymes by using a target sound or creating new rhymes. This is wonderful way to practice a new sound in a fun way (e.g., "No noodles, no knees, no naughty noses, no neck, no nurses need knock at my door").

Books, nursery rhymes, fingerplays, audiotapes and videotapes that include words with the targeted sounds are useful play materials. Cooking activities can be tailored to give the child practice with a particular sound. For example, if the target sound is "n," the adult and child can make "noodles" and play silly rhyme games to describe the noodles (e.g., "no noodles for poodles").

INTERVENTION GUIDELINES

PLAY MATERIALS AND OPPORTUNITIES

DEVELOPMENTAL LEVEL

> • Intelligibility: 100% of words will be understood although speech contains errors
> (4–5 years)

The suggestions provided for the previous developmental level are also appropriate here.

INTERVIEW GUIDELINES

The materials and opportunities provided on page 328 are also appropriate for children at this developmental level.

PLAY MATERIALS AND OPPORTUNITIES

DEVELOPMENTAL LEVEL

> • Intelligibility: 100% of words will be understood
> (5–6 years)
> (6½–7 years)

The guidelines suggested on pages 327 and 372 are also appropriate for children at this developmental level.

INTERVENTION GUIDELINES

The suggestions on page 328 are also appropriate for this developmental level.

PLAY MATERIALS AND OPPORTUNITIES

EXAMPLE

Moi C. is a 4-year-old girl. She was abandoned in the streets of Korea at birth and then adopted by her parents and brought to the United States when she was 2 years of age. She was born with a cleft palate, which has been repaired.

A TPBA revealed that Moi is shy and interacts minimally with peers or adults. She stays close to her mother and cries for extended periods of time if her mother leaves the room.

According to Mrs. C., Moi is an only child and has limited opportunities to play with other children because there are few children in their neighborhood.

During the TPBA, Moi engaged in play with her mother. She appeared to enjoy playing with dolls, the kitchen set, and at the water table. She demonstrated several steps in a schema (e.g., picked up the doll, gave her a bottle, and put her down; put a pan on the stove, poured water in the pan, and stirred). Moi did not seem to integrate schemata into a script.

Moi answered simple questions and commands. Expressively, she appeared to talk with her mother with a soft, whispered voice. She appeared to produce simple four- to five-word sentences. The majority of her utterances included requestives and commands, and few other functions were noted.

Moi's speech intelligibility was 70% when context was known. The speech-language therapist reported that Moi presented a phonological impairment. Moi also demonstrated poor oral awareness and control. She did not elevate her tongue tip and presented limited lip movements.

The team determined that Moi needed to develop social skills with her peers and begin to separate from her parent. It was also suggested that her play be expanded to include integrating schemata into a script. The speech-language therapist recommended Moi's lip and tongue strength and control be increased. The Hodson phonological approach was implemented. The speech-language therapist suggested that the team emphasize and highlight a specific phonological pattern each week during play and routine activities (e.g., stridency, clusters, velars, liquids).

It was recommended that Moi attend preschool 3 days a week. She would also receive speech-language services in the classroom to increase her phonological skills.

The team recommended that Moi be given toy props for developing various scripts (e.g., house, doctor). Adults in Moi's environment could help Moi integrate the schemata through modeling and providing cues and prompts. During these play scenarios, the adult could also help Moi develop other functions (e.g., commenting on an object/action) by prompting or cuing Moi. For example, the adult and child could read a story to the baby doll. The adult could use a "cloze technique" to increase Moi's ability to comment on objects and actions (e.g., "Moi, let's read for the baby. Here's a _____ and oh, look this puppy is _____.") Adults could provide materials that included each phonological process. The adult could model the practice words while playing.

Activities that would help Moi increase awareness and control of her articulators could be introduced. Moi and the children in the classroom could play in front of the mirrors, put on face makeup, and make funny faces in the mirror. They could also blow bubbles, blow paint on a paper with straws, or blow musical instruments. The teacher could also introduce "tongue walk" games, in which the teacher would place Cheerios and peanut butter on the children's lips and they could look in the mirror and lick them off.

OBSERVATION GUIDELINES FOR COMMUNICATION AND LANGUAGE DEVELOPMENT: SEMANTIC AND SYNTACTIC UNDERSTANDING

IV. Semantic and Syntactic Understanding
- A. What cognitive level of understanding is demonstrated in the child's language?
  1. Referential (specific objects)
  2. Extended (more than one object)
  3. Relational (relations between objects)
  4. Categorical (discrimination and classification)
  5. Metalinguistic (talking about language)
- B. What types of words are used?
  1. Nouns
  2. Verbs
  3. Adjectives
  4. Adverbs
  5. Prepositions
  6. Negatives
  7. Conjunctions
- C. What semantic relations are expressed in the child's language?
  1. Agent (*baby*)
  2. Action (*drink*)
  3. Object (*cup*)
  4. Recurrence (*more*)
  5. Nonexistence (*all gone*)
  6. Cessation (*stop*)
  7. Rejection (*no*)
  8. Location (*up*)
  9. Possession (*mine*)
  10. Agent–action (*baby drink*)
  11. Action–object (*drink juice*)
  12. Agent–action–object (*baby drink juice*)
  13. Action–object–location (*throw ball up*)
  14. Other
- D. What type of sentences are used by the child?
  1. Structure
     a. Declarative
     b. Imperative
     c. Negative
     d. Questions
  2. Level of complexity
     a. Simple
     b. Compound
     c. Complex

(continued)

OBSERVATION GUIDELINES FOR COMMUNICATION AND LANGUAGE DEVELOPMENT: SEMANTIC AND SYNTACTIC UNDERSTANDING

IV. Semantic and Syntactic Understanding
    E. What morphological markers does the child use?
        1. Present progressive (*-ing*)
        2. Prepositions (*in, on*)
        3. Regular and irregular past tense (*-ed, came*)
        4. Possessives (*'s*)
        5. Contractible and uncontractible copula (*dog's little*; *he is*—in response to question, "*Who is happy?*")
        6. Regular and irregular third person (*jumps, does*)
        7. Contractible and uncontractible auxiliary (*Mommy's drinking*; *he is*—in response to the question, "*Who is combing his hair?*")
    F. What is the child's mean length of utterance?

INTERVENTION IMPLICATIONS

Semantics and syntax are components of expressive language and represent different ways a child's verbal utterances can be classified or described. *Semantics refers to the meaning reflected by words or groups of words.* "*Syntax refers to the rule system for combining words or symbols into meaningful phrases and sentences, including the parts of speech, word order, and sentence structure*" (Dickson, Linder, & Hudson, 1993, p 176). *A thorough assessment of a child's expressive language skills should include the knowledge level expressed by words, the parts of speech employed, the semantic relations utilized, the types of sentences used by the child, the morphological markers used, and the child's mean length of utterance.*

Semantic Understanding

Each of the aspects of the assessment are interrelated and are listed in the outline in a developmental sequence. For example, when a young child first begins to use words, his or her cognitive level reflects an understanding of specific objects. Referential nouns comprise 60%–65% of the child's first words (Schwartz & Leonard, 1984) and include names of animals, foods, and toys. The child then progresses to use extended, relational, categorical, and metalinguistic language.

The words that a child produces reflect his or her conceptualization of the world. By 18 months of age, a child has had increased experience with persons, objects, and events and his or her vocabulary has expanded to 20 words. At this developmental level, a child begins to extend meanings of words to include various objects with specific attributes. For example, a bottle is any bottle and not just his or her bottle. A child produces nouns, verbs (e.g., go, eat), modifiers (e.g., your, mine), personal–social words (e.g., please, thank you), and function words (e.g., this, that) (Nelson, 1973). A child's lexicon expands and includes a variety of words (e.g., adjectives, adverbs, prepositions, negatives, conjunctions). If a child produces a limited number and type of words, intervention should emphasize increasing a variety of words. For example, if a child produces mostly nouns, intervention should emphasize action verbs and modifiers.

Before establishing an expressive language goal, it is important to be certain the child has the necessary prerequisite cognitive and linguistic skills. For example, if the adult wants to teach the child the color "blue," the child must first be able to match blue objects, then identify a blue truck when asked, "Which truck is blue?," and then be able to say, "blue" when asked, "What color is the truck?" Before expecting a child to know the name of a "cup," he or she must understand and demonstrate the use of a cup. Before the child answers "when" questions or adds tense makers to verbs (e.g., ing, ed), he or she must understand time concepts.

An intervention principle is to increase the child's skill level by providing an enriched environment and facilitating language development through natural conversational interaction. The adult must provide an interesting and motivating environment with toys and objects that are appropriate for the child's overall developmental needs. The adult should observe the child manipulating objects and interacting with adults and other children and then take advantage of these opportunities to model conversational discourse and semantic and grammatical constructions. Children learn words and rules for joining words together when the words match the event. *The INREAL conversational strategies can be used to facilitate language development in a natural conversational manner.* The adult must use silence, understanding, and listening (S.O.U.L.) when observing the child's play. By using S.O.U.L., the adult understands the child's communicative intention and can then respond to the child in a meaningful manner. For instance, when the adult uses self-talk (e.g., "Mama will get your *bottle*"), the child hears the parent's words and sees the object. After many repeated experiences, he or she begins to associate the words with the object. When a parent uses parallel talk (e.g., "You're sad"), the child associates the feeling with the word that he or she hears repeatedly. When the parent mirrors, (e.g., child points and the parent imitates pointing) the child's actions, the child learns how to be a conversational partner. With vocal monitoring and reflecting (e.g., child says "do" for "go" and the adult says "go"), the child feels acknowledged as a conversational partner and learns how to take turns and correct language forms. If a parent listens to the child, uses the child's words, and adds information (i.e., expansion), the child feels validated because the adult uses his or her words. The child also hears new information and acquires new language forms. The child learns how to use language forms and acquires new knowledge with modeling. For example, if a child fails to say, "Thank you" after receiving a cookie, the adult can model the response for the child. Another type of modeling includes asking the child questions that promote thought and problem-solving. For instance, if the child and adult are reading a book, the adult may say, "I wonder what will happen to John?"

Syntactic Understanding

Syntax can be described in terms of word order, inflections, and relationships among words. Once the child's intentions are understood, his or her semantic relations are present and the child has progressed to multiword utterances and syntactic skills can be emphasized.

To increase semantics and syntactic understanding, the same principles that were noted on pages 303–304 apply. These principles are summarized here:

1. The adult should respond to the child's communicative attempts in a timely and thoughtful manner.
2. The adult should develop keen observational skills and begin to understand the child's communicative attempts by using contextual cues (i.e., practice S.O.U.L.).
3. The adult must understand the child's "intention" (e.g., protesting, commenting, requesting) whether it is expressed verbally or nonverbally and respond in a meaningful manner (e.g., self-talk, parallel talk, expansion, mirroring, vocal monitoring, modeling).
4. The adult should create a need for the child to communicate, as all communicative interaction should occur in meaningful contexts.
5. Intervention should aim toward "bumping" the child up to the next higher-level skill by modeling and by providing prompts and implementing INREAL strategies.

The adult must consider the child's goals and then set up the environment with toys and experiences that will provide an opportunity for the targeted concepts and constructions to occur. It is especially important to select activities that will motivate and interest the child. For instance, for a child who enjoys dinosaurs and needs to express the semantic relations "recurrence" (more), the adult could place dinosaurs in a bag and introduce the water and sand table. The adult could show the child the dinosaur as it is removed from the bag. As the child explores the use of the object, the adult could watch and observe him or her. When appropriate, the adult could shake the bag and ask for "more." When the child reaches for the bag and nonverbally indicates "more," the adult can model the word "more" and give the child the dinosaur. After repeatedly hearing the word "more" and associating "recurrence" with the event, children typically begin to vocalize a close approximation of the word. The adult must observe the child exploring objects and interacting with others. The child's communicative intention is interpreted and then the adult adds meaning to the child's acts by using INREAL strategies. For example, if a child picks up a ball, starts to throw it, and says, "Ball," the adult can "expand" the utterance by saying "Throw ball," "Bounce ball," or "Kick ball." If a child needs to formulate "wh" questions, the adult could fail to give all of the children a snack item or necessary tools for completing an art project. When a child in the group asks, "Where's my cookie?," or "Where's my crayon?," the child with a language delay has an opportunity to hear a model of a "wh" question. The adult can also repeat the question, "Where's Maria's cookie?" The adult can wait for the child with a language delay to ask the question. If the child inappropriately formulates a question, the adult can provide a model and correctly formulate the question. For example, if the child asks the question with rising intonation, "Cookie?," the adult could say "Where's the cookie?" (i.e., expansion).

To increase use of morphological constructions, the adult sets up the environment and listens to the child's utterances and then waits for an appropriate time to interject examples and use of morphological markers. For example, if a child says, "Dog jump" when watching a pet dog jump up for food, the adult can expand the utterance and increase the child's understanding by saying,

"Yes, that dog's jumping. He's jumping high." By repeating the targeted construction several times, the child has a greater opportunity to hear the ending on the word and associate the grammatical form with the event and time concept.

- Referential knowledge: A particular word represents a specific item (e.g., "bankie" refers to the child's blanket only)
  (9–15 months)

DEVELOPMENTAL LEVEL

To increase a child's knowledge of the world and expressive verbalizations, the facilitator must *name* and *label objects* and *events in the environment.* Words that are meaningful to the child and pertain to the immediate environment should be emphasized. Labels for referents should be *repeated* so the child has many opportunities to hear the name. Young children should be encouraged to *make choices* as this will facilitate initiation and verbal output. Initially, children will only produce close approximations of words. These productions should be expected and accepted.

    Caregivers can help children learn the correct productions of words by accepting their vocalizations as meaningful and modeling the correct pronunciation of the word. When the child points to a ball and says "ba," the adult can give the child the ball and repeat "Ball, ball, here's your ball."

INTERVENTION GUIDELINES

The adult must name and label common objects and toys in the child's environment as the child explores them. Objects frequently used include blankets, bottles, shoes, coats, cookies, babies, balls, cups, crackers, dogs, diapers, blocks, and books.

PLAY MATERIALS AND OPPORTUNITIES

- Extended knowledge: A word represents various kinds of objects (e.g., "chair" can mean many types of chairs)
  (9–15 months)

DEVELOPMENTAL LEVEL

Observe the child as he or she explores the environment. Objects that appear to interest the child should be named. The facilitator can extend the child's knowledge by presenting or pointing out different objects that share the same names.

INTERVENTION GUIDELINES

The adult should have several types of objects available for the child to manipulate and explore (e.g., cups, balls, shoes, dolls, books). The adult can name and label the items as the child explores them. Pictures of objects should also be introduced so the child sees several examples of the objects that match a word.

PLAY MATERIALS AND OPPORTUNITIES

- Relational knowledge: A word understood to relate to itself or something else
  (18 months +)

DEVELOPMENTAL LEVEL

INTERVENTION GUIDELINES

A child's expressive vocabulary reflects his or her knowledge base. Words within a child's lexicon reveal how he or she is learning object concepts, relational concepts, and new vocabulary. As the child acquires cognitive skills of object permanence, object constancy, and causality, he or she begins to express relational meanings in words (i.e., children recognize how one word can relate to another) (Sinclair, 1970; Werner & Kaplan, 1963). For example, knowing "open" in relation to "box" is to understand the relational meaning between words that refer to an action and an affected object (Bloom & Lahey, 1978). Relational categories include utterances pertaining to existence, nonexistence, disappearance, action, location, possession, and characteristics of objects, persons, and situations (Owens, 1988).

Understanding of *existence* (i.e., "there," "uh," "oh") occurs when the child wants to point out objects. When the child says, "no" to comment on a missing object, he or she is demonstrating the relational understanding of *nonexistence*. To comment on the disappearance of an object that had existed in context, the child comments, "away," which exemplifies *disappearance*. If a child extends his or her arms and says, "up," he or she is requesting an *action*. The same word, "up," when used to describe where something is located in space, indicates *location*. If a child holds a doll and says, "mine," the relational function indicates *possession*.

DEVELOPMENTAL LEVEL

- Reflexive-relational knowledge: Mark existence, nonexistence, disappearance, and recurrence: "this," "all gone," "more"
  (18 months +)

INTERVENTION GUIDELINES

The reflexive-relational category includes words that mark existence (e.g., "this"), nonexistence (e.g., "no"), disappearance (e.g., "all gone"), and recurrence (e.g., "more"). The facilitator must arrange the environment so that the relationships among objects can be manipulated. When the opportunity arises, the adult can describe events and model appropriate verbal utterances.

PLAY MATERIALS AND OPPORTUNITIES

Snacktime and other events in which the child must request "more" provide opportunities for the child to learn the concept of "recurrence." The adult can offer small amounts of an item so the child must request or indicate "more" (e.g., raisins, Cheerios, small pieces of cookie or cracker, milk, bubbles, blocks, cars). The adult can model the word "more" and wait for the child to use a gesture or word. If a child says, "More," the adult can increase the length of the utterance by expanding the child's comment and by repeating, "More _____" (e.g., bubbles, cookies) and adding the appropriate word. The adult can also use a cloze technique and ask a question (i.e., "More _____?") and wait for the child to complete the phrase, "More bubbles."

To teach the concept of "disappearance," the adult can model the words "all gone" when the child's food or toys disappear. Children also enjoy hiding toys in pockets, sand, oatmeal, cornmeal, beans, popcorn, Jell-o, and boxes and under washcloths.

- Action-relational knowledge: Movement implied: "up," "down," "bye-bye," "do")
  (18 months +)

The facilitator must arrange the environment and create a need for the young child to communicate wants. One must observe the child for communicative attempts. The adult can describe or model the response (e.g., gestures, words) or expand the response as the child masters a skill at one level. For example, when the child extends his or her arms to indicate "up," the adult can accept the gesture and expand the response by saying the word "up." When the child produces the word "up," the adult can expand the response to two words by saying, "Pick me up."

Children learn by doing and associating words with movement. The adult should arrange situations so the child must ask to be lifted "up." For example, tape balloons out of reach on a wall, look out a high window and describe some exciting event, or place toys on a high shelf.

To increase the use of "bye-bye," the adult can create opportunities for the child to use this construction (e.g., the child can go in and out of a large cardboard box and say "bye"; when putting toys in a toybox, the adult can say "bye-bye"; when leaving a room the adult can model saying "bye-bye" to the objects and people in the room).

- Location-relational knowledge: Direction or spatial relationship— object is located
  (18 months +)

The environment must be structured so the child needs to communicate (e.g., place a toy "up" and out of reach). The adult prompts or cues the child by posing questions (e.g., Where's Teddy?) and waits for the child to express the answer. If the child doesn't initiate, the facilitator can model the appropriate communicative act (e.g., a gesture, word). After the child responds, the facilitator must accept the child's communicative efforts and use appropriate INREAL strategies to increase communication skill development.

The adult can encourage the child to respond with location-relational comments by posing "where" questions. For example, when searching for a bottle, diaper, or blanket, the adult can ask, "Where's _____?" and wait for the child to respond. If the child does not respond, the adult can say the response, "Here's bottle" or "There's bottle," or "in box."

- Possessional-relational knowledge: Object associated with a person: "mine"
  (18 months +)

INTERVENTION GUIDELINES

To facilitate the child's understanding of possessional-relational concepts, the adult can direct the child's attention to events that depict this form. The adult can model the appropriate construction in a contextually meaningful manner.

PLAY MATERIALS AND OPPORTUNITIES

The adult can find opportunities to model and demonstrate possessional-relational concepts. For instance, the adult can stack coats or shoes together and encourage each child to find his or her possessions. The adult can say the construction when finding his or her coat (e.g., "my coat"). When a child takes another child's toy, the adult can demonstrate possession (e.g., "Julie's car," "my car"). A parent can play with toys and clothes and periodically query the child (e.g., "Mama's sock?") to prompt a response (e.g., "my sock," "mine"). During mealtime the parent can place dishes and food before each family member and say, "Here's Mama's cup" or, "Here's Daddy's cup."

DEVELOPMENTAL LEVEL

- Categorical knowledge: The semantic category of words demonstrating the awareness of common aspects among objects (e.g., the word "toys")
  (2 years +)

INTERVENTION GUIDELINES

By organizing the environment and providing external structure, the facilitator can support the child's ability to classify and group objects appropriately. Through natural conversational interaction, the adult can prompt problem-solving skills that will support development of organizational thought.

PLAY MATERIALS AND OPPORTUNITIES

An adult can facilitate categorical knowledge by storing toys in baskets or buckets and organizing the environment so the child can place all of the "animals" in a box or sort dolls, blocks, books, trucks, dishes, and cars. The adult can model the names of items while playing with them and then putting them away. Children can be encouraged to help with household chores (e.g., throwing away trash, putting pots and pans in a drawer, placing clothes in hamper). Asking children questions promotes thought organization (e.g., "Where do animals live?", "What do we eat?", "What things can cut?").

DEVELOPMENTAL LEVEL

- Metalinguistic knowledge: The ability to think about language and comment on it as well as produce and comprehend it (e.g., the child states that "ball" begins with a "b")
  (4–5 years)

INTERVENTION GUIDELINES

While interacting with children, the adult can comment on the characteristics of language (e.g., sounds that rhyme, sounds that are alike, words with double meanings, definitions of words). *Follow the interests of the children and find teachable moments that will expand their knowledge bases.*

The adult can prompt and encourage the child to talk about language by modeling responses. For example, when reading a book, reciting a rhyme, or introducing a new word, the adult can comment on the word and associate it with something else (e.g., "That's a silly word. It sounds like _____"; "That has your sound in it—_____"; "These words rhyme"). Discuss the meanings of words as they arise in storybooks and daily events. Adults can prompt thought and discussion by posing questions (e.g., "I wonder what word rhymes with *mad*"; "The tree has bark, and an animal barks. Do you know what animal barks?").

PLAY MATERIALS AND OPPORTUNITIES

Parts of Speech

An intervention principle is to follow a normal developmental sequence when planning remediation goals. Expect a child to point toward objects and vocalize before he or she begins to label and name them. First vocabulary words should include referential nouns and items from the categories of animals, foods, and toys (Benedict, 1979, Nelson, 1973; Schwartz & Leonard, 1984). Nouns, verbs, adjectives, prepositions, and negatives emerge during the second year of life. Adverbs and conjunctions are seen in the third and fourth year (Dickson, Linder, & Hudson, 1993). A child first produces one-word utterances, then two words, and eventually multiword sentences. As linguistic and cognitive skills increase, he or she adds morphological endings (e.g., *-ing*, *-ed*).

INTERVENTION IMPLICATIONS

Semantic Relations

As a child's cognitive and linguistic skills emerge, nonverbal and verbal expressive language reflects the child's unfolding knowledge of the relationships between objects, people, and events. At first, the child expresses his or her needs and wants with gestures, single words, and inflection but as thinking skills and vocabulary expand, more words are added to reflect the child's thoughts. Like developmental building blocks, the child learns how to create sentences to express more complex ideas.

One-, two-, and three-word telegraphic utterances are presentence structures. Because these early comments do not meet the criteria for a sentence, they are not described in terms of the adult syntactic model. Bloom and Lahey (1978) and Brown (1978) found that these early presentence structures reflect the child's rule system for joining words together. The messages reflect the content of a child's thoughts and are described as "semantic-syntactive" (Bloom & Lahey, 1978) constructions or "semantic relations" (e.g., agent, action, recurrence, nonexistence). These forms are the foundation for future longer utterances. For example, a child may say, "Mommy, bye-bye" when the parent leaves and again when the parent gets her purse and keys. In the first example, the two-word phrase reflects the semantic relation of nonexistence because the child is describing the disappearance of the parent. In the second utterance, the child is requesting action as he or she wants to go someplace with the parent. As cognition and language skills expand, the child uses an increased number of words to communicate these messages (e.g., "Mama go bye-bye," "I go bye-bye").

Intervention should emphasize increasing a variety of age-appropriate seman-tic relations. If a child does not exhibit a specific semantic relational form, a goal should be established to develop this construction. One-word utterances should be expanded to two- and then three-word utterances by using a variety of INREAL strategies (e.g., vocal monitoring/reflecting, expansion, modeling, self talk, parallel talk).

Sentence Types

The types of sentences a child generates is another indicator of syntactic devel-opment. Semantic relations and longer utterances can be described and classi-fied as declarative, imperative, negative, or question forms. For example, early question forms do not contain wh- words but are marked by rising intonation. When a child searches for a cookie after it drops out of view, he or she formu-lates a question "Cookie?" The intonation indicates he or she is asking, "Where's the cookie?"

Another way to analyze syntactic development is to determine whether a sentence is a simple, compound, or complex form. A simple sentence includes a subject and verb phrase. Compound sentences contain two independent clauses (e.g., "I brushed my teeth and went to bed.") Complex sentences in-clude an independent and dependent clause. Sentences increase in complexity as the child acquires more abstract thought processes. Developmentally basic sentence forms, which include a subject and a verb, emerge between 18 months and 3 years of age. Compound sentences appear between 2 and 2½ years of age. Complex sentence structures develop between 2 and 3 years of age (Trantham & Pedersen, 1976).

Morphology

Development of grammatical morphemes follows a developmental sequence. Morphemes are the smallest meaningful units of language. There are two differ-ent types of morphemes—lexical (e.g., free morphemes) and grammatical (e.g., bound morphemes). Lexical morphemes include root words such as "dog" and "cat." Grammatical morphemes include word endings, such as "s" and "ed," that indicate pluralization and past tense. Brown (1973) identified a developmental sequence for the acquisition of morphological grammatical units. For example, irregular past tense verbs (e.g., fell, broke, sat, went) emerge before regular past tense verbs (e.g., pulled, walked). Self-talk, parallel talk, vocal monitoring and reflecting, modeling, and expansion techniques can be used to increase usage of morphological endings. For instance, if a child says, "Mama, I eated it all up," the caregiver could respond "Yes, you *ate* it all."

Morphological Markers

Roger Brown (1973) identified five developmental stages and described gram-matical morphemes and sentence types that emerged at each level. His 14 mor-phemes are listed in Table 3. After the developmental stage has been identified, intervention goals can be developed to move the child to the next develop-mental level. For example, if a child produces negative sentences with the word "no," intervention should emphasize increasing use of two-word sentences by

Table 3. Brown's 14 morphemes

Age of mastery[a] (in months)	Morpheme	Example
19–28	Present progressive -ing (no auxiliary verb)	"Mommy driving."
24–33	Regular plural -s	"Kitties eat my ice cream." Forms: /s/, /z/, and /ɪz/ Cats (/kæts/) Dogs (/dogz/) Classes (/klæsɪz/), wishes (/wɪʃɪz/)
25–46	Irregular past	"Came," "fell," "broke," "sat," "went"
26–40	Possessives	"Mommy's balloon broke." Forms: /s/, /z/, and ɪz/ as in regular plural
26–46	Regular third person -s	"Kathy hits." Forms: /s/, /z/, and /ɪz/ as in regular plural
26–48	Regular past -ed	"Mommy pulled the wagon." Forms: /d/, /t/, ɪd/ Pulled (/puld/) Walked (/wɔkt/) Glided (/g l aɪ d ɪ d/)
27–30	In	"Ball in cup."
27–30	On	"Doggie on sofa."
27–39	Uncontractible copula (verb *to be* as main verb)	"He is." (response to "Who's sick?")
28–46	Articles	"I see a kitty." "I throw the ball to Daddy."
28–50	Irregular third person	"Does," "has"
29–48	Uncontractible auxiliary	"He is." (response to "Who's wearing your hat?")
29–49	Contractible copula	"Man's big." "Man is big."
30–50	Contractible auxiliary.	"Daddy's drinking juice." "Daddy is drinking juice."

[a]Used correctly 90% of the time in obligatory contexts
Source: Brown (1973); Miller (1981); Owens (1988).

using parallel talk, self-talk, modeling, expansion, and vocal monitoring and reflecting. If a child says, "No" when the parent offers more milk, the adult could expand the utterance by saying, "No more milk." If the child generates "what" questions but does not use "where" or "when" forms, the adult can model these questions while reading books or playing games (e.g., "Where's that boy going?," "When is his mama coming back?," "Maybe we should ask Billy, 'where's the bike?'").

Mean Length of Utterance

An average length of a child's utterances can be used to predict syntactic abilities. When a child's MLU is greater than 4.5, content and sentence structure are better indicators of language development. Brown (1973) identified five stages in the growth of language that correspond to an increase in the child's mean length of utterance (MLU) (Table 4). The (MLU) can be calculated from

Table 4.   Predicting chronological age from mean length of utterance

Brown's stage	MLU	Predicted chronological age[a]	Predicted age ± 1 SD middle 68%
Early Stage I	1.01	19.1	16.4–21.8
	1.50	23.0	18.5–27.5
Late Stage I	1.60	23.8	19.3–28.3
	2.00	26.9	21.5–32.3
Stage II	2.10	27.7	22.3–33.1
	2.50	30.8	23.9–37.7
Stage III	2.60	31.6	24.7–38.5
	3.00	34.8	28.0–41.6
Early Stage IV	3.10	35.6	28.8–42.4
	3.50	38.7	30.8–46.6
Late Stage IV/ Early Stage V	3.60	39.5	31.6–47.4
	4.00	42.6	36.7–48.5
Late Stage V	4.10	43.4	37.5–49.3
	4.50	46.6	40.3–52.9
Post Stage V	4.60	47.3	41.0–53.6
	5.10	51.3	46.9–59.7
	5.60	55.2	46.8–63.6
	6.00	58.3	49.9–66.7

Reprinted with the permission of Macmillan Publishing company from *Assessing Infants and Pre-schoolers with Handicaps* by Donald B. Bailey, Jr. and Mark Wolery. Copyright © by Macmillan College Publishing Company, Inc.
[a]Age is predicted from the equation: Age (in months) = 11.199 + 7.857 (MLU). Computed from obtained standard deviations.

the child's language sample. One hundred utterances should be obtained. The total number of morphemes is calculated (e.g., rid/ing = 2 morphemes; dog/s = 2 morphemes). Then the total number of morphemes is divided by the total number of utterances. For a 100-utterance sample that contains 200 morphemes, the MLU would be calculated as 2.0. According to Brown's (1973) stages, this score would be expected for a child 26.9 months and at the Late Stage I Level. Characteristics of a child's syntactic abilities are described at each stage (I–IV). For example, at late Stage I, children typically produce negative statements with a single word, "No." An interrogative may be expressed as, "What + this/that" or "What" + noun phrase or verb phrase?

To facilitate the development of longer utterances, the interventionist can implement modeling, VMR, expansion, parallel talk, and self-talk. For example, if a child says, "*No* like that," the adult can say, "You *don't* like that." When the child points to something, the adult can produce the appropriate comment that matches the child's gesture. If the child points to a big truck, the adult could say, "That's a truck." If the child jumps up and down, the adult can comment, "You're jumping." When completing tasks, the caregiver can describe his or her actions (e.g., "I'm vacuuming.")

INTERVENTION GUIDELINES

Intervention should focus on increasing cognitive and pragmatic skills. Increased mean length of utterance and more advanced grammatical structures will follow. The adult can facilitate cognitive development by providing opportunities to learn relationships among people, objects, and events and by organizing relationships among people, objects, and events. The adult needs first to identify the child's communicative intent (e.g., requestive, command) and then to model the linguistic structure that is developmentally appropriate for the child. For instance, if the child is watching a dog do tricks at the circus and comments on an action (e.g., "Doggie jump"), the adult can interpret the child's intention based on the context of the situation and expand the utterance by adding another linguistic unit (e.g., "Dog's jumping high"). The adult has *listened to the child's comment, responded in a natural conversational manner, and added information* (e.g., time concept—"ing"—and semantic concept—"high").

Toys that are appropriate for the child's developmental play level must be selected. *All learning experiences must be meaningful to the child.* Communication will occur if the child feels motivated to interact and is rewarded by appropriate toys at each developmental level. To master the prepositions "in" and "on," children enjoy getting into boxes and climbing on small toy gyms. When children reach the top of a nursery apparatus, the adult can use parallel talk and say "You're *on* the top." When the child hides inside a box, the adult can say, "Where's Tommy? There he is. He's *in* the box."

PLAY MATERIALS AND OPPORTUNITIES

Children can learn the present progressive "ing" when they are jumping, kicking, climbing, smiling, and laughing. The past tense of verbs can be elicited by discussing something that was just read in a book or something that occurred at the end of the day to recall events of the day.

Plural forms can be taught with toys or during snack. The facilitator can count the number of cookies, peas, or crackers the child has on his or her plate. Plates, cups, and utensils can be counted and identified.

When a child omits a morphological marker, the adult can use communication strategies to facilitate development. For instance, if a child omits the auxiliary (e.g., "I wearing hat"), the adult can repeat the child's words with a corrected form (e.g., "I am wearing a hat.").

OBSERVATION GUIDELINES FOR COMMUNICATION AND LANGUAGE: COMPREHENSION OF LANGUAGE

V. Comprehension of Language
  A. What early comprehension is demonstrated?
    1. What is the child's reaction to sounds?
    2. Does the child exhibit joint referencing with an adult?
      a. With visual regard
      b. With verbal cue
      c. With physical cue
    3. Does the child respond to common routines or statements?
      a. With contextual cues
      b. Without contextual cues
  B. What comprehension of language forms is demonstrated?
    1. To which semantic relations does the child respond?
    2. To which questions does the child respond?
      a. Yes/no questions
      b. Simple "wh" questions (*where, what, who*)
      c. Advanced "wh" questions (*which, when, why, how*)
    3. What commands can the child follow?
      a. Complexity (one-step, multistep)
      b. With/without contextual cues
    4. What prepositions can the child understand?
      a. Simple (*in, on*)
      b. Advanced (*next to, behind, in front of*)
    5. What temporal terms does the child understand?
    6. What relational terms does the child understand?

INTERVENTION IMPLICATIONS

The Hierarchical Development of Language Comprehension

Receptive language, or language comprehension, involves receiving and understanding spoken words, associating the word with its referent, and understanding a word's meaning or function (Weiss & Lillywhite, 1981). The items listed in the TPBA outline represent developmental skills that usually emerge in a hierarchial manner; for the most part, one skill builds upon another. For instance, in order for a child to associate a word with an object, he or she must hear the word repeated innumerable times and associate the word with the event. Before this associative learning can occur, the child must pay attention to the event (e.g., shared joint attention or gaze behavior directed toward an object). A child usually comprehends gestures and routines before he or she comprehends words. For example, a child reaches for a bottle and understands its purpose before he or she comprehends the word "bottle."

The developmental sequence of language acquisition is definable and predictable. For instance, the first words an infant typically comprehends include his or her name, "no," "bye," and "mama." Initial receptive vocabulary consists of single-syllable words that are concrete and pertain to the immediate environment. Developmentally, the child comprehends body parts, names of family members, clothing, and selected names of toys before he or she understands more abstract concepts such as numbers, colors, and feelings. A child follows simple commands with gestures before commands without gestures. The child follows simple commands with one verb (e.g., "Get a book") before following a two-step command (e.g., "Get a book and open it").

Clark (1973) found that children acquire prepositions in a specific sequence. For instance, children acquire spatial terms as they are related to self before acquiring those not related to themselves. A child first develops vertical spatial words (e.g., up, down), then horizontal-frontal words (e.g., in front of), and then horizontal-lateral words (e.g., in back of). Children comprehend "yes" or "no," "what," and "where" questions before they decode more complex interrogatives, such as "which," "why," and "how." Piaget (1926) noted that children must understand cause, manner, and time to decode these questions.

Intervention Principles that Promote Language Comprehension

Although a child learns language through all of the senses, the primary means of acquiring the language of one's culture is by hearing it. *Therefore, if a child presents a delay in language acquisition or comprehension, a hearing loss must be ruled out before intervention can proceed. The child must be referred to his or her physician or an audiologist for a hearing screening.*

Develop Goals Based on the Developmental Sequence

After the team has identified a delay in the area of language comprehension, goals should be planned using a developmental sequence as a guide. These goals should consider the child's cognitive abilities and functional needs. For example, expect a child to search for an object when it is hidden from view (i.e., object permanence) before he or she knows the name of the referent. Children localize to sound before responding to their names. Expect the child to comprehend gestures (e.g., extended hand cue) before following commands without gestural cues (e.g., "Give me the cup"). One would expect a child to follow one command and direction (e.g., "Give me the cup") before remembering more complex directions that include two units of information (e.g., "*Give* me a cup and *put* it on the table").

For safety purposes it is important for the child to recognize and localize to sound, respond to his or her name, and understand the concept "no." These goals should be established before expecting the child to identify body parts or point to common objects.

Encourage Concurrent Comprehension and Expression

Historically, receptive language development has been thought to always precede expressive language development. This rule appears to be true before a child acquires words. However, after words have emerged, research has shown that children use words and structures that are beyond their comprehension because they remember and repeat phrases within an appropriate context. For example, children with autism often repeat and echo sentences and requests they hear. They do not, however, comprehend the words they repeat. As young children are learning language, they may repeat words before they comprehend the meaning of the concepts. Consequently, some researchers recommend that intervention stress production rather than comprehension (Bloom & Lahey, 1978). Other researchers believe the traditional approach of training comprehension before expression is preferred (Schumaker & Sherman, 1978). A third alternative is to plan an intervention program that provides both comprehension and production concurrently (Siegel & Spradlin, 1978). This is the preferred intervention strategy for transdisciplinary play-based intervention because it is a holistic method that follows a natural method of acquiring language.

The adult's role in this intervention strategy includes the following: 1) to provide an enriched environment and establish routines, 2) to provide prompts and cues, 3) to name and label objects and events, and 4) to expand the child's knowledge base by utilizing a variety of interaction strategies. One of the most important roles that the adult performs is to offer an enriched learning environment and conversational interaction. A child does not know about the world unless he or she is given an opportunity to experience a variety of stimuli. The child needs exposure to a variety of toys, books, videotapes, audiotapes, sensory stimuli, and outings to the zoo, library, grocery store, park, and other interesting places.

Label Objects and Events   Without a language model that offers information, the child does not benefit from the enriched environment. In the early stages of language development, the facilitator must label and name objects and events and provide prompts and cues to facilitate language development. For instance, if a child's hearing acuity has been tested and found to be satisfactory but the child does not attend to environmental events or verbalizations, goals must focus on increasing the child's sound awareness and focusing his or her attention on the event so that he or she begins to associate sounds and words with objects. When the telephone rings, the adult must stop, look, and point toward the object. If the child does not respond, additional prompts and cues may be needed to direct or focus the child's attention (e.g., physical prompts—touch the child or turn his or her head toward the object). As the child begins to respond, fewer prompts and cues are necessary and should be gradually decreased. For instance, after the child consistently looks toward the telephone when gesturally cued (i.e., adult points and directs child's attention), the adult should wait 3–4 seconds for the child to look toward the telephone before giving more prompts. Adults should avoid using indefinites (e.g., this, that, it) excessively when talking with a child because children need to hear the names of the objects. If the child does not respond, the prompts could be reintroduced. Because children learn language in conjunction with events, it is important that the child have a set routine in the learning environment (e.g., home, school), and that the same words and phrases be used to describe the environment and the objects in the environment. For example, when a parent drove her preschooler to school, they passed a school playground. The parent always pointed to the swingset and said "bye-bye, swings" as they passed them. The child would look toward the swings but did not say anything. After repeated trips, the child began to wave at the swings as they passed them. After 10–15 trips, the child initiated a wave "bye-bye" and said an approximation of "swing." It is apparent that children attend to and interpret environmental cues and routines before they comprehend actual words.

Strengthen New Words Along with naming and labeling, one can also use another technique for strengthening new words (Weiss & Lillywhite, 1988). After a child has said a word for the first time, the adult can bombard the child with the word and reinforce its use. For instance, if a child says, "Ball" the adult could say, "Yes, ball. Big ball. Jimmy's ball."

Use a Simplified Language Style In the early stages of language development, the facilitator increases the child's comprehension by talking to the child with a simplified language style. It is important to "match" the child's behavior (e.g., act and communicate in ways similar to those used by the child). The adult provides a model for the child and facilitates interaction. For instance, when talking with a 2-year-old who produces mostly single-word utterances, the adult could describe events and talk with the child using two- to three-word phrases. As the child begins to produce mostly two- to three-word phrases, the adult could "bump the child up" by interacting with three- to five-word phrases. This strategy is called "progressive matching" because the adult communicates and interacts at an active and communicative level similar to that of the child while simultaneously showing the child the next developmental step (McDonald & Carroll, 1992). At this time, there is very little evidence to suggest whether an adult should talk with a child who has a language impairment with short simple utterances that lack grammatical details (e.g., "baby cat," "doggie sleep") or if simple, but grammatically well-formed, sentences should be used. Fey (1986) suggests the adult speak with the child with grammatically complete utterances. He states that a child's comprehension might exceed production, and the child would expect to hear function words (e.g., copula, articles, morphological endings). Children who do not have knowledge of certain linguistic forms probably filter them out and attend to parts of utterances they understand. Hearing the additional linguistic forms probably does not interfere with learning. INREAL interaction strategies including self-talk, parallel talk, and expansion, can be implemented to facilitate both increased receptive and expressive language skills (see pp. 290–291).

Use Questions Appropriately Questions can be used to facilitate language development, but if used inappropriately can actually hinder language skills. Adults frequently use questioning to the exclusion of other communication techniques. For example, to encourage naming skills, adults point to objects and ask the child to name them. At other times, adults choose to interact and gain information from children by asking many questions such as, "What are you doing?," "What did you do at school today?," and "Where are you going?" These types of questions require the child to answer with single words and do not promote conversational discourse. If an adult asks many questions of this nature, the child will feel like he or she is being tested and pressured to talk. Excessive questioning limits opportunities for the child to express thoughts and ideas. Adults should monitor the number and types of questions they ask. Particular types of questions should be used less often. For example, yes or no questions (e.g., "Are you hungry?") and tag questions (e.g., "That's a scary monster, isn't it?") require a single answer. Other types of questions can be posed in such a manner that they promote language development.

For example, adults can ask rhetorical questions while reading books or playing with the child (e.g., "I wonder what will happen next?," "I wonder how we can fix the torn picture?"). These types of questions invite the child to interact and problem-solve with the adult. Instead of starting a conversation with the child by asking "What are you doing?," the adult could make statements that invite the child to talk (e.g., "Looks like you're drawing").

DEVELOPMENTAL LEVEL

- Responds to sound frequencies
- Anticipates routines when sees familiar objects (bottle)
- Responds to sound frequencies within varying environment
  (3–6 months)

INTERVENTION GUIDELINES

With the adult's encouragement and loving support, the child begins to learn about the world. At this stage, it is important to help the child to develop an awareness of various sounds in the environment and to associate sounds with objects. The infant also associates a referent with a routine (e.g., bottle with eating, extended hands and arms with someone who will pick him or her up). Thoman, Becker, and Freese (1978) describe this stage as "affective communication." The caregiver and infant are integrated through expression, reception, and reaction to the affective behaviors of the other. Therefore, it is important that the adult appear animated when interacting with the child (e.g., This should include an animated facial expression and an expressive intonation in the voice to develop communicative interaction). These are the communication cues the child first comprehends. It is also important to establish "mutual" eye gaze as this is a precursor skill for "shared joint attention" on an object.

PLAY MATERIALS AND OPPORTUNITIES

Provide one-to-one interaction during feeding, diapering, and holding. Provide toys that produce sound and are visually appealing (e.g., rattles, squeeze toys, musical toys) so the child begins to explore objects. Take advantage of environmental noises such as the telephone, airplanes, family pets, and siblings' voices. Show the child objects and name or label them. Show the infant a bottle and place it just out of reach. Name and label the object and repeat several times, (e.g., "Bottle, bottle, want bottle"). Wait 3–4 seconds for the child to reach for the bottle. Repeat the sequence each time the bottle is presented.

DEVELOPMENTAL LEVEL

- Responds to own name
- Recognizes words like "bye-bye," "mama"
- Looks, stops, or withdraws in response to "no"
- Recognizes family members' names
- Responds with appropriate gestures (e.g., "up") and familiar routines
- Appears to listen to conversations of others
- Stops activity when name called
- Recognizes names of familiar objects
  (6–9 months)

When playing with the child, frequently call him or her by name and play peekaboo. When he or she turns and looks, the adult can reward this action with a warm smile. Play interactive games and call other family members by name and play "gonna get you, _____." Fill in the blank as appropriate (e.g., Daddy, Bobby, Sissy). When a child reaches for a hot stove or electrical outlet, say, "No" with emphatic intonation and an accompanying head gesture and remove the child from the situation. When playing with a jack-in-the-box, watching toys disappear, or leaving a situation, the adult can model waving and saying, "bye-bye." The adult should closely observe the child, attempt to understand the child's "intention," and name and describe actions and wants. Use mirroring, self-talk, and parallel talk. A child first understands events by responding to contextual cues (e.g., expected routines, parents' intonation, facial expressions). The child first understands words that are most meaningful and that have occurred frequently (e.g., bottle, Mama, no).

Increase comprehension by repeating words. For instance, when dressing the child, name clothing (e.g., "shoes, shoes on"; "diaper, diaper off"). When bathing the child, say, "tickle nose," "tickle mouth." Emphasize vocabulary that is concrete, includes single syllables, and pertains to the here and now.

Provide toys that can be manipulated in various ways and help develop object permanence and an understanding of cause and effect. These types of items include balls, dolls, rattles, soft blocks, jack-in-the-boxes, musical telephones, Busy Boxes, C-links, spoons, and buckets or containers. Toys and objects can be hidden under blankets or washcloths.

- Looks at objects that mother looks at
- Identifies individuals in their own environment
- Appears to understand simple commands or requests ("Give me _____," "Where's the _____?")
  (9–12 months)

The adult must provide toys and one-to-one interaction. *Observe the child closely and strive to understand communicative intention. Respond to the child's behavior in meaningful ways* (e.g., INREAL strategies). *Direct the infant's attention toward objects, people, and events and name and label them* (e.g., "Bobby see doggie"). Accompany commands with simple gestures and slowly decrease use of the gestures as the child begins to understand the words. Periodically, ask the child to find family members, common objects, toys, and body parts. If the child does not respond, direct his or her attention to the referent. When the child is playing, request toys with an extended hand, "Please give it to me."

At this stage, children enjoy emptying things out of containers. It is important to give them a handbag, bag, or box. Common objects that they can explore can be put in the containers (e.g., spare keys, small purse, toys, cup, postcards, hair brush, mirror). The adult can observe the child exploring the items and periodically request an item with an extended hand "Please give me _____."

**DEVELOPMENTAL
LEVEL**

- Responds to facial expressions of emotion
- Will look for and find objects not in view
- Recognizes names of various body parts
  (12–18 months)

**INTERVENTION
GUIDELINES**

The adult must observe the child and interpret communicative intention. When the child points to or gazes toward an object, the child can name and label the referent and repeat the name several times. The adult can use self-talk to describe his or her actions with parallel talk to describe the child's actions. When the child exhibits a motor behavior, the adult can mirror the nonverbal behavior. If a child produces close approximations of words, the adult can respond with vocal monitoring and reflecting to increase the child's ability to interact and learn new words. When the child says a single word, the adult can use expansion to help the child learn to combine words. Modeling can also be used to help the child learn new linguistic forms.

Exaggerate facial expressions and utilize animation when playing with children. Smile frequently and make sure there is congruence between the facial expressions, vocal interactions, and the messages one wants to convey. For instance, when telling a child not to touch a dangerous object or to stop some dangerous activity (e.g., jumping from high furniture) the adult should not smile but should exhibit a concerned facial expression.

**PLAY MATERIALS
AND
OPPORTUNITIES**

Children at this stage demonstrate sensorimotor and relational and functional play. They enjoy taking objects in and out of containers. They are more aware of themselves and comprehend emotions. They can find objects that are out of view.

Use simple toys that can be functional (e.g., drums, telephones, toy cars, balls). Also, provide toys that can be related spatially by putting objects "in" (e.g., boxes, cans, bottles) and "on" (e.g., hats, blocks) other objects.

Play games, tickle body parts, and encourage the child to "find your nose." Use puppet washcloths during bathtime and name and tickle body parts. Encourage children to "get _____" when there are several toys on the floor.

At this level, children are learning how to use common objects functionally, developing object permanence, and discovering cause-and-effect. Toys should be selected to meet these needs. The adult can play peekaboo with the child and hide toys under blankets or washcloths. A jack-in-the-box also helps to develop the concept of object permanence. Cause-and-effect toys include various Busy Boxes and pop-up toys. Common objects make great toys to explore and investigate (e.g., cups, spoons, keys, bowls). Children at this age also enjoy soft, furry toys, musical toys, balls, and squeaky books.

- Comprehends action words
- Can carry out 2-step directions
- Identifies familiar objects from a group
- Identifies pictures
- Understands complex sentences
- Uses prepositions *in* and *on*
    (18–24 months)
- Follows simple one-step commands
    (18–30 months)
- Comprehends numbers (see one-to-one correspondence)
    (18 months +)

DEVELOPMENTAL LEVEL

The adult should observe the child and interpret behavior (e.g., comment, request, protest). To increase auditory comprehension, the adult can begin to encourage the child to follow commands with playful games. At first, the child follows command with only one verb and then commands with two and more. The adult can say, "Jimmy, find _____" or, "Get Mama's comb." If the child does not comprehend, the adult can take the child, "show" him or her the object, and repeat the command with the action.

INTERVENTION GUIDELINES

The adult can expand the child's communicative intentions and comprehension by providing a variety of experiences. Children learn action words by *doing*. Offer the child many opportunities for activity.

Offer the child a variety of toys and experiences. Take him or her to the park to learn about swinging, sliding, running, and jumping. Give him or her practice opportunities with toys that move (e.g., balls, merry-go-rounds, toy cars). Describe the child's routine actions (e.g., eat, drink, potty, cry, walk, and talk). Look at colorful picturebooks that depict action. Introduce music and dance. Clap and sing.

PLAY MATERIALS AND OPPORTUNITIES

Find opportunities to introduce counting in fun ways. For example, before swinging a child or giving him or her a snack such as cereal, count to three. Occasionally, say, "Please, give me one."

- Understands possessives such as "mine," "yours," and "his"
- Uses preposition *under*
- Understands words through function (what you eat with)
- Understands common verbs
- Understands common adjectives
    (24–36 months)

DEVELOPMENTAL LEVEL

The adult should observe the child during play, interpret his or her communicative intention, and provide new information by implementing INREAL strategies.

INTERVENTION GUIDELINES

Possessives and Ownership

Children learn by doing, and it is important that they have a variety of experiences. They begin to understand possessives when they have private space (e.g., a cubby, a room, a drawer) and their own possessions (e.g., cup, coat, shoes). They learn about what belongs to others by hearing statements such as "That's his" and "That's yours."

Spatial Concepts

Children learn about spatial words by experiencing the concept. They can learn the concept "in" when they are "in" boxes, rolling barrels, or tunnels. They also learn about putting objects "in" water, sand, or buckets. To learn the concept "on," they can put on hats, shoes, and coats. They can also place objects "on" tables, chairs, and the floor. For "under," they can crawl "under" tables, trees, and slides.

Association of Words with Function

Adults can help children expand their knowledge by sharing new information during play. For example, during a tea party, the adult could request, "I need something to *eat with*." The child begins to associate words with function. These concepts can also be introduced while looking at picturebooks. The adult can pose statements such as, "I wonder what that boy will wear."

Verbs and Adjectives

Use of verbs can be increased by providing opportunities for action. The child needs to explore various materials and tools (e.g., paper, scissors, paints, paintbrushes, crayons, hole punches). By exploring various materials, he or she also discovers number concepts, colors, and common adjectives (e.g., big, little, rough, heavy). By placing snow or ice in one water table and warm water in another, children will discover the concepts "warm" and "cold."

PLAY MATERIALS AND OPPORTUNITIES   Provide various materials and tools that can be explored (e.g., paper, scissors, a garlic press, glue, tape, hole punch, ice tongs, paintbrushes, crayons, sand, Styrofoam peanuts, water, cornstarch, paints, cotton). Provide toys that encourage imaginative play (e.g., dolls, puppets, dishes, a kitchen set, cars and trucks, blocks). To facilitate literacy, the adult can model reading and writing and offer the child frequent opportunities to explore these activities.

- Uses preposition *next to*
  (36–40 months)
- Follows complex multistep commands
- Uses preposition *behind, in front of*
- Wants explanation of "why," "how"
- Can follow three-step commands given in a complex sentence
  (36–48 months)
- Temporal terms *before* and *after*
- Uses preposition *above, below, at the bottom*
  (48–60 months)
- Locational prepositions in temporal expressions such as "in a week"
- Locative directions in reference to the body (*left* and *right*)
  (60 months +)

The adult should set up the environment, observe the child, interpret intention, and facilitate language learning by implementing INREAL strategies and providing prompts and cues. With verbal children, the adult frequently uses expansion and modeling. To increase the child's ability to remember more information and follow complex commands, the adult can ask the child to help with tasks. The adult could say, "Jerome, please go *get* the paintbrushes and

Parental reactions to the child's words and actions build turn-taking and lead to pleasurable interactions.

then come *sit down*" or, "Savannah, please *get* the cups, *give* me one, and *give* Hannah one." *Commands should always be functional and meaningful for the situation.*

Spatial and Locational Concepts

To increase the child's comprehension of spatial and locational concepts, words could be introduced during fine and gross motor play (e.g., "Simone, you can stand *next to* Ahmad"; "Jerena, stand *in front* of Ramone"). When children do not understand the concepts, the adult can model the response for the child. At the water or sand table, children learn about putting things *in, on, in front,* and *between.* When a child is learning a new concept, it is important to repeat it several times in a natural conversational manner (e.g., "Simone's *next to* Ahmad, I'm *next to* Jerena, and Talisha is *next to* Ernesto"). Children could learn concepts *above, below* and *at the bottom* while on a playground, climbing a ladder, or looking at a picturebook.

Use of Questions

When increasing the use of questions, such as "why" and "how," the adult can *model the questions when they are meaningful during play.* For instance, when reading a story about a little boy who is going on a bear hunt, the adult could pose questions such as, "How will he get there?" and, "How can he get over the water?." The same type of modeling could be used with "why" questions. Questions can also be posed during role playing with puppets or dolls (e.g., adult could cue the child, "Let's ask the dragon why he looks so sad").

Time Concepts

Time concepts can be presented by incorporating special events into the daily routine. For instance, the adult could discuss upcoming events such as going to the zoo, a show, or the library. The event could be discussed repeatedly (e.g., "We're going *in* a week," "We're going *tomorrow*"). The adult could also describe *what* will happen *before* the event and then *after* the event (e.g., "*Before* we go, we'll get money, and *after* the zoo, we'll get a Happy Meal").

Temporal concepts can also be discussed in terms of regular routine activities such as cooking, bedtime, and going to a doctor. For instance, the parent could say, "*Before* bedtime, you take a bath. *After* the bath, we read a book."

PLAY MATERIALS AND OPPORTUNITIES

Children need experiences to talk about. Take them to the zoo, park, library, grocery store, restaurants, and swimming. *Give them opportunities to engage in imaginative play.* They need props such as dress-up clothes, dishes, dolls, puppets, blocks, and a kitchen area. To develop decontextualization abilities, children need miniature props and replica toys (e.g., doll houses, miniature dolls, playsets). They also need someone to model role playing and integrating schemes into a script (e.g., play house and grocery shop, cook and wash dishes).

Children learn about their bodies and materials by having experiences with fine and gross motor activities. *Give them a variety of art materials and time to explore* (e.g., paper, markers, clay, paints).

Books increase children's knowledge of the world and help them to develop abstract thinking. *Provide a variety of books and time to read every day.*

EXAMPLE

Hannah L. is a 4-year-old who was born 2 months prematurely and has a complicated medical history, including frequent bouts of pneumonia and ear infections. She has speech-language and cognitive deficits.

Hannah links multischeme combinations into meaningful sequences and complex scripts (e.g., she makes tea, pours it into cups, and then washes the dishes). She enjoys imaginary play and re-enacts tea parties with her dolls and stuffed animals.

Hannah demonstrates difficulty in problem-solving, as she does not place graduated sizes in order. She counts to three and understands the concept of one. The ability to classify objects as "big" or "little" is not present.

In the area of communication, Hannah inconsistently localizes to sound. She follows two related auditory commands and points to common objects and animals in a picturebook. Her communicative intentions are easy to understand, and she produces a variety of functions with gestures and simple sentences. She frequently initiates conversational discourse and interacts well with her peers. Hannah produces three- to four-word sentences that are telegraphic in nature because she produces few morphological markers. She substitutes the pronouns me and I, him and he, and her and she. Her articulation is mildly affected; she substitutes "t" and "k" sounds, "d" and "g" sounds, and "p" and "f" sounds. Her overall speech is judged to be 70%–75% intelligible when context is known.

Goals for Hannah include increasing cognitive skills in the areas of sequencing objects by size, comprehending the concepts "big" and "little," rote counting to 10, and counting three to four objects. Communication goals include increasing Hannah's comprehension of concepts and mean length of utterance, use of morphological marker "ing" and regular plural "s," and speech intelligibility. She is scheduled to receive speech-language therapy and intervention in the classroom. The therapist said she would emphasize the "k" and "g" sounds in the first position of words. Because Hannah inconsistently turns and localizes sounds, it was recommended she have a hearing screening.

The team determined that Hannah could increase cognitive and language skills during her tea party scenario. Additional props could be added to the play area at school and home. It was decided that when an adult plays with Hannah, he or she would find opportunities to count cups, plates, spoons, cookies, and so forth. Various sizes of cups and plates could be introduced and Hannah could be encouraged to stack the objects after washing them and match big and little objects and clothes with dolls. The size relationships could be discussed through natural conversation. The consonant "k" could also be emphasized during play.

To increase mean length of utterance and use of morphological markers and pronouns, the adult could use vocal monitoring and reflecting, expansions, and "modeling" during the course of play.

OBSERVATION GUIDELINES FOR COMMUNICATION AND LANGUAGE DEVELOPMENT: ORAL MOTOR DEVELOPMENT

VI. Oral Motor Development
   A. What cup-drinking skills does the child demonstrate?
      1. Is the head aligned with the body?
         a. Midline
         b. Head extension or retraction
      2. What degree of lip control is seen?
         a. Degree of lip seal when cup to lips
         b. Ease with which jaw and lips meet cup
         c. Lip control when cup removed from mouth
      3. What degree of tongue control is seen?
         a. Degree of tongue protrusion under cup
         b. Lack of tongue thrust forward
      4. How does the child coordinate suck/swallow?
         a. Sequence of suck/swallow
         b. Amount child can drink without pause
         c. Can inhibit breathing while swallowing
         d. Frequency of coughing and choking
   B. How adept is the child at chewing and swallowing solids?
      1. Can the child sustain and control a bite?
      2. What jaw movement is observed?
         a. Bite release
         b. Rotary pattern—diagonal
         c. Rotary pattern—circular
      3. To what degree does the tongue assist in moving food from side to side?
      4. What degree of lip control is seen?
         a. Movement is independent of jaw
         b. Mouth closure
         c. Amount of food loss or salivation while chewing

INTERVENTION IMPLICATION[1]

Oral motor development is important for both feeding and the accurate production of speech sounds. The lips, tongue, jaw, and palate are important for both eating and articulation. As with speech sound production, oral motor skills emerge in a defined and organized manner. Oral motor problems may affect a child's ability to produce intelligible speech. Depending on the degree of involvement, oral motor difficulties may influence speech production slightly or may preclude the development of oral communication. In severe cases, a child may never acquire speech and needs an alternative form of communication (e.g., sign language, a communication board, a computerized device).

Assessment of Oral Motor Skills

By the time intervention is considered, oral motor skills have been screened. If a problem was identified, further assessment is completed by an occupational

---

[1]Information included in this section relies heavily upon material found in PRE-FEEDING SKILLS (#7406) by Suzanne Evans Morris and Marsha Dunn Klein, copyright 1987, published by Therapy Skill Builders, a division of Communication Skill Builders, Inc., P.O. Box 42050, Tucson, Arizona 857330.

and/or speech-language therapist. At the conclusion of these assessment procedures, the child's abilities and strengths in movement, feeding, breathing, and communication are identified. The team knows the areas that are difficult for the child and is able to explore possible reasons for the problem(s). Intervention goals and specific strategies can be identified from this data.

Intervention Principles that Promote Oral Motor Development

Goals and specific intervention techniques differ according to the problem and the child. The principles discussed here can be used to plan intervention for oral motor problems that interfere with nourishment intake and may affect speech development.

Combine Sensory Exploration and Sound Play with Feeding

One intervention principle is to incorporate sensory exploration and sound play into feeding. Many researchers deny that there is a causal relationship between the motor control used for eating and that used for speech production. Bosma (1975) found that for typically developing children, there does not appear to be a direct relationship between feeding and early speech development. However, Love, Hagerman, and Taimi (1980) studied the relationship between feeding problems and speech mastery in children with cerebral palsy. This study revealed a possible relationship between abnormal reflexes (e.g., sucking, rooting, feeding difficulties) and speech proficiency. Clinical experience has shown that when a child exhibits difficulty with oral control with eating, there are similar oral control problems in speech sound production. For example, children who do not have satisfactory lip closure when eating may also have difficulty producing speech sounds that are made with the lips (e.g., "p," "b," "m"). Children who have decreased tongue mobility and exhibit difficulty cleaning their upper lip or removing food from the roof of the mouth often exhibit difficulty producing speech sounds that are produced with the tongue elevated (e.g., "d," "t," "n," "l"). Yet early interventionists cannot be assured that simply working on feeding will resolve the child's difficulty with motor control for speech. An intervention program must include learning experiences that facilitate development of both systems in an integrated and holistic manner.

Vocalization and sound play and sensorimotor exploration can be encouraged before, during, and after feeding. The adult can engage the child with physical activities, such as playfully moving the chin and touching the lips and tongue with a spoon, pacifier, fingers, or a washcloth. These playful interactions encourage the child to produce sounds and offer opportunities for sensorimotor exploration. The adult can encourage the child to vocalize by imitating reflexive noises, vowels, and consonants, or by modeling specific sounds and movements. For example, when a young child is eating a sticky substance that adheres to the lips, the facilitator could use this experience to increase lip strength and encourage development of bilabial sounds (e.g., "b," "m," "p"). When the child smacks his or her lips, the facilitator could imitate the lip smacking and say, "mmm." If the child blows on the food, the facilitator could imitate the blowing and say, "bu, bu." For some children, an oral stimulation activity could routinely precede snacktime and mealtime. Children could engage in a variety of activities that would increase awareness (e.g., blow bubbles, wash their faces, brush teeth). With some infants and children who are developmentally under the age of 5 months and for children who cannot produce voice because of a tracheostomy or severe neuromotor damage, the adult may produce sounds to get the child's attention without requiring vocal interaction. With older infants and children who can vocalize, one would expect some direct vocalizations and imitation.

Plan New Behaviors Based on the Development Sequence

After identifying the child's developmental level in speech and feeding, the team should plan the next behaviors to be learned based on the developmental sequence. For instance, a child who has not mastered cup drinking should not be expected to suck through a straw, as this is a more difficult task and is usually not introduced until cup drinking is emerging. If this child has not mastered earlier developing sounds (e.g., "m," "b," "p") in words, he or she should not be expected to produce later developing speech sounds that require more precise lip control (e.g., "f," "v"). For children who are tube fed, who present hypersensitivity, or cannot tolerate oral stimulation, the goal may first be to desensitize the child to touch. Before introducing oral feedings, the adult provides pleasurable interaction with toys and various textures. The adult could introduce a puppet or stuffed animal and encourage the child to hold, touch, kiss, or orally explore the objects.

Position the Child Appropriately

To facilitate both speech and feeding, the child should be positioned appropriately. If a child is not correctly positioned, he or she may not be able to breathe optimally, vocalize, or swallow. There are relationships and connections between the oral and respiratory systems and movement in the neck, shoulders, trunk, pelvis, hips, arms, and legs. Positioning varies with each child and depends on the child's motor abilities, needs, and muscle tone. The occupational, physical, and speech-language therapists can explore total body changes that may affect functioning of the oral mechanism. In some instances, adaptive equipment may be necessary. For example, in some cases a facilitator should not try to control the child's head by placing a hand behind the neck because that may cause the child to tense and resist positioning by pushing the head back (Mueller, 1975). If the child has poor head and neck control, he or she may need an adaptive chair that has both head, arm, and feet supports. When the child's body is aligned and positioned appropriately, he or she has greater stability and oral motor control for eating and speaking.

Use Mealtimes and Snacktime To Develop Communication Skills

Mealtime and snacktime can also be opportunities to acquire and refine communication skills. These routine events occur frequently and can provide the need and motivation for communication. Pragmatic communication, such as seeking attention, requesting, and protesting, occurs naturally during these times. When the adult is aware of the importance and opportunities for developing basic communication skills during a meal, communication skills increase. The adult should assume the roles of initiator and responder and understand the concept of turn-taking. Adults should routinely eat with children so they can model eating as well.

Early Infant Feeding
- Oral reflexes (suck/swallow, rooting, gag)
- Suckling (tongue moves up and down, in and out)
- Loses liquid from sides of mouth, incomplete lip closure
    (0–4 months)

The suggestions provided here are aimed at developing normal oral motor patterns by increasing oral awareness and facilitating movement. For the child with a poor feeding posture (e.g., high or low tone) during feeding, the adult should identify the best feeding posture when the child is held on the adult's lap. The shoulders should be forward with abduction of the scapulae. The neck should be elongated and the chin slightly tucked.

Reduce Confusing Sensory Input

If an infant or child is stressed by an overstimulating environment, he or she reverts to more immature or limiting movement patterns. In this case, the adult should reduce the confusing sensory input (e.g., problem-solve with the family to choose an appropriate feeding time when the environment is quiet and has few distractions, introduce quiet background music with 60 beats per minute to create a calm environment). The infant could be swaddled in a soft blanket to reduce the effects of random touch and body movement.

Offer Oral Stimulation

While the child is held, the adult can offer oral stimulation. For example, for oral stimulation, the adult can gently tap the lips, stroke the tongue with downward–forward movements, and then touch the lips again to initiate a coordinated suckle pattern. For a young infant, formula can be placed on the adult's fingers. For an older child, different tastes can be placed on the adult's fingers.

When the child produces a rhythmical suck, the procedure can be repeated using the nipple or a bottle. (If touch to the tongue causes retraction or disorganized movement, only the lips should be stimulated.) During oral stimulation, the child can also be rocked in a rocking chair to the rhythm and tempo of the music.

If a child's suckling pattern becomes disorganized from touch to the tongue, a suckle or sucking pattern can be developed by stimulating the lips. In this instance, the child may move directly to a cup because the nipple touching the tongue elicits disorganized movement. For this technique, drops of liquid are placed on the adult's finger and the fingers tap and stroke the lips outward and with a circular motion to initiate the suckle from the lips. When the suckle can be easily initiated from the lips, a spoon or medicine cup can be placed on the lower lip. The child can be encouraged to suckle the liquid from the spoon or cup.

Provide Vocal Stimulation

For vocal stimulation, the adult can imitate the child's vocalizations. For example, if the child vocalizes "uh-uh," the adult can wait for 3 seconds after the child vocalizes and then imitate the child's sounds. This "imitative" interaction can continue until the child ends the interaction. The adult can also sing to the child and increase the child's awareness of sound.

PLAY MATERIALS AND OPPORTUNITIES

Toys should stimulate sucking and reduce hypersensitivity of the mouth. They should also increase tolerance of objects coming toward the face, oral stimulation and exploration, and tongue, lip, and jaw movements. For example, a Lanco Soft Latex Squeak Toy can be mouthed by the child. The toy has a gentle "squeak" that does not startle a hypersensitive child. For children who have motor problems, adults must help the child to explore his or her hands and to mouth toys.

Children can also be encouraged to mouth pacifiers, rattles, and washcloths. The pacifier and bottle nipple must be selected to fit the child's mouth and motor needs (e.g., Mini Mom Orthodontic Newborn Pacifier for a premature infant or Passy Pacifier for an older child). For children who exhibit motor patterns that interfere with the ability to feed in a semi-reclined position, an adapted bottle might be necessary. For example, a Correcto Feeding Bottle is often used for infants who tend to hold their heads in extension and those who feed best in sidelying or prone positions.

DEVELOPMENTAL LEVEL

- Cup drinking introduced, tongue may thrust
- Mouth opens for spoon
- Tongue thrusts when spoon withdrawn, food ejected
  (4–6 months)

INTERVENTION GUIDELINES

Cup Drinking

The adult should support the child's jaw and facilitate drinking from a neutral position. While the child is drinking, the adult can provide jaw support (Figure 2) and provide greater stability. If a child exhibits hypersensitivity, it is helpful to maintain constant contact of the cup and lower lip (i.e., tip the cup down for drinking and up for pauses) rather than taking it away from the child's mouth. In some cases, the child can be encouraged to hold onto the edge of the glass with the teeth while drinking. Using thickened substances facilitates learning to drink because the child has greater control than with thin liquids. In some cases, special adaptive cups should be used (e.g., Solo clear 9-ounce cup; bell-shaped cup, cut-out cups).

It is always important to talk with a child during feeding and describe the

Feeder's Position	Finger	Placement	Purpose
To the side or from behind	Middle	Under the jaw just behind the chin	To assist upward jaw movement and reduce tongue protrusion
	Index	• On the chin	• To assist downward jaw movement
		• Below the lower lip	• To stabilize the lower lip
	Thumb	At the temporomandibular joint	To stabilize the feeder's hand
From in front	Middle	Under the jaw just behind the chin	To assist upward jaw movement and reduce tongue protrusion
	Index	At the temporomandibular joint	To stabilize the feeder's hand
	Thumb	• On the chin	• To assist downward jaw movement
		• Below the lower lip	• To stabilize the lower lip

These feeding positions help the child to experience a closed-mouth sensation and provide greater stability for the jaw and temporomandibular joint. This procedure, which provides jaw stability and support, can be done from the side, back, or front positions.

 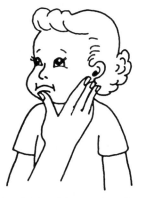

Gradually release the amount of control or assistance as the child is able to reduce the amount of jaw thrust. Criteria: Jaw control or oral-control techniques are helpful only after reducing extensor patterns of the body through handling and positioning. They are of limited value when the jaw thrust is extremely strong or when jaw thrust is triggered by touch to the face.

Figure 2. A jaw support technique. This procedure to provide jaw stability and support can be done in at least two ways—from the side or back, and from the front. (From PRE-FEEDING SKILLS, by Suzanne Evans Morris and Marsha Dunn Klein, copyright 1987, by Therapy Skill Builders, a division of Communication Skill Builders, Inc., P.O. Box 42050, Tucson, AZ 85733. Reprinted with permission.)

actions. This verbal mediation is especially important for children with visual impairments. The adult needs to tell the child what is happening so the child is not startled and begins to understand the process.

To facilitate development of communication skills, it is important for the adult to imitate the child's vocalizations and vocal play. For example, if the child blows bubbles in a cup, it is important to imitate the sound the child makes and encourage this exploration. The adult can demonstrate turn-taking and facilitate the development of intention by stopping between sips and waiting for the child to signal that he or she is ready for another drink.

Spoon Feeding

For spoon feeding, children need to maintain an open-mouth position with a still tongue. Jaw support can be provided for the child (see Figure 2) to help him or her understand that the mouth can be still and ready before the spoon enters the mouth. If it is difficult for the child to keep the mouth quiet as food approaches, the activity can begin by touching the child's mouth with a toy and then moving it away. Gentle pressure on the tongue with the spoon often stimulates a downward movement of the upper lip. (This approach is not appropriate when the stimulation triggers increased hypertonicity and lip or tongue retraction or thrusting.)

The child's individual motor patterns should be assessed with feeding. In some cases, a special adapted spoon might be necessary to facilitate feeding (e.g., rubber or coated spoon for a child who presents a bite reflex). Normally, a child opens the mouth for food, but in the case of a child with visual impairments, this may not be the case because he or she can not see the object. In some instances, a penlight or small flashlight can be attached to a spoon to increase visual awareness for blind children and children with visual impairments.

Exaggerated Tongue Protrusion and Tongue Thrust

The adult can help the child achieve and maintain the tongue position in the mouth by placing a hand on the child's jaw and providing jaw support. This reduces forward movement of the base of the tongue. For children who present low tone in the tongue, the bowl of the spoon can be placed on the middle of the tongue and then pressed evenly downward using a vibratory movement. Slowly removing the spoon from the mouth encourages the lips to close and assists with food removal from the spoon. (This approach is effective with low tone but not recommended when a child presents a tonic bite or hypertonicity in the tongue.)

Before and after the feeding, the adult can encourage oral stimulation by offering the child a toy that can be explored orally (e.g., squeaky toy, rattle). Washing the child's face with a washcloth or soft sponge also encourages oral stimulation. The child can be given the washcloth or sponge and encouraged to explore and suck on it. For children with hypersensitivity (e.g., increased postural tone and abnormal reflexes), it is important to limit sensory input before and during feeding. For example, a child who has been tube fed for several months may avoid oral intake. For this child, the adult might introduce the Lanco Duck and play with it and encourage the child to explore it with the mouth. If the child enjoys the toy, the adult could place some pleasant food on the toy and encourage the child to taste it. Feeding with a spoon could be introduced slowly.

To facilitate strength and use of the lips and cheeks for drawing in food and liquid, it is important to develop tone in the face with playful games. The adult can play pat-a-cake on the cheeks, vocalize, pat the lips to make interesting sounds, and *firmly* apply face lotion to the cheeks. Stroking firmly with a circular motion around the lips encourages lip activity and a forward posturing for the suck. These activities can be presented in a communicative and interactive manner. The adult can stimulate the mouth while making funny sounds such as smacking, blowing raspberries, and clicking the tongue.

DEVELOPMENTAL LEVEL

- Jaw moves up and down
- True suck, stable jaw
- Tongue lateralization begins
- Upper lip comes down well on spoon
      (6–12 months)

Jaw Movement

Children sometimes present jaw thrust, jaw clenching, jaw retraction, and jaw instability. The etiology for each varies. If children have difficulty with jaw movement, medical attention should be sought to rule out dental and orthopedic problems. During feeding, it is important to support the child's jaw to facilitate eating. If abnormal patterns appear in response to an overstimulating environment, it is important to limit sensory input during feeding (e.g., turn the television off, limit the number of people present, wait until the child is calm and relaxed before feeding him or her). For a child who presents hypersensitivity when the face or oral structures are touched, it is important to desensitize him or her before and during feeding by providing firm pressure to the face, gums, and teeth while maintaining the jaw in a closed position. It is also important to achieve better body movement by positioning the child to maximize his or her ability to eat and speak.

Playful sensory games to provide oral motor input can be integrated into snacktime.

To increase communication skills, *feeding time should be used as an interactive time*. The child and adult should take turns vocalizing and offering and accepting food. The adult should encourage the child to explore the smells, textures, and temperatures of foods. Children enjoy smearing food on the trays of high chairs and on their faces. This *exploration is important and should be nurtured*.

Between feedings, the adult can support the child's oral exploration by touching and playing with the lips, tongue, and jaw. When the child vocalizes, the adult can touch the mouth with the palm of the hand and make an "OO-OO" sound. The adult can allow and encourage the child to touch and explore his or her mouth.

Tongue Lateralization

Tongue lateralization occurs when the child moves the tongue from side to side inside or outside of the oral cavity. If the child fails to lateralize the tongue, it may be helpful to assess different positions and consider how each affects the child's ability to move the lips, tongue, and jaw. Providing jaw support when the child chews gives him or her added support and stability and he or she experiences a sensation of rhythmical chewing. An electric toothbrush, toy, or finger can be used to stimulate the lateral borders of the tongue and encourage lateralization. Depending on the child's cognition and motor skills, the adult could introduce small bites of food (e.g., graham cracker, Cheerio) and play "Hide and seek" with the food; the adult places food on the tongue and the child "hides" it, or the food is placed in the side of the mouth and the child "finds" it with the tongue. With this game, the adult can take a turn and demonstrate for the child.

DEVELOPMENTAL LEVEL

Cup Drinking
- Lip seal intact when cup to lips
- Jaw and lip meet cup easily, may bite edge of cup (stability or fun)
- Tongue may or may not protrude under cup (a cupper tongue position expected)
- No tongue thrust forward
- No head extension (thrust forward accompanies swallow)
- Infrequent coughing/choking
         (12–18 months)

INTERVENTION GUIDELINES

The guidelines on pages 378–381 regarding cup drinking, tongue protrusion, and spoon feeding are also appropriate for improving the feeding skills of children at this developmental level. It is also important to provide play activities that help the child develop oral motor awareness and control to facilitate feeding and speech. For example, the child can be given whistles and simple musical instruments, bubbles, different toothbrushes, and so forth. During feeding, the adult should name objects and actions to increase the child's vocabulary skills. The adult should watch the child for pragmatic communications (e.g., protesting, requestives) and respond to these behaviors in a meaningful manner.

Continue to encourage the child to explore objects and toys in the environment. Provide toys that have different textures (e.g., toys made of rubber, cloth, and plastic, wooden blocks, toothbrushes). Children normally explore everything around them (e.g., buttons, cups, spoons, bowls, textures) and begin to discover the differences in properties. Children with disabilities often can not explore these objects because they have motor or cognitive deficits that prevent exploration. Consequently, the adult must introduce these items and help the child to mouth and explore them.

PLAY MATERIALS
AND
OPPORTUNITIES

Chewing/Swallowing Solids
- Sustained, controlled bite
- Jaw movement: bite release
                              rotary pattern — diagonal
                              rotary pattern — circular
          (12–18 months)

DEVELOPMENTAL
LEVEL

Facilitating a Normal Controlled Bite Pattern

Bite Patterns

INTERVENTION
GUIDELINES

The child who fails to demonstrate a sustained, controlled bite may present any of the following symptoms: jaw thrust, jaw clenching or tonic bite when foods are presented for biting, associated movements and tension in the rest of the body triggered by biting, inability to exert enough biting force to bite through soft or hard food, sucking or suckling all food, and a rapid phasic bite pattern rather than a controlled bite. Possible causes for these problems include increased or decreased postural tone, an overstimulating environment, hypersensitivity, edentulousness (i.e., toothlessness), a developmental level below 9–12 months, or the inability to inhibit tongue movement.

For children whose biting is influenced by high or low muscle tone and whose oral patterns include jaw thrust, jaw clenching, or tonic bite reflex, the adult can evaluate various postures that reduce the affects of hypertonicity or hypotonicity. For children who show signs of sensory integration and sensory overload (e.g., poor eye contact, rhythmical self-stimulation, hyperactivity), the adult can work toward reducing confusing sensory input. The environment should be quiet and calming. The television and radio should be turned off. The amount of activity in the room should be decreased. People in the environment should use softer voices.

When children exhibit difficulty developing jaw stability in an open position, the adult can help desensitize the child and introduce a toy and touch the child's mouth with it. The toy can be moved away and the child encouraged to remain calm even when the food is presented. A cookie could be used instead of the toy. For older children, instructions such as, "Now, the cookie will touch your mouth, but it's not time to eat it. This is time to practice keeping the mouth calm" could be offered. Older children can also be encouraged to keep their mouths calm until the adult touches the lips with a spoon. When the children feel the spoon, they can open their mouths and take a bite.

Because the ability to stabilize the jaw in a closed position while holding food occurs in normal development before the ability to use a controlled bite, the adult can help the child acquire this skill by asking the child to hold a soft cookie between his or her gums. The adult can say, "I'll break off the outside piece while you hold the part that is in your mouth." This approach should be used only if the child does not have a tonic bite reflex.

When children present low tone in the facial area and cannot sustain holding pressure for a bite or exhibit hypersensitivity, they can benefit from firm and regular sensory stimulation. The adult can play pat-a-cake, peekaboo, and other children's games that incorporate tapping, stroking, and other soft tactile and proprioceptive stimulation around the jaw area. Folk music that has a clear rhythm and regular tempo can be used when providing tapping and other sensory input to the muscles. Children often enjoy singing when the adult touches or taps the face. During feeding, the adult can support the child's jaw (see Figure 2) so the child develops the sensation of greater stability.

Chewing

A diagonal rotary pattern is a chewing pattern characterized by downward and lateral or central movement of the jaw. These jaw movements are observed as food is moved by the tongue to the side or from the side to the middle of the mouth.

A circular rotary pattern is a chewing pattern characterized by circular or semi-circular jaw patterns. These jaw movements occur as the tongue moves food from one side of the mouth across the middle to the other side. This pattern typically is used with harder and tougher food because the molars are used for grinding food. If the child fails to develop these chewing patterns, intervention should address precursor skills in the tongue, lips, cheeks, jaw, and overall body muscle tone.

PLAY MATERIALS AND OPPORTUNITIES

Use folk music with a regular tempo. Children can play with toys that help increase muscle strength in the lips and jaw (e.g., bubbles, toy horns, whistles). Adults can play imitative games and move the tongue in and out of the mouth, side-to-side, and up and down. These fun and silly games can be played in front of a mirror so the child can see and feel the movements. The adult can also use simple language to describe the movements so the child associates words with the movements and names with the body parts.

DEVELOPMENTAL LEVEL

Cup Drinking
- Lip control when cup removed from mouth
- Does sequence of suck–swallow
- Drinks 1 ounce from cup without pause
- Can inhibit breathing while swallowing
    (18–24 months)

INTERVENTION GUIDELINES

Before a child can drink from a cup, he or she must demonstrate the ability to swallow without choking or aspirating (i.e., aspiration indicates liquid of food has gone into the lungs secondary to a swallowing disorder). If an abnormal swallow is observed and it appears that the child is aspirating, medical management is necessary. The child must have normal tone in the lips, tongue, jaw, and cheeks. To strengthen or normalize tone in these structures, the facilitator must increase the child's awareness of these muscles by touching and massaging the cheeks, gums, lips, and tongue. If a child presents hypersensitivity and gags when seeing, tasting, or smelling foods or does not enjoy touch to the face, the interventionist must desensitize the child. By providing pleasant experiences (e.g., firm touch to the face, pleasant tastes of chocolate and various flavors) the adult can decrease the negative responses.

The child must be positioned optimally to decrease tone and facilitate body alignment, which will facilitate a swallow. Specific individualized verbal instructions can be provided (e.g., "Let's take a drink," "Keep your tongue still," "Open your mouth").

The facilitator can offer small sips and facilitate a swallow with the chin support (see Figure 2). If a child exhibits hypersensitivity, it is helpful to maintain constant contact of the cup with the lower lip (i.e., tip the cup down for pauses and up for drinking), rather than taking it away from the child's mouth. In some cases, the child can be encouraged to hold onto the edge of the glass with the teeth while drinking.

To facilitate development of communication skills it is important for the adult to imitate the child's vocalization and encourage vocal play. The adult can encourage communication by waiting between sips for the child to signal that he or she is ready to have another drink.

PLAY MATERIALS AND OPPORTUNITIES

As mentioned previously, toys and activities that encourage the child to use his or her lips for control (e.g., straws, horns) are also helpful for breath control. Playful activities that desensitize and increase tone (e.g., face painting, making funny faces) are helpful.

DEVELOPMENTAL LEVEL

- Tongue lateralizes when food is at side of mouth
- Lips move independently of jaw
- Chews with lips closed
- Chews with mouth closed
- No loss of food or saliva while chewing
  (18–24 months)

INTERVENTION GUIDELINES

To increase tongue lateralization, the suggestions on pages 282–283 are appropriate. To facilitate strength and use of the lips and cheeks it is important to develop tone in the face through playful games. The adult can play pat-a-cake on the cheeks, vocalize, pat the lips to make interesting sounds, and firmly apply face lotion to the cheeks. Stroking firmly with a circular motion around the lips encourages lip activity. These activities can be presented in a communicative or interactive manner. The adult can stimulate the mouth while making funny sounds like smacking, blowing raspberries, or clicking the tongue. The adult can also play "funny face" games and protrude the lips and tongue. Cheerios can be placed on the lips with peanut butter or honey and child encouraged to "find" the Cheerios with his or her tongue.

To help the child achieve mouth closure the adult can provide chin support (see Figure 2). This helps the child achieve jaw stability and begin to sense how it feels to close the mouth and chew. It is important to talk with the child and describe the action so he or she begins to integrate the information.

PLAY MATERIALS AND OPPORTUNITIES

Choose toys and play activities that help the child develop awareness of the oral structures and gain increased motor control and strength. Eating and playing in front of a mirror can be helpful. Children often enjoy vibrators and will touch their lips, tongue, and cheeks with these devices.

DEVELOPMENTAL LEVEL

- Cheeks assist in holding food
- Can easily transfer food from one side of the mouth to other (24–36 months)
- Child has all basic movement components of oral motor function (36 months)

INTERVENTION GUIDELINES

The guidelines suggested on pages 383–385 are also appropriate at this developmental level for increasing strength and awareness in the lips, tongue, and jaw.

PLAY MATERIALS AND OPPORTUNITIES

Continue to provide toys and activities that increase the child's overall muscle tone, strength, and endurance. Increasing strength in the shoulders, upper body, and abdomen increases the child's ability to vary the loudness of his or her voice. Playing with various toys that increase oral motor skills facilitates eating and speech (e.g., bubbles, pinwheels, painting with straws). Play activities should always encourage development of speech and language skills as well as oral motor abilities (e.g., pragmatic skills, speech sound development).

EXAMPLE

Ernesto H. is 3-year-old who sustained a spinal cord stroke when he was 2 years of age. He is paralyzed from the neck down. He uses a respirator because he cannot breathe on his own. Ernesto cannot eat orally but receives nutrition through a tube placed in his stomach. He is tactilely defensive and does not like touch to his face or around his mouth. Ernesto is very shy and minimally talks with strangers. His mother reports that he says short sentences to her and his father, but becomes quiet when anyone comes to the home. She also noted that he demonstrated difficulty coordinating his voice with the respirator. At times, he would mouth words and use his voice.

The team recommended that Ernesto receive speech-language and occupational therapy while attending the preschool 3 days a week. Due to his shyness, it was recommended that the therapists first establish a rapport with Ernesto before he comes to the preschool. The plan included slowly making a transition into the new setting. For example, he could initially come for a visit and then extended visits with his mother or father.

The occupational therapist noted that Ernesto needed to use his mouth for playing with toys and that a computer would be critical for learning. The computer could be accessed with a mouth switch, and environmental controls (e.g., turn lights and music on and off) could be developed to interface with the computer.

Before any of the recommended intervention could occur, Ernesto would have to be less orally sensitive. To orally desensitize Ernesto, the occupational therapist recommended that the family place Ernesto's favorite stuffed toys and objects with other textures beside his head and face when he is in bed or in his wheelchair. His parents were encouraged to kiss Ernesto and playfully touch his face with various toys.

The occupational therapist provided cause-and-effect toys (e.g., penguins that climb a ladder, a bear that plays music) that could be operated with a chin switch. By turning his head and touching the switch, Ernesto could activate the toy. The speech-language therapist provided various toothbrushes and soft rubber toys that the parents could introduce. Pleasant tastes, (e.g., chocolate, mint, banana) could be placed on the toy and Ernesto encouraged to taste the flavors and explore the different textures.

When Ernesto joined the children in the classroom, it was recommended that he be offered adaptive tools so he could join the fun (e.g., a paintbrush he could hold comfortably with his mouth, a mouth stick he could use to move animals into a barn or to move rocks and plants to make an aquarium).

The speech-language therapist also recommended that the family talk with Ernesto about "listening" for his "air" so he could talk and coordinate the ventilator with voicing.

OBSERVATION GUIDELINES FOR COMMUNICATION AND LANGUAGE DEVELOPMENT: OBSERVATIONS RELATED TO OTHER AREAS—HEARING, VOICE QUALITY, COGNITIVE DEVELOPMENT

VII. **Observations Related to Other Areas**
    A. **Hearing**
    B. **Voice quality**
    C. **Cognitive development**
        1. **What level of imitation is indicated in the child's language?**
            a. **Motor acts**
            b. **Oral motor acts**
            c. **Speech and nonspeech sounds**
            d. **Word approximations**
            e. **Words (one-syllable, two-syllable, multisyllable)**
            f. **Word combinations (two-word, three-word, etc.)**
            g. **Complete sentences**
            h. **Morphological markers**
        2. **What cognitive prerequisites to language are evident?**
            a. **Object permanence (ability to represent objects and events not perceptually present)**
            b. **Means-ends behaviors (actions to achieve a goal)**
            c. **Functional object use and object classification (perception of relationships)**
            d. **Symbolic behavior (ability to internalize and reproduce information)**

Hearing

Children who do not respond to sounds in their environment, produce many articulation errors, or fail to develop language skills at expected developmental levels should have their hearing evaluated. Because hearing is critical to the development of language, a hearing screening should be implemented before intervention is initiated.

Voice Quality

For the child who presents an unusual vocal quality (e.g., high or low pitch, soft or loud voice, breathiness, harshness, hoarseness, unusual vocal resonance such as hypernasality or hyponasality), it is recommended that he or she be referred for medical evaluation and/or management.

Cognitive Development

The relationship between language and cognition has been highlighted in this chapter and in Chapter 8. Imitation skills and cognitive prerequisites are two specific areas that warrant further discussion.

Imitation

Nonverbal and verbal imitations are two types of imitation skills that are described in the literature. Nonverbal imitation usually includes gross and fine motor imitation, while verbal imitation generally refers to vocal imitation (i.e., repeating nonmeaningful sounds, groups of sounds, and words or larger linguistic units such as word combinations, sentences, and morphological markers).

The exact role imitation plays in language acquisition is widely debated. Some theoreticians (Bates et al., 1977; Piaget, 1952) believe language or symbolic development emerges from a base of imitation skills. When a child imitates the motor and vocal behaviors of others, he or she begins to internalize these behaviors and is later able to represent them independently without a model. Children appear to imitate linguistic components they are in the process of learning, and imitation appears to function as a means to practice new constructions. After 2 years of age, as language becomes more complex and imitation appears to be used less often as a learning technique. However, if imitation is a key component to language acquisition, it would be necessary for children to imitate everything they hear. This is not the case because children frequently create new linguistic units they have never heard, (e.g., "Where go Mom?"). Risley, Hart, and Doke (1972) stated that regardless of whether imitation is important to the development of language, all language intervention programs should include it as a key procedure. In behavioral or operant programs, children are required to imitate constructions they hear. With this type of approach children exhibit difficulty generalizing behavior. Bloom and Lahey (1978) reported that imitation must be *functional* or it is not useful in an intervention program (i.e., imitation must be supported by context and the child's intention). *This means that it is important to imitate the child, model both verbal and nonverbal behaviors, and wait for the child to imitate the behaviors he or she finds to be meaningful.* The adult should avoid direct demands and requirements, such as "Bobby, you say _____?" Imitation serves a more useful purpose if the child selects and imitates the behavior he or she feels is meaningful.

Cognitive Prerequisite

Bates et al. (1977) and Bowerman (1974) stated that many of the cognitive skills that emerge in the first year of life affect language development. Skills such as object permanence, means–end behavior, functional use of objects, and object classification, are necessary prerequisites that appear before physical and verbal symbolic behavior. The reader is encouraged to review Chapter 8 and plan a remediation program that facilitates development in these areas.

OBSERVATION GUIDELINES FOR COMMUNICATION AND LANGUAGE DEVELOPMENT: OBSERVATIONS RELATED TO OTHER AREAS—SOCIAL-EMOTIONAL DEVELOPMENT

D. Social-emotional development
1. See pragmatic skills related to social interaction
2. Are topics of communication appropriate?
3. Does the child communicate in a similar manner with all partners?

INTERVENTION IMPLICATIONS

The development of language is dependent on cognitive skills, motor abilities, and social-emotional well-being. Children who present social-emotional problems may present difficulty with social interaction and pragmatic skills (Bates, 1976). *When children present social-emotional problems that affect development in other areas, a referral to or consultation with a psychologist or counselor is recommended.*

OBSERVATION GUIDELINES FOR COMMUNICATION AND LANGUAGE DEVELOPMENT: OBSERVATIONS RELATED TO OTHER AREAS—SENSORIMOTOR DEVELOPMENT

E. Sensorimotor development
1. Visual-motor skills
2. Muscle tone and postural control
3. Reflexes
4. Fine motor skills
5. Motor planning

INTERVENTION IMPLICATIONS

Children who present difficulty with sensorimotor abilities may also exhibit problems with speech-language and communication development. When children present fine and gross motor problems such as hypertonia or hypotonia, the abnormal strength and movement patterns can affect breathing, voicing, articulation, and feeding. Limited motor movements can also affect the child's ability to use hand or facial gestures. When a child can not move his or her body, exploration and discovery of concepts such as "in," "on," and "under" are affected.

Children who are hypersensitive to touch and avoid exploring new materials may experience difficulty learning concepts such as "rough," and "smooth." Similarly, visual motor problems can affect a child's ability to establish eye contact with a parent, establish joint referencing, and later develop reading and writing abilities. For these and other reasons, *the interventionist must consider the child's sensorimotor problems and how they can affect the development of speech-language and communication skills when planning a remediation program.*

ACKNOWLEDGMENTS

The age ranges provided in this chapter are based on recognized data and the work of the following researchers: for Development of Intentionality, Owens (1988); for Communicative Intentions Expressed in Prelinguistic, One-Word, and Multiword Utterances, Coggins and Carpenter (1981), Dore (1974), and Roth and Spekman (1984); for Articulation, Creaghead & Newman (1989) and Weiss and Lillywhite (1981); for Semantic-Knowledge Levels Reflected in Words, Bloom and Lahey (1978); for Brown's 14 Morphemes, Brown (1973), Miller (1981), and Owens (1988); for Language Comprehension, Bzoch and League (1970), Clark, Morgan, and Wilson-Vlotman (1984), and Owens (1988); for Oral/Motor Skills, Hall, Cirriello, Reed, and Hylton (1987), and Morris (1982); for Development of Speech/Sound Production, Bankson and Bernthal (1981), Eisenberg, Murkoff, and Hathaway (1989), and Weiss and Lillywhite (1981); and for Piaget's sensorimotor stages, Dunst (1981).

REFERENCES

Ainsworth, M.D., & Bell, S.M. (1972). Infant crying and maternal responsiveness. *Child Development, 43,* 1171–1190.

Argyle, M., & Ingram, R. (1972). Gaze, mutual gaze, and proximity. *Semiotics, 4,* 32–49.

Bailey, D., & Wolery, M. (1989). *Assessing infants and preschoolers with handicaps.* Columbus, OH: Merril.

Ayres, J.A. (1979). *Sensory integration and the child.* Los Angeles, CA: Western Psychological Services.

Barataz, J. (1968). Language in the economically disadvantaged child: A perspective. *Asha, 10,* 145–146.

Bates, E. (1976). Pragmatics and sociolinguistics in child language. In M. Morehead & A.E. Morehead (Eds.), *Language deficiency in children: Selected readings* (pp. 411–463). Baltimore: University Park Press.

Bates, E., Benigni, L., Bretherton, I., Camaioni, L., & Volterra, V. (1977). From gesture to the first word: On cognitive and social prerequisites. In M. Lewis & L. Rosenblum (Eds.), *Interaction, conversation, and the development of language* (pp. 247–302). New York: John Wiley & Sons.

Bates, E., Camaioni, L., & Volterra, V. (1975). The acquisition of performance prior to speech. *Merrill Palmer Quarterly, 21*(3), 205–226.

Benedict, H. (1979). Early lexical development: Comprehension and production. *Journal of Child Language, 6,* 183–200.

Bernthal, J., & Bankson, N. (1981). *Articulation disorders.* Englewood Cliffs, NJ: Prentice Hall.

Betances, S. (1991). Diversity. *Vocational Education Journal, 66,* 21–23.

Bloom, L., & Lahey, M. (1978). *Language development and language disorders.* New York: John Wiley & Sons.

Bos, B. (1983). *Before the basics.* Roseville, CA: Turn the Page Press.

Bosma, J.F. (1975). Anatomic and physiologic development of the speech apparatus. In D.B. Tower (Ed.), *The nervous system: Human communication and its disorders* (Vol. 3, pp. 469–480). New York: Raven Press.

Bowerman, M. (1974). Discussion summary—Development of concepts underlying language. In R. Schiefelbusch & L. Lloyd (Eds.), *Language perspectives—Acquisition, retardation, and intervention* (pp. 191–209). Baltimore: University Park Press.

Brandes, P., & Brewer, J. (1977). *Dialect clash in America: Issues and answers.* Metuchen, NJ: Scarecrow Press.

Brown, R. (1973). *A first language: The early stages.* Cambridge, MA: Harvard University Press.

Bruna, D. (1972). *Looking at animals.* London: Methuen Children's Books.

Bruner, J. (1977). Early social interaction and language acquisition. In R. Schaeffer (Ed.), *Studies in mother–infant interaction* (pp. 271–289). New York: Academic Press.

Bzoch, K., & League, R. (1970). *Receptive-expressive emergent language scale.* Baltimore: University Park Press.

Carle, E. (1969). *The very hungry caterpillar.* Cleveland, OH: Collins-World.

Chapman, R.S., & Miller, J.F. (1980). Analyzing language and communication in the child. In R.L. Schiefelbusch (Ed.), *Nonspeech language and communication: Analysis and intervention* (pp. 159–196). Baltimore: University Park Press.

Chomsky, N. (1965). *Aspects of the theory of syntax.* Cambridge, MA: The M.I.T. Press.

Clark, E. (1973). What's in a word? On the child's acquisition of semantics in his first language. In T. Moore (Ed.), *Cognitive development and the acquisition of language* (pp. 65–110). New York: Academic Press.

Clark, T.C., Morgan, A.L., & Wilson-Vlotman, C. (1984). *The INSITE model: A model for home intervention for multiply handicapped sensory impaired infants.* Logan, UT: The SKI*HI Institute.

Clarke-Stewart, K.A. (1973). Interactions between mothers and their young children: Characteristics and consequences. *Monographs of the Society of Research in Child Development, 38*(6–7, Serial No. 153).

Coggins, T.E., & Carpenter, R.L. (1981). The Communication Intention Inventory: A system for observing and coding children's early intentional communication. *Applied Psycholinguistics, 2,* 235–251.

Collier, V. (1989). How long? A synthesis of research on academic achievement in a second language. *TESOL Quarterly, 23*(3), 509–531.

Creaghead, N., & Newman, F. (1989). *Assessment and remediation: Articulatory and phonological disorders* (2nd ed.). New York: Macmillan.

Cummins, J. (1984). *Bilingualism and special education: Issues in assessment and pedagogy.* Clevedon, England: Multilingual Matters.

Cummins, J. (1984b). Language proficiency, bilingualism, and academic achievement. In J. Cummins (Ed.), *Bilingualism and special education: Issues in assessment and pedagogy* (pp. 130–151). San Diego: College-Hill.

Cummins, J. (1986). Empowering minority students: A framework for intervention. *Harvard Educational Review, 56*(1), 18–36.

Cummins, J. (1989). *Empowering minority students.* Sacramento, CA: Jim Cummins and California Association for Bilingual Education.

Damico, J. (1992a). *Acquiring and using a second language: Implications for speech-language pathologists.* Paper presented at the Colorado Speech-Language Hearing Association Convention, Lakewood, Colorado.

Damico, J. (1992b). *Language assessment and intervention in a multicultural context.* Paper and presentation, Colorado Speech-Language Hearing Association Convention, Lakewood, Cognition and Communication in Infancy. New York: Academic Press.

DeAvila, E.A., & Duncan, S.E. (1980). The language minority child: A psychological, linguistic, and social analysis. In J.E. Alatis (Ed.), *Georgetown University round table on language and linguistics 1980: Current issues in bilingual education* (pp. 104–137). Washington, DC: Georgetown University Press.

Dejoy, D. (1988). Disfluent speech behavior in children. In M. Schrader (Ed.), *Parent articles* (pp. 107–109). Tucson, AZ: Communication Skill Builders.

Diaz, R. (1983). Thought and two languages: The impact of bilingualism in cognitive development. *Review of Research in Education, 10,* 23–54.

Dickson, K., Linder, T.W., & Hudson, P. (1993). Observation of communication and language development. In T.W. Linder, *Transdisciplinary play-based assessment: A functional approach to working with young children* (rev. ed.): Baltimore: Paul H. Brookes Publishing Co.

Dore, J. (1974). A pragmatic description of early languagae development. *Journal of Child Language, 2,* 21–40.

Dulay, H., Hernandez-Chavez, E., & Burt, M. (1978). The process of becoming bilingual. In S. Singh &

J. Lynch (Eds.), *Diagnostic procedures in hearing, language, and speech* (pp. 251–305). Baltimore: University Park Press.

Dunst, C. (1981). *Infant learning: A cognitive-linguistic intervention strategy.* Allen, TX: DLM Teaching Resources.

Dyson, A., & Paden, E.P. (1983). Some phonological acquisition strategies used by 2-year-olds. *Journal of Child Communication Disorders, 7,* 6–18.

Edwards, M.L., Magiuk, M.K., & Louko, L.J. (1991). *Preschool phonology group: Maximizing remediation effects.* Paper presented at the annual meeting of ASLHA, Atlanta, Georgia.

Eisenberg, A., Murkoff, H., & Hathaway, S. (1989). *What to expect the first year of life.* New York: Workman.

Fey, M. (1986). *Language intervention for young children.* Boston, MA: College Hill Press.

Fillmore, L.W. (1991). When learning a second language means losing the first. *Early Childhood Research Quarterly, 6*(3), 323–347.

Froschl, M., & Sprung, B. (1983). Providing an anti-handicapist early childhood environment. *Interracial Books for Children Bulletin, 14*(7–8), 21–23.

Gardner, A. (1986). *Talking together.* Comox, British Columbia: Cartwright Printers.

Garton, A.F., & Pratt, C. (1989). *Learning to be literate.* Great Britain: Oxford Basil Blackwell.

Goodman, K. (1986). *What's a whole in whole language?* Portsmouth, NH: Heinemann.

Goodwin, M.H. (1990). *He said, she said.* Indianapolis: Indiana University Press.

Gordon, D., & Ervin-Tripp, S. (1984). The structure of children's requests. In R. Schiefelbusch & J. Pickar (Eds.), *The acquisition of communicative competence* (pp. 295–321). Baltimore: University Park Press.

Greenspan, S. (1990). *Floor time tuning in to each child: A professional program guide.* New York: Scholastic.

Grice, H. (1975). Logic and conversation. In D. Davidson & G. Harmon (Eds.), *The logic of grammar* (pp. 64–75). Encino, CA: Dickinson Press.

Hakuta, K. (1990). Language and cognition of bilingual children. In A. Padilla, H. Fairchild, & C. Valadex (Eds.), *Bilingual education: Issues and strategies* (pp. 47–60). Newbury Park, CA: Sage.

Hall, S., Cirriello, N., Reed, P., & Hylton, J. (1987). *Considerations for feeding children who have a neuromotor disorder.* Portland, OR: Health Science University, Crippled Children's Division.

Harris, S.L. (1975). Teaching language to nonverbal children with emphasis on problems of generalization. *Psychology Bulletin, 82,* 565–580.

Heublein, E., Weiss, R., Gaar, S., Kelly, M., Zelazo, J., & Becker, B. (1991). *INREAL Training Evaluation Model (ITEM).* (Available from the INREAL/Outreach Center, University of Colorado, Boulder, Campus Box 409, Boulder, Colorado 80309).

Hodson, B.W. (1991). *Targeting intelligible speech* (2nd ed.). San Diego, CA: College Hill Press.

Ingram, D. (1976). *Phonological disability in children.* London: Arnold.

INREAL/Education Center. (1978). *The Essence of INREAL Educational Approach.* Boulder: University of Colorado, Boulder.

Kaye, K., & Charney, R. (1981). Conversational asymmetry between mothers and children. *Journal of Child Language, 8,* 35–49.

Keenan, E. (1975). Evolving discourse—The next step. *Papers and Reports on Child Language Development, 10,* 80–87.

Khan, L., & Lewis, N. (1986). *Phonological analysis.* Circle Pines, MN: American Guidance Service.

Lee, V. (Ed.). (1979). *Language development.* New York: Halstead Press Book, John Wiley & Sons.

Leonard, L., Bolders, J.G., & Miller, J.A. (1976). An examination of the semantic relations reflected in the language usage of normal and language-disordered children. *Journal of Speech and Hearing Research, 19,* 371–392.

Liebman, R. (1977). Feeding therapy and speech: Some problems of oral motor control. In A. Golbin (Ed.), *Cerebral palsy and communication: What can parents do* (pp. 27–44). Washington, DC: Washington University.

Linder, T.W. (1993). *Transdisciplinary play-based assessment: A functional approach to working with young children* (rev. ed.). Baltimore: Paul H. Brookes Publishing Co.

Love, R.J., Hagerman, E.L., & Taimi, E.G. (1980). Speech performance, dysphagia and oral reflexes in cerebral palsy. *Journal of Speech Hearing Disorders, 45,* 59–75.

Low, G., Newman, P., & Ravsten, M. (1989). Pragmatic considerations in treatment: Communication-centered instruction. In (Eds.), *Assessment and remediation, articulation, and phonological disorders* (2nd edition) (pp. 217–238). New York: Macmillan.

Lucas, E. (1980). *Semantic and pragmatic language disorders: Assessment and remediation.* Rockville, MD: Aspen Systems Corporation.

Martin, B. (1967). *Brown bear, brown bear, what do you see?* New York: Holt, Rinehart, & Winston.

McCord, S. (1993). *A storybook journey: Pathways to literacy through life and play experiences.* Englewood, CO: Teacher Ideas Press.

McDonald, J., & Carroll, J. (1992). A partnership model for communicating with infants at risk. In J. Blackman (Ed.), *Infants and young children* (pp. 20–30). Gaithersburg, MD: Aspen.

McDonald, J., & Gillette, Y. (1982). *Ecological communication assessment: Assessment of language through conversation.* Columbus: Nisonger Center, Ohio State University.

McKissack, K.P. (1986). *Flossie and the fox.* New York: Dial Books for Young Readers.

McLean, J.E., & Snyder-McLean, L.K. (1978). *A transactional approach to early language training: Derivation of a model system.* Columbus, OH: Charles E. Merrill.

McLaughlin, B. (1978). *Second language acquisition in children.* Hillsdale, NJ: Lawrence J. Erlbaum.

Miller, J. (1981). *Assessing language production in children.* Austin, TX: PRO-ED.

Montague, A. (1990). *Apple seeds: Thoughts for teachers.* IA: Thoughtul Books Sta-Kris Inc.

Morris, S.E. (1982). *The normal acquisition of oral/feeding skills.* New York: Therapeutic Media Inc.

Morris, S., & Klein, M. (1987). *Pre-feeding skills.* Tucson, AZ: Therapy Skill Builders.

Mowrer, O. (1954). The psychologist looks at language. *American Psychologist, 9,* 660–694.

Mueller, H. (1975). Feeding. In N.R. Finnie (Ed.), *Handling the young cerebral palsied child at home* (pp. 113–132). New York: E.P. Dutton.

Musselwhite, C., & St. Louis, K.W. (1982). *Communication programming for the severely handicapped: Vocal and nonvocal strategies.* San Diego, CA: College Hill Press.

Nelson, K. (1973). Structure and strategy in learning to talk. *Monographs of the Society for Research in Child Development, 69,* 409–415.

Norris, J., & Hoffman, P.R. (1990). Language intervention within naturalistic environments. *Journal of Language, Speech, and Hearing Services in Schools, 21,* 72–84.

Owens, R. (1988). *Language development.* Columbus, OH: Charles E. Merrill.

Oxenbury, H. (1987). *Say goodnight.* New York: Alladin Books.

Padilla, A., & Lindholm, K. (1976). Acquisition of bilingualism: A descriptive analysis of the linguistic structures of Spanish/English speaking children. In G. Keller (Ed.), *Bilingualism in the bicentennial and beyond* (pp. 97–142). New York: Bilingual Review Press.

Porter, R.E., & Samovar, L.A. (1976). Communicating interculturally. In L.A. Samovar & R.E. Porter (Eds.), *Intercultural communication: A reader* (p. 7). Belmont, CA: Wadsworth.

Pendergast, K., Dickey, S.E., Selman, J.W., & Soder, A. (1969). *Photo articulation test.* Austin, TX: PRO-ED.

Piaget, J. (1926). *Language and thought of the child.* London: Routledge and Kegan Paul.

Piaget, J. (1951). *Play, dreams, and imitation in childhood.* New York: Norton.

Piaget, J. (1952). *The origins of intelligence in children.* New York: International Universities Press.

Piaget, J. (1954). *The construction of reality in the child.* New York: Basic Books.

Powell, A., & Mahoney, G. (1986). *Transaction intervention program: A child-centered approach to developmental intervention with young handicapped children.* Ypsilant, MI: High Scope Educational Research Foundation.

Prizant, B.M., & Duchan, J.F. (1981). The function of immediate echolalia in autistic children. *Journal of Speech and Hearing Disorders, 46,* 241–249.

Ramey, C.T., Sparling, J., & Wasik, H. (1981). Creating social environments to facilitate language development. In R. Schiefelbusch & D. Bricker (Eds.), *Early language acquistion and intervention* (pp. 449–469). Baltimore: University Park Press.

Risley, T., Hart, B., & Doke, L. (1972). Operant language development: The outline of a therapeutic technology. In R. Schiefelbusch (Ed.), *Language of the mentally retarded* (pp. 107–141). Baltimore: University Park Press.

Roth, F., & Spekman, N. (1984). Assessing the pragmatic abilities of children: Part I. Organizational framework and assessment parameters. *Journal of Speech and Hearing Disorders, 49,* 2–11.

Rowe, M.B. (1986). Wait time: Slowing down may be a way of speeding up. *Journal of Teacher Education, 37,* 42–50.

Schiefelbusch, R. (1978). Introduction. In R. Schiefelbusch (Ed.), *Base of language intervention* (pp. 3–33).

Baltimore: University Park Press.

Schiefelbusch, R., & Bricker, D. (1981). *Early language: Acquisition and intervention*. Baltimore: University Park Press.

Schumaker, J.B., & Sherman, J.A. (1978). Parent as intervention agent: From birth onward. In R. Schiefelbusch (Ed.), *Language intervention strategies* (pp. 237–315). Baltimore: University Park Press.

Schwartz, R., & Leonard, L. (1984). Words, objects and actions in early lexical acquisition. *Journal of Speech and Hearing Research, 27*, 119–127.

Secord, W. (1989). *Assessment and remediation of articulatory and phonological disorders* (2nd ed.). New York: Macmillan.

Shuy, R.W. (1984). Language as foundation for education: The school context. *Theory into Practice, 23*(3), 167–173.

Siegel, G., & Spradlin, J. (1978). Programming for language and communication therapy. In R. Schiefelbusch (Ed.), *Language intervention strategies* (pp. 357–398). Baltimore: University Park Press.

Sinclair, H. (1970). The transition from sensorimotor to symbolic activity. *Interchange, 1*, 119–126.

Skinner, B.F. (1957). *Verbal behavior*. New York: Appleton-Century-Crofts.

Skinner, B.F. (1959). *Cumulative record*. New York: Appleton-Century-Crofts.

Sparks, L.D., and the A.B.C. Task Force. (1989). *Anti-bias curriculum tools for empowering young children*. Washington, DC: National Association for the Education of Young Children.

Spradlin, J.E., & Siegel, G.M. (1982). Language training in natural and clinical environments. *Journal of Speech and Hearing Disorders, 47*, 2–6.

Stern, D. (1977). *The first relationship: Infant and mother*. Cambridge, MA: Harvard University Press.

Stern, D., Jaffe, J., Beebe, B., & Bennet, S. (1975). Vocalizing in unison and in alteration: Two modes of communication within the mother–infant dyad. In D. Aaronson & R. Rieber (Eds.), *Developmental psycholinguistic and communication disorders* (pp. 89–99). New York: New York Academy of Sciences.

Thoman, E.B., Becker, P.T., & Freese, M.P. (1978). Individual patterns of mother–infant interaction. In G.P. Sackett (Ed.), *Application of observational/ethological methods to the study of mental retardation*. Baltimore: University Park Press.

Trantham, C.R., & Pedersen, J. (1976). *Normal language development*. Baltimore: Williams & Wilkins.

VanRiper, C. (1978). *Speech correction principles and methods*. Englewood Cliffs, NJ: Prentice Hall.

Weiss, C., & Lillywhite, H. (1981). *Communicative disorders: Prevention and early intervention*. St. Louis: C.V. Mosby.

Weiss, R.S. (1981). INREAL intervention for language handicapped and bilingual children. *Journal of the Division of Early Childhood, 4*, 40–41.

Werner, H., & Kaplan, B. (1963). *Symbol formation: An organasmic development approach to language and the expression of thought*. New York: John Wiley & Sons.

Westby, C.E. (1980). Assessment of cognitive and language abilities through play. *Language, Speech, and Hearing Services in Schools, 11*, 154–168.

Wilson, L. (1990). *Infants and toddlers: Curriculum and teaching*. Albany, NY: Delmar.

Winitz, H. (1983). Use and abuse of the developmental approach. In H. Winitz (Ed.), *Treating language disorders: For clinicians* (pp. 25–42). Baltimore: University Park Press.

11

Facilitating
Sensorimotor Development

Anita C. Bundy and Jane C. O'Brien

Sensorimotor abilities are important both in their own right and because they enhance other aspects of development (cf. Connolly, 1975; Greenspan & Greenspan, 1985; Morris, 1987; Piaget, 1954). Thus, the improvement of a child's motor skills and tolerance for, and ability to use, sensory information can have important ramifications for development as a whole.

However, while sensorimotor development is important, it is only one aspect of development. Often, choices must be made regarding the most important objectives on which to concentrate in early intervention. Those choices should be made carefully; they can be difficult because they may have long-term implications. Sometimes choices must be made about what to emphasize with a particular child—social interactions, the pleasure of play, quality of movement, or cognitive use of materials. It may be necessary to prioritize. For example, when working with a child who rarely initiates play and seems to derive little pleasure from it, developing intrinsic motivation and the desire to master may be a greater priority than is remediating the child's motor disabilities. Furthermore, developing a desire to interact and master may be an important first step toward helping the child *want* to play and then *want* to move in order to play. These important decisions about where to place emphasis in early intervention are best made by a transdisciplinary team of individuals who know the child well; the most important members of this team are the child and his or her parents or caregivers.

This chapter, like the previous three, is meant to be used in a transdisciplinary way. Not only must objectives be prioritized according to what the child is most ready for, but objectives that address more than one domain at a time may be written. In this way, the holistic nature of development and learning can be emphasized. For example, an objective relating to refining the child's grasp could be integrated with problem-solving skills using cause-and-effect toys and materials; talking about movements and actions integrates language; and activities that require two persons may address specific social interactions with peers as well. Priority, functional use, and holistic integration should be emphasized as a program plan is developed.

The sensorimotor area is also important for writing the last page of the TIP Sheet. Frequently, specific preparatory activities, positioning techniques, sensory adaptations, or adaptive materials or devices may be suggested. These suggestions may be derived from the sensorimotor observations but generally apply to many of the activities in which the child engages.

Observation Guidelines for sensorimotor development from Hall, S. (1993). Observation of sensorimotor development. In T.W. Linder. *Transdisciplinary play-based assessment: A functional approach to working with young children* (rev. ed.). (pp. 201–246). Baltimore: Paul H. Brookes Publishing Co; reprinted by permission.

OBSERVATION GUIDELINES FOR SENSORIMOTOR
DEVELOPMENT: GENERAL APPEARANCE OF MOVEMENT

I. General Appearance of Movement
    A. Physical appearance
        1. Is there anything unusual about the child's body?
        2. When plotted on a chart, are the child's height and weight appropriate for age?
    B. Motor activity
        1. Is the child able to get from one play area to another alone?
        2. What is the child's primary means of moving during play (crawling, walking, running, etc.)?
        3. Does the child appear to move more often or less than other children?
        4. What positions does the child choose for play?
        5. How often does the child use each position for play?
        6. Are there any motor skills that the child seems to avoid?

INTERVENTION IMPLICATIONS

If the child feels comfortable in the assessment environment, it is likely that he or she will use positions and patterns of movement typical of those used daily. Thus, observations of a child's ability to move from one play environment or object to another and to play have important implications for the home and intervention environments. The skills a child demonstrates spontaneously and independently during free play generally reflect those the child has mastered or is in the process of mastering. Much also can be learned about the child's temperament, interests, and ability to focus attention.

Independent Movement

For a child to be able to play optimally, he or she must be able to move independently and reasonably efficiently. This means that the child must have control over a form of locomotion (e.g., rolling, crawling, walking, wheelchair use) and that the environment must support those movements (e.g., paths wide enough, toys at proper height). If the child cannot move independently from one play area to another, he or she must depend on a caregiver for opportunities to play. This dependence can set up a difficult dynamic between the child and others. The child who is nonverbal as well as immobile is doubly at risk for failure to develop skills in and for play.

Variety in Positioning and Movement

Variety is the hallmark of normal movement. Typically developing young children assume many different body positions during play. They move easily into and out of these positions. While young children sometimes seem to be in perpetual motion, their movements are directed and purposeful. They have likes and dislikes and favorite toys, games, and people. They are able to focus their attention and to become absorbed in activity. Although their movements during play sometimes seem awkward or inefficient, they are capable of, and often demonstrate, highly coordinated movements. They enjoy movement and moving.

Children who have motor disabilities often move in stereotyped ways. Their movements often lack the variety seen in typically developing children; they may be fearful of movement. Different patterns of atypical movement are associated with different kinds of developmental disabilities (e.g., cerebral palsy, spina bifida, congenital anomalies). Familiarity with the cause of particular atypical movements assists team members in determining: 1) which approach(es) to employ in intervention in order to promote the child's sensorimotor development, and 2) the expected outcomes from that intervention. Clearly, both intervention and the expected outcomes of that intervention differ markedly for the child who has athetoid cerebral palsy, the child who is hyperactive, and the child with a congenitally absent limb.

OBSERVATION GUIDELINES FOR SENSORIMOTOR DEVELOPMENT: MUSCLE TONE/STRENGTH/ ENDURANCE—FEATURES OF NORMAL MUSCLE TONE

II.   Muscle Tone/Strength/Endurance
   A.   Features of normal muscle tone
     1.   Do body parts on the right and left side look and move the same?
     2.   Does the child assume a wide variety of positions?
     3.   Does the child look coordinated when moving from one position to another?

Muscle Tone

INTERVENTION IMPLICATIONS

Muscle tone affects the amount and type of movement (Bobath, 1985). Furthermore, muscle tone may affect the amount and type of sensory information a child receives from the environment, including toys and play materials. When a child's muscle tone is low (i.e., hypotonia), it is likely the child takes in less information; when it is too high (i.e., hypertonia), it is likely that the child perceives abnormal information. Thus, the "normalization" of muscle tone is important preparation for early intervention directed toward improving sensorimotor abilities.

Addressing a child's abnormal muscle tone is a complex and difficult task for many reasons. First, any one child may manifest symptoms of more than one type of abnormal muscle tone simultaneously. For example, a child may be hypotonic in certain body parts and hypertonic in others; a child who has fluctuating muscle tone in certain body regions may have hypertonia and/or hypotonia in other body regions. Furthermore, the quality of a child's muscle tone may change in different positions (e.g., sitting, standing) and often depends on the child's level of excitation and fatigue and the amount of effort required to perform a particular task (Ingram, 1966; Scherzer & Tscharnuter, 1990). For these reasons, techniques designed to normalize muscle tone must be used judiciously. There are many techniques for addressing abnormal muscle tone. The choice of techniques depends on: 1) the type of abnormal muscle tone manifested, and 2) the training and expertise of the early interventionist.

Handling

The most common procedure for modifying muscle tone involves physically "handling" the child. Through handling,

> sensory input and appropriate support for a movement may be provided through the use of 'key points of control' (Bobath & Bobath, 1972). The therapist places his or her hands on specific body parts, such as the trunk, hips, or shoulders, and guides the child's movements. External assistance from the therapist is kept to a minimum, however, so that the child learns to control the body independently. (Hall, 1993, p. 205)

As important as they can be, specific handling techniques designed to normalize muscle tone should not be used alone. Effective intervention involves *simultaneous* inhibition of abnormal muscle tone and facilitation of desirable movements. Furthermore, techniques to normalize muscle tone are most effective when they are done in conjunction with meaningful activity.

Specific handling procedures designed to facilitate a child's ability to perform skilled motor actions, while simultaneously inhibiting abnormal muscle tone, generally are prescribed by an occupational or physical therapist. However, therapists frequently instruct other team members to perform techniques in order to promote specific abilities (including play) in a child. In this way, the child is able to experience maximum benefits from procedures that normalize muscle tone because all caregivers use the same approach to handling the child.

Environmental Factors

In addition to specific techniques, many environmental factors also influence muscle tone. These include, for example, temperature of the surroundings and quality of the lighting. In general, colder and more stimulating surroundings promote higher muscle tone. Warmer temperatures, subdued lighting, and quiet, rhythmic voices help to calm the child and to reduce high muscle tone.

Positioning

Proper positioning is another way to ensure that the child experiences more normal muscle tone as he or she interacts with toys, objects, or people in the environment. The objective of proper positioning is to put the child in a position in which abnormal patterns of movement are minimized or prevented. Optimal positioning for play and other daily life tasks often is accomplished through the use of therapeutic equipment or adapted furniture. As with handling and all procedures designed to alter muscle tone, positioning equipment should be prescribed and monitored by a trained therapist.

OBSERVATION GUIDELINES FOR SENSORIMOTOR DEVELOPMENT: MUSCLE TONE/STRENGTH/ ENDURANCE—COMMON FEATURES OF UNUSUAL MUSCLE TONE

B.   Common features of unusual muscle tone
1.   What behaviors indicate the presence of low tone?
a.   Does the child have difficulty holding the head up?
b.   Is the child's posture slumped?
c.   Is there a wide base of support?
d.   Is there a tendency to lock joints?
e.   Is there a tendency to lean against supports?
f.   Is there a tendency to "W" sit?

INTERVENTION IMPLICATIONS

Two types of movement experiences are useful for promoting more normal muscle tone in children with hypotonia. These are the following: 1) rapid, non-repetitive movements; and 2) resistance to movement (Fisher & Bundy, 1989; Fisher, Murray, & Bundy, 1991). It is quite easy to incorporate these techniques into play. It is important to reiterate, however, that activities designed to increase muscle tone should be carefully planned and implemented. When engaging in these activities, *the amount and type of sensory input and the child's body alignment should be carefully monitored.* If activities are not carefully monitored, they can do more harm than good.

PLAY MATERIALS AND OPPORTUNITIES

Activities such as jumping up and down on cushions or a bouncer form the basis for many fun-filled interactions that also may contribute to building muscle tone. Very young children and children with disabilities who lack the skills needed to jump independently may enjoy bouncing up and down on an adult's knee or lying (sitting) on a bouncer while an adult gently bounces the surface.

Pushing and pulling heavy objects and playing games that incorporate wooden or metal (rather than plastic) toys and solid (rather than hollow) toys can be used to provide resistance to the child's movements for building muscle tone. Magnetic toys and toys with parts that attach by Velcro can be used similarly. Activities such as digging in and pouring with sand also provide resistance to movement. Lentils, beans, or rice (or a combination) often are used as a substitute for sand; lentils provide a particularly appealing texture. Water also can be used similarly; adding a few drops of food coloring to the water makes it more interesting and provides an opportunity for children to experiment with mixing colors. Clay and Play-Doh provide differing degrees of resistance to movement.

OBSERVATION GUIDELINES FOR SENSORIMOTOR DEVELOPMENT: MUSCLE TONE/STRENGTH/ ENDURANCE—COMMON FEATURES OF UNUSUAL MUSCLE TONE

2. What behaviors indicate the presence of high tone?
   a. When the child moves, does the body get stiffer?
   b. At rest, do the arms or legs appear to be stiff?
   c. Is there fisting in one or both hands?
   d. Does the child stand or walk on the toes?
   e. Does the child have balance problems?

INTERVENTION IMPLICATIONS

As when attempting to increase muscle tone, movement experiences can be used carefully in the context of play activities to decrease muscle tone in children with hypertonia. Movement experiences used to inhibit hypertonia, generally involve slow, repetitive, linear stimulation. Play activities done in various body positions (e.g., lying down, sitting) that incorporate gentle rocking and slow swinging can be very effective for reducing hypertonia. Again, it is important that these activities be carefully planned and implemented so the desired effects are recognized.

Some children appear hypertonic in the arms and legs, but hypotonic in the trunk. With children whose muscle tone varies, slow movement may seem to facilitate, rather than inhibit, the hypertonia. When tone is increased by techniques designed to decrease it, the child may be voluntarily "fixing" body parts in order to act more effectively on objects in the environment. With children whose hypertonia is not normalized or is made worse by slow, repetitive movement, the *judicious* use of more rapid or irregular movement often seems to be most effective for normalizing muscle tone (Fisher & Bundy, 1989).

PLAY MATERIALS AND OPPORTUNITIES

Creating activities that incorporate slow, repetitive movements can be a challenge to facilitators because slow means *very slow* (less than 6 cycles per minute) (Fisher & Bundy, 1989). Rocking the child in a chair or in your lap, especially in tempo with a slow beat or slow music, can be successful, although facilitators must take care not to continue for so long that the child goes to sleep.

Activities that incorporate neutral warmth (i.e., neither hot nor cold) are very useful for normalizing muscle tone. Swimming and playing in water are particular favorites of many children.

In contrast with the heavy or resistive toys and activities typically used with children with hypotonia, facilitators generally should seek lightweight toys and activities that are highly responsive to children's efforts. Breaking bubbles blown by the facilitator, spreading shaving cream or pudding on a table or mirror, and batting at a beach ball suspended from a string are examples of such activities. Some children enjoy battery-operated toys powered by switches. However, facilitators should remember that many of these toys do only one thing and may have to be exchanged frequently to prevent boredom.

OBSERVATION GUIDELINES FOR SENSORIMOTOR DEVELOPMENT: MUSCLE TONE/STRENGTH/ ENDURANCE—COMMON FEATURES OF UNUSUAL MUSCLE TONE

3. What behaviors suggest the presence of fluctuating tone?

INTERVENTION IMPLICATIONS

Fluctuating muscle tone is particularly characteristic of children with athetoid cerebral palsy (Bobath & Bobath, 1975). The degree to which tone fluctuates (e.g., between hypotonia and normal, between hypotonia and hypertonia) varies from child to child. The child's clinical picture determines whether techniques to reduce or increase tone are most appropriate.

PLAY MATERIALS AND OPPORTUNITIES

In general, children who have fluctuating muscle tone benefit from using heavy toys and toys and activities that provide resistance described for use with children with hypotonia. In addition to helping build sustained muscle tone, heavy and resistive toys are less apt to "get away" as a result of the extraneous movements or tremors commonly seen in children with athetoid or ataxic muscle tone. Toys that are suspended or secured to a surface and toys that do not break easily also make play more enjoyable for children who have fluctuating muscle tone.

OBSERVATION GUIDELINES FOR SENSORIMOTOR DEVELOPMENT: MUSCLE TONE/STRENGTH/ ENDURANCE—COMMON FEATURES OF UNUSUAL MUSCLE TONE

4. Can any pattern of unusual tone be detected?
    a. Does one side of the body appear to be stiffer than the other?
    b. Do the legs appear to be stiffer than the arms?

INTERVENTION IMPLICATIONS

Children with hypertonia commonly have greater involvement on one side of their bodies or in one set of extremities (i.e., legs, arms) than in the other. Typically, when these children use their lesser involved extremities in play or other activities, they experience associated reactions. Associated reactions manifest themselves as increased stiffness in the more involved extremities. Positioning and proper weight bearing (in addition to techniques for reducing muscle tone) can be used to decrease the effects of associated reactions. For example, the child with hemiplegia can be instructed to side-sit toward his or her affected side while playing on the floor. When the child sits at a table, his or her chair can be turned so that the involved side is next to the table surface. In so doing, the child is encouraged to bear weight on the involved arm and body side. The child with diplegia (i.e., greater involvement in legs than arms) can sit on a small box or wedge to prevent rounding of the back and minimize the extensor spasticity that is apt to develop in the legs. Children with more complicated clinical pictures may require more individualized prescriptions for seating.

These are best developed in conjunction with an occupational or physical therapist.

OBSERVATION GUIDELINES FOR SENSORIMOTOR DEVELOPMENT: MUSCLE TONE/ STRENGTH/ENDURANCE—STRENGTH AND ENDURANCE

C. **Strength and endurance**
    1. **Does the child get tired if a motor activity is performed over and over?**
    2. **Are there indicators of decreased cardiovascular function?**
        a. **Skin changes?**
        b. **Blue lips and fingernails?**
        c. **Breathing difficulty?**

INTERVENTION IMPLICATIONS

Distress Signs

Generally, if a young child is involved in a play activity in which he or she can become completely absorbed (Csikzimentihayli, 1975), the child does not fatigue easily. In fact, some children become so absorbed in play their parents say, "The house could fall down around him (or her). He (or she) would never hear it." When a child becomes easily fatigued or shows other signs of distress (e.g., skin changes, blue lips or fingernails, breathing difficulties), he or she should be checked by a physician.

A child who is known to have decreased cardiovascular function or serious musculoskeletal disorders (e.g., muscular dystrophy) should be monitored carefully for signs of distress. An activity should be terminated at the earliest sign of such distress. Many children self-monitor (i.e., they spontaneously discontinue activities when they feel tired). However, young children should not be given such responsibility, especially when health and safety are concerned. Terminating an activity in which a child has become very involved can be very difficult. If such situations occur frequently, there is a risk that they may negatively affect the relationship between the child and the caregiver. The caregiver needs the assistance of other team members to develop strategies for handling such situations successfully.

Skeletal and Musculoskeletal Abnormalities

Some children with Down syndrome have atlantoaxial dislocation (i.e., a skeletal abnormality at the junction between the spinal column and the cranium). For these children, certain movements involving flexion of the neck (e.g., somersaults) are contraindicated. All children with Down syndrome should have cervical spine X rays prior to participating in any form of intervention or vigorous physical activity (Harris, 1984).

Many other children, particularly those with genetic syndromes, have other musculoskeletal abnormalities that contraindicate certain physical activities. Team members should be certain they have familiarized themselves with children's medical records and with literature pertaining to those conditions before initiating intervention.

EXAMPLE

Timothy G. is 36 months old with a developmental delay of unknown etiology. Timothy especially enjoys playing with cars and trucks and is interested in many toys and objects. However, Timothy's low muscle tone and decreased strength interfere with his ability to play with many of the toys his classmates enjoy. He is easily frustrated when playing with toys that offer too much resistance to movement. For example, he does not have enough strength to put Legos together; he cannot pull the string on the See 'n Say or separate pop beads. When Timothy is unable to play with a toy in the desired way, he generally throws it in a fit of anger. A temper tantrum commonly ensues.

To improve Timothy's ability to use toys and other objects (e.g., buttons, silverware, crayons), activities to increase muscle tone and strength were developed. His mother, his teacher, and the occupational therapist were involved in the creation of the activities. Team members were certain to create lots of activities that did not require adult supervision and that Timothy could do alone or with a friend.

The activities provided graded resistance to movement but, in order to reduce Timothy's frustration, did not have clearly specified outcomes. Team members created both gross motor and fine motor activities because Timothy's low muscle tone interfered with his attempts to master many developmental skills.

Activities included sponge and water play, pouring sand, using squirt bottles, whipping soap and water mixtures with an egg beater, hiding and locating objects in beans and rice, building with Play-Doh, tug-of-war, running, being pulled on a scooter board, riding toys, swinging, and playing with magnetic blocks and a Velcro mit and ball.

With access to so many activities that enabled him to succeed, Timothy's frustration levels decreased markedly. Because he engaged so frequently in activities that provided graded resistance to his movement, his strength began to improve. Thus, when he chose to do so, he began to be able to utilize successfully some of the same toys that, 3 months previously, led to temper tantrums.

OBSERVATION GUIDELINES FOR SENSORIMOTOR DEVELOPMENT: REACTIVITY TO SENSORY INPUT

III. **Reactivity to Sensory Input**
  A. **Touch**
    1. **Does the child respond to tactile stimuli?**
    2. **Does the child seem to have a pleasurable reaction to tactile input?**
  B. **Movement**
    1. **Does the child respond to movement?**
    2. **Does the child seem to have a pleasurable reaction to movement?**
  C. **Auditory**
    1. **Does the child respond to auditory stimuli?**
    2. **Does the child seem to have a pleasurable reaction to auditory stimuli?**
  D. **Visual**
    1. **Does the child respond to visual stimuli?**
    2. **Does the child seem to have a pleasurable reaction to visual stimuli?**

INTERVENTION
IMPLICATIONS

In recent years, theorists, researchers, and clinicians have become increasingly interested in atypical responses to sensory input (cf. Fisher et al., 1991). Atypical responses to sensory input can include either of two opposite ends of a continuum. The child may: 1) fail to "register," or respond, in a very delayed manner; or 2) overreact (usually negatively) to the input.

Sensory Modulation Disorders

Disorders of responsiveness to sensory input commonly are referred to as sensory modulation disorders (i.e., they are thought to result from the child's inability to modulate incoming sensory information) (Fisher et al., 1991). While it is possible for a child to have a sensory modulation disorder in response to only one type of sensory information, it is far more common for these children to respond atypically to many kinds of sensory information. Because of their nature, sensory modulation disorders can be particularly confusing to caregivers and children. On one day or at one particular moment, the child might respond quite normally to sensory information; on the next day, or at the next moment, that same child might fail to respond, have a significant delay in responding, or overreact to seemingly minor sensory information.

Children who have sensory modulation disorders (particularly those who overreact to sensory input) frequently avoid experiences in which they are apt to become overwhelmed by sensory information. Thus, they may avoid cuddling from a parent, "messy" art activities, certain kinds of food, certain clothing, or playground equipment. They may become inordinately distressed by having their hair washed or cut or their faces wiped. The avoidance of such sensory experiences is problematic for many reasons. First, bathing and grooming activities are a part of daily life. When they become a "battleground" between parents and children, these unpleasant interactions often spill over into other aspects of their relationship. Second, sensory input accompanies the execution of all fundamental motor skills. The development of sensorimotor abilities requires practice. While sensory modulation disorders do not cause sensorimotor deficits, *the child who avoids sensory experiences because they overwhelm him or her may be at a disadvantage for developing fundamental abilities to interact with objects and people* (Fisher et al., 1991).

Cravings for Sensory Input

In contrast to children with sensory modulation disorders are children who seem to crave certain types of sensory experiences. While such craving is often seen in children who have sensory or cognitive impairments, it also occurs in typically developing children. For example, some typically developing children (particularly preschool-age boys) seem to like the vestibular and proprioceptive sensations generated by running, jumping, and crashing into things. They will turn virtually every play activity into an opportunity to run, jump, or fall. Thus, the observation that a child craves a particular sensory input does not necessarily have any implications beyond a statement of the child's preferences.

Early interventionists should seek to: 1) utilize sensory experiences children find pleasurable to promote their sensorimotor development; and 2) when necessary, minimize a child's negative experiences with particular sensory information. With regard to the former, *children themselves are the best judges of what they find pleasurable. They reveal those preferences in many ways, including asking for or repeatedly seeking certain toys and experiences.* Sensory experiences can be highly motivating for most children. Often they can be used to draw children into other, more difficult, activities.

Children who have sensory modulation disorders require carefully planned and monitored intervention in order to minimize the child's negative experiences with sensory information. This intervention generally is prescribed by an occupational or physical therapist trained in sensory integration theory (Ayres, 1972; Fisher et al., 1991) or in utilizing the more invasive sensory stimulation procedures described as highly effective by Wilbarger and Royeen (1987). The procedures prescribed by the therapist are often implemented by a parent or another facilitator.

EXAMPLE

Michael T. is a 30-month-old toddler who does not like to be held or cuddled. He often gags when he eats textured foods. His mother also reports that Michael does not like baths, playing in the sand, or the feel of some clothing against his skin. In addition to difficulties with touch, Michael also reacts negatively to noises and movement. He moves cautiously and with effort and becomes tearful when his balance is challenged even slightly. Michael does not enjoy swinging and refuses to climb. His parents report that Michael frequently becomes carsick after short rides, such as to the grocery store.

Michael's parents were very confused by Michael's behavior. They saw him as a difficult child with a behavior problem, and they questioned their ability to parent him successfully. When the occupational therapist explained many of Michael's behaviors as negative reactions to sensory input, she cast a whole new light on the situation.

As they came to understand Michael's behavior in a new way, his parents worked on their own and with the therapist to structure the environment to minimize Michael's negative experiences with touch, movement, and noise. They used firm touch when they held him and made sure he was expecting to be touched. When they could, they respected his need to determine when he wanted to be touched. When they had to impose touch (e.g., to brush his teeth or wash his face or hair), they warned him ahead of time, acknowledged that they knew he didn't like it, and let him know how long the experience would last. They also helped him to develop strategies for dealing with uncomfortable situations, such as taking a favorite toy into the bathtub.

Michael's occupational therapist also worked directly with Michael while at the same time demonstrating to his parents how to reduce his sensitivity to sensory input. The combination of consultation and direct and indirect intervention resulted in dramatic improvements in Michael's behavior and his parents' abilities to interact with him.

OBSERVATION GUIDELINES FOR SENSORY
DEVELOPMENT: STATIONARY POSITIONS USED FOR PLAY—PRONE

IV.   Stationary Positions Used for Play
   A.   Prone (lying on the abdomen)
      1.   Is the child able to raise the head in prone?
      2.   Can the child prop on the forearms?
      3.   Can the child bring the hands together and look at them while propped on the forearms?
      4.   Can the child reach for a toy and play with it while lying on the stomach?
      5.   Are the legs widely spread apart or close together?

INTERVENTION
IMPLICATIONS

Cephalocaudal Development

Typically developing children generally gain control of their movements in prone earlier than they gain such control in supine, sitting, hands and knees, or standing. Furthermore, typical development generally proceeds cephalocaudally (i.e., from head to "tail"). Thus, in prone, a child generally gains control of the head earlier than of the shoulders and trunk. However, it is important to remember that children do not gain total control of their movements in prone before beginning to gain control in supine or sitting. Similarly, children do not gain total control of their heads in prone before beginning to gain control of their shoulders, arms, and trunk. Because sensorimotor development occurs simultaneously in many positions, it is important that facilitators provide children with opportunities that will encourage their total development.

Weight Bearing

Some theorists and clinicians (Boehme, 1988) have emphasized that children should bear their body weight on their arms and hands while in prone to promote the development of palmar arches and general hand skill. However, other researchers (cf. Case-Smith, Fisher, & Bauer, 1989) have found little relationship between proximal and distal development. Even if there is a relationship between weight bearing on the arms and hands and the development of skilled hand use, prone may not be the position in which children find it easiest to use their hands to manipulate objects. Bilateral manipulation and exploration of objects are virtually impossible in prone unless the hands are relieved of their weight bearing function (e.g., lying the child on a wedge; using the prone-on-elbows position).

Gravitational Demands

When a child is lying in the prone position, he or she must resist the full force of gravity in order to lift the head. The need to resist gravity makes prone a particularly important position for working on the development of extension and head control. However, for children who have abnormal muscle tone or weakness, gravity may present too much challenge to their attempts to lift the head.

Thus, the facilitator may be able to help children with abnormal muscle tone or weakness develop control of their heads more effectively from an upright position in which the demands of gravity are fewer. Generally, that control is gained in the context of activities in which the facilitator supports the child's trunk and upper chest and gently tips the child from side to side and forward and backward. Children usually gain control of the head first in response to slight forward tipping and later in response to slight side-to-side tipping. The ability to control the head in response to backward tipping is acquired last. After the child begins to gain control of the head while upright, he or she is more ready to begin work in prone where the demands of gravity are greater.

Play in Prone

The use of play is particularly important when promoting development in prone because this position is so physically demanding. When playing, a child becomes totally absorbed in the transaction. Prone is a physically demanding position. Thus, if the child can become absorbed in play while prone, he or she is likely to be willing to remain longer than if the child is not playing.

However, while play may increase a child's willingness to remain in prone, children will not bear weight on their arms and hands for more than a few seconds at a time. Typically developing children shift their weight from one arm to another and backward and forward, on and off their arms. Children with disabilities, particularly those children with abnormal muscle tone or weakness, also need to be able to shift their weight in the prone position. For many, this may require physical handling by the facilitator.

- Head turns side to side
- Head lifts momentarily
- Hips bent with bottom in air
        (0–2 months)
- Lifts head and sustains in midline
- Rotates head freely when up
- Able to bear weight on forearms
- Able to tuck chin and gaze at hands in forearm prop
- Attempts to shift weight on forearms, resulting in shoulder collapse
        (3–4 months)

Head and Neck Extension

One important difference between the child functioning at the 0- to 2-month level and the child functioning at the 3- to 4-month level, with regard to development in prone, is the child's increasing ability to extend the head and neck against gravity. This is accomplished, in part, because the physiological flexion characteristic of the newborn infant is disappearing. Physiological flexion resulted in the child's hips bending and the weight of the body shifting forward onto the head and shoulders; this increased weight, coupled with the strong pull of gravity, prevented the infant from lifting his or her head.

When attempting to assist a child to lift and control the head in prone and to bear weight on forearms, *the facilitator can place a hand on the child's bottom and shift the child's weight toward the feet.* This weight shift often results in the child spontaneously lifting the head and upper trunk. These same procedures can also be done carefully on a large ball or wedge. When a ball is used, the weight shifting can be accomplished by tipping the ball slightly toward the child's feet.

As the child lifts the head, the facilitator can *present an interesting toy in the child's line of vision* (usually, slightly *lower* than the head). Children often find the face of another person to be highly motivating, especially when the other person talks or makes faces at the child.

Prone-on-Elbows Position

In addition to head lifting, the facilitator often wants to encourage the child to assume and maintain the prone-on-elbows position. The most desirable prone-on-elbows position includes the child's forearms being vertical. If the child does not spontaneously place the forearms vertically, it may be necessary for the facilitator to reposition them. *Shifting the child's weight slightly toward the feet also may help the child to assume and maintain a good prone-on-elbows position.*

Hypertonia

Some children who have hypertonia become quite stiff as they attempt to perform difficult tasks such as lifting the head in prone. They may draw their arms and hands tightly against their bodies or their legs may extend and move tightly together. If the facilitator notices increased stiffness in response to any movement, he or she should consult the occupational or physical therapist.

Withdrawal of Support

As with the facilitation of any movement, the facilitator should withdraw support as quickly as possible to enable the child to be as independent as possible in the prone-on-elbows position. *The ultimate aim is that the child assume and maintain positions totally independently.*

DEVELOPMENTAL LEVEL

- Weight shift on forearms and forward reach
- Weight bearing and weight shifting on extended arms
- Legs closer together and thighs roll inward toward natural alignment
- Hips flat on surface
- Equilibrium reactions present
    (5–6 months)

INTERVENTION GUIDELINES

Two major changes characterize the shift from the previous developmental level to this one: 1) increased spontaneous shifting of weight backward; and 2) increased control of head, arms, and trunk. In addition, the child is beginning to gain control of hips and legs. To assist the child in assuming and maintaining the more high-level prone positions described here, the facilitator can again work with the child on the floor or on a wedge or ball. The wedge or ball usually make fewer demands on the child; thus, it is easier for the child to assume and maintain these positions. However, the ultimate aim is for the child to be able to assume and maintain these positions on the floor without assistance.

As mentioned previously, the interventionist can place a hand on the child's bottom and assist with shifting the child's weight toward the feet. Gentle side-to-side rocking also assists the child in shifting weight to free one arm for reaching. While shifting the child's weight side-to-side to enable reaching, the facilitator must be sure to maintain the backward weight shift; otherwise, the child's arm may remain trapped by body weight. Facilitators again are cautioned that *children can be expected to bear most of their body weight in the prone-on-hands position for only a few seconds before shifting their weight backward off their arms.*

As the child's weight is shifted, attractive toys or another person can be used, as described previously, to facilitate the child's assumption and maintenance of the prone-on-hands position and reaching. Placement of these objects should be *slightly below* the child's head in the line of vision. *If the objective of the intervention session is for the child to attain a toy, that toy must be within the child's reach.*

Equilibrium Reactions

Equilibrium reactions generally develop in prone at this developmental level, first when the child is lying flat and later when the center of gravity is higher (i.e., prone-on-elbows, prone-on-hands). Equilibrium reactions are compensatory movements of the limbs and head that enable the child to maintain a particular body position. They occur in response to alterations of the support surface or because of a change in the center of gravity brought on by the child's reaching or changing position (Weisz, 1938). The adult can facilitate the child's equilibrium reactions by gently rocking the child so the center of gravity moves slightly beyond the base of support. If the child does not respond automatically by moving the uphill limbs (i.e., side opposite the direction of the tilt), it is possible to facilitate these reactions more directly. However, an occupational or physical therapist should be consulted to ensure that the proper techniques are utilized.

DEVELOPMENTAL LEVEL

- Airplane posturing in prone, chest and thighs lift off surface (5–8 months)

INTERVENTION GUIDELINES

The significance of the airplane posture is an indicator that the child has attained the ability to fully extend the head, arms, trunk, and legs against gravity. While it represents a significant accomplishment for the child (Stockmeyer, 1967) and can be incorporated into a number of games that are fun for both the child and the parent or facilitator, the airplane posture is not a particularly functional position. Because the child's hands and arms are drawn back, the child is unable to explore or manipulate toys or other objects.

This position is most easily facilitated when the facilitator grasps the child firmly with both hands around the child's lower trunk. The lack of a support surface under most of the body surface often causes the child to lift the total body against gravity spontaneously and assume the airplane position. Gently raising and lowering the child's body provides vestibular input that may further facilitate the child assuming the posture.

PLAY MATERIALS AND OPPORTUNITIES

As its name suggests, facilitation of this posture lends itself nicely to games of "airplane." The parent or facilitator can make motor noises as he or she moves the child up and down. Many adults like to play this game as they lie supine (i.e., on the back) on the floor. In that way, they can maintain eye contact with the child and help to decrease fear of falling.

DEVELOPMENTAL LEVEL

- Increased variety of positions
    (7–8 months)

INTERVENTION GUIDELINES

Because development at this level is characterized by greater variety in the prone position rather than by the child's developing new abilities, all of the previously mentioned guidelines apply well here.

PLAY MATERIALS AND OPPORTUNITIES

In general, toys used in the process of assisting a child to become more capable in the prone position should possess two characteristics. First, for the child who is not very mobile in prone, toys should be relatively stable (i.e., they should not move easily out of the child's reach). Toys, such as Koosh balls, that do not roll easily and toys that can be readily suspended near the ground are ideal. Second, *the toys or play materials utilized should capture the child's interest and reflect the level of the child's cognitive development.* In addition, *the toys should reflect the child's sensory preferences.* If the object of intervention is to facilitate the child's lifting his or her head rather than reaching, the toys can be relatively larger. Music boxes with revolving pictures capture some children's interest at least for brief periods of time. If the object of the intervention is that the child should reach for a toy, the toy should be responsive to the child's contact with it. It should be easy to knock it over or create a noise with it. If the object of intervention is that the child attain a toy while prone, the toy should be small enough to fit easily in the child's hand (e.g., small blocks, Fisher-Price people). Most children prefer toys that have an element of surprise associated with them. Toys that do only one thing do not capture a child's attention for long. If a child is expected to meet the physical demands of prone, the child must have some good reason for doing so. The creation of truly playful interactions is one way to motivate the child to perform difficult tasks.

OBSERVATION GUIDELINES FOR SENSORIMOTOR DEVELOPMENT: STATIONARY POSITIONS USED IN PLAY—SUPINE

B. Supine (lying on the back)
1. Can the child maintain the head in midline and turn it to both sides?
2. Does the child bring the hands together on the chest?
3. Does the child reach above the chest for objects? (with one or both hands?)
4. Are the legs together or apart?
5. Can the child play with the feet (e.g., put the hands on the knees, play with the feet, bring the feet to the mouth)?

INTERVENTION IMPLICATIONS

Unlike prone, supine is a very good position for some children to explore and manipulate toys. In supine, the floor provides support to the child's trunk and shoulder girdle, thus enabling the very young or unskilled child to use higher-level hand skills than might be possible in positions in which there is less proximal support (e.g., sitting). Furthermore, supine is a particularly good position for working on head control and the ability to flex against gravity. However, as with prone, when the child is in supine, the full force of gravity is acting on the child's head and body, making it particularly difficult to lift the head, arms, trunk, and legs. Thus, when a child has abnormal muscle tone or weakness, it may be easiest to begin developing control of flexion by tilting the child gently backward from an upright position or by creating activities that require the child to flex from a semi-reclined position.

DEVELOPMENTAL LEVEL

- Head held to one side
- Able to turn head side to side
        (0–3 months)
- Head held in midline
- Chin tucked, neck lengthens in back
- Legs come together
- Lower back flat against the floor
        (3–4 months)

INTERVENTION GUIDELINES

Much of the development of ability that occurs during this 4-month period is the result of the lessening of physiological flexion and the downward shifting of the child's weight. These changes result in lengthening of the muscles in the back of the neck and in the lower back coming down against the support surface to provide a wider base of support. When these changes fail to occur spontaneously, a physical therapist may need to develop and implement procedures for lengthening particular muscles. Given that the child has sufficient length in his or her neck muscles, but is unable to tuck the chin or maintain the head in midline, the facilitator can assist these movements by placing a hand on the child's upper chest and pulling toward the child's feet. This helps the child to shift his or her body weight toward the feet, thus freeing the head for movement.

Not much purposeful reaching is expected of a child 4 months of age or younger. However, as children get involved in play interactions, they often begin to wave their arms in excitement and may touch a toy accidentally. Many purposeful movements happen first as "accidents." The pleasure derived from contact with the object and the facilitator's delight may lead the child to repeat the motion, an added bonus.

PLAY MATERIALS AND OPPORTUNITIES

As the child's weight is shifted downward, the facilitator can encourage the child to tuck the chin by resting a small stuffed animal, doll, or puppet on the child's stomach and helping them to "converse." Another way to encourage the child to tuck the chin and look down is to make the "raspberries" sound on the child's stomach. Whatever game the facilitator chooses to initiate, he or she should be certain to *watch the child's cues carefully and give the child sufficient time to respond.* Children with disabilities often require considerable time and effort to respond to verbal or physical prompts. If the facilitator does not allow enough time before repeating the prompt, the child may become overstimulated or frustrated. *Infants and nonverbal children often say, "I've had enough," by actively turning their heads or eyes away from the facilitator or by developing the hiccups.* If the child does not respond in the desired way to the game, it should be discontinued at least temporarily.

DEVELOPMENTAL LEVEL

- Head lag gone when pulled to sit
- Hands together in space
  (4–5 months)

INTERVENTION GUIDELINES

Because pull-to-sit, (i.e., facilitator holds child's hands and pulls child from supine to sitting) is very stressful and demanding for a child, and because it is not a very functional activity, generally, intervention does not directly involve pull-to-sit activities. Rather, observation of a child's ability to perform pull-to-sit during assessment is indicative of that child's ability to flex the head, neck, and upper trunk against gravity. Flexion can be facilitated by playing games with the child in which the adult supports the seated child's trunk and slowly tips him or her backward in increasingly greater arcs. The child is tilted only as far as he or she is able to maintain control of the head. Another way to encourage flexion is to entice the child to lift his or her head from supine in order to see or attain an object that the child finds to be highly motivating. The parent or facilitator can assist the child by placing a hand on the child's chest and moving the child's weight toward the feet.

PLAY MATERIALS AND OPPORTUNITIES

The same principles for toy selection mentioned on page 412 with regard to promoting the prone position apply here. When the child is supine, it generally is best to suspend or hold toys above the child's arms or stomach at the desired height.

- Lifts head independently
- Feet to mouth
- Hands to feet
- Able to reach for toy with one or both hands
- Hands predominantly open
     (5–6 months)

**INTERVENTION
GUIDELINES**

At approximately the same time they have gained relatively good control of the head, shoulders, and arms in supine (i.e., can lift them independently against the full force of gravity), many children begin to play with their feet and bring them to the mouth. When the child is supine holding onto the feet, his or her hips are bent more than 90 degrees while the knees, back, and elbows are straight. This is the same relative position of body parts that the child maintains when sitting. The difference is only that the child's entire body is rotated 90 degrees. Because so many children spend a considerable amount of their time lying supine and playing with their feet at the same time that they are learning to sit, it seems very likely that the two positions are related. Because children with abnormally high muscle tone often have difficulty sitting due to increased extensor tone in their hips, which makes bending them to 90 degrees difficult, many facilitators use the supine hands-on-feet position (in conjunction with techniques for reducing muscle tone) to prepare a child for sitting. Playing with and mouthing feet also seems to be an important way infants learn about their bodies.

Children with abnormally high muscle tone may need assistance to assume the supine hands-on-feet position. Facilitators should never push or pull against tight muscles. Pushing or pulling generally results in increased tightness at the very least; it may result in injury. The child's occupational or physical therapist can assist other team members to develop safe ways to facilitate this position.

In order to assume the supine hands-on-feet position, a child must have low enough muscle tone to bend the hips fully. However, the child must have enough tone to move the legs and arms against the full force of gravity. Thus, children with low muscle tone may have difficulty assuming this position. Facilitators should be aware that, as with all developmental positions, children usually can maintain the supine hands-on-feet position before they can assume it. When specific techniques are needed to build muscle tone in order to enable the child to assume or maintain this position, the child's physical or occupational therapist should be consulted.

**PLAY MATERIALS
AND
OPPORTUNITIES**

Most infants find playing with their feet to be fun. Facilitators can turn this position into a game by grabbing the child's feet and hands and moving the child into and out of sitting. *Be sure to observe vigilantly for signs that the child may be losing head control.* Another way to encourage active foot movements is for the facilitator to tickle, blow on, or "make raspberries" on the child's stomach or one or both of the feet.

DEVELOPMENTAL
LEVEL

- Equilibrium reactions present
  (7–8 months)

INTERVENTION
GUIDELINES

After a child begins to develop the ability to sit independently, he or she probably will not voluntarily spend much waking time in supine. Thus, the development of equilibrium reactions in supine is rarely an objective for intervention. However, when equilibrium in supine *is* the intervention target, the same principles, techniques, and play opportunities described previously for developing equilibrium reactions in prone also apply here (see pp. 411–412).

PLAY MATERIALS
AND
OPPORTUNITIES

The same suggestions recommended for development in prone (see p. 412) are also effective at this developmental level.

OBSERVATION GUIDELINES FOR SENSORIMOTOR DEVELOPMENT: STATIONARY POSITIONS USED FOR PLAY—SITTING

C. Sitting
1. Does the child need to be held in sitting?
2. How much support does the child need when held in sitting?
3. Is the child able to hold the head up?
4. Is the child able to freely turn the head? (to both sides, up and down?)
5. Is the back rounded or straight?
6. Is the child able to sit by propping on the arms?
7. Does the child sit independently without support?
8. Can the child bring the hands together in front of the body?
9. Can the child use the arms and hands to play with toys in sitting?
10. Does the child turn the upper body to reach for or watch objects, keeping the lower body stationary?
11. Is the child able to cross the center of the body with the arms when reaching for a toy?
12. Does the child use the arms to catch him- or herself when falling (forward, sideways, backward)?
13. Are the legs spread widely apart or maintained more closely together?
14. How many different sitting positions are used?
15. When sitting in a chair, does the child's body droop forward?
16. Does the child's bottom slide forward in a chair?

INTERVENTION
IMPLICATIONS

Sitting is one of the most important developmental positions because, in sitting, the child's arms and hands are free for exploration of toys and other objects in the environment. Furthermore, when sitting, the child is at a height more conducive to interactions with family members and others than when the child is lying on the floor. Thus, the ability of the child to sit is frequently a target of intervention. In sitting, as with other body positions, the child gains control of the head before the trunk and the trunk before the hips, and so forth. Of course, the child does not gain total control of any body part before working on the next. Sitting independently with the arms free for play requires considerable ability; the typically developing child often does not fully attain this ability for 8–10 months.

Because sitting is so important and so difficult, many children with abnormal muscle tone or weakness require adapted furniture to provide support and minimize the development of deformity. Such furniture usually is prescribed by an occupational or physical therapist. The therapist, in turn, teaches family members and other facilitators about the proper use and care of the furniture.

- Head bobs in sitting
- Back rounded
- Hips apart, turned out and bent
    (0–3 months) (held in sitting)
- Head steady
- Chin tucks, able to gaze at floor
- Sits with less support
- Hips bent, shoulders in front of hips
    (3–4 months) (held in sitting)
- Sits alone momentarily
- Increased extension in back
- Sits by propping forward on arms
- Wide base, legs bent
- Periodic use of "high guard" position
- Protective responses present when falling to the front
    (5–6 months) (supports self in sitting)

The aim of early intervention across the developmental levels of sitting is to enable the child to gain sufficient control of the head, shoulders, arms and hands, and hips so that he or she can: 1) support him- or herself and 2) catch him- or herself when falling forward. Two problems commonly interfere with a child's ability to acquire these skills: 1) insufficient flexion at the hips (i.e., the child tends to sit on the lower spine rather than the buttocks); and 2) insufficient muscle tone in the trunk. These two problems often occur together and result in poor alignment of the head, trunk, and hips.

Insufficient Hip Flexion

Insufficient flexion at the hips is often caused by tightness in muscles in the backs of the legs. This tightness should be addressed directly by a physical therapist. However, the negative effects of this tightness on the child's ability to sit with a straight back can be minimized by sitting on a short bench or roll. The actual height of the surface depends on the child's height, but the aim of a raised surface is for the child to sit with the back straight and the knees extended. A child at this stage of development is not able to prevent him- or herself from falling. Thus, *the child should never be left unattended while sitting on a raised surface.*

When the child is sitting on a raised surface, the child is too far from the floor to be able to play with objects placed there. Thus, a small table may be useful as a playing surface. The child also can use the table as a support surface if he or she begins to fall forward.

Hypotonia in the Trunk

The problem of insufficient muscle tone in the trunk can be addressed using techniques suggested for hypotonia on page 401. Again, a physical or occupational therapist should select the techniques most appropriate for the child and teach these to family members and other facilitators. Because techniques to increase muscle tone commonly include bouncing and other means of providing vestibular and proprioceptive input, it is easy to incorporate them into games. However, these games must be implemented carefully, heeding the precautions noted by the therapists.

Not all of the intervention techniques designed to improve a child's ability to sit must be done in sitting, although parents and facilitators should not neglect the sitting posture. When activities conducted in prone and supine require that the child move the head, trunk, and arms actively against gravity, they also assist the child in developing some of the abilities needed for sitting.

DEVELOPMENTAL LEVEL

- Sits alone steadily, initially with wide base of support
- Able to play with toys in sitting
    (5–10 months) (sits alone)
- Equilibrium reactions present
- Able to rotate upper body while lower body remains stationary
- Protective responses present when falling to the side
    (7–8 months)
- Sits well without support
- Legs closer, full upright position, knees straight
- Increased variety of sitting positions, including "W" sit and side-sit
- Difficult fine motor tasks may prompt return to wide base of support
    (8–10 months)

INTERVENTION GUIDELINES

When sitting is functional, the child is able to rotate the trunk while reaching for toys scattered within arm's reach on the floor. If the child misjudges his or her capabilities, he or she can use equilibrium reactions, or protective responses, to prevent falling. A child can be helped to develop sitting skills by scattering toys in a circle around the child and encouraging the child to retrieve the toys and deposit them in a strategically placed container. The container can be placed in the child's lap, beside or in front of him or her, or at a slight distance, depending on the desired reaction from the child. As the game progresses, the facilitator can move the container slightly to change the postural demands. If the objects make noise when dropped into the container, the child may be more highly motivated. Another way of promoting the child's ability to move around while sitting is to play a game in which the facilitator gives the child an object and then asks for it. The facilitator can vary the placement of his or her hand so the child is encouraged to reach toward it. The facilitator can give the toy back to the child or hide it under another strategically placed object. If the child wants to play with an object he or she has reached for and attained, the facilitator should encourage this. After a short time, the facilitator can try to entice the child to reach for a different object by offering another equally desirable toy to the child.

The key to success of activities such as this one is for *the facilitator to remember that he or she is playing with the child*. The game should be fun for both of them and the facilitator should continually give the child verbal and nonverbal (e.g., facial) cues indicating that, "This is play" (Bateson, 1971). In games such as these, the facilitator should follow the child's lead. Sometimes the placement of the object should be within easy reach of the child. Sometimes placement should make the child "stretch" his or her skills a little.

Not all of the activities done to promote a child's sitting ability must be done in sitting. Another way to foster trunk control is to carry the child with his or her back toward the adult's chest (i.e., the child facing away from the adult). The adult can support the child around the hips and, if necessary, around the lower trunk. As the child and adult walk through the environment, the child can be encouraged to reach for toys or other objects. By modifying the distance he or she stands from objects, the adult can control the amount the child must move the trunk. If the adult also shows interest in the object the child is trying to reach, the child may persist longer with this game.

DEVELOPMENTAL LEVEL

- Protective extension backward, first with bent elbows then straight elbows
      (10–12 months)
- Trunk control and equilibrium responses fully developed in sitting
- Further increase in variety of positions possible
      (11–12 months)

INTERVENTION GUIDELINES

These developmental levels represent a refinement of the child's abilities in sitting. Thus, the activities listed on pages 418–419 can be used with a child at this level also. The degree of challenge these activities present can be varied to match the child's abilities and needs. The facilitator should remember that a child at this level of skill in sitting is probably able to crawl. Thus, objects scattered too far from the child may encourage the child to assume the hands-and-knees position.

PLAY MATERIALS AND OPPORTUNITIES

The characteristics of toys used to promote a child's ability to sit depend on three things: 1) the preferences of the child (which, in turn, may depend on the child's cognitive level); 2) the degree of mobility the child has in sitting; and 3) the level of the child's hand skill. When a particular sensorimotor activity presents a significant challenge to the child, he or she may be more willing to engage in that activity if the facilitator can truly make the session playful. Children respond best to toys that are flexible and somewhat unpredictable; they get bored easily by a toy that does only one thing. If the child is not very mobile in sitting, the best play materials are those that remain relatively stationary, but at the same time are highly responsive to the child's efforts (e.g., pop-up toys, activity centers, toys that stand up automatically when they've been knocked over). Children are often as fascinated by objects they see around the house (e.g., pans, diapers, a purse) as by actual toys. As the child becomes more mobile, the toys also can be more mobile (e.g., balls, toy cars).

DEVELOPMENTAL LEVEL

- Seats self in small chair
  (18–19 months)

INTERVENTION GUIDELINES

Although this developmental level represents sitting, it is very different than the previous sitting items. Typically, children walk before they begin to seat themselves in chairs. Thus, the attainment of this skill really is better described in the section pertaining to mobility in standing. Of course, some nonambulatory children have as a goal for intervention the ability to seat themselves in a small chair from the floor or from a wheelchair. When this is the case, procedures specific to the needs and abilities of the particular child must be utilized. The physical or occupational therapist should teach other team members to use these procedures.

OBSERVATION GUIDELINES FOR SENSORIMOTOR DEVELOPMENT: STATIONARY POSITIONS USED FOR PLAY—HANDS AND KNEES

D. Hands and knees
    1. Can the child hold the head up when playing on hands and knees?
    2. Can the child reach for a toy while on hands and knees?

INTERVENTION IMPLICATIONS

Children most often assume the hands-and-knees position for crawling. Therefore, a more extensive discussion of this position appears in the section on mobility (see pp. 429–430). However, while in the hands-and-knees position, a child should be able to shift the body weight enough to "free" one hand to reach for a toy. If a child has difficulty doing this, the facilitator can assist the child by placing a hand on the child's back or hips and *gently* shifting the child's weight toward one side and toward the feet. The amount of weight shift necessary to free one hand is very small. Thus, *the facilitator should take care not to move the child too far in either direction as this may result in the child losing balance.*

**OBSERVATION GUIDELINES
FOR SENSORIMOTOR DEVELOPMENT:
STATIONARY POSITIONS USED FOR PLAY—STANDING**

E.   **Standing**
  1.   **Does the child need to be held to stand?**
  2.   **How much support is needed when held in standing?**
  3.   **Can the child hold the head up in standing?**
  4.   **Does the child stand alone at a low table or support, steadying by leaning against the table?**
  5.   **Can the child stand without support, and for how long?**
  6.   **How far apart are the legs when standing?**
  7.   **Are the arms in "high guard"?**
  8.   **Do both sides of the body appear to function equally well?**

Standing is a position that holds tremendous significance for parents and children because standing independently suggests the child will walk soon. Furthermore, the upright position is important for musculoskeletal development and for digestive and circulatory system functioning. Thus, *even if a child cannot stand independently, it is important that he or she spend time in the standing position.* This generally is accomplished by means of adaptive furniture prescribed by the occupational or physical therapist. The therapist, in turn, should teach other team members to use and maintain the equipment properly.

**INTERVENTION
IMPLICATIONS**

**DEVELOPMENTAL
LEVEL**

- When held in standing, takes some weight on legs
        (0–3 months)
- When held in standing, legs may give way
        (2–3 months)
- Bears some weight on legs, must be held proximally
- Head up in midline, no chin tuck
- Pelvis and hips behind shoulders
- Legs apart and turned outward
        (3–4 months)
- Increased capability to bear weight
- Decreased support needed, may be held by arms or hands
- Legs still spread apart and turned outward
        (5–6 months)
- Stands holding on
        (5–10 months)
- Stands alone momentarily
        (9–13 months)

INTERVENTION GUIDELINES

Standing, even when holding on, requires the same abilities required for sitting—and more. In standing, the child's center of gravity is higher and, thus, balance must be better. While holding on, the child may bear a portion of his or her body weight on the arms, but to be able to stand alone, the child must bear total body weight on the legs and feet. Because difficulties with the head and trunk have been discussed previously (see pp. 408–419), this section concentrates on intervening for problems related to the legs.

Abnormal Muscle Tone or Weakness

Hypotonia

The most common problem interfering with a child's ability to stand is abnormal muscle tone or weakness. Some children do not have sufficient muscle tone and strength to support their total body weight. If these children can maintain any semblance of standing (usually while holding on), they tend to keep their feet spread widely apart and lock their knees to prevent falling. They also tend to lean forward on the supporting surface, bending at the hips. The specific procedures for addressing problems with low tone and weakness discussed on page 401 are also relevant here. A physical therapist is needed to prescribe procedures tailored to the needs of a particular child. However, the therapist often can teach other team members to implement these procedures so that the child is able to spend as much time standing as is indicated.

Hypertonia

Children who have hypertonia (especially children's whose arms are less involved than their legs) tend to stand on their toes with their feet close together and their legs stiffly extended at the knees. Usually the hips are bent. This stiff extension is spasticity and should not be misconstrued as strength. As with hypotonia, a physical therapist is needed to prescribe specific procedures for reducing muscle tone and helping the child to stand more normally. These procedures generally are taught to all team members who then can assist with their implementation.

For the child who has abnormal muscle tone or weakness, the job of standing is a very difficult one. Thus, as with the earlier developmental stages, play can serve a very important role. If the child is engaged in a playful transaction that requires standing, the child is much more likely to want to remain in standing for prolonged periods of time. Thus, all of the guidelines discussed previously for helping a child to become totally involved in play apply equally well here.

PLAY MATERIALS AND OPPORTUNITIES

Toys to promote the child's ability to stand should be selected based on the child's preferences, cognitive level, and degree of hand skill. If the child is not very mobile in standing, the toys should be relatively stationary to minimize the chances that the child will become frustrated. Toys that do not roll readily (e.g., dollhouses, simple puzzles, activity centers) or that can be suspended just above a table surface work well. When the child is working on standing while holding on, toys that can be held and manipulated primarily in one hand (e.g., Fisher-Price people) are most effective as the child must hold on with the other hand. If the table surface is of a height that the child can rest the forearms against the surface, bilateral manipulation is possible. However, toys that are too large may be difficult to handle.

EXAMPLE

Maureen B. is an 8-month-old infant with right hemiplegia. Maureen sits independently and is beginning to pull herself to standing, but she neither assumes nor maintains a hands-and-knees position. In fact, she refuses to bear weight on her right arm and becomes tearful when placed on hands and knees. Maureen also seems frustrated by her inability to move around a room to pursue toys or people.

A decision was made to work on Maureen's ability to maintain the hands-and-knees position for two reasons. First, this position was a necessary prerequisite to creeping, which would be a good way for Maureen to move through her environment. Second, the hands-and-knees position "forced" Maureen to bear weight on her right arm, which in turn also provided sensory input to the arm.

Because Maureen was so reluctant to assume and maintain a hands-and-knees position, any intervention that required her to do so would need to be done in the context of a highly motivating activity or experience. Maureen loved movement and roughhousing. Thus, games in which the facilitator or parent placed Maureen head first over a roll and encouraged her to catch herself on her hands helped entice Maureen to work on weight bearing on her hands, a necessary prerequisite to the hands-and-knees position. Maureen also enjoyed rocking back and forth (i.e., right side to left side or hands to knees) over her parent's or the facilitator's knee. Another activity that Maureen and her father enjoyed involved him holding her up in the air by her left arm and leg and swinging her gently back and forth. Periodically, her father lowered Maureen to the floor to rest on her right arm and leg so that he could take a break.

Another favorite activity to encourage Maureen to maintain the hands-and-knees position included placing her in that position on a water-filled transparent mat containing plastic fish. As Maureen shifted her weight from one arm to the other (with help from a parent or facilitator) or from knees to hands, the fish moved inside the mat. Maureen really enjoyed this activity; she could stay with it for 30–40 minutes and seemed never to tire of repeating it. Thus, this activity was particularly useful for promoting both her ability to maintain the hands and knees position and to shift her weight while in it.

OBSERVATION GUIDELINES
FOR SENSORIMOTOR DEVELOPMENT:
MOBILITY IN PLAY—MOVEMENTS IN PRONE AND SUPINE

V. **Mobility in Play**
   A. **Movements in prone and supine**
      1. In stomach-lying, can the child roll onto the side or over to the back?
      2. In back-lying, can the child roll onto the side or over to the stomach?
      3. Does the body appear rigid during rolling ("log roll")?
      4. Does the trunk twist during rolling, so that the hips and shoulders do not move as a unit?
      5. Does the child's body arch backward during rolling?
      6. Does the child roll toward both the left and right?
      7. Can the child control rolling, stopping at any point in the sequence?
      8. Is the child able to move forward while lying on the stomach?

INTERVENTION IMPLICATIONS

Rolling requires somewhat less effort than other means of locomotion in prone (e.g., crawling on the belly). Thus, rolling can be a good means for some children to travel short distances. However, when other means of locomotion that generally occur later in development (e.g., moving forward in prone) are available, the child usually abandons rolling as it is quite difficult to position oneself in the precise location desired when rolling.

As with the facilitation of any movement, *the facilitator should give only as much assistance to the child as is necessary to accomplish rolling or moving forward in prone.* If the child is to master these movements, they must be repeated many times, gradually lessening the amount of assistance given. Facilitation should not be done too quickly. The child must be given ample time to control the movements of body parts not being guided by the facilitator.

Teaching a child to roll or move forward in prone is more successful if it is done in the context of play. *The child should have a good reason to want to move.* Attractive toys or a playful facilitator can provide just such a reason. No matter what is used to entice the child to move, he or she should have the opportunity to attain the object and to interact with it. If a child repeatedly moves to attain an object, only to have it taken out of his or her hands and be made to move to get it again, the child soon stops being interested in moving. *Most children are much less interested in learning to perform a specific movement than they are in attaining a desired play object.* The facilitator must follow the child's lead.

- Rolls prone to side accidentally, due to poor control of weight shift
- Rolls supine to side
        (3–4 months)
- Rolls prone to supine
- Rolls supine to side with right and left leg performing independent movements
- Rolls supine to prone with right and left leg performing independent movements
        (5–6 months)
- Rolls segmentally with roll initiated by head, shoulder, or hips
        (6–14 months)

Generally, rolling is accomplished first from prone to supine and later from supine to prone. The earliest rolling is accidental and caused by poor control of weight shifts. Later, the child voluntarily initiates rolling, often by collapsing one shoulder and flexing the opposite hip and knee. The optimal form of rolling is segmental rolling, in which the child initiates the roll with head, arm, or leg and the rest of the body follows, section by section, rather than in one piece like a log.

Children who have abnormally high muscle tone usually use lesser involved body parts to initiate rolling (i.e., if the legs are more involved than the arms, they initiate rolling with the head, shoulder, or arm). If the child is more involved on one body side, he or she initiates rolling by using the sound side. This choice may not be desirable as it results in little or no active movement of the more involved extremities and often triggers associated reactions.

When learning to roll is an objective for children who have abnormally high muscle tone, the precise means for facilitating that movement should be decided by the physical or occupational therapist who, in turn, teaches other team members to implement these procedures so the child can receive the optimal benefit from intervention. Of course, rolling supine to prone is more difficult than rolling prone to supine. Thus, the two types of rolling can not always be mastered at the same time.

- Pivots in prone
- Crawls forward on belly
- Moves from prone to sit
- Begins to dislike supine and rolls to another position
        (7–8 months)

Pivoting in prone, crawling on the belly, and moving from prone to sit are difficult because they require the child to do different things simultaneously with the two sides of the body. Because children with abnormally high muscle tone tend to move in an all-or-none fashion, doing different things with different limbs (or even with different segments of the same limb) is extraordinarily difficult. Children with abnormally high muscle tone often are not taught to crawl on their bellies because the effort of doing so tends to make their muscles very stiff. Generally, the potential losses far outweigh the gains. The ability to pivot in prone sometimes *is* an objective for intervention. The ability to rise from prone to sitting is such an important skill that it almost always is included in an objective at some time during the course of a child's intervention. However, because abnormally high muscle tone manifests itself in a number of ways, it is not possible to give general guidelines for teaching these skills. Rather, an occupational or physical therapist should be consulted to discern the optimal ways to teach these skills to particular children.

Children with abnormally low muscle tone often find pivoting, crawling, and rising to sit to be difficult because: 1) the total force of gravity is acting on them, and 2) the increased contact of the body with the support surface provides considerable resistance to movement.

Children with normal or slightly low muscle tone can be helped to crawl on their bellies by grasping one foot and carefully flexing the knee and flexing and externally rotating the hip. Leaving a hand on the child's foot, the facilitator can then provide resistance as the child straightens the leg. After the child has moved forward by pushing with one leg, the facilitator can repeat the procedure with the other foot and leg. *The child is far more willing to perform these movements if there is something interesting toward which to move.*

It is difficult to physically assist a child with normal or slightly low muscle tone to pivot in prone. This movement is usually best facilitated by playing with the child from the front or slightly to one side. If the child and the facilitator are playing with toys that readily roll a little, it is possible, once the child has become absorbed in the play, for the facilitator to roll the toys *slightly* out of the child's reach. If the facilitator is patient, the child is apt to turn a small amount to continue the game. As the child becomes more capable of pivoting, the distance the facilitator rolls the toys can be increased.

The facilitator can assist the child with normal or slightly low muscle tone to rise from prone to sitting by placing a hand along one of the child's sides. The base of the facilitator's hand should be at the child's hip. Being careful to monitor the child's opposite shoulder, the facilitator rotates the child's pelvis backward and, as the hips come into the sidelying position, pulls the child's weight in the direction of the buttocks. With the weight shifted backward, the child should rise spontaneously into sitting. The facilitator should move slowly enough to enable the child to control movements of the head, upper trunk, and arm. The movement must be repeated frequently, giving the child greater control as he or she is ready to take it. Because the child is moving from one plane to another, it is difficult to use toys to entice the child to move from prone to sitting. A playful interaction is usually the thing that most effectively motivates the child.

PLAY MATERIALS AND OPPORTUNITIES

As with toys used to promote any form of sensorimotor development, toys used to promote movement in prone should reflect the child's preferences, cognitive level, and degree of skilled hand use. Because, in this case, the child is being asked to move, the toys also can move easily (e.g., balls, push cars). In that way, movement becomes a natural part of the game rather than something contrived. Of course, the toys should not move so easily that they move out of the child's range or the flow of the game will be disrupted and the child may become frustrated.

OBSERVATION GUIDELINES FOR SENSORIMOTOR DEVELOPMENT: MOBILITY IN PLAY—MOVEMENTS IN SITTING

B. **Movements in sitting**
1. **Does the child pivot in a circle in sitting?**
2. **Does the child scoot on his or her bottom in sitting?**
3. **Does the child move in and out of sitting alone?**
    a. **From stomach to sitting and sitting to stomach?**
    b. **From sitting into hands and knees and vice versa?**
    c. **To both sides (to the right and to the left)?**

Sitting is a very functional position because the child can freely use his or her hands to explore toys and other objects in the environment. Sitting becomes more functional as the child becomes increasingly mobile (i.e., when the child is able to move in and out of sitting at will).

INTERVENTION IMPLICATIONS

- Gets to sitting from prone
    (6–11 months)
- Able to move in and out of sitting into other positions
    (11–12 months)

DEVELOPMENTAL LEVEL

When children move voluntarily out of sitting, they generally move into sidely-ing, prone (including prone-on-elbows and prone-on-hands), or onto hands and knees, depending on the location of a desired toy or object. If the toy is reasonably close or very far away (e.g., across the room, in another room), the child may choose a hands-and-knees position. If the toy or object is too far away to be reached by assuming a hands-and-knees position or a variation of it, but not so far away as to require crawling to it, the child may assume a prone or sidelying position to get to it. The facilitator should experiment with placing toys at different distances and in different positions relative to the child to see the elicited responses. If the transaction between the child and the facilitator is a playful one, the child may be more apt to move in and out of sitting. He or she should be encouraged to move to both sides, except in the case of children who tend to move to one side; these children should be encouraged to move toward their nonpreferred sides.

INTERVENTION GUIDELINES

The facilitator can assist the child to move by placing a hand on the child's hip and gently shifting the child's weight toward the toy. The movement should be done slowly enough to ensure that the child maintains control over move-ments of the head, trunk, and arms. It is particularly important that the child be able to catch him- or herself while moving toward the floor.

PLAY MATERIALS AND OPPORTUNITIES

Toys that move easily provide very natural media when movement out of sitting is an objective. Although the choice of toys depends on the child's preferences and skills, push cars and balls can be used in a number of ways. Playing "catch" with a rolled ball or car is a favorite of many child–facilitator dyads. Catch also provides opportunities for the facilitator to occasionally roll the toy in such a way that the child has to move to get it. Another favorite for children is to knock over a stack of blocks by rolling a toy. The harder the child rolls the toy, the more widely the blocks scatter. The child can be encouraged to move out of sitting to help the facilitator to retrieve the scattered blocks. Wind-up toys also encourage children to move out of sitting; many children do not have the skills necessary to activate the toys themselves, but they enjoy chasing them. A third game, popular with many children, involves encouraging the child to throw and then retrieve a handful of balls, beads, puzzle pieces, or blocks. Again, it is not important that the child have the skills to use the retrieved objects (e.g., string the beads, stack the blocks); the facilitator can do that. The objective of this game is for the child to have a number of opportunities to move into and out of sitting.

DEVELOPMENTAL LEVEL

- Rises from supine by first rolling over to stomach then pushing up into four-point
  (9–18 months)
- Rises from supine by first rolling to side then pushing up into sitting
  (11–24 months +)
- Seats self in small chair
  (18–19 months)
- Some children able to come straight up to sit from supine
  (5–6 years)

INTERVENTION GUIDELINES

The difference between the requirements for rising to sit from prone and side-lying is in how much the child must laterally flex the head and trunk to rise against gravity. Lateral flexion requires a balance of flexor and extensor muscles. Both of these patterns of rising to sit are intermediary methods, used until the child is able to rise directly to sitting from supine.

When helping a child to learn to rise to sit from supine, it usually is best to help the child rise through the sidelying position. This movement is facilitated by reversing the movements described for assisting a child to move from sitting to prone on page 427. The facilitator places a hand on the child's hip and helps the child roll to sidelying. Then the facilitator pulls downward toward the child's buttocks, shifting the weight to the child's bottom and freeing the head, trunk, and arms so that the child can rise spontaneously into sitting. As with moving from prone to sitting, it is difficult to place toys within the child's line of sight in order to entice him or her to rise to sitting. The playful facilitator usually is the best tool for encouraging the child to move. Of course, if the child is involved in play and must move out of sitting to retrieve a toy, it is likely that the child will be intrinsically motivated to return to sitting where it is easier to use the toy.

Virtually any toy or object that is of a size the child can handle easily and is motivating to the child can be used to facilitate movement into, out of, or in sitting. Because movement is the desired outcome, the toy should not "pull for" stationary sitting (i.e., it should not be a toy that the child simply holds on the lap and manipulates there). However, if the child is unable to creep on hands and knees, the toy also should not move too easily away from the child. Often, it is easier to use more than one toy simultaneously to facilitate a child's moving in sitting. When several toys are close by, the facilitator can offer to trade toys with the child, *strategically placing the toy so that the child must move slightly to get it. However, the facilitator should take care not to frustrate or tease the child by taking toys away too quickly and disrupting the child's play.* When movement is the desired outcome of intervention, movement should be built naturally (rather than in a contrived way) into the interaction.

PLAY MATERIALS AND OPPORTUNITIES

Creating activities that enable the child to work repeatedly on rising to sit can be quite a challenge. Most children are highly motivated to move into sitting where they can play. However, once in sitting, they may be happy to play for some time. Thus, the creation of activities that entice the child to move *out of sitting*, such as those specified in the next section, also can be used to create opportunities to practice assuming the sitting posture again.

In addition to creating activities in which the child moves into or out of sitting, the facilitator also might be interested in creating activities that promote mobility of the head, trunk, and arms (and, to a lesser extent, of the legs) in the seated position.

Games in which a child retrieves several relatively small (of a size to be held in one hand) toys or objects and places them in a container lend themselves easily to working on mobility in sitting. Many children find dumping the container to be more motivating than filling it. Filling is a necessary prerequisite to dumping. Of course, when dumping is a part of the activity, the facilitator must be certain that the objects do not move beyond the child's range of movement. The social skill of turn-taking can be encouraged by the adult taking every other turn in the filling process, leaving the joy of dumping to the child.

OBSERVATION GUIDELINES FOR SENSORIMOTOR DEVELOPMENT: MOBILITY IN PLAY— MOVEMENTS IN THE HANDS-AND-KNEES POSITION

C. Movements in the hands-and-knees position
  1. Does the child rock back and forth while on hands and knees?
  2. Does the child move forward while on hands and knees?
  3. How mature is the child's creeping pattern?
      a. Do the arm and leg on the same side of the body move forward simultaneously?
      b. Do the arm and leg on the opposite side of the body move forward simultaneously?
  4. How does the child move from hands and knees into sitting?
      a. Does the bottom drop straight back, between the thighs?
      b. Does the bottom drop to one side, into side-sitting?
      c. Does the child move in both directions (to the right and to the left)?
  5. Can the child rise from hands and knees up into kneeling?

INTERVENTION IMPLICATIONS

Creeping on hands and knees is a very effective means of getting around for some children. However, many children who have abnormally high muscle tone are not taught to creep, both because it is difficult for them to do different things simultaneously with their two legs and because they are at risk for developing hip and knee deformities; the creeping position can contribute to that risk. A physical therapist should be involved in the determination of whether creeping is a good objective for a particular child.

DEVELOPMENTAL LEVEL

- Reciprocal creep
  (7–10 months)
- Creeps on hands and feet
  (10–11 months)
- Creeps well
  (11–12 months)

INTERVENTION GUIDELINES

Before children learn to creep, they generally go through a stage in which they rock back and forth on their hands and knees. This allows them to practice weight shifting forward and backward, a necessary prerequisite for creeping. If a child is not able to creep, but is able to assume the hands-and-knees position, the facilitator can assist the child to rock back and forth by placing a hand on the child's back and gently shifting the child's weight to and fro in very small arcs. The facilitator also should shift the child's weight side to side gently, as this weight shift also is necessary for creeping. By shifting the weight simultaneously slightly backward and to one side, the facilitator can free one of the child's arms. After the arm is free, the facilitator can shift the child's weight gently but quickly in the direction of the free arm. The objective is to get the child to use the free arm and hand to catch him- or herself and to move forward. The hand should land slightly in front of its initial position. The same movements can be performed on the other side to get the child to move the other hand. After the hands are forward, the child usually spontaneously brings the knees closer to the hands. The facilitator should watch to be sure the child moves only one leg at a time.

PLAY MATERIALS AND OPPORTUNITIES

Several different kinds of toys can be used to facilitate creeping. Unless the child is very proficient at the movement, the toys should not move too readily (e.g., motorized cars). Any toy that the child finds appealing can be used. Again, *the child should be encouraged to play with the toy after it has been reached.* This generally is most easily accomplished by moving back into the sitting position. Some children are motivated to creep by seeing themselves in a full-length mirror attached to a wall. The mirror alone may be enticing to children at some levels of development, but mirrors also can be made more appealing by squirting Crazy Foam, Silly String, or shaving cream on them. Some children are most effectively enticed to creep if a family member or playful facilitator is sitting a few feet away. Cooperative family pets also can entice some children to creep.

OBSERVATION GUIDELINES FOR SENSORIMOTOR DEVELOPMENT: MOBILITY IN PLAY—MOVEMENTS IN STANDING

D. Movements in standing
  1. Does the child bounce up and down when held in standing?
  2. Is the child able to pull up into standing by holding onto furniture?
  3. When pulling up, do both legs push together or does the child plant one foot and come up through half-kneel?
  4. Can the child walk sideways while holding onto furniture?
  5. Does the child demonstrate the ability to walk without support?
      a. Are the arms in "high guard" or down by the child's side?
      b. How far apart are the legs?
  6. Is the child able to rise to standing from the floor, without the use of furniture? (Does the child need to place the hands on the floor for support when rising to standing?)
  7. Can the child squat in play?
  8. Is the child able to lower to the floor from standing?
  9. Is the child able to run?
      a. Is there a moment when both feet are off the ground?
      b. Are the arms in "high guard"?
      c. Does running appear stiff and awkward, or coordinated?
      d. Can the child stop quickly, avoid obstacles, and change directions?
      e. Can the child run on varied surfaces (grass, gravel, tile)?

INTERVENTION IMPLICATIONS

Mobility in standing includes a variety of movements from simple (e.g., bouncing up and down while being held) to complex (e.g., walking heel-to-toe). Clearly, these movements reflect variation in the amount of control the child needs in order to execute them successfully. Thus, it is not surprising that development of fundamental movements in standing occurs throughout infancy and toddlerhood and well into the preschool years.

The Significance of Mobility in Standing

Mobility in standing, particularly walking, holds tremendous significance in American culture. The first steps of typically developing children are celebrated. When parents of very young children with disabilities are asked about their goals for their child, walking is among those most commonly listed. The goal of walking often seems to have both symbolic and practical significance. Walking often signifies "normalcy" as well as the lessening of the need to carry the child everywhere. Because the goal of walking often seems to be imbued with deep meaning, other team members must take particular care to listen and respond to parents' explicit and implicit feelings regarding their child's ability to walk. The decision about whether to work toward functional ambulation with a child is complicated; it cannot be made lightly.

Walking

For many children with disabilities, walking is an extraordinarily difficult task that consumes a considerable amount of energy. When the decision to work on walking is made, the physical therapist usually guides the child and other team members in the development of therapeutic techniques. However, all team members should become aware of those techniques so intervention is most effective. Furthermore, the development of mobility in standing requires considerable practice. Young children are most easily enticed to practice difficult skills in the context of enjoyable activity. Thus, all team members may want to develop a repertoire of play strategies that can be used to help a child practice the skills necessary for developing mobility in standing. Some suggested strategies are discussed in the following sections.

DEVELOPMENTAL LEVEL

- Bounces in standing
  (5–6 months)
- Pulls to stand at furniture
  (6–12 months)
- Cruises sideways
- Rotates the trunk over the lower extremities
  (8 months)
- Lower extremities more active in pull to stand
- Pulls to stand through kneeling, then half-kneel
  (8–9 months)
- Walks with two hands held
  (8–18 months)
- Cruises around furniture, turning slightly in intended direction
  (9–10 months)
- Pulls to stand with legs only, no longer needs arms
  (9–13 months)

INTERVENTION GUIDELINES

Pulling To Stand

The development of pulling to stand and cruising generally precede walking in typically developing children. However, children with disabilities, particularly those with abnormally high muscle tone, may learn to walk before they learn to rise to stand independently.

To work on pulling to stand, place toys or objects known to motivate the child on top of a surface a little beyond the child's reach from the floor, but not out of sight. The actual surface to be used depends on the child's height and the amount of support he or she needs to pull to stand; a physical or occupational therapist can help to identify the best surface when team members have questions. A coffee table often works well for small children.

Pulling to stand requires considerable energy expenditure by the child. Thus, if the child is totally absorbed in a play transaction, he or she is likely to be thinking about the play rather than the difficulty of rising to stand. Children vary in the kind of games in which they become most involved; facilitators should always attempt to use the type of games known to motivate the child.

Some children need special assistance from the facilitators in order to be able to assume the standing position. As noted previously, such techniques should be developed in conjunction with the physical therapist. The parents, caregivers, or facilitators who implement these techniques may require considerable practice administering them before they are able to play with the child simultaneously. The same is true for techniques used to facilitate cruising. The physical or occupational therapist may offer significant support in this area.

Cruising

After the child is standing, he or she can be enticed to cruise by movement of the objects on the table surface. If the objects move easily, cruising becomes a natural part of the game rather than a maneuver contrived by the facilitator. Generally, children should be encouraged to cruise in both directions (right and left); of course, some children (especially those with motor asymmetries) need more help to move in one direction than the other.

It is easy to incorporate both cruising and pull-to-stand into the same game. However, *the facilitator should remember the primary goal for the child.* Cruising is easier than pulling to stand; pulling to stand generally requires more time and energy from the child. If pull-to-stand is the important goal, then more dropping of toys should be incorporated into the game. If cruising is the important goal, the facilitator should retrieve any dropped toys or relatively immobile toys should be incorporated into the game.

Games involving "capture" or "keep away" themes with toys lend themselves to working on pull-to-stand as they encourage the child to move quickly. In addition, it is easy for both children and adults to get involved in games of these types.

If several small toys that move easily are incorporated into the game, it is very likely that they will land on the floor periodically. When that happens, the child can be encouraged to "go get them." Of course, after the child has retrieved the missing toys, the child can be enticed to return to standing and the game can begin again.

PLAY MATERIALS AND OPPORTUNITIES

DEVELOPMENTAL LEVEL

- Walks with one hand held
- Reaches for furniture out of reach in cruising
- Cruises in either direction, no hesitation
    (11 months)
- Takes independent steps, falls easily
    (9–17 months)
- Walking—stoops and recovers in play
    (10–14 months)
- Equilibrium reactions present in standing
    (12 months)

Equilibrium Reactions

INTERVENTION GUIDELINES

Shortly after a child is able to assume and maintain standing, equilibrium reactions develop in that position. Equilibrium reactions are compensatory movements of the arms, legs, head, and trunk that enable the child to maintain a position even when the support surface changes or the child is jostled gently (Weisz, 1938). The development of equilibrium reactions is, perhaps, the most important component of mobility that occurs during this time. Although equilibrium reactions are not necessary for walking, they are necessary for stopping, negotiating obstacles, reaching, bending, and other such movements performed in standing.

Promoting the Development of Equilibrium Reactions

Specific "handling" techniques for promoting the development and use of equilibrium reactions (and other skills in standing) often are developed as a part of a child's physical or occupational therapy program. However, as with the development of all important sensorimotor components, movements in standing (e.g., equilibrium reactions, cruising, bending) must be practiced repeatedly. That practice is most effective if it is done in the context of naturally occurring play activities.

PLAY MATERIALS AND OPPORTUNITIES

Through play activities, the facilitator seeks to provide the child with many different opportunities to practice emerging skills in standing. In many ways, these games are extensions of those described on page 433 for the promotion of cruising as the child and the facilitator play games in which the child must reach for and retrieve toys and play materials. The child can be expected to move more frequently and with greater confidence. The facilitator also can vary the support surface on which the child plays. Carpet, bare floor, foam rubber, and pillows make different demands on the child's abilities in standing. Furthermore, children who are able or who need only a little assistance to walk independently sometimes enjoy pushing a cart, doll stroller, or even a child-size chair as they move from place to place in play.

It is important to follow the child's lead in all play activities. If the child seems frightened, timid, easily angered, or frustrated, the activity may be beyond his or her skill level. *The facilitator can reduce the sensorimotor demands of the activity by bringing objects closer to the child or playing on a firm support surface.* The facilitator also must ensure that he or she is not "teasing" the child by not allowing him or her enough time to play with a toy once he or she has acquired it.

DEVELOPMENTAL LEVEL

- Able to start and stop in walking
  (15 months)
- Seldom falls
- Runs stiffly, eyes on ground
  (18 months)
- Squats to play
  (21 months)
- Runs, whole foot contact, stops and starts
  (2–2½ years)
- Runs around obstacles, turns corners
  (3–4 years)
- Walks with a heel to toe pattern
  (3½–5 years)

The ability to execute relatively high-level components of walking and running (e.g., stopping, avoiding obstacles, walking heel-to-toe) depends on many skills and abilities. These include, but are not limited to, balance, motor planning, and an accurate body scheme. Usually, difficulties with these underlying abilities are identified and addressed directly by an occupational or physical therapist. However, in addition to specific therapeutic techniques that may be used to facilitate acquisition of high-level components of walking and running, each child needs considerable practice using these abilities before he or she masters them. Thus, team members should create situations in which the child is encouraged to run, negotiate obstacles, and walk in novel ways (e.g., on toes, on heels, heel-to-toe). Obstacle courses and games such as "Simon says," "Tag," and "Red light, green light" appeal to many preschoolers. Younger children often enjoy simple games of chase with an adult who can ensure the child's safety. Pull toys and lightweight push toys (i.e., not stable enough for the child to lean on) provide other ways of varying walking skills for toddlers. In order to navigate successfully through the environment, the child must learn to use push or pull toys as though they were an extension of his or her own body; this presents a special challenge to the child's motor planning abilities. In addition, children often turn around to walk as they use pull toys; this promotes the development of another variation on basic walking skills.

There are three basic categories of toys or objects that can be used to promote the development of mobility in standing. These are: 1) toys and objects that give the child a reason to move, 2) toys or objects a child can push or pull, and 3) objects that can be used to vary the support surface. Because these categories of toys serve very different purposes in the promotion of walking and running skills, the characteristics of desirable toys from these categories have been described more fully in the sections to which they pertain.

EXAMPLE

Keith T. is a 22-month-old child with Down syndrome. He is able to creep, walk with one hand held, cruise around furniture, and pull-to-stand. Mrs. T., Keith's mother, is expecting a second child and is experiencing difficulty lifting and carrying Keith. Thus, one primary objective for Keith is that he learn to walk independently.

While the physical therapist has developed specific handling techniques to work on walking, Mrs. T. currently is unable to carry out a home program that includes those techniques. Thus, because of Mrs. T.'s needs and the importance of the objective, the amount of direct intervention Keith receives from the physical therapist has been increased temporarily. However, there are many activities Keith and his mother *can* do at home that will enable him to practice components of walking. For example, Keith enjoys pushing a child-size grocery cart from room to room. His mother encourages him to fill the cart with toys so that it is more stable and provides him with the extra support he needs to move independently. Small riding toys provide another alternative for independent mobility when creeping is impractical (e.g., outdoors). These toys also have the added benefit of promoting the same pattern of movement necessary for rising from squat to stand.

OBSERVATION GUIDELINES
FOR SENSORIMOTOR DEVELOPMENT:
OTHER DEVELOPMENTAL ACHIEVEMENTS—JUMPING

VI.   Other Developmental Achievements
    A.   Jumping
        1.   What movements demonstrate the child's ability to project the body in space?
            a.   Does the child jump down from a bottom step?
            b.   Does the child jump up from the floor?
            c.   Are the arms in "high guard" during jumping?
            d.   Does the child crouch in preparation for jumping?

INTERVENTION IMPLICATIONS

Jumping, hopping, and skipping are fundamental motor skills that begin to develop after the child can walk fairly well. However, children continue to develop these fundamental motor skills until they are approximately 7 years old (Keogh & Sugden, 1985; Williams, 1983). A child's ability to run, skip, and hop reflects the child's balance, strength, bilateral coordination, and motor planning ability. At more advanced levels, when the child can jump, hop, or skip around obstacles, these skills reflect the child's ability to perform anticipatory motor skills. This means that the child must be able to alter the course of his or her actions *before* encountering the obstacles.

Running, jumping, and hopping are a part of many common childhood games. Thus, they are important to a child's social-emotional, as well as sensorimotor, development.

DEVELOPMENTAL LEVEL

- Jumps down from step
      (17–21 months)
- Jumps off floor with both feet
      (17 months–2½+ years)
- Jumps from bottom step
      (19 months–2½+ years)
- Jumps over objects
      (2–5 years)

INTERVENTION GUIDELINES

Children generally begin to learn how to jump by jumping off low surfaces, such as a bottom step. Initially, they may need to hold a railing or the facilitator's hand, but very soon they master simple jumps. Most children are eager to demonstrate their "physical prowess" by attempting jumping feats. Children who show persistent and inordinate fear of jumping and other tasks in which the feet must leave the ground, especially in the absence of obvious postural difficulties (e.g., poor balance), should be evaluated by an occupational or physical therapist trained in sensory integration theory (Fisher et al., 1991) and testing procedures (Ayres, 1989).

The facilitator can assist the child in learning to jump by providing supervised opportunities for jumping. When the child asks for or requires assistance, the facilitator should position him- or herself in front of the child and offer his or her hands to the child. The facilitator should be cognizant of how much of the child's body weight he or she is bearing during the jump and gradually turn that support over to the child. This can be done in a number of ways, including offering only one hand instead of two. Perhaps the best way to assist the child in taking control of the jump is by the facilitator keeping his or her arms limp. In that way, the facilitator provides a little assistance to the child's balance, but the child does the majority of the "work." The amount of control needed for jumping can also be varied by increasing (or decreasing) the height of the surface from which the child is jumping.

As the child begins to master jumping off a low surface, he or she can begin a game of jumping over an object placed on the floor. At first, the object to be jumped over should be at or slightly above floor level. Pieces of colored tape work very well. The height and width of the object can be increased as the child becomes more proficient. The facilitator can assist the child in the same ways described above for jumping off a low surface.

DEVELOPMENTAL LEVEL

- Hops on one foot, few steps
    (2½+ years)
- Hops on one foot
    (3–5 years)
- Skips on one foot
    (3–4 years)
- Gallops, leading with one foot and transferring weight smoothly and evenly
    (5–6 years)
- Hops in straight line
    (6 years)
- Skips on alternating feet, maintaining balance
    (6–7 years)

INTERVENTION GUIDELINES

Hopping on one foot, galloping, and skipping are variations of jumping. However, they require greater bilateral coordination and balance. Hopping is jumping on one foot. Skipping is basically hopping reciprocally, first on one foot and then the other. Galloping generally represents an intermediate stage of development between hopping and skipping. Girls usually can be expected to learn to skip before boys of the same age.

Hopping and skipping are reasonably difficult skills that require a considerable amount of practice before they are mastered. After the child has the idea of what it means to hop or skip, the best assistance the facilitator can provide to the child is plenty of opportunities for practice. This easily can be incorporated into active games outside or inside a classroom. Hopping and skipping fit easily into obstacle courses and simple relay races.

The child who finds hopping difficult because of poor balance can be assisted to develop better one-legged standing balance through many activities.

Kicking a ball requires that the child stand briefly on one foot. Similarly, stepping over large obstacles (e.g., a pile of cardboard bricks or a tire tube) requires that the child maintain balance for brief periods of time on one foot.

PLAY MATERIALS AND OPPORTUNITIES

Toys and play materials are unnecessary in the development of jumping, hopping, and skipping. The child needs many opportunities to practice in places that are safe and, occasionally, the child may need a model. As the child begins to master these skills, he or she also may enjoy the presence of a spectator who cheers enthusiastically (Sutton-Smith, 1980).

OBSERVATION GUIDELINES FOR SENSORIMOTOR DEVELOPMENT: OTHER DEVELOPMENTAL ACHIEVEMENTS—CLIMBING

B. Climbing
  1. **What method does the child use to climb stairs?**
      a. **Does he or she creep on hands and knees or hands and feet?**
      b. **If upright, is a rail or adult support needed?**
      c. **Does the child place both feet on each step (marking time) or alternate feet?**
  2. **What size and length of stairs can the child manage?**
  3. **What other types of climbing are demonstrated (onto a foam block, up a ladder, on a jungle gym)?**

INTERVENTION IMPLICATIONS

Climbing is a part of everyday life, especially for the young child. Children climb stairs; they climb onto chairs and into bed; and they climb on the playground. Thus, the development of a child's ability to climb safely and independently is an important objective for many children's intervention. Because the motor patterns for climbing up stairs and climbing on furniture and playground equipment differ markedly, each is discussed separately.

DEVELOPMENTAL LEVEL

- Creeps up stairs
    (15 months)
- Walks up stairs, holding on
    (12–23 months)
- Walks down stairs, holding on
    (13–23 months)
- Creeps backward down stairs
    (18–23 months)
- Walks up stairs without support, marking time
    (18–2½+ years)
- Walks down stairs without support, marking time
    (19 months–2½+ years)
- Walks up stairs, alternating feet
    (28 months–3 years)
- Walks down stairs, alternating feet
    (2½+ years)

A child's ability to safely navigate stairs is of tremendous concern for many families. This is particularly true because children learn to go up stairs independently before they are able to go down stairs. The young child eager to explore the environment may climb a set of stairs and find him- or herself with no way to get back down. If the child becomes distressed at being separated from others who have remained downstairs (perhaps unaware of the child's departure), the child may attempt to go down the stairs head first. The results of these attempts can be disastrous.

There are two important abilities regarding stair climbing that commonly are addressed through intervention. These are: 1) creeping backward down stairs, and 2) ascending and descending by alternating feet.

Depending on their cognitive level and motor planning skills, some children need only be shown how to turn around and creep down the stairs feet first. However, a significant number of children require physical guidance as they learn to creep backward down the stairs. Whatever method is selected for teaching the child, the facilitator should be certain that the child can safely and reliably go down the stairs. If the child requires physical guidance, the facilitator should remember that *passive movements are not as effective as active movements for learning a skill* (Evarts, 1985; Kalaska, 1988). Thus, while some passive movements initially may be required to give the child the idea of how to move, the child should be encouraged to take over the movements as soon as possible.

To learn to descend the stairs by alternating feet, a child often needs only a model and some coaching. As the facilitator walks down the stairs with the child, he or she can say something like, "This foot first. Now the other foot first. Now the other foot first." If the facilitator holds the child's hand, he or she can control the speed with which the child descends the stairs and can gently "hold the child back" until he or she alternates feet. Some children require that the facilitator gently touch the leg that is to lead at each stair.

INTERVENTION IMPLICATIONS

DEVELOPMENTAL LEVEL

- Climbs into adult chair
    (18 months)
- Climbs down from adult chair
    (21 months)
- Climbs up and down furniture independently
    (2–2½ years)

INTERVENTION GUIDELINES

To climb onto and off of adult-size furniture, the child must be able to shift his or her body weight onto a horizontal surface that is somewhat higher than the child's own center of gravity. The exact amount of the shift depends on the child's height; the shorter the child, the greater the shift required. The greater the necessary weight shift, the more relative strength is required from the child. Most children approach the task of climbing onto adult-size furniture by laying their upper bodies on the seat, lifting one knee onto the surface, and using the knee and arms to pull the rest of the body onto the support surface. The facilitator can assist the child to get onto the furniture by assisting the child to get the upper body and knee in place. Once there, the facilitator can place a hand on the bottom of the child's raised foot and resist the extension of the child's leg as he or she attempts to climb onto the furniture.

Once on the furniture, the child must move from prone into the sitting position. Generally, this is accomplished in much the same way as the child moves from prone to sitting on the floor. If the furniture is soft, the surface does not resist the child's movements well, making it more difficult than rising to sit than on the floor. The longer the surface (e.g., sofa compared with chair), the more turning room the child has and thus the easier it is to get to sit. However, once the child is in sitting, there may be somewhat less support on the sides. The facilitator can assist the child to rise to sitting on furniture by using the same procedures used on the floor.

DEVELOPMENTAL LEVEL

- Climbs easy nursery apparatus
  (2½–3 years)
- Climbs ladder
  (4–5 years)

INTERVENTION GUIDELINES

Climbing equipment, such as ladders, jungle gyms, and sliding boards hold special appeal for most preschool-age children. Two things commonly interfere with a child's ability to use this equipment effectively: 1) fear, and 2) lack of maneuverability caused by poor motor planning ability. The child who is 4 years of age or older who manifests either of these problems (especially the child who has an inordinate amount of fear in the absence of obvious postural dysfunction) on equipment that seems easy for peers to maneuver should be evalu-

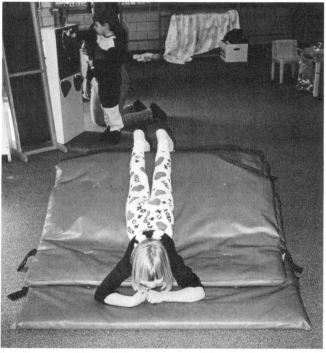

Experimentation with how the body moves over different surfaces can help the child to develop equilibrium responses and motor-planning skills.

ated by an occupational or physical therapist trained in sensory integration theory (Fisher et al., 1991) and evaluation procedures (Ayres, 1989).

There are many things that any facilitator can do to help a fearful child develop skills to use simple climbing equipment. The facilitator can climb the ladder of the sliding board behind the child and sit the child in his or her lap to slide down. If the sliding board is too small for the facilitator, he or she can hold onto the child's hand throughout the process. When the child is ascending the ladder and sitting down, it is best to be positioned behind him or her. As the child slides down, it is best to be in front of him or her to be able to catch the child. The amount of assistance can be graded according to the child's needs, but *the child's fear should be respected.*

The child who has difficulty maneuvering the body on climbing equipment usually has difficulty shifting the body weight appropriately. This may be particularly evident on small jungle gyms. When the child reaches the corner, he or she may not be able to figure out how to shift the weight away from the corner and still go around it. The facilitator can help by making sure the child's feet are close together, placing both hands on the child's hips, and shifting the weight very slightly over the foot that will move second, thus freeing the other foot to move around the corner. Bringing the feet together and shifting the child's weight slightly may be sufficient to enable the child to move around the corner. If more assistance is needed, the facilitator can tell the child to move the hands and feet and, if necessary, can help the child place the foot and hands and transfer weight onto them. As with all movements, control should be returned to the child as soon as possible. Mastery of these movements requires considerable practice and the facilitator should provide the child with ample time.

PLAY MATERIALS AND OPPORTUNITIES

As with running, hopping, and skipping, no toys are really necessary for teaching the child to climb. It is usually best to do this teaching by using the actual stairs, furniture, or climbing equipment the child uses at home and school. If necessary, favorite toys or playmates can be used to entice the child to climb. However, this is generally unnecessary as these activities seem to be highly motivating in themselves. The names of companies that manufacture simple, safe climbing equipment can be given to parents who are seeking advice about the purchase of such equipment. Because playground equipment varies and some manufacturers are locally operated businesses, it is not possible to recommend manufacturers here. However, since this equipment can be expensive, a physical or occupational therapist should spend time talking to parents or caregivers about the desirable traits of the actual piece of equipment they are seeking.

OBSERVATION GUIDELINES
FOR SENSORIMOTOR DEVELOPMENT:
OTHER DEVELOPMENTAL ACHIEVEMENTS—BALL SKILLS

C. Ball skills
  1. Throwing
     a. What size balls is the child able to throw?
     b. Do the feet remain firmly planted?
     c. Does the foot on the same side of the body as the throwing arm step forward as the ball is thrown?
     d. Does the foot on the opposite side of the body step forward as the ball is thrown?
  2. Catching
     a. What size balls is the child able to catch?
     b. Can the child trap a ball that has been rolled to him or her?
     c. From a straight elbow position, do the elbows bend and trap the ball against the chest?
     d. Can the child catch the ball with the hands, without making contact with other parts of the body?
     e. Does the child change the placement of the feet in preparation for the catch?
  3. Kicking
     a. Does the child walk into the ball in an attempt to kick it?
     b. Does the kicking leg actually swing in preparation for and follow through on the kick?

INTERVENTION IMPLICATIONS

Ball skills are another example of fundamental motor skills that most children find highly motivating. As with running, jumping, and skipping, children develop ball skills over a period of time. While most children have developed basic skills by 7 years of age (Williams, 1983), children who play sports continue to develop their skills well into adolescence.

Many factors contribute to the development of mature ball skills. Among the most important of these are motor planning abilities. Ball skills represent a particular kind of high-level motor planning tasks known as *projected action sequences* or *anticipatory movements* (Fisher et al., 1991). In order for a child to be successful catching or kicking a ball or throwing it at a moving target, the child must be able to get the hands or foot to the place where the ball will arrive *before* the ball gets there. If the child waits to stretch out the arms or leg until the ball is an arm's or leg's length away, he or she will be unsuccessful at catching or kicking. Rather, if the ball is coming directly toward the child, it is likely to hit the child.

Some general principles of the development of spatial and temporal accuracy (Keogh & Sugden, 1985) can assist the facilitator to develop programs to help children develop throwing, catching, and kicking skills. Ball activities are easiest when the child and the ball (or the target) are stable. In the next stage of development, either the child or the ball can be moving. Finally, the child is able to intercept a moving ball (or hit a moving target) while the child also is moving. For the purpose of this discussion, the developmental levels and age ranges regarding ball skills are separated. First, throwing is addressed; catching is discussed on page 444; and kicking is examined on pages 445–446.

- Visually tracks ball
    (2–5 years)
- Retains or releases without reference to the examiner
    (9 months)
- Plays ball
    (9 months)
- Definite fling of ball
    (9–18 months)
- Throws ball overhead
    (15 months–2½ years)
- Throws ball in standing without falling
    (2–2½ years)
- Throws, guiding the course of the ball with the fingers
    (3–5 years)

Keogh and Sugden (1985) noted that children must resolve three movement problems in order to throw a ball accurately and efficiently in the standing position. First, the child must be able to generate and impart sufficient force to the ball. Second, the child must be able to properly direct the ball. Finally, the child must be able to counteract the force of throwing in order to maintain balance.

Clearly, the rudiments of throwing are visible in young infants who forcibly release objects. Toddlers (approaching 2 years) can approximate an overhand throw in standing, but lack the ability to direct the ball and to modulate force. Thus, the ball may not go to the intended location and is probably thrown with so much force as to preclude another from catching it. Very young children throw with the arm only, by forearm extension or by bringing the ball overhead and throwing it forward without bending the elbow. The feet and body remain stationary (Keogh & Sugden, 1985).

The young child moves from using only the arm to also rotating the upper body when throwing. As the child gains greater control over direction and force, the child also adds a step forward with the ipsilateral leg (i.e., same side as the throwing hand). The pattern of the arm remains similar; the arm is brought over the head with the elbow extended. Many people use this pattern of throwing throughout their lives (Keogh & Sugden, 1985).

In a more effective and mature throwing pattern, the child rotates the entire throwing side (i.e., arm, leg, and trunk) backward. As the child brings the arm and hand forward to release the ball, he or she steps onto the contralateral foot (i.e., opposite the throwing hand). The movements of the wrist and fingers just before and during release influence the direction and velocity of the ball (Keogh & Sugden, 1985).

Young children require a great deal of practice in order to master ball throwing. Thus, *facilitators should provide children with ample time and space to engage in practice.* Because young children often are not able to reliably control either the direction or the force of their throws, they need wide open spaces in which to practice throwing. *Small balls are easier to throw than large balls; the ball should fit the size of the child's hand.* Balls made of lightweight rubber are the safest for objects and other people in the environment. However, children with abnormally high muscle tone sometimes have difficulty releasing balls that do not provide resistance to squeezing (e.g., Nerf balls). Young children who are being helped to move from an immature pattern of throwing to a more mature one can be prompted verbally or visually (by a model) to move their upper bodies or one leg while throwing.

DEVELOPMENTAL LEVEL

- Catches ball from straight arm position, trapping ball against chest
  (30–35 months)
- Catches ball with elbows bent in front of body
- Throws ball using shoulder and elbow
  (3–4 years)
- Catches ball with elbows at sides
  (54–59 months)
- Bounces and catches tennis ball
  (60–71 months)

INTERVENTION GUIDELINES

Like throwing, the ability to catch a ball begins to develop in infancy and continues to develop over a long period of time. However, because of individual differences, the ages by which children are expected to move through stages of maturity with regard to catching are not well specified (Williams, 1983). In general, by 1 year of age, children are expected to be able to intercept a small object slowly rolling toward them while they are seated (Keogh & Sugden, 1985). As Keogh and Sugden (1985) indicated:

> This is an important achievement that indicates that the basics for moving in a moving environment are in place, even though children must develop further before they can deal with the more rapid requirements of moving in playgame and other movement situations. (p. 121)

Keogh and Sugden (1985) also indicated that there are two important challenges to the child learning to catch (or kick) a ball. First, the child must be able to look at the ball in flight and know where it is going and when it can be intercepted. Second, the child must be able to move to the interception point in time to catch (or kick) the ball.

In preparation for catching the ball, the very young child may stand with outstretched arms, but wait for the ball to bounce off the chest before chasing it. Later, the child is apt to bend the outstretched elbows to try to "trap" the ball against the body as the ball contacts the arms and hands. The child often turns his or her head as the ball approaches to avoid being hit in the face (Williams, 1983).

With greater maturity and skill development, the child learns to relax the arms in preparation for catching the moving ball, to track the ball visually, and to catch the ball in the hands. These changes in performance lead to the development of adult-like catching skills. Williams (1983) described these skills as follows:

> The catcher (a) adjusts her body and hand/arm positions to accommodate the trajectory of the oncoming object; and (b) receives the object with coordinated, well-timed movements that result in proper absorption of force and skillful control of the ball. (p. 238)

As with throwing and the other fundamental motor skills described in this chapter, the development of catching skills requires considerable practice. Thus, facilitators must be certain to provide children with ample time and space for practicing. Williams (1983) described two general factors that can assist facilitators in creating and implementing practice sessions to help young children develop better catching skills. These are size and flight characteristics of the ball.

Young children generally are more successful at catching large balls than small balls. However, smaller balls (that can be cupped in the child's hands) tend to elicit a more mature pattern of catching than do large balls. Large balls tend to elicit a "trapping" pattern (Williams, 1983).

The speed of the ball in flight, the angle at which it travels, and whether the ball has been bounced also affect the child's ability to catch it. In general, Williams (1983) concluded that both tossing a ball directly to the child and bouncing the ball elicits the child's best performance. The more slowly the ball is thrown, the easier it is to catch. Furthermore, children learn to move to the side to catch a ball before they learn to move forward or backward.

DEVELOPMENTAL LEVEL

- Walks into large ball to push it forward
  (15–18 months)
- Kicks ball forward
  (20–24 months)

INTERVENTION GUIDELINES

Clearly, children cannot begin to develop kicking skills until they are able to walk. However, as with all the fundamental motor skills, kicking skills continue to develop until a child is at least 5 years old; for children who develop an interest in soccer or football, kicking skills can continue to develop for many years. Keogh and Sugden (1985) described three movement problems that children must solve in order to become proficient at kicking; these are similar to those encountered in developing throwing skills. First, a child must control the sequence of movements of the joints of the leg and foot while maintaining balance. Second, the child must move the leg in the direction and path of the ball so as to contact the ball in the desired position. Finally, the child must coordinate the sequence of the movements of the joints of the leg and foot so as to finish the movement at the point of contact.

In the earliest stage of the development of kicking, the child merely walks into the ball, propelling it with the foot or the lower leg. Later, the child begins to move the kicking leg backward prior to initiating the kick. As the child develops greater proficiency, the amount of swing of the kicking leg increases; this allows the child to impart greater force to the ball (i.e., to kick it harder).

Children can kick a stationary ball before they can kick a moving ball. After a child is able to stand in front of a stationary ball and kick it, the next stage is to have the child move toward the stationary ball. Only after the child has developed considerable skill can he or she be expected to run up to a moving ball and kick it.

As with the development of all of the fundamental motor skills, the development of kicking requires considerable practice. *Facilitators must allow ample time and space for such practice to occur.* Children are frequently more motivated to engage in all ball tasks if an adult or a skillful older child plays with the child. Stacking up cardboard bricks or other light objects as targets also can be highly motivating to children. The crash of the objects following a successful kick provides a powerful form of feedback to the child.

PLAY MATERIALS AND OPPORTUNITIES

The only toys necessary for the development of ball skills are balls. These must be carefully chosen as the properties of the balls have considerable effect on the child's ability to throw, catch, or kick them. As noted previously, small lightweight balls (e.g., Nerf balls, Koosh balls) usually are easiest for throwing unless the child has difficulty releasing objects. In that case, a ball made of more resistive material is more desirable. For catching, the ball should be larger; balls just large enough to be cradled in the child's two hands probably elicit the most mature catching pattern. Bigger balls are easier than smaller balls for kicking. Again, balls meant for kicking should be fairly lightweight. However, if these balls are to be used outside with very unskilled kickers, they should not be so lightweight that they are blown away easily by the wind.

EXAMPLE

Jay C. is a 7-year-old with motor incoordination and learning disabilities. Jay's parents would like him to develop some of the motor skills he needs to play "sandlot" sports with his friends; they have specifically named ball skills. Jay is highly motivated to learn to catch and throw as his father and older brothers are active in Little League; significant portions of their weekends are devoted to practice and games. However, when he tries to catch, Jay stands with his arms stretched stiffly out in front of him. In fear of being hit by the ball, he usually closes his eyes when the ball comes at him.

Through extensive evaluation, the occupational therapist determined that Jay has sensory integrative dysfunction that manifests itself as a motor planning disorder. She has begun to provide direct intervention to Jay to address his underlying disorder. In addition to this direct intervention, the therapist and Jay's parents have developed a home program designed to teach Jay the skills to catch a small ball.

The first step in learning to catch the ball involved Jay overcoming his fear of being hit so that he could keep his eyes open. Jay donned a large Velcro vest to which Ping-Pong balls, thrown gently underhand, would stick. With practice and encouragement from his father and brothers, Jay learned to keep his eyes open and to move *into*, rather than out of, the path of the oncoming ball. Because Jay could succeed at this activity, both he and his family had a good time playing it. Often another family member would wear the vest while Jay threw the balls. This enabled Jay to practice throwing and also added to the enjoyment of the game.

OBSERVATION GUIDELINES FOR SENSORIMOTOR DEVELOPMENT: PREHENSION AND MANIPULATION—MUSCLE TONE AND STRENGTH AND HEAD AND TRUNK CONTROL

VII. Prehension and Manipulation·
   A. Muscle tone and strength
      1. Muscle tone
         a. Does the opposite arm get stiff while one hand plays with a toy?
         b. Does the tongue move or come out of the mouth when the child is concentrating?
         c. Is the mouth open or closed when the child is concentrating?
         d. Are the hands generally open or closed?
      2. Strength
         a. What is the child's ability to lift heavy objects?
         b. Is the child able to pull apart and push together resistive toys?
         c. Is the child able to pull up a zipper or pull off tube socks?
         d. Does the child demonstrate fatigue with increasing repetitions of the same activity?
   B. Head and trunk control during prehension and manipulation
      1. Is the child able to keep the head and trunk upright when playing with objects?
      2. Does the child use the arms for support when reaching?

INTERVENTION IMPLICATIONS

Prehension and manipulation enable the child to grasp, explore, and use objects in the environment. These movement patterns underlie a myriad of activities ranging from writing, drawing, and coloring to cutting, pasting, and manipulation of small objects and instruments (Williams, 1983). Frequently, for the purposes of discussion and observation, prehension and manipulation are subsumed under the broader categories of fine motor control and visual-motor (eye–hand) coordination.

> Development of fine motor control or eye–hand coordination skills represents an important and integral part of the total motor development of the young child and clearly reflects the increasing capacity of the CNS (central nervous system) to pick up and process visual input and to translate that input into skillful, well-executed motor behaviors—behaviors that are necessary if the child is to be able to interact effectively with the practical as well as the communication aspects of his object-laden school and home environments. (Williams, 1983, p. 171)

Fine Motor and Visual-Motor Abilities

Many functions and abilities contribute to the development of eye–hand coordination skills; muscle tone and strength are among these. Thus, the previous discussion of muscle tone and strength (see pp. 401–405) applies equally well to intervention aimed at improving a child's fine motor and visual-motor ability.

Furthermore, a child's ability to engage successfully in a fine motor or visual-motor activity depends, in part, on the child's ability to control the movements of the head and trunk. However, as noted previously, recent research (cf. Case-Smith et al., 1989; Loria, 1980) has found little relationship between the development of proximal and distal function in children. The results of these studies suggest that facilitators should not wait to work with a child on the development of fine motor ability until the child has attained head and trunk control.

While there may be little neurological or statistical relationship between the development of distal and proximal function, there is a functional relationship between the child's control of gross movements of the head, trunk, shoulders, and hips and the child's ability to use the eyes and hands together to explore and use objects. A child cannot explore or use an object unless he or she can attain that object and place it in desired locations. Attaining and placing objects usually involve reaching; reaching seems, at least intuitively, to be more closely related to proximal function than do prehension or manipulation. Thus, it may be necessary to use adapted positioning equipment to provide external stability to a child who has intervention needs in the areas of fine motor or visual-motor control, but who lacks proximal stability. Furthermore, some tasks that reflect a child's cognitive ability but are too demanding for the child's motor abilities may require adaptation to enable the child to accomplish them easily.

Stress and Fatigue

Fine motor and visual-motor activities demand fairly precise motor control; many also have significant cognitive and perceptual demands. For these reasons, fine motor and visual-motor activities can be very difficult for a child. Signs of stress, such as an open mouth, protruding tongue, increased drooling, and increased muscle tone, may suggest that an activity is very difficult. The child is likely to fatigue quickly when engaged in stress-producing activities. Some children begin to "droop" when they are fatigued; they may rest the head and trunk on the supporting surface. Other children increase their activity level as a result of fatigue; they may begin to act silly, run around the room, or become highly distractible. *When a child begins to show signs of stress or fatigue, it is time to change the activity or to give the child permission to rest for a few minutes.*

OBSERVATION GUIDELINES
FOR SENSORIMOTOR DEVELOPMENT:
PREHENSION AND MANIPULATION—REACHING SKILLS

C. Reaching skills
   1. Accuracy of reach
      a. Does the child over-reach?
      b. Does the child go directly to the target, or use wide, sweeping motions or corralling of the object?
   2. Visual guidance of reach
      a. Does the child look before reaching?
      b. Does he or she watch the hand or the object while reaching?
      c. Does he or she look away while contacting the object?
   3. Is the child able to position the hand and arm, accommodating them to an object's orientation?

Accurately placing the arm and hand in space in preparation for grasping or releasing an object seems to depend on at least two components: 1) vision and 2) motor control. Williams (1983) indicated that there seem to be four major stages that strongly involve vision in the early development of eye–hand coordination. She labeled the first of these *static visual exploration*, which is predominant from birth to 4 months of age.

INTERVENTION IMPLICATIONS

> The infant, during this stage of development, seems to have a genuine visual predilection for his hands and spends a large percentage of his waking time fixating intently on his hands while he lies in the crib. Typically this infant will look at an object in his crib or playpen and then immediately look back at his hands. At this point the eyes tend to immobilize and fixate on the hands while the arms and legs activate in rather spontaneous activity. (Williams, 1983, p. 177)

The second stage, predominant from the 17th to the 28th week, is characterized by *active and repeated visual exploration of objects* in the environment (Williams, 1983).

> For example a twenty-week old infant, lying in a supine position, will intently watch a dangling ring held above him. He looks at the object and then at his hand and then back at the object, and he does this repeatedly. All at once, while the eyes are on the object, all bodily activity stops and shortly thereafter the arms are flung outward in a crude attempt to make contact with the ring as it swings near his hands. Contact may or may not be made . . . , but when it is and the infant actually grasps the object, it goes immediately to his mouth for further exploration. Interestingly, even while the object is in the mouth the infant tries to fixate it visually. (Williams, 1983, p. 177–178)

In the third stage, predominant from weeks 28 to 40, *the visual mechanism seems to take the lead in helping the child to adapt reaching, grasping, and manipulation* (Williams, 1983).

> During this stage the child seems first to locate an object or toy with his eyes. He then initiates a movement toward the toy. As he reaches for the object, his visual fixation relaxes. Frequently this initial movement is in error, and when it is the child's visual fixation of the object intensifies and he adjusts or corrects his reaching response. Focus on the toy is maintained throughout this time, and when the hand finally comes into contact with the toy, visual fixation becomes even more intensified. As the object is grasped and manipulated, the eyes continue to explore it visually. (Williams, 1983, p. 178)

The final stage of the development of eye–hand coordination involves its *refinement and generalization*. This stage begins at approximately 40 weeks and continues throughout middle childhood (Williams, 1983).

While vision plays a dominant role in the development of reaching, a child also must have the motor capacity to act on information gained visually. Control for reaching comes more from proximal muscles, especially the shoulder. Control for prehension and manipulation comes primarily from the wrist, hand, and forearm.

Reaching occurs in all developmental positions. However, because the arms and hands often are involved in weight bearing when the child is prone, the requirements for reaching in that position differ somewhat from those of supine or upright. Thus, reaching in prone is discussed in a separate section (see p. 452).

DEVELOPMENTAL LEVEL

- Visual regard of objects
    (0–2 months)
- Swipes at objects
    (1–3 months)
- Alternating glance from hand to object
    (1–4½ months)
- Alternating gaze from one hand to the other
    (1–5 months)
- Inspects own hands
- Reaches for, but may not contact object
    (2–6 months)
- Visually directed reaching
    (3½–4½ months)
- Hands oriented to object
- Rapid reach for object without contact
    (3½–6 months)
- Circuitous reach, out to side
- Straight approach in reach
    (3½–12 months)
- Shoulders come down to natural level
- Hands together in space
- Sitting: bilateral backhand approach with wrist turned so thumb is down
    (4 months)
- Elbow in front of shoulder joint
- Developing isolated voluntary control of forearm rotation
    (5–6 months)
- Trunk adapts in reaching by leaning
    (7½ months)
- Experiments with forearm rotation by stabilizing against rib cage
    (7–8 months)
- Unilateral direct approach, reach and grasp single continuous movement
    (8–9 months)
- Controls supination with upper arm in any position, if trunk stable
    (9 months)
- Wrist extended, appropriate finger extension
    (10 months)
- Voluntary supination, upper arm in any position
    (11–12 months)

INTERVENTION GUIDELINES

Reaching occurs in all body positions. However, early reaching skills may be most easily developed in supine or semi-reclining positions because the arms and hands are free and the shoulder girdle, trunk, and head are well-supported. Sometimes placing two small (in diameter) towel rolls or half bolsters, one behind each shoulder, can provide additional support and assist the child to bring the shoulder girdle forward for reaching. Sitting also is a good position for reaching if the child has adequate proximal control or if such control can be provided externally by furniture or, preferably, by the facilitator's body. If the facilitator chooses to use his or her own body, it probably is easiest to sit behind the child. The child should sit squarely on his or her bottom with the back aligned. The facilitator can place attractive toys and objects in various locations near the child and entice the child to reach; other people, especially a parent, also can provide a "target" for the child's reach. If needed, the facilitator can support the child's upper arm to assist with the reaching movement. However, *assistance should be minimized or eliminated as soon as possible.*

Varying Object Placement

Varying the placement of objects helps the child to develop a repertoire of reaching abilities. Although reaching is accomplished with the arm, the trunk and shoulder girdle also move in support of the arm. If the child is reaching forward, the trunk moves forward; if the child reaches a long distance forward, balance reactions occur in other body parts. If the child is reaching to the side, the child's weight is shifted to that side and the trunk usually bends away from the reach to enable the child to balance. If the child reaches on a diagonal, the weight shifts toward the reaching side and the trunk rotates. The farther away the object, the more trunk movement is required. It may be necessary for the facilitator to assist the child with these movements. A physical or occupational therapist can be very helpful in teaching other facilitators to perform these complex types of facilitation successfully.

Varying Spatial Orientation of Objects

Varying the spatial orientation of toys and objects facilitates the child's rotation of the forearm to contact or acquire the object. The most difficult orientation of the hand to attain is palm up; this is the last to be acquired developmentally and is particularly difficult for children who have abnormally high muscle tone.

The child learns spatial orientation and prehension and manipulation skills through active problem-solving.

Sometimes children can be motivated to reach with a palm-up orientation by placing a sticker (or other object that does not need to be grasped) in the child's palm and asking the child to show it to someone sitting in front or to the side at arm's length away. *Never try to force a child's hand into the palm-up position as there are many tendons, ligaments, and muscles that could be accidentally injured in this way.*

Many children with abnormally high muscle tone in their hands, arms, and shoulders need assistance with the development of reaching. Before (or in the context of) intervening with these children to develop reaching skills, it often is necessary to normalize the muscle tone around the shoulder girdle and in the arms and hands. A physical or occupational therapist is needed to prescribe the best techniques for altering tone. These techniques often can be taught to other facilitators to maximize the child's developmental outcomes.

DEVELOPMENTAL LEVEL

- Prone: bilateral approach, hands sliding forward
- Two-handed corralling of object
    (5 months)
- Prone: reaches with one hand while weight bearing on other forearm
- Elbow extended, wrist straight, midway between supination and pronation
    (6 months)
- Prone: reaches with one hand while weight bearing on other extended arm
    (7 months)

INTERVENTION GUIDELINES

Prone can be a very difficult position for reaching and hand usage. In order for the child to be able to reach while in prone, the body weight must be far enough back that the arms and upper trunk are free of the need to support the body's weight. Thus, suggestions from the earlier sections on prone and mobility in prone (see pp. 408–412) apply equally well here.

PLAY MATERIALS AND OPPORTUNITIES

The focus of this section is on the development of reaching rather than grasping or manipulation. If the child is able to grasp objects easily, the facilitator has access to a wider range of toys and games to play with the child. For children who cannot grasp easily, toys should be selected for their reactivity to the child's contact. Suspended toys (e.g., balloons) work well for this as do toys that can be knocked over readily. Cars or small balls placed on the top of a "road" that goes downhill also can be highly motivating. The child merely needs to touch the object to begin its descent. Shaving cream on a mirror or other surface can be used to entice a child to reach and to control arm movements without the need to grasp. Switch-operated toys can be used in the same manner. Children become much more easily absorbed in activities that are unpredictable than in those that always have the same outcome; unpredictable activities usually occupy a child for prolonged periods of time. The child often provides many ideas about ways to vary a game to attain the same desired results. Even nonverbal children provide many such cues if the facilitator vigilantly observes for them.

> ## OBSERVATION GUIDELINES
> ## FOR SENSORIMOTOR DEVELOPMENT:
> ## PREHENSION AND MANIPULATION—GRASPING SKILLS
>
> D. **Grasping skills**
>   1. **Is the total hand or fist being used?**
>   2. **Is the thumb involved?**
>   3. **What are the actions of the fingers?**
>   a. **Do all the fingers move as a unit?**
>   b. **Is the child able to point or poke with one finger?**
>   4. **What is the grasping action of the thumb and index?**
>   a. **Mostly at the side of the index**
>   b. **Pads of the index and thumb contact**
>   c. **Very tips of the index and thumb contact**
>   5. **Is the child able to grasp more than one object at a time?**

INTERVENTION IMPLICATIONS

The ability to grasp an object (i.e., to attain and retain it) develops over a prolonged period of time. Many of the movement patterns necessary for grasping develop very early in response to tactile and proprioceptive stimulation to the hand (cf. Twitchell, 1970, 1979). Gradually, these movement patterns come under increasingly voluntary and visual control. From approximately 5 or 6 months, grasping patterns become extremely varied in response to the characteristics of the object to be grasped and the action the infant intends to perform with or on the object (Corbetta & Mounoud, 1990). In general, the development of grasping proceeds from gross or whole-hand grasping patterns to grasping patterns involving primarily the fingers (Corbetta & Mounoud, 1990). Grasp also develops from the little finger side of the hand to the thumb side. The young child is able to pick up relatively larger objects (e.g., rattles, cubes, small balls) earlier than he or she can pick up very small objects (e.g., Cheerios, raisins).

"The hand represents one of the most elaborate organs of the human body" (Corbetta & Mounoud, 1990, p. 188). Because control of the hand is so complex, the development of grasp, release, and manipulation is often delayed in children with disabilities. In children who have abnormally high muscle tone, the early grasping and avoidance reflexes sometimes are retained for several years or even across the lifespan. These early reflex behaviors can cause the child to open or close the hand involuntarily when someone pulls on or touches the arm or hand, or even when the child touches an object. Reflexive behavior of the hand can preclude the child being able to grasp voluntarily. However, these behaviors are not always easy to identify. If a child seems to have excessive difficulty grasping objects, a physical or occupational therapist should evaluate the child.

While proximal control tends to develop earlier than grasping and other fine motor or visual-motor skills, proximal control is not a prerequisite for the acquisition of fine motor skills. Furthermore, grasping and manipulation are the primary means by which children interact with objects. Thus, *it is important that work on fine motor skills begin as soon as possible.* When a child clearly has difficulty with the development of fine motor and visual-motor skills, the intervention team should utilize some of the technological devices that have been developed to enable children with disabilities to play with (e.g., switch-operated toys) and use objects (e.g., adapted and switch-operated environmental controls), and to communicate with others (e.g., electronic communication devices) (cf. Musselwhite, 1986).

DEVELOPMENTAL LEVEL

- Hands predominantly closed
  (0–3 months)
- Object is clutched between little and ring fingers and palm
  (2–7 months)
- Hands clasped together often
  (3–3½ months)
- Able to hold a small object in each hand
  (3–7 months)
- Hands partly open
  (4 months)
- Hands open in anticipation of contact
  (4–4½ months)
- Hands predominantly open
  (4–6 months)
- Partial thumb opposition on a cube
- Attempts to secure minute objects
  (4–8 months)
- Picks up cube with ease
  (4–8 months)
- Raking or scooping minute object
  (5–9 months)
- Object held in palm by fingers and opposed thumb (radial palmar grasp)
  (6–7 months)
- Picks up minute object with several fingers and thumb
  (6–10 months)
- Precisely picks up minute object
  (7–12 months)
- Minute object held between side of index and thumb (lateral scissors)
  (8 months)
- Object held with opposed thumb and fingertips, space visible between palm and object
  (8–9 months)
- Small object held between thumb and index, first near middle of index (inferior pincer), later between pads of thumb and index with thumb opposed (pincer)
  (9–10 months)
- Pokes with index
  (10 months)
- Small object held between thumb and index, near tips, thumbs opposed (fine pincer)
  (12 months)

At least two guidelines can be useful for facilitators working with a child to improve grasping ability. First, it may be difficult for a child to control the trunk, arm, and hand simultaneously. Thus, *when a child is working on the development of grasp* (or any fine motor or visual-motor skills), *it is important that the child be positioned such that he or she has as much support as is necessary*. Furthermore, it may be helpful for the facilitator to support the child's arm in order that the child is able to concentrate fully on grasping the object. By supporting the arm, the facilitator can also assist the child to orient the hand in the optimal way for grasping the object. *The amount and type of support the child needs is individually determined*. Usually, an occupational or physical therapist is the team member best qualified to make recommendations about positioning and physically assisting the child and to train other team members. In general, however, the nearer to the shoulder the facilitator places his or her hands, the more the child is controlling the arm and hand movements. The nearer to the wrist the facilitator places his or her hands, the more support he or she is providing for the child.

Second, control of the hand develops from the little finger side toward the thumb side. Control of the thumb side of the hand enables the child to grasp very small objects between the thumb and the first and second finger. When working with a child to develop grasping of small objects, the facilitator can sometimes assist the child by curling the child's ring and little finger into the palm of the hand and holding them there as the child attempts to attain a desired object. Resting the child's forearm on the support surface also assists the child to grasp small objects.

Most children seem to have considerable motivation to grasp and manipulate toys and other objects in their environments. However, because control of the hand is so difficult, attempts to attain objects can elicit considerable stress in children. This stress often is seen as increased drooling or muscle tone. Facilitators should try to minimize this stress by selecting objects that are of a manageable size (neither too small nor too large). Furthermore, *the facilitator can assist the child by minimizing verbal instructions and other distractors in the immediate working area*.

Any relatively small toy can be used to encourage children to work on developing grasping skills. The choice of toys depends primarily on the child's cognitive level, preferences, and the type of grasp desired. As the child gains greater skill in grasping, a variety of toys should be offered. Blocks, small balls, stickers, colorforms, Fisher-Price people, pegs, bubble wands, small dolls or stuffed animals, small cars, playing cards, and clay are examples of toys that many children find to be motivating objects to grasp.

INTERVENTION GUIDELINES

PLAY MATERIALS AND OPPORTUNITIES

DEVELOPMENTAL LEVEL

- Crayon held in fist with thumb up
    (12–18 months)
- Crayon held with fingers, hand on top of tool, forearm turned so thumb is directed downward (digital pronate)
    (2–3 years)
- Pencil held with mature grasp, but no isolated movements within the hand (static tripod)
    (3½–4 years)
- Mature grasp on pencil, fine localized movements present in the hand (dynamic tripod)
    (4½–6 years)

INTERVENTION GUIDELINES

Crayons and pencils are examples of the myriad of tools that children learn to grasp and use. The developmental sequence specified above represents the most commonly described grasp patterns utilized by children with writing implements. Schneck and Henderson (1990) have more fully described these and other grasp patterns commonly used by children. Facilitators working with children to improve their abilities to grasp writing implements should pay careful attention to these sequences and recognize that children pass through many stages before they grasp a pencil or crayon in a mature fashion. *Children who are ready to move to a more mature grasp can sometimes be assisted to do so through verbal reminders or the facilitator's physically repositioning of the writing implement in the child's hand.* However, facilitators are encouraged not to turn children's pencil or crayon grasp into a "battleground" or power struggle. Generally, it is more important to encourage the child to draw than it is to worry that he or she uses the most mature grasp on the writing implement. If a child seems very delayed in developing grasp patterns or if the child is only able to grasp a writing implement by using a motor pattern that is very undesirable, an occupational therapist should evaluate the child. Simple devices often can be attached to the pencil or crayon in order to enable the child to utilize a more desirable grasp pattern.

PLAY MATERIALS AND OPPORTUNITIES

Of course, the most direct way for children to practice grasping writing implements is by using the implements themselves. In general, the larger the pencil or crayon, the easier it is to grasp. Furthermore, because grasping pencils or crayons can be difficult, some children do well to practice with paintbrushes or markers first. The grasp required for paintbrushes and markers is similar to that required for pencils or crayons, but "scribbling" or creating a picture may be easier with these implements as they provide less resistance to the child's movements. Klein (1982) and Myers (1992) also have offered numerous suggestions for activities related to the development of prewriting skills.

**OBSERVATION GUIDELINES
FOR SENSORIMOTOR DEVELOPMENT:
PREHENSION AND MANIPULATION—RELEASING SKILLS**

E. **Releasing skills**
   1. **Is the child able to release objects by transferring them from one hand to the other (left to right and right to left)?**
   2. **In order to release with one hand alone, does the child need to support the arm on a surface or press down with the object?**
   3. **Is the child able to smoothly release objects in free space?**

Precise release of objects is necessary for placement of objects in a desired location. The smaller or the more precarious the desired location for placement (e.g., when stacking blocks), the more refined the release pattern must be if the child is to be successful. The development of precise release of objects develops later than does grasping. Thus, initially, the child either flings the object or removes it from one hand by grasping with the other hand.

Children learn to release objects onto a surface first by pressing the object down on the surface. As they gain greater control, they need only stabilize the base of the hand on the edge of the container. Later, they develop enough control to be able to release the object in free space, above a container or surface.

When a child has developed a mature releasing pattern, he or she is able to move the limb toward the target and release the object precisely as a smoothly integrated part of the whole limb movement. When the ability to release is fully developed, the child does not stop the movement of the arm and hover over the desired location before releasing the object. Thus, a certain degree of anticipatory motor control is required for precise release of objects. The child must initiate the release *before* the hand is over the desired location of placement or he or she will overshoot the target.

**INTERVENTION
IMPLICATIONS**

DEVELOPMENTAL LEVEL

- No release, grasp reflex strong
  (0–1 month)
- Involuntary release
  (1–4 months)
- Mutual fingering in midline
  (4 months)
- Transfers objects hand to hand
  (4–8 months)
- Two stage transfer, taking hand grasps before releasing hand lets go
  (5–6 months)
- One stage transfer, taking hand and releasing hand perform actions simultaneously
  (6–7 months)
- Volitional release
  (7–9 months)
- Presses down on a surface to release
  (7–10 months)
- Release above a surface with wrist flexion
  (8 months)
- Release into a container, wrist straight
  (9–10 months)
- Clumsy release into small container, hand rests on edge of container
  (10–14 months)
- Precise controlled release into small container, wrist extended
  (12–15 months)

INTERVENTION GUIDELINES

The facilitator can use the same strategies discussed in the section on reaching to assist the child to develop more mature releasing patterns. This involves the facilitator: 1) positioning the child so that the trunk, head, shoulders, and legs are well supported; 2) supporting the child's upper arm, forearm, or wrist as needed; and 3) assisting the child in maintaining the ring and little fingers curled into the palm of the hand. Furthermore, *the facilitator should wait patiently for the child to release the object rather than "prying" the child's fingers open.* Sometimes bending the child's wrist slightly assists the child to release.

PLAY MATERIALS AND OPPORTUNITIES

Releasing objects can be a very difficult task. Thus, the facilitator should be certain that the practice of this skill is done in the context of highly motivating activity. *Adding an element of unpredictability to the activity often makes it more fun* (Caillois, 1979). Releasing toys into cans or water so they create a noise or a splash when they land can be highly successful. Many children find releasing small objects (e.g., marbles) down cardboard tubes so they fall into a container to be highly motivating. Some children enjoy toys such as shape sorters, mailboxes, pegboards, banks, and simple puzzles with pegs attached to the pieces. *Objects to be released should vary in size, shape, and texture; the size of the opening of the containers into which the objects are released also should vary.* Tweezers and eye droppers also can be incorporated into games for children who need to work on the development of high-level abilities related to releasing (and grasping). In addition to all of the other components of release, tools such as tweezers and eye droppers require that the child precisely control the amount of opening of the fingers during release so as not to drop the tool.

OBSERVATION GUIDELINES
FOR SENSORIMOTOR DEVELOPMENT:
PREHENSION AND MANIPULATION—BILATERAL DEVELOPMENT

F. Bilateral development
   1. **Is the child able to bring both hands together in front of the body?**
   2. **Can the child reach across the front of the body to get a toy on the other side?**
   3. **Is there a preference for one hand?**
      a. **No difference?**
      b. **Strong dominance?**
   4. **If there is a preference, is the nonpreferred hand also readily used (i.e., to stabilize a toy)?**

Bilateral coordination is defined as the use of both sides of the body together in a well-coordinated fashion. Often the term refers to use of two extremities (i.e., arms or legs) together. However, whenever the extremities are involved in a bilateral task, the trunk and more proximal body parts also are involved. Here, two issues related to the development of bilateral coordination (hand preference and crossing the midline) are discussed. Other related issues are discussed in relation to manipulative prehension (see p. 447) and ball skills (see p. 442).

INTERVENTION IMPLICATIONS

Hand Preference

Handedness usually is evident in children by approximately 5 years of age (Tan, 1985), although there may be some normal cultural variations. Furthermore, children who are left-handed may be somewhat slower to develop a hand preference. Hand preference refers to a child always using or leading with the same hand when performing a specific task (e.g., writing, eating); it does not refer to performing all tasks with the same hand. When a child who is 6 years of age or older sometimes uses one hand to eat (or write, etc.) and sometimes uses the other, he or she demonstrates signs of delayed hand preference and should be evaluated by an occupational or physical therapist trained to observe signs of subtle motor dysfunction. Conversely, the infant or very young child who seems to use only one hand also should be evaluated for signs of asymmetry by a therapist and a pediatric neurologist.

Crossing the Midline

The ability to cross the midline enables the child to use one (generally the preferred hand) or both hands to attain an object located on either side of the body. Crossing the midline is thought to depend, in part, on the child's ability to rotate the trunk (Fisher et al., 1991). In turn, the child who has limited trunk rotation and difficulty crossing the midline also may tend to be delayed in developing clear hand preference because that child tends to reach for an object with the hand closest to it. However, poor trunk rotation is not the only, or perhaps even the primary, cause of delayed development of hand preference.

Intervention for a child who has delayed development of bilateral coordination or hand preference can be complicated. Facilitators must guard against a tendency to contrive activities designed to improve bilateral coordination or develop hand preference (i.e., if a child is being asked to perform a play activity with both hands, the activity itself must require bilateral usage). Otherwise, the likelihood of the skill being generalized to daily use is minimal. If a child tends to use only one arm and hand because the other arm and hand have abnormally high muscle tone, the picture is even more complicated, and an occupational or physical therapist should be involved in developing strategies for facilitating the development of bilateral skills.

PLAY MATERIALS AND OPPORTUNITIES

Many toys are used more effectively if the child stabilizes with one hand and manipulates the toy with the other hand. However, many children are quite adept at turning bilateral tasks into unilateral tasks. When promoting bilateral hand usage, larger toys are more likely to require two hands to manipulate. Furthermore, positioning, such as side-sitting, can be used to encourage children to stabilize with one hand and manipulate with the other or to facilitate crossing the midline. These have been described in earlier sections. Many kinds of gross motor play also encourage a child to use both body sides. Tricycles, swings, climbers, jump ropes, and roller skates are examples of toys that can be used effectively to promote children's use of both body sides in a well-coordinated fashion.

OBSERVATION GUIDELINES FOR SENSORIMOTOR DEVELOPMENT: PREHENSION AND MANIPULATION—MANIPULATIVE PREHENSION

G. Manipulative prehension
1. When holding an object in one hand, is the child able to reposition it within the hand?
2. What is the quality of the child's motor control when coloring?
3. Does the child attempt to color within a confined space?
4. What other examples of higher-level tool use are demonstrated (scissors, turning key on a shape sorter, unscrewing lids)?

INTERVENTION IMPLICATIONS

Manipulative prehension, perhaps more than any other skill, enables a child to utilize objects and make them do whatever he or she wants. Thus, *when working on the development of manipulative prehension, the facilitator needs to offer toys of many different sizes, shapes, and textures and to provide tools (e.g., crayons, scissors, keys) that have many different uses and require many different hand and arm movements.* Facilitators can use the following information as guidelines for developing activities. The child's cognitive level and preferences for play materials also have considerable influence on the nature and type of activities created. For children who lack the motoric abilities necessary, but who have the cognitive ability and desire to perform tasks requiring manipulative prehension, adaptations must be made. Klein (1982, 1983, 1987) has described a number of useful adaptations to equipment and teaching strategies that can be used with children with various types of developmental disabilities.

Toward the end of the first year of life, the child begins to use both hands together in tasks of manipulative prehension (Corbetta & Mounoud, 1990). Midair banging of objects (beginning at approximately 9 months of age) appears to precede true collaborative hand usage in which the child simultaneously performs different actions with each hand. Between 9½ and 11 months, the child begins to be able to accomplish such tasks as holding onto a box with one hand and withdrawing an object from the box with the other hand. Complementary use of the two hands develops over a considerable period of time; this development does not culminate until at least 6½ years of age (Williams, 1983).

Keogh and Sugden (1985) identified three levels of difficulty with regard to the development of coordinated use of two hands for manipulative prehension.

> Holding an object with one hand and manipulating another with the second [e.g., holding bolt while twisting on a nut] is at the first level and means that the first hand provides support while the second hand does the manipulating. Buttoning is at the second level of difficulty and requires the manipulation of cloth and button by both hands. Tying shoelaces is at the third level of difficulty, in which both hands manipulate the laces without the solid resistance of the material as a cue to regulating the movements. Shoelaces are flexible and do not have a stable form to provide an external resistance, whereas bolts and buttons are solid and stable in form. The adjustment of one hand movement in tying shoelaces is made in relation to the movement of the other hand, with the material providing very little useful information. (p. 50)

Activities that require a child to perform in-hand manipulation skills (i.e., repositioning an object in the hand without using the other hand or a support surface), such as moving an object from the fingers to the palm (e.g., picking up pennies from the table one at a time and storing them in the palm) or the palm to the fingers (e.g., moving a penny from the palm to the fingertips to deposit it in a bank) (Exner, 1989, 1990), represent a particular class of manipulative prehension. The ability to perform these activities is very important, but often is neglected by facilitators. In-hand manipulation is a difficult skill; activities requiring in-hand manipulation generally are appropriate for children with fine motor skills equivalent to those of typically developing children between the ages of 3 and 6 years.

**DEVELOPMENTAL
LEVEL**

- Separates pop beads
- Snips paper with scissors
  (18–25 months)
- Strings 3–4 beads
  (18–41 months)
- Folds paper in half
  (22–30 months)
- Uses forearm rotation to turn door knob
  (24–29 months)
- Unbuttons large buttons
  (24–35 months)
- Snips on line using scissors
  (28–35 months)
- Cuts paper in half with scissors
  (30–35 months)
- Buttons one or two buttons alone
  (30–47 months)
- Holds paper with one hand while writing with the other hand
  (36–47 months)
- Uses scissors to cut paper on a line
  (36–59 months)
- Cuts circle with scissors
  (42–47 months)
- Places paper clips on paper
- Opens small padlock with key
  (48–59 months)
- Colors within lines
  (60–71 months)

**INTERVENTION
GUIDELINES**

Although the developmental levels presented above provide a list of activities representative of manipulative prehension, this list is not exhaustive. *Any activity in which a child is asked to handle or reposition a toy after it has been grasped includes manipulative prehension.* Generally, the more complex the activity, the more different types of manipulative prehension are utilized and practiced. Several books are available that address the prerequisites of activities to promote some of the most common skills requiring manipulative prehension (cf. Benbow, 1990; Case-Smith & Pehoski, 1992; Klein, 1982, 1983, 1987).

In order to enable a child to perform activities involving manipulative prehension, the facilitator first must analyze the requirements (motor and cognitive) of the activity, determine whether the child has the necessary prerequisites, and then develop a strategy for helping the child. An occupational therapist usually is the team member responsible for identifying specific patterns of manipulation to be practiced by a particular child. The occupational therapist, in turn, describes the pattern to other team members and helps them to develop activities likely to promote that pattern of movement. An occupational or physical therapist also develops any handling techniques necessary to enable the child to succeed at the activity and teaches those to other team members.

Many commercially available toys can be used to promote manipulative prehension. These include Legos, shape sorters, cash registers, fishing games, dress-up clothes, Fisher-Price people and settings, dolls for dressing or feeding, and puzzles. Tools commonly used by preschoolers also promote manipulative prehension. These include scissors, crayons, forks, and spoons.

PLAY MATERIALS AND OPPORTUNITIES

EXAMPLE

Judy P. is a 24-month-old who has ataxic cerebral palsy. Judy has typical cognitive ability. Like most 2-year-olds, she is active and interested in everything. However, Judy's motor skills are not always adequate to enable her to engage in the play activities she chooses. While she walks independently, Judy's balance is poor. The muscle tone in her trunk is slightly low and in order to play with objects, she often stiffens her arm muscles. Judy tends to keep her hands slightly fisted and she has difficulty extending her fingers fully. During fine motor skills, she keeps her shoulders elevated and retracted. Judy has bilateral tremors.

During the evaluation, Judy demonstrated fine motor skills typical of a 12- to 15-month-old child according to the guidelines from *Transdisciplinary Play-Based Assessment* (Linder, 1993). She was able to point with her index finger and scribble spontaneously. She built towers of two cubes with some difficulty. Judy used an inferior pincer grasp to pick up small objects, which she was able to release (with an exaggerated movement) into a large container.

Judy's parents and the other members of the evaluation team predicted that Judy would be able to be integrated into general education. The team recommended that, in order to succeed in school, Judy needed intensive work on fine motor skills. Furthermore, her family and teacher expressed a need for help in developing strategies to minimize the fine motor demands of school and play activities.

Judy's fine motor control improved with postural support. Therefore, the occupational therapist suggested that Judy perform activities with many fine motor demands while sitting in a high-backed chair with lateral supports. Furthermore, heavy toys and objects that provided resistance were easier for her to manipulate than were lightweight toys. Thus, her family and teacher sought magnetic and Velcro toys; they added weights to some objects.

Team members also created a number of highly motivating play activities that provided opportunities for Judy to practice various fine motor skills. For example, to improve her ability to let go of objects voluntarily, Judy was encouraged to drop heavy toys into empty metal pans and pans filled with water. As her ability to let go of objects improved, Judy began to engage in activities that required her to pick up small objects and place them into progressively smaller containers. Judy's motivation to participate in these activities was enhanced through the use of pretend. For example, at first she pretended to feed large animals (i.e., large container). Eventually, as her skills improved she fed tiny pieces of food (i.e., cracker crumbs) to small animals (e.g., ants).

OBSERVATION GUIDELINES FOR
SENSORIMOTOR DEVELOPMENT: MOTOR PLANNING

VIII. **Motor Planning**
  1. **What behaviors are demonstrated that indicate the child's awareness of the body in space?**
    a. **Can the child perform a motor task following modeling or a demonstration?**
    b. **Can the child move the body up, on, through, around, under, and into the gross motor equipment?**
    c. **Can the child change directions in movement?**
    d. **Is there excessive visual monitoring of movements?**
  2. **What motor activities indicate the child's ability to sequence movements?**

INTERVENTION
IMPLICATIONS

Clumsiness, in the absence of obvious neurological or cognitive deficits, has been described by many authors (Ayres, 1972, 1985; Cermak, 1985; Fisher et al., 1991; Gubbay, 1975, 1985). One type of clumsiness described in sensory integration theory is labeled *developmental dyspraxia* (i.e., motor planning deficits). Developmental dyspraxia is thought to result from a disordered body scheme (i.e., a poor sense of how body parts relate to one another or of how the body is moving in space) that, in turn, is caused by inefficient central nervous system processing of somatosensory (i.e., touch and muscle sense) and/or ves-

The use of tactile materials allows the child to develop tactile tolerance and fine motor materials, incorporates cognitive problem-solving, and encourages the use of words to describe the materials.

tibular–proprioceptive (i.e., inner ear and muscle) information (Fisher et al., 1991).

Children who have motor planning deficits seem to have difficulty figuring out how to perform new tasks that have a motor component; they require more repetitions than their peers for learning motor tasks. Because most play, adaptive skills, and school tasks for young children have a motor component, developmental dyspraxia can have a considerable effect on a child's development. If a child is suspected of having developmental dyspraxia, he or she should be evaluated by an occupational or physical therapist trained in the evaluation of sensory integrative dysfunction (Ayres, 1989). Developmental dyspraxia and other forms of clumsiness are complex problems with many potential causes. Thorough evaluation helps to ensure that the optimal plan for intervention can be developed for each child.

Although formal evaluation enables team members to formulate specific plans tailored to the individual needs of each child, some general guidelines can be helpful for assisting team members who parent, teach, or intervene with children who are clumsy.

1. Give the child ample opportunities to engage in motor activities that are at, or *slightly* above, the child's current level of motor ability. Encourage the child to practice skills that are important to him or her; repetition is the key to learning.

2. Ensure that the child is physically safe as he or she engages in motor activities. Be sure that, if the child falls, he or she will fall onto relatively soft surfaces (e.g., mats, mattresses, sand) and that corners or other protruding surfaces are padded. All children fall and bump into things; clumsy children may fall or bump into things more frequently than other children. Vigilance and planning on the part of the adult usually are more effective than verbal warnings or reprimands to the child.

3. Ensure that the child is emotionally safe as he or she engages in motor activities. The clumsy child sometimes is the target of other children's teasing. Because the child has a poor sense of the body, he or she is at risk for spilling food and breaking toys. *Adults can offset some of the potentially devastating emotional consequences of clumsiness by their actions and reactions to "accidents."* An adult and child can set up "code words" that can be used to warn a child of impending "disaster." One mother–child team discovered that less spilling of milk occurred if the child's glass was placed at the 12 o'clock position on the placemat. They called this the "head." When the mother noticed that the child was at risk for knocking over her milk glass, she would quietly remind the child, "Put it on the head." This code language saved considerable embarrassment and many spills. Likewise, when adults seek out clumsy children as partners for play, other children often follow their lead.

4. Build many sensory experiences into the child's day. This provides the child with many opportunities to process information about body scheme. Activities such as fingerpainting, playing in sand, playing in water, "painting" body parts with lotion, rolling in the grass or on the carpet, swinging, sliding, pushing, pulling, and roughhousing provide a lot of sensory information. Furthermore, because activities selected primarily for sensory experience usually do not have a predetermined outcome, the child's motor incoordination does not prevent the child from succeeding.

5.   Play with the child; allow the child to choose the activity; follow his or her lead. Give the child verbal and nonverbal messages that he or she is important as are his or her opinions and preferences.

6.   When the child must perform a difficult or frustrating motor activity, assist the child unobtrusively. Be clear about what exactly the child is attempting to learn or produce in the activity and minimize other demands. For example, if the primary purpose of making a collage is for the child to express feelings, it may be important to minimize or eliminate the demands created by cutting out pictures with scissors. The child could tear the pictures out or the adult could hold the paper, turning it as necessary, while the child handles the scissors.

7.   Talk honestly and openly with the child about his or her difficulties. One father told his daughter, "You're really smart in your head, but your body is not always so smart." Help the child figure out easier ways of doing difficult things and develop interests that match the child's developmental strengths and preferences.

EXAMPLE

Lynne G. is a 4-year-old with developmental delays and poor motor planning abilities. Her parents reported that Lynne is clumsy and has difficulty moving quickly. She seems to need time to think about how to do what she wants to do. Lynne is not a particularly playful child. She does not enjoy gross motor play with other children and is fearful of roughhousing. She prefers to spend her time coloring or playing with her doll. In general, it is difficult to engage her in play activities. However, Lynne's parents reported that she recently developed an interest in imitative kitchen play with a slightly younger neighbor child.

On the transdisciplinary play-based assessment (Linder, 1993), Lynne's scores ranged from 18 months on some observations in the sensorimotor domain to 3 years on some cognitive abilities. In the sensorimotor domain, Lynne was observed to make transitions in and out of positions with difficulty. She had delayed balance reactions and fell several times during the evaluation. She was unable to get into an adult chair (18 months) and ascended the stairs by marking time (18 months–2½ years). Lynne could not jump down from a step (17–21 months).

At the recommendation of the evaluation team, Lynne was enrolled in a preschool program for children with disabilities. However, even in that setting it was somewhat difficult to get her involved in play activities. One day, capitalizing on Lynne's enjoyment of imitative kitchen play, the teacher and two of the children created a successful activity in which Lynne and a friend went through an obstacle course to "find foods that belong in the kitchen." Interspersing language concepts with the motor activity, the teacher hid foods *under* tables, *on top* of the refrigerator, and *inside* the tunnel. Sometimes Lynne or her friend had to go through an obstacle course to get to the grocery store and back through the course to get to the kitchen. At various stages of the game, the girls pretended to pour liquids into cups and put decorations on Play-Doh cookies.

Although the teacher was instrumental in the creation and implementation of this activity, Lynne and her friend also had important roles in shaping the activity. The teacher followed their lead, carefully watching for cues as to how to interact with them and how to help them modify the activity.

ACKNOWLEDGMENTS

The age ranges provided in this chapter are based on recognized data and the work of the following researchers: for Development in Prone, Bly (1983), Chandler (1979), and Scherzer and Tscharnuter (1982); for Development in Supine, Bly (1983) and Chandler (1979); for Development in Sitting, Bly (1983), Chandler (1979), Gilfoyle, Grady, and Moore (1981), and Scherzer and Tscharnuter (1982); for Development in Standing, Bly (1983) and Chandler (1979); for Mobility in Prone and Supine, Bly (1983), Chandler (1979), Connor, Williamson, and Siepp (1978), and Scherzer and Tscharnuter (1982); for Mobility in Sitting, Bly (1983), Chandler (1979), Gilfoyle et al. (1981), and Scherzer and Tscharnuter (1982); for Mobility in Hands and Knees, Bly (1983), Furono, O'Reilly, Hosaka, Zeisloft, and Allman (1984), and Scherzer and Tscharnuter (1982); for Mobility in Standing, Bly (1983) and Chandler (1979); for Jumping, Chandler (1979), Folio and Fewell (1983), and Hellebrandt, Rarick, Glassow, and Carns (1961); for Development of Climbing, Chandler (1979); for Development of Ball Skills, Chandler (1979), Folio and Fewell (1983), and Scherzer and Tscharnuter (1982); for Development of Reaching Skills, Boehme (1988), Chandler (1979), Erhardt (1982), Espenschade and Eckert (1980), and Gilfoyle et al. (1981); for Development of Grasp, Chandler (1979), Erhardt (1982), and Gilfoyle et al. (1981); for Development of Release; Chandler (1979) and Erhardt (1982); and for Development of Manipulative Prehension, Folio and Fewell (1983), Furono et al. (1984), and Newborg, Stock, Wnek, Guidibaldi, and Svinicki (1984).

REFERENCES

Ayres, A.J. (1972). *Sensory integration and learning disorders.* Los Angeles: Western Psychological Services.

Ayres, A.J. (1985). *Developmental dyspraxia and adult-onset apraxia.* Torrance, CA: Sensory Integration International.

Ayres, A.J. (1989). *Sensory integration and praxis tests.* Los Angeles: Western Psychological Services.

Bateson, G. (1971). The message "this is play." In R.B. Heron & B. Sutton-Smith (Eds.), *Child's play.* New York: John Wiley & Sons.

Benbow, M. (1990). *Loops and other groups: A kinesthetic writing system.* Tucson, AZ: Therapy Skill Builders, a division of Communication Skill Builders.

Bly, L. (1983). *The components of normal movement during the first year of life and abnormal motor development.* Oak Park, IL: The Neuro-Developmental Treatment Association (P.O. Box 70, Oak Park, Illinois, 60303).

Bobath, B. (1985). *Abnormal postural reflex activity caused by brain lesions* (3rd ed.). London: Wm. Heinemann Medical Books Ltd.

Bobath, B., & Bobath, K. (1975). *Motor development in the different types of cerebral palsy.* London: Wm. Heinemann Medical Books Ltd.

Bobath, K., & Bobath, B. (1972). Diagnosis and assessment of cerebral palsy. In P.H. Pearson & C.E. Williams (Eds.), *Physical therapy services in the developmental disabilities* (pp. 31–185). Springfield, IL: Charles C Thomas.

Boehme, R. (1988). *Improving upper body control: An approach to assessment and treatment of tonal dysfunction.* Tucson, AZ: Therapy Skill Builders, a division of Communication Skill Builders.

Caillois, R. (1979). *Man, play and games.* New York: Schocker.

Case-Smith, J., Fisher, A.G., & Bauer, D. (1989). An analysis of the relationship of proximal and distal motor control. *American Journal of Occupational Therapy, 45,* 657–662.

Case-Smith, J., & Pehoski, C. (Eds.). (1990). *Development of hand skills in the child.* Rockville, MD: American Occupational Therapy Association.

Cermak, S. (1985). Developmental dyspraxia. In E.A. Roy (Ed.), *Neuropsychological studies of apraxia and related disorders* (pp. 225–248). New York: North Holland.

Chandler, L. (1979). Gross and fine motor development. In M.A. Cohen & P.J. Gross, *The developmental resource: Behavioral sequences for assessment & program planning* (Vol. 1) (pp. 119–153). New York: Grune & Stratton.

Connolly, K. (1975). Movement, action and skill. In K.S. Holt (Ed.), *Movement and child development: Clinics in developmental medicine #55* (pp. 102–110). Philadelphia: J.B. Lippincott.

Connor, F.P., Williamson, G.G., & Siepp, J.M. (Eds.). (1978). *Program guide for infants and toddlers with neuromotor and other developmental disabilities.* New York: Teachers College Press.

Corbetta, D., & Mounoud, P. (1990). Early development of grasping and manipulation. In C. Bard, M. Fleury, & L. Hay (Eds.), *Development of eye-hand coordination across the lifespan* (pp. 188–216). Columbia: University of South Carolina Press.

Csikzimentihayli, M. (1975). *Beyond boredom and anxiety.* San Francisco: Jossey-Bass.

Erhardt, R.P. (1982). *Developmental hand dysfunction: Theory assessment treatment.* Laurel, MD: Ramsco.

Espenschade, A.S., & Eckert, H.M. (1980). *Motor development* (2nd ed.). Columbus, OH: Charles E. Merrill.

Evarts, E.V. (1985). Sherrington's concept of proprioception. In E.V. Evarts, S.P. Wise, & B. Bousfield, (Eds.), *The motor system in neurobiology* (pp. 183–186). New York: Elsevier/North Holland.

Exner, C.E. (1989). Development of hand functions. In P.N. Pratt & A.S. Allen (Eds.) *Occupational therapy for children* (2nd ed.) (pp. 235–259). St. Louis: C.V. Mosby.

Exner, C.E. (1990). The zone of proximal development in-hand manipulation skills of nondysfunctional 3- and 4-year-old children. *American Journal of Occupational Therapy, 44,* 884–891.

Fisher, A.G., & Bundy, A.C. (1989). Use of vestibular stimulation in the treatment of postural and related disorders. In O. Payton, R.P. DiFabio, S.V. Paris, E.J. Protas, & A.F. Vansant (Eds.), *Manual of physical therapy.* New York: Churchill Livingstone.

Fisher, A.G., Murray, E.A., & Bundy, A.C. (1991). *Sensory integration: Theory and practice.* Philadelphia: F.A. Davis.

Folio, M.R., & Fewell, R.R. (1983). *Peabody developmental motor scales and activity cards.* Allen, TX: DLM Teaching Resources.

Furono, S., O'Reilly, K., Hosaka, C., Zeisloft, B., & Allman, T. (1984). *Hawaii early learning profile.* Palo Alto, CA: VORT.

Gilfoyle, E.M., Grady, A.P., & Moore, J.C. (1981). *Children adapt.* Thorofare, NJ: Charles B. Slack.

Greenspan, S., & Greenspan, N.T. (1985). *First feelings.* New York: Viking Penguin.

Gubbay, S.S. (1975). *The clumsy child.* Philadelphia: W.B. Saunders.

Gubbay, S.S. (1985). Clumsiness. In P.J. Vinken, G.W. Bruyn, & H.L. Klawans (Eds.), *Handbook of clinical neurology* (rev. series) (pp. 159–167). New York: Elsevier/North Holland.

Hall, S. (1993). Observation of sensorimotor development. In T.W. Linder, *Transdisciplinary play-based assessment: A functional approach to working with young children* (rev. ed.). Baltimore: Paul H. Brookes Publishing Co.

Harris, S. (1984). Down syndrome. In S.K. Campbell (Ed.), *Pediatric neurologic physical therapy.* New York: Churchill Livingstone.

Hellebrandt, F.A., Rarick, G.L., Glassow, R., & Carns, M.L. (1961). Physiological analysis of basic motor skills: I. Growth and development of jumping. *American Journal of Physical Medicine, 40,* 14–25.

Ingram, T.T.S. (1966). Spasticity in cerebral palsy. *Clinical Orthopedics, 46,* 23–26.

Kalaska, J.F. (1988). The representation of arm movements in postcentral and parietal cortex. *Canadian Journal of Physiology and Pharmacology, 66,* 455–463.

Keogh, J., & Sugden, D. (1985). *Movement skill development.* New York: Macmillan.

Klein, M.D. (1982). *Pre-writing skills.* Tucson, AZ: Communication Skill Builders.

Klein, M.D. (1983). *Pre-dressing skills.* Tucson, AZ: Communication Skill Builders.

Klein, M.D. (1987). *Pre-scissor skills.* Tucson, AZ: Communication Skill Builders.

Linder, T.W. (1993). *Transdisciplinary play-based assessment: A functional approach to working with young children* (rev. ed.). Baltimore: Paul H. Brookes Publishing Co.

Loria, C. (1980). Relationship of proximal and distal function in motor development. *Physical Therapy, 60,* 167–172.

Morris, S. (1987). Therapy for the child with cerebral palsy: Interacting frameworks. *Seminars in Speech and Language, 8*(1), 71–86.

Musselwhite, C.R. (1986). *Adaptive play for special needs children: Strategies to enhance communication and learning.* San Diego: College-Hill Press.

Myers, C.A. (1992). Therapeutic fine motor activities for preschoolers. In J. Case-Smith & C. Pehoski (Eds.), *Development of hand skills in the child.* Rockville, MD: American Occupational Therapy Association.

Newborg, J., Stock, J.R., Wnek, L., Guidibaldi, J., & Svinicki, J. (1984). *Battelle Developmental Inventory.* Allen, TX: DLM Teaching Resources.

Piaget, J. (1954). *Origins of intelligence.* New York: Basic Books.

Scherzer, A.L., & Tscharnuter, I. (1982). *Early diagnosis and therapy in cerebral palsy: A primer on infant developmental problems.* New York: Marcel Dekker.

Scherzer, A.L., & Tscharnuter, I. (1990). *Early diagnosis and therapy in cerebral palsy: A primer on infant developmental problems* (2nd ed.). New York: Marcel Dekker.

Schneck, C.M., & Henderson, A. (1990). Descriptive analysis of the developmental progression of grip position for pencil and crayon control in nondysfunctional children. *American Journal of Occupational Therapy, 44,* 893–900.

Stockmeyer, S.A. (1967). An interpretation of the approach of Road to the treatment of neuromuscular dysfunction. Proceedings of an exploratory and analytical survey of therapeutic exercise: Northwestern University Special Therapeutic Exercise Project (NUSTEP). *American Journal of Physical Medicine, 46*(1), 900–956.

Sutton-Smith, B. (1980). A sportive theory of play. In H. Schwartzman (Ed.), *Play and culture* (pp. 10–19). West Point, NY: Leisure.

Tan, L.E. (1985). Laterality and motor skills in four-year-olds. *Child Development, 56,* 119–124.

Twitchell, T.E. (1970). Reflex mechanisms and the development of prehension. In K. Connolly (Ed.), *Mechanisms of motor skill development* (pp. 25–62). New York: Academic Press.

Twitchell, T.E. (1979). Development of motor control in the presence of cerebral lesions. In Development of Motor, Learning and Cognitive Behaviors. *Neurosciences Research Program Bulletin, 12,* 565–569.

Weisz, S. (1938). Studies in equilibrium reactions. *Journal of Nervous and Mental Disease, 80,* 150–162.

Wilbarger, P., & Royeen, C.B. (1987, April). *Tactile defensiveness: Theory, applications and treatment.* Paper presented at the Annual Interdisciplinary Doctoral Conference, Sargent College, Boston University.

Williams, H.G. (1983). *Perceptual and motor development.* Englewood Cliffs, NJ: Prentice Hall.

III

Pulling It All Together

12

TPBI for Maria

$\mathbf{M}$aria F.'s transdisciplinary play-based assessment has just been conducted, and the Summary Sheets for each of the four developmental domains have been completed (Figures 1–4). An assessment report has been written (see Appendix, beginning on p. 515, or p. 521 for a shorter alternative), and a videotape of the TPBA is available as well. Maria's parents and the rest of the team are ready to plan her transdisciplinary play-based intervention program. They have scheduled a 2-hour time period to meet.

Because Maria, who recently celebrated her fourth birthday, attends a 4-day-a-week, half-day preschool program, the team will need to develop TIP Sheets for both home and school intervention. Prior to the intervention planning meeting, several of the team members chose to review the TPBI Planner and to watch the TPBA videotape once more.

THE TPBI PLANNING MEETING

At the beginning of the meeting, the team briefly discussed the results of the TPBA. Because very little time had elapsed since the assessment, most of the information contained on the summary sheets and in the assessment report was still fresh in everyone's minds. However, they paid particular attention to the summary sheet columns labeled "Strengths" and "Things I'm ready for." The team then designated a member to take notes, and that person found several sheets of blank paper for preliminary planning notations.

Mr. and Mrs. F. first identified what they would like to see as goals for Maria. Maria's parents said they would like to see their daughter "talk better, using more words," "play with other kids," "walk better," and "tell us when she needs to use the bathroom."

Having selected family goals for Maria, the team then began a discussion of objectives related to these goals. Because the family's goals included language, social, motor, and adaptive skills, these areas were addressed first. In discussing how Maria could be helped to "talk better," the team again looked at the Summary Sheet for communication and language guidelines. They also watched a segment of the TPBA videotape. One of the team members pointed out that most of Maria's comments were in response to an adult's initiations or were requests for objects or actions from an adult. In other words, the team members summarized, "Maria doesn't seem to offer or seek information from others." Mrs. F. commented that Maria usually spoke when spoken to at home as well, but that she hadn't thought about that as important to Maria's language development. Mary, the teacher, added that Maria seemed to speak more and used longer sentences when the adult playing with her asked fewer questions and followed Maria's lead, commenting on her play. Mary found a segment on the videotape in which she, as the play facilitator,

Summary Sheet for Cognitive Guidelines

Name of child: __Maria F.__ Date of birth: __1-3-88__ Age: __4 years, 4 days__

Name of observer: _____ Discipline or job title: _____ Date: __1-7-92__

Observation categories	Areas of strength	Rating	Justification	Things I'm ready for
I. Categories of play	Demonstrates simple, dramatic play; seems to prefer sensorimotor and functional play; beginning construction play.	−	Primarily engages in functional/relational play even in dramatic play areas (24-36 mo. level)	Provide stimulating props for higher-level play in dramatic play sequences and construction activities
II. Attention span	Prolonged attention span in one-to-one setting	+	Is very capable of staying with a task for a long period of time; persistent	Facilitate using attention span to learn new activities
III. Early object use	Used a variety of objects and schemes; simple combination of schemes	−	Object use is limited to two to three steps with single movements (24-36 mo.)	Increase sequence of actions on objects to three to four steps
IV. Symbolic and representational play	Uses beginning dramatic play actions that are seen at home.	−	Limited steps in sequencing of ideas, need real objects (18-36 mo.)	more experience and stimulation in symbolic and dramatic play scenes. Increase to two events
V. Gestural imitation	Uses imitation in play as a means of learning	−	Dependent on adult's model to imitate. Doesn't modify creatively	Needs to imitate peers, increase deferred imitation, and modification

Figure 1. Maria's Summary Sheet for cognitive development.

Summary Sheet for Cognitive Guidelines

Name of child: __Maria F.__   Date of birth: __1-3-88__   Age: __4 years, 4 days__

Name of observer: _____   Discipline or job title: _____   Date: __1-7-92__

Observation categories	Areas of strength	Rating	Justification	Things I'm ready for
VI. Problem-solving approaches	Very persistent in problem-solving	—	Persistent but perseverative; doesn't use trial-and-error (24-30 mo.)	Give wait time, cue possible solutions, then provide model. Use peers. Increase trial and error
VII. Discrimination/ classification	Able to match and group by shape, color, and size	—	Is not able to group by characteristic (abstract) or function (30-48 mo.)	Provide more labeling and classification problems; Increase discrimination of characteristics
VIII. One-to-one correspondence	Can count consistently to 5 by rote	—	Has one-to-one correspondence to two (24-30 mo.)	Incorporate one-to-one correspondence of three to four objects
IX. Sequencing ability	Can sequence up to three steps. Understands some size concepts	—	See early object use (24-36 mo.) Size concepts (36-42 mo.)	Increase sequencing of ideas in play and integrate ordering concepts
X. Drawing ability	Seems to enjoy drawing and painting	—	Drawing skills limited to lines, arcs, and circles (24-36 mo.)	Model and take turns with drawing controlled lines. Increase fine motor strength and tone

475

Summary Sheet for Social-Emotional Guidelines

Name of child: _Maria I._   Date of birth: _1-3-88_   Age: _4 years, 4 days_

Name of observer: _____   Discipline or job title: _____   Date: _1-7-92_

Observation categories	Areas of strength	Rating	Justification	Things I'm ready for
I. Temperament	Very flexible and adaptive; sustained attention level	−	Overall low activity level; good with adults, shy with peers; passive interactions	Add tactile- and motor-alerting activities to increase movement; use high animation and variations in inflection to increase affect
II. Mastery motivation	High degree of persistence; responds well to challenging tasks; chooses tasks with a variety of difficulties	+	Perseveration in problem-solving; does not use trial-and-error in problem-solving	Expose to new stimuli that requires problem-solving; facilitate problem-solving strategies without direct intervention to increase working toward goal.
III. Social interactions with parent	Good attachment	−	Low-intensity; limited repertoire of interactions; mostly responds rather than initiates	Increase M.'s initiations with mom; turn-taking; and conversations
IV. Social interactions with facilitator				

Figure 2.   Maria's Summary Sheet for social-emotional development.

Summary Sheet for Social-Emotional Guidelines

Name of child: _Marie F._ Date of birth: _1-3-88_ Age: _4 years, 4 days_

Name of observer: _____ Discipline or job title: _____ Date: _1-7-92_

Observation categories	Areas of strength	Rating	Justification	Things I'm ready for
V. Characteristics of dramatic play	Able to share joint topics of attention; play doctor theme	–	Limited themes; sequences rote or by imitation	Increase themes used in play and sequences
VI. Humor and social conventions	Smiled and laughed with adults; good social behaviors	+	Appropriate social behaviors but limited intensity of expression	Increase affective range through modeling; increase pleasurable interactions with peers
VII. Social interactions with peers	Demonstrated sharing	–	Demonstrated only isolated and parallel play	Increase imitation, turn-taking, and associative play with peers

477

Summary Sheet for Communication and Language Guidelines

Name of child: _Maria F._

Name of observer: _____

Date of birth: _1 - 3 - 88_

Discipline or job title: _____

Age: _4 years, 4 days_

Date: _1 - 7 - 92_

Observation categories	Areas of strength	Rating	Justification	Things I'm ready for
I. Communication modalities	Uses words and gestures	+	Average utterance is 2.2 (24-30 mo.)	Expand current usage to three to four words
II. Pragmatics A. Stages	Locutionary stage	+	Age appropriate, Uses words	Increase vocabulary and frequency of communication
B. Range of meaning	Gives response upon request	−	Limited pragmatic functions and lack of initiation of communication (2-3 years)	Expand functions to include commenting, requesting, information; increase initiation of dialog
C. Functions	Requests actions or assistance	−	Limited pragmatic functions and lack of initiation of communication (2-3 years)	Expand functions to include commenting; requesting information; increase initiation of dialog
D. Discourse skills	Interacts through 1-2 turns, primarily in response to adult	−	Primarily responsive; limited to one to two turns (2 to 3 years)	Expand turn-taking by three to extending topic through four turns; increase initiation
E. Imitation/echolalia	Repeats often		Few statements are self-generated. Imitations at a 2-3 year level	Move into spontaneous speech, with imitation of difficult words or sentences

Figure 3.   Maria's Summary Sheet for communication and language development.

Summary Sheet for Communication and Language Guidelines

Name of child: Maria F.

Date of birth: 1-3-88

Age: 4 years, 4 days

Name of observer: _____

Discipline or job title: _____

Date: 1-7-92

Observation categories	Areas of strength	Rating	Justification	Things I'm ready for
III. Phonology: Sound production system	Intelligible in context and by familiar adults	—	Nasal condition affects ability to make sounds. Many omissions, deletions, assimilations (30-40 mo.)	Check sinus/breathing problems; increase oral motor stimulation; practice sounds in context
IV. Semantic and syntactic understanding in verbal expression	Showed categorical understanding of many types of words	—	Classification and use of higher-level structures is limited (2-3 years)	Increase use of classification, categorical, and metalinguistic language
V. Comprehension of language	Understands basic sentences and wh- questions		Responds to simple wh- words	Increase response to open-ended questions. Administer vocabulary/concept test
VI. Oral motor	Good rotary patterns and tongue control	—	Open lip chew, weak lip control, lacks sensitivity, low tone in facial area	Oral motor exercise to increase lip and tongue control; increase awareness of facial movements and tactile input
VII. Other concerns (identify):			poor breathing is affecting eating and talking	Further evaluation by specialist

479

Summary Sheet for Sensorimotor Guidelines

Name of child: Maria F.

Name of observer: _____

Date of birth: 1-3-88

Discipline or job title: _____

Age: 4 years, 4 days

Date: 1-7-92

Observation categories	Areas of strength	Rating	Justification	Things I'm ready for
I. General appearance of movement	Arm and leg movements were purposeful but awkward	−	Movements for fine and gross motor activities were awkward; hands held in claw position; W-sit and wide stance when walking	Practice activities to promote fine and gross motor development
II. Muscle tone/ strength/endurance	Maria demonstrated and attempted a wide variety of activities which required tone and strength	−	Low tone demonstrated in legs, arms, and hands	Gross and fine motor play activities to develop coordination and increase strength; do facilitation before activities to increase tone
III. Reactivity to sensory input	Responded with alertness to visual and auditory stimuli	+	Responds to tactile, auditory, visual and movement stimuli. Prefers visual and auditory. Oral area lacks sensitivity	Activities to increase oral sensitivity. Vestibular and tactile activities to increase tone.
IV. Stationary play positions	Was able to maintain sitting positions for extended time periods	−	Balance in standing poor, needs support in sitting to maintain fine motor control	Provide positions that give trunk and leg support

Figure 4.   Maria's Summary Sheet for sensorimotor development.

Summary Sheet for Sensorimotor Guidelines

Name of child: Maria F.

Name of observer: _____

Date of birth: 1-3-88

Discipline or job title: _____

Age: 4 years, 4 days

Date: 1-7-92

Observation categories	Areas of strength	Rating	Justification	Things I'm ready for
V. Mobility in play	Relatively good fine motor skills and she attempted gross motor skills	—	Lack of balance and awkward movements when standing and changing positions	Develop balance and practice coordination of upper and lower body. Work on weight shifting and rotation
VI. Other developmental achievements	Maria climbs, runs, and throws	—	Throwing and catching were uncoordinated; she cannot jump or kick	Increase anticipation, motor planning, balance, and bilateral coordination
VII. Prehension and manipulation	Reach and release movements adequate; performed many manipulative activities	—	Raking grasp; prehension movements are awkward due to low tone and lack of shoulder stability	Improve grasp, move to pincer; increase shoulder stability and improve tone
VIII. Motor planning	Planned motor activities to climb slide and complete fine motor sequences	—	M. has difficulty with movements that are unfamiliar, such as throwing	Plan activities requiring M. to coordinate unfamiliar movement patterns in both fine and gross motor play

had asked Maria a question and gotten a one-word response. Mary then contrasted that interaction with another segment of the videotape in which Maria used a four-word sentence in imitation of the teacher's comment.

As the discussion continued, the team reiterated that Maria communicated with peers much less than she did with adults, partially because she primarily played in proximity to, but not with, peers. The team reinforced the importance of Maria playing with peers for social, language, and cognitive development as Maria could learn much through imitation and taking turns with peers. Because the assessment indicated that Maria understood many different types of words and sentences, including simple "what" and "where" questions, and that Maria had used sentences and phrases of two to three words, the team decided that increasing her sentence length by modeling the addition of another word was appropriate.

Both Mr. and Mrs. F. indicated concern about Maria's articulation skills. Colleen, the speech-language pathologist, pointed out that some of Maria's articulation errors were normal for children her age, but agreed that Maria was often difficult to understand. Colleen suggested that Maria's allergies might be affecting her breathing patterns and influencing sounds that should be made through the nose. Colleen offered to talk to Maria's allergist about the prescribed medications and additional treatments that might make Maria more comfortable and increase her ability to form sounds. Colleen also described some oral motor difficulties she had noticed during Maria's TPBA and talked about techniques for increasing sensitivity in the mouth area.

The team's discussion of communication and language naturally led to talk about Maria's social-emotional skills. The team commented about Maria's easy temperament and adaptability. Mr. F. said that sometimes he would like to see Maria "get a little more excited" and show more enthusiasm. The rest of the team agreed, and someone added that increased emotional response would also attract other children to play with Maria. The teacher noted the need for comprehension and expression of a range of emotions in different social situations, and Lisa, the occupational therapist, added that lack of emotional expression could be related to Maria's low tone in the facial area as muscles are needed to make different expressions. Attempting to increase facial expressions, she said, would be beneficial to muscle control in Maria's face as well.

The team then talked about increasing Maria's turn-taking in play as a means of increasing social interactions with adults and peers, increasing communication, and improving imitation of problem-solving skills. Observation of peers and initiation of conversation were also suggested as important for Maria's social interactions.

Motorically, Maria had been observed to walk and run awkwardly. During the TPBA, she had demonstrated a wide base of support and easily lost her balance. Mr. and Mrs. F. said they would like to see Maria "move better" so she could play more active games with the neighborhood kids and her cousins. They commented that Maria did not interact with the neighborhood kids when they were out "running around" and suggested that part of the problem might be due to her inability "to keep up with them." Lisa said that Maria's lack of stability probably did keep her from interacting in motor activities and proceeded to explain which components of movement were influencing Maria's walking and running, such as the ability to shift her weight, rotate her body, and keep her body balanced in space. Lisa also discussed Maria's low tone and her need to increase strength and endurance so she could more fully participate in activities. She also commented that low tone and lack of strength contributed to Maria's difficulty in manipulating objects.

Lisa's last comment led to a discussion of cognitive skills. Mary reminded the team of how persistent Maria was in trying to manipulate and figure out tasks requiring combining objects (e.g., stringing beads). She said that Maria's persistence and level of problem-solving seemed lower in higher-level play activities requiring her to think about finding a new object or step in a sequence (e.g., play in the house area). The team found a segment of the videotape in which

Maria played in the house area by primarily interacting with toys in a repetitive way (e.g., stirring in a pot, feeding the baby). Mary suggested that increasing the number of steps in Maria's play would lead to both longer play sequences and more opportunity to comment on her play actions and take turns with peers. The team discussed modeling, suggestion, gesturing, and using nondirective cues as ways of increasing the number of steps in Maria's play while allowing her to remain in control of the play. Because Maria showed good functional use of objects, Mary felt it would "bump her up" to a higher level of play to move those functional activities into dramatic play, which would require Maria to think about another series of actions hooked together in a meaningful sequence. Another team member suggested moving her into sequencing two dramatic play events.

It was then suggested that problem-solving could be incorporated into dramatic play by encouraging Maria to examine, explore, and find different ways of using objects. Imitation of problem-solving by a peer or adult could be encouraged if Maria's spontaneous efforts were unsuccessful. Mary noted that Maria showed stronger skills in identifying colors and shapes and was ready to classify other types of concepts, including grouping by function and categories. Maria also seemed ready to increase her understanding of number by moving from rote counting to being able to count actual objects accurately up to two.

Then Lisa brought up drawing, which, for Maria, was at a sensorimotor level. Maria could draw arcs, lines, and circles, but was not yet indicating that these lines had any meaning. When Mrs. F. said that Maria liked to color at home, it was suggested that drawing could be a good turn-taking activity for Maria to do with family members.

Mr. and Mrs. F. then guided the discussion to their goal of Maria telling them when she needed to use the bathroom. Overall, Maria's adaptive skills were a relative strength, and she did go to the bathroom when taken. The team discussed how this also reflected Maria's lack of initiative and tendency to respond rather than lead. They developed a plan for reinforcing her when she said she needed to go to the bathroom, first when they took her there, then when asked, and finally when she initiated the behavior.

From this discussion of Maria's abilities, the team phrased several objectives, relating developmental areas where possible. These objectives were then prioritized according to the family's goals for Maria.

Because the team members had examined the Planner before the meeting, they were ready to present ideas during the conference. To locate guidelines and ideas for Maria throughout the meeting, a team member identified the domain in question and the corresponding subcategory from the Summary Sheets and then the developmental behaviors closest to Maria's observed behaviors. Because the objectives cross developmental domains, it was often possible to find useful suggestions in more than one area. For instance, the first objective on Maria's TIP Sheet was, "Maria will initiate dramatic play with a peer and initiate conversation with the peer in 25% of her interactions." This objective crosses three areas: the cognitive domain, in that dramatic play is desired; the communication and language domain, in that initiation of conversation is desired; and the social-emotional domain, in that initiation of play with a peer is desired.

By referring to these sections of the Planner, the team arrived at ideas and talked about the basic principles that helped Mr. and Mrs. F. to understand why certain intervention approaches are effective. Maria's team used the Planner for the first and second objectives, as Mr. and Mrs. F. were interested in learning more about increasing Maria's use of language. They also referred to the Planner for ideas related to walking. Mr. and Mrs. F. requested photocopies of several of the pages of principles for intervention. Table 1 illustrates each of Maria's objectives and identifies where ideas may be found in the Planner related to that objective.

The note-taking team member then got two TIP Sheets out of a folder (Figures 5 and 6). At the top of each, she circled TIP and then entered Maria's name, date of birth, and age, along with

Table 1.   Cross-referencing Maria's objectives to TPBI Planner ideas

Objective	Domain and subcategory	Curriculum ideas
1. Maria will initiate dramatic play with a peer and initiate conversation with the peer in 25% of the interactions within the dramatic-play area.	Cognitive—imitation	Use interesting toys that peer can demonstrate.
	Cognitive—imitation	Have two of various objects to encourage imitation and parallel play.
	Cognitive—symbolic/representational	Use props for common routines and activities; plan two- to three-step scenarios that can be acted with a peer. Practice scenario several times; then give them props and let them do it.
	Communication—pragmatics	"Sabotage" by removing needed props so child will need to request.
		Encourage discourse and initiating conversations by using toys where turn-taking is implied (e.g., phones, coffee pot and cups)
		Encourage joint-referencing to objects to get children on "same topic."
	Social-emotional—social interactions with peer	Cue peer to get Maria's attention and to model.
		Use challenging toys to encourage asking for assistance from peer.
2. Maria will initiate conversations by providing information or commenting on actions, using three to four words.	Communication—pragmatics	Start with encouraging her to initiate by using forms she demonstrates (e.g., requesting objects, actions), and move into higher levels.
		Provide interesting objects.
		Look expectant; wait for comment; use toys that require assistance to operate.
		Use "cloze" procedure (see comment on object).
		Expand utterances by one word and model three to four words; context and objects should be motivating and cause her to want to interact; use turn-taking in actions simultaneously.
3. Maria will take turns in conversation and in play sequences through three to four turns.	Cognitive—imitation	Imitate Maria's actions; when she repeats, imitate again.
	Cognitive—problem-solving	Use mechanical cause-and-effect toys—objects that present solvable problems that are motivating to encourage taking turns activating mechanism.
	Communication—pragmatics	Use words she commonly uses; imitate her actions, then comment, imitate again, then comment again; as she repeats action to get adult to do it again, add comments; wait; look at her—*wait* for her to comment to get adult to repeat action; repeat and comment.
4. Maria will initiate interactions with a peer that result in laughing and smiling.	Cognitive—attention preferences	Maria likes tickling and rough-housing; encourage these type of activities.
	Social-emotional—social interactions with peers	Use peer modeling and peer imitation—place in situations where peers are having fun so she will join.
	Social-emotional—social interactions with parent/facilitator	Adult can initiate and get turn-taking going; let her tickle adult, then substitute peer.

(continued)

Table 1.   *(continued)*

Objective	Domain and subcategory	Curriculum ideas
		Add enthusiasm, model affect; use high energy peers to model.
		Respond to affect, reflecting feelings to develop awareness of emotional response.
5. Maria will demonstrate increased balance and ability to shift her body weight from side to side in climbing and moving through an obstacle course.	Sensorimotor—other developmental achievements	Provide support to hips; tilt to shift weight in climbing.
		Bring feet closer together.
		Practice running, climbing, and jumping games through various positions, and starting and stopping.
	Sensorimotor—motor planning	Ensure safety.
		Do activities to develop body awareness.
		Add sensory component to activities.
		Place objects so she must manuever around them.
6. Maria will show increased hand and arm strength as demonstrated by her ability to push and pull heavy objects and push objects together and pull them apart.	Sensorimotor—prehension	Manipulation of "heavy" objects (or add weights).
		Use toys requiring strength to combine (e.g., pop beads, cookie cutters and clay, Legos).
		Incorporate push toys (e.g., carts) into obstacle courses.
		Use bilateral toys (requiring two hands or feet), such as tricycles or clay.
7. Maria will show an increased ability to isolate and control finger movements in problem-solving with small objects.	Cognitive—problem-solving	Model more complex actions; use toys requiring a sequence of actions including turning, poking, and pulling.
		Put small objects into small containers; then remove.
		Use small blocks (e.g., Legos) requiring her to problem-solve (e.g., Duplo blocks).
		Encourage use of both hands in exploring and manipulating objects.
8. Increase Maria's functional/relational play within dramatic play to a three- to four-step sequence in 75% of sequences.	Cognitive—functional/relational Cognitive—object use	Use sets of materials or use peer in parallel play with sets of toys.
		Use language to stimulate sequential ideas (e.g., "now the baby is dirty"); model or suggest additional related step in action sequence.
9. Given a challenging cause-and-effect toy, Maria will spontaneously use visual exploration and trial-and-error manipulation of key parts.	Cognitive—object use	Use materials that are motivating and toys requiring skills she demonstrates; then change in some way to make more challenging (e.g., put tape over mechanism).
		Include visual or tactile cues to direct visual search for operating mechanisms or key parts.
10. Maria will be able to sort objects by function and category.	Cognitive—discrimination	Place sets of objects or pictures together in categories (e.g., boxes of food, vegetables).
		Provide objects and pictures that can be grouped or matched.
		Encourage sorting toys by function (e.g., "I need toys that roll").

(continued)

Table 1.   *(continued)*

Objective	Domain and subcategory	Curriculum ideas
		Use language to point out attributes (all are food).
		Encourage adjectives, relational words, and noun categorical words.
		Set up play situations illustrating these types of words.
11. Maria will indicate when she needs to go to the bathroom by statement or request.	Social-emotional	Reinforce approximations of behavior.
		Help her become aware of cues (sensations).
		Structure environment so she's successful (timing).

the current date, in the identifying information section of the form. In the blank labeled location, she wrote "home" on one form and "school" on the other. Then, at the bottom of each form, she wrote the names and roles of each team member in relation to Maria (e.g., Mary—teacher, Colleen—speech-language pathologist).

She then wrote the goals Mr. and Mrs. F. had identified in the family goals portion of each sheet. She was careful to retain the words they had used and the order in which they had prioritized them. The prioritized objectives were then entered in the left column of each sheet. The team then spent some time re-phrasing these objectives to explain why each had been chosen and why it would help Maria. These re-phrasings were then written in the columns of each form adjacent to the objectives column, which is labeled "Rationale/things I'm ready for."

Mr. and Mrs. F. then described Maria's daily routine at home. Each key period of the day was written across the horizontal axis of the Home TIP Sheet. Maria is in preschool from 9 A.M. to 12 P.M. and in child care from 12 P.M. to 5:30 P.M. each day. Her Home TIP Sheet thus included morning and evening activities. Mrs. F. said she would share information on the TIP Sheets with the child care staff and see if they would like more input from the team. Mary and Bev, the teacher assistant, then listed each of the types of preschool play centers across the top of the School TIP Sheet. They combined centers that required similar skills (e.g., the theme area and house area into representational play). The team then took a short break while each form was photocopied and set aside to be used as TAP Sheets later.

When the meeting resumed, the team began to plan play activities to address each objective in each of the environments listed in the horizontal axis. The team worked first on the Home TIP Sheet (see Figure 5) and then the School TIP Sheet (see Figure 6). As the activities were planned, they were written in the appropriate block of the grid. Occasionally, a team member consulted the TPBI Planner to get an idea for an activity. The idea was then modified to match Maria's interests and the family's lifestyle.

The team made a point of noting that the objectives included on the TIP Sheets were just a few of the skills and learning processes that would be addressed in the classroom. Each of the team members would be working on component skills as the children engaged in play. Articulation, balance and equilibrium, number concepts, and other skills also would be included. The team chose a limited number of objectives to evaluate to keep the process from becoming unwieldy. They made it clear that these objectives could be modified as Maria accomplished them or as anyone felt that a new focus was needed.

When the grid was filled, the team then addressed other aspects related to learning, including preparation, cues and prompts, and adaptations. For Maria, the team recommended doing

Team Ideas for Play (TIP)/Team Assessment of Play (TAP) Sheet

Name of child: **Maria F.** Date of birth: **1-3-88** Age: **4 years, 4 days**

Location: **Home** Date: **1-7-92**

Family goals:
1. Talk better and use more words to communicate
2. Play with other kids
3. Walk better
4. Tell adult when she needs to use the bathroom
5.
6.

Time frame: **6 months**

Areas of intervention/assessment

Objectives	Rationale/things I'm ready for	Eating—Breakfast/Dinner	Solitary play	Watching T.V.	Storytime/bedtime
1. Maria will initiate the dramatic play of the peer and initiate conversation with the peer in 25% of interactions within the dramatic-play area.	Maria responds to questions and is ready to initiate conversation. She will pick up higher-level skills if she initiates with peers.	N/A	N/A	Have brothers initiate actions of characters; then Maria initiates to brother.	Have brother look at books with Maria and act out some parts.
2. Maria will initiate conversations by providing information or commenting on activities, using 3-4 words.	Maria uses her words to respond to questions. She is ready to comment, provide information, or ask a question. She currently uses 2-3 words.	Open cupboards and point. Let Maria choose what she wants for breakfast. Hold out food. Wait for comment. Try not to ask yes or no questions.	Put out some toys with missing parts or pieces (naked doll, or shape box without shapes). Let Maria tell you what she needs.	Sit and wait for Maria to tell you to turn it on. Have toy near that she can play with. She may talk to doll, etc. Then comment as if she initiated conversation.	

Figure 5. Maria's TIP Sheet for home.

(continued)

Figure 5. (continued)

Team Ideas for Play (TIP)/ Team Assessment of Play (TAP) Sheet

Name of child: _Maria F._   Date: _1-7-92_

Objectives	Rationale/things I'm ready for	Eating/ Breakfast/Dinner	Solitary play	Watching T.V.	Storytime/ bedtime			
					Areas of intervention/assessment			
3. Maria will take turns in conversation and play sequences through 3-4 turns.	Turns are basic to conversation and learning through observation and imitation. Maria takes two turns; she is ready for longer sequences.	Take turns with activities like passing or taking a bite. Comment on food. Try to keep on topic through 3-4 comments.	N/A	Comment on action on T.V.; ask open-ended questions. "What happened? Repeat her comments; add another comment, etc.	Take turns "reading" the page. Mommy's turn," "Mommy's turn. Have her ask you "what's that?" Then play, "what's that game?" "What's he doing?"			
4. Maria will initiate inter-actions with a peer that result in laughing and smiling.	Maria smiles at adults, but does not enjoy peers. She will be more interested in peers if she finds play fun.		Outdoors on swing set, practice climbing, jumping and travelling through; use bikes.	Play tickle games with Dad and brother. Get Maria to tickle others. Show big response.	Do funny faces or silly action games with brother.			
5. Maria will demonstrate increased balance and ability to shift her body weight from side to side in climbing and moving through obstacle course.	Maria's move-ments will look less awkward and she will move more easily if she can shift her weight easily.	Climbing into chair; provide support at hips and slight shift of body. Same for getting down. Climb stool.	Outdoors on swing set, practice climbing, jumping and travelling through; use bikes.	Place T.V. controls high; have her get them by climbing up, or reaching on toes. Imitate.	Practice walk-ing on bed, blankets, or pillows; climb-ing into bed, or onto chair. Assist with weight shift, if needed.			

(continued)

Name of child: __Marie F.__   Date: __1-7-92__

Objectives	Rationale/things I'm ready for	Areas of intervention/assessment						
		Eating: Breakfast/Dinner	Solitary play	Watching T.V.	Storytime/ bedtime			
6. Marie will show increased hand and arm strength as demonstrated by her ability to push and pull heavy objects and push objects together and pull them apart.	Using large and small heavy objects will improve her arm and back strength required for moving her body and objects in environment.	Carry heavy (unbreakable) objects to table. Push cart to table. Pull self up to counter to help. Use can opener.	Leave heavy objects in cart or wagon. Put out heavier toys to play with.	Push chair over to sit. Push footstool.	Carry blankets and pillows to bed. Put weights on dolls to rock and put to bed. Get pile of books.			
7. Marie will show an increased ability to isolate and control finger movements in problem-solving with small objects.	Finger isolation, combined with strength (above) will help with drawing, manipulation, and problem-solving.	Finger foods. Place raisins in small container. Push buttons on mixer, disposal, lights, etc. Open lids on jars, pans, etc.	Use cause-and-effect toys, blocks, puzzles, crayons, tubes, and sticks, wind-up toys, and button play toys.	Push buttons on T.V. controls. Turn up and down channels, volume, etc.	Turn lights off and on. Turn pages with fingers. Use flashlight to find way around bedroom or bathroom.			
8. Increase Marie's functional/relational play within dramatic play to thru a four-step sequences as in 45% of play.	Marie currently uses two to three steps in her play. She relates objects in isolation and is ready to incorporate these actions into dramatic play, too.	N/A	Put out "sets" of toys that go together: broom and dustpan; pots, pans, dishes, and silverware; or dolls, clothes, combs and toothbrushes. Suggest what needs to be done.	N/A	Use props (e.g., three bears) for stories with objects. Act out after reading and using props.			

(continued)

Figure 5. (continued)

Team Ideas for Play (TIP)/Team Assessment of Play (TAP) Sheet

Name of child: __Maria F.__   Date: __1-7-92__

Objectives	Rationale/things I'm ready for	Areas of intervention/assessment						
		Eating—breakfast/dinner	Solitary play	Watching T.V.	Storytime/bedtime			
9. Given a challenging cause-and-effect toy, Maria will spontaneously use visual exploration and trial-and-error manipulation of key parts.	Maria typifies what she sees. She needs to visually search for solution and use more than one alternative to solve a problem. Let observation and exploration develop.	Let her open jars, boxes, lids, etc. Don't help her too quickly. Let her study it and work at it a little.	Put colored lines or tactile strips glued to mechanisms or switches.	Let her experiment with T.V. controls to see what it does while adults watch, give Maria cause-and-effect toys to with which to play.	Tell a "story" with "barn" or other action toy with figures (barn, garage).			
10. Maria will be able to sort and describe objects by function and category.	Maria's language and thinking skills will increase as she understands how things are alike, how things have more than one name, and the functions of things.	Label different categories like food or cereal; request objects—something to eat, something we clean with, etc.	N/A	Talk about what's on T.V., Labeling actions (fruits and cars like Dad drives, or "Oh—there's something you ___")	Label pictures. Talk about categories—toys, animals; what things do, or characteristics.			
11. Maria will indicate when she needs to go to the bathroom by statement or request.	This will increase Maria's independence and also reflect an increased initiative on her part in both language and thought relating to consequences.	Use the same process all day. Reinforce when she states she has to go, when you take her: give her a gummy bear.	Same.	Same.	Same.			

Team Ideas for Play (TIP)/Team Assessment of Play (TAP) Sheet

Name of child: _Marie F._

Date: _1-7-92_

Preparations:
1. Do activities to increase tone before engaging in tasks requiring stability —
   e.g., bouncing, running, swinging, tickling, etc.
2. Have duplicate materials for imitation and turn-taking.

Cues and prompts:
1. Give Marie plenty of wait-time so she will initiate play and conversation.
2. Show excitement and look expectant.
3. Use gestural cues to prompt exploration, rather than directions.

Adaptations:
1. Add weight to objects or use heavier toys and materials.
2. Add visual or tactile cues to unused parts or mechanisms.
3. Increase intensity of sensory input and model increased affect.

Evaluation schedule:
1. Do TAP sheets once a month in school.
2. Do TAP sheets once a month at home.

**Other state requirements
(e.g., funding source):**

Team members:
Mr. and Mrs. F.   parents
Mary J.   teacher
Coleen R.   speech-language pathologist
Lisa W.   occupational therapist
Bev L.   teacher assistant

491

Team Ideas for Play (TIP)/Team Assessment of Play (TAP) Sheet

Name of child: _Maria F._   Date of birth: _1-3-88_   Age: _4 years, 4 days_

Location: _School_   Date: _1-7-92_

Family goals:
1. Talk better and use more words to communicate   4. Tell adult when she is ready to use the bathroom
2. Play with other kids   5. _____
3. Walk better   6. _____

Time frame: _6 months_

Objectives	Rationale/things I'm ready for	Areas of intervention/assessment					
		Sensory	Gross motor	Representational	Manipulatives	Music/books	Snack
1. Maria will imitate the dramatic play of the peer and initiate conversation with the peer in 25% of interactions within the dramatic play area.	Maria responds to questions and is ready to initiate conversation. She will pick up higher-level skills if she imitates peers.	N/A	Create theme scenarios in motor area. Have peer initiate sequence; Maria imitate. Leave out prop so Maria needs to ask peer.	In house or theme area, have peer play next to Maria with one piece of "bait" so Maria needs to ask or comment.	In miniature play houses, farms, etc., have peer play with Maria and model higher-level play.	Act out songs. Imitate peers.	Incorporate dramatic play into snack eating in restaurant, or eating with cradle. Imitate peers. Wait for Maria to request snack.
2. Maria will initiate conversations by providing information or commenting on actions, using 3-4 words.	Maria uses her words to respond to questions. She is ready to comment, provide information, or ask a question. Use "I need" statements. Uses 2-3 words.	In sand or water, task with clay or paints. Have missing tools for Maria to request. Comment on actions, wait for Maria to comment. Use "I need" statements. Imitate her words and actions.	Motor is difficult for Maria. Language will be depressed during actions. Talk about actions before and after. "What do you think will happen? you went through the tunnel."	Have sets of functional toys both familiar and new. Imitate her actions (comment, model actions). Wait. Take away some needed props.	Use highly stimulating toys that are motivating to Maria and have a big effect. Model actions. Wait for Maria to request again. Model, actions. Wait. Model 3-4 words. Have Maria cause an effect.	Turn pages of book - look expectant; gesture, wait for comment. Model 3-4 words.	Place unusual props or foods before Maria (e.g. chopsticks). Wait for comment.

Figure 6.   Maria's TIP Sheet for school.

Team Ideas for Play (TIP)/Team Assessment of Play (TAP) Sheet

Name of child: __Maria F.__   Date: __1-7-92__

Objectives	Rationale/things I'm ready for	Areas of intervention/assessment					
		Sensory	Gross Motor	Representational	Manipulatives	Music/books	Snack
3. Maria will take turns in conversation and play sequences through 3-4 turns.	Turns are basic to conversation and learning through observation and imitation. Maria takes turns; she is ready for longer sequences.	Set up situations in sensory centers. Imitate Maria - turn into game. Modify and bump up. Take turns again.	On one piece of equipment imitate Maria and take turns. Then substitute a peer.	Use props that require turns (cups and coffee, doctor's office, etc.). Follow her lead. Start with imitation; then model a new turn.	Use toys that have many pieces so turns can be taken - marble shoots, puzzles, games, or blocks.	Take turns turning pages, "reading" pictures. Take turns in action songs.	Initiate a discussion during snack about foods, T.V., or movies. "I like..." Take turns through several rounds.
4. Maria will initiate interactions with a peer that result in laughing and smiling.	Maria smiles at adults, but does not enjoy peers. She will be more interested in peers if she finds play fun.	Play squirt gun games, painting, or tickling.	Play chase games with peer. "Bumper cars" in inner-tubes.	Pretend actions that are funny - dress the clown, walk your "dog", or feed baby with peer.	Build towers and knock down. Hide funny objects in container with lid.		Make faces.
5. Maria will demonstrate increased balance and ability to shift her body weight from side to side in climbing and moving through obstacle course.	Maria's movements will look less awkward and she will move more easily if she can shift her weight easily.	Use stool at water table. Place materials around sensory centers so Maria has to reach up, to sides, and shift weight.	Obstacle courses with motivation to reach, climb, pull self up, crawl, run, etc.	Place props at different levels requiring movement of body, up and to sides. Put step stool in to climb.	Put some toys on low bench. Use bench, kneel-stand and objects on ends of bench.	Dancing and moving in action songs requiring movement side-to-side, up and down, and around motions.	Research for snacks, get table set, or reach across table for more snack.

(continued)

Figure 6. (continued)

Team Ideas for Play (TIP)/Team Assessment of Play (TAP) Sheet

Name of child: __Maria F.__   Date: __1-7-92__

Objectives	Rationale/things I'm ready for	Areas of intervention/assessment					
		Sensory	Gross motor	Representational	Manipulatives	Music/books	Snack
6. Maria will show increased hand and arm strength as demonstrated by her ability to push and pull heavy objects and push together and pull apart.	Using large and small heavy objects will improve her tone and build strength required for moving her body and objects and environment.	Use heavy or weighted toys or real tools that are heavy. Put toys in that pull apart or push together.	Pull set up rope, pull peer in wagon, or drag objects (prop) through obstacle course.	Set up theme area; move furniture, and arrange props and toys.	Have Maria get container of toys down off shelves.	Carry books in wagon or in pile to distribute to kids. Carry boxs, etc. over to "read" to them.	Move chairs so all have seat. Carry snack on heavy tray.
7. Maria will show an increased ability to isolate and control finger movements in problem-solving with small objects.	Finger isolation combined with strength (above) will help with drawing, manipulation, and problem-solving.	Use toys with small lids. Plungers, tubes, sticks, marbles, sticky substances, etc.	N/A	Incorporate props with activating devices, buttons, snaps, keys, or zippers.	Use cause-effect toys requiring pushing, pulling, or turning.	Push recorder buttons; turn pages.	Practice cutting or putting small pieces on plates.
8. Increase Maria's functional/representational play within dramatic play to three-to-four-step sequences in 75% of play.	Maria currently uses two to three steps in her play. She relates objects in isolation and is ready to incorporate those actions into dramatic play, too.	Incorporate sensory into house and theme area with soap and brushes.	Use toys in gross motor theme (going camping with dolls). Put "uses" of toys interspersed with gross motor equipment (mountains, etc.)	Model use of "sets" within theme area. (Demonstration actions. Invite Maria; then modify and add new action.) through 3-4 turns.	Move into miniatures when ready.	Relate musical instruments in rhythmic sequences. (Drum and stick, xylophone and stick, triangle, etc.)	Role-play of different testing situations. (Picnic, camping, or restaurant.)

494

Team Ideas for Play (TIP)/Team Assessment of Play (TAP) Sheet

Name of child: Marie F.   Date: 1-7-92

Objectives	Rationale/things I'm ready for	Areas of intervention/assessment					
		Sensory	Gross Motor	Representational	Manipulative	Music/books	Snack
9. Given a challenging cause and effect toy, Marie will spontaneously use usual exploration and trial-and-error manipulation to solve a problem of key parts.	Marie explores what she does. She needs to visually search for solutions and use more than one alternative to solve a problem. Observation and exploration are key.	Act problems into sensory centers—e.g. find, open, clean, pick-up, use tools, etc.	Use large puzzle blocks to build structure.	Within theme or house are place objects needing manipulation; or leave out key prop—have to find it.	Sabotage toys that usually work by substituting, covering part, or leaving out battery. Have Marie "fix it".	Look for props to go with music or books.	Have Marie find missing things for snack time.
10. Marie will be able to sort and describe objects by function and category.	Marie's language and thinking skills will increase as she understands the ways things are alike, how things are more than one name, and the functions of things.	Label discrete emotions. Model mushy, squishy, soft, lucky, etc. Objects that float or blow.	Use and label objects that are high, tall, wide, heavy, etc. Incorporate problem-solving. "we need a heavy block."	Depending on theme—identify, key function, classification, and attribute words.	Depending on theme—identify, key function, classification, and attribute words.	Label concepts in books—relate to other concepts. Model use of words in them.	Label foods, tools, etc. Talk about functions.
11. Marie will indicate when she needs to go to the bathroom by statement or request.	This will increase Marie's independence and also reflect an increase initiative on her part in both language and thought-relating to consequences.	Use reinforcement and increase required imitation until need is stated outside of bathroom spontaneously.	Use reinforcement and increase required imitation until need is stated outside of bathroom spontaneously.	Use reinforcement and increase required imitation until need is stated outside of bathroom spontaneously.	Use reinforcement and increase required imitation until need is stated outside of bathroom spontaneously.	Use reinforcement and increase required imitation until need is stated outside of bathroom spontaneously.	Use reinforcement and increase required imitation until need is stated outside of bathroom spontaneously.

(continued)

495

Figure 6. (continued)

Team Ideas for Play (TIP)/Team Assessment of Play (TAP) Sheet*

Name of child: _Marie F._ Date: _1-7-92_

Preparations:	1. Do activities to increase tone before engaging in tasks requiring stability — e.g., bouncing, running, swinging, tickling, etc. 2. Have duplicate materials for imitation and turn-taking.
Cues and prompts:	1. Give Marie plenty of wait-time so she will initiate play and conversation. 2. Show excitement and look expectant. 3. Use gestural cues to prompt exploration, rather than directions.
Adaptations:	1. Add weight to objects or use heavier toys and materials. 2. Add visual or tactile cues to unused parts or mechanisms. 3. Increase intensity of sensory input and model increased affect.
Evaluation schedule:	1. Do TAP sheets once a month in school. 2. Do TAP sheets once a month at home.
Other state requirements (e.g., funding source):	
Team members:	Mr. and Mrs. F. parents Mary J. teacher Colleen R. speech-language pathologist Lisa W. occupational therapist Bev L. teacher assistant

activities to increase muscle tone before conducting activities requiring fine and gross motor skills. These included bouncing and tickling. Another preparation the team suggested to increase imitation included having two of various materials available in the play area. These recommendations were written on each TIP Sheet. In the cues and prompts block, the team wrote suggestions such as giving Maria wait time to encourage her to initiate play and communication and to use gestural cues to encourage exploration and alternative actions. Proposed adaptations were to add weight to objects to build strength, to add visual or tactile cues to complex objects to encourage exploration of unused parts, and to increase the intensity of affect associated with activities to increase responsivity.

The team then discussed a time frame for checking on Maria's progress. The team indicated that re-evaluations would be conducted every 6 months, but that this could be modified. The team leader asked how soon the parents would like to do a check on progress. Mrs. F. suggested 3 months. The team believed that this time frame would probably be appropriate for the intervention plans they had discussed. The meeting concluded with Mr. and Mrs. F. thanking the team for their input and commenting that they were anxious to try the ideas on the TIP Sheets. Mary, Maria's teacher, indicated that the information about Maria contributed by Mr. and Mrs. F. was extremely helpful and that their ideas for intervention greatly enriched the plan. They agreed to keep in touch by telephone and notes, and Mary said she would make a home visit to review and update the plan in 3 months.

INTERVENTION FOR MARIA

During the next 3 months, the team developed numerous storybook units for the class. Examples are shown in Figures 7, 8, and 9. As play activities were integrated into the themes, the team addressed Maria's objectives, incorporating the ideas from the TIP sheets into each day. After only a few days, team members remembered most of the objectives for each of the children, but an occasional review of the TIP Sheets notebook during weekly planning sessions was helpful.

Throughout the year, the team did videotaping in the classroom, usually at the end of a storybook unit when the children have become immersed in the various play activities. A parent volunteer came in on Thursday or Friday and videotaped the children interacting with each other and team members interacting with children in various activities. These videotapes were then used individually with parents to illustrate what was happening in class with their child and in group parent meetings to illustrate the curriculum or specific topics (e.g., facilitation of language development). Occasional videotapes of Maria were thus made during the ensuing months.

The team implemented Maria's plan throughout the day in each of the play activities. When team members facilitated Maria's play they attempted to foster her language and interactions with peers. They enticed her to play in areas with peers at higher levels so that she could model their actions and encouraged her to take the lead and initiate play and communication with peers in her immediate play area. For example, in the story of *The Three Bears*, Maria played the part of the baby bear, which allowed her to observe and model the actions of the Papa and Mama bear. They facilitated increasing the length of Maria's play sequences in her use of schemes on objects, sequencing of events, and creating dramatic story sequences. For instance, when Maria played with Maggie in the house area and spontaneously began to cook "porridge," the teacher modeled blowing on it because hers was too hot. She stated, "I need something to cool down my porridge." When Maggie ran to the refrigerator to get "milk," Maria followed and brought some back, too. Maria then poured milk on her porridge, blew on it, and ate it. Maggie and Maria repeated this sequence the next day without the presence of the teacher. As the team tried to increase play sequences, they also worked on increasing her sequence of ideas and related comments on her actions and the conceptualization and discrimination of classes of objects.

Play-Based Curriculum Planning Sheet: Preschool/Kindergarten

Date: _____ Theme (optional): Bears Book title (optional): The Three Bears

Play area	Monday	Tuesday	Wednesday	Thursday	Friday
Home Area: Living Room; Bedroom	Set up house for three bears. Arrange props by size.		Three bears' living room: 1. Too hard. 2. Too soft. 3. Just right.	Three bears' bedroom: 1. Too high. 2. Too low. 3. Just right.	Assessments; planning meetings; home visits.
House Area: kitchen	Arrange pots, bowls, and spoons by size.	Act out the Three Bears, scene 1: kitchen— 1. Too hot. 2. Too cold. 3. Just right.	Same.	Same.	
Motor Area:	the woods: have kids hang streamers for trees. Hang high; use ladder.	Obstacle course through woods— picking flowers.	Bears looking for honey; move like bears.	Teddy bear games. Rolling over bears; passing bears.	
Blocks:	Make trees from big blocks and sticks.	Legos; Lincoln Logs; add miniature bears.	Marble runs.	Same as previous two days.	
Floor Play:	Puzzles of bears; Legos; Lincoln Logs.	Bear miniatures and blocks.	Teddy bear counters and egg cartons.	Lacing bear cards and previous day's toys.	
Sensory Play:	- Sensory box—feel hard/soft; wet/dry.	Water table with measuring cups, bowls, spoons, etc.	- Glue fake fur onto mural. - Finger paint.	- Paint faces to be bear. - Paint fingernails like claws.	
Art Area:	Color mural of woods and three bears' house.	Make "bearskin" hats from fake fur.	Make bear puppets from felt or paper bags.	easel/paint; crayon/paper-tracing bears	

Figure 7. A Play-Based Curriculum Planning Sheet for a week of programming at Maria's preschool.

Play-Based Curriculum Planning Sheet: Preschool/Kindergarten

Date: _____

Theme (optional): _Bears_

Book title (optional): _The Three Bears_

Play area	Monday	Tuesday	Wednesday	Thursday	Friday
Woodworking:	Make beds for bears from boxes.	Work on making a new chair for baby bear (Volunteer Dad).	Make a bed for your bear at home.	Same as previous.	
Table Play:	- Stamp pad drawings. - Make bear tracks.	Templates for tracing plus previous.	Puzzles plus previous.	Same as previous.	
Music Area:	Story and tape of "the Teddy Bears' Picnic."	"Five Little Bears Jumping on the Bed" (jump and sing).	Dancing bear to lumbering music.	Teddy Bear, Teddy bear turn around.	
Book Area:	The Three Bears and tape of Brown Bear, Brown Bear.	Bring bear from home; read it Polar Bear, Polar Bear.	The Bears' Picnic plus tape.	The Bear Party plus tape.	
Science:	Make Oatmeal. Measure water and oatmeal.	Measuring and mixing flour and water to make goop.	Weighing teddy bears from home.	Measure the different bears from home.	
Outdoors:	Fill cans with dirt and sticks for trees.	Place bear traps around playground; hide packets of honey.	Bear tag.	Free play.	
Snack:	Oatmeal with different-size bowls and spoons. Kids choose size and match to spoon.	Honey and Toast	Teddy grahams.	Matt-o-meal.	

(continued)

499

Play-Based Curriculum Planning Sheet: Preschool/Kindergarten

Date: _____   Theme (optional): _Castles, knights and dragons_   Book title (optional): _The Knight and the Dragon by Tommy DePaola_

Play area	Monday	Tuesday	Wednesday	Thursday	Friday
Theme area: Castle	Build castle out of brick blocks. Costumes for knights and princesses. Big pot in fireplace. Moat	Act out sequence: 1. I see a dragon. 2. Get the knight. 3. Knight fights dragon.	Act out sequence again.	Add injured dragon— need Merlin.	Assessments; parent meetings; planning.
House Area: Restaurant	Knight and dragon serve barbecue.	1. Customer orders. 2. Cook food. 3. Serve it.	Same as previous day.	Add paying check and cleaning up.	
Motor Area:	Dinosaur egg roll.	Hunting the dragon through obstacle course.	Follow dragon-footprints trail.	Beanbag throw at mural of dragon. Cost is two dragon tokens.	
Blocks:	Large blocks for castle.	Add magnetic blocks.	Add Lego and Duplo blocks for castle	Add bristle blocks.	
Floor Play:	Make beads for princess.	Toilet paper roll cannons and marbles.	Miniature of knights. Catapult ever-to shoot pading peanuts.	Same as previous day.	
Sensory Play:	Sand table with hidden Lego knight figures.	Finger paint dragon feet, and dragon breath.	Same as Monday and Tuesday.	Play-doh dragons and knights plus previous.	
Art Area:	Make pointed hat for princess. Paint flag for castle.	Cut doh and paper scales for dragon. Glue these and sequins on paper for big paper dragon.	- Cut up knights into puzzles. - Color mural of dragon.	Easel painting plus previous choices.	

Figure 8.   A Play-Based Curriculum Planning Sheet for a week of programming at Maria's preschool.

Play-Based Curriculum Planning Sheet: Preschool/Kindergarten

Date: _____ Theme (optional): <u>Castles, knights and dragons</u> Book title (optional): <u>The Knight and the Dragon</u> by Tomny DePaola

Play area	Monday	Tuesday	Wednesday	Thursday	Friday
Woodworking:	Make drawbridge out of big piece of cardboard box. Hook ropes to it and pulleys to castle.	Make shields and cardboard swords.	Make armor from cardboard box.	Same.	
Table play:	Lego and Duplo castles. Make dragon feet.	Stamping insignia on paper.	All of previous columns.	Knight puzzles made in Art Area.	
Music Area:	Puff the Magic Dragon.	Movie - Reluctant Dragon with songs.	A Hunting We Will Go.	The Crocodile.	
Book Area:	<u>The Knight and the Dragon</u> - book and tape.	<u>The Popcorn Dragon</u> - book and tape.	<u>There's no such thing as a Dragon</u> - book and tape.	<u>Dragonling</u> - book and tape.	
Science:	Pictures of Komodo Dragon. Computer: Dinosaurs are forever.	Pictures of dinosaurs.	Weighing egg and rocks. Same as previous.	Measuring your height and that of dragon on mural. Same as previous.	
Outdoors:	Chasing the dragon through countryside.	Make jungle gym into castle. Role-play climbing in.	Knight and dragon runs and relays.	Free play.	
Snack:	Dragon eggs.	Popcorn: Make like in the <u>Popcorn Dragon</u>.	Dinosaur Spaghettios.	Miniature hot dogs to dip into barbeque sauce.	

501

Play-Based Curriculum Planning Sheet: Preschool/Kindergarten

Date: _____ Theme (optional): _Exploring_ Book title (optional): _Henry the Explorer_

Play area	Monday	Tuesday	Wednesday	Thursday	Friday
Theme area:	Make cave out of refrigerator box. Put big stuffed bear in cave; flashlights.	Role-play: –Explore motor area. –Find and explore caves.	Reenact _Henry the Explorer_.	Reenact _Henry the Explorer_; add new props (sleeping bags, etc.)	
House Area:	Picnic supplies for making picnic.	1. Pack picnic lunch. 2. Put in backpack; pack flashlight.	Same.	Same.	
Motor Area:	Make into jungle with hanging vines and trees.	Walk through jungle on mats, pillows, textures, and paper.	Let kids explore jungle and ride in "boat" across river on scooter-board.	Plant flags around room; track flags (up, over, under, and through) to find lost peer.	
Blocks:	Build farmhouse Henry passed.	Use various types of blocks to make paths, towers, and stairs.	Same as previous day's.	Same as previous day's.	
Floor play:	Incorporate people-figures into block area.	Make shadows on sheets with flashlights, hands, and objects.	Playmobile Eskimo	Playmobile camping set.	
Sensory Play:	Feet painting; Use different materials to make footprints.	"Quicksand" in wading pool (oatmeal). Then cross river (pool).	Water table–different sizes, shapes, and textures of rocks; make water-fall.	Wet sand in sand table–make animal tracks with different tools.	
Art Area:	–Make flags with your initials on them.	Bear-foot stamps; make feet for cave hanging from rubber band.	Sponge painting to make tracks.	Trace feet.	

Figure 9. A Play-Based Curriculum Planning Sheet for a week of programming at Maria's preschool.

Date: _____

Theme (optional): _Exploring_   Book title (optional): _Henry the Explorer_

Play-Based Curriculum Planning Sheet: Preschool/Kindergarten

Play area:	Monday	Tuesday	Wednesday	Thursday	Friday
Table Play:	Animal home lotto.	Match footprints to animals.	Teddy bear counters and toilet-paper roll caves.	Feely-box with fur, rocks and plastic spiders. Match to picture.	
Music Area:	Going on a Bear Hunt.	The Bear Went Over the Mountain	The Ants Go Marching.	She Waded in the Water.	
Book Area:	Henry the Explorer book and tape.	Corduroy book and tape.	Winnie the Pooh and tape.	Polar Bear, Polar Bear and tape.	
Science:	Look through binoculars.	Study insects under magnifying glass.	Weigh rocks and dirt.	Measure footprints and hand prints.	
Outdoors:	Ropes to climb up mountains.	Follow bear-tracks around playground.	Wagons full of camping gear outside to set up camp.	Set up tents, climb mountain, fish.	
Snack:	Peel and eat carrots.	Peanut butter sandwiches	Trail mix.	Beef jerky.	

503

Through the strategies of commenting, gesturing, modeling or suggesting, they also tried to increase her ability to scan, explore, investigate, and solve problems. They gave her plenty of wait time to allow her time to process information and formulate a response; they set up situations so that Maria had to request materials or actions from the team members or peers; and they provided sensory input prior to play activities to stimulate her sensory system and increase her tone and sensory awareness. They modified toys and materials to increase the amount of weight Maria handled and placed objects to require her to shift and rotate her body in order to gain access to them. The team also worked with Maria to notify them when she had to go to the bathroom, first reinforcing her when she went on a scheduled bathroom trip and also by making her aware of how she felt when she needed to go.

At home, Mr. and Mrs. F. encouraged Sean to include Maria in his dramatic play and helped him to understand that it was good for her to imitate him and play a role in his stories. He let her dress up in a cowboy hat and gave her a stick horse to ride. He then chased her, and they played "hide and seek" on the horses. Mr. F. played roughhouse games with both children in the evening after dinner, let Maria operate the TV controls, and tried to get Maria to talk about what was happening on their favorite shows. Mrs. F. involved Maria in the planning and preparation of meals and spent time before bed reading to both children. They made a game out of taking turns turning the pages of the book they were reading and pointing out what they saw on the page before they read it. Mrs. F. would ask, "What do you think is going to happen?" Mr. and Mrs. F. also engaged Maria in doing the household chores by identifying and finding the items they needed. For example, to do the laundry Maria found the laundry soap and a measuring cup, and to hang a picture, she located a hammer and nails with her father.

THREE MONTHS LATER: EVALUATION AND PROGRAM MODIFICATION

After 3 months, Mary, Maria's teacher, sent home a blank TIP Sheet with a note that indicated that the team was planning to check on Maria's progress during the upcoming week. They asked Mr. and Mrs. F. to observe Maria in their normal activities during the next week and make notes of behaviors that she was doing in relation to each of the objectives they had developed. They sent home a "sample" TAP Sheet to serve as an example of the type of behaviors to note. Mary then followed up the note with a telephone call and discussed the TAP Sheet with Mrs. F., answering all of her questions and telling her that they would also be doing a TAP Sheet at school. Mary said she would then make a home visit or have a conference at school, whichever Mrs. F. preferred, to discuss how things were going and to make program modifications.

During the ensuing week, Mr. and Mrs. F. and the team completed their respective TAP Sheets. At home, Mrs. F. kept the TAP Sheet close by, so that she could jot down things Maria said or did (Figure 10). In school, the teacher assistant moved around the room with Maria during the day and took notes on behaviors relating to her objectives (Figure 11). The children had been involved in activities related to *The Knight and the Dragon* (DePaola, 1980) during the week and had the story and related activities in mind. This gave the team an opportunity to review Maria's abilities after she had experimented and practiced with props and materials during the week. In this way, her highest level skills could be observed. The planning sheet for *The Knight and the Dragon* is shown in Figure 8.

After completing the TAP Sheet for the classroom, the team met to discuss Bev's (the teacher assistant) observations. They noted that although Maria was observing and imitating peers more frequently, she still was not initiating conversation on a consistent basis. She was using three-word phrases to comment on her actions, to indicate location, to request an action, and to provide information. This showed growth in her pragmatic language usage. The team felt the objective to use three to four words to comment and offer information was still appropriate, as

Team Ideas for Play (TIP)/Team Assessment of Play (TAP) Sheet

Name of child: Maria F.
Location: Home

Date of birth: 1-3-88
Date: 4-17-92
Age: 4 years, 3 months, 14 days

Family goals:
1. Talk better and use more words to communicate
2. Play with other kids
3. Walk better
4. Tell adult when she needs to use the bathroom
5.
6.

Time frame: 6 months

Objectives	Rationale/things I'm ready for	Areas of intervention/assessment			
		Eating, Breakfast/Dinner	Solitary Play	Watching T.V.	Storytime/Bedtime
1. Maria will initiate the dramatic play at the peer to peer level (initiate conversation with the peer) in 25% of interactions within the dramatic play area.	Maria responds to questions and is ready to initiate conversation. She will pick up higher-level skills if she imitates peers.	N/A	N/A	Imitated Sean when he acted out commercial. Imitated Sean in play with his Batman dolls. Said "Give me one." "me too."	Sean & Maria have been acting out 3 Bears and Cat in the Hat. Now wants Sean to do storytime every night.
2. Maria will initiate conversations by providing information or commenting on information, or ask a question, using actions, using 3-4 words.	Maria uses her words to respond to questions. She is ready to comment. She currently uses 2-3 words.	Now asks "I want Cheerios" or whatever. She helps me cook and has been telling me what we're making.	Now she's helping me set up play area. Tells me what she wants to pull out.	Says "Turn it on, Mom." Doesn't comment while she plays.	With book we've read several times, will say something if I wait and don't read.

Figure 10.   A TAP Sheet completed by Maria's mother at home.

(continued)

Figure 10. (continued)

Team Ideas for Play (TIP)/ Team Assessment of Play (TAP) Sheet

Name of child: __Maria F.__   Date: __4-17-92__

Objectives	Rationale/things I'm ready for	Areas of intervention/assessment						
		Eating Breakfast/Dinner	Solitary Play	Watching T.V.	Storytime/bedtime			
3. Maria will take turns in conversation and play sequences through 3-4 turns.	Turns are basic to conversation and learning through attention and imitation. Maria takes two turns; she is ready for longer sequences.	Still at a turn at talk. But will do 3-4 turns in imitation play like building blocks and drawing.	N/A	If family initiates she will comment back. Still not a conversation.	Now she and I take turns asking "what that?" or "What's happening?" She likes to ask me. Will answer when I ask.			
4. Maria will initiate interactions with a peer that result in laughing and smiling.	Maria smiles at adults, but does not enjoy peers. She will be more interested in peers if she finds play fun.	She imitates her brother opening his mouth with food in it. Then they laugh. Now she's imitating this. How do I stop it?	N/A	David + Sean play rough-house every night. She now will start the game by poking them and laughing.	Likes big bashing game. Laughs when it this off the board.			
5. Maria will demonstrate increased balance and skill in shifting her body weight from side to side in climbing and moving through obstacle course.	Maria's movements will look less backward and she will move more easily if she can shift her weight easily.	Doing better— I still shift her weight or she pulls up on one side.	She swings on her stomach, will climb up on merry-go-round. Won't climb slide.	We now keep controls on shelf with stool for Maria. She likes to get it for us.	Sean + Maria love to jump on "big bed" (ours). We play games with pillows, blanket tents. She falls when she does these— but laughs.			

(continued)

Name of child: __Maria F.__   Date: __4-17-92__

Objectives	Rationale/things I'm ready for	Eating Breakfast/Dinner	Solitary play	Watching T.V.	Abstaining T.V.	Storytime/Bedtime	Areas of intervention/assessment		
6. Maria will show increased hand and arm strength as demonstrated by her ability to push and pull heavy objects and push objects together and pull them apart.	Using large and small heavy objects will improve her coordination and build strength required for moving her body and objects in environment.	She pushes chair over to table, pushes stool to counter. Needs help.	Maria avoids heavy objects. I put things in wagon - so she didn't play with it.	She's getting into pushing things. Pushed coffee table - but it wouldn't move.		Drags blanket to bed. Tries to put pillow in (carries 3-4 books).			
7. Maria will show an increased ability to isolate and control finger movements in problem-solving with small objects.	Finger isolation, combined with strength (above) will help with drawing, manipulation and problem-solving.	Is using thumb and finger now to put things in. Can't get jar top open unless I start.	Maria likes new wind-up toys. Does easy puzzles.	Maria has become the T.V. controller (much to Dad's dismay).		Maria climbs on stool to turn off light. Then we use her flashlight to get into bed. She likes this game (we had to get Sean one too).			
8. Increase Maria's functional/relational play with dramatic play to three- to four-step sequences in 75% of play.	Maria currently uses two to three steps in her play. She relates objects in isolation and is ready to incorporate these actions into dramatic play, too.	N/A	Maria is putting many things together. Favorites - combing baby's hair or washing baby. Cooks with pots and pans.	Will play with dolls while we watch T.V.		We use props for 3 bears and "Lost in the Nest."			

(continued)

Figure 10. (continued)

Team Ideas for Play (TIP)/Team Assessment of Play (TAP) Sheet

Name of child: _Maria F._   Date: _4-17-92_

Objectives	Rationale/things I'm ready for	Eating, Breakfast/Dinner	Solitary play	Watching T.V.	Storytime/bedtime			
					Areas of intervention/assessment			
9. Given a challenging cause-and-effect toy, Maria will spontaneously use visual exploration and trial-and-error manipulation of key parts.	Maria explores what she sees. She needs to visually search for solutions and use more than one alternative to solve a problem. Observation and exploration are key.	Maria is now trying to open milk carton, cereal boxes. She knows what to do but lacks strength and needs help.	We have put colored tape on tape recorder and T.V. controls. She can work these now.	She works T.V. controls, but loses interest in other things without adult.	We haven't done this (TIP.) We do stories at bedtime.			
10. Maria will be able to sort and describe objects by function and category.	Maria's language and thinking skills will increase as she understands how things are alike, how things have more than one name, and the functions of things.	Says "It's good food." Will imitate us when we say "I like fruit" or "I like meat."	N/A	She's labeling when I say "Oh look, there's a ____"	She knows bears are animals and can identify people, toys, boys, girls.			
11. Maria will indicate when she needs to go to the bathroom by statement or request.	This will increase Maria's independence and also reflect an increased initiative on her part in both language and thought relating to consequences.	She's now saying she has to go when she's in the bathroom (She sometimes doesn't make it).						

508

Team Ideas for Play (TIP)/Team Assessment of Play (TAP) Sheet

Name of child: _Maria_   Date of birth: _1-3-88_   Age: _4 years, 3 mo., 16 days_
Location: _School_   Date: _4-19-92_

Family goals:
1. _Talk better and use more words to communicate_   4. _Tell adults when she needs to use the bathroom_
2. _Play better with other kids_   5. _____
3. _Walk better_   6. _____

Time frame: _6 months_

Objectives	Rationale/things I'm ready for	Areas of intervention/assessment					
		Sensory	Gross motor	Representational	Manipulatives	Music/books	Snack
1. Maria will imitate the dramatic play of the peer and initiate conversation with the peer in 25% of interactions within the dramatic-play area.	Maria responds to questions and is ready to initiate conversation. She will pick up higher-level skills if she imitates peers.	Maria grabbed Tom along knights in sand and imitated him. Didn't imitate his higher-level knights jousting play. Mostly buried, dug up and reburied with Pepe. Just out-of-up.	Enjoyed buying tickets and throwing. When type of throwing shifted M. didn't imitate — had to be prompted. Didn't initiate conversation, except to buy ticket.	Loves dressing as princess. Doesn't want to be knight. Imitated Maggie cheering the flight.	Didn't want to make knights — want to find beads to make necklace for her princess outfit.	Sat with Jose in book area and read Dracula with for hot dogs. Tried tape. Tried to work tape recorder. Jose helped her.	Imitated peers in "taking order" for hot dogs.
2. Maria will initiate conversations by providing information or commenting on actions, using 3-4 words.	Maria uses her words to respond to questions. She is ready to comment, provide information, or ask a question. She currently uses 2-3 words.	Said "mine all gone," "Here it is." Said 4 3-word phrases.	"I want ticket" "my turn." Didn't comment or provide information.	"Give me hat" "Mine is pretty." "Mine is blue." 10 3-4 words.	Named colors of beads on necklace. Concentrated on task, didn't talk to peers.	"Push this." "I do it." Turn the page (in imitation).	Imitated "you want." "I want hot dogs."

Figure 11. A TAP Sheet completed at Maria's preschool during a week of storybook curriculum programming.

(continued)

Figure 11. (continued)

Team Ideas for Play (TIP)/Team Assessment of Play (TAP) Sheet

Name of child: __Maria F.__   Date: __4-19-92__

Objectives	Rationale/things I'm ready for	Areas of intervention/assessment					
		Sensory	Gross motor	Representational	Manipulatives	Music/Books	Snack
3. Maria will take turns in conversation and play sequences through 3-4 turns.	Turns are basic to conversation and learning through observation and imitation. Maria takes two turns; she is ready for longer sequences.	Imitated twice, then did her own thing.	Took turns, but needed adult support.	Maria on her own, not taking turns.	Isolated play.	Took turns turning page with 1st teacher prompt, then peer.	Said "I like hot dogs" after peer said, then said again after another peer repeated.
4. Maria will initiate interactions with a peer that result in laughing and smiling.	Maria smiles at adults, but does not enjoy peers. She will be more interested in peers if she finds play fun.	No smiling or laughing observed.	Jumped up and down and smiled when she hit dragon - not in interaction with peer.	Laughed when knights fell down. Smiled and cheered when Maggie did (in imitation).	Concentrated on task - no smiling until completed then said "Look" and smiled.	No affect in interaction with Jose.	Smiled when Jose laughed at R's funny face.
5. Maria will demonstrate increased balance and ability to shift her body weight from side to side in climbing and moving through obstacle course.	Maria's movements will look less awkward and she will move more easily if she can shift her weight easily.	Lisa held objects up to sides for Maria to reach. Maria switches hands rather than rotates. Needed assistance.	Lisa had Maria stand sideways to throw. Couldn't do it. Kept turning toward front unless Lisa assisted.	shifted to watch knights run.	When C. moved beads to side, shifted to get them. Didn't rotate.	Leaned for wand and rotated and shifted to hit buttons on recorder.	Rotated to pass the dip.

Team Ideas for Play (TIP)/Team Assessment of Play (TAP) Sheet

Name of child: __Maria F.__   Date: __4-19-92__

Objectives	Rationale/things I'm ready for	Areas of intervention/assessment							
		Sensory	Gross motor	Representational	Manipulatives	Music/books	Snack		
6. Maria will show increased hand and arm strength as demonstrated by her ability to push and pull heavy objects and push objects together and pull them apart.	Using large and small heavy objects will improve her tone and build strength required for moving her body and objects in environment.	Pushed stool over to water table.	Maria helped dress knights in cardboard boxes. Couldn't be left alone.	Helped rebuild castle when wall got knocked over by a knight. Pulled up draw bridge.	Carried book of beads to table braced against body.	Carried toys, reordered and put on floor.	Helped push chairs under table.		
7. Maria will show an increased ability to isolate and control finger movements in problem-solving with small objects.	Finger isolation combined with strength (above) will help with drawing, manipulation, and problem-solving.	Uses whole hand primarily — did use fingers to pull knight out of sand.	N/A	Needed help with buttons and gloves.	Used all fingers to string beads. Occasional thumb-fore-finger.	Pushed recorder button with fingers.	Wrote "orders" with thumb-finger grasp.		
8. Increase Maria's functional/relational play within dramatic play to three- to four-step sequences in 75% of play.	Maria currently uses two to three steps in her play. She relates objects in isolation and is ready to incorporate these actions into dramatic play, too.	Mostly dug up and buried with seeds with ____. I gave tools and she used. Put objects in pail. 1-2 steps.	Climbed mountains to throw, threw, and retrieved bean bags to give to peer.	Got dressed, helped knights get in horses (with prompting and modeling). Watched and cheered.	Repetitive scheme used — no modifications.	Pushed button. Turned pages with Jose.	Took orders. Served hot dogs (with assistance).		

(continued)

Figure 11. (continued)

Team Ideas for Play (TIP)/Team Assessment of Play (TAP) Sheet

Name of child: __Marie F.__   Date: __4-19-92__

Objectives	Rationale/things I'm ready for	Areas of intervention/assessment					
		Sensory	Gross motor	Representational	Manipulatives	Music/books	Snack
9. Given a challenging cause-and-effect toy, Marie will spontaneously use visual exploration and trial-and-error manipulation of key parts.	Marie explores what she sees. She needs to visually search for solutions and use alternative to solve a problem. Observation and exploration key.	Was able to find with visual cues (bumps in sand) searched with hands - no plan.	Adjusted throw after it went up into the air.	Searched for hat, gloves, dress.	Not cause-effect but did try to find colors to make a pattern.	Tried wrong button on tape, Jose showed her, then she pushed it.	Looked for pencil and paper.
10. Marie will be able to sort and describe objects by function and category.	Marie's language and thinking skills will increase as she understands how things are alike, how things have more than one name, and the functions of things.	Said "men", "blocks", tried to put Legos together for castle.	L. said "let's find things we can throw" at the dragon Marie found bells, bean bags.	Mary said "where are the animals?" Marie went to the horses. Knight injured. C. said he need something to fix him up. M. "call doctor."	In art area Mary said "look at all the things you can use to paint." Marie narrated all of them.	Labeled pictures in book - but not by category or function.	Knew snack was "food." Mary asked "what else do we eat at a restaurant?" Marie said "french fries."
11. Marie will indicate when she needs to go to the bathroom by statement or request.	This will increase Marie's independence and also reflect an increased initiative in her part in both language and thought relating to consequences.	Marie is starting to give physical cues - wiggles when she needs to go to bathroom. When asked if she has to go, she'll nod.					

Maria was limited to two to three words and her comments were still primarily related to posses-sion and labeling of objects. Maria was taking turns when prompted, but did not persist in turn-taking without adult support. Maria showed increased affect when she accomplished a task and smiled and laughed when unexpected events occurred (e.g., the knight on a cardboard horse fell over) or when other peers laughed and she laughed in imitation. Weight shifting and body rota-tion was still difficult for Maria. She needed the adult to manipulate the environment to encour-age her to move her body to the sides or to shift weight from one side to the other. Maria still demonstrated low tone and lack of strength, but was attempting to lift and move objects willingly. The occupational therapist suggested that this was still an appropriate technique for Maria and should be continued. Maria's fine motor skills were improving, and she was using her fingers more and using a slightly higher-level grasp. Continued encouragement of problem-solving using her fingers, particularly with cause-and-effect toys, was recommended. The team talked about not having enough opportunities in this area and the need to incorporate more cause-and-effect problem-solving into their planning. The team also noted that Maria needed more opportunities to relate objects in the various themes as she did most of her functional relational play in the house area. The teacher said she would work on facilitating more relational play in the sensory and manipulative areas. The speech-language therapist, who had been con-sulting in a different room on the day Maria was observed, studied the TAP Sheet and agreed that Maria was using more categorical words. She had said "men," was able to identify things to throw at the dragon, and said, "call the doctor," when the knight was injured and the teacher said, "We need something to fix him up." She also gave examples of other words she had heard her use at other times. The team also commented that Maria was making progress on her bath-room skills. She was beginning to recognize and give physical cues when she needed to go to the bathroom and would then respond positively if asked by a team member if she needed to go.

The teacher then arranged for a home visit to see how Maria was doing at home and to make modifications in the plan. She took a portable VCR and tapes of Maria made during class to show Mrs. F. examples of what Maria was doing in class.

Mrs. F. first discussed how Maria was playing more with Sean and imitating everything he did. She said Sean was enjoying his role as teacher. She stated that Maria was helping her in the kitchen and relating many objects. She felt Maria was initiating more conversation and asking for things. She said that making her aware that it was important for Maria to initiate and not always respond to a question had really helped her interact differently with Maria, and she believed Maria was doing more talking and turn-taking. The teacher laughed and commented on Mr. F.'s idea to place the television controls out of Maria's reach so that she would need to climb to get them. Mrs. F. said, "Actually, he used to put them up there so she couldn't get them. Now he gives her the stool so she can." The teacher discussed all of the areas on the TAP Sheet with Mrs. F. and related what Mrs. F. was seeing at home to what the team was seeing at school. She noted that Mrs. F. had incorporated creative ideas for cause-and-effect and using dramatic play with stories at bedtime. Mrs. F. also felt that Maria was making progress in indicating when she needed to go to the bathroom. She wasn't yet consistent, "but at least she knows what that room is for," said Mrs. F.

Mrs. F. said that she hadn't incorporated all of the ideas on the original TIP Sheet into Maria's day; but she felt that Maria was making progress in all areas. Mary assured her that the TIP Sheet was not meant to be work, only ideas for things that could be included naturally into the day with Maria. Mrs. F. said that was how she had used them and had found them to be "good reminders."

Mary then showed Mrs. F. cuts of videotape of Maria from the classroom storybook units. Mary summarized what the team had discussed from the TAP Sheets and related that to what Mrs. F. had described about Maria's behaviors at home. Mrs. F. and Mary then talked about modifications. They felt that most of the objectives were still appropriate, as Maria still needed to expand and refine her skills. Mary suggested that the grocery store was another good place to work on concepts and discrimination. Mary had brought a new blank TIP Sheet, so they added a new "shopping" column. They added new ideas that Mrs. F. had tried and ideas that Mary suggested. Mrs. F. believed that they could change the language objective to have Maria use four words as she was now consistently using three words. Mary made this change on the original TIP Sheet. When the visit was over Mrs. F. had two sets of TIP Sheets, the modified original sheets, and a new set with several new ideas added to complement the original set. The home visit took an hour. Mrs. F. commented as Mary was leaving that she loved watching the videotape of the class and that she appreciated the notes that came home telling her about what was happening at school. They discussed setting up another observation at the end of the school year, and Mrs. F. said that she believed that would be fine. She was pleased with Maria's progress and appreciated the input from the entire team.

MARIA'S STORY CONTINUES . . .

Maria's story doesn't end here. Because the TPBI process is cyclical, it will continue throughout Maria's placement in preschool. At the end of the school year, TAP Sheets again will be used, along with other measures, to summarize her progress. The team may decide to do another transdisciplinary play-based assessment, or it may choose to wait until the beginning of the school year, so that they will begin the year with a fresh baseline on Maria's behavior levels. At the end of the following year, Maria will be transitioned into kindergarten. A TPBA will be done at this time, and the videotape will be sent to her receiving kindergarten program. If the kindergarten she attends uses the process as well, the transition from preschool to kindergarten will be easier for Maria and her family. They understand this process and have incorporated it into their lifestyle, so the shift to kindergarten will not have to be a traumatic event. If the kindergarten Maria attends uses more traditional approaches, the videotape will still be a valuable addition to their information about Maria.

CONCLUSION

As can be seen from Maria's case study, TPBI is a cyclical process of evaluation and intervention. Transdisciplinary play-based intervention is a dynamic tool that can be integrated into numerous play models or other curricula. Like the transdisciplinary play-based assessment model, TPBI is meant to be flexible and can be modified to meet the needs of the children and families for whom it was intended; specifically, all infants, toddlers, preschool and kindergarten children, with or without disabilities, between infancy and 6 years of age. Regular review of the TPBI Planner, particularly in areas that are unfamiliar, serves to remind even the most knowledgeable professional of principles and practices that are often not in the forefront of memory. Discussion of these principles and practices with family members and other team members ensures an integrated, holistic approach to facilitation of child growth and development.

REFERENCE

DePaola, T. (1980). *The knight and the dragon*. New York: G.P. Putnam's Sons.

Appendix

REPORT: MARIA F.
Name: Maria F.
Sex: Female
Parent(s): Carmen and Louis F.
Address:
Telephone:
Examiners: Mary Jones, E.C.E. teacher
James Smith, psychologist
Colleen Rodriguez, speech-language pathologist
Lisa White, occupational therapist

Date of birth: 1/3/88
Date of testing: 1/7/92
Age at testing: 4 yr., 4 days

Reason for Referral:

Maria was evaluated for an IEP review and update.

History:

Developmental and social history were obtained from previous records. Mrs. F. reported a normal pregnancy, but stated that Maria was delivered at 33 weeks gestation, which was about 6 weeks early. Maria weighed 4 pounds, 8 ounces at birth. Mrs. F. stated that Maria was in the neonatal intensive care unit for 12 days following her birth, during which time she was in an incubator for 10 days and on a respirator for 5 days.

Maria's mother stated that Maria has had bronchitis on a yearly basis, but that she has had no other childhood illnesses. Dr. Summers is her pediatrician. At 2 years of age, Maria was diagnosed as having food allergies. The primary food allergies are to milk, chocolate, citrus, tomatoes, fish, nuts, and sweet potatoes. She takes Attarex, a prescription allergy medication in liquid form, daily.

Maria lives with both of her natural parents and her 6-year-old brother, Sean. Mrs. F. is a part-time secretary, and Mr. F. is a carpenter. Mrs. F.'s mother also lives with them part of the year. Mrs. F. reported that Maria crawled at 10 months of age, walked at 21 months of age, and began talking between 2½ and 3 years of age. Mrs. F. also stated that Maria currently wears tennis shoes with an orthopedic arch. Mrs. F.'s major concerns are related to Maria's motor and speech skills.

Maria has attended the infant and toddler and preschool programs at the center, beginning when she was 16 months old. She is currently enrolled in a 4-day-a-week preschool program with both age peers and other children with delays. Mrs. F. participates in observing Maria at school, plays with her at home, and participates in school activities with Maria (e.g., going on field trips). Maria receives occupational and speech-language therapy as an integrated part of her preschool program.

Method of Assessment:

Maria was assessed in a transdisciplinary play-based assessment session at Brantley Elementary School, where she attends the Center for Early Education. The room contains a house area with a kitchen and other household props, a doctor area with a doctor kit, beads, a sand-and-water table, a slide and a dry wading pool, crayons, markers, a paint easel, tricycles, scooters, puzzles, Play-Doh, and other toys appropriate to a preschool. The play session consisted of observations of Maria interacting with a play facilitator (who was also her teacher), her mother, and a peer. All aspects of the assessment were completed by the team members listed above. Maria's mother completed a developmental questionnaire, and both parents participated in the discussion of Maria's play assessment.

INTERPRETATION OF ASSESSMENT RESULTS

Cognitive Development:

Categories of Play   Maria was observed to participate in sensorimotor, relational, and dramatic play. She preferred functional play with objects over more complex forms of play.

Attention Span   Maria's longest play time was 15 minutes, which she spent stringing beads and interacting with the facilitator. In general, Maria demonstrated a long attention span with most tasks. She moved to a new area of play only when the facilitator moved her through a transition.
    Maria was distracted by sounds, but returned to task and did not need external prompting or reinforcement to stay focused on her play.

Object Use   Maria tends to use simple actions with objects and links schemes together in simple combinations of two-step processes, consisting primarily of imitative play. She tends to prefer very simple manipulative toys. She enjoyed stacking and lining up blocks, threading beads, and simple dramatic play, such as putting the doctor's stethoscope on her ears and placing it on her bear. Maria's use of objects is within the 2- to 3-year range. Much of her play is repetitive and lacks variation and problem-solving.

Symbolic/Representational Play   Maria engages in simple dramatic play with actions directed toward self and a doll or other inanimate object. She uses real or realistic objects in play and was not observed to be able to use symbolic substitutes. Her dramatic play was primarily in imitation of the facilitator. She needed support to maintain dramatic play. Maria is functioning at the 18- to 36-month level in this area, with the lower-level skills in spontaneous dramatic play and the higher-level with facilitation.

Imitation   Imitation is the chief means through which Maria plays and interacts with others. She imitated stringing beads, playing in the seeds, and using the doctor tools. She imitated using the basketball, playing with blocks, and making "tea" after an extended time. Maria showed turn-taking, but her passive style makes it difficult to determine whether she is intentionally taking turns or passively allowing the other person to interject an action.

Problem-Solving   Maria uses persistence in solving problems but does not often demonstrate the ability to try an alternative when she is having difficulty. For example, in threading beads, she had difficulty keeping the string in the hole and pulling it through the other side. She was very persistent in repeating the action, but did not try other ways of holding the bead or string to make it easier. Her problem-solving approaches appear to be in the 24- to 30-month range.

Discrimination/Differentiation   Maria demonstrates her highest level of cognitive skills in this area. She names and matches colors, shapes, and sizes. She can name animals, and "M" for her name, but does not recognize or label any other letters or numbers. Discrimination of these concepts is an area that receives much attention from parents, preschool teachers, and programs such as "Sesame Street." Her skills in this area reflect this practice and are at the 30- to 48-month level.

One-to-One Correspondence   Maria can count by rote to five and inconsistently to 10. She has a rudimentary understanding of one-to-one correspondence and was observed counting to 2 with the blocks. However, this was not observed in other contexts. Her number and one-to-one correspondence skills are at the 24- to 36-month level.

Sequencing Ability   Maria's sequences are limited to two-step processes. She tends to repeat the same actions without variation or thinking of another step in a sequence of actions. Her highest-level behavior was observed in the "hospital" area, where she ministered to the bear with two steps. She was able to understand size sequencing, such as big and little. Her skills in this area range from 24 to 36 months in action sequencing and from 36 to 42 months in ordering sizes.

Drawing Ability   Maria drew arcs, circles, and lines spontaneously. She enjoyed scribbling and painting. She was unable to draw a named shape. Her drawing skills are at the 24- to 36-month level.

In conclusion, Maria's cognitive abilities appear to be predominantly in the 2- to 3-year age range, with some practiced skills at a higher level. A strength is her persistent, good-natured attempts to complete tasks. She has strong imitative skills and interacts pleasantly with others. Labeling, matching, and rudimentary counting are also strengths and can serve as a foundation for developing more concepts. A focus for intervention should be on increasing her initiative and problem-solving strategies, increasing the sequences in her play, moving her into dramatic play and representational play in drawing and construction, and adding to the depth of her conceptual understanding.

Social-Emotional Development:

Temperament   Maria's activity level was low. She had to be encouraged to move around the room. This may be related to her low tone and other motor difficulties, which make moving a struggle.

Maria was flexible and adaptable to each new play situation. She responded with interest, smiles, and verbalizations to the facilitator and her mother. Maria was not as adaptive with peers. She returned to isolated and parallel play and became very quiet.

Maria demonstrated positive, but low, intensity of reactions to stimuli. Her affect was also low and showed a restricted range of emotion. More intense stimulation did get her to smile.

Mastery Motivation   Maria's activities were mainly purposeful and goal-oriented. She was persistent and focused, even with challenging tasks. She primarily selected tasks that were not too difficult.

Social Relations with Parent   Maria appeared to enjoy the structured activity with her mother as demonstrated through her attention and persistence with the task, but she did not smile or show other positive affect. Maria directed her attention toward the object and responded to her mother's directions. She did not take turns in actions or dialogue.

Reaction of Child to Parent with Facilitator Present   Maria was able to function well independently. She did not need to "check in" with her mother, but occasionally looked in her direction. Maria continued to play comfortably when her mother left the room and returned. She seems relaxed in this familiar environment.

Social Interaction with Facilitator   Maria was a bit more animated when the facilitator used verbal inflection, high animation, and enthusiasm. She shared good eye contact, had verbal interactions, and smiled more frequently. Turn-taking increased when the facilitator imitated

Maria's behaviors. More spontaneous language was observed when the facilitator used fewer questions and more commenting and waiting.

Relation to Peers   Maria was observed in play with a familiar peer from her class. Limited spontaneous verbal interaction occurred. Maria was aware of the peer's presence and played first in isolation and then with the facilitator. With the facilitator's assistance, Maria joined the peer in parallel play. Maria appeared more passive and less animated with the peer.

Sense of Humor   Maria smiled and occasionally laughed at appropriate events and physical tickling. Fairly intense stimulation was needed to provoke these responses. She did not use words to describe emotions or pleasant experiences (e.g., that's funny, this is fun).

Social Conventions   Maria demonstrated social conventions such as greeting the facilitator and eating nicely at the table. Her mother reported that she does not use "please" and "thank you" unless prompted. Maria did not exhibit any unusual or maladaptive behaviors.

In conclusion, socially, Maria is ready to move into more interactions with peers. As in the cognitive and communication and language areas, she is ready to initiate more interactions, take turns, and move toward associative play. At this time, parallel play with initiation of verbal interactions is appropriate. Imitation of Maria and wait time will be important to help her with turn-taking. A less directive and more responsive approach is recommended. Increased affect and enthusiasm on the part of adults is also important.

Communication and Language Development:

Modality   Maria communicates chiefly with gestures and words. She was also able to pair gestures with words and use eye contact to enhance communication.

Pragmatics   The use of words to communicate meaning places Maria in the locutionary stage of language development, which is appropriate for her age. Maria primarily uses language to regulate the behavior of others and to respond to adults' requests. She did not use words to provide or seek information from others. She demonstrated the following pragmatic intentions: requesting objects, requesting action, protesting, acknowledging, and answering.

Although Maria demonstrates a range of intentions, her discourse, or dialogue, skills are limited. Her communication seems confined to direct response to specific inquiry. She rarely initiates a verbal interaction. Initiation of a topic is restricted to requests for assistance. Turn-taking in conversation was observed most with the facilitator and was limited to one or two turns. With a peer, even less initiation and turn-taking was observed. Maria's pragmatic communication and discourse skills are at the 2- to 3-year level.

Much of Maria's interactive speech is repeating statements. She will modify statements, however, demonstrating her comprehension of what was said. Her imitative level is also at the 2- to 3-year level.

Phonology   Maria's phonological system is approximately at the 3-year level. Her speech is nasal and difficult to understand. Her mother reported that this nasality is due to her allergies, which keeps her nose stuffed up. Maria demonstrated some initial omissions (e.g., 'ellow/yellow), deleted consonants (e.g., coooor/color), and made some assimilations (e.g., ta ang go/triangle).

Semantic and Syntactic Understanding   *Semantics* refers to Maria's ability to understand the meaning of signs, symbols, and words. The words she uses demonstrate her understanding of referential knowledge (understanding that a word refers to a specific thing [e.g., Mommy, pull ups]), extended knowledge (e.g., block or bead means various types of blocks or beads), relational knowledge (i.e., understanding of how things relate [e.g., in, on, same]), and categorical knowledge (i.e., discriminating by attributes [e.g., green one, big one]). Maria uses nouns (e.g., necklace, car, money), verbs (e.g., pull, goes), adjectives (e.g., green, big), adverbs (e.g., fast), prepositions (e.g., on, in), negatives (e.g., no, don't), and pronouns (e.g., I, her, it, he.)

Maria also uses a variety of structures in her syntax. She combines agent and action (e.g., it broke) and agent, action, and location (e.g., you sit there). Maria also uses possessives, contractions, and the third person. Her semantic and syntactic structures are at the 2- to 3-year level.

Comprehension of Language   Maria responds to visual, verbal, and physical cues. She comprehends statements, yes and no, and wh- questions. A further assessment on the Preschool Language Scale revealed receptive language at the 3- to 4-year level.

Oral Motor   Maria drank juice from a cup and ate a cracker. Her lips sealed adequately on the cup while drinking. She has a slight tongue thrust while drinking and chooses to drink small amounts. This may also be related to her allergies, which negatively influence her breathing patterns. Breathing during eating and drinking appeared laborious. Maria used a rotary chew, but her lips do not close and she drools when eating. She showed a lack of sensitivity to food or drool on her lips and chin. Her overall tone in the facial area appeared low.

Other Concerns   Maria's voice quality is very soft. This also may be related to breathing difficulty.

In conclusion, Maria demonstrates good language comprehension and is able to imitate most semantic and syntactic structures. She seldom initiates conversations and limits her sentence length to two to three words. Maria is ready to use longer sentences, initiate conversations, take turns in a dialogue with two to three turns, and use words to comment and request information. As in the cognitive area, Maria is ready for words related to higher-level concepts (e.g., functions, classifications). Her vocabulary will grow through exposure to a variety of experiences.

Sensorimotor Development:

General Appearance of Movement   Maria's body proportions appear normal; however, her weight and height are significantly less than age peers. Maria appears awkward in both her gross and fine motor movements.

Muscle Tone/Strength/Endurance   Maria's movements lack fluidity and control indicative of normal muscle tone. She walks with a wide base of support and frequently uses a W-sit or a long-legged sit. She prefers sitting in a stable chair to standing or moving. Her arms are stabilized against her sides for fine motor tasks. She has limited strength in her upper body and hands. She was unable to pull herself up on the slide or up a pole. In order to get the top on the magic marker, she leaned her whole body over the magic marker and pushed down with all of her weight on the top.

Reactivity to Sensory Input   Maria appeared to enjoy activities that involved manipulation with her hands. She initiated activities such as stringing large beads, placing plastic coins in a cash register, painting with a brush, and playing with Play-Doh. She enjoyed being tickled by the facilitator. Maria tried many types of tactile and motor activities, including riding a tricycle, climbing up and sliding down a slide, and throwing and catching a basketball. She was alert to auditory and visual stimuli.

Stationary Play Positions   Maria most frequently sat in a chair or on the floor with her legs outstretched. She was observed to squat to play once. Several times she sat in a W-sit. When playing at the table, she frequently stabilized herself by holding onto the table edge and leaning forward. In standing Maria appeared to use the wide base of support, with feet spread apart.

Mobility in Play   Maria was motivated to try a variety of motor activities; however, she seemed to prefer fine motor activities. Walking appeared awkward, with legs somewhat stiff. She had difficulty changing positions, especially when going from a floor sit to standing, when she would use a "bear" stand. Maria could roll both ways on the floor, but did not have a good segmental roll. She was observed to squat to play with a toy.

Other Developmental Achievements   Maria was not able to jump off a step; instead, she stepped down one foot at a time. She was also unable to climb the ladder on the slide by stepping up and pulling herself up. She attempted to kick a ball, but was unsuccessful. When throwing and catching the small basketball, Maria demonstrated straight-arm movements. She held the ball over her head with both arms and then threw it in a downward motion. She was able to catch the ball with straight arms by capturing it between her chest and chin. She frequently turned her head and closed her eyes when the ball came toward her. She had difficulty with riding a tricycle due to lack of strength and coordination.

Prehension and Manipulation   Maria's hands were generally held in a claw-like position, but she attempted a more sophisticated grasp with crayons. Her fingers, which are short, were held somewhat apart. Although Maria manipulated objects well, her movements were awkward. Maria was able to reach, grasp, and release easily. She tends to stabilize her arms against her body or on the table when concentrating on a fine motor task.

Maria was observed to perform the following manipulative tasks: stringing beads, playing with a cash register by putting in coins and punching buttons, taking off and replacing the Magic Marker cap, drawing with Magic Markers and crayons, squeezing and forming Play-Doh, putting a puzzle together, opening a food packet, picking up food, cutting Play-Doh, using both hands to paint with a brush, putting seeds in a funnel, and putting a stethoscope on her ears.

Motor Planning   Maria was able to do better with fine motor than gross motor tasks, although problem-solving was limited. Her motor planning for activities such as kicking a ball or maneuvering through an obstacle course is slow. Maria needs time to process and react.

In conclusion, Maria shows overall delays in motor development and needs to increase tone, strength, rotational and weight-shifting abilities, hip and shoulder stability, balance and coordination, and motor planning. Refinement of fine motor grasp is also recommended.

SUMMARY

Maria has many strengths. She is easy going, pleasant, and adaptable. She is persistent and can focus on a task for an extended period of time. Her lack of initiation affects her cognitive, communication and language, social-emotional, and sensorimotor abilities. Her low tone and lack of strength also have a negative impact on her ability to demonstrate more sophisticated skills. A medical follow-up is recommended to see if breathing can be improved. Continued placement in the Center for Early Education with integrated therapy is recommended.

Things Maria Is Ready for:

1. Initiation of play with peers
2. Initiation of dialogue with adults and peers, including commenting and providing and requesting information
3. Extension of functional play with objects into three- to four-step play sequence in dramatic play
4. Increased turn-taking in conversation and play to 3–4 steps
5. Increased spontaneous use of language, including words for categories, emotions, functions, and relations
6. Increased understanding of number—to 2 and 3
7. Increased response to open-ended questions
8. Increased range of emotional expression
9. Improved problem-solving skills, including visual search and trial-and-error
10. Increased tone and strength in body, limbs, and hands
11. Increased balance and coordination, including weight-shifting and rotation
12. Increased facial sensitivity and tongue and lip control
13. Improved breathing patterns while talking and eating

REPORT: MARIA F.
Name: Maria F.
Sex: Female
Parent(s): Carmen and Louis F.
Address:
Telephone:
Examiners: Mary Jones, E.C.E. teacher
James Smith, psychologist
Colleen Rodriguez, speech-language pathologist
Lisa White, occupational therapist

Date of birth: 1/3/88
Date of testing: 1/7/92
Age at testing: 4 yr., 4 days

Reason for Referral:

Maria was evaluated for an IEP review and update.

History:

Developmental and social history were obtained from previous records. Mrs. F. reported a normal pregnancy, but stated that Maria was delivered at 33 weeks gestation, which was about 6 weeks early. Maria weighed 4 pounds, 8 ounces at birth. Mrs. F. stated that Maria was in the neonatal intensive care unit for 12 days following her birth, during which time she was in an incubator for 10 days and on a respirator for 5 days.

Maria's mother stated that Maria has had bronchitis on a yearly basis, but that she has had no other childhood illnesses. Dr. Summers is her pediatrician. At 2 years of age, Maria was diagnosed as having food allergies. The primary food allergies are to milk, chocolate, citrus, tomatoes, fish, nuts, and sweet potatoes. She takes Attarex, a prescription allergy medication in liquid form, daily.

Maria lives with both of her natural parents and her 6-year-old brother, Sean. Mrs. F. is a part-time secretary, and Mr. F. is a carpenter. Mrs. F.'s mother also lives with them part of the year. Mrs. F. reported that Maria crawled at 10 months of age, walked at 21 months of age, and began talking between 2½ and 3 years of age. Mrs. F. also stated that Maria currently wears tennis shoes with an orthopedic arch. Mrs. F.'s major concerns are related to Maria's motor and speech skills.

Maria has attended both the infant and toddler and preschool programs at the center, beginning when she was 16 months old. She is currently enrolled in a 4-day-a-week preschool program with both age peers and other children with delays. Mrs. F. participates in observing Maria at school, plays with her at home, and participates in school activities with Maria (e.g., going on field trips). Maria receives occupational and speech-language therapy as an integrated part of her preschool program.

Method of Assessment:

Maria was assessed in a transdisciplinary play-based assessment session at Brantley Elementary School, where she attends the Center for Early Education. The room contains a house area with a kitchen and other household props, a doctor area with a doctor kit, beads, a sand-and-water table, a slide and a dry wading pool, crayons, markers, a paint easel, tricycles, scooters, puzzles, Play-Doh, and other toys appropriate to a preschool. The play session consisted of observations of Maria interacting with a play facilitator (who was also her teacher), her mother, and a peer. All aspects of the assessment were completed by the team members listed above. Maria's mother completed a developmental questionnaire, and both parents participated in the discussion of Maria's play assessment.

This report is provided as an example of a short form, integrated approach. This method is gaining popularity.

INTERPRETATION OF ASSESSMENT RESULTS

Maria has a nice attention span for all activities, particularly simple tasks requiring repetition of a simple action (e.g., stringing beads). Lack of strength and low muscle tone in her hands and arms are affecting her fine motor abilities. Maria is ready to increase the sequence of her play actions to two to three different actions in a sequence. She also is ready to use observation and manipulation for problem-solving.

Maria uses imitation in both her play and her language. She imitates the facilitator in dramatic play, but does not initiate a dramatic play sequence of more than two steps. In the same way, she imitates statements, but will not initiate comments or request information. She is ready to increase her initiations of interactions with language and play. Her play sequences in dramatic play could be increased to three to four steps. She is also ready to increase her spontaneous sentence length to three to four words and begin to comment, provide, and request information, and respond to open-ended questions (i.e., questions requiring a statement, rather than yes or no).

Maria's play interactions are primarily with the facilitator. She watches but does not initiate conversation or play with a peer. She is ready to increase her parallel and interactive play with peers and increase her communication with peers through increased turn-taking. Increasing her enjoyment and expression of pleasure in play with adults and peers will also improve her use of words to express emotions.

Maria enjoys gross motor activities with peers, which may be an avenue for increasing social, motor, and communication skills. She has low tone and lacks strength to pull her self or heavy objects around, but enjoys trying. She likes tactile input, although she would prefer to be in control, giving herself the stimulation rather than participating with an adult or peer. Her movements are awkward due to lack of balance, poor weight shifting (i.e., ability to shift weight from one side of the body to another), and poor rotation skills (i.e., ability to move and rotate the top half of the body separately from the bottom half of the body). She is ready to increase her coordination through practice of motor skills that require the use of these skills. Turn-taking and motor planning could be incorporated into motor activities (e.g., climbing, jumping, catching, throwing, kicking).

Maria lacks tone and sensitivity around the mouth area. In addition, allergies affect her breathing and swallowing patterns. Language and eating skills could be improved through increasing Maria's awareness of her tongue and lips as well as improving her breathing pattern.

SUMMARY

Maria has many strengths. She is easy going, pleasant, and adaptable. She is persistent and can focus on a task for an extended period of time. Her lack of initiation affects her cognitive, communication and language, social-emotional, and sensorimotor abilities. Her low tone and lack of strength also have a negative impact on her ability to demonstrate more sophisticated skills. A medical follow-up is recommended to see if breathing can be improved. Continued placement in the Center for Early Education with integrated therapy is recommended.

Things Maria Is Ready for:

1. Initiation of play with peers
2. Initiation of dialogue with adults and peers, including commenting and providing information and requesting information
3. Extension of functional play with objects into three- to four-step play sequence in dramatic play
4. Increased turn-taking in conversation and play to 3–4 steps

5.   Increased spontaneous use of language, including words for categories, emotions, functions, and relations
6.   Increased understanding of number—to 2 and 3
7.   Increased response to open-ended questions
8.   Increased range of emotional expression
9.   Improved problem-solving skills, including visual search and trial-and-error.
10. Increased tone and strength in body, limbs, and hands
11. Increased balance and coordination, including weight-shifting and rotation.
12. Increased facial sensitivity and tongue and lip control
13. Improved breathing patterns while talking and eating

Index

Page numbers followed by "f" indicate figures; those followed by "t" indicate tables.

Order these innovative tools today!

Transdisciplinary Play-Based Assessment: **A Functional Approach to Working with Young Children, Revised Edition**
By Toni W. Linder, Ed.D., with invited contributors
This hands-on guide shows you how to conduct play sessions that combine the insight of parents with the expertise of a transdisciplinary team. Using specific observation guidelines presented in this manual, you'll be able to assess a child's cognitive, social-emotional, communication and language, and sensiormotor development - all at play time. A dynamic, comprehensive, and user friendly assessment instrument!
Stock #1626/$41.95/1993/352 pages/illustrated/7x10/spiral-bound/ISBN 1-55766-162-6

Transdisciplinary Play-Based Assessment and Intervention: **Child and Program Summary Forms**
By Toni W. Linder, Ed.D.
Attractive, convenient, and easy to use, this single product incorporates all of the forms you'll need throughout the TPBA/TPBI process! Use these forms to save time, energy, and money, and to ensure the consistency of your observations and your program. Each 58-page tablet of forms includes instructions and a template for implementing TPBA/TPBI.
Stock # 1634/$27.00 (package of 5 tablets)/1993/58 pages each/81/2 x 11/ISBN 1-55766-163-4 (Opened packages are nonreturnable.)

Video
And You Thought They Were Just Playing: Transdisciplinary Play-Based Assessment
Produced & written by Toni W. Linder, Ed.D. Directed & edited by Rebecca S. Newman
Through captivating footage of two play sessions, this training video shows you how to use the TPBA approach. Plus, you'll learn how to transfer assessment information onto time-saving TPBA summary forms (sold separately - see above) that organize data and help you understand individualized instruction.
Stock #2223/purchase price $175.00/preview price $25.00*/1995/65 minutes/VHS/ISBN 1-55766-222-3

Video
Observing Kassandra: A Transdisciplinary Play-Based Assessment for a Child with Severe Disabilities
Produced & written by Toni W. Linder, Ed.D. Directed & edited by Matt Walker
A companion to *And You Thought They Were Just Playing*, this training tape provides a firsthand opportunity to practice taking notes during a real-life TPBA. You'll observe Kassandra—a preschooler with severe disabilities and health impairments—and complete the summary forms that accompany the tapes. Then, you'll compare your observations and recommendations to those discussed in Kassandra's actual summary forms and final TPBA report (also included with the video). A great source of effective and affordable practice!
Stock #2665/purchase price $165.00/preview price $25.00*(includes video and accompanying booklet of forms)/1996/60 minutes/ VHS, 48 page booklet and one tablet of Child & Program Summary Forms/ISBN 1-55766-266-5

*VIDEO ORDERING POLICY: Videocassettes costing more than $50.00 are nonreturnable. They may be previewed, however, for a nonrefundable fee of $25.00 per video. To preview a video, write "Preview" on the order form, fill in the preview price of $25.00, and send a check or money order payable to Brookes Publishing Co. If you decide to keep the video, then the preview fee will be credited toward the purchase price of the video, and you will be billed for the balance. All returns of previewed videos must be received within 10 days of the original invoice and must be in resalable condition. Videos costing less than $50.00 can be returned for refund or credit within 30 days. Videos must be accompanied by the invoice and be in resalable condition and rewound. Duplication in whole or in part of any videotape is strictly prohibited.

PLACE YOUR ORDER NOW! Free shipping and handling on prepaid check orders.

Please send me ___ copy(ies) of **Transdisciplinary Play-Based Assessment/Stock #1626/$41.95**
Please send me ___ copy(ies) of **TPBA & TPBI Child and Program Summary Forms/Stock #1634/$27.00**
Please send me ___ copy(ies) of **And You Thought They Were Just Playing (Video)/Stock #2223/$175.00/Preview $25.00***
Please send me ___ copy(ies) of **Observing Kassandra (Video)/Stock #2665/$165.00/Preview $25.00***

___ Bill my institution (purchase order must be attached)   ___ Payment enclosed (make checks payable to Brookes Publishing Co.)

___ VISA   ___ MasterCard   ___ American Express   Credit Card # _____ Exp. date _____

Signature _____   Daytime telephone _____
Name _____
Address _____
City/State/Zip _____
Yours to review 30 days risk-free. Prices subject to change without notice. Prices may be higher outside the U.S. Maryland orders add 5% sales tax.

Photocopy this form and mail or fax it to Brookes Publishing Co., P.O. Box 10624, Baltimore, MD 21285-0624, Fax 410-337-8539. Or call toll-free (8 A.M.–6 P.M. ET) 1-800-638-3775. Or e-mail custserv@pbrookes.com.